Handbook of Strategic
Environmental Assessment

Handbook of Strategic Environmental Assessment

Edited by

Barry Sadler, Ralf Aschemann, Jiri Dusik,

Thomas B. Fischer, Maria R. Partidário and Rob Verheem

publishing for a sustainable future

London • New York

First published in 2011 by Earthscan

Earthscan
2 Park Square, Milton Park, Abingdon, Oxfordshire OX14 4RN
Simultaneously published in the USA and Canada by Earthscan
711 Third Avenue, New York, NY 10017
Earthscan is an imprint of the Taylor & Francis Group, an informa business

Earthscan publishes in association with the International Institute for Environment and Development

ISBN: 978-1-84407-365-8 hardback

Typeset by OKS Prepress
Cover design by Andrew Corbett

A catalogue record for this book is available from the British Library

Library of Congress Cataloging-in-Publication Data

Handbook of strategic environmental assessment / edited by Barry Sadler ... [et al.].
    p. cm.
  Includes bibliographical references and index.
  ISBN 978-1-84407-365-8 (hardback)
1. Environmental impact analysis—Handbooks, manuals, etc. 2. Strategic planning—
Environmental aspects—Handbooks, manuals, etc. I. Sadler, Barry.
  TD194.6.H36 2010
  333.71'4—dc22   2010027870

At Earthscan we strive to minimize our environmental impacts and carbon footprint through reducing waste, recycling and offsetting our CO_2 emissions, including those created through publication of this book.

Contents

Part II SEA Application

Part III SEA Linkage to Other Instruments

Part IV Cross-Cutting Issues in SEA

List of Figures, Tables and Boxes

Figures

Tables

Boxes

Acknowledgements

This handbook was prepared and produced with help and inputs from many people. First and foremost, the editors acknowledge the substantive contribution made by the authors of the individual chapters included in this volume, which were originally drafted for the International Conference on Strategic Environmental Assessment (SEA) organized by the International Association for Impact Assessment (Prague, September 2005). In that context, we are grateful to all the participants who variously helped to provide information and to develop perspectives, either specifically through contributed papers or generally through participating in the various working dialogues. Thanks are also extended to those who helped to plan the conference and to shape the agenda, particularly: Urszula Rzeszot who served with the editors on the programme steering committee; Ausra Jurkeviciute and Simona Kosikova Sulcova, the executive secretariat; and the members of international advisory committee, namely Hussein Abaza, Virginia Alzina, John Ashe, Michelle Audoin, David Aspinwall, Elvis Au, Ingrid Belcakova, Olivia Bina, Aleg Cherp, Ray Clark, Barry Dalal-Clayton, Jenny Dixon, Carlos Dora, Linda Ghanimé, Kiichiro Hayashi, Miroslav Martis (Chair), Nenad Mikulic, Sibout Noteboom, Wiecher Schrage, Riki Thérivel, Martin Ward and Christopher Wood. Appreciation is also extended to the local organizing committee, namely Ivana Kasparova (Co-Chair), Vera Novakova, Martin Smutny, Vaclav Votruba and Vladimir Zdrazil (Co-Chair), and to the Czech University of Agriculture, which hosted the conference. Many other people worked on the long and often frustrating process to get from there to here with particular thanks to Rob West, Nicki Dennis, Claire Lamont, Camille Bramall and Nick Ascroft at Earthscan who stayed with this when there were times that it looked as if this would never get to press.

The SEA conference programme included a tribute to Norman Lee of the EIA Centre, University of Manchester, who died in the previous month (August 2005). Dr Lee was internationally renowned for his work in environmental assessment and a major intellectual force in the development of SEA in the European Union. His impact on the field was significant, both directly through his research activities and indirectly through his teaching of a generation of students. A number of them are represented in the list of contributors to this volume and readers need look no further for his legacy.

List of Acronyms and Abbreviations

AAPC	Anglo American Platinum Corporation
ADB	Asian Development Bank
ADF	Australian Defence Force
AEAM	adaptive environmental assessment and management
AEE	assessment of environmental effects
AFMA	Australian Fisheries Management Authority
ANSEA	analytical strategic environmental assessment
ASEAN	Association of Southeast Asian Nations
BAP	biodiversity action plan
BCLME	Benguela Current Large Marine Ecosystem
BEACON	Building Environment Assessment Consensus (EC)
BEE	Black Economic Empowerment
BLM	Bureau of Land Management (US)
BPA	Bonneville Power Administration
CAMP	coastal area management plan
CAPE	Cape Action Plan for People and the Environment
CBA	cost benefit analysis
CBBIA	capacity-building for biodiversity and impact assessment
CBD	Convention on Biological Diversity (UN)
CCME	Canadian Council of Ministers of the Environment
CEA	cumulative effects assessment
CEAA	Canadian Environmental Assessment Agency
CEQ	Council on Environmental Quality
CESD	Commissioner for Environment and Sustainable Development (Canada)
CIA	cumulative impact assessment
CIDA	Canadian International Development Agency
CNSOPB	Canada-Nova Scotia Offshore Petroleum Board
CPRGS	Comprehensive Poverty Reduction and Growth Strategy (Vietnam)
CSR	corporate social responsibility
CZM	coastal zone management
CZMP	coastal zone management plan
DAC	Development Assistance Committee

DEAT	Department of Environment Affairs and Tourism (South Africa)
DEH	Department of the Environment and Heritage (Australia)
DEMP	Decentralized Environment Management Project
DfID	Department for International Development (UK)
DG	Directorate General
DGENV	Directorate General Environment (EC)
DHS	Department of Homeland Security (US)
DISR	Department of Industry, Science and Resources
DPSIR	driver-pressure-state-impact-response
DTI	Department of Trade and Industry (UK)
EA	environmental assessment
EAA	environmental assessment addendum
EAAIA	Eastern African Association for Impact Assessment
EARP	Environmental Assessment and Review Process (Canada)
EBS	environmental baseline study
EC	European Commission
EDPRS	Economic Development and Poverty Reduction Strategy (Rwanda)
EEB	European Environmental Bureau
EECCA	Eastern Europe, Caucasus and Central Asia
EIA	environmental impact assessment
EIR	environmental impact report
EIS	environmental impact statement
ELC	European Landscape Commission
ELP	ecological landscape plans
EMF	environmental management framework
EMPR	environmental programme management report
EMS	environmental management system
EOAR	Ecosystem Overview and Assessment Report (Canada)
EP & EP	Environmental Protection and Enhancement Procedures (New Zealand)
EPA	Environmental Protection Agency
EPAA	Environment Planning and Protection Act (Australia)
EPBC Act	Environment Protection and Biodiversity Conservation Act (Australia)
ETC	EIA Transportation Centre
EU	European Union
FMA	Fisheries Management Act (Australia)
FTIP	Federal Transport Infrastructure Plan (Germany)
GDP	gross domestic product
GHG	greenhouse gas
GIS	geographical information system
GMI	Global Mining Initiative
GPRS	Ghanaian Poverty Reduction Strategy
GTZ	German Technical Cooperation
GWP	Global Water Partnership
HEFRMS	Humber Estuary Flood Risk Management Strategy

HIA	health impact assessment
HIMI	Heard Island and McDonald Islands
IA	impact assessment
IAIA	International Association for Impact Assessment
IBA	impact benefit agreement
ICMM	International Council on Mining and Metals
ICZM	integrated coastal zone management
IDP	integrated development plan
IIRIRA	Illegal Immigration Reform and Immigration Responsibility Act (US)
ILM	integrated landscape management
IMF	International Monetary Fund
INS	Immigration and Naturalization Service (US)
IPA	integrated policy appraisal
IPPC	Integrated Pollution Prevention and Control
IT	information technology
IUCN	International Union for Conservation of Nature
IWRM	integrated water resources management
JPOI	Johannesburg Plan of Implementation
LCA	life cycle analysis
LEP	local environmental plan
LFP	landscape framework plan
LHA	landscape heritage assessment
LMM	landscape management models
LOMA	large ocean management area
LP	landscape plan
LPOE	land ports of entry
LTCCP	long-term council community plan
MDG	Millennium Development Goal (UN)
MEA	Millennium Ecosystem Assessment
MLT	Ministry of Land, Infrastructure and Transport (Japan)
MMSD	Mining, Minerals and Sustainable Development
MoD	Ministry of Defence (UK)
MOE	Ministry of the Environment (Japan)
MOP	meeting of the parties
MPA	marine protected area
MRC	Mekong River Commission
NAAEC	North American Agreement on Environmental Cooperation
NAFTA	North American Free-Trade Agreement
NBSAO	National Biodiversity Strategy Action Plan
NCEA	Netherlands Commission for Environmental Assessment
NDPC	National Development Planning Commission
NEPA	National Environmental Policy Act (US)
NEPAD	New Partnership for Africa's Development
NEPC Act	National Environment Protection Council Act (Australia)
NEPM	National Environmental Protection Measures (Australia)
NES	national environmental standard

NGO	non-governmental organization
NHS	National Health Service
NIMBY	not in my backyard
NIS	Newly Independent State
NPS	national policy statement
NSDS	national sustainable development strategy
NSGRP	National Strategy for Growth and Reduction of Poverty (Tanzania)
NSSD	National Strategy for Sustainable Development
NTT	National Task Team
NWT	Northwest Territories (Canada)
ODPM	Office of the Deputy Prime Minister (UK)
OECD	Organisation for Economic Co-operation and Development
OVOS	Assessment of Environmental Impacts (Russian abbreviation)
PARPA	Action Plan for the Reduction of Absolute Poverty (Mozambique)
PCO	Privy Council Office (Canada)
PEI	Poverty Environment Initiative
PEIA	plan environment impact assessment
PEIS	programmatic environmental impact statements
PEP	protection of the environment policy
PERS	Prior Environmental Review System (South Korea)
PHAC	Public Health Advisory Committee (New Zealand)
PI	public involvement
POP	persistent organic pollutant
PPP	policy, plan and/or programme
PRSC	Poverty Reduction Support Credit
PRSP	Poverty Reduction Strategy Paper
PSIA	poverty and social impact assessment
PSL Act	Petroleum (Submerged Lands) Act (Australia)
RAC	Resource Assessment Commission (Australia)
RBMP	River Basin Management Plan
RCEP	Royal Commission on Environmental Pollution
REC	Regional Environmental Centre
REDSO	Regional Economic Development Services Office (USAID)
REP	regional environmental plan
REIA	regional environmental impact assessment
RFA	Regional Forest Agreement
RIA	regulatory impact assessment
RISDP	Regional Indicative Strategic Development Plan
RLTS	regional land transport strategy
RMA	Resource Management Act (New Zealand)
RMP	regional marine plan
ROD	Record of Decision
RPS	regional policy statement
RSA	regional sectoral assessment
RSEA	regional strategic environmental assessment
RSP	regional strategic plan

RUL	Rössing Uranium Limited
SA	sustainability assessment
SADC	South African Development Community
SAIEA	Southern African Association for Impact Assessment
SAR	Special Administrative Region
SD	sustainable development
SDF	spatial development framework
SEA	strategic environmental assessment
SEACAM	Secretariat for Eastern African Coastal Area Management
SEAN	strategic environmental analysis
SEDP	strategic environmental development plan
SEIA	social and environmental impact assessment
SEMP	strategic environmental management plan
SEPA	State Environmental Protection Administration (China)
SEPP	state environment protection policy
SER	State Environmental Review (EECCA)
SFA	substance flow analysis
SI	strategic initiative
SIA	social impact assessment
SIDA	Swedish International Development Cooperation Agency
SLP	social and labour plan
SMP	strategic master planning
SPREP	South Pacific Regional Environmental Programme
SWOT	strengths, weaknesses, opportunities and threats
TEA	transboundary environmental analysis
UN	United Nations
UNDP	United Nations Development Programme
UNECE	United Nations Economic Commission for Europe
UNEP	United Nations Environment Programme
UNU	United Nations University
USAID	United States Agency for International Development
USFWS	United States Fish and Wildlife Service
US-VISIT	United States Visitor and Immigrant Status Indicator Technology
VEC	valued ecosystem component
WFD	Water Framework Directive (EU)
WHO	World Health Organization
WMP	waste management plan
WSSD	World Summit on Sustainable Development

1

Taking Stock of SEA

Barry Sadler

Strategic environmental assessment (SEA) is undertaken, both formally and informally, in an increasing number of countries and international organizations. This field has developed rapidly in the past decade and is now the subject of a voluminous literature, which continues to grow apace with the extension and diversification of SEA practice into new areas. Much of the emphasis still focuses on what might be termed the standard model based on environmental impact assessment (EIA), enshrined in the European SEA Directive (2001/42/EC) and the United Nations Economic Commission for Europe (UNECE) SEA Protocol (2003). Internationally, however, this is only one of a number of forms of SEA that are applied to policy, and planning level initiatives and further variants and institution-specific adaptations, often with their own brand name, are being rolled out all the time, particularly in relation to lending and aid instruments used by donor agencies. These trends, in pushing the boundaries of SEA practice, expose new and residual issues about its role, theory and methodology.

This handbook is intended to provide a state-of-the-field review of SEA, bringing together a wide range of perspectives that both frame and focus the ongoing discourse on its role and contribution to decision-making. It has three interrelated objectives: to take stock of international experience with SEA; to highlight key aspects and areas of process development and application; and to probe issues related to the quality and effectiveness of SEA practice. Collectively, the chapters that follow provide a comprehensive, thematic survey of the dimensions and dynamics of the field. They document the multifaceted, cross-sectoral nature of SEA activity, the variety of institutional and policy contexts within which it is undertaken and the emerging linkages to other assessment, planning and decision-making instruments. Individually, the contributors take stock of SEA trends and issues through their own particular lens on the field, reflecting nuanced interpretations of the conventional wisdom and, in some cases, trenchant critiques of prevailing concepts and underlying assumptions.

This chapter provides an introduction to the handbook. It begins with a brief primer on the basic characteristics of the SEA process. Next, there is an overview of the background and structure of the book. A review of the main themes and chapter highlights follows. Such an upfront synthesis of the key messages of the book seemed the best way to introduce readers to a large body of information organized into 35 chapters written by nearly 50 contributors. In addition, more detailed thematic overviews have been prepared by their respective editors for certain sections that were considered to need greater definition, namely the linkages of SEA to other tools that are applied to similar purpose (Fischer) and SEA capacity development (Partidário). For other sections, readers may want to refer back to this chapter.

A brief profile of SEA

At base, SEA is a simple and straightforward concept, although perhaps deceptively so given the massive body of commentary and qualification that can be found in the critical literature of the field and in many of the pages in this book. Before starting down this ever widening road with its many branches and diversions (and the odd blind alley), it may be helpful to briefly identify the departure point, represented by some key dimensions of the SEA process that are more or less commonly understood and often drawn on in answering basic questions such as what is SEA, why is it important and how is it related to decision-making? In this section, these elements are taken to include the premise and purpose of SEA and the core precepts of application, leaving it to the next and subsequent chapters to discuss their elaboration and argumentation.

Broadly stated, the rationale of SEA is to ensure that environmental considerations are taken into account and inform higher levels of decision-making, including policies, plans and programmes (terms which mean different things in different contexts). The introduction of SEA has been an integral part of the development of EIA (although this is not the only evolutionary source) and, from that perspective, it responds partly to the limitations of EIA as traditionally applied only or largely to projects and specific actions. By excluding public policy and plan-making from examination, EIA on its own manifestly did not cover the range of government initiatives that matter environmentally. SEA rounds out and scales up the scope of review to the tier of development proposals above the project level, most importantly to genuinely strategic, agenda and direction setting decisions that shape the trajectory of economic growth with potentially significant implications for the use of land, resources and ecosystems. In that context, SEA can be applied to positive purpose as a means of promoting environmentally sound and sustainable development, shifting from a 'do least harm' to a 'do most good' approach.

This shift also reflects a hierarchy of aims of SEA, corresponding to progressively deeper levels of environmental integration in policy and plan-making, which may be represented as a transition from pale to dark green. In moving from one to the other, the progression of aims is more difficult to accomplish. A commonly accepted objective of SEA is to analyse and evaluate the potentially significant effects of a proposed initiative on the environment in order to support informed decision-making. Some commentators approximate SEA to this role of information-conveying and decision-assisting, emphasizing that environmental effects form only part of the broad mix of considerations addressed in policy and plan-making. By itself, however, this objective correlates with a relatively shallow (pale green) level of environmental integration (although potentially acting as a vector for long-term value change). Other commentators go beyond this minimalist stance and consider SEA should be undertaken to deliver more substantive objectives of contributing to environmental protection and sustainable development (variously cited in SEA legislation). If taken at face value, these aims (which are interrelated but not the same) reflect a deeper (dark green) and more challenging level of environmental integration.

Within any jurisdiction, a relatively standardized process typically is applied to meet the objectives enshrined in law or policy, for example, as exemplified in Directive 2001/42/EC. This approach varies institutionally and methodologically across the extended family of SEA procedures and diagnostic tools but there is broad agreement on certain characteristics or principles that are common or defining. For example, as a generic process, SEA is understood to be a systematic, proactive approach to analysing the potential environmental consequences of a proposed policy, plan or programme in order to ensure they are considered in decision-making. It is undertaken as an integral part of this process, beginning at an early phase of proposal formulation and identification of alternative courses of action. The SEA process itself follows a number of well-known steps that are organized sequentially, undertaken iteratively, tailored to purpose and thus carried out in full or in part. Commonplace elements of approach include consulting stakeholders, identifying likely environmental effects, evaluating their significance, determining measures to mitigate adverse impacts or enhance positive ones and reporting the findings to decision-makers. In addition, there are widely accepted principles of SEA good practice that are discussed in the next chapter and elsewhere in this volume.

Background and structure of the volume

In the last decade, the SEA literature has grown enormously and frequent conferences and workshops continue to be held on the subject. Despite considerable progress, there is a range of outstanding issues related to SEA process, practice and performance, including deep-rooted concerns and questions regarding the extent to which SEA achieves its aims, contributes to decision-making or leads toward positive outcomes. These matters have been a long-standing subject of critical evaluation and, more recently and particularly, have focused on the role and potential of SEA in facilitating sustainable development, moving along the spectrum from environmentally-specific to integrative approaches.

For more than a decade, annual meetings of the International Association for Impact Assessment (IAIA) have provided a forum for discussing these and related issues and collectively have contributed in no small measure to advancing the larger agenda of SEA theory and practice. In 2005 in Prague, IAIA held its first theme-specific conference additional to annual meetings to review progress with SEA. The intent was to hold an interactive forum covering key aspects and areas of the field. Although variously modified, all the chapters in this book are based on keynote papers or other materials prepared for the Prague conference (widely cited in the pages that follow). In that context, as many contributors note, they have drawn upon and benefited from the information and perspectives in supplementary papers and working discussions that took place at their specific topic sessions. The chapters of this book thus reflect, to varying degrees, some distillation of expert opinion as well as information from the usual sources.

The book is organized into six main parts, prefaced by this introduction. Part I covers the SEA systems that are in place in specific countries (Australia, Canada, New Zealand and the US), in developing regions (Africa, Asia, Latin America and Newly Independent States), within the European Union (EU) and under the UNECE SEA Protocol to the Espoo Convention on EIA in a Transboundary Context. The focus of Part II is on SEA practice in selected sectors (extractive industries, transport, water and coastal zone management) and the application of indicators in these and other areas. In Part III, the emphasis is on the use and linkages of SEA to other related fields and instruments (environmental management, spatial planning, landscape planning, biodiversity conservation and poverty reduction strategies). Part IV deals with cross-cutting issues in SEA (tiering, public participation and addressing health, cumulative effects and transboundary considerations, respectively). The concern in Part V is with ways and means of SEA process and capacity development (theory and research, knowledge building, guidance, follow-up, organizational strengthening and professional and institutional capacity-building). In Part VI, the focus is on sustainability assessment or appraisal and the relationship to SEA and EIA (theoretical frameworks and case applications). As the next section draws out, the boundaries between the above sections are arbitrarily drawn and there are many overlaps among the themes and subjects discussed in this book.

Part I: SEA frameworks and their implementation

In this section, the focus is on SEA legal and institutional frameworks and experience with their implementation in selected countries and regions including the EU. Within any jurisdiction, these arrangements constitute the foundations of the SEA regime and can be thought of as enabling conditions of good practice. As the chapters in this section attest, in the last decade especially, SEA legal and procedural developments have been considerable and extensive, reaching a critical mass that represents international take off. The European Directive (2001/42/EC) and its subsequent transposition into national law by 27 member states was a major impetus in that regard, approximately doubling the number of countries that then had provision for SEA. The conclusion of the UNECE SEA Protocol (signed by 35 countries and the EU at Kiev 2003) has added further momentum to this trend, although at the time of writing it had yet to come into force. However, as illustrated by the experience of a number of countries, SEA frameworks are one thing and their implementation is another matter again.

Australia: Ashe and Marsden describe the range of federal and state legislation under which SEA is carried out in Australia, where SEA experience dates back more than 30 years. At the national level, the Environment Protection and Biodiversity Conservation Act (1999) provides for discretionary (general) and mandatory (fisheries specific) application of SEA. Limited use of SEA has been made for general purposes to date but Ashe and Marsden consider its application to marine fisheries management plans has been highly successful, resulting in the certification of some 120 plans as ecologically sustainable (which, at first glance, appears to be an exemplary approach with few peers internationally). They also describe other SEA arrangements and elements that are applied federally or in different states (where development is reported to be uneven). Despite such progress, Ashe and Marsden conclude that SEA is still underutilized in Australia and see its future development as potentially converging with sustainability appraisal.

Canada: Sadler describes the SEA system established by the federal government under a Cabinet Directive (introduced 1990, various amendments). Nationally, this system has no strictly comparable provincial or territorial counterparts and, internationally, it may be of interest as the first of the 'new generation' of SEA frameworks established separately from EIA. As set out in the guidelines, the emphasis is on a flexible approach to SEA, tailored to the policy or planning circumstances of federal agencies and integrating environmental, economic and social considerations. This flexibility, as a series of evaluations and audits document, has a major downside, reflected in patchy compliance with the provisions of the Directive, basic weaknesses in process implementation and little or no monitoring of the consistency and quality of SEA practice. Despite several attempts at incremental reform, progress remains unsatisfactory and Sadler contends that, after nearly two decades, the Canadian SEA system has systemic failings that make it unfit for purpose. After more than 15 years of ineffective application, this system needs a radical overhaul.

New Zealand: Wilson and Ward describe the SEA-type arrangements that have been introduced in New Zealand under various provisions including legal frameworks such as the Resource Management Act (1991) and the Local Government Act (2002) or as elements of mandatory or *ad hoc* planning instruments such as, respectively, regional land transport strategies or urban growth strategies. SEA practice in New Zealand is said to typify an integrative approach that is seamlessly threaded or embedded in policy and plan-making, rather than separately named or delineated as such. In principle, Wilson and Ward consider this approach has considerable potential in terms of its scope and application, particularly as a sustainability instrument. In practice, however, they argue that too much is left to planners and analysts who lack the knowledge, tools and resources for the task and the absence of specific provision and formal requirements for SEA is becoming increasingly problematic. Building the skills base will help but the authors conclude that legal and institutional reforms may ultimately be needed to bolster the current integrative approach.

The US: Clark, Mahoney and Pierce describe SEA procedure and practice under the 1969 US National Environmental Policy Act (NEPA). NEPA regulations apply to all major actions proposed by federal agencies but, in practice, policies, plans and programmes go largely unexamined. Specifically, Clark et al note that only a 'handful' of programmatic environmental impact statements (PEIS), the main form of SEA implemented under NEPA, are completed each year. As their analysis suggests, the underuse of PEIS is deeply rooted in the institutional structure and political culture of decision-making within the US government and reinforced by recent legislative and regulatory developments, which have lessened NEPA requirements. Despite these trends, Clark et al present two innovative examples of SEA practice that illustrate business-case and ecosystem-based applications. They also dissect ten main challenges to the wider use of SEA in US policy-making (from poor understanding of the concept to disagreement about the merits of an integrative approach) and conclude that SEA must be flexibly adapted to the realities of decision-making, possibly through procedures outside those of NEPA.

Asian region: Hayashi, Song and Au describe the SEA systems and processes that have been introduced and implemented in the Asia region with a particular focus on east and southeast Asian countries where rapid changes are taking place. They underline the increasing recognition of SEA in this region and the diversity of approaches that have emerged in response to regional conditions and circumstances, such as variations in economic growth, political culture and institutional capacity. So far, SEA systems have been established in only a few countries or jurisdictions (for example, China, Hong Kong, South Korea and Vietnam) but more are in the process of doing so (for example, Indonesia, Malaysia and Thailand) or apply some form of SEA on a pilot or *ad hoc* basis (for example, Laos and Cambodia). Hayashi et al analyse SEA developments individually for this first group of countries (plus Japan) and comparatively for a larger group of east and southeast Asian countries, and distil key trends, issues and characteristics of SEA in this region. Despite increasing formalization of SEA in legislation, they conclude that many reservations and obstacles remain to be overcome and, among other things, call for greater regional cooperation and self-help.

Eastern Europe, Caucasus and Central Asia (EECCA): Cherp, Martonakova, Jurkeviciute and Gachechiladze-Bozhesku review the development of SEA systems in the newly independent states of Eastern Europe, Caucasus and Central Asia (EECCA). As former republics of the Soviet Union, these countries inherited a common machinery of centralized planning including EIA-type procedures that apply to project and strategic-level proposals. Cherp et al describe the evolution and reform of these so-called State Environmental Reviews (SER) and Assessment of Environmental Impacts (OVOS in the Russian abbreviation) systems and compare them to SEA frameworks and arrangements as internationally recognized. Their discussion highlights the persistence of SER/OVOS features with varying degrees of modification in the hybrid systems of SEA introduced in different EECCA countries, some relatively unchanged, others incorporating internationally accepted elements (for example, Moldova, Russia and Armenia). A profile of existing strengths, weaknesses, opportunities and threats that characterize SEA systems in the region indicates relatively slow progress towards meeting international standards and largely unfavourable trends in governance that hinder further improvements. In response, the authors call for a more discriminating, needs-focused approach to build SEA capacity in the EECCA region.

The EU: Sadler and Jurkeviciute profile the SEA systems of EU member states, focusing particularly on experience with the transposition and implementation of Directive 2001/42/EC. Long in the making, the SEA Directive covers certain plans and programmes and establishes the minimum procedural requirements that must be applied, including a number of member states that previously had made no provision for SEA. The authors note that initial progress in bringing the Directive into EU-wide force (post-2004) was uneven and slow and that questions remain about the compliance of legislation of some member states. In addition, Sadler and Jurkeviciute categorize the sizeable differences among member states in numbers of assessments being processed, relating them to underlying geopolitical divisions in approaches to governance. More tellingly, they enumerate emerging concerns about the state and quality of SEA practice, for example in undertaking key stages of the process such as determining scope and alternatives to be considered. At the same time, it is acknowledged that information on these issues is incomplete and, in that regard, much awaits the European Commission's review of the implementation of the Directive.

Southern Africa: Audouin, Lochner and Tarr review the development of SEA in southern Africa and the socio-ecological and geopolitical contexts that have shaped its evolution. They underline the dependency of the rural poor on natural resources that are under increasing pressures and stresses from human activities and the post-colonial trends that slowed acceptance of the concepts of environmental governance and sustainable development. While SEA frameworks have been introduced in what Audouin et al term 'a surprising number' of countries in the southern Africa region, their application is not necessarily supported by detailed requirements and is often found wanting. They profile the evolving body of examples of SEA-type processes that have been applied to policies, plans and programmes, notably in South Africa and as part of regional or transboundary initiatives, and argue that there is huge unrealized potential for SEA to have a much greater impact than it does at present on ecosystem and resource management in support of sustainable development and poverty reduction initiatives. More than in any other region, this relationship is pivotal to improving the livelihoods of poor people (see also Part III).

The SEA Protocol: Bonvoisin describes the background, requirements and characteristics of the SEA Protocol to the UNECE Espoo Convention on EIA in a Transboundary Context (1991). He outlines the scope of the Protocol, emphasizing its potential as a global legal instrument to which countries outside the UNECE region can accede and its mandatory application to plans and programmes and, on a discretionary basis, to policies and legislation beyond just a transboundary context. Although heavily influenced by the prior conclusion of European Directive 2001/42/EC, the Protocol has a number of important differences that are annotated by the author. In this context, Bonvoisin focuses specifically on what he calls 'operative provisions', such as those relating to objectives, means or elements of procedure and fields of application, namely policies and legislation, which are outside the scope of the Directive. He also annotates future directions for the implementation of the Protocol, such as promoting its ratification by the signatories, its accession by states outside the UNECE and its application to policies and legislation.

Part II: SEA application in certain sectors

In Part II, the focus is on SEA practice in a sector context. By many accounts, this is the most common area of SEA application and the sectors represented here are only a subset of those now covered. Transport and water, both represented here, are among the sectors where experience with SEA is most extensive. The reviews of both sectors are not so much concerned with SEA-specific applications as with how this process is embedded in sector planning, part of new approaches to transport planning and water management. By contrast, there is less experience with SEA application to pre-clear or regulate hydrocarbon or mineral development in a particular region or its use in coastal zone management. However, as indicated in this section, SEA practice is evolving in both areas and the early examples cited here may be taken as harbingers of the groundswell of interest in regional level assessment to help reconcile development opportunities with resource potentials.

SEA and transport planning: Tomlinson examines the evolving integration of SEA and transport planning, arguing that the transport sector is better placed than most to accommodate SEA and employ its potential to policy service. In that context, he notes the changing approach to transport planning that has taken place in many countries in response to common economic, environmental and social trends. Specifically, Tomlinson emphasizes the shift toward broader, community-based transport goals and consideration of a wider array of options to meet them, moving slowly away from the traditional reliance on building road infrastructure to cater for ever-increasing private vehicle use (often the focus of public opposition) toward the management of multi-modal networks. In this more integrated approach to transport system planning, Tomlinson considers SEA can provide a robust analytical tool to identify equity and environmental effects, highlight policy conflicts, trade-offs and alternatives to resolving them, and possibly serve as a mechanism for consensus building. He also recognizes that much needs to be done to fully embed SEA in transport planning including dealing with many issues identified already in SEA practice such as tiering EIA to SEA, appropriate participative processes and effects monitoring.

SEA and water management: Nooteboom, Huntjens and Slootweg describe the contribution that SEA can make to water management, which is rapidly emerging as one of the most urgent global issues of resource availability and potential conflict. They emphasize that the scale, jurisdictional complexity and asymmetry of water issues often resist efforts to find cost-effective technical solutions and instead require integrated, cooperative approaches to river basin and watershed management that encompass the linkages of land-use and water supply and quality. Nooteboom et al use the term 'water systems' to describe the institutionalized arrangements and practices for management and decision-making, enumerate their important characteristics including the value of SEA in providing sound information and facilitating transparent, participative planning, and draw lessons from several cases on how conditions for success in these key elements are created. Specifically, they are concerned not so much with SEA as with the role of cooperative instruments that support integrated water resource management and identify key areas where further progress is required. These include participative methods for multi-stakeholder participation and dialogue, integration of water management with spatial planning, climate change adaptation strategies and economic analysis, and new ways of bridging science, policy and implementation.

Regional sectoral assessment and extractive industries: Baker and Kirstein outline approaches to regional sectoral assessment (RSA), focusing on its application in the extractive sector. They use this term instead of SEA, arguing that current terminology does not adequately describe the different characteristics of RSA and notably its more limited scope in taking account of strategic alternatives in relation to energy or mining development in a defined geographical area. Specifically, Baker and Kirstein indicate that RSA (also called regional environmental impact assessment) may be used to evaluate the area-wide environmental effects of alternative development scenarios in order to establish the conditions to guide, but would not extend to examining whether mining or energy use represented an optimum use of a given area. The authors describe examples of RSA application (for example, in relation to the offshore oil and gas industry), enumerate its benefits for environmental protection and highlight key challenges including the need for improved methods for predicting regional impacts and moving towards integrated assessment of the impact of multi-sector development and use of an area.

SEA and coastal zone management: Govender and Trumbic discuss the potential of SEA to enhance coastal zone management (CZM), notably by identifying environmental opportunities and constraints for sustainable development of an intensively used, highly valued and relatively confined area. Specifically, they examine how SEA can be used to address issues of port planning as an integral part of CZM, using case examples from different parts of the world. As with water management, an integrated approach is considered essential to take account of the multiple uses and interactions in this zone and to ensure resource use that is both sustainable and adapted to local conditions and needs. In this context, Govender and Trumbic emphasize that SEA should be applied to strengthen CZM, building on steps and tools that both processes have in common, such as vulnerability mapping. To date, experience with SEA application has been in relation to CZM in general and port planning in particular, but the authors review several cases to distil emerging lessons and identify key challenges (such as the use of SEA to generate knowledge rather than to influence decision-making, for example).

Part III: SEA linkage to other instruments

In Part III, the focus is on functional linkages of SEA with other comparable or complementary instruments and tools that are deployed to similar purpose. SEA is widely understood to encompass a family of approaches and to form part of a broader set of ex ante and ex post strategic instruments for environmental planning and management. At this level, new tools have evolved and existing ones have been modified to address environmental impacts that have become more intensive or extensive and to respond to the sustainable development agenda. The concern here is to gain a better understanding of the potential and practical relationship among selected instruments, particularly how SEA fits into this spectrum and what are the pros and cons of seeking closer linkages with these tools, recognizing that much will depend on the policy context and jurisdictional arrangements that are in force.

Such issues have been the subject of increasing interest in SEA literature. The chapters in this section highlight key linkages of SEA and other tools, particularly in addressing major cross-cutting issues. Specifically, they highlight two broad themes: the role and contribution of SEA in responding to bellwether issues of biodiversity conservation and poverty reduction, which are the focus of dedicated strategies and specific tools; and the relationship and potential integration of SEA with more broadly based processes for spatial and landscape planning and environmental management. In the first category, the approaches and their linkages to SEA have been driven largely by international legal and policy obligations, enshrined, respectively, in the United Nations Convention on Biological Diversity (CBD) and the Millennium Development Goals (MDGs); in the second category, the processes are an established part of the public policy regime of many countries.

Thematic overview: Fischer takes stock of the instruments and perspectives discussed in this section (namely environmental management, landscape planning, biodiversity conservation, poverty reduction strategies and spatial planning). He underlines their individual and collective contribution in elevating the profile of environmental and equity issues that typically are under-represented in development policies, plans and programmes and suggests there is considerable benefit to linking SEA with closely related instruments in support of decision-making, provided the cultural context and institutional capacities are taken into account. In this regard, both the tools and scope of application are relatively diverse, encompassing issue-oriented and place-based or environmentally-grounded approaches to assess and manage the impacts of development in developed and developing countries.

SEA and environmental management systems (EMS) and beyond: Sheate discusses the importance of the relationship of SEA and EMS in facilitating follow-up and as a stepping stone to a wider analysis of linkages to other strategic instruments. He notes that the benefits of integration, widely touted in SEA literature, are not automatic, and emphasizes the need to maximize the benefits of using existing tools and approaches effectively. Sheate is adamant that the seemingly constant effort to 'develop' new tools (or less generously, 'to rename or reinvent the wheel') is counterproductive and wastes much time and energy to no discernable purpose. This is arguably a maxim for SEA process development generally and underlines the particular need for institution strengthening and capacity-building to secure the benefits of integration of tools and processes (see also Part V).

SEA and landscape planning: Hanusch and Fischer examine the linkages between SEA and landscape planning, drawing on the experience of four countries (Germany, Canada, Ireland and Sweden), focusing particularly on Germany where both instruments have statutory force and are widely implemented. They emphasize the contribution that landscape planning instruments can make to SEA, for example, in establishing environmental baselines and evaluating alternatives; note the main challenges of such approaches, such as more limited consideration of environmental impacts than is normally required for SEA; and caution that landscape ,planning is 'susceptible to the same general limitations and challenges of SEA'.

SEA as a biodiversity instrument: Treweek et al explore the use of SEA as a tool for biodiversity conservation and sustainable use of ecosystem goods and services, drawing on international experience and examples from a number of countries, particularly South Africa and India, to identify trends, issues and requirements for making this application more systematic and effective. Despite considerable progress, they emphasize that 'mainstreaming' biodiversity in development decision-making remains a major challenge and that there is little consensus about the merits of formalizing SEA for this purpose, although there is agreement on the value of adopting SEA-type approaches (for example, along the lines of guidance issued to support the CBD).

SEA as a poverty reduction instrument: Ghanimé, Risse, Levine and Sahou analyse evolving approaches to the application of SEA to Poverty Reduction Strategy Papers (PRSPs) as a key macro-policy instrument to identify the structural reforms and programmes needed to reduce poverty and achieve other MDGs. They focus on the lessons of case experience gained in several African developing countries (Benin, Ghana, Rwanda and Tanzania) and emphasize the role of SEA in mainstreaming the environment and integrating it with social equity, health and development considerations in recent versions of the PRSP process. But many issues remain outstanding and Ghanimé et al describe a series of measures needed to improve the application of SEA to PRSP.

SEA and spatial planning: Nelson evaluates the evolving relationship of SEA and spatial or land-use planning and profiles the current state of practice, drawing on the general literature and case studies presented at Prague to describe key aspects and dimensions of approach in what is probably the most extensive area of SEA application and experience. He stresses the range of national models and systems of spatial planning that have been established and the different types of SEA that apply to or are integrated into the process of plan-making, and notes the ongoing debate on how to best link them and to what purpose. Despite considerable variation in their context and focus, Nelson unpacks the common issues and lessons from the cross-section of international experience tabled at Prague, identifying key components for successful application of SEA for spatial planning.

Part IV: Cross-cutting issues in SEA

In Part IV, the focus is on a range of issues that cut across or underlie SEA implementation and practice. These comprise development and use of indicators, the role of public participation, consideration of health impacts and aspects, addressing cumulative effects and transboundary issues, respectively, and the tiering of SEA at different levels of application, including the relationship to EIA. By definition, these aspects and issues are well-known and the papers here can be loosely grouped into three main sections that refer respectively to: (a) matters bearing on the scope of SEA (the role of public participation and the consideration of health effects); (b) how to come to grips with old and new issues (cumulative and transboundary effects); and (c) aids to improving SEA practice in the form of indicators (analysis) and tiering (process and substantive integration).

Environmental indicators in SEA: Donnelly and O'Mahony describe the critical role and potential of environmental indicators in supporting a robust approach to SEA. They underline the complex process of developing and selecting appropriate, multifunctional indicators that track or predict change associated with plans or programmes against relevant objectives or criteria for environmental reporting (such as those listed in Annex I of Directive 2001/42/EC). According to the authors, little published material is available on the effective use of environmental indicators in SEA, much of the work on this subject is theoretical rather than practical and robust and rigorous frameworks still remain to be developed. In response, Donnelly and O'Mahony propose a 'simple and logical' methodology for developing plan-specific objectives, targets and indicators and list criteria against which to evaluate them for quality assurance (for example, to ensure their policy relevance and to cover a range of environmental receptors). Finally, they also consider the application of indicators to review SEA quality as represented in the environmental report (as required under Article 12 of Directive 2001/42/EC), drawing on Irish experience to identify lessons learned.

Public participation in SEA: This is a perennial theme of analysis and discussion in SEA literature, much of which centres around what constitutes good practice for this activity and how best to consult with stakeholders and the public at large in SEA of proposed policies and plans (which are often perceived by many citizens has having little or no immediate impact on their environment or well-being as compared to an EIA of a major project in a nearby location). Elling ploughs new theoretical ground in reflecting on the fundamental challenges of public participation in the SEA process and the underlying issues and matters that must be taken into account in conduct of this activity. He argues that the strategic and abstract character of SEA explains why public participation is so important and requires a different approach than that used in the EIA process. In his view, citizens are a means of activating a multidimensional concept of rationality that includes ethics and aesthetic values and not just the technical instrumentalism that remains the predominant model of SEA. The chapter moves the discourse beyond the conventional and repays careful reading.

SEA and health: Bond, Cave, Martuzzi and Nuntavorakarn discuss the trends, issues and options associated with integrating health into SEA as compared to developing a separate approach to strategic health assessment, recognizing that response will vary from country to country. In recent years, there has been increasing discussion of the relationship of SEA and health impact assessment (HIA). This debate has been driven by two key developments: the application of HIA at the policy level and the inclusion of health aspects in SEA, which is listed in the SEA Directive and features prominently in the SEA Protocol. Yet, the authors also point to the larger, underlying set of institutional and professional capacity issues that hinder progress on this front, such as the limited engagement of health experts in SEA process, and suggest areas for further work to address them. In that regard, future work on the implementation on the SEA Protocol (once ratified) could become an important driver for practical consideration of the relationship of SEA and health.

SEA and cumulative effects: Dixon and Thérivel describe cumulative impact assessment (CIA) as a counterpart to SEA, focusing on the resource and the impact on a receiving environment of the totality of activities rather than only assessing a proposed plan or programme. They recognize that analysing cumulative impacts is also an integral aspect of SEA legal frameworks, although practice is wanting, 'carried out half-heartedly and sporadically at best'. In addition, Dixon and Thérivel consider CIA methods to be 'in their infancy', particularly in relation to the urgency of addressing large-scale, significant cumulative impacts, such as climate change, biodiversity loss and imbalances in water supply and demand. Managing cumulative effects, in their view, represents the critical and hardest challenge; it involves complex issues of how to initiate behavioural change, bring together multiple actors with different mandates and reconcile divided jurisdictional responsibilities. So defined, cumulative effects management is best improved by reforms in governance and capacity-building initiatives, which are more difficult than giving effect to analytical improvements.

SEA and transboundary issues: Bonvoisin describes the use of SEA to take account of transboundary issues, distinguishing between SEA of national plans and programmes that have potentially significant environmental effects on the territory of another country and SEA of large-scale regional plans that extend over the boundaries of two or more countries. In the first case, the EU SEA Directive and UNECE SEA Protocol both include requirements for undertaking transboundary consultations with the affected country. These provisions, according to Bonvoisin, may also be used for the second type of transboundary issue, for management of shared resources such as lake or river basin, for example. While experience with SEA of transboundary effects is relatively limited, Bonvoisin analyses a mix of cases to draw lessons on difficulties encountered in practice and proposes ideas and procedures for their resolution including bilateral and multilateral arrangements and their facilitation through joint bodies, established either on a permanent or *ad hoc* basis.

Tiering to link SEA and EIA: Arts, Tomlinson and Voogd argue that tiering of SEA and EIA is an important notion in the literature of the field that has yet to be discussed critically. They note that the notion of 'tiering' a sequence of assessments, from statements of broad scope to those of narrower scope, has been long been championed, particularly as an approach to focus and relate EIA to prior order SEA of plans and programmes (for example, as indicated in article 3.2(a) of Directive 2001/42/EC). But, in their view, the concept of tiering as conventionally understood assumes a linear planning process and does not come to grips with the complexity of strategic decision-making processes that encompass horizontal and diagonal as well as vertical linkages, and the practice of tiering SEA and EIA has not yet become standard operational practice. Arts et al unpack issues related to tiering practice, identify SEA follow-up and 'onward scoping' as linked means for more effective transfer of information and issues, and use imagery and metaphor to describe the characteristics and enabling conditions of successful tiering (for example, 'bridging islands of assessment in a sea of decisions').

Part V: SEA process development and capacity-building

SEA process development has been a perennial theme of discussion in the literature on the field, dating from its early form under NEPA and continuing through its subsequent evolution and adaptation within more and more jurisdictions. This discussion has been and still is wide-ranging; it cuts across or touches on many areas and aspects of SEA study and analysis and this volume is no exception. Many chapters, other than those in this section, contribute to our understanding of SEA process development (for example, reviews of institutional arrangements in different countries or regions of the world). The emphasis in Part V is on certain underlying components and challenges of SEA process development, including how to address them through capacity-building programmes and measures. Overall, perhaps what stands out most is the scope and diversity of elements that now enter into consideration as part of discourse on how to strengthen the SEA process or to improve its implementation, and the variety of perspectives that are brought to bear.

Thematic overview: Partidário discusses the main themes and areas of concerns with regard to SEA process development and capacity-building. She highlights the key themes and core messages from Part V and the actions and priorities that can be taken to advance the common objective of SEA improvement. These are analysed under three main headings: improving standards for SEA; better capacity for decision-making towards sustainable development; and acknowledging diverse interpretations of the rationale of SEA. Noting there is much still to learn about SEA, Partidário calls for greater clarification of its purpose, including the need to sort out the overlap with EIA. In doing so, she emphasizes the importance of recognizing the rich legacy of SEA practice and experience in multiple contexts, the emerging use of SEA as a sustainability tool and the richer understanding of SEA development that can be gained from probing decision theory and models of governance among other areas.

SEA theory and research: Bina, Wallington and Thissen argue that very little attention has been given to the conceptual basis of SEA although there have been continuing calls to do so. In their view, the ambiguities and contradictory interpretations concerning the role and future direction of this process threaten its viability and need to be resolved as a matter of priority. From that perspective, they discuss the issues related to three connected themes relevant to theory development, namely the substantive purposes of SEA, the strategies for achieving them and methods and tools for their operational implementation. After dissecting these issues, the authors endorse environmental sustainability as the substantive key 'to carving out a definitive space' for SEA in policy and plan-making, which requires a strategy that combines interactive and analytical processes and selects or adapts appropriate techniques to a particular situation.

SEA capacity-building: Partidário and Wilson outline current trends and issues of SEA capacity-building, review examples and lessons of experience in this area that were discussed at the Prague workshop and summarize principles and measures to strengthen professional and institutional capabilities in applying SEA to inform decision-making. They define the objective of capacity-building as developing the process and methodology of SEA and the scope of activities includes strengthening SEA frameworks, structures and participating organizations through guidance and training of practitioners. Drawing on a range of experience, including chapters from other sections in this book, Partidário and Wilson identify policy, institutional and technical drivers in SEA capacity-building, principles for improving its influence on decision-making and priorities for addressing problem areas.

SEA guidance: Schijf reviews SEA guidance documents and manuals and considers their role and contribution in supporting SEA good practice. Noting these materials have been rolled out in ever greater numbers in recent years, Schijf describes the different types and levels of formal guidance from implementation of legal and procedural requirements established by national jurisdictions to SEA application in relation to specific sectors or spatial plans and the resource manuals and toolkits that supplement them (particularly at the international level). The author also makes the case both for customizing SEA guidance to purpose and the targeted audience and for better harmonization among different approaches. She also outlines lessons and examples of good practice in preparing SEA guidance, recognizing that there has been little systematic evaluation of such documents and their impact on effective application.

SEA institutional challenges and the search for appropriate organizations: Kørnøv and Dalkmann discuss the social and organizational dynamics that influence SEA process development and implementation and shape the use that is made of reports and findings. These interactions have been given increasing attention recently in SEA discourse and the authors dissect the key factors at play. Specifically, Kørnøv and Dalkmann analyse the role of formal and informal institutional structures, the use and influence of political power and the relationship among key actors (politicians, administrators, stakeholders and consultants), and emphasize the importance of communication and learning processes that bridge differences in knowledge and preferences among these groups. In their view, for the SEA process to have an impact on decision-making, these four institutional challenges need to be better understood and reflected in a search for appropriate organizational arrangements.

SEA follow-up: Cherp, Partidário and Arts discuss the role of follow-up in SEA process development, beginning with the recognition that it is derived from similar principles and rationale to EIA follow-up but addresses more complex challenges, taking account of factors such as uncertainty and deviation between the formulation and implementation of strategic initiatives. They review the key elements of SEA follow-up and the multiple tracks that may be followed in linking strategic decision processes and different types of implementation activities. In this context, SEA follow-up is seen as particularly important for integrating environmental considerations into implementation activities, balancing the traditional emphasis on strategy formulation (which is considered a non-linear process). As the authors note, the ideas and models discussed remain to be tested empirically and they provide some pointers on practice such as the benefit of undertaking SEA follow up throughout the life cycle of an initiative.

SEA knowledge: Van Gent reviews the role of SEA knowledge centres and networks for professional exchange, describes their function and activities and profiles the resource, guidance, training materials and toolkits that are available. Specific details on the types of information and services of selected SEA knowledge centres are organized in a series of boxes. In addition, van Gent discusses issues of sourcing, financing and assuring quality of web-based information and considers future directions for interactive learning and sharing of ideas and experiences. As she emphasizes, although these centres serve different groups and interests, a common, larger challenge is how to keep information up-to-date, to facilitate knowledge exchange among SEA practitioners, and to create synergies with particular regard to SEA training where different manuals have been developed by international agencies for use in development cooperation. Here van Gent suggests that content sharing through licensing could facilitate the design of training courses that are tailored to needs.

Part VI: Toward integrated sustainability assessment

The emergence of sustainability assessment (or appraisal as some prefer) may be seen as both the next phase of SEA and a more encompassing, generic approach that integrates the economic, environmental and social dimensions of sustainable development in all forms of public policy analysis and review (rather than only applied as part of an EIA or SEA regime). In either case, SEA can be seen as an important procedural and analytical stepping stone toward a more systematic consideration of sustainable development issues in policy and planning options and decisions. Aspects and elements of an integrated, sustainability-directed approach are evident already in SEA concept and practice, although this dimension can be overstated or exaggerated. The relationship of SEA and sustainability assessment was the focus of active debate at the Prague conference and afterwards as the subject of special issues of journals of the field. In Part VI, there are two perspectives on sustainability assessment concepts and methodology and their application; they conclude the volume on a theme that many consider to be a future orientation of SEA development and capacity-building.

From SEA to sustainability assessment: Pope and Dalal-Clayton describe this shift as an attempt to direct decision-making at all levels toward sustainability purpose. They explore the concept of sustainability, taking pains to expose the limitations of the 'three pillar' approach as reductionist rather than truly integrative in relating economic, social and environmental considerations. In considering alternatives to this approach, Pope and Dalal-Clayton focus on process design to promote integration using broad steps that are embedded already in assessment methodology and making more effective use of governance and consultative procedures (while also recognizing that institutional reforms may be required in some jurisdictions). The authors pitch the discussion 'largely at a conceptual level', reflecting their view of sustainability as a concept that challenges notions of assessment and what constitutes good practice and recognizing that much remains to be done in translating sustainability assessment into operational terms. They provide initial pointers on how this can be done, citing emerging experience and cases (for example, in the UK and western Australia).

Assessment for sustainable development: Hacking and Guthrie also discuss how assessment could be redirected towards sustainable development by delineating a theoretical framework and illustrating its application to the mining sector, using six case studies. Based on the literature of the field, they identify three key features of 'strategicness', 'comprehensiveness' and 'integratedness' that distinguish sustainable development-directed assessment. As normative concepts, Hacking and Guthrie recognize these are largely untested; however, they argue there is empirical evidence to indicate that the use of EIA, SEA and other forms of assessment have contributed to positive outcomes including elements of sustainable development. Specifically, they analyse and compare several mining projects that exemplify 'best practice' but incorporate different forms of assessment (for example, SEA, cost benefit analysis) to test for the representation of sustainable development-directed features. The authors focus particularly on the concept of 'strategicness' and its relationship to project-level assessment, which can have SEA-type features but cannot be stretched too far in that direction unless an effective tiering mechanism is in place (recognizing these are more promoted than applied).

Retrospect and prospect

This volume brings together a considerable body of information and many different perspectives on the state of SEA practice and its theoretical and methodological underpinnings. In taking stock of the field overall, three major trends stand out:

1   SEA is a fast-moving and diversifying field reflected in legal innovations, process developments, new areas of application and take up in developing countries.
2   SEA now encompasses an extended family of instruments which have the same basic aim (integrating environment into policy and plan-making) but vary in provision, scope and process elements, particularly notable is the difference between the entrenchment of EIA-based procedure in the

European SEA Directive and the UNECE SEA Protocol and the array of SEA-type tools that have evolved within multilateral and bilateral aid agencies in support of policy-based lending and development cooperation.
3   Emerging directions include the shift toward a more integrative approach (sustainability appraisal) that seems to be generally welcomed, provided environmental concerns are not downplayed in the process (which some see as a serious threat).

Despite considerable progress, many concerns remain regarding the overall state of SEA practice. Three common areas of shortfall are:

1   Inconsistent implementation of the SEA process, reflected in failures to meet basic requirements within individual jurisdictions (a low clearance bar) or, more generally, to approximate to internationally agreed principles (a higher standard that, among other things, calls for SEA to be adapted to the context and content of specific proposals).
2   Unsatisfactory quality of SEA inputs and outputs, reflected in analytical weakness and insufficient reports that do not provide the information necessary for decision-making (thereby failing to meet a basic test of SEA effectiveness).
3   Little or no evidence of performance in delivering positive results and outcomes, reflected by the lack of follow-up and research on the linkage of SEA, decision-making, policy and plan implementation and delivery and environmental benefits (which represents an important area for further research).

PART I

SEA FRAMEWORKS

2
SEA in Australia

John Ashe and Simon Marsden

Introduction

Australia has a federal system of government with nine separate jurisdictions, comprising the Australian (federal or Commonwealth) government, six state governments and two self-governing territories. Each has its own environmental impact assessment (EIA) legislation and procedures. Formal provision for strategic environmental assessment (SEA) varies between jurisdictions. There are, however, many examples of environmental assessment of policies, plans and programmes (PPP) not explicitly described as SEA that are part of the broader SEA family. They include public inquiries, assessments conducted under land-use planning and environmental protection legislation, and assessments of natural resource use.

In this chapter, we focus principally on the forms of SEA that are conducted under legislation and that involve the assessment of a PPP that includes the preparation and public exhibition of an impact statement or similar document. The chapter begins with an examination of SEA at the Australian government level. It is followed with an examination of SEA at the state–territory level. At the end of the chapter, our conclusions and a summary statement are presented.

SEA at the Australian government level

SEA under Section 146 of the EPBC Act

The Environment Protection and Biodiversity Conservation Act 1999 (EPBC Act) is the principal piece of environmental assessment legislation at the Australian government level. Under Section 146 of the EPBC Act, the Environment Minister may agree with a person responsible for the adoption or implementation of a PPP that an assessment be made of the impacts of actions under a PPP on a matter protected by a provision of Part 3 of the Act. Part 3 identifies seven matters of national environmental significance. They are:

- World Heritage properties.
- National Heritage places.

Table 2.1 *Profile of SEA in Australia*

Main trends and issues	Australia has substantial experience over the last 30 years with assessments of PPPs. These assessments have been conducted under a variety of legislative mechanisms.
	Federal EIA legislation (EPBC Act) includes discretionary SEA provisions of general application and mandatory provisions for SEA of fisheries. Little use has been made of the mandatory provisions but more than 120 fisheries have been assessed.
	Strategic assessments are also required for proposed National Environment Protection Measures and for Australia's overseas aid programme.
	Australia's oceans and the marine environment have been the focus of considerable SEA-type activity in recent years. This includes fisheries assessments, the SEA of petroleum exploration, the preparation of regional marine plans and the strategic assessment of defence activities in the Great Barrier Reef Marine World Heritage Area.
	A recent development at the federal level is the commencement of trials of a number of non-statutory regional strategic plans in areas with high development pressure and potential impacts on matters of national environmental significance.
	SEA provisions at the state and territory level vary greatly between jurisdictions ranging from explicit to non-existent. A number of jurisdictions have provision for SEA-type assessment of environment protection policies, land-use plans and other types of management plans.
Key findings and conclusions	Although there are many examples of SEA-type assessment in Australia over a long period of time, much of this has been *ad hoc* in nature, has not used the language of SEA and in some instances may best be characterized as 'para SEA'.
	The mandatory SEA provisions for fisheries at the federal level have been very successful and may be contrasted with the limited use of the discretionary provisions intended for more general application. Recent amendments to the discretionary provisions may provide greater incentive and payoff to proponents and industry sectors to encourage their involvement in strategic assessment.
	Strategic assessment also seems to be working well in some niche areas, for example, in relation to National Environment Protection Measures and Australia's overseas aid programme.
	The assessment of natural resources is an area where successful and innovative strategic assessments have been conducted and provide models suitable for wider application.
	Australian experience suggests to some participants in the SEA process that SEA can be extremely successful and that successful SEA can be mandatory or voluntary. The perceived benefits of SEA determine greatly the willingness of stakeholders to become involved and the quality of inputs to the process.

Table 2.1 *(continued)*

	Overall, it would appear that SEA is being underutilized in Australia despite the existence of specific SEA legislation. The use of SEA is particularly uneven at the state and territory level.
Future directions	The Australian government views strategic assessment of fisheries as being a particularly successful element of the federal legislation but has been concerned about the limited use of the discretionary provisions in the legislation and has recently introduced amendments to encourage greater take-up of strategic assessment.
	The future development of SEA, both at the federal and state–territory level is likely to reflect the trend in EIA and other environmental legislation of incorporating sustainability objectives. It is likely that we will see a convergence of SEA and sustainability appraisal in coming years.

- Ramsar wetlands of international significance.
- Listed threatened species and ecological communities.
- Listed migratory species.
- The Commonwealth marine environment.
- Nuclear actions.

Part 3 also protects the environment on Commonwealth land and the environment generally in relation to actions by the Commonwealth or Commonwealth agencies anywhere in the world.

The SEA provisions in the EPBC Act apply to the relevant impacts of 'actions' implemented or adopted under a PPP. The Act (Section 523) defines an 'action' as including:

(a) a project;
(b) a development;
(c) an undertaking;
(d) an activity or series of activities; and
(e) an alteration of any of the things mentioned in (a), (b), (c) or (d).

As with all legislation, the EPBC Act is subject to judicial interpretation. In recent years, decisions have been handed down on the meaning of several key terms that may affect the interpretation of SEA provisions in the Act (McGrath, 2005).

The EPBC Act specifies the matters to be provided for in a Section 146 agreement. In certain circumstances, a Section 146 agreement may also provide for the assessment of the impacts of actions on matters not protected by Part 3 which are to be taken in a state or self-governing territory and there is agreement between the Environment Minister and the appropriate State or Territory Minister to do so (Section 146(1A)). A strategic assessment may reduce or remove the need for subsequent environmental assessment for actions under a PPP. Under Section 87 of the EPBC Act, the Minister, when deciding on the assessment approach for a controlled action,[1] must take into account the information about the impacts of the action included in a strategic assessment report on the PPP under which the action is to be taken. If the impacts of an action have already been assessed during a strategic assessment, the Minister could decide, for example, that the impacts should be assessed by means of preliminary documentation rather than a more onerous form of assessment such as a public environment report or an environmental impact statement. Also, if the Minister endorses a PPP embodied in a management plan in force under a law, the Minister may make a declaration under Section 33, or make a bilateral agreement, declaring that actions approved in accordance with the management plan do not need approval for the purposes of a specified provision of Part 3.

Marsden (2002) has evaluated Section 146 against the 'Principles of SEA' identified in a report prepared for the International Study into the Effectiveness of Environmental Assessment (Sadler and Verheem, 1996, p79). Although concluding that the legal implementation of SEA requirements by the Commonwealth is a step in the right direction, he identifies a number of weaknesses in the legislation. They include, for example, the voluntary nature of the SEA provisions and the dependence on ministerial discretion, and the limitations on the scope of environmental matters that may be considered in an SEA.

Although the EPBC Act commenced in July 2000, by June 2006 only two discretionary strategic assessments had been initiated under Section 146, and neither of those assessments had been completed. The two assessments are: (a) a strategic assessment of the environmental impacts of offshore petroleum exploration and appraisal activities in Commonwealth marine waters (see Box 2.1); and (b) a strategic assessment of major military exercises. It would appear that little use has been made of these provisions because of a perceived lack of benefit to proponents and industry sectors. In light of the poor take-up of the SEA provisions, the government introduced amendments to the EPBC Act in late 2006,[2] designed to provide greater incentives to authorities and proponents to engage in strategic assessments, bioregional planning and conservation agreements under the EPBC Act. These amendments are intended to make it easier for developments to be considered earlier in the planning process and in strategic and regional contexts. New Section 146B enables the Minister to approve an action or class of actions without further environmental assessment provided it is undertaken in accordance with the requirements of a PPP that has been endorsed under a Section 146 strategic assessment.

Strategic assessment of fisheries

Part 10 of the EPBC Act includes provision for the mandatory strategic assessment of Commonwealth fisheries.[3] The Act requires that the Australian Fisheries Management Authority (AFMA) must make agreements under Section 146 for the assessment of the impacts of actions in fisheries managed under the Fisheries Management Act 1991 (FMA). Under the FMA, AFMA must determine plans of management for all fisheries unless it determines that a plan of management is not warranted for a particular fishery. A Section 146 agreement must be made whenever it is proposed to make a plan of management for a fishery or a determination not to have a plan. An agreement

Box 2.1 *Strategic assessment of offshore petroleum exploration and appraisal activities*

On 27 September 2001, the Minister for Industry, Science and Resources and the Minister for the Environment and Heritage agreed to undertake a strategic assessment of offshore petroleum exploration and appraisal activities in Commonwealth marine waters. The assessment is examining the environmental effects of all aspects of exploration activities that fall within the jurisdiction of the Commonwealth government under the Petroleum (Submerged Lands) Act 1967 (PSL Act). The scope of the assessment covers the selection and release of offshore petroleum exploration acreage, the award of exploration titles, exploration activities (airborne surveys, seismic surveys, exploration drilling) and appraisal activities.

The terms of reference for the assessment were finalized in September 2002. They include, among other things, a requirement to describe the potential relevance of the strategic assessment to decision-making under the EPBC Act in relation to a proposed action under the Offshore Petroleum Program and the scope for accreditation under the EPBC Act of assessment processes under the PSL Act.

The draft strategic assessment report, prepared by the Department of Industry, Science and Resources (DISR) was released for public comment in January 2005 for a six-week period. It identifies five areas for further consideration through the Standing Committee on Environment and Approval Processes for Offshore Acreage.[4] They relate principally to the assessment processes to be followed in relation to proposed petroleum exploration and appraisal activities.

A central issue in the assessment has been the impact of offshore seismic activities on whales and other cetaceans. In May 2007, the Department of the Environment and Water Resources issued EPBC Act Policy Statement 2.1 – Interaction Between Offshore Seismic Exploration and Whales, replacing the October 2001 guidelines.

was required within five years of the commencement of the EPBC Act (by 16 July 2005) for all fisheries that did not have a plan at that commencement date.

The EPBC Act also requires that the Minister administering the Torres Strait Fisheries Act 1984 must make agreements under Section 146 for the assessment of actions permitted by policies or plans for managing fishing in Torres Strait. All policies or plans were required to be covered by an agreement within five years of the commencement of the EPBC Act. A further agreement for strategic assessment must be made if the Environment Minister and the Minister administering the FMA agree that the impacts of actions in a fishery are significantly greater than previously assessed.

Fisheries assessments conducted under Section 146 agreements also include assessment of impacts required for other purposes under the EPBC Act; that is, Part 13 – interaction with protected species; and Part 13A – export of native species. In addition to assessments of Commonwealth fisheries conducted under Part 10, fisheries assessments are also conducted for State and Northern

Territory fisheries for the purposes of Parts 13 and 13A. All fisheries assessments, whether conducted under Part 10 or otherwise, are conducted against the *Guidelines for the Ecologically Sustainable Management of Fisheries* (Environment Australia, 2001).

The Act makes provision for the Minister to accredit a fisheries management plan or policy for the purposes of Part 9, Part 13 and Part 13A of the Act. Fisheries operations conducted in accordance with an accredited management plan or policy are thereby approved for the purposes of these Parts of the Act.

As of June 2006, more than 120 fisheries assessments had been conducted. Box 2.2 illustrates the operation of the strategic assessment of fisheries for the Heard Islands and McDonald Islands (HIMI) fishery.

Box 2.2 *Strategic assessment of Heard Island and McDonald Islands (HIMI) Fishery*

On 31 May 2001, the Minister for the Environment and Heritage signed an agreement with AFMA under Section 146 for a strategic assessment to be carried out of the draft HIMI Fishery Management Plan. Terms of reference required inclusion of the following:

- A description of the potential impacts on the environment.
- An analysis of the nature and extent of the likely impacts.
- An assessment of whether impacts are likely to be unknown, unpredictable or irreversible.
- An analysis of the significance of the potential impacts.

Any environmental effects were to be evaluated against *Guidelines for the Ecologically Sustainable Management of Fisheries* (Environment Australia, 2001), consisting of objectives and overarching principles. Principle 1 is concerned with overfishing and Principle 2 with minimization of impacts upon the ecosystem, including by-catch, endangered, threatened and protected species.

On 1 September 2001, the draft SEA Report and Management Plan were released for public comment. After consultation ended, the Report was amended to take account of submissions received. A final Assessment Report and the draft Management Plan were submitted to the Department of the Environment and Heritage (DEH) for an evaluation against the Guidelines on 19 December 2001, to ensure that the assessment had been carried out correctly and in order for the DEH to advise the Minister whether the draft Management Plan should be accredited. In April 2002 the assessment by the Marine and Water Division of the DEH was released.

The assessment commented only to the extent to which the (trawl) fishery currently impacts on target and non-target species and the broader marine environment. If fishing methods change in the future (to longlining, for example), another assessment will be required. Overall it concluded that the fishery is well managed and operates in accordance with the Guidelines. The management regime was considered sufficiently precautionary and capable of controlling, monitoring and enforcing the level of take from the fishery, while ensuring stocks are fished sustainably.

However, concerns were expressed regarding impacts on a number of by-catch species, with a recommendation that risk assessments and mitigation strategies are completed for these species. The most significant concern is the illegal, unreported and unregulated fishing of the Patagonian toothfish, with a recommendation made to investigate the extent to which HIMI and neighbouring island groups (the Kerguelen Islands) share straddling stocks. Habitat protection for benthic communities was another concern and partly as a result, it was recommended that a Category 1A marine protected area (MPA) should be established in order to protect the ecological sustainability of the fishery.

In the light of all of the above, the DEH considered that the actions of the fishery would not have an unacceptable or unsustainable impact on the marine environment and recommended the accreditation of the draft Management Plan. Following the Minister's accreditation it was necessary for the Management Plan to be tabled in Parliament; as there were no objections the Plan came into force. The HIMI Marine Reserve (which includes the MPA) was subsequently established in October 2002. The 65,000km² reserve provides for the protection of the benthic communities, land-based predators and protected species, as well as providing reference areas for impact monitoring.

The SEA of the HIMI fishery can be contrasted with measures for the management of Australia's islands and oceans. Although Sections 147–153 of the EPBC Act require strategic assessments of Australia's fisheries, Section 146 is discretionary for other strategic assessments, including those of management plans for protected areas. Following the declaration of the HIMI Marine Reserve, a management plan was required under Section 362 of the EPBC Act. Taking into account submissions received during an initial public comment period from March–May 2003, the draft Marine Reserve Management Plan (prepared by the Australian Antarctic Division) included the following:

- Comprehensive measures to prevent the introduction of alien species from human activities.
- Measures to ensure protection of important terrestrial and marine species, habitats and ecosystems.
- Measures to interpret the cultural heritage values associated with 19th century sealing activities and the earliest Australian Antarctic Research Expedition.

Despite acknowledgement in the Plan that the relationship between the reserve and the fishery is vital to the maintenance of the values of both, the Reserve Management Plan was neither assessed individually nor in combination with the AFMA Fisheries Plan, the assumption being that there is no need to do so because the former is designed to avoid environmental impacts. In 2005, the Minister approved the Marine Reserve Management Plan and, following the Plan being tabled in Parliament, it subsequently came into force.

Regional marine planning

Australia's Oceans Policy, released in 1998, commits Australia to integrated ecosystem-based management of Australia's oceans and the preparation of regional marine plans (RMPs). The Oceans Policy identifies strategic assessment as a key mechanism in the development, endorsement and implementation of RMPs. RMPs are designed to integrate sectoral commercial interests and conservation requirements to prevent conflict regarding resource access and allocation.

In October 2005, the Minister for the Environment and Heritage announced that the regional marine planning process would be brought directly under federal environmental law. Under this approach, regional marine plans will be prepared as bio-regional plans under Section 176 of the EPBC Act. As the Minister must have regard to a bio-regional plan in making any decision under the Act to which the plan is relevant, the change means that RMPs will now have statutory force (Section 176(5)). The changes announced by the Minister are part of moves to give new impetus to Australia's Oceans Policy and to bring the development of MPAs within the broader regional marine planning programme.

RMPs are prepared by the National Oceans Office, now part of DEH. Work on the Southeast Regional Plan has been completed (see Box 2.3). Work is underway on the Northern Region and Torres Strait Plans.

Box 2.3 *Southeast Regional Marine Plan*

The Southeast Marine Region comprises marine areas off Victoria, Tasmania (including Macquarie Island), southern New South Wales and eastern South Australia, comprising some 2 million square kilometres. Development of the Southeast Regional Marine Plan began in April 2000 and included the following components:

- **Scoping:** Including the release of a scoping paper and a 'snapshot' document providing an overview description of the region.
- **Assessment:** Preparation and release of assessment reports in relation to six themes: (a) biological and physical characteristics; (b) resource uses; (c) impacts on the ecosystem; (d) community and cultural values; (e) indigenous uses and values; and (f) management and institutional arrangements.
- **Discussion paper:** Release of a discussion paper to assist public input to the planning process.
- **Draft plan:** Release of the draft Southeast Regional Marine Plan, for a three-month public consultation period.
- **Final plan:** Released in April 2004.

The plan was developed by the National Oceans Office with extensive input from government and interest groups, and with public consultation at all stages of the process.

Box 2.4 *SEA of defence activities in the Great Barrier Reef World Heritage Area*

The Great Barrier Reef region is used by the Australian Defence Force (ADF) and other agencies for a wide variety of military activities. These activities are subject to the Great Barrier Reef Marine Park Act 1975, the EPBC Act and other Commonwealth and Queensland legislation.

An SEA, based on risk assessment, undertaken by the Australian Department of Defence was finalized in January 2006. The overall objective of the assessment was to facilitate sustainable military activities in the Great Barrier Reef World Heritage Area and contiguous areas.

The three components of the assessment were:

1   Description and quantification of the full range of defence activities undertaken in the Great Barrier Reef World Heritage Area by the ADF and defence contractors.
2   Consideration of the environmental implications of these activities, particularly with respect to World Heritage values and the regulatory framework within which they are controlled.
3   Review of the management framework within which these activities are planned, assessed and controlled to reduce environmental risk.

The assessment concluded that defence activities in the Great Barrier Reef World Heritage Area are unlikely to have significant negative effects on the World Heritage values of the area or upon socio-economic values of the Great Barrier Reef region. The Great Barrier Reef Marine Park Act accepted the SEA in March 2006. In light of the favourable outcome of the assessment, the Authority and the Department of Defence have agreed that routine military training exercises will not need to be individually referred if they meet agreed requirements.

SEA of defence activities in the Great Barrier Reef World Heritage Area

As a separate exercise from the SEA of major military exercises under the EPBC Act (see above) a strategic assessment of defence activities in the Great Barrier Reef World Heritage Area was completed in early 2006 (see Box 2.4).

SEA of National Environment Protection Measures[5]

The National Environment Protection Council (NEPC) is a Commonwealth–State–Territory statutory body with law-making powers established under the National Environment Protection Council Act 1994 (Commonwealth) (NEPC Act) and corresponding state and territory legislation. The Council members are Ministers appointed by the participating jurisdictions. The Council has two primary functions: (a) to make National Environment Protection Measures (NEPMs); and (b) to assess and report on their implementation and effectiveness in participating jurisdictions. NEPMs are described by the Council as 'broad framework-setting statutory instruments defined in NEPC legislation' (NEPC, 2005, p101). They outline agreed national objectives for protecting particular aspects of the environment and may consist of any combination of goals, standards, protocols and guidelines.

As of May 2006, seven NEPMs had been prepared, dealing with ambient air quality, national pollutant inventory, movement of controlled waste, used packaging materials assessment of site contamination, diesel vehicle emissions and air toxins.

Before making an NEPM, the NEPC must prepare a draft and an impact statement dealing with a range of matters, including environmental and social impacts.[6] Impact statements are prepared in accordance with an NEPC protocol. The draft NEPM and the impact statement are made available for public consultation for a period of at least two months The NEPC must have regard to the impact statement and submissions received during public consultation in deciding whether to make an NEPM.

SEA of Australia's overseas aid programme

Under Section 160 of the EPBC Act, Australia's overseas aid agency (AusAID) must obtain and consider advice from the Environment Minister when entering into a contract, agreement or arrangement for the implementation of a project that has, will have or is likely to have a significant impact on the environment anywhere in the world. In order to meet its obligations under the EPBC Act and its own policy requiring potential environmental impacts to be considered when designing and implementing aid activities, AusAID has adopted an environmental management system (EMS). The EMS includes a 'strategic environmental assessment' component, requiring an evaluation of the environmental impacts of a policy, programme, plan, country or regional strategy or sector strategy or its alternative and incorporation of the SEA findings into the policy, programme, plan or strategy (AusAID, 2003).

Keen and Sullivan (2005, p646) comment that the introduction of the EPBC Act has forced a closer relationship between AusAID and DEH for the purpose of undertaking strategic assessments. They observe that the coordinated and strategic assessment of several large regional projects, such as the recent Pacific programme concerning the removal of persistent organic pollutants (POPs) involved several government agencies, the South Pacific Regional Environment Programme (SPREP) and partner countries. Their view is that such an assessment forestalls unexpected demands for referrals, alerts DEH to potentially significant activities, facilitates a consistent 'whole of government' perspective from Australia, and opens the early assessment process to regional partner participation. They consider internal reviews of the POPs programme have been extremely positive, suggesting that strategic assessment has helped to build a strong programme design and environmental management plan (Keen and Sullivan, 2005, p646).

Regional strategic plans (RSPs)

RSPs are non-statutory strategic assessments by DEH of regional areas identified as areas with high developmental pressures and potential impacts on matters of national environmental significance. DEH is conducting the trials in an effort to engage more proactively in key regions than is possible through the application of project-level EIA under the EPBC Act.

As of June 2006, four trial RSPs were in progress, covering the Bunbury–Busselton region in southwest Western Australia; the Greater Geelong area in Victoria; Magnetic Island, Queensland; and Mission Beach, Queensland. Impacts of particular concern include impacts on Word Heritage areas, Ramsar sites and threatened species and ecological communities.

Among other things, it is hoped that the development of RSPs will facilitate proactive interaction between the Commonwealth's responsibilities under the EPBC Act and land-use planning at the state, regional and local level. There is potential for RSPs to become vehicles for strategic assessments under Section 146 of the EPBC Act or bio-regional plans under Section 176 of the EPBC Act.

Strategic assessments of forest resources

Australia has for many years conducted natural resource planning processes which have many of the characteristics of SEA. Of particular note are the public inquiries conducted by the Resource Assessment Commission (RAC) and the Regional Forest Agreement (RFA) process.

Resource Assessment Commission (RAC)

Between 1989 and its disbandment in 1993,[7] the RAC conducted three major inquiries, concerning: (a) the use and management of Australia's forests and timber resources; (b) mining in the Kakadu Conservation Zone; and (c) the use and management of coastal zone resources (Stewart and McColl, 1994).

The Forest and Timber Inquiry was a very wide-ranging inquiry, which sought to identify and evaluate the options for the use of Australia's forest and timber resources. Dalal-Clayton and Sadler (2005, p57) comment that 'although now more than ten years old, the inquiry remains one of the reference points for integrated strategic, environmental and sustainability assessment'. The options identified by the RAC were influential in the drafting of the National Forest Policy Statement 1992 and in the conduct of the RFA process (described below).

Regional Forest Agreement (RFA) process

The RFA process took place over 5–6 years beginning in the mid-1990s. It has been described as 'the most comprehensive and expensive resource and environmental planning exercise ever undertaken in Australia' (Dargavel, 1998, p133). Ten RFAs were signed between 1997 and 2001, encompassing most of the native forest wood production areas in Australia. Although not formally described as SEA, the RFA process has many strong affinities with forms of SEA that have a sectoral focus or which integrate environmental, social and economic assessments into policy development and natural resource decision-making (Ashe, 2002).

Strategic assessment at the state and territory level[8]

New South Wales
The Environmental Planning and Assessment Act 1979 (EPAA) provides the legislative framework for an integrated land-use planning and environmental assessment system, which has some SEA type elements. The Act requires the preparation of environmental studies when preparing draft regional environmental plans (REPs) and local environmental plans (LEPs). These studies are placed on exhibition as part of the public consultation process for making REPs and LEPs.

Amendments to the EPAA, which took effect in August 2005, include provision for 'concept approvals' for major projects, plans and programmes. Concept approvals have statutory force and are intended to provide up-front certainty for projects or programmes, which are either long-term or complex, or where overarching strategies require statutory endorsement. Examples of possible application include road programmes for major highways or an infrastructure plan such as the Freight Strategy.[9]

Under the Protection of the Environment Operations Act 1997, the Environmental Protection Agency (EPA) may prepare, or be directed by the Minister to prepare, draft protection of the environment policies (PEPs). In preparing a draft PEP, the EPA must take into account, among other things, the environmental, economic and social impact of the policy and must prepare an impact statement relating to the draft PEP. The EPA must release the draft PEP and the impact statement for public comment.

Victoria
Under the Environment Protection Act 1970, the Governor-in-Council may, on the recommendation of the EPA, declare State Environment Protection Policies (SEPPs). Before a SEPP is declared or varied, the EPA must prepare a draft policy and a policy impact assessment, both of which must be placed on public exhibition. The policy impact assessment must include, among other things, an assessment of the possible financial, social and environmental impacts of the alternative means by which the purposes of the policy or variation may be achieved. The Minister may appoint a review panel to review the policy impact statement and report to the EPA on the adequacy of the draft policy or variation.

Western Australia
Amendments to the Environmental Protection Act 1986 in 2003 enable the EPA to assess 'strategic proposals'. A proposal is a 'strategic proposal' if and to the extent to which it identifies:

(a) A future proposal that will be a significant proposal; or
(b) future proposals, likely, if implemented in combination with each other, to have a significant effect on the environment (Section 37B).

Referral of a 'strategic proposal' by a proponent is voluntary. The benefit for a proponent is that a subsequent proposal which was identified in a strategic proposal may be declared by the EPA to be a 'derived proposal' not requiring further assessment. The Minister may determine legally binding conditions of approval for the strategic proposal, but these do not take effect until the Minister has declared that a subsequent proposal is a derived proposal. The conditions are then binding on the derived proposal (Section 45A(2)). As of June 2006, two strategic proposals had been referred, which were still at the early stages of the assessment process.

The Environmental Protection Act has specific provisions for the assessment of planning schemes. Legislative amendments, which came into effect in 1996, require that all statutory town and regional planning schemes and redevelopment schemes and any amendments thereof must be referred to the EPA by the responsible authority for a decision by the EPA as to whether to assess them under the formal EIA process (Malcolm, 2002). The relevant planning Acts define when and how a referral to the EPA shall be made. Statements of planning policy under the Town Planning and Development Act 1928 may optionally be referred to the EPA by the Western Australian Planning Commission (WA EPA, 2005).

Tasmania

The Resource Management and Planning System of Tasmania includes legislation, policies and administrative arrangements that aim to achieve sustainable outcomes from the use and development of the state's natural resources. The Resource Planning and Development Commission has a central role within the system, which includes the conduct of assessments and preparation of reports in relation to policies and plans prepared under these Acts. Included are assessments and reviews concerning:

• The making of state policies under the State Policies and Projects Act 1993 concerning sustainable development of natural and physical resources, land-use planning, land management, environmental management, environmental protection and any other matter that may be prescribed.
• The certification and approval of draft planning schemes, the approval of draft amendments to planning schemes and the issue of planning directives under the Land Use Planning and Approvals Act 1993.
• The preparation of water management plans under the Water Management Act 1999.

The assessment processes include public exhibition of the policy or plan and may include public hearings. Representations must be considered before a policy or plan is finalized.

Under the Environmental Management and Pollution Control Act 1994, the Environment Protection Policy Review Panel is established to conduct assessments of draft environment protection policies. The review process includes public exhibition of the draft environment protection policy and an impact statement, and may include public hearings.

The Marine Farming Planning Act 1995 establishes the Marine Farming Planning Review Panel to conduct assessments of draft marine farming development plans. The review process includes public exhibition of the draft plan and an environmental impact statement and may include public hearings.

Conclusions

Australia has substantial experience with SEA-type assessments over the past 30 years. These assessments have been conducted under a variety of legislative mechanisms. Some of these assessments have been *ad hoc* in nature and have generally not used SEA terminology. Some are recognized as good examples of mainstream SEA while others may be better seen as examples of 'para SEA' (as defined in Dalal-Clayton and Sadler, 2005).

At the Australian government level, strategic assessments are conducted under a range of legislation. The mandatory provisions for assessment of fisheries have been particularly successful, perhaps in part because they are mandatory but also because in some instances they provide positive incentives by facilitating the obtaining of export licenses and in relation to interaction with protected species.

By contrast, the discretionary SEA provisions in Section 146 of the EPBC Act cannot be seen as successful to date, given that only two SEA agreements have been signed since the provisions came into effect in July 2000 and neither of the agreements has delivered a final product. The recent amendments to the Act may help to overcome the reluctance by proponents and government authorities to refer proposals for assessment under Section 146.

Outside the EPBC Act, there are examples of SEA that appear to be working well within niche areas, for example, the assessment of National Environment Protection Measures and of Australia's foreign aid programme.

The assessment of natural resources is an area where successful and innovative strategic assessments have been conducted and continue to provide models suitable for wider application. The assessments conducted by the RAC and as part of the RFA process are noteworthy as are the preparation of regional marine plans. The conduct by DEH of trial regional strategic plans is another area of innovation.

At the state and territory level, the experience with strategic assessment is uneven. Some states have a range of mechanisms for assessment of PPP; in other states and in the two self-governing territories there is little to report.

The future development of SEA, both at the federal and state–territory level is likely to reflect the trend in EIA and other environmental legislation of incorporating sustainability objectives. It is likely that we will see a convergence of SEA and sustainability appraisal in coming years.

Notes

1 A controlled action is one that requires approval under Part 9 of the EPBC Act.
2 Environment and Heritage Legislation Amendment Act (No 1) 2006.
3 The Australian Fisheries Management Authority (AFMA) manages Commonwealth (commercial) fisheries. These fisheries are in the Australian Fishing Zone, an area of waters between 3–200 nautical miles seaward of the Australian coastline.
4 The Standing Committee on Environment and Approval Processes for Offshore Acreage is a committee of senior officers from the Industry Department and the Environment Department, which meets on a regular basis to examine and work through areas of overlap between the two portfolios as they relate to offshore oil and gas.

5 For further information on National Environment Protection Measures, see the NEPC website, www.ephc.gov.au.
6 NEPC Act 1994 (Commonwealth), Section 17.
7 Although the RAC was disbanded as an organization in 1993, the Resource Assessment Commission Act 1989 has not been repealed.
8 For a more extended treatment of SEA legislation in Australian States and territories than that provided here, see Marsden and Ashe (2006).
9 Second Reading on Environmental Planning and Assessment Amendment (Infrastructure and Other Planning Reform) Bill, 27 May 2005.

References

Ashe, J. (2002) 'The Australian Regional Forest Agreement Process: A case study in strategic natural resource assessment', in Marsden, S. and Dovers, S. (eds) *Strategic Environmental Assessment in Australasia*, The Federation Press, Sydney

AusAID (2003) *Environmental Management Guide for Australia's Aid Program*, www.ausaid.gov.au, accessed June 2006

Dalal-Clayton, B. and Sadler, B. (2005) *Strategic Environmental Assessment: A Sourcebook and Reference Guide to International Experience*, Earthscan, London

Dargavel, J. (1998) 'Regional forest agreements and the public interest', *Australian Journal of Environmental Management*, vol 5, pp133–134

Environment Australia (2001) *Guidelines for the Ecologically Sustainable Management of Fisheries*, www.deh.gov.au, accessed June 2006

Keen, M. and Sullivan, M. (2005) 'Aiding the environment: The Australian Development Agency's experience of implementing an environmental management system', *Environmental Impact Assessment Review*, vol 25, pp628–649

Malcolm, J. (2002) 'Strategic Environmental Assessment: Legislative developments in Western Australia', in Marsden, S. and Dovers, S. (eds) *Strategic Environmental Assessment in Australasia*, The Federation Press, Sydney

Marsden, S. (2002) 'Strategic Environment Assessment and fisheries management in Australia: How effective is the Commonwealth legal framework?', in Marsden, S. and Dovers, S. (eds) *Strategic Environmental Assessment in Australasia*, The Federation Press, Sydney

Marsden, S. and Ashe, J. (2006) 'Strategic Environmental Assessment legislation in Australian States and Territories', *Australasian Journal of Environmental Management*, vol 13, pp205–215

McGrath, C. (2005) 'Key concepts of the EPBC Act 1999', *Environmental and Planning Law Journal*, vol 22, pp20–39

NEPC (National Environment Protection Council) (2005) *Annual Report 2004–2005*, www.nepc.gov.au, accessed June 2006

Sadler, B. and Verheem, R. (1996) *Strategic Environmental Assessment: Status, Challenges and Future Directions*, Ministry of Housing, Spatial Planning and the Environment, The Hague

Stewart, D. and McColl, G. (1994) 'The Resource Assessment Commission: An Inside Assessment', *Australian Journal of Environmental Management*, vol 1, pp12–23

WA EPA (Environmental Protection Authority of Western Australia) (2005) *Draft Guidance Statement No 33*, (June 2005), www.epa.wa.gov.au/accessed June 2006

3
SEA in Canada

Barry Sadler

Introduction

Strategic environmental assessment (SEA) in Canada encompasses a number of non-statutory processes, some long-standing, others still emerging. In 1990, Canada became the first country to introduce a dedicated, formal system of SEA of government policies, plans and programmes (PPPs), separate from project-level environmental assessment (EA). This process, which applies only to federal decision-making, has been subject to several, increasingly critical reviews and currently its future may lie in the balance. So far, there are no fully operational provincial or territorial counterparts, although other strategic processes have been or are being introduced. For example, joint-federal SEA regimes are in place to review oil and gas drilling off the eastern coast, Alberta is introducing regional strategic environmental assessment (RSEA) as a tool for cumulative effects management and similar approaches and elements are in place or proposed in other jurisdictions. These developments and particularly the future of the federal system and prospects for RSEA are the subject of active debate in Canadian assessment circles and may be of wider, international interest.

In this chapter, these issues and related aspects of Canadian experience with SEA are examined against international trends in law, policy and practice, drawing on the general literature as well as the papers and discussion at the Prague workshop.[1] The chapter is organized into three main parts:

1 Background on the development of SEA in Canada and the frameworks and elements that are used federally and provincially.
2 Review of the federal system of SEA of government PPPs, which is the bellwether of Canadian practice and its standing internationally.
3 Profile of new directions in SEA policy and methodology and particularly the consideration now being given to RSEA, notably by the Canadian Council of Ministers of the Environment (CCME).

Background on SEA development

SEA in Canada encompasses both formal procedures and informal, *ad hoc* arrangements that are embedded in land and resource use planning regimes. These are Canadian variations of forms of approach to SEA that are common internationally, although there is no equivalent to the legal frameworks that are in place in the US (Chapter 5) or member states of the European Union (EU) (Chapter 8). In this section, the main dimensions of SEA development in Canada are briefly explained in relation to:

- The geopolitical realities imposed by a vast land and the divided jurisdiction for resource and environmental management between the federal and provincial or territorial governments, which are reflected in a mix of SEA instruments and permutations.
- The evolution of EA initially toward a more strategic focus and eventually to federal provision for a separate system of SEA that operates under different arrangements from and parallel to the Canadian Environmental Assessment Act, which applies only to designated projects.
- The relationship of this and other emerging systems of SEA to international trends, experience and concepts of good practice.

Geopolitical context

In Canada, the primary powers and responsibilities for environmental assessment and management are divided between two main orders of government and undertaken, respectively, by the federal government, ten provinces and three territories. All of these jurisdictions have enacted EA frameworks that apply only or predominantly to projects, although some have provisions that can apply to plans or programmes, for example, class assessment in Ontario (Gibson, 1993) or the regional impact of industry sectors (such as salmon aquaculture in British Columbia). In addition, separate EA systems are in place in a number of municipalities (for example, National Capital Region) and in native land claim settlement areas in Northern Canada (for example, Mackenzie Valley Environmental Impact Review Board).[2] Other EA regimes have been established jointly through federal-provincial agreements to harmonize processes in cases where projects are subject to overlapping jurisdiction. These arrangements provide for a diverse range of EA processes and applications, although to date SEA frameworks and elements as internationally understood are a relatively limited part of this jurisdictional profile (Dalal-Clayton and Sadler, 2005).

Evolution of SEA

The history of SEA in Canada is variously told and interpreted (for example, Sadler, 2005a; Noble and Harriman, 2008). In this account, it is abbreviated into two interrelated phases using the formal provision of SEA at the federal level as a dividing dateline. Although an important milestone, this is also an artifice in that many of the trends and directions that influenced the introduction of SEA continue to play out in the application of project-specific assessment. Most notably, they include the emergence of ecosystem-based, regional-scale approaches to address cumulative effects, which were an early, *de facto* response to the limitations of analysing them on a project-by-project basis (Sadler, 1986). Some now consider cumulative effects assessment (CEA) to be a distinctive branch of Canadian practice (for example, Duinker and Grieg, 2006), one that was and is instrumental in introducing a strategic, regional dimension and presaging a case for its formalization (Sadler, 1990; Noble, 2003).

SEA precursors and prototypes 1973–1990

SEA in Canada has a number of antecedents, some dating back to the early and mid-1970s. It was prefaced in the 1973 Cabinet directive to establish the federal Environmental Assessment and Review Process (EARP), which referred to projects and programmes. However, in practice, only projects were subject to EARP and programmes were not. Despite this *de facto* exclusion, strategic issues were addressed directly on an *ad hoc* basis and particularly in the first generation of federal environmental inquiries and reviews of major northern and offshore energy projects, which typically took place under poorly developed and incomplete policy and planning frameworks. Several of these processes established important precedents for SEA well before the term itself became widely used (Sadler, 1986, 1990). Three major examples are outlined in Box 3.1.

Box 3.1 *SEA antecedents in Canada 1974–1984*

Public inquiries and reviews of the environmental impact of major oil and gas projects in Northern Canada have been influential agents of change in introducing a strategic dimension into EA process. Early environmental inquiry and review processes that included consideration of related policy and planning issues:

- The Mackenzie Valley Pipeline Inquiry (1974–1977) established an early and enduring benchmark for scope and procedure of impact assessment, including an examination of policy and planning issues that set the course of northern development for a generation. Key recommendations to postpone building the pipeline to allow for the settlement of native land claims, entrenching aboriginal rights, and the abandonment of a pipeline connection across northern Yukon and its designation as a wilderness reserve (Berger, 1977) had a major impact on public policy that few other environmental reviews have approximated, either in Canada or internationally.
- The EA panel on exploratory oil and gas well drilling in Lancaster Sound, a unique High Arctic ecosystem, found that 'a meaningful assessment ... cannot be made 'in isolation from the broader issues that affect all uses of the area' and required 'a comparison of the benefits and dis-benefits of all policy options' (FEARO, 1979, p73). In deferring its ruling, the panel recommended that the federal government should 'address on an urgent basis the best use(s)' of the Lancaster Sound region,

which initiated a lengthy and protracted planning process (see Jacobs and Fenge, 1986).

- The scope of the EA review of oil and gas production and transportation from the Beaufort Sea (1982–1984) was unprecedented. It addressed the potential issues and effects of a multicomponent proposal at an early stage of definition, encompassing a range of potential alternatives and scenarios, and the capacity of governments to manage and regulate development, which required statements of relevant policies and programmes from specific agencies (FEARO, 1984, pp140–141). Often called a concept review, this mandate and its prosecution made a strong case for SEA of development policies and its regional integration into northern land-use planning (Sadler, 1990, pp58–60).

In the mid to late 1980s, elements of approach that prefigure the emergence of SEA were also evident in certain EA panel reviews of east and west coast offshore energy development that today are subject to SEA when new areas are opened to lease. Most notable in terms of the precedent set was the two-year EA panel review of potential environmental and socio-economic effects of renewed west coast offshore exploration jointly commissioned by the governments of Canada and British Columbia (1986). Although focused on the regulatory terms and conditions under which this activity could proceed, it was a *de facto* regional assessment covering a large area of the continental shelf (approximately 75,000 km^2), which made reference to several documents (rather than a single impact statement) and recommended the designation of protection and impact exclusion zones (although still falling far short of a resource plan or management strategy).[3] In the event, the development moratorium was not lifted and almost two decades later, the same issues and measures were replayed (with remarkable continuity) in perhaps the most extended procedure conducted to date under the current federal regime of SEA.

SEA provision and premises 1990–2007

Formal provision for SEA was first made in Canada in 1990 as part of a comprehensive reform of the federal EARP. In this package, EARP was replaced by the Canadian Environmental Assessment Act (1992, in force 1995), which applied only to designated projects, and a separate EA process was established under Cabinet Directive[4] for policy and programme proposals (until that time included in principle but excluded *de facto* from EARP).[5] This new process was based on the premise that policy assessment required 'very different' procedures from those used for project review and that they provided a 'much enhanced and progressive' approach (FEARO, 1990, p1). At the time, the first proposition had a measure of support in Canadian assessment circles and subsequently in other countries that established a non-statutory, SEA-specific system (Sadler and Verheem, 1996). Much of the promise of a progressive approach rested on the application of SEA to policy and programme proposals submitted to the federal Cabinet, the highest level of political decision-making in Canada.

Two decades later, it is clear that this regime has not lived up to initial hopes or expectations in meeting procedural requirements or achieving its policy objectives (see next section). In the interim, there has been no shortage of measures to strengthen the support or strengthen the SEA process, for example, as described by Wilburn (2005) and Canadian federal officials who made presentations at the Prague workshop (see note 1). Key developments include:

- The 1999 *Cabinet Directive on the Environmental Assessment of Policy, Plan and Program Proposals* revised the original Directive to provided clearer context and direction on when SEA was necessary.
- The *Guidelines for Implementing the Cabinet Directive* updated the 1993 'blue book' to provide more detailed information on procedural considerations such as scoping, public involvement and documentation.
- The 2004 *Cabinet Directive on the Environmental Assessment of Policy, Plan and Program Proposals* introduced further amendments to strengthen transparency and departmental accountability, notably in public reporting of the results of SEA.

In large part, these changes were introduced in response to a series of independent reviews and audits of the performance of federal departments in implementing requirements and delivering against the objectives of the SEA Directive. The most authoritative and influential have been the reports of the parliamentary Commissioner for Environment and Sustainable Development (CESD, 1998, 2004, 2008) who derives his/her functions from the Auditor-General Act (as amended 1995).[6] The Commissioner's focus on SEA comes from a broader, strategic concern that the government is not making good use of available decision-making tools that provide information on the environmental and sustainability effects of proposed actions. It also reflects a particular recognition of the importance of SEA as a means of addressing these at the highest level. Yet for a decade – or longer if earlier reviews are taken into account (for example, CEAA, 1996; LeBlanc and Fischer, 1996) – most federal departments and agencies have been found consistently to be deficient in their compliance with the Cabinet Directive and limited in their use of SEA and integration of findings into decision-making (see Box 3.2). These basic shortcomings are examined further, together with other issues, in the next section.

Box 3.2 *Key findings of SEA audits conducted by the parliamentary Commissioner for Environment and Sustainable Development (CESD)*

The Commissioner has carried out four audits of SEA compliance and performance by federal departments and agencies. A brief annotation of their headline results affords a relatively bleak profile of progress in SEA implementation:

- Initial audits of SEA (1998, 2000) were relatively limited investigations that were conducted as part of a larger review of the statutory application of EA. The 1998 audit identified major weaknesses in the implementation of the Directive and the 2000 follow-up found 'no evidence of improved of improved compliance' despite an updated directive issued in 1999.

- The 2004 audit was the first in-depth, cross-government example of SEA administration and practice in selected federal agencies and departments. It found that most still had not made 'serious efforts' to apply the Directive and that there was no assurance that environmental effects of strategic proposals were being assessed systematically or that ministers had sufficient information on which to base informed decisions
- The latest audit (2008) reported unsatisfactory progress in addressing the deficiencies reported in 2004. Despite some improvements, basic weaknesses were identified in accountability and transparency; mechanisms to enforce these obligations were not in place; and most departments are not preparing public statements of their assessments as required by the Cabinet Directive (as amended 2004).

The federal SEA system

Overall, as reported above, the predominant trends in SEA implementation at the federal level in Canada are less than positive and fall short of what is required. At best, progress has been slow and uneven and the quality and outcomes of SEA practice are open to serious question. Yet the federal SEA system, like others, is multifaceted rather than monolithic, encompassing a mix of strengths and weaknesses including institutional aspects that may be considered as innovative and elements of approach that correspond to good practice as understood internationally. In this section, the lineaments of the SEA system and its application are analysed, focusing on the framework, process and products of SEA and their relationship to decision-making and, by extension, to environmentally sound and sustainable development. This analysis updates an earlier evaluation of the federal SEA system (Sadler, 2005a), drawing on recent sources of information (notably CESD, 2008).

Foundations: Purpose, scope and role in policy-making

The major aim of SEA is framed in the Cabinet Directive as an expectation that PPP programme proposals with potential environmental effects are considered consistent with the government's commitment to sustainable development (Government of Canada, 2004, p1). It is also expected that SEA 'should contribute to the development of policies, plans and programmes on an equal basis with economic or social analysis' and 'environmental considerations should be fully integrated into the ... options developed' for decision-making (Government of Canada, 2004). By doing so, the government considers federal departments and agencies will be better able to deliver on what could be called secondary objectives including optimizing positive and minimizing adverse environmental effects of proposed actions, implementing sustainable development strategies, saving time and money by drawing attention to potential environmental liabilities and streamlining project-level assessments through elimination of issues that are best addressed at the strategic level (Government of Canada, 2004, p2). As described, this is fairly typical list of SEA functions that Canada holds in common with those established for many other countries.

In this case, the link to sustainable development strategies stands out as a particularly important, presaging a potentially significant role for SEA in policy-making. Certainly other frameworks identify SEA as a means to give effect to sustainable development, notably the European Directive (see Chapter 8). Arguably, this relationship is explicit rather than generic under the Canadian regime, where federal departments and agencies have a statutory obligation to prepare sustainable development strategies and update them every three years. Moreover, the amendment made to the Cabinet Directive in 1999 was intended to reinforce the role of SEA in promoting and implementing the strategies, and this relationship is a recurrent theme of the accompanying guidelines. In reality, however, the wording of the guidance on this matter is exhortatory rather than advisory and provides little or no direction on how SEA of specific proposals should or could be related to departmental policies and priorities for sustainable development. This is a missed opportunity to give effect to a concrete, dedicated role for applying SEA to policy purpose.

The scope of application of SEA in relation to the process of government decision-making also frames its policy role and importance. SEA is required only for PPP proposals that are submitted to Cabinet or to individual ministers and that have potentially important environmental effects, although departments and agencies are also 'encouraged' to conduct assessments for other selected proposals 'as circumstances warrant' (for example, to help implement sustainable development goals or address public concerns about environmental issues) (Government of Canada, 2004, pp1–2). So while circumscribed, the Canadian SEA system is positioned at the apex of federal policy-making, which, internationally, distinguishes it from most others (Sadler, 2005b). Most notably, SEA forms part of the documentation that accompanies memoranda to Cabinet,[7] and, at first glance, this niche allows environmental leverage on major policy and programme initiatives that are approved at the very highest level. That said, in keeping with the constitutional convention of Cabinet confidentiality, this process is secret and the reach of SEA is a matter of conjecture using circumstantial information – most of which suggests its impact on decision-making is limited (Sadler, 2005a, p57; discussed below).

Institutional framework: SEA provision, requirements and obligations

As noted earlier, the provision for SEA is made under Cabinet Directive (1990, as amended 2004). The non-statutory basis of the Canadian federal system was a response to strongly expressed concerns in Ottawa policy circles and to the particular secrecy and sensitivity that surrounds the flow of information to Cabinet. While this approach made sense at the time it was introduced, the Directive has proven to be an ineffective instrument for ensuring departmental compliance and accountability in carrying out the provision for SEA. Despite two amendments, in 1999 and 2004, and improved guidance, these basic functions are not yet enforced under the framework of the Directive as exemplified by the latest findings of the Commissioner of the Environment and Sustainable Development (CESD, 2008). Seventeen years after the Directive was introduced, their absence signals a need for fundamental reform and a further Agency-commissioned evaluation is underway at the time of writing.

The Directive as now written is a brief, one-page document that sets out the basic responsibilities and requirements for federal departments and agencies to conduct a SEA of PPP proposal. It nevertheless establishes a clear obligation on federal departments and agencies to comply with its terms under writ of ministers and the Clerk of the Privy Council, the head of the public service. As such, the Directive might be reasonably assumed to have binding, quasi-legal force. The reality is otherwise. The language of the Directive is general and permissive, framed in terms of ministerial expectations and what should be done (the sole exception is an edict that departments and agencies 'shall prepare a public statement') and there is no central mechanism to ensure accountability for non-compliance or limited commitment by departments and agencies.

In effect, the Directive is an institutional framework without a clear locus of quality control other than self-policing of responsibilities. Support and assistance responsibilities are decentralized among a number of participants notably Environment Canada (which provides expert advice), CEAA (which provides guidance and training) and the CESD (who reviews compliance and performance). None of them have powers of enforcement (although reports of the Commissioner command attention and response from audited departments). The Privy Council Office (PCO), as a central power-broking agency, has declined to take a lead to establish authorities for monitoring compliance and quality of assessments as recommended by the Commissioner (CESD, 2004). The upshot is ongoing basic weakness in SEA compliance and accountability noted earlier (Box 3.3).

Box 3.3 *SEA compliance and accountability: Findings of the CESD*

In 1998, 2000 and 2004, CESD audits identified the evident weaknesses and a low level of commitment toward SEA resulted from 'insufficient commitment by senior management, lack of central ownership, and no assignment of responsibility and authority to ensure the quality and consistency of the assessment process'. For the 2008 follow-up audit, the CESD expected to find an acceptable accountability framework including 'clear roles and responsibilities, clear performance expectations, credible reporting, and reasonable adjustment and review'. What the audit found was that many departments and agencies examined had made unsatisfactory progress. Specifically they 'did not provide information on their compliance with the Cabinet directive in the documents that they tabled in Parliament. For those that provided some information on their SEA activities, most of the information was insufficient to demonstrate compliance with the Cabinet directive.'

Source: CESD (2008, pp12–13)

SEA principles and guidance on implementation

The Cabinet Directive is supplemented by guidelines that provide advice for policy analysts and senior managers of federal departments and agencies on how to conduct SEA consistent with the obligations and requirements described above. In nine pages, the guidelines provide only a brief description of the basics of implementing the Directive. Although commensurate with a terse provision, SEA practitioners likely will find Canadian guidance short on specifics especially by comparison to those issued by other countries and open-ended in encouraging departments and agencies to refine the document to support their needs in developing PPPs (Government of Canada, 2004, p2).

Key areas addressed comprise guiding principles, procedure and methodology for analysing environmental effects, understanding public concerns and documentation, and reporting of findings. Other aspects covered include 'special cases' for which no SEA of a proposal is required (emergency responses, matters of urgency or issues previously assessed), summary of roles and responsibilities, and interpretive definitions. In that last regard, two aspects are of note: the broad definition of an environment effect, for example, to include health and socio-economic conditions;[8] and the use of policy assessment as a generic term that covers policies, plans and programmes (in effect not defining or differentiating these instruments).

Seven core principles form a cornerstone of the guidance (Box 3.4). As described, these principles correspond in orientation if not wording to internationally accepted statements such as the SEA performance criteria issued by the International Association for Impact Assessment (IAIA, 2002), notably in their call for early integration into policy or plan development, examination of alternatives, appropriate level of analysis and instilling accountability through an open process that involves stakeholders. These four principles are instrumental to good practice and, if applied conscientiously, should focus and structure the other three principles of flexibility, self-assessment and use of existing mechanisms (which emphasize the discretion available to departments and agencies in conducting assessments). In that context, flexibility in adapting and applying tools to the particular circumstances is endorsed in the SEA literature; self-assessment may strike some as more a premise than a stated core principle in most SEA systems but few would argue against it; and encouraging departments and agencies to use existing mechanisms for analysis and reporting makes sense within the federal policy context and the particularities of Cabinet memorandum procedure (discussed above). As always, the real test is the use made of the principles to deliver fit-for-purpose assessments.

SEA process and methodology

Canadian guidance emphasizes that there is no single 'best' methodology and encourages departments and agencies 'to apply appropriate frameworks and techniques and to develop approaches tailored to their particular needs' (Government of Canada, 2004, p4). It thus outlines general guidelines which are presented as flexible (applicable in different policy settings), practical (applicable by non-specialists) and systematic (based on logical, transparent analysis). The guidance also posits the 'real challenge' to policy analysts as

---

Box 3.4 *Guiding principles for SEA*

In implementing the Cabinet Directive, federal departments and agencies should be guided by the following principles:

- **Early integration:** The analysis of environmental considerations should be fully integrated into the development of a PPP ... beginning early in the conceptual planning stages of the proposal, before irreversible decisions are made.
- **Examine alternatives:** One of the most critical aspects [is to] evaluate and compare the environmental effects of alternatives in the development of a new PPP which will help identify how modifications or changes ... can reduce environmental risk.
- **Flexibility:** Departments and agencies have discretion in determining how they conduct strategic environmental assessments, and are encouraged to adapt and refine analytical methodologies and tools appropriate to their circumstances.
- **Self-assessment:** Each individual department and agency is responsible for applying strategic environmental assessments to its PPPs as appropriate, determining how an assessment should be conducted, performing the assessment and reporting on the findings of the assessment.
- **Appropriate level of analysis:** The scope of analysis of potential environmental effects should be commensurate with the level of anticipated effects.
- **Accountability:** Strategic environmental assessment should be part of an open and accountable decision-making process within the federal government. Accountability should be promoted through the involvement of affected individuals and organizations, when appropriate, and through documentation and reporting mechanisms.
- **Use of existing mechanisms:** Departments and agencies should use existing mechanisms to conduct any analysis of environmental effects, involve the public if required, evaluate performance and report the results.

Source: Government of Canada (2004, p4)

---

thinking more broadly about a proposal and its interaction with the environment and integrating SEA with ongoing economic and social analyses, rather than conducting it as an add-on or separate process. These propositions are in keeping with the mainstream literature on SEA methodology.

A two-stage SEA process is outlined in the guidelines, comprising a preliminary scan to determine whether or not a proposal is likely to have significant environmental effects, followed if necessary by a detailed analysis. The preliminary scan is a non-standardized screening procedure to identify 'strategic considerations' using tools such as matrices, checklists and expert opinion and taking account of the criteria listed in Box 3.5. In principle, this methodology appears to be appropriate to task in the federal process and consistent with the flexible approach called for in the guidelines (particularly

---

Box 3.5 *Criteria for conducting the preliminary scan*

- The proposal has outcomes that affect natural resources, either positively or negatively.
- The proposal has a known direct or a likely indirect outcome that is expected to cause considerable positive or negative impacts on the environment.
- The outcomes of the proposal are likely to affect the achievement of an environmental quality goal (for example, reduction of greenhouse gas (GHG) emissions or the protection of an endangered species).
- The proposal is likely to affect the number, location, type and characteristics of sponsored initiatives that would be subject to project-level environmental assessments, as required by the Canadian Environmental Assessment Act or an equivalent process.
- The proposal involves a new process, technology or delivery arrangement with important environmental implications.
- The scale or timing of the proposal could result in significant interactions with the environment.

Source: Government of Canada (2004, p4)

---

needed in conducting a preliminary scan of broad scale policy initiatives for which immediate outcomes may be difficult to determine). However, its application is neither appropriate nor consistent, According to a recent report, in the period since 2004, preliminary scans were completed for less than half of all proposals prepared since 2004 by the 12 departments and agencies audited, several had screened less than one third of their proposals and systems did not adequately identify PPPs that require detailed assessment (CESD, 2008, p9).

For proposals with potentially important environmental effects, a detailed and iterative analysis is conducted for each policy or planning option developed, As shown in Figure 3.1, this process should address five main considerations: scope and nature of potential environmental effects; need for mitigation/ opportunities for enhancement; potential importance of residual effects; need for monitoring and follow-up; and identification of public and stakeholder concerns. Key criteria to be taken into account in assessing effects and determining the level of effort include magnitude, frequency, location and risk. This process is broadly in keeping with internationally recognized steps and measures that are used for quality control. However, the lack of compliance and accountability mechanisms noted previously means that much is left to the discretion of departments and agencies in developing the flexible approach encouraged in guidance. At best, process application and the quality of analysis can be said to be uneven. In the worst cases, departments are not preparing detailed assessment of proposals that have potentially important effects such as export and import of hazardous waste (CESD, 2008, p8), thereby undermining the basic purpose of SEA.

Preliminary scan

- Identify the direct and indirect outcomes of the proposal for resource or environmental quality or policy
- Determine whether these are likely to have potentially important environmental consequences.

>> If no, further process completed
>> If yes, go to next stage

Analysis of environmental effects

- Describe the scope and nature of potential effects from implementing the proposal.
- Consider the need for mitigation measures to reduce or eliminate these effects.
- Describe the scope and nature of residual effects in the short and long term.
- Consider the follow-up measures to monitor the effects on the environment or to ensure implementation supports government sustainable development goals.
- Identify the concerns of affected and interested parties for decision-makers.

Source: Based on information in Government of Canada (2004)

Figure 3.1 *Canadian SEA process*

Public concerns and documentation

The guidelines devote considerable space to these matters. Where appropriate, analysis of potential environmental effects should identify the concerns of those likely to be most affected, other interested stakeholders and the public. This understanding can strengthen the quality and credibility of decision-making in a number of ways, for example, by avoiding delays because of a need for further analysis, as well as developing credibility and trust over time in the process. Sources of information regarding public concerns could include economic and social analysis, ongoing public consultation using existing mechanisms, expert departments and agencies and outside experts and organizations. As stated in guidance, public and stakeholder involvement is only one avenue to identify the concerns of affected or interested parties. At first glance, it has a less visible role than in other SEA systems and in many applications, public involvement is absent entirely, although there some notable examples that approximate to or exceed international standards of good practice (Sadler, 2005a, see Box 3.6; also Noble, 2009).

The most recent amendment of the Cabinet Directive (2004) was made to strengthen transparency of the SEA process and includes a requirement to prepare public statements of environmental effects whenever a detailed assessment has been conducted. Public statements are intended to demonstrate that environmental factors have been considered during decision-making and to describe the outcome of a proposal. A separate or dedicated report is not required, rather statements 'should be integrated into existing reporting mechanisms to the fullest possible extent' with their content and extent reflecting the circumstances of each proposal (Government of Canada, 2004, p4). In effect, public statements summarize any SEA report that accompanied a memorandum to Cabinet (all such documents are confidential). However, for some proposals, particularly those with significant adverse effects or public

---

Box 3.6 *SEA good practice: Public review of the policy moratorium on British Columbia offshore oil and gas development*

Federal guidelines call for the level of public involvement in SEA to be commensurate with and to make use of any activities 'that may be underway as part of the proposal' (Government of Canada, 2004, p7), which in many cases includes none at all. In practice, public involvement is much talked about but little used in the federal SEA system, although there are important exceptions. An example of good practice was the 'extended' SEA of the British Columbia Offshore Oil and Gas Moratorium (imposed by in the early 1970s and since then subject to a series of environmental reviews). This process was undertaken as a multi-phase, independent public review comprising:

- **Science review** undertaken by an independent expert panel in accordance with the precautionary principle to evaluate and report on information and knowledge gaps and their implications for offshore oil and gas regulation.
- **Public hearings and consultation** conducted by a review panel to canvass views and concerns on environmental and socio-economic issues related to the moratorium and following the five step procedure outlined in federal SEA guidelines.
- **First Nations' engagement** through a separate, independently facilitated dialogue to explore the issues of specific and unique interest to coastal indigenous peoples, notably their traditional use of marine resources and any potential infringement.

Source: Natural Resources Canada

---

concerns, departments or agencies 'may choose' to release a more detailed report on these to accompany the public statement of environmental effects. In either case, Canadian procedure is less than that required in most other SEA systems and, in practice, falls short of even these minimum arrangements.[9]

According to the latest CESD audit, most of the departments and agencies audited 'do not comply with the directive's public reporting requirement' (CESD, 2008, p10). In conducting the audit, the Commissioner expected to find that departments and agencies publicly report the results of all their detailed assessments and that these statements 'are sufficient to assure stakeholders and the public that environmental factors have been appropriately considered' (CESD, 2008). However, 5 of the 12 organizations audited had not issued any public statements on their detailed assessments and only 3 had complied fully with this provision of the Directive. In addition, many statements are incomplete, failing to identify the potential environmental effects of a proposal or how these were factored into decision-making. There has also been unsatisfactory progress toward establishing a central, easily accessible public registry of statements on detailed assessments, a commitment made by the federal government in response to previous audit findings (CESD, 2004).[10] Only a small number of departments had links to the central website maintained by the CEAA (www. ceaa-acee.gc.ca) and less than a quarter of all detailed assessments completed since 2004 were readily accessible to the public. By any reasonable standard, these statistics suggests that the implementation of the Cabinet Directive on SEA fails to meet even a basic test of transparency.

SEA quality and outcomes

The procedural shortcomings and uneven application of SEA in the federal government augur poorly for achieving a high level of quality or positive outcomes from the application of the Canadian SEA system. A good process does not automatically guarantee these results but a poor one is unlikely to do so. In this context, public statements of environmental effects serve as the main record of the quality of input to decision-making although, as noted above, it provides a second-hand and often flawed summary of the information SEA reports that accompany a Memorandum to Cabinet. As the primary decision document, the analytical section of a Memorandum is expected to include a discussion of the results of any SEA and to state how the PPP relates to the department's sustainable development strategy with further details contained in an accompanying SEA report (Government of Canada, 2004, p8). Whether or not it does so is a matter of conjecture but circumstantial evidence dating back over more than a decade suggests there are few grounds for optimism (CEAA, 1996; LeBlanc and Fischer, 1996; CESD, 1998).

Recently, issues regarding the quality and effectiveness of SEA practice in the federal government have been brought into sharper focus through independent audits conducted by the CESD (2004, 2008). In 2004, for example, the Commissioner reported that in most cases departments and agencies do not know how their assessments have affected the decisions made or what is likely to be the ultimate impact on the environment; and that there is little assurance that environmental issues are assessed systematically or that ministers and the Cabinet receive sufficient information to make informed decisions on proposals put before them. Four years later, little had improved in the fundamentals of SEA practice that would lead to a different conclusion and, additionally, the Commissioner reported that public statements 'often do not contain sufficient information to assure ... that environmental factors have been integrated into the decision-making process – the stated objective [of the Directive]' (CESD, 2008). Some may be inclined to read this as an epitaph for a SEA system that is broken and not worth fixing.

Other SEA developments

Despite the fraying credibility of the federal system, there is increasing interest in SEA in Canada, particularly in regional level, spatial approaches. A number of activities and initiatives are underway in RSEA or related areas. In approximate order of their development, these include:

- Provision for regional assessment under the Canadian Environmental Assessment Act.

- Role of SEA in joint federal-provincial regulatory regimes for offshore oil and gas.
- Use of ecosystem assessment in integrated oceans planning and management.
- Introduction of RSEA as a component of land-use planning in Alberta.
- RSEA working party of the CCME.

Discretionary provision for federal regional assessment

Recently, under Section 16.2 of the Canadian Environmental Assessment Act (1992, as amended 2003), discretionary provision was made for regional studies defined as follows:

> *The results of a study of the environmental effects of possible future projects in a region, in which a federal authority participates, outside the scope of this Act ... may be taken into account in conducting an environmental assessment of a project in the region, particularly in considering any cumulative environmental effects that are likely to result from the project in combination with other projects or activities that have been or will be carried out.*

The potential role that such a study could play in supporting project-level EA to address the perennial problem of cumulative effects is evident and includes a means of tiering currently absent from Canadian practice. Whether or how this approach is to be applied is not evident. As a discretionary provision, Section 16.2 might be expected to lack an explicit triggering requirement but it is vague on the basis for undertaking a regional study conducted outside the scope of the Act and on its subsequent relationship to a project subject to the Act. There appears to be little or no incentive for a responsible authority to undertake a regional study that 'may be taken into account' and (as far as I can determine) no supplementary guidance or informal advice on this matter. For example, what is understood by 'a study of the environmental effects of possible future projects in a region' (scope and content), which federal processes might qualify as a fit for purpose instrument and how can their results be tiered or otherwise taken into account (including to reduce or eliminate the need to address cumulative effects at the project level)? At the time of writing, no explicit use seems to have been made of this moot provision, although a pilot demonstration of regional environmental assessment in support of potential offshore oil and gas development in the Beaufort Sea is now underway.

Joint regimes for offshore oil and gas exploration and development

In the past decade, several assessments have been conducted by joint offshore petroleum boards established by Canada and Nova Scotia and Canada and Newfoundland and Labrador, respectively. These boards are independent regulatory agencies with a responsibility, among other things, to ensure the protection of the environment during all phases of offshore petroleum activity. SEA is used to identify environmental issues prior to opening marine zones for exploration bids, for example, SEA of Potential Exploration Rights Issuance for the Eastern Sable Island Bank, Western Banquereau Bank, the Gully Trough and the Eastern Scotian Slope, which encompasses ecologically significant areas and species including critical fish habitat (CNSOPB, 2003; also CNSOPB, 2005). This process generally follows the requirements of the Cabinet Directive and assessment documents can be accessed online (www. cnsopb.ns.ca). All subsequent projects in an area covered by an SEA, including seismic programmes and exploratory wells, still require project-specific environmental assessments under the Canadian Environmental Assessment Act and this provision allows for tiering (although, as elsewhere, the benefits from this aspect of SEA practice reportedly are less than anticipated). Based on this experience, the government of Quebec is in the process of establishing a SEA process for offshore oil and gas exploration and development, beginning with the maritime estuary and north-western basin of the Gulf of St Lawrence (BAPE, 2004).

Ecosystem assessment for large ocean areas

At the federal level, there are also spatially explicit, SEA-comparable processes that are applied outside the remit of the Cabinet Directive (Sadler, 2010). Most notable perhaps is the Ecosystem Overview and Assessment Report (EOAR), which is an initial step in a comprehensive process of integrated planning and management for marine regions undertaken by the Department of Fisheries and Oceans (DFO, 2005a). It is used, in part, to gain purchase on cumulative impact of multiple activities on ecosystem functions and properties of large ocean management areas (LOMA). Specifically, the EAOR provides baseline information on ecosystem states and trends and identifies ecologically significant areas, species and properties, analyses threats and impacts from multiple activities and stressors within a driver–pressure–state–impact–response (DPSIR) framework, and delineates areas and species of concern in terms of their deterioration and depletion, respectively, and pathways of effects. This process draws on best-estimate ecosystem science and knowledge of the relative significance of valued ecosystem components (DFO, 2004) to document and synthesize the interactions and considerations that need to be taken into account in preparation of LOMA plans, such as those for the Eastern Scotian Shelf, covering an area of 325,000 km² offshore Nova Scotia (DFO, 2005b). At the time of writing, other EAORs are incomplete and it is too early to determine the extent to which they will provide a satisfactorily accounting of cumulative threats to ecosystem structure, resource productivity and environmental quality.

RSEA, land-use planning and cumulative effects management in Alberta

Currently, the government of Alberta is in the process of introducing RSEA as part of a major overhaul of its land-use planning and environmental assessment and management systems. This reform responds to the accelerating scale and intensification of development, particularly evident in the Alberta oil sands where the spatial and temporal concentration of major projects has resulted in a massive environmental impact footprint. RSEA is being positioned as a proactive instrument to inform the development of regional land-use plans that will provide the framework for cumulative effects management. As with the CCME approach (below), RSEA will be applied to analyse and compare multiple development scenarios to identify the best or preferred option that will realize 'sustainable regional outcomes and/or objectives weighted according to public values (trade-offs)',[11] using a combination of spatially explicit models, methods and decision support tools[12] (Alberta Environment, undated). At the front-end of the RSEA/planning process, prior to the assessment of cumulative effects, preferred development paths and outcomes will be identified by reference to baseline information on the current state

Table 3.1 *Profile of SEA in Canada*

Main trends and issues	Canada was the first country to establish a wholly separate, dedicated SEA system, using a non-statutory framework to ensure its flexible application to federal policies and plans. Since then, there has been an unsatisfactory record of SEA application, characterized by basic and persistent weaknesses in compliance and contribution to decision-making. The fundamental issue centres on whether and how to reform this process.
Main perspectives	SEA provision federally is made under a Cabinet Directive, supplemented by guidance on its implementation, which, respectively, provide a brief statement of basic requirement and general advice on how to conduct and adapt SEA to circumstances.
	Core potential strengths of this SEA system are its application at the highest level of policy-making and its link to statutory sustainable development strategies (largely unrealized).
	Audits have shown that most departments and agencies have a low level of commitment to SEA; ongoing weaknesses in systems for ensuring transparency and accountability; inconsistencies in SEA application; deficiencies in reporting and tracking assessments; and lack of oversight and enforcement mechanisms.
	These limitations have compromised the quality and effectiveness of SEA. No assurance that the SEA system provides Cabinet or ministers with the information needed for decision-making.
Key lessons	Institutional weaknesses arise from the non-onerous, bare minimum administrative basis of SEA, which works only if agencies are committed and environmentally responsible.
	Low level of compliance reflects the lack of central mechanisms for ensuring transparency, accountability and quality.
	Marginal contribution to decision-making undermines the basic purpose of undertaking SEA and compromises environmental and sustainability policies of the government.
Future directions	Legislative reform of SEA at the federal level – current system is moribund and dysfunctional.
	Institution and skills building to support emerging process of RSEA, nationally and provincially.

of the environment, social and economic trends and public values, preferences and priorities, reflecting different regional contexts and thresholds. This process will be challenging to implement but promises to provide overall direction to development and environmentally-sound zoning of land and resource use (recasting a framework that Alberta abandoned in the early 1980s). Ultimately, it should also help reduce the duplication and inefficiencies of project assessment and regulation, although whether it will eliminate the need for addressing cumulative effects at this level as hoped is highly debatable.

Towards a Canada-wide understanding of RSEA

The Environmental Assessment Task Group (EATG) of the CCME, an inter-governmental body, has identified RSEA as an important work priority (CCME, 2007). It has issued guidance on the principles and criteria for undertaking this approach (CCME, 2009), which, among other things, attempts to establish a consolidated procedural and methodological framework for RSEA practice, recognizing that there is a range of ideas and initiatives being considered or applied by federal and provincial agencies (see also Noble and Harriman, 2008). Given the mandate of CCME, this thrust promises to advance the SEA agenda by clarifying the benefits of this approach, although a drawback is that there are no recommendations regarding how it should be taken up or moved forward. A further reservation is that the proposed process is ambitious and may be seen by some practitioners as methodologically complex,[13] although others likely see this differently given the emphasis on these tools and the push for greater national capacity in using them (PRI, 2005a, b).

Conclusions

As the first country to make specific provisions for SEA, Canada was recognized internationally as an early leader in process innovation. By establishing a non-statutory procedure, the federal government wanted to ensure that SEA would be flexibly adapted to the context and content of high level policies and plans. This principle still has resonance in the literature but Canadian federal experience also exposes a considerable downside of inadequate compliance and non-performance under an administrative framework that relies overly on the good faith of proponents. In reality, independent audits have documented a low level of commitment to SEA among many departments, as well as persistent weaknesses in applying a process that has no clear mechanism for ensuring accountability. Given these deficiencies, the quality of many completed assessments and their contribution to decision-making are questionable.

The federal system of SEA currently stands at a crossroads, with the form and structure of the Cabinet Directive subject to pending review. Federal officials, including those in attendance at Prague, understandably point to the positive aspects of this system including case examples of good practice and the actions taken to strengthen the Cabinet Directive and guidance on its implementation. Despite these measures, the track record of SEA has shown little measurable improvement and remains poor. On the basis of the evidence of independent audit reports cited in this chapter, an impartial observer would conclude that the current system is unfit for purpose and not worth fixing. What type of SEA system could or should replace it is another matter entirely. Legal provision is probably the best option, either through a separate act or an amendment to the Canadian Environmental Assessment Act. In either case, the concern should be to integrate SEA more closely with project-level assessment, for example, capitalizing on opportunities for tiering and securing process efficiencies, and with departmental sustainable development strategies, perhaps as a means of assurance that proposed policies and plans are aligned with stated objectives.

Internationally, Canada has regressed from an international leader to a laggard in SEA, although there is no shortage of wishful thinking to the contrary in federal circles. The stark gap between Canadian and international legal frameworks is exemplified by the relationship of the Cabinet Directive and the SEA Protocol (see Chapter 10), adopted in Kiev in 2003 by 35 member states of the United Nations Economic Commission for Europe (UNECE) region (that includes North America). Canada was not one of the signatories to the SEA Protocol and it is unlikely to become one so long as current arrangements remain in force. In this case, the incompatibility of federal and international obligations is at issue since to date Canadian provinces and territories have made no formal provision for SEA.[14] However, this situation may be changing given the emergence of RSEA in Alberta and the prospect of its promotion nationally by the CCME. If this approach becomes institutionalized, the profile of SEA in Canada (summarized in Table 3.1) will be significantly heightened, perhaps bringing new momentum to reform the moribund federal process.

Notes

1   The Prague workshop on legal and policy frameworks for SEA in Canada was organized by the Canadian Environmental Assessment Agency (CEAA) in cooperation with other federal agencies. It comprised a series of short statements from members of the Canadian delegation on: SEA arrangements and guidance (Gerard Aubry, CEAA); SEA audits of the Commissioner for Environment and Sustainable Development (George Steutz); departmental experience with SEA application in relation to agriculture (Kathy Wilson), transport (Cara McCue) and trade (Jaye Shuttleworth); the relationship of SEA and the environmental rights of indigenous peoples (Merrill-Anne Phare); and a wrap-up session facilitated by Irene Gendron (CEAA). The author has drawn on and gratefully acknowledges these inputs but the opinions expressed here do not reflect and should not be attributed to the officials, who almost certainly would have written a very different chapter to this one.

2   Comprehensive agreements of settlement cover sizeable tracts of Northern Canada. For example, the first such settlement, the Inuvialiut Final Agreement (1984), gave the (then) 2500 Inuvialiut of the Mackenzie delta region full or partial title to approximately $90,000\,km^2$ of their area of traditional use. It also confirmed Inuvialiut hunting and trapping rights to the entire area ($435,000\,km^2$ or almost twice the size of the UK).

3   On the east coast, in comparison, contemporary EA panel reviews were conducted on a more restricted basis; for example, the EA review of the Hibernia offshore oil and gas project was restricted to the footprint of the field ($130\,km^2$) despite its

location on the Grand Banks, a fishery resource of major importance (Canada-Newfoundland, 1985). In large measure, the differences in scope of assessment on the two coasts reflected the geopolitical regime with a cooperative federal-provincial accord on offshore oil and gas development in Atlantic Canada compared to a federal policy moratorium on offshore oil and gas development on the Pacific shelf.

4 *Cabinet Directive on the Environmental Assessment of Policy and Program Proposals (1990)*, Federal Environmental Assessment and Review Office, Government of Canada, Ottawa.

5 The Canadian Environmental Assessment Act was narrower in scope than the EARP Guidelines Order (1984), which, among other things, stated that 'the Process shall ... ensure that the environmental implications of **all proposals** for which it [the initiating department] is the decision-making authority are fully considered and where the implications are significant, refer the proposal to the Minister for public review by a Panel' (emphasis added).

6 The mandate of the Commissioner is to provide objective, independent analysis of government activities to deliver on policy commitments on the environment and sustainable development. Reviews and audits of progress in specific areas and aspects are described in the Commissioner's annual report to the House of Commons. They serve as an important means of ensuring accountability on environmental and sustainable development matters, and, as noted, the reports of the Commissioner on SEA compliance and practice have been instrumental in changes made to the Cabinet Directive and guidelines.

7 Couch (1998) has described the place of SEA in the policy context and process of preparing memoranda to Cabinet, emphasizing the steps and measures that were taken to integrate this requirement into a central mechanism for government decision-making (see also Wilburn, 2005). Cabinet memorandum are written in accordance with the strict specifications of the Privy Council Office (PCO), which calls for: 'Brief, clearly worded decision documents; thorough, integrated analysis of all relevant factors; full accounting of costs; clearly identified risks and opportunities; appropriate consultation, where necessary; and linkages to broader government priorities, such as sustainable development. In addition ... Privy Council analysts expect thorough environmental assessments, where necessary, and clear accounting of relevant environmental considerations' (Taylor, 2004). However, the CESD has found no evidence the PCO exercises this function (CESD, 2008, p3).

8 As described in the Guidelines (Government of Canada, 2004, p10), an environmental effect is:

a. any change that the policy, plan or program may cause in the environment, including any effect of any such change on health and socio-economic conditions, on physical and cultural heritage, on the current use of lands and resources for traditional purposes by Aboriginal persons, or on any structure, site or thing that is of historical, archaeological, paleontological or architectural significance, and any change to the policy, plan or program that may be caused by the environment, whether any such change occurs within or outside Canada.

9 Guidance on public statements further suggests that public statements summarize the SEA results, including whether environmental effects are positive or negative; what enhancement, mitigation, or follow-up measures need to be taken; and what are the results of any consultations. In principle, this proviso brings Canadian SEA closer to internationally accepted standards, although practice still falls short as discussed in the text.

10 The CEAA website contains hyperlinks to the public statements of other departments and agencies. Several were listed at the time of writing (www.ceaa-acee.gc.ca).

11 With regard to its expected application in Alberta, RSEA is defined as follows: 'RSEA is a strategic, region-based, future-focused systematic information-gathering and analytical process. It is a tool that can be used in support of regional planning through assessment of cumulative effects associated with alternative development scenarios and identification of the suite of management approaches and land-use strategies that best balances desired environmental outcomes' (Alberta Environment, undated, p10).

12 For example, approximately 20 candidate models have been identified for consideration in developing an integrated modelling framework. ALCES, a terrestrial landscape disturbance model that has particular currency in the province for addressing cumulative effects, is recommended for use in tandem with other spatial models and decision support tools, such as MARXAN or another Multi-Objective Land Allocation (MOLA) tool for vulnerability and suitability mapping to aid land/water zoning (Alberta Environment, undated, p33).

13 That said, the guidance is an improvement over an earlier draft reviewed, which championed quantitative models that are 'capable of processing vast spatial data sets and running multiple scenario iterations while simultaneously considering complex pathways and VEC interactions' (which is true) and exemplified the conventional, 'exhaustive approach' to impact assessment that has stymied cumulative effects assessment in the past. From that perspective, RSEA would be better positioned by taking a risk-based, precautionary approach to identify and compare the potentially significant cumulative effects and consequences associated with the interaction of human activities with key properties of the particular (geographically defined) ecosystem, in other words, those that determine its structure and functioning. This of course brings its own challenges.

14 This comment alludes to the fact that Canada is a party to the UNECE Espoo Convention on EIA in a Transboundary Context (to which the SEA Protocol is supplementary) only in the right of the federal government, in other words, without binding provinces and territories (all of which have established EIA systems). This is a curious anomaly since countries are supposed to sign treaties as nation states. Despite questioning by other parties, the UNECE (and Canada) appear content to let this irregularity stand. Whether it establishes a precedent for a future Canadian accession to the SEA Protocol is left to legal scholars or jurisprudence.

References

Alberta Environment (undated, c2007) 'A Guide to Undertaking Regional Strategic Environmental Assessment', Alberta Environment, Edmonton, Oil Sands Environmental Management Division, draft paper

BAPE (Bureau d'Audiences Publiques sur l'Environnement) (2004) *Les enjeux liés aux levés sismiques dans l'estuaire et le Gulf of St Lawrence*, BAPE Report 193

Berger, T. (1977) *Northern Frontier, Northern Homeland: The Report of the Mackenzie Valley Pipeline Inquiry* (2 vols), Minister of Supply and Services Canada, Ottawa

Canada-Newfoundland (1985) *Hibernia Development Project*, Report of the Environmental Assessment Panel, Ministry of Supply and Services, Ottawa

CCME (Canadian Council of Ministers of the Environment) (2007) *CCME Action on Environmental Assessment*, CCME Environmental Assessment Task Group, Statement of 30 November 2007, Winnipeg

CEAA (Canadian Environmental Assessment Agency) (1996) *Review of the Implementation of the Environmental Assessment Process for Policy and Program Proposals*, CEAA, Ottawa

CESD (Commissioner of the Environment and Sustainable Development) (1998) 'Chapter 6: Environmental Assessment – A Critical Tool for Sustainable Development', *Report of the Commissioner of the Environment and Sustainable Development to the House of Commons*, Office of the Auditor General of Canada, Ottawa

CESD (2004) 'Chapter 4: Assessing the Environmental Impact of Policies, Plans, and Programs', *Report of the Commissioner of the Environment and Sustainable Development to the House of Commons*, Office of the Auditor General of Canada, Ottawa

CESD (2008) 'Chapter 9: Management Tools and Government Commitments – Strategic Environmental Assessment', *Report of the Commissioner of the Environment and Sustainable Development to the House of Commons*, Office of the Auditor General of Canada, Ottawa

CNSOPB (Canada-Nova Scotia Offshore Petroleum Board) (2003) *Strategic Environmental Assessment of Potential Exploration Rights Issuance for the Eastern Sable Island Bank, Western Banquereau Bank, the Gully Trough and the Eastern Scotian Slope*, CNSOPB, Halifax, NS

CNSOPB (2005) *Strategic Environmental Assessment of the Misane Bank Area*, CNSOB, Halifax, NS

Couch, W. (1998) 'Strategic Environmental Assessment within Canada's Memorandum to Cabinet Procedure: Some Personal Reflections', in Kleinschmidt, V. and Wagner, D. (eds) *Strategic Environmental Assessment in Europe: Fourth European Workshop on Environmental Impact Assessment*, Kluwer Academic

Dalal-Clayton, B. and Sadler, B. (2005) *Strategic Environmental Assessment: A Sourcebook and Reference Guide to International Experience*, Earthscan, London

DFO (Department of Fisheries and Oceans) (2004) *Identification of Ecologically and Biologically Significant Areas*. DFO, Canadian Science Advisory Secretariat, Ecosystem Status Report 2004/006, Ottawa

DFO (2005a) *National Technical Guidance Document: Ecosystem Overview and Assessment Report*. Ottawa, draft report, Oceans Directorate, DFO

DFO (2005b) 'The Eastern Scotian Shelf Integrated Ocean Management Plan', DFO, Dartmouth, NS, www.mar.dfo-mpo.gc.ca/oceans/e/essim/essim-intro-e.html

Duinker, P. and Greig, L. (2006) 'The impotence of cumulative effects assessment in Canada: Ailments and ideas for redeployment', *Environmental Management*, vol 37, no 2, pp153–161

FEARO (Federal Environmental Assessment Review Office) (1979) *Report of the Environmental Assessment Panel: Lancaster Sound Drilling*, Federal Environmental Assessment Review Process 7, Government of Canada, Ottawa

FEARO (1984) *Beaufort Sea Hydrocarbon Production and Transportation: Final Report of the Environmental Assessment Panel*, Federal Environmental Assessment Review Process 25, Government of Canada, Ottawa

FEARO (1990) 'Environmental Assessment of Policies and Programs', Factsheet no 7, Federal Environmental Assessment and Review Office, Ottawa

Gibson, R. B. (1993) 'Ontario's class assessments: Lessons for policy, plan and program review', in Kennet, S. (ed) *Law and Process in Environmental Management*, Canadian Institute of Resources Law, Calgary

Government of Canada (2004) *Strategic Environmental Assessment: The Cabinet Directive on the Environmental Assessment of Policy, Plan and Program Proposals –*

Guidelines for Implementing the Cabinet Directive, Government of Canada, Privy Council Office and Canadian Environmental Assessment Agency, Ottawa

Government of Canada and Province of British Columbia (1986) *Offshore Hydrocarbon Exploration, Report and Recommendations of the West Coast Offshore Exploration Environmental Assessment Panel*, Ministry of Supply and Services, Ottawa

IAIA (International Association for Impact Assessment) (2002) *Strategic Environmental Assessment Performance Criteria*, Special Publication Series No 1, IAIA, Fargo, ND

Jacobs, P. and Fenge, T. (1986) 'Integrating resource management in Lancaster Sound: but on whose terms?', in Lang, R. (ed) *Integrated Approaches to Resource Planning and Management*, University of Calgary Press, Calgary

LeBlanc, P. and Fischer, K. (1996) 'The Canadian federal experience', in de Boer, J. J. and Sadler, B. (eds) *Environmental Assessment of Policies: Briefing Papers on Experience in Selected Countries*, Publication 53, Ministry of Housing, Spatial Planning and the Environment, The Hague

Noble, B. (2003) *Regional Cumulative Effects Assessment: Toward a Strategic Framework*, Research and Development Monograph Series, Canadian Environmental Assessment Agency, Ottawa

Noble, B. (2009) 'Promise and dismay: The state of strategic environmental assessment systems and practices in Canada', *Environmental Impact Assessment Review*, vol 29, pp66–75

Noble, B. and Harriman, J. (2008) 'Strengthening the Foundation for Regional Strategic Environmental Assessment in Canada', draft report for CCME, Winnipeg

PRI (2005a) *Integrated Landscape Management Models for Sustainable Development Policy Making*, Sustainable Development Briefing Note, PRI, Ottawa

PRI (2005b) *Towards a National Capacity for Integrated Landscape Management Modelling*, Sustainable Development Briefing Note, PRI, Ottawa

Sadler, B. (1986) 'Impact assessment in transition: A framework for redeployment', in Lang, R. (ed) *Integrated Approaches to Resource Planning and Management*, University of Calgary Press, Calgary

Sadler, B. (1990) *An Evaluation of the Beaufort Sea Environmental Assessment Panel Review*, Federal Environmental Assessment Review Office, Ottawa

Sadler, B. (2005a). 'Canada', in Jones, C., Baker, M., Carter, J., Jay, S., Short, M. and Wood, C. (eds) *Strategic Environmental Assessment and Land Use Planning: An International Evaluation*, Earthscan, London

Sadler, B. (2005b) 'The status of SEA systems with application to policy and legislation', in Sadler, B. (ed) *Recent Progress with Strategic Environmental Assessment at the Policy Level*, Czech Ministry of the Environment for UNECE, Prague

Sadler, B. (2010) 'Spatial approaches to integrated management for sustainable development', *Horizons*, vol 10, no 4, pp95–105 (special issue on sustainable places available at www.policyresearch.gc.ca/page.asp?pagenm=2010-0022_01)

Sadler, B. and Verheem, R. (1996) *Strategic Environmental Assessment: Status, Challenges and Future Directions*, Publication 53, Ministry of Housing, Spatial Planning and the Environment, The Hague

Taylor, L. (2004) 'The Privy Council and integrated decision making: Proceedings of the First Strategic Environmental Assessment (SEA) Workshop', CEAA, Ottawa, www.ceaa.gc.ca/016/001/0_e.htm

Wilburn, G. (2005) 'SEA Experience at the Federal Level in Canada', in Sadler, B. (ed) *Recent Progress with Strategic Environmental Assessment at the Policy Level: Recent Progress, Current Status and Future Prospects*, Czech Ministry of the Environment for UNECE, Prague

4
SEA in New Zealand

Jessica Wilson and Martin Ward

Introduction

Strategic environmental assessment (SEA) is not a term in common use within New Zealand's policy and planning communities. Given the lack of any specific legislative requirement for SEA, the term is likely to be unfamiliar to many practitioners. While New Zealand has more than 30 years experience with environmental assessment (EA), this process is only gradually gaining a foothold at policy level. For the most part, the analysis of policies and plans as envisaged by SEA internationally is not common practice.

To date, the trend in New Zealand has been to integrate general principles of EA into planning laws rather than to explicitly introduce SEA under legislation or policy directive. As a result, where they can be found, requirements for SEA tend to be implicit rather than explicit. This trend can be traced back to the Resource Management Act 1991 (RMA), New Zealand's key statute for managing air, land and water resources. More recently, it has found expression in land transport and local government laws.

A number of commentators have described New Zealand arrangements as typifying an integrative approach to SEA, where EA is 'embedded' within policy and plan-making (for example, Sadler, 2001, 2005). On paper, this approach has attractions, not least in the way it seamlessly connects policy development and EA process. In practice, however, the absence of explicit provisions for SEA has proved increasingly problematic. As Dixon (2002, p195) observes, without formal requirements, much remains dependent on 'the extent to which planners and decision-makers embrace the principles of SEA in preparing policies and plans, and institutional support given for its implementation'.

This chapter examines New Zealand's experience with SEA integration, looking at recent developments and existing issues of practice. To provide context, the chapter begins by examining the history of EA in New Zealand. It then looks at how SEA principles have been integrated into legislation, focusing on laws relating to resource management, land transport and local government. Recent examples of SEA-type practice in the development of non-statutory policies and plans are also outlined.

Background

New Zealand's experience with EA can be traced back to 1974 and the introduction of the Environmental Protection and Enhancement Procedures (EP & EP). These procedures were introduced in response to a climate of increasing concern regarding the state of the environment. In New Zealand, as elsewhere, the 1960s and 1970s had seen growing public concern about the environmental impacts of increasingly major, unchecked development schemes. International events, such as the 1972 United Nations (UN) Conference on the Human Environment, also served to focus domestic attention on these limitations of planning processes.

The EP & EP were aimed at raising the status of environmental considerations in government decision-making and were based loosely on the US National Environmental Policy Act (1969). The procedures required all government organizations to carry out an environmental impact assessment (EIA) in respect of any works and management policies that affected the environment and any projects that required a government licence or received government funding. State agencies were, however, allowed significant discretion in determining the extent of any EIA carried out. A full environmental impact report (EIR) was required only where major environmental impacts were expected.

In practice, government organizations proved to be reluctant users of the EP & EP. Between 1974 and 1985, on average, only nine EIRs were released per year (Wells and Fookes, 1988). Most were for major development projects rather than government policies. Among certain departments, the procedures were seen as interference in their internal affairs. They particularly resented the requirement for public comment on the EIR. At the time, this was one of the few opportunities the public had to participate in resource management processes. They also resented the scrutiny of the Commission for the Environment, New Zealand's first environmental agency, which was required to audit EIRs. As a result, the relationship between the Commission and certain government departments was often acrimonious.

A major reform of New Zealand's environmental management framework in the 1980s eventually led to the demise of the EP & EP and the disbanding of the Commission for the Environment. Technically, the EP & EP have never been withdrawn and ostensibly remain in force. However, as the procedures were not enacted in legislation but instituted under Cabinet directive, they have no statutory basis. As a result, government organizations have not used the EP & EP for some time.

The reforms of the 1980s also established the Office of the Parliamentary Commissioner for the Environment, a new Ministry for the Environment and led to the introduction of the RMA. With the passage of the RMA, EA entered a new phase. The RMA repealed more than 60 laws and brought together requirements for air, land and water management under a single statute. One of the objectives in drafting the RMA was to try to integrate EA and statutory planning processes. Rather than maintain a separate assessment process, as in the EP & EP, the aim was to include key principles and components of EA within the RMA.

The motivations behind this approach were mixed. At the time the RMA was introduced, there was a strong political desire to improve the efficiency of planning processes. Combining EA and planning procedures was seen as more cost-effective than maintaining separate processes (Wells and Fookes, 1988). To a degree, the approach was also influenced by a desire of those involved in drafting the legislation to make EA less prominent and thereby reduce its political vulnerability (Fookes, 2000a). As Fookes explains:

> *Experience with EIA in New Zealand and Australia had shown that where it was successful at addressing environmental problems, and consequently halting developments, governments reacted by reviewing its procedures ... In other words, a separate statute for EIA left it vulnerable to being reduced in its effectiveness once powerful interests began to be affected by this procedure. (Fookes, 2000a, p81)*

Since the RMA's introduction, legislation in other areas has followed a similar approach. Increasingly, New Zealand's planning laws have incorporated requirements to assess the environmental effects of proposed actions. Rather than prescribe specific SEA processes, the trend has been for legislation to place general obligations on decision-makers to consider environmental impacts when policies and plans are being developed. In theory, this kind of integrated approach suggests it may be possible to gain the benefits of SEA without the need for specific legislation. In practice, however, New Zealand's experience suggests this is not necessarily the case. In the sections that follow, this experience is discussed in more detail.

SEA and the RMA

When it was introduced, the RMA was lauded in some quarters as a revolutionary Act of Parliament. Former environment minister Geoffrey Palmer went as far as claiming the RMA placed New Zealand 'in the vanguard of international reform' (Ministry for the Environment, 1988). Much of this early praise of the RMA focused on the enactment of sustainable management as its governing principle (see Box 4.1).

RMA mandate for SEA: Aspects and issues

For SEA researchers, a key focus of attention has been the RMA framework for policy and plan development. The Act establishes a hierarchy of policies and plans to achieve its purpose of sustainable management. At the top of the hierarchy are national policy statements (NPSs) on matters of national significance and national environmental standards (NESs) for nationally significant issues. Preparation of both NPSs and NESs is optional and subject to the discretion of the Minister for the Environment.

At the regional level, the RMA requires all regional councils to prepare a regional policy statement (RPS) to provide 'an overview of the resource management issues of the region and policies and methods to achieve integrated

Box 4.1 *Sustainable management in the RMA*

Section 5 of the Resource Management Act defines sustainable management as: 'Managing the use, development and protection of natural and physical resources in a way, or at a rate, which enables people and communities to provide for their social, economic and cultural well being and for their health and safety while:

- Sustaining the potential of natural and physical resources (excluding minerals) to meet the reasonably foreseeable needs of future generations.
- Safeguarding the life supporting capacity of air, water, soil and ecosystems.
- Avoiding, remedying or mitigating any adverse effects of activities on the environment.'

management of the natural and physical resources of the whole region' (Section 59). Regional councils may also prepare regional plans to assist in carrying out their functions. Sitting beneath RPSs and regional plans are district plans, which are mandatory and must be prepared by every district and city council. They identify significant resource management issues for the district and sets out objectives, policies, and methods to address these issues.

In theory, EA is intended to underpin both policy and plan development and project approval. Within the Act, EA requirements can be readily identified at the project level in provisions relating to resource consent applications. Resource consent is required to use air, land or water resources where that use is not expressly permitted in a plan. Every consent application must be accompanied by an assessment of environmental effects (AEE).

In policy and plan development, however, the requirements for EA are more implicit. Components of strategic EA that can be identified include:

- Requirements to consider alternatives and evaluate proposed actions (Section 32).
- Requirements for environmental monitoring (Section 35).
- Requirements for public participation in policy and plan development (First Schedule).

In particular, SEA researchers have drawn attention to the provisions of Section 32, which obliges decision-makers to evaluate all proposed policies, plans and standards before they are adopted. The Act does not prescribe a specific process for this evaluation. Rather, it states the matters that the evaluation must examine, which are:

- The extent to which each proposed objective (in the policy, plan or standard) is the most appropriate way to achieve the purpose of the Act.
- Whether, having regard to their efficiency and effectiveness, proposed policies and rules are the most appropriate way for achieving objectives.

The evaluation must also take into account:

- The benefits and costs of policies, rules or other methods.
- The risk of acting or not acting if there is insufficient information about the subject matter of the policies, rules or other methods.

Memon (2004) argues that section 32 is equivalent to SEA and believes it has effectively institutionalized SEA in environmental planning. However, other commentators take a more circumspect view (Dixon, 2002; Ward et al, 2005a). Section 32 has been amended several times since the Act's introduction in an attempt to improve its clarity. Practitioners have found the intent of the section confusing. Its use of terms such as 'efficiency and effectiveness' and 'benefits and costs' has led to evaluations that its focus was more on economic than environmental outcomes. Environmental groups also have criticized the section, stating it has presented a barrier to environmental regulation.

Dixon (2002, p199) describes Section 32 as requiring a type of policy assessment but argues the RMA's 'mandate for SEA is partial at best'. She points out that there are gaps between the RMA provisions and what might be expected in an ideal SEA system. Several key components of SEA are not specifically provided for in the Act. For example, there is no provision for an independent quality review process. The main opportunity for some form of review is through the public submission process once the policy or plan has been publicly notified. Dixon (2002, pp198–199) also observes it is significant that 'the term SEA, or any variant of it, does not appear in the Act'.

In looking at the RMA as an SEA statute, it also needs to be emphasized that the Act does not cover all resource uses and provides a framework only for the management of air, land and water resources. Fisheries and minerals are excluded from the provisions of the Act. Management of issues such as transport also takes place under separate legislation. Although specific road-building projects will generally require resource consent under the RMA, transport policy development and planning takes place outside of the Act. This means policy issues that may have significant implications for air, land and water management may not be considered under the RMA.

Implementing the RMA: SEA in practice?
While there are different readings of RMA requirements for SEA, opinion is less divided when it comes to questions of practice. To date, implementation of the RMA has fallen short of expectations for enhanced EA outcomes. In part, problems associated with implementation have been due to poor practice. Limited resources of local government, lack of guidance from central government and barriers to public participation have been identified as key impediments to good practice. However, the lack of clarity of the Act's requirements for EA has also proved a problem.

In their review of policy statements and plans prepared under the RMA, Ericksen et al (2004) rated most as only fair to poor in quality, describing them as 'lacklustre'. They cited limited staff resources and poor understanding of the legislation as among the key factors contributing to this outcome. Not surprisingly, these factors have impacted on the quality of evaluations carried out under Section 32. For the most part, the evaluation process has been used to justify decisions rather than to comprehensively assess alternative courses of action. Environmental monitoring has also been affected by resource issues. Figures from the Ministry for the Environment show only 53 per cent of councils undertake state of the environment monitoring (Ministry for the Environment, 2009).

To a significant extent, these problems have been exacerbated by lack of guidance and support from central government. For much of the RMA's history, responsibility for implementation has fallen on local government while central government has taken a back seat. The Ministry for the Environment, responsible for the Act's implementation, has had a very limited budget to carry out its functions. Successive environment ministers have also been disinclined to develop national policy statements, which have the potential to enhance environmental outcomes. Work to develop national environmental standards has progressed slowly, with the first standards only released in 2004, some 13 years after the Act's introduction.

With regard to public participation, there are significant barriers that affect the ability of some sectors of the community to take part in policy and planning processes. Opportunities to participate in policy development tend to be dominated by industry, which is able to maintain its involvement more readily than public interest groups that are hampered by a lack of resources (Local Government Rates Inquiry Panel, 2007; Wilson, 1996). Given current arrangements rely heavily on the public to monitor the implementation of environmental legislation, this remains an important issue.

SEA in other legislation

Since the introduction of the RMA, planning legislation in other areas has increasingly incorporated requirements to assess the environmental impacts of proposed actions. As noted above, the trend has been for legislation to place general obligations on decision-makers to consider environmental impacts within policy and plan development. For example, the Fisheries Act (1996), which governs fisheries management, sets out duties to avoid, remedy or mitigate adverse environmental effects. Similarly, the Hazardous Substances and New Organisms Act (1996) contains a general duty on decision-makers 'to protect the environment, and the health and safety of people and communities, by preventing or managing the adverse effects of hazardous substances and new organisms' (Section 4). Changes to land transport and local government legislation provide further examples of this trend. They also highlight some of the key issues with New Zealand's approach to EA.

EA and land transport legislation

Requirements for transport planning in New Zealand are set out primarily in the Land Transport Act (1998). Similar to RMA provisions for the development of national policy statements, the Land Transport Act provides for a national land transport strategy to be prepared by the Minister of Transport. Like the

RMA, however, the Act gives the Minister the discretion to decide whether or not to prepare a strategy. To date, no strategy has been developed.

In the absence of a national strategy, regional land transport strategies (RLTS) provide one of the main mechanisms through which transport policy is set. They are mandatory planning documents and must be prepared by every regional council in consultation with the public. In essence, RLTS identify desired outcomes for land transport in the region and the means by which these outcomes will be achieved.

Recognition of the growing environmental impacts of transport has led to changes to transport legislation. These changes strengthen the obligations on regional councils to address environmental issues in RLTS development. Under amendments introduced in the Land Transport Management Act 2003, regional councils are now required to prepare RLTS that contribute to a sustainable land transport system and to environmental sustainability. Mirroring SEA principles, every RLTS must also:

- Avoid, to the extent reasonable in the circumstances, adverse effects on the environment.
- Take into account the need to give early and full consideration to land transport options and alternatives.
- Take into account the need to provide early and full opportunities for public participation in strategy development.

In addition, legislation now requires RLTS to be independently audited. Regional councils are also obliged to monitor RLTS implementation.

The Act also includes reference to a set of consultation principles (Box 4.2) that emphasize the importance of actively encouraging community involvement in RLTS development. They also highlight the need to provide the public with reasonable access to information, relevant information, a reasonable opportunity to present their views and the reasons for decisions made.

EA and local government legislation

The Local Government Act (2002) sets out the structure and powers of local authorities (regional councils, district and city councils). It requires local authorities to take a 'sustainable development approach' in fulfilling their functions and, in doing so, they must take into account:

- The social, economic and cultural well-being of people and communities.
- The need to maintain and enhance the quality of the environment.
- The reasonably foreseeable needs of future generations.

One of the key components of the Act is the requirement for local authorities to develop a long-term council community plan (LTCCP). These plans are a new requirement and oblige councils to consult with their communities to identify desired community outcomes. All councils were required to prepare a ten-year LTCCP by 30 June 2006, which must be reviewed every three years.

Box 4.2 *Consultation principles referred to in the Land Transport Management Act 2003*

Consultation must be undertaken in accordance with the following principles:

- That persons who will or may be affected by, or have an interest in, the decision or matter should be provided with reasonable access to relevant information in a manner and format that is appropriate to the preferences and needs of those persons.
- That persons who will or may be affected by, or have an interest in, the decision or matter should be encouraged to present their views.
- That persons who are invited or encouraged to present their views should be given clear information concerning the purpose of the consultation and the scope of the decisions to be taken following the consideration of views presented.
- That persons who wish to have their views on the decision or matter considered should be provided with a reasonable opportunity to present those views in a manner and format that is appropriate to the preferences and needs of those persons.
- That the views presented should be received with an open mind and should be given, in making a decision, due consideration.
- That persons who present views should be provided with information concerning both the relevant decisions and the reasons for those decisions.

In developing their LTCCPs, local authorities are required to identify and assess 'all reasonably practicable options' before making decisions (Local Government Act, Section 77). This assessment of options must include consideration of the present and future environmental benefits and costs of each option. In respect of water services provided by district and city councils (water supply and wastewater treatment), the Act contains a specific duty to assess both current and future demands and consider the 'full range of options and their environmental and public health impacts' (Local Government Act 2002, Section 128).

In parallel with the Land Transport Act, the Local Government Act requires the LTCCP to be audited and for plan implementation to be monitored. Both acts also share requirements to assess alternatives, consider environmental impacts and provide opportunities for public participation in policy and plan development. These provisions mirror key principles of SEA and imply a need for this process. However, both acts stop short of specifying an explicit EA process or using the term.

Evaluating implementation

To date, in-depth research on how well local government is fulfilling its obligations under land transport and local government legislation has not been carried out. At this stage, it is still too early to examine comprehensively council responses to the legislation. As with the RMA, however, the implementation of

EA provisions is likely to be dependent on the resources and skills available to councils and support provided by central government.

In the context of transport planning, research has indicated that EA skills are not yet well-developed (Ward et al, 2005b). Specifically, for RLTS developed prior to 2003, EA practice was characterized by:

- Limited environmental analysis of options.
- Limited opportunities for public participation.
- Insufficient monitoring to assess whether strategies are achieving desired environmental outcomes (Ward et al, 2005b).

This analysis suggested that regional councils may need to invest significantly in EA to respond effectively to new legislative requirements. There are also indications that implementation of the Local Government Act may prove challenging for councils. A survey of local authorities reported that just under a third have found implementation of the Act's provisions 'difficult or very difficult' and identified council capability and the availability of resources and guidance as among the main factors affecting implementation (Borrie and Memon, 2005, p67). Resourcing issues persist today.

These findings highlight one of the key issues with New Zealand's framework for EA: the absence of explicit requirements for SEA and the lack of its adequate recognition in policy and planning processes. As a result, appropriate resources are not provided, the skill base remains limited and professional development and practice is inadequate. In this respect, the integrated approach may result in EA becoming effectively 'hidden'. Effective SEA practice depends significantly on both clear legislation and appropriate guidance and support.

Other SEA initiatives

While the integration of EA requirements within planning legislation remains problematic, several commentators suggest there are some examples of emerging SEA practice in non-statutory policy and planning processes (Dixon, 2002; Fookes, 2000a; Ward et al, 2005a). Ward et al (2005a) identify elements of SEA in the process used to develop Auckland Regional Council's growth strategy (Box 4.3) and in a Parliamentary Select Committee inquiry into the environmental effects of transport (Box 4.4). Dixon (2002) has highlighted reports by the Parliamentary Commissioner for the Environment on possum management and rabbit calicivirus as examples of SEA of government policy proposals. Recent initiatives relating to policy-level health impact assessment may also provide an opening for SEA-type approaches (Box 4.5).

However, these examples of SEA tend to be *ad hoc*. For the most part, evidence of SEA application is difficult to find. At central government level, most policy decisions with environmental implications are not subject to any requirement for EA. A case in point is the government's 1998 decision to eliminate tariffs on imported motor vehicles. This decision, which led to a significant rise in vehicle imports and associated increases in emissions and

---

Box 4.3 *Auckland regional growth strategy*

The greater Auckland region is home to 30 per cent of New Zealand's population. The former Auckland Regional Council was responsible for preparing a regional policy statement to guide the integrated management of the natural and physical resources of the region. In response to growing development pressures, it began preparation of a growth strategy for the region. This process, carried out through an *ad hoc* body called the Regional Growth Forum, brought together the region's four city councils and three district councils that are responsible for controlling land use.

Project teams drawn from contributing councils worked on the following areas: regional planning overview; national and physical resource constraints; transport capacities; physical and social infrastructure; growth management techniques; intensification; employment location; and rural issues.

Options for accommodating future growth were considered by reference to desired outcomes as follows: safe, healthy communities; diversity of employment and business opportunities; housing choices; amenity of urban environments; protection and maintenance of the character of the region's natural environment; sustainable use and protection of the region's resources (including infrastructure); and efficient access to activities and appropriate social infrastructure for all.

Each step of the process was associated with public consultation. In the first stage, preliminary consultation with groups and the wider public helped to establish a draft strategy. In the second stage, the draft strategy was released for submissions and public hearings were held.

Source: Adapted from Ward et al (2005a)

---

other environmental impacts, was made without any reference to the RMA (Ward et al, 2005a). The same decision could also be taken now, more than a decade on, without any requirement for policy-level EA.

In the absence of specific requirements, SEA relies on guidance provided in strategy documents such as the government's *Programme of Action* for sustainable development, which built on New Zealand's response to the 2002 World Summit on Sustainable Development (Department of Prime Minister and Cabinet, 2003). It set out a list of principles intended to underpin all policy development in the public sector. The principles state that the economic, social, environmental and cultural consequences of decisions should be taken into account by:

- Considering the long-term implications of decisions.
- Seeking innovative solutions that are mutually reinforcing.
- Using the best information available to support decision-making.
- Addressing risks and uncertainty when making choices and taking a precautionary approach.
- Working in partnership with local government and other sectors and encouraging transparent and participatory processes.

- Considering the implications of decisions from a global as well as a New Zealand perspective.
- Decoupling economic growth from pressures on the environment.
- Respecting environmental limits, protecting ecosystems and promoting integrated management of land, water and living resources.
- Working in partnership with appropriate Maori authorities to empower the Maori people in development decisions that affect them.
- Respecting human rights, the rule of law and cultural diversity.

These principles reflect a number of aspects common to SEA such as ensuring decision-making is informed by quality information and encouraging transparent

---

Box 4.4 *Select Committee inquiry into the environmental effects of road transport*

In 1998, New Zealand's Parliamentary Transport and Environment Select Committee, comprising Members of Parliament from government and opposition parties, conducted an inquiry into the environmental effects of road transport. In conducting its inquiry, the Committee's terms of reference were to:

- Consider the nature and scale of the environmental effects of road transport.
- Review work currently undertaken by the government to investigate these effects.
- Consider the management option being recommended by the Roading Advisory Group.
- Identify possible mechanisms for minimizing the environmental effects of road transport.
- After examining these matters, report to the House with recommendations to the government.

The Committee was assisted by the Office of the Parliamentary Commissioner for the Environment and an independent adviser. It met regularly and invited submissions and reports from relevant government departments and agencies. However, it did not invite public or expert submissions outside of government.

In an unusual but not unprecedented act, the Committee sought to bring a dimension into the policy-making arena that was not being addressed by the lead policy agencies. In an interim report in 1998, it noted that the Resource Management Act can have only limited influence in the management of environmental effects of transport and that it is not integrated with transport planning. It concluded that the lack of an integrated legislative framework for managing the environmental effects of road transport poses risks to the environment.

Source: Adapted from Ward et al (2005a)

Box 4.5 *Health impact assessment (HIA) at the policy level*

Policy-level HIA is identified as an objective of the New Zealand Health Strategy, a government statement of public health goals. To support its delivery, a guide on HIA for policy-makers has been developed by the Public Health Advisory Committee (PHAC, 2004), a government advisory body. The guide was also developed in response to concerns that central government policies are not taking sufficient account of their effect on population health and well-being (Thornley et al, 2004). It is designed to offer practical approaches to HIA and aims to promote an understanding of the wider socio-economic and environmental determinants of health.

More than 45 HIAs are underway or have been completed. The majority have been carried out by or for local government rather than central government, the primary target of the PHAC guide (Quigley and Ward, *forthcoming*). Sixteen of the assessments focus on different aspects of urban planning and ten on transport. An HIA was also carried out by the Parliamentary Commissioner for the Environment to examine the health impacts of potential energy options (Quigley and Ward, *forthcoming*).

For the most part, HIA applications have not addressed environmental issues explicitly and therefore do not meet the SEA 'test'. However, the process followed in the HIAs of the Christchurch Urban Development Strategy illustrates the potential to use HIA as a tool to move towards SEA (Stevenson, 2006). The Christchurch process included consideration of a range of both environmental and socio-economic determinants of health, assisting a far wider consideration of issues and options comparable to SEA.

---

and participatory approaches. However, it is important to note that the *Programme of Action* has no legislative basis and is not binding. State departments cannot be legally challenged for failing to observe the principles. Following a change of government in 2008, the *Programme* has effectively been set aside.

Conclusion

Key conclusions are summarized in Table 4.1. On paper, New Zealand's integrated approach to SEA gives the appearance of an almost seamless connection between EA and policy processes. In the RMA and in land transport and local government legislation, SEA components have the potential to be an integral part of policy and plan development. In theory, 'embedding' SEA within these processes holds the promise of delivering both environmental and efficiency gains.

In practice, however, the absence of specific requirements for SEA can mean EA is not adequately recognized in policy and planning processes. As a result, resources are not made available to support implementation and the skill base for SEA remains limited. In this regard, the integrated approach may result in EA being 'hidden' – or at least obscured – limiting its effectiveness.

Table 4.1 *Profile of SEA in New Zealand*

Main trends and issues	New Zealand's experience with EA began in the 1970s with the introduction of the Environmental Protection and Enhancement Procedures. The procedures introduced an environmental impact assessment framework for government policies and projects. In practice, however, application focused primarily on projects.
	Major reform in the 1980s led to significant changes in environmental management. Key principles and components of EA were integrated into the RMA (1991), New Zealand's key environmental legislation. Elements of EA have subsequently been included in other environmental and planning laws such as land transport and local government legislation. However, New Zealand has not yet developed any specific SEA legislation.
Main perspectives	New Zealand's integrated approach is attractive in the way it links EA with policy development. However, the absence of specific SEA provisions has drawbacks. Without formal requirements, SEA implementation relies on the knowledge and skills of policy and planning communities and the resources available to them.
	To date, experience of SEA has been limited. Where it occurs, EA is often restricted by limited resources and skills. Critical elements of effective SEA such as monitoring remain under-resourced. This means there is often limited information to assess whether environmental goals are being achieved.
Key lessons	New Zealand's experience suggests EA requires a prominent place in policy and planning processes if it is to gain resources. Specific legislative provisions for SEA may be needed to provide this prominence. Guidance and expertise are also required to ensure effective SEA practice.
Future directions	In the immediate future, efforts need to be focused on developing the knowledge and skill base of policy and planning communities at both central and local government level. Attention also needs to be given to removing barriers to public participation. Current arrangements rely significantly on the public and advocacy groups to monitor the implementation of environmental legislation. In the medium term, attention will need to focus on improving the legislative base for integrated SEA.

To gain prominence in policy and plan development, SEA may demand specific legislative enactment.

Without formal requirements, SEA implementation in New Zealand relies heavily on the knowledge and skills of policy and planning communities. While some examples can be found where practice is improving, these tend to be the exception rather than the rule. To date, local government has carried much of the legislative responsibility for EA. However, evidence of local government planning practice under the RMA and land transport legislation suggests SEA processes are limited, critical elements of effective practice, such as monitoring, remain poorly developed and guidance and expertise needed to support them are also lacking.

At central government level, most policy development continues without any consideration of the need for EA. Mounting evidence of environmental problems, particularly climate change, may force a more proactive approach in the future. International influences may also have an impact. New Zealand sees itself as a good international citizen and is a signatory to many international environmental agreements. To date, overseas developments in SEA have had little influence domestically and there is considerable scope for New Zealand to take advantage of international experience with SEA good practice.

Past experience suggests progress is likely to occur in small steps. It is doubtful that New Zealand will see any SEA legislation in the short-term. In the immediate future, progress will depend on efforts to develop the skill base of New Zealand's policy and planning communities at both central and local government level. In turn, these efforts will depend on the willingness of central government to provide resources and other support to ensure existing legislation is being implemented effectively. In the medium term, attention will need to focus on improving the legislative base for integrated SEA to provide a clear mandate for its application.

References

Borrie, N. and Memon, A. (2005) *Long-Term Council Community Plans: A Scoping Survey of Local Authorities*, International Global Change Institute, University of Waikato, Hamilton

Department of Prime Minister and Cabinet (2003) *Sustainable Development for New Zealand: Programme of Action*, Department of Prime Minister and Cabinet, Wellington

Dixon, J. (2002) 'All at SEA? Strategic environmental assessment in New Zealand', in Marsden, S. and Dovers, S. (eds) *Strategic Environmental Assessment in Australasia*, The Federation Press, Sydney

Ericksen, N., Berke, P., Crawford, J. and Dixon, J. (2004) *Plan-making for Sustainability: The New Zealand Experience*, Ashgate, London

Fookes, T. (2000a) 'Environmental assessment under the Resource Management Act 1991', in Memon, P. A. and Perkins, H. C. (eds) *Environmental Planning and Management in New Zealand*, Dunmore Press, Wellington

Local Government Rates Inquiry Panel (2007) *Funding Local Government – Report of the Local Government Rates Inquiry*, Wellington

Memon, P. A. (2004) 'SEA of Plan Objectives and Policies to Promote Sustainability in New Zealand', in Schmidt, M., João, E., Eike, A. and Knopp, L. (eds) *Applied Strategic Environmental Assessment*, Springer-Verlag, Berlin

Ministry for the Environment (1988) *RMLR Analysis of Existing Statutes: Legal Analysis, Part 1: Town and Country Planning Legislation and Procedures*. Working Paper No 7, Ministry for the Environment, Wellington

Ministry for the Environment (2009) *Resource Management Act: Two-yearly Survey of Local Authorities 2007/2008*, Ministry for the Environment, Wellington

New Zealand Parliament Transport and Environment Select Committee (1998) *Inquiry into the Environmental Effects of Road Transport: Interim Report of the Transport and Environment Committee*, New Zealand House of Representatives, Wellington

PHAC (Public Health Advisory Committee) (2004) *A Guide to Health Impact Assessment: A Policy Tool for New Zealand*, PHAC, Wellington

Quigley, R. and Ward, M. (*forthcoming*) *Health and Well-Being Impact Assessment: The New Zealand Experience*, Wellington

Sadler, B. (2001) 'Environmental impact assessment: An international perspective with comparisons to New Zealand experience', in Lumsden, J. (ed) *Assessment of Environmental Effects: Information, Evaluation and Outcomes*, Centre for Advanced Engineering, Christchurch

Sadler, B. (2005) 'The status of SEA systems with application to policy and legislation', in Sadler, B. (ed) *Recent Progress with Strategic Environmental Assessment at the Policy Level*, Czech Ministry of the Environment for UNECE, Prague

Stevenson, A. (2006) *Health Impact Assessment of the Greater Christchurch Urban Development Strategy*, Community and Regional Public Health, Christchurch

Thornley, L., Dixon, J. and Ward, M. (2004) 'Policy tools for health impact assessment: A report on a New Zealand initiative', paper presented to the International Association of Impact Assessment Annual Conference, Marrakech, Morocco

Ward, M. (2006) 'Health impact assessment in New Zealand: Experience at policy level', report to the New Zealand Public Health Advisory Committee, Wellington

Ward, M., Dalziel, A. and Wilkie, R. (2005a) 'SEA experience and opportunities in New Zealand', in Sadler, B. (ed) *Strategic Environmental Assessment at the Policy Level: Recent Progress, Current Status and Future Prospects*, Czech Ministry of the Environment for UNECE, Prague

Ward, M., Wilson, J. and Sadler, B. (2005b) *Application of Strategic Environmental Assessment to Regional Land Transport Strategies*, Land Transport New Zealand, Wellington

Wells, C. and Fookes, T. (1988) *Resource Management Law Reform: Impact Assessment in Resource Management*, Working Paper No 20, Ministry for the Environment, Wellington

Wilson, J. (1996) *Public Participation and the Resource Management Act 1991: Participation for Whom?*, thesis submitted to Victoria University of Wellington in fulfilment of the requirements for the degree of Master of Arts (Applied) in Environmental Studies

5
SEA in the US

Ray Clark, Lisa Mahoney and Kathy Pierce

Introduction

The US was the first country to introduce environmental impact assessment (EIA) as a part of the 1969 National Environmental Policy Act (NEPA).[1] NEPA includes provision for applying this process to major actions at the strategic or non-project level, commonly termed programmatic EIA by US federal agencies. Yet traditionally this form of strategic environmental assessment (SEA) has been underused in NEPA applications. Since 1987, less than 100 programmatic environmental impact statements (PEIS) have been filed with the US Environmental Protection Agency. This trend still continues with only a handful of the 500 draft, final and supplemental environmental impact statements filed each year described as 'programmatic'.

In this chapter, SEA provision, procedure and practice under NEPA are analysed. The chapter is organized into four main parts. First, the context of NEPA implementation is described, particularly the institutional arrangements and policy-making processes that explain why there has been only limited use of programmatic and other strategic level analysis. Second, recent legislative and regulatory developments to further waive or dilute NEPA provisions at both strategic and project levels are summarized. Third, two innovative examples of SEA practice are cited to illustrate how this approach can contribute to informed decision-making and provide a framework for subsequent NEPA applications. Finally, ten main challenges to the practical application of SEA in US policy-making are identified, followed by a concluding statement.

Background

The US Congress passed NEPA in 1969 amid growing evidence of significant degradation of the quality of the human environment. Environmental awareness throughout the country was growing in response to visible examples of major environmental events, such as the Santa Barbara oil spill off the coast of southern California. In response, Congress enacted a national environmental policy, a tool to implement that policy and an oversight agency to ensure its implementation. The Council on Environmental Quality (CEQ), the oversight agency, developed implementing regulations in 1978 that established the basic procedures that federal agencies must follow in implementing NEPA (CEQ, 1978). These regulations provide substantial flexibility to agencies which are relatively free to develop their own approach to compliance.

NEPA was a landmark statute and was the first of its kind to be adopted by any government. It has since served as a model for legislation around the world, but in the US today NEPA is under attack. In particular, the use of strategic analysis under NEPA is being questioned by many and embraced by only a few. In order for the US to achieve the maximum benefit from this landmark legislation, more agencies must embrace the flexibility inherent in NEPA and the particular benefits of strategic analysis.

NEPA requires the preparation of a detailed statement for all federal proposals that may have a significant effect on the quality of the human environment. It delegates to CEQ the responsibility to develop the definitions and procedures for how to conduct these evaluations. CEQ regulations state that all policies, plans and programmes (PPPs) should be assessed for their environmental effect if it is thought PPPs may have a significant effect on the quality of the human environment.[2] While about 500 draft, final or supplemental environmental impact statements (EIS) are completed each year (and about 50,000 less comprehensive environmental assessments (EAs)), it is rare for an agency to prepare a Programmatic EIS (PEIS) and even rarer for an agency to prepare a Policy EIS.

Traditionally, federal agencies in the US have conducted environmental analysis at the project level of implementation. This focus has been growing in recent years and is reflected in a recent trend on the part of some federal agencies to refute the provision that NEPA requires an EA or EIS for plans or policies (and even worse, to eliminate environmental review for some projects). However, there are still some good examples of agencies using PEIS or strategic analyses to their advantage in improving their decision-making processes.

The framework

CEQ has encouraged agencies to employ a programmatic approach through its regulations and its periodic reviews of NEPA. CEQ Regulations provide for the preparation of a programmatic analysis when it is useful to evaluate proposals that can be grouped: (a) generically, including actions that have common timing, impacts, alternatives, subject matter; (b) geographically, including those that occur in the same general location; or (c) by stage of technological development.[3] In 1997, CEQ issued a report on the effectiveness of NEPA that, among other things, identified the failure of federal agencies to use the strategic opportunities inherent in the programmatic approach (CEQ, 1997). In 2003, the NEPA Modernization Task Force again recommended that federal agencies should take advantage of the programmatic approach in order to make NEPA process more efficient (NEPA Modernization Task Force, 2003). This report noted that, while some agencies apply the programmatic approach to address cumulative effects and to formulate mitigation strategies, others struggle with how to use it. Importantly, it is solely within the discretion agency decision-makers to choose the analysis best suited for the decision at hand. Despite this discretion, few agencies choose to prepare a PEIS.

In 2003, CEQ convened a series of round tables with experts from business, industry, academia and non-governmental organizations (NGOs) to review the report of the NEPA Modernizing Task Force. The final report from the round tables concluded: 'Confusion still looms about what a Programmatic NEPA analysis really is, which creates many opinions on their utility and worth.' It is even unclear how many PEIS are undertaken in any given year. Environmental Protection Agency figures in 2006 showed that only about 75 programmatic EIS had been written since 1987. However, that number is disputable because all PEIS filed are self-labelled as to their scope and some not described as a PEIS could be interpreted as such (such as an EIS for forest or land resource management plans). So there is a clear need to define what constitutes a programmatic analysis and its role in agency planning. CEQ was encouraged by the round table experts to conduct pilot projects that explored the use of programmatic analyses within and across agencies and within ecosystems.

There remain sharp divisions regarding their worth and intent among NEPA practitioners, politicians and the general public. Programmatic analyses are sometimes characterized by the public as a 'shell game' where agencies defer issues to subsequent tiered analyses and then, when issues arise for specific projects, tell the public that 'these have been addressed already'. On the other hand, some public comments received during the round tables described programmatic analyses as valuable because of their ability to best assess the cumulative effects of agency actions.

The decision-making process

Initial decisions regarding US policy or strategy are most often made by appointed officials at the secretarial and assistant secretarial level of federal departments. These individuals are the political appointees who arrive with every new presidential administration along with their vision of how the world should work and come to make policy decisions that will put their stamp on society. Their decisions are made in consultation with Members of Congress and the staff within the legislative branch of government, often in consultation with the industries, associations and public interest groups most affected by these decisions. Many major policy decisions made at the departmental level by these political appointees are not influenced by the project level staff responsible for their implementation or the broad public most likely to be impacted by them.

For example, in the National Energy Strategy (1992), the Secretary of the Department of Energy noted that more than 90 of the strategy initiatives could be implemented without new legislation. While many of these initiatives were environmentally-friendly, no NEPA analysis was completed for the strategy. The Department of Energy's reasoning was that the strategy did not contain any initiatives requiring analysis because there were no specific proposals in the strategy. The 2001 White House Energy Task Force, led by then Vice-President Dick Cheney, was even less inclined to prepare any environmental impact analysis or even divulge who was giving advice to the Task Force. Its purpose was to expedite energy-related projects, including acceleration of the permitting process. In May 2001, the White House released the National Energy Strategy without any associated environmental impact analysis. After later criticism from many environmental NGOs and litigation following a request under the Freedom of Information Act,[4] in 2002, a federal judge ordered the Department of Energy to release some of the documents that informed the energy policy. The released documents showed participation in the process from many industry officials, including oil company executives,[5] but no public involvement or NEPA analysis took place.

Many analysts have concluded that the most effective way to improve the quality of impact assessment and influence the outcome of decisions is through political and administrative action to build environmental impact analysis into the regular business of agency policy and decision-making. Andrews (1997) makes the argument that one of the most fundamental limitations of NEPA has been the rarity of its influence on truly major federal decisions at the policy, programmatic and legislative levels. Many reasons for the failure of agencies to integrate NEPA into early strategic planning have also been identified. They range from inadequate communication among planning and environmental staff to the difficulty inherent in defining and analysing a strategic level decision (Keysar et al, 2002). Whatever the reason, the adverse consequences of this failure to integrate are becoming increasingly evident. Although the EIS is most often completed at the project level, policies and legislative initiatives and the appropriations bills that underlie them are major federal actions that create far more pervasive impacts that typically are not analysed under NEPA. Examples identified by Andrews (1997) include government policies with perverse environmental effects such as agriculture crop payment formulas, below cost timber sales, fossil fuel and mining subsidies, and differential investments in highways as opposed to mass transit. In addition, the NEPA process is triggered too late to be fully effective, undermining its basic purpose, which is to consider alternatives, weed out poor proposals, and support innovation in order to avoid or minimize environmental impacts. The stifling of NEPA by the late timing of the analysis was a major finding of the report on NEPA effectiveness study (CEQ, 1997).

The public clearly wants to be more involved in the strategic decisions made by federal agencies but public involvement is rarely part of the discussions and decisions at the time when assistant secretaries and other high-level policy-makers are screening and choosing among options. While there is a true desire among many policy-makers to consult with the public, there is a belief among some that the public needs a concrete proposal to react to rather than a mere conceptual notion. They are reluctant to involve the public in such amorphous discussions for fear of appearing ill-prepared or, worse, possibly being sued. Unfortunately, these proposals are shaped over time only by consultations among high-level policy-makers who often foreclose options long before the public is even aware of the policy or programme. At this level, relatively few people are involved and conflict is worked out among political elites with political agendas. Few of these strategic decisions get revisited, and therefore the public involvement that occurs at the project level becomes essentially meaningless.

Generally speaking, most EIS appear to have been prepared after someone had made the decision about strategic paths. For example, very few of the EIS prepared by the Department of Transportation address a strategy for transport. More often, an EIS is prepared for a specific mode of transport, such as a road, a railroad or an airport, after the decision on which type of transport will be used has already been made.

Every six years, the US Congress passes a multibillion dollar transportation bill and the secretaries of transportation in the 50 states eagerly await their share of the appropriations. By far, the largest percentage of the money is always spent on the nation's highway system. Strategic questions (such as how much should be spent expanding the highway system to relieve congestion versus how much should go to maintaining the systems which are already in place?) are settled in the Legislative Branch. While the Executive and the Legislative Branches work out the amount of funding and agree upon some earmarked projects, state officials make most of the decisions regarding projects and prepare the EIS or EA required under NEPA. At this level, there is public involvement, controversy and litigation over the effects of highway building on the ever-increasing sprawl but little discussion about the broader issues such as the possibility of alternative modes of transportation. The funding formula that the US uses to help the states favours large capital improvements, rather than maintenance of existing roads.

The 2005 transportation bill, Safe, Accountable, Flexible, Efficient Transportation Equity Act: A Legacy for Users (SAFETEA-LU),[6] tried to simplify transportation planning. It directs the Secretary and heads of other federal agencies to presume that the results of the transportation planning process form the basis for environmental reviews, provided that certain conditions are met. One of the major goals of the bill was to expedite the project-level environmental review process. The new bill does add environmental programmes and funding for certain mitigation, but fundamentally it remains a highway bill with the goal of supporting the implementation of highway projects. As a result, US transportation projects move ever closer to minimizing the environmental review process at every level.

This bifurcation in decision-making is being noticed by the governmental institutions charged with reporting on the effectiveness of government. The General Accounting Office, an oversight arm of the US Congress, issued a report on the Forest Service's decision-making process and concluded that there are major inefficiencies in the current practice of developing forest plans to reach project level decisions. The study suggested that environmental analysis accompanying a plan or project be 'tiered' or linked to a broader-scoped environmental study. Yet, the US Forest Service is currently proposing to eliminate forest plans as an 'action' for the purposes of NEPA. Similarly, a study by the Army Environmental Policy Institute found that despite the potential benefits of fully integrating NEPA with master planning at army installations, 'concurrent preparation of land-use planning documents and their required NEPA documents is the *exception* at Army installations' (Keysar et al, 2002).

Recent trends undermining NEPA

Recently, the very heart of the NEPA process has been undermined by numerous legislative, regulatory, and agency decisions. Laws have been passed exempting certain agencies or projects from the requirement to comply with NEPA, and proposals to eliminate the need for NEPA compliance on broad initiatives have been raised by some agencies. Examples are described below.

The REAL ID Act (2005)

In 1996, Congress passed the Illegal Immigration Reform and Immigration Responsibility Act (IIRIRA)[7] that provided the authority to waive NEPA and the Endangered Species Act for the construction of a 14-mile border fence near San Diego, California, as well as other barriers in the vicinity of the border. This is the same law that set forth the requirements for an entry-exit programme that is now part of the US Visitor and Immigrant Status Indicator Technology (US-VISIT) and is discussed below. Despite this waiver authority, the agency responsible for implementation of this fence and barriers chose to complete an EIS on the project. However, the project was essentially halted as a result of objections from the California Coastal Commission in 2004 and has never been completed. The Coastal Commission had authority to review the project under the Coastal Zone Management Act, a law that was not waived under IIRIRA. In response, the US Congress expanded on the waiver authority in IIRIRA.

On 11 May 2005, the REAL ID Act[8] was passed and essentially granted the new Secretary of the Department of Homeland Security (DHS) the authority to waive any and all laws as necessary to allow for the construction of roads and barriers on the border. Notably, this provision was added as a rider to the Iraq war supplemental appropriation and thus reduced the likelihood of any opposition to the waivers. In a change from previous policies, on 14 September 2005, the Secretary of DHS announced his intention to apply the new waiver authority and subsequently the department gave notice in the federal register officially declaring their intent to waive not only NEPA, but at least seven other federal environmental laws. Completion of the San Diego Fence project is now underway and plans for a fence along the Arizona Border are also moving forward (Garcia et al, 2005). This change in direction reflects a broader trend occurring throughout the US with respect to NEPA.

The Energy Policy Act (2005)

As evidence of the continuing trend in the US away from environmental analysis, Section 390 of the Energy Policy Act of 2005[9] categorically excludes numerous activities from environmental review:

- Individual surface disturbance of less than five acres so long as the total surface disturbance on the lease is not greater than 150 acres and site-specific analysis in a document prepared pursuant to NEPA has been previously completed.
- Drilling an oil and gas location or well pad at a site at which drilling has occurred within five years prior to the date of spudding the well.

- Drilling an oil or gas well within a developed field for which an approved land-use plan or any environmental document prepared pursuant to NEPA analysed drilling as a reasonably foreseeable activity, so long as such plan or document was approved within five years prior to the date of spudding the well.
- Placement of a pipeline in an approved right-of-way corridor, so long as the corridor was approved within five years prior to the date of placement of the pipeline.

The Healthy Forests Restoration Act (2003)

This Act provides a categorical exclusion which will allow the Forest Service to conduct large-scale logging projects without considering any alternatives or their relative environmental impacts. The geographic scope of the bill is very broad, potentially applying to most National Forest and Bureau of Land Management (BLM) lands. Instead of specifying a distance limitation from communities, the bill generally allows expedited logging projects anywhere in the 'proximity' of wildland-urban interface and intermix areas. Consequently, the agencies could log many miles away from any community, as long as the Forest Service thought that there was 'significant risk' that a fire could spread and threaten human life and property. The bill would allow the agencies to ignore any alternatives to their proposed fuel reduction projects, regardless of the size, environmental impacts and level of public controversy. The agency would not even be required to consider a 'no action' alternative to compare a project's impacts to the environmental status quo. According to the CEQ regulations, the evaluation of alternatives is 'the heart of the environmental impact statement' and serves to provide 'a clear basis for choice among options by the decision-maker and the public'.[10] Thus, the bill would effectively cut the heart out of the NEPA process.

Applying the tool: Good practice examples

Despite these trends, a number of agencies have embraced NEPA as a sustainability tool and have used programmatic approaches to save time and money and help agency decision-making. Two specific examples stand out as approaches that skirt the academic issue of SEA, but embrace the practical benefits of a strategic approach.

Bonneville Power Administration (BPA)

In the early 1990s, BPA needed to balance its responsibilities as a business with its responsibilities as a federal agency. The agency clearly needed a sound business plan to compete in the electric utility market and to continue to fund its public responsibilities. The BPA business plan was intended to set policy direction for pricing, power marketing, transmission and other necessary activities such as conservation and fish and wildlife administration activities (BPA, 1995). Such a business plan would clearly be a major federal action requiring the preparation of an EIS, but prior to 1995, very few US agencies had successfully completed this type of strategic policy analysis and the very idea of whether such a strategic analysis met the intent of NEPA was being questioned. From a global perspective, in the early 1990s, even fewer practitioners or legislators had embraced the idea of SEA. BPA's undertaking was therefore a considerable achievement in that it was one of the earliest examples of the successful application of SEA principles. They have been challenged in court on their approach[11] and the courts have upheld their EIS. BPA never titled their EIS 'programmatic' or 'strategic', but it stands out as a great example of what this level of analysis can achieve.

The challenge that faced BPA was how to prepare an EIS when there were so many different variables, when the affected environment was changing rapidly, and when so much information was incomplete or unavailable. BPA met this challenge by successfully preparing a Business Plan EIS, which was scoped broadly and included a wide range of alternatives that provided support if the agency needed to change its business direction later on. A framework for environmental impact analysis based on a review of previous environmental analyses that showed the many variables that needed to be considered made predictions of specific numbers uncertain but the fundamental relationships behind the numbers held true. A qualitative analysis was undertaken to illustrate those fundamental relationships.

The BPA EIS relied on the use of 20 different policy modules to help frame six alternatives and allowed sufficient flexibility to choose any number of options for implementation. The EIS stated that the action BPA ultimately takes 'may not correspond exactly to a single alternative and its intrinsic modules'. However, the six alternatives and the 20 modules 'are designed to cover the range of options for the important issues affecting BPA's business and the impacts of those options' (BPA, 1995). This approach to impact assessment was difficult for many in the EIA community to embrace. As discussed below, one of the major challenges to SEA is the uncertainty inherent in the process, the conceptual nature of the analysis, and in the NEPA context, the problem of no proposal. Although BPA's approach allowed the agency substantial flexibility in its decision-making process, it also adequately assessed the potential environmental impacts of its proposals and alternatives.

The Business Plan EIS was designed to be a living document accommodating BPA's needs in the evolving electric utility markets and providing guidance for a number of future decisions through a tiered Record of Decision (ROD) strategy. Although these innovative methods were controversial at the time, the BPA approach has survived numerous challenges and has resulted in approximately 25 decisions that have demonstrated the utility of this approach. This strategic approach allowed BPA to reduce the cost and time associated with NEPA compliance by addressing long-term issues up front and thereby eliminating the need for multiple environmental analyses each year. The cost and time savings garnered the support of programme managers for the EIA process while the strategic approach ensured adequate consideration of potential environmental impacts early in the planning process. The Business Plan EIS has served as a decision-making framework for more than ten years, and has therefore been embraced by senior leadership in BPA.

US-VISIT programme

The US-VISIT programme was established in 2003 as part of DHS. US-VISIT, along with the rest of DHS, was in large part a response to the terrorist attacks of 11 September 2001. The major requirement of the programme is to enhance security for US citizens and visitors while facilitating legitimate travel and trade across US borders. This entry-exit programme was originally based on legislation passed in 1996 (IIRIRA), which required the former Immigration and Naturalization Service (INS) to ensure that visitors to the US complied with the provisions of their visas. The programme was designed to facilitate the legitimate flow of foreign travellers to and from the US. However, the programme at INS suffered for a number of years from a lack of funding and political will. After the creation of DHS and the renewed emphasis on border security initiatives, US-VISIT was created to implement the initiative at all air, sea and land ports of entry. The mission is to help secure borders, facilitate the entry and exit process and enhance the integrity of the immigration system while respecting the privacy of visitors. The US has around 12,000 km of border, 153,000 km of shoreline and 330 air, sea and land border ports of entry, making the challenge of implementing this requirement overwhelming.

Since its formation, US-VISIT has been developing new technology and business processes in order to meet these goals. However, when the programme was initiated, there was little shape to the technology or solution as the programme managers and industry worked quickly to develop a system. The need for efficiency and speed in the development of all areas of the programme was clear since the programme was established in response to growing threats to the US. In order to ensure that potential environmental impacts were considered without preventing the rapid deployment of the needed solutions, the environmental programme manager developed the idea of a 'strategic environmental appraisal' or SEA. The SEA was developed to identify the environmental resources and authorities for those resources long before a specific project or programme was identified, using the ecosystem as the geographical boundary for appraisals.

Based on the stated goals of US-VISIT, the difficult problems of correctly identifying travellers to and from the US and maintaining the integrity of the data safeguarding personal privacy have been and continue to be analysed. Solutions include the use of different types of technology and biometrics, the addition of new business processes and the construction or modification of facilities to house the new technologies and processes. The SEA concept was developed prior to any decisions on what system would be placed at the borders. The only known factors were that there would be one and that there would be change. Depending upon the system and operations chosen, the environmental team concluded that the changes could potentially cause delays in port passage with subsequent environmental impacts to air quality; that changes could require modifications to existing port facilities with possible alterations to historic structures and possible impacts on existing land-uses; and that changes could require the purchase or exchange of lands around the port.

The US-VISIT programme used the flexibility of NEPA and the discretion accorded the agency decision-makers to design a 'strategic environmental appraisal' process for all of the land ports of entry. This appraisal was a 'pre-NEPA' approach to environmental planning. The intent was to inform future NEPA analyses and decision-making processes by understanding what the environmental baseline conditions were that could be affected by the programme's implementation. The SEA considered the potential natural, physical and human environmental consequences of a proposed programme in a broad context. Early on, US-VISIT did not have enough information about the systems or goals that would ultimately be considered to prepare a programmatic or strategic NEPA-compliant analysis. They used SEA to inform future analyses through environmental planning prior to reaching the point of a decision that was ripe for NEPA analysis.

Although the programme was to be implemented at air, sea and land ports of entry (LPOE), the latter were most notable locations in terms of environmental sensitivity. The first step in this SEA process was the collection of environmental baseline data. The 166 LPOE were grouped by ecosystem based on the US Fish and Wildlife Service (USFWS) classifications, and site surveys resulted in baseline information for each port within an ecosystem. Environmental baseline studies (EBS) included data on air quality, wetlands and other ecological components, information on historic and cultural properties and an inventory of the laws and authorities governing existing resources. The EBS reports summarized these findings and identified site-specific environmental constraints within, and in the vicinity of, each LPOE, and evaluated potential cumulative impacts concerns within each ecosystem. Each port was assigned a final assessment score of green, amber or red. Green meant that the LPOE-affected environment contains no resources that could be significantly impacted. Amber meant that the LPOE-affected environment contains resources that, if impacted, could result in issues of concern but at this time were unquantifiable or unknown. Red meant that the LPOE-affected environment contained resources that, if impacted, would result in potentially significant impacts depending on their intensity. These ratings served as guidance for planning purposes but were not intended to replace any impact analysis required under NEPA.

The second step in the process was the development of SEA reports, which provided a higher level screening than the EBS reports and further analysis on the resources of most concern in each ecosystem. Fifteen SEA reports were prepared, one for each of the USFWS-classified ecosystems. This process was effective in helping to inform decision-makers about the direction that they should take, even before any concepts had been formed, to implement the entry-exit requirements. For example, some of the earliest concepts included ideas about an infrastructure-heavy solution at the border. The SEA reports showed that in many areas, both urban and rural, sensitive resources were present in the vicinity of the land border ports. An understanding of the potential environmental consequences of such an approach helped to inform the decision-makers and begin to focus the programme in the pursuit of a technology-driven solution. While the ultimate decision about which approach to take did not occur until a few years later, after the completion of a Programmatic EA (US-VISIT, 2006), early assessment and planning helped push the decision-makers to consider less environmentally damaging alternatives and ultimately laid the foundation for their support of the subsequent programmatic NEPA analysis.

Ten challenges to implementing SEA in the US

While SEA is a promising avenue for incorporating environmental considerations into the highest levels of decision-making, it is still at a relatively early, formative stage. Many practical questions remain about the procedures, methods, and institutional frameworks that will be applied in SEA. Meanwhile, policy-makers are being urged to make decisions at larger and larger scales, even global in nature. Although EIA practitioners recognize this phenomenon, the profession has not been very successful in adapting EIA to the enormous task. There are ten major challenges that must be overcome in order to make SEA attractive to policymakers and successfully incorporated into practice:

Definition

In any new approach, the first problem is to define exactly what the notions are and get a general understanding of the concept. Thérivel et al (1992) and others have moved the profession a long way toward a common definition of SEA. Perhaps the definitional flexibility shown in this chapter could be codified. To be attractive to decision-makers in the US, SEA *must* be differentiated from programmatic EIS, which, albeit misunderstood by many, is not an attractive proposition for many decision-makers. On average, data show that programmatic EIS take an average of about five additional months to complete and are around four times as expensive. Alternatively, the SEA approach is an integrated decision-making approach that can help to reduce timelines and minimize costs while providing for more informed decisions that can help to reduce adverse environmental impacts.

Organizations

Current organizations, at least within the US, are not cohesive enough to work at a strategic level within one sector. For example, transportation projects are often *proposed* by individual states. The Legislative Branch (particularly the transportation committees) and the Executive Branch (particularly the Secretary of Transportation) make incremental decisions regarding whether to pursue these proposals. Transportation decisions are collaboratively made among the individual states, the Legislative Branch and the Executive Branch (the President and his cabinet), but are not based on cohesive strategic plans.

In order for organizations to support SEA implementation, programme managers will need to look across agencies and think in terms of cumulative effects within a particular ecosystem. It is at an ecosystem level where it is likely that most of the species and environmental resources are affected by the combination of different federal and non-federal activities within a particular region. However, current organizational frameworks, such as in the transportation community, lead to individual consideration of federal and non-federal projects scattered over various ecosystems. Organizational frameworks and thinking need to evolve to support SEA.

Data

Data and information feed the environmental impact analysis necessary for good decision-making. Currently in the US, analysts can rarely provide all of the data that leaders believe they need for decision-making. Even with existing data, federal and state agencies do not have the infrastructure to coordinate the sharing of data or information. At a strategic level, there is even less data, interpretation is foggier, and acceptance by decision-makers is less certain. It is difficult for an analyst or a policy-maker to assess the environmental effects of a conceptual idea absent a setting and time. But often there may be sufficient information to judge the consequences of strategic decisions on several key macro-issues: (a) the use of natural resources, including energy and raw materials; (b) the quantity and quality of waste streams; (c) emissions to air, water and soil; (d) human health and safety; and (e) use of space (Verheem, 1994). The higher level the decision is, the less likely an environmental analyst will be able to quantify impacts or even predict the probability of some impacts.

Uncertainty

Lack of data is often cited as a reason that EIA cannot be prepared at a higher level. Although data is important for good decisions, analysts sometimes crave data too much and forget that some levels of decision-making are possible and necessary even if not all the facts are known. There will always be risk-adverse people unwilling to make decisions or allow decisions to be made without virtual certainty. Indeed, there are points in the decision-making stages when more detail (such as engineering drawings) is required. Usually, however, the need for specific data is at a tier (or two) following the strategic decision. As the EIA profession gains sophistication, SEA will incorporate monitoring and adaptation strategies that can accommodate the reality of unavailable data, rather than insisting upon up-front certainty.

Litigation

In the US, NEPA has been used as a tool to stop or alter federal projects, to avoid environmental impacts and to establish a body of case law that recognized the environment was a paramount concern in agency decision-making. While the courts have said that NEPA creates a procedural obligation on government agencies to consider the environment, the Supreme Court (the third co-equal branch of government) has instructed lower courts not to substitute its judgments for that of the federal agency. As long as the agency has taken a 'hard look' at the environmental consequences of their decisions, they will likely prevail in court. In 1979, the court ruled in Andrus versus Sierra Club[12] that an EIS is not required as part of the budgetary process, thereby foreclosing an early opportunity to think strategically about environmental obligations. Although the court observed that if environmental concerns are not interwoven into the fabric of agency planning, the action forcing characteristics would be lost, it played a major role in closing such analysis. Strategic EIA, as many authors define it, has many pitfalls and decision-makers are reluctant to embrace it now. The lack of a concrete proposal or 'mere speculation' is already explicitly exempted from NEPA review through case law and voluntary exposure to potential litigation would be seen as unnecessary treated by staff and agency leadership. What may attract US policy-makers to SEA is the opportunity to use the benefits of EIA without the procedural traps, particularly litigation. Litigation should not drive policy. There is, after all, no irreversible commitment of resources at the strategic decision-making level and that may be the largest benefit of SEA over project level EIA.

No proposal problem

Is spending resources toward the development of a new generation of nuclear power plants a 'proposal'? If there is no location attached to it, there will be no direct indication of the potential site specific impacts of the proposal. Even so, it should be possible to assess the difference among alternate strategies. At a macro-level, for example, assessment might focus on the relative impact of proposed alternatives on the environment, comparing which would occupy more or less land, result in more or less habitat loss, generate more or less emissions of air pollutants, consume more or less energy, and have more or less acceptable risks. Through appropriate public engagement at the earliest stages in strategy development, it is also possible to determine the public's willingness to accept risks.

Capacity, knowledge and skills

Preparing an EIA at the project level requires advanced skills and the current pool of qualified professionals is low. SEA is another rung up the ladder of complexity and closer to the policy level of decision-makers with high expectations and the pool of qualified professionals is even lower. EIA practitioners have not yet mastered strategic analyses and concepts such as carrying capacity and sustainability thresholds. This new approach requires analysts who understand not only SEA but the policy or business sector being studied. With some successes (seen through the eyes of policy-makers), the profession can advance this part of EIA. Along with these analytical skills, SEA practitioners must have the ability to bring closure to the process at a reasonable cost and in a reasonable time frame.

Political will

Policy-makers do not take unnecessary risks, but they will take risks that they can manage. They seek as a reward breaking new ground in the advancement of the organization's core goals. Practitioners know that EIA can be a tool that turns rhetoric into action; many policy-makers do not yet believe that.

Role of the public

How early to involve the public in EIA remains one of the most vexing questions. Public acceptance of playing a role at a stage when there is no proposal and high uncertainty, and agree not to sue because the policy-maker is proposing an ill-formed, half-baked idea is critical to the success of SEA in the

US. When this happens, policy-makers should see SEA and public involvement as a useful and helpful product, not a therapeutic process for people devoted to procedure.

Integration

There has always been an argument within the EIA community in the US regarding whether EIA is an objective analytical tool or an integrative planning tool, synthesizing economic, social and environmental concerns into one analysis for decision-makers. SEA has the opportunity to combine economic development, environmental protection and community well-being into one cohesive analysis and move the analysis toward a discussion of sustainability.

Conclusion

Policy development is a dynamic process and it is inevitable that policy issues will never be as precise as the EIA profession has assumed them to be. Because decisions are incremental and there is not always a precise stage at which government decides public policy, so too should EIA evolve to a tiered, incremental approach. SEA moves the focus from one place, one site, to a more strategic level so that policy-makers can see how their entire operation fits in a national or even global context. In the current NEPA framework, by the time a project is assessed, there are few decisions left to be made regarding whether a proposal will proceed. This approach is appropriate for some types of projects but not for the development of sustainable strategies.

Do we need different procedures for SEA than EIA? The answer is yes. While the principal analytical elements are similar, there are significant differences. SEA must be more flexible, allowing the decision-maker to take those elements that are useful and apply it to their process. For example, the inception and extent of public involvement will be up to the decision-maker who must see the benefit of SEA. It should embrace the concept of adaptive management where decisions are made without perfect information, incorporate monitoring as an essential element and allow the programmes to move forward. SEA is significantly more complex than EIA and it will require developing a professional capacity to ensure its success and acceptance. It provides an iterative, continuous look at the environmental effects of a proposed action.

This emphasis on monitoring rather than certainty will yield new information that under ordinary circumstances would procedurally call for a new EIA. Because SEA should lead to a shorter, simpler, more open process, perhaps it should have no procedural requirements. The new model performs analysis at a different time, covering a different scope, while maintaining the science and art of EIA. SEA eliminates the obstacles to performing EIA earlier in the process and should result in improved decision-making with a focus on sustainability rather than process. In the US, this will happen only when the benefits of this model are apparent to the EIA community and those making the decisions regarding PPPs.

Notes

1   42 USC § 4321 et seq
2   40 CFR § 1508.18
3   40 CFR § 1502.4
4   5 USC. § 552
5   www.washingtonpost.com/wp-dyn/content/article/2005/11/15/
    AR2005111501842_pf.html
6   23 USC § 507
7   Pub. L. No. 104-208
8   Pub. L. No. 109-13
9   Pub. L. No. 109-58 (119 Stat. 594)
10 40 CFR § 1502.14
11 *Association of Public Agency Customers v Bonneville Power Administration*, 126
    F.3rd 1158, 1997
12 442 U.S. 347, 1979

References

Andrews, R. (1997) 'The unfinished business of national environmental policy', in Clark
    R. and Canter L. (eds) *Environmental Policy and NEPA: Past, Present and Future*,
    St Lucie Press, Boca Raton, FL
BPA (Bonneville Power Administration) (1995) 'Business plan: Final environmental
    impact statement', BPA
CEQ (Council on Environmental Quality) (1978) 'Regulations for implementing the
    procedural provisions of the National Environmental Policy Act', US Government
    Printing Office, Washington, DC
CEQ (1997) *The National Environmental Policy Act: A Study of its Effectiveness After
    Twenty-five Years*, Washington, DC
Garcia, M., Lee, M., Tatleman, T. and Eig, L. (2005) *Immigration: Analysis of the Major
    Provisions of the REAL ID Act of 2005*, Congressional Research Service Report
    32754 for US Congress, Washington, DC
Keysar, E., Steinemann, A. and Webster, R. (2002) *Integrating Environmental Impact
    Assessment with Master Planning at Army Installations*, Army Environmental Policy
    Institute, AEPI-IFP 0902A, Atlanta
NEPA Modernization Task Force (National Environmental Policy Act) (2003)
    'Modernizing NEPA Implementation', report to the Council on Environmental
    Quality, Washington, DC
Thérivel, R., Wilson, E., Thompson, S., Heaney, D. and Pritchard, D. (1992) *Strategic
    Environmental Assessment*, Earthscan, London
US-VISIT (US Visitor and Immigrant Status Indicator Technology) (2006) *Programmatic
    Environmental Assessment on Potential Changes to Immigration and Border
    Management Processes*, Washington, DC
Verheem, R. (1994) *SEA of Dutch Ten Year Programme on Waste Management*, paper to
    IAIA 1994, Quebec City

6
SEA in the Asia Region

Kiichiro Hayashi, Young-il Song, Elvis Au and Jiri Dusik

Introduction

Strategic environmental assessment (SEA) is now widely recognized and increasingly applied in the Asian region. However, SEA systems and implementation in Asian countries lags behind that in advanced regions such as Europe and North America. Asian SEA practice is still limited to a relatively few nations and jurisdictions. Hong Kong Special Administrative Region (SAR) is one of the leading jurisdictions in terms of establishing and implementing an SEA system as part of its planning processes. Other nations, such as South Korea and China, have made recent advances in this field.

This chapter reviews SEA systems and their implementation in the Asian region and particularly in east and southeast Asian countries. It is based on the results of the Prague SEA conference in 2005 and a survey of developments in this region conducted by the authors and others. The paper is organized into three main sections: background on the region and its history of EIA and SEA development; analysis of SEA systems and their implementation in selected countries and comparative review of progress on key measures and procedures; and discussion of key issues and future directions for promoting SEA in Asia.

Background

Asia houses half of the world's population and is a very diverse region in terms of level and type of economic development, institutional capacity and political, cultural, social and environmental conditions. For example, Japan is a developed nation and is a member of the Organisation for Economic Co-operation and Development (OECD). On the other hand, the current gross domestic product (GDP) per capita of several Asian countries are around US$1000–2000 per year. Recently, Asian countries, especially China, South Korea and Association of Southeast Asian Nation (ASEAN) member states, have become a major engine of world economic development, growing at a rate of approximately 10 per cent of GDP growth per year.

The Asian region is also very diverse with regard to the types and complexity of policy-making systems and the decision-making processes for projects and developments that are applied in different countries and jurisdictions. These varying conditions call for a highly flexible, diversified approach in applying strategic environmental conditions to suit different social and economic circumstances.

EIA implementation in Asia

Most Asian nations/economies have already introduced environmental impact assessment (EIA) systems in one form or another. Also many different forms of EIA legislation are in place. Some examples are cited below, recognizing that EIA has been a precursor to SEA development in this region.

The EIA system in South Korea started from the establishment of the Environmental Preservation Act in 1977. Subsequently, in 1990, the Framework Act on Environmental Policy was established including the requirement for environmental impact assessment of major projects. In addition, the Environmental Impact Assessment Act (passed in 1993 and revised in 1997) was the first independent statute requiring EIA for projects. Currently, the Act on Assessment of Impacts of Works on Environment, Traffic and Disasters (Act No 6095, 1999, revised 2003) is enforced.

In Japan (see MOE-J website), an EIA concept was first initiated in 1972 through a cabinet directive on the Environmental Conservation Measures Relating to Public Works. Then the cabinet directive on the Implementation of Environmental Impact Assessment was approved in 1984, which standardized the rule on EIA process for large development projects. EIA legislation was enacted in 1997 for full implementation in 1999.

Hong Kong enacted its own EIA legislation in 1997 to formalize an administrative EIA system that had been in place since the mid-1980s, and brought the law into full operation in April 1998, with provisions for EIA of major development plans. In 2003, China passed an EIA law with provisions for applying the EIA process to plans and strategies as well as to projects. Other South Asian countries that have a record of EIA implementation include Indonesia, Lao PDR, Malaysia, the Philippines, Thailand and Vietnam and the EIA system is being established also in Cambodia (see Dusik and Xie, 2009).

SEA in Asia: Analysis and review

As in other parts of the world, SEA has been gaining greater attention in Asia over the past few years, largely because of the increasing challenges being posed by the cumulative or large-scale environmental implications arising from major strategies or policies. But there have not been many examples of SEA, consistent with internationally accepted practice, although this is beginning to change. Many Asian nations are still grappling with institutional, technical and administrative difficulties in order to make the EIA system fully effective.

Several developing and transitional countries of east and southeast Asia (for example, China, Vietnam, the Philippines and Malaysia) have pilot-tested environmental assessment processes for various plans since the early 1990s. Since 2003, SEA has become institutionalized in the region and undertaken as either as an application of EIA principles to plans or programmes (as, for example, in China, the Philippines and Thailand) or as a more flexible approach for integrating environmental considerations into planning processes (for example, Indonesia, Malaysia). Vietnam has since 2005 established an autonomous SEA system which in many ways resembles the SEA regime in the European Union. Other developing and transitional countries in Asia (for example, Lao PDR, Cambodia and Fiji) have started pilot-testing SEA or similar assessment processes with donor support since 2005 (see Dusik and Xie, 2009).

Examples of SEA systems in Asian countries

In this section, the focus is on several selected SEA systems and their implementation in the planning processes of Asian countries and jurisdictions. The examples cited represent the more developed SEA frameworks and elements that are applied in the region. However, it also needs to be noted that this area is rapidly changing as a result of institutional developments being introduced undertaken by Asian countries and capacity-building initiatives undertaken through international development cooperation processes.

Hong Kong SAR

Among all Asian jurisdictions, Hong Kong is probably one of the few to have established actual practice and examples of SEA application since the 1990s. The EIA Ordinance includes a statutory requirement for EIA to be conducted for the feasibility study of major development plans. The recent completion of several major strategic environmental assessments of strategies or policies has fuelled greater recognition and acceptance of the importance and usefulness of this process in Hong Kong. Some of the earlier examples of SEA are shown in Table 6.1.

SEA development in Hong Kong has gone through three main phases. The first phase, from 1988–1992, encompassed the formative years for applying the EIA process to major new towns. The second phase started in 1992, when the then governor announced a major government initiative requiring the EIA process to be applied to all major policies, strategies and plans through a government directive. From 1992–1997, Hong Kong learned to apply SEA to various major strategies and territorial plans such as the Territorial Development Strategy, the transport strategy and the railway development strategy. Such applications produced very tangible outcomes and benefits, and created greater acceptance of the usefulness of SEA In particular, the application of SEA to the Territorial Development Strategy resulted in the evolution and development of a sustainable development system for Hong Kong.

Since 2000, SEA has been applied to more sectors and different types of plans and strategies such as waste management, a territory-wide energy conservation scheme, and so on. A recent application of SEA was for the long-term planning until 2030. This SEA is different from the previous applications in that it is sustainability driven and has incorporated the concept of continuous public involvement, making the process far more transparent with multi-stakeholder participation throughout.

Another advance in Hong Kong was the launch of a bilingual web-based SEA knowledge centre (www.epd.gov.hk/sea) in December 2005 by the Director General of State Environmental Protection Adiminisation in China,

Table 6.1 *Examples of SEA experience in Hong Kong*

Study	Key sectors involved	Scale	Dimension of environmental issues	Strategic environmental concerns and foci
Territorial land-use planning				
Territorial Development Strategy Review (1995)	Territorial land-use, transportation	Territory-wide population from 6.8 million in mid-1999 to 8.1 million in 2011	Territorial, district	Potential environmental implications and acceptability of various development options. Key concerns were air, water, traffic noise and conservation.
Transportation strategies				
The Third Comprehensive Transport Study (1997)	Transportation	Territory-wide cross-boundary population from 6.8 million in mid-1999 to 8.9 million in 2016	Territorial, district and local	Environmental implications due to different transport modes, polices and major development identified. Key concerns were air pollution and traffic noise.
The Second Railway Development Study (2000)	Transportation fuel, consumption, land-use	Territory-wide cross-boundary population from 6.8 million in mid-1999 to 8.9 million in 2016	Territorial, district and local	Potential environmental implications due to the railway development options, including indirect effects and benefits on reducing air pollution comparing with the use of road transport.
Electronic Road Pricing Study (1993)	Road transport, economic and equity, charging technology	Territory-wide 960,000 private cars by 2016 if unrestrained	Territorial, district and local	Environmental performance of and potential benefits of various charging schemes. Key concerns were air quality and traffic noise.
Strategic proposals and options evaluation				
1800MW Power Station (1999)	Power supply, local land-use, fuel supply, power-generation technology	1800MW power generation capacity	Global, regional, territorial, district and local	Potential environmental implications and acceptability of various fuel, technology and site options. Key concerns were greenhouse gas (GHG), regional and local air quality, and ecological impacts.

Source: Au (2003)

the Permanent Secretary for the Environment in Hong Kong SAR, and the Chairman of the Advisory Council on the Environment. The Hong Kong SEA Manual was published in October 2004 to promote wider application of SEA in Hong Kong SAR and Southern China. There is also good cooperation with mainland China in applying SEA to the Pearl River Delta Region and other regions in China. SEA has become an important catalyst for experience and knowledge-sharing, and a platform for cooperation.

China

The PRC was one of the earliest developing countries to introduce EIA requirements in 1979. Trial Environmental Protection Law in 1979 and subsequent environmental laws on air, water, noise and solid waste led to the development of a series of supporting documents on project EIA. These requirements focused on EIA projects and did not extend to plans, programmes and policies. At the same time, the significance of SEA has attracted increasing attention from EIA experts and officials since the 1990s. For instance, already in 1996 the State Council proposed environmental impact analysis for territorial and resources plans, urban and industrial development plans or making momentous decisions on economic construction or social development involving industrial structure and productivity layout (Li Tianwei, 2008)

SEA elements in regional EIAs in the 1990s: The practice of SEA in China has evolved from the practice of regional environmental impact assessment (R-EIA). In January 1993, a Circular on Strengthening the Management of Environmental Protection of the Construction Projects was issued by the State Environmental Protection Administration (SEPA) This process was in 1998 formalized by the State Council in Regulations on the Administration of Construction Project Environmental Protection. These required R-EIAs for the development of river basins, economic development zones, construction of new urban areas and reconstruction of old urban districts (Li Tianwei, 2008). The key purposes of R-EIA in development zones were defined as follows: (a) to assess the environmental quality and calculate the environmental carrying capacity for development, (b) elaborate environmental management plans, and (c) to simplify future EIA requirements for planned construction activities in such zones. Da Zhu and Jiang Ru (2008), however, observed that development plans were always a given and government agencies would hire scholars and experts to perform R-EIAs to identify and mitigate the possible environmental impacts of such plans. Results of R-EIA studies were then fed into agencies' decision-making processes, but the use of R-EIA results in making decisions was left to agencies' discretion.

SEA elements in EIA for mega-scale projects in the 1990s: In addition to R-EIA and EA for development zones, two other types of EA are believed to contain elements of SEA. The first type concerns EIAs conducted by several large industrial firms in relation to their development plans. The purpose of these EIAs was to identify environmental remedies for planned industrial activities. For example, EIAs for five-year development plans of three large iron and steel companies; EIA and environmental protection plan for the Integrated Agricultural Development Project at the Three-Rivers Plain; the West-to-East Electricity Transmission Project; the West-to-East Natural Gas Transmission Project; and the South-to-North Water Transfer Project. Da Zhu and Jiang Ru (2008) note that similar to R-EIA, all these EIAs were conducted to find remedies for identified environmental problems, but they did not determine the environmental feasibility of the proposed projects. Public participation was also limited to experts selected by the responsible agencies.

SEA provisions in the 2003 EIA Act and their fields of application: The new EIA Law (effective since 2003) applies to projects and certain plans as well. Initial drafts of the EIA Law also included SEA obligations for policies. However these proposals were met strong objections from sector government departments (Li Wei, 2006). The Ministry of Environmental Protection (the MEP) is fully aware that SEA should not be limited to the plans as these often have narrow scope and small influence; the MEP tries to extend the SEA applications to macro and directive plans and policies, such as industrial policy, trade policy and macro-development plans for a region or for the whole nation. To this end, the MEP for instance successfully organized the international workshop 'SEA in China' in October 2007, which attracted significant attention of the General Affairs Office of State Council and relevant government sectors. Under the EIA Law, the coverage of plans is divided into two categories: general plans for land-use, regions, watersheds and offshore waters; and specific plans, such as for agriculture, industry, livestock, breeding, forestry, natural resources, cities, energy, transportation and tourism (see Table 6.2). For general plans, SEA is used to integrate environmental considerations into plan preparation and is required to prepare an EA chapter or statement that is part of the proposed plan. There are no provisions for consultation with other relevant authorities or with the public.

For specific plans, SEA is required to analyse the impacts of draft development plans before their adoption and to prepare a separate Plan EIA Report (P-EIA). The EIA law requires public consultation on the draft plan and report prior to its submission for approval and review by the relevant environmental agency, which must convene an expert panel for this purpose. The agency responsible for approving the plan must consider both the findings of the Plan EIA Report and review inputs in making its decision.

A number of regulations to implement the EIA law and its SEA provisions have been issued by the Ministry of Environmental Protection, including review of Plan EIA Reports, and technical guidelines have also been prepared, for example, for undertaking Plan EIA and preparing EA chapters. In addition, many of the provinces have issued comparable regulations or guidance relating to these components (see Wei, 2005a). However, there is relatively little information available on how the SEA process is implemented in practice, particularly in regard to integrating environmental considerations into spatial plans. One interest may be a large pilot SEA that in 2008–2009 tested the application of EA and stakeholder participation in urban planning on the example of the Master Plan of Dali Municipality (Yang et al, 2009; YEPB and Ramboll Natura, 2009). To date, more than 13 provinces (cities and regions) including Shanghai, Hebei, Inner Mongolia, Jiangsu, Shandong, Hubei, Shaanxi, Guangxi, Yunnan and Xinjiang have issued relevant regulations for SEA in the form of local regulations and government documents (Li, 2008). These regulations have stipulated the process, review methods and financial resources of SEA taking into consideration the local conditions. In addition, the MEP has developed a series of technical guidelines, such as a trial version of the Technical Guideline on SEA for Development Programs.

There is also increasing research on SEA concepts and cases by Chinese scholars, and an extensive programme of SEA piloting is underway focusing on

Table 6.2 *Comparison of SEA requirements for general plans and special plans*

SEA elements	General plans and 'guidance' plan in special plans	Special plans
Field of application	General plans such as the land use plan, the plans for the development and utilization of regions, river basins and sea waters and also 'guidance' plans among the 'special' plans	Special plans for industry, agriculture, animal husbandry, forestry, energy, water conservancy, transportation, urban construction, tourism and natural resources development
Reporting requirements	A chapter or statement on environmental impacts	A separate Plan EIA report (P-EIA report).
Linkage to planning process	Assessment shall be carried out during the period of the plan drafting	Assessment shall be carried out before the submission of the draft plan for approval. It is normally done after the draft plan is prepared and before it is submitted for review and approval
Main focus of the assessment	• An analysis, prediction and appraisal of the environmental impacts that might occur if the plan or programme is implemented • Measures for preventing or mitigating the unfavorable environmental impacts	• An analysis, prediction and appraisal of the environmental impacts that might occur if the plan or programme is implemented • Measures for preventing or mitigating the unfavorable environmental impacts • Conclusion of the P-EIA report
Stakeholder engagement	Not required	For those special plans that are deemed to induce negative environmental impacts and thus directly affect the public interest, the proponent authority must hold discussion meetings, public hearings or some other forum to solicit comments on the draft P-EIA report prior to submitting draft plans for review and approval. However, classified plans under national security regulations are excluded from this obligation.
Review	The chapter or statement on environmental impact shall be submitted together with the plan to a relevant authority for examination and approval	The plan and respective P-EIA report is submitted to the relevant environmental protection department or other departments designated by the government When these authorities receive draft plans, they must convene a review panel of representatives of relevant departments and environmental experts to examine the P-EIA report
Legal liabilities	The department in charge of drawing up plans	The authority for review and approval of plans

Source: Adapted from Li Tianwei (2008) and Tao Tang et al (2005)

different types of plans and applications and this is expected to shed more light on the state of practice and the issues of concern (Dusik and Xie, 2009). The future priorities of the MEP regarding the SEA system development include: amendment of EIA law to ensure EIA applications for all decision-making with significant impacts on the environment; development of technical guidance on P-EIA for key fields and industries; training of SEA professionals and officials; and establishing several national SEA research centres (Li, 2008).

South Korea

In South Korea, the Prior Environmental Review System (PERS) was introduced in 1993 and restructured in 2005 to identify and minimize environmental impacts at an early stage for specific plans and programmes. The target of the PERS is a policy, plan and programme (PPP) that affects the determination of projects that will require EIA. The objective of the PERS is to overcome the limitations of EIA as well as achieve environmentally-sound sustainable development.

As noted, the scope of plans and programmes subject to PERS is determined by their subsequent connection to types of development projects subject to EIA. Specifically, the revised PERS system is applied to more than 100 administrative and development plans and programmes that are related to the 63 types of development projects subject to EIA. The plans and programmes subject to the PERS are divided into two groups, high-level and low-level plans, according to their characteristics (Table 6.3). The new PERS system is expected to encourage systematic environmental assessment through its step-by-step application from plans and programmes to development projects.

A PERS report is prepared during the preparation of a plan or programme before either its adoption or its submission to the legislative procedure (there are variations in review procedure and timing of consultation for each process). Public and authority consultation must be conducted within a period that ensures the consultees are given effective opportunities to express their opinion on the PERS report.

The PERS report must provide certain required information including the results of scoping, consideration of alternatives and public consultation. The

Table 6.3 *Characteristics and number of high and low-level plans and programmes*

Classification	Characteristics	Number of plans
High-level plans and programmes	Mid to long-term plans with policy and strategic characteristics. Plans that have indirect impacts on development projects of subsequent plans.	16 plans and programmes under 11 laws
Low-level plans and programmes	Plans that have direct impacts on development projects. Plans that have concrete geographical boundaries. Plans that are directly implemented into subsequent development projects.	72 plans and programmes under 48 laws

responsible authority prepares a draft report in consultation with the PERS committee on alternatives, scoping, public consultation procedures and level of public participation. The draft report contains all the information required in a final PERS report except for the consultation results. It should be open to the public for the period of at least 20 days and public hearing and meetings can be held if the PERS committee decides that these procedures are appropriate.

The responsible authority should inform the public of the contents of the draft report, the address at which a copy of the report may be viewed or obtained, the period of public consultation and invite the public to express opinions on the report, specifying how they must be sent, by publishing the information in a daily newspaper more than once. If a public hearing or meeting is held, the responsible authority should inform the public by publishing a notice in more than one national and regional daily newspaper more than once at least 14 days before the date of the hearing or meeting.

The draft report does not need to be open to the public if the committee decides the following reasons apply: the sole purpose of a plan or programme is to serve national defence; it is prohibited by a law to make the plan or programme open to the public; or it causes serious difficulties in achieving administrative objectives to make the plan or programme open to the public.

With regard to the role of the PERS committee, it helps the responsible authority to prepare the report by providing its expertise on establishing alternatives and conducting scoping. The current PERS system does not allow the PERS results to be applied to the final plan or programme. The committee will allow environmental aspects to be considered in the early stage of making plans and programmes. The composition of the PERS committee is made up of a chair (civil servant of the responsible authority) and members (fewer than ten members consisting of experts, members of environment groups, civil servants of the responsible authority and related authorities, resident representatives or local assembly members nominated by the head of the region).

Japan

Japan is the major developed country in the Asia region but it does not have a national legislation-based SEA system except for harbour planning, which is subject to current EIA law. However, recent research projects and initiatives commissioned by the Japanese Ministry of the Environment (MOE) laid the groundwork for developing an SEA system that complements the project level EIA system. The MOE has issued a preliminary guideline on SEA in the formulation of municipal waste management plans. In 2007, new developments toward establishing a national SEA system in Japan were initiated by the MOE in the form of a new guideline on SEA focusing on a programme stage of projects subject to the EIA law. The third National Environmental Plan prescribes the development of the SEA guideline. In 2010, after ten years of implementation of the EIA law, the discussion of revision of the current EIA law is now ongoing. The main point for discussion is the introduction of SEA into the national legislative system. (See MOE-J website for national and local SEAs/EIAs)

At the local government level, several SEA systems have been introduced already, for example in Saitama prefecture, Tokyo Metropolitan Area, Hiroshima and Kyoto.

In addition, the Japanese Ministry of Land, Infrastructure and Transport (MLIT, see MLIT website) has introduced guidelines for promoting public involvement (PI) for road, airport, harbour planning and river planning. This so-called PI system considers environmental, social and economic aspects as well as alternative development. With regard to road planning, the PI system is applied just before the stage of a road construction project that is subject to environmental impact assessment under the EIA law. At this stage, route alternatives and road structure alternatives, such as skyway or underground, are presented by the proponent and discussed from economic, social and environmental perspectives.

For example, the PI system has been applied to the Yokohama northwest circle highway road in Kanagawa prefecture near Tokyo (see Yokohama northwest line website). An expert meeting, questionnaire survey of the public and firms, public hearing, specific website and publication and distribution of summary documents were all used as consultation tools in this process. Environmental assessment focused on quantitative and qualitative impacts on air, noise, fauna and flora, groundwater, soil landscape and solar rights, although both scope and methods of analysis were relatively limited. The PI system might be recognized as a similar approach to SEA. After the implementation of the SEA guideline, the MLIT has revised its PI systems to fit the requirement of the SEA guideline.

Vietnam

Policy commitments: The SEA has already been contained conceptually in the Vietnamese legislative framework since the 1990s, for example in the 1993 Law on Environmental Protection, its implementing Government Decree 175 and Circular No. 490, which defined that 'EIA not only must be carried out at project level, but also for master plans for development of regions, sectors, provinces, cities and industrial zones'. However, only a few pilot SEAs were carried out before 2005 and they resembled large-scale EIAs. Various 'pilot SEAs' were undertaken in Vietnam before 2005. Many of these studies have used primarily EIA techniques focusing on environmental mitigation aspects rather than more strategic-level interventions into the planning process (ICEM, 2006). They were undertaken as separate analyses that were performed after the finalization of the respective plans, and a lack of legal imperative for SEA integration has reduced their ability to influence the decision-making process.

The momentum for developing an SEA framework in Vietnam has been growing since the beginning of the millennium with several government policy initiatives calling for strategic-level evaluation of policies, programmes and plans and the integration of environmental considerations into development planning. Of particular importance is a Comprehensive Poverty Reduction and Growth Strategy (2002), which calls for a full and active integration of 'environment and natural resource issues into the master plan for socio-economic development in provinces, districts, [to] ensure that development is sustainable and does not cause degradation in natural resources' and a National Strategy for Environmental Protection to 2010 and Vision to 2020 (2003), which placed a high priority on the 'integration of environmental considerations into socio-economic planning' by 2010 and included a call for the introduction of strategic environmental assessment.

The Law on Environment Protection (LEP) has been revised in 2005 and it includes mandatory provisions for a wide range of national, provincial and inter-provincial strategies and plans. Developed proposals for which SEA is always required include national and provincial socio-economic development strategies and plans; national sector development strategies and plans; plans for land use, forest protection and development; exploitation and utilization of other natural resources in inter-provincial or inter-regional areas; plans for development of key economic regions and planning of inter-provincial river watersheds.

The LEP stipulates that SEA reports need to be prepared by agencies that formulate the relevant strategies or plans. The LEP requires that the SEA report must constitute an integral content of the planning document and must be prepared concurrently with the formulation of the strategy or plan. These framework requirements were further refined in the MONRE Circular No. 05 which lays down detailed SEA procedure and the required content of SEA reports. The circular requires the proponents to set up a working group which includes environmental specialists and relevant scientists to conduct a SEA. The circular requires assessment of the respective environmental issues but also calls for provision of information of social and economic background and implications of the planning proposals.

The SEA Reports are to be appraised by a review council and the results of the review shall serve as basis for their approval. MONRE is in charge of organizing review councils for the strategies and plans approved by the National Assembly, the government and the Prime Minister. Line ministries, ministerial-level agencies and government bodies set up review councils for strategies and plans approved within their competencies. Lastly, Provincial Peoples Committees organize review councils for strategies and plans that are decided on provincial levels.

The Law of Environmental Protection also gives right to organizations and individuals to submit their comments during the review of SEA Reports. Comments can be submitted to relevant environmental protection agencies, to agencies that are responsible for establishing the SEA review council or to agencies that are responsible for approval of the proposed strategies and plans. However, the initial experience with the first domestic pilot SEAs that used the local resources in Vietnam indicates that public participation will be perhaps the most challenging part of any SEA (Nam and Dusik, 2008).

In 2006–2008, the Ministry of Natural Resource and Environment used the Sida-funded SEMLA programme to develop a General Technical Guidance for SEA (MONRE, 2008). The elaboration of the guidance included its pilot testing within various SEA pilots sponsored in Vietnam by Sida, GTZ, ADB and the World Bank. The guidance stipulates that SEA aims to integrate consideration of environmental impacts in the planning process and recommends that SEA should be carried out through flexible integration of

Table 6.4 *Examples of donor-supported pilot SEAs in Vietnam undertaken after passage of 2005 Law on Environment Protection*

SEA project name	Donor support
SEA of the Vinh Phuc Province Socio-economic Development Plan (SEDP) 2006–2010	GTZ
SEA of the Son Duong District (Tuyen Quang Province) Socio-economic Development Plan (SEDP) 2006–2011	GTZ
SEA of the National Power Development Plan IV – Hydropower sub-sector with a focus on impacts on biodiversity	World Bank
Prior SEA for the Forestry Master Plan 2010–2020	World Bank
SEA for socio-economic development master plan for the Red River Delta	World Bank
SEA of the Quang Nam Hydropower Development Plan	ADB
SEA of the Hydropower Master Plan within the Vietnam Power Development Plan IV	ADB
SEA for socio-economic development plan of Quang Nam Province	Danida
SEA of socio-economic planning for the coastal corridor in the Gulf of Tokin	Sida
SEA of land-use planning in key economic zone in the Northern Region	Sida
SEA of industrial development planning in key economic zone in the Central Region	Sida
SEA of the Con Dao Socio-economic Development Plan (SEDP) and the Con Dao National Park Tourism Development Plan	UNDP / WWF

the following tasks, as and when these are deemed relevant, into the various stages of the planning process:

1 Broad SEA scoping and elaboration TOR for the relevant SEA.
2 Determination of key environmental issues and environmental objectives related to the strategy or plan.
3 Identification of key stakeholders and preparation of a stakeholder engagement plan.
4 Analysis of environmental trends without the strategy or plan.
5 Assessment of proposed development objectives and scenarios of strategy or plan.
6 Assessment of future environmental trends as influenced by the actions proposed in the strategy or plan.
7 Concluding overview of the proposed mitigation/enhancement measures and proposed environmental-monitoring arrangements.
8 Compilation of the SEA Report and its submission to the relevant authorities for appraisal.

The guidance suggests that SEA could use simple techniques such as matrices, expert judgements, calculations and comparisons with relevant points of reference or trend analyses that can operate even in situations constrained by significant data gaps. Trends can be presented through: i) storylines that describe the overall trends, their main drivers, their territorial dimensions and key concerns and opportunities arising from these trends; ii) maps showing spatial development patterns; iii) graphs that illustrate the evolution of key issues overtime.

In response to this issue, MONRE initiated in November 2005 a process of donor coordination and harmonization aimed at more affectively focusing long-term capacity building support for SEA implementation in Vietnam. This mechanism which involved Sida, GTZ, Swiss Development Cooperation, Danida and the World Bank facilitated exchange of lessons learnt and coordination (see examples in Table 6.4). Donors also launched a multi-donor National SEA Training Program that supported capacity-building activities in various sectors and agreed to use the MONRE General SEA Technical Guidelines as the basic reference document for the elaboration of sector SEA technical guidelines within their various programmes (Nam and Dusik, 2008).

In 2009, the Ministry of Construction adopted specific technical SEA guidelines for urban planning; and the Ministry of Planning and Investment drafted SEA guidelines for socio-economic development planning. In 2010, additional SEA guidelines were under development for fisheries and agriculture. The latest development at the time of writing this article (October 2010) was the elaboration of the Prime Minister's Decree on SEA which aims to specify roles of sector authorities and differentiate SEA requirements for various planning processes.

During 2005–2010, for successful SEA implementation in Vietnam, it is critical that the first pilot projects are successfully adapted to local capacities and planning contexts and cover a wide spectrum of planning levels and sectors. Targeted support activities in the next 2–5 years will therefore be important in assisting Vietnam develop its capacity.

The knowledge and experience of SEA in line ministries and especially at a provincial level is still only partly developed given the wide scope of SEA with respect to sectors, planning levels and geographic locations. Further capacity building support will be needed to increase training coverage at provincial levels and in sectors that are not currently exposed to pilot activities.

Indonesia

The Ministry for Environment (the MOE) has shown a strong interest in the application of SEA as an environmental mainstreaming tool since 1998. The concept of SEA started gaining wider acceptance during post-tsunami reconstruction programmes when the various donors and authorities called for a more rigorous consideration of environmental risks and constrains during the planning process.

The MOE considered it important that the relevant authorities and public do not see SEA as a bureaucratic obstacle to approval of policies, plans and programmes, but rather as a flexible tool which facilitates planning and decision-making. In 1996, the MOE and the National Development Plan Agency (Bappenas) and the Ministry for Home Affairs (MOHA) started working together on developing a SEA system within the Indonesia-Denmark Environment Support Program. The ESP2 programme promotes cross-ministerial consultations on SEA; supports implementation of real-life SEAs in various planning processes on national, provincial and local levels; develops regulatory framework for SEA and guidance materials, and undertakes extensive awareness raising and capacity building throughout Indonesia.

The major impetus for the development of the SEA system was the adoption of Law No. 32/2009 on Environmental Protection and Management in September 2009. The enactment of this law was a remarkable achievement and the culmination of much effort since 2007 to promote and develop SEA system in Indonesia. This law stipulates mandatory obligations for conducting SEA for spatial plans, long-term development plans and medium-term development plans at national, provincial and local levels. It also requires discretionary SEA application for policies, plans or programmes which may pose significant environmental impacts and/or risks. It defines mandatory and optional analyses that may be conducted during such assessments and requires stakeholders' engagement in the SEA process. The law explicitly requires that SEA shall contain assessment of at least:

- the environmental carrying capacity and accommodating capacity for development;
- expected environmental impact and risk;
- ecosystem service performance;
- efficiency of natural resources utilization;
- vulnerability to climate change and capacity for adaptation; and
- biodiversity.

The law stipulates that SEA should become a basis for developing the relevant plans. It instructs authorities not to allow continuation of any undertaking and/or activity which exceed the environmental carrying capacity.

The main challenge in the future application of the new legal framework is the flexibility of the planning process in Indonesia and the limited appreciation of environmental issues in decision-making. The lessons from review of the first ten pilot SEAs applied during 2007–2009 indicate that plans, programmes and policies in Indonesia are usually prepared through a very flexible negotiation process which can be influenced only through facilitation from SEA experts, not by provisions of technical inputs alone (Dusik, 2010a).

SEA provisions laid down in the Environmental Protection Law were, in 2010, being refined in the Government Regulations on SEA and in the MOE's General Guidance on SEA. According to the guidance, SEAs should be conducted by teams that involve representatives of relevant authorities. SEA can use – depending on the needs of decision-making – quick appraisals or more detailed assessments to facilitate consultations on indentified concerns between the relevant authorities. External consultants, if engaged, will likely play a role of process facilitators or providers of specific technical inputs on key decision-making concerns (Dusik et al, 2010; Setiawan et al 2010). The aim of the SEA is to improve the planning proposal and to facilitate learning among relevant agencies, and the entire SEA process has many similarities with the institution-centred SEA approach promoted by the World Bank.

In 2010, Bappenas successfully tested the consultative approach to SEA proposed in the General Guidance on SEA in the palm oil sector. Subsequently, Bappenas started developing SEA guidance for national development plans and national sectoral plans that will further detail the consultative elements of the

SEA process (Sucofindo, 2010). The Ministry of Home Affairs has been preparing their own a ministerial regulation on SEA and also a guidance for an integrated SEA approach (Wibowo, 2010) that would allow assessment of multiple planning processes within one assessment process. In 2010, five such integrated SEA processes have being pilot-tested on provincial and local levels.

Experience in other countries

In east and southeast Asia, SEA also has been introduced or used in several countries other than those described above. Vietnam has established and implemented an SEA system under the Law on Environment Protection (revised in 2005, came into force in 2006). This process applies to socio-economic development and sector strategies and plans at national and provincial levels and land and resource use plans for inter-regional areas. It must be undertaken concurrently with the planning process and the preparation of a SEA report must be subject to review that serves as a basis for plan or strategy approval. The requirements for conducting SEA are outlined further in Circular No 05/2008 of the Ministry of Natural Resources and the Environment.

Other countries where SEA process development is underway include (see also Dusik and Xie, 2009):

- Malaysia: SEA is being developed as a process for sustainability appraisal of plans.
- Philippines: SEA legislation is pending (before Congress).
- Thailand: SEA guidance is under preparation, focusing on common procedures but flexible scope of application reflecting the nature of the proposal, level of detail required.

Box 6.1 *Status of SEA systems in east and southeast Asia region*

The development of SEA systems in this region with particular reference to developing countries can be divided into five main categories:

1 Countries that have introduced and implemented SEA systems including legal frameworks, specific guidance and increasing practice, namely China and Vietnam.
2 Countries that are developing proposals to introduce for SEA (Malaysia, Thailand and the Philippines).
3 Countries that are at an early stage of SEA use or experimentation with the support of donor agencies, namely Laos and Cambodia.
4 Countries that have little or no nationally driven or donor supported SEA activities (all other low-income or transitional countries in the region).

Source: Adapted from Dusik and Xie (2009)

Comparative review

In this section, some comparative analysis of SEA process development in countries of the east and southeast Asia region is presented, including:

- Overall status of SEA systems, level of process development and state of practice (Box 6.1).
- Key factors of SEA implementation and their evolution as at 2005 (Table 6.5).

In summary, based on the outcome of the Prague SEA conference, the main characteristics of SEA implementation in the Asian region are as follows:

- A great diversity in the status, quality and effectiveness of SEA in Asia.
- Strengths include the advantages of geographical proximity and some similarities in cultures and ways of thinking; and the flexibility and adaptability of SEA processes to suit different circumstances and socio-economic settings, which is reflected by the emergence of a variety of SEA approaches and practices.
- Weaknesses include lack of regional cooperation on SEA and insufficient information, experience and knowledge sharing across different settings. Except for a few places in Asia, there is a general lack of commitment, capacity and knowledge in actually managing and enforcing SEA of PPPs.
- Benefits of SEA as a tool for sustainable development are being gradually recognized.

Main trends and issues are summarized as below:

- There is increasing formalization of SEA in legislation and regulation but resistance, reservations and obstacles remain in some parts of Asia to the adoption of SEA at the national level.

Table 6.5 *SEA implementation in the Asian region (as of 2010)*

	Political Will	Legal Mandate	Institutions	SEA Procedure	Public Participation	SEA Application
Japan	O	×	O	□	O	□
Korea	O	O	O	□	O	□
China	□	O	O	□	□	□
Hong Kong	O	O	O	O	O	O
Mongolia	□	×	O	×	×	×
Singapore	□	×	O	×	□	×
Indonesia	□	×	O	×	×	×
Philippines	O	×	O	□	□	□
Thailand	□	×	O	×	□	×
Vietnam	O	□	□	□	□	□
Cambodia	□	×	O	×	×	×
Lao PDR	□	×	O	×	□	×

O Minimal; □ Present; × Absent;
Source: Adapted from Xie (2005)

- There has been increasing attention paid to public participation.
- There has been increasing attention paid to the linkage between SEA and sustainable development.
- Building capacity, gaining actual experiences and enforcing existing requirements for SEA remain major issues.

Conclusion

The key findings of this chapter are summarized in Table 6.6. Although now widely recognized in the Asian region, SEA practice is still limited to a relatively few nations or jurisdictions such as Hong Kong SAR, South Korea, China, Japan and Vietnam. Asia is very diverse in terms of the level and types of economic development, institutional capacities and political, cultural, social and environmental conditions. It is also very diverse with regard to the types and complexity of the policy-making and decision-making processes. These varying conditions call for a flexible, diversified approach in applying SEA conditions to suit different social and economic circumstances.

In Asia, SEA needs to be integrated with and linked to a wider government agenda for sustainable development and poverty reduction. This will be critical

Table 6.6 *SEA in the east and southeast Asia region*

Main trends and issues	There is a trend of increasing formalization of SEA in legislation and regulation. But resistance, reservations and obstacles remain in some parts of Asia to the adoption of SEA at the national level. There has been attention paid to public participation and the linkage between SEA and sustainable development. Building capacity, gaining experiences and enforcing the requirements continue to be issues.
Main perspectives	Strengths: There are the advantages of geographical proximity and some similarities in cultures and ways of thinking. There is also the flexibility and adaptability of SEA processes to suit different circumstances in different socio-economic settings. Weaknesses: There is a lack of cooperation in Asia on SEA and insufficient information, experience and knowledge sharing across different settings. Except for a few places in Asia, there is a general lack of capacity and knowledge in managing and enforcing SEA of PPPs.
Key lessons	SEA needs to be integrated with and linked to government agendas such as sustainable development and poverty reduction. Greater attention needs to be given to the practices rather than just getting legislation or regulations in place. More efforts need to be given to enable individual institutions and practitioners to learn, and to develop good success stories for capacity-building and for gaining acceptance of the use of the SEA instrument.
Future directions	Promote the development of a network of SEA professionals and international agencies. Promote SEA knowledge exchange. Promote mutual help and sharing of experiences to assist those who conduct pilot or actual application of SEA.

to overcome the lack of implementation of SEA. Greater attention needs to be given to the actual practices on the ground, rather than just getting legislation or regulations in place. Then much more effort needs to be given to enable individual institutions and practitioners to learn by doing, and to develop good success stories for capacity-building and for gaining wider acceptance of the use of the SEA instrument.

References

Au, E. (2003) *International Trend of Strategic Environmental Assessment and the Evolution of Strategic Environmental Assessment Development in Hong Kong*, Hong Kong Environmental Protection Department

Dusik, J. and Xie, J. (2009) *Strategic Environmental Assessment in East and Southeast Asia: A Progress Review and Comparison of Country Systems and Cases*, World Bank, Washington, DC

Dusik, J. (2010) 'SEA as a dialogue and planning support tool: Lessons from pilot projects in Indonesia', Indonesia-Denmark Environmental Support Programme, Ministry of Environment in Indonesia, Jakarta

Dusik, J. and Nam, L.H. (2008) 'Status of SEA in Vietnam', Workshop on Strategic Environmental Assessment in East Asia and Pacific Region, World Bank Institute and ADB-GMS Environment Operations Center, Hanoi, December

Dusik, J., Setiawan, B., Kappiantari, M., Argo, T., Nawangsidi, H., Wibowo, S.A. and Rustiadi, E. (2010) 'Making SEA fit for the political culture of strategic decision-making in Indonesia: Recommendation for general guidance on SEA', Environmental Support Programme, Ministry of Environment of Indonesia, Jakarta, June

ICEM (2006) 'Strategic environmental assessment in the Greater Mekong subregion—status report', GMS Environment Operations Centre, Bangkok, Thailand

Li, Tianwei (2008) 'Status of SEA development in the People's Republic of China', Workshop on Strategic Environmental Assessment in East Asia and Pacific Region, World Bank Institute and ADB-GMS Environment Operations Center, Hanoi, December

Setiawan, B. et al (2010) 'General guidance of SEA (draft 3)' (in Bahasa Indonesian), Jakarta 25 September

Sucofindo (2010) 'Draft SEA for national mid-term development plan for one sector', Bappenas, Jakarta, 15 September

Tang, T., Zhu, T., Xu, H. and Wu, J. (2005) 'Strategic environmental assessment of land-use planning in China', *Environmental Informatics Archives*, vol 3, pp41–51

Wei, L. (2005a) 'Progress of SEA in China', presentation at the OECD/DAC workshop on SEA, Vietnam, January 2005 (CD Rom)

Wei, L. (2005b) 'SEA of Grand Western Development Strategy', presentation at the OECD/DAC workshop on SEA, Vietnam, January 2005 (CD Rom)

Wei, L. (2006) 'Status of SEA development in the People's Republic of China', Planning Workshop on Strategic Environmental Assessment of Economic Corridors and Sector Strategies in the Greater Mekong Subregion, ADB/EOC, 9–10 August

Wibowo, S.A. (2010) 'SEA application for spatial and development plans: West Sumatra Province and its districts/municipalities', Ministry of Home Affairs, Jakarta, September

World Bank (2006) *Environmental Impact Assessment Regulations and Strategic Environmental Assessment Requirements: Practices and Lessons Learned in East and Southeast Asia*, World Bank, Washington, DC

Xie, J. (2005) 'A cross-country review of EIA regulations, SEA requirements and practice in east and southeast Asia', paper presented at the IAIA SEA conference, Prague

Yang, Y., Luo, S., Yu, Y., Li, Z. and Zhang, H. (2009) 'Overview of pilot SEA for the Dali Urban Development Master Plan till 2025', Yunnan Appraisal Center for Environment and Engineering, April

YEPB and Ramboll Natura (2009) 'Core training material on strategic environmental assessment: Version 2', Yunnan Environmental Protection Bureau, April

Zhou, T., Wu, J. and Chang, I. (2005) 'Requirements for strategic environmental assessment in China', *Journal of Environmental Assessment Policy and Management*, vol 7, no 1, pp81–97

Zhu, D. and Ru, J. (2008) 'Strategic environmental assessment in China: Motivations, politics, and effectiveness', *Journal of Environmental Management*, vol 88, pp615–626

Websites

Environmental Protection Department Hong Kong Special Administrative Region Government, Hong Kong SEA Manual and Web-based SEA Knowledge Centre, www.epd.gov.hk/epd/sea

Ministry of the Environment Government of Japan, www.env.go.jp/policy/access/index.html (in Japanese)

Ministry of Land, Infrastructure and Transport Government of Japan (MLIT), www.mlit.go.jp and www.mlit.go.jp/tec/kanri/process.html (in Japanese)

Yokohama northwest line, www.ktr.mlit.go.jp.yokohama/nwline (in Japanese)

7
SEA in Eastern Europe, Caucasus and Central Asia

Aleh Cherp, Henrietta Martonakova, Ausra Jurkeviciute and Maia Gachechiladze-Bozhesku

Introduction

This chapter reviews the development of strategic environmental assessment (SEA) systems in the Eastern Europe, Caucasus and Central Asia (EECCA) countries that were once part of the former Soviet Union. Although diverse, these countries share a number of similar structures that have influenced the evolution of their SEA systems. Specifically, SEA in the EECCA region is based on State Environmental Reviews (SER) and Assessment of Environmental Impacts (OVOS in the Russian abbreviation) procedures inherited from the Soviet era. Their main features, and implications for recent reforms aimed at incorporating internationally accepted standards of SEA practice, are presented, providing essential background to understand regional issues and challenges of introducing effective SEA systems. These perspectives are further developed through a strengths, weaknesses, opportunities and threats (SWOT) analysis of the status of SEA systems in EECCA countries and an evaluation of key requirements and directions for targeted efforts to build the capacity for SEA in this region. Our review is based on the studies cited and particularly on papers and discussions at the EECCA regional session of the Prague SEA conference.[1]

Regional context

The EECCA region includes 12 countries that used to be constituent republics of the Soviet Union and acquired their independence at the end of 1991. The region contains three geographically, culturally and economically distinct sub-regions: Eastern Europe (Belarus, Moldova and Ukraine), Caucasus (Armenia, Azerbaijan and Georgia) and Central Asia (Kazakhstan, Kyrgyzstan, Tajikistan, Turkmenistan and Uzbekistan). The Russian Federation – dominating this part of the world – can be considered as a large and diverse region of its own.

Despite its diversity, the region has many similar conditions that affect its SEA systems. Its administrative structures were inherited from the Soviet Union and still bear some features of a centrally planned economy. Most countries experienced severe economic decline in the 1990s, but some of them (for example, Russia, Kazakhstan and Azerbaijan) underwent vigorous recovery largely based on export of natural resources. Economic conditions of the region still vary widely with some countries (for example, Russia) being middle-income economies and some (for example, Moldova and Tajikistan) comparable in their income per capita to Third World countries. Some of these nations (most notably Georgia, Moldova and Ukraine) have expressed their commitment to integration into European institutions whereas others (for example, Belarus, Turkmenistan and Uzbekistan) have adopted a more cautious stance towards the West.

Evolution of environmental assessment in the EECCA region

SER and OVOS procedure

Environmental assessment (EA) systems in the EECCA region cover both projects and higher level actions such as plans, programmes, 'strategies', and so on. These systems are largely based on the so-called State Environmental (Expert) Review (SER or 'ecological expertise') system introduced in the USSR in the late 1980s. SER is a process of reviewing environmental aspects of proposed activities by 'expert' commissions appointed by environmental authorities. It was largely a government procedure, non-transparent for outside

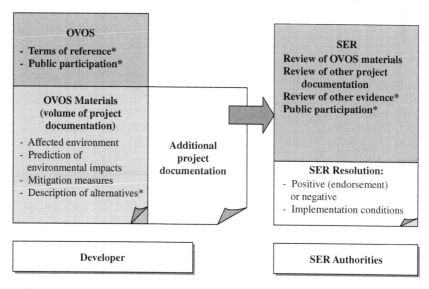

Note: *elements not always legally required and/or rarely implemented
Source: OECD (2003), see also Dusik et al (2006)

Figure 7.1 *Typical simplified content of and relationship between OVOS and SER in an EECCA country*

parties and not subject to independent checks. SER resulted in a mandatory 'Resolution' which might endorse or prohibit the proposed development and lay out certain implementation conditions.

The concept of OVOS was also developed in the USSR starting from the mid-1980s, largely inspired by EA in developed countries. OVOS is a procedure implemented by the developer to document potential environmental impacts arising from planned activities. However, in contrast to SER, the concept of OVOS has not figured prominently in legislative documents and there was little public awareness of this requirement. As a result, developers often neglected OVOS requirements. The relationship between OVOS and SER has not always been clearly delineated, though in most systems, findings of OVOS should be included in the project documentation that is reviewed by SER. The most typical content of and links between OVOS and SER are shown, in a simplified form, in Figure 7.1. Thus, EA systems of Newly Independent States (NIS) are often called SER/OVOS systems (Cherp and Lee, 1997).

EA Reform in the EECCA region

Following the disintegration of the USSR, all EECCA countries have undergone an unprecedented change in their political and economic regimes. In parallel, they had to tackle the vast legacy of environmental problems and struggle with threats to the environment arising from their accelerating integration into the global economy. These circumstances prompted a reform of EA systems in EECCA, largely inspired by international experience and promoted by internal and external pressures for environmental responsibility and transparency in decision-making. Particularly important for EECCA countries were EA procedures of the World Bank, European Bank for Reconstruction and Development and Asian Development Bank, as well as the UNECE Espoo Convention on EIA in a Transboundary Context (1992) and the UNECE Åarhus Convention on Access to Information, Public Participation in Decision Making and Access to Justice in Environmental Matters (1998) to which most EECCA countries are parties. With respect to SEA, the main driving force for the reform of SEA systems in the region has been the UNECE 'Kiev' Protocol on Strategic Environmental Assessment (2003), which four countries of the region (Armenia, Georgia, Moldova and Ukraine) had signed by the time of preparing this chapter (whereas some others, for example, Belarus, were seriously considering signing).

The general goal of EA reform has been to reduce the gap between the SER/OVOS systems and the internationally accepted EA standards. This intention has been reflected in more than 50 EA-related legal provisions adopted in EECCA during the 1990s. However, depending upon driving forces, capacities and circumstances in particular EECCA countries, these reforms have proceeded at various speeds and in various directions. Framework environmental protection laws that exist in all EECCA countries require SER and almost all EECCA countries have specific parliamentary acts regulating SER (and in some cases OVOS). However, some of these laws do not provide for significant modification of the SER/OVOS system, whereas others (for example, in Moldova, Russia and Armenia) have introduced prominent elements of the internationally accepted EA process.

Differences between regional and international practice of SEA

In nearly all EECCA countries, the SER (and in some cases OVOS) procedure applies not only to project-level activities, but also to strategic initiatives. However, in most cases, no formal distinction is being made between projects, plans, programmes and other activities. As a result, existing SEA arrangements significantly diverge from the international best practice and requirements of international conventions such as the Kiev SEA Protocol. These differences have been analysed in a number of studies (for example, Cherp, 2001; Dalal-Clayton and Sadler, 2005; Dusik et al, 2006) and can be briefly summarized as follows:

- **'Focusing' elements of SEA** (screening and scoping) are virtually absent from formal provisions in EECCA countries. On paper, SER is typically required for all planned activities and should address all environmental issues. In practice, the first requirement is unrealistic, especially in view of the limited capacity for undertaking SEA. As a result, SERs have been conducted discretionally for only a small proportion of arbitrarily selected plans and programmes and almost never for policies (Cherp, 1999, based on SER statistics for strategic activities in Belarus). Most of the SEAs documented so far have been pilot studies undertaken with the support and involvement of international organizations such as the Regional Environmental Centre for Central and Eastern Europe (REC) and the United Nations Development Programme (UNDP). The absence of scoping procedures have typically led either to the omission of significant environmental impacts from EA or, alternatively, to overambitious attempts to include too many.
- **'Analytical' elements of SEA** (impact prediction and analysis of objectives and other environmental implications) have been addressed under the implicit assumption that they are identical to project-level impact predictions. Accordingly, SEA practitioners have often struggled to predict impacts under conditions of considerable uncertainty typical for strategic initiatives and, as a result, they have been disappointed in the utility of SEA. For example, during the SEA of the 2006–2010 National Tourism Development Programme of the Republic of Belarus:

> *National experts – even those who successfully executed EIAs – struggled trying to identify likely significant consequences of a programme implementation for the environment and human health and to come up with relevant recommendations. To the great extent [this] can be attributed to the fact that the approaches and techniques used in SEA are different [from] those used in EIA. The national specialists also lack knowledge pertinent to managing of SEA process. (Tchoulba, 2005)*

The deficiencies of such an approach have been further aggravated by the traditional focus of the SER/OVOS system on verifying the compliance of planned activities to 'environmental requirements', sector and media-specific technical standards. Such standards are not applicable in the case of many strategic initiatives, which has hindered interpretation and application of environmental assessment findings in the EECCA region. In addition, the focus of SERs is largely on negative effects rather than positive effects and how these can be enhanced.

- **'Integration aspects of SEA'** have been dramatically underdeveloped. SER is sometimes called an 'outcome-oriented' approach to EA that has an ultimate purpose of deciding whether to permit or not to permit a planned activity (the so-called 'SER Resolution'). It is focused on final project, plan or programme *documentation*, not on the *process* by which such documentation is prepared. Such an approach is ill-suited to integrate environmental considerations into design of strategic initiatives because this should happen at a much earlier stage of planning. At the stage of formally documenting a strategic initiative, neither SER nor environmental authorities have sufficient mandate and influence to affect its shape. As a result, strategic initiatives have been rarely modified as a result of SER/OVOS-based EA.
- Finally, the **'participation aspect of SEA'** also has been neglected even with respect to the most basic requirements such as ensuring that EA reports and related documents are open to the public. In general, the EECCA countries have struggled to ensure participation even in project-level EIA, which has been viewed as a little more than state permitting procedure where no other parties except the authorities and the developer should be involved.

Most of these deficiencies arise from a mechanistic extension of project-level requirements to strategic initiatives in the EECCA countries. This can be traced back to the centrally planned economy of the USSR, where planning was considered a purely technical exercise not significantly different from project design and governed by essentially the same types of rules (including environmental rules). Most of the current SER/OVOS legislation in the EECCA region does not recognize the terms 'plan' and 'programme', and if it does (as, for instance, in Georgia), it does not treat them separately from 'projects' and requires the same type of environmental assessment provisions. This approach inevitably results in significant practical problems and discourages practitioners and officials from engaging in SEA, so that practical applications of strategic-level SER (or OVOS) remain very rare.

Key challenges of SEA system development in the EECCA region

In view of the current challenges of introducing workable SEA systems in the region, the session on SEA in EECCA at the IAIA Conference in Prague focused on the following questions:

- **Do EECCA countries need SEA?** Is introducing SEA a priority or should attention first be given to existing environmental regulation (including the project-level EIA), given that scarce resources and capacities cannot be spread too thin?

- **Can SEA effectively function within the current planning systems of the region?** SEA is best integrated with either 'rational', analysis-based planning or 'participatory' planning based on identifying and reconciling different interests. But do current planning processes in EECCA countries fit into any of these definitions? Many current plans are not based on either analysis or participation and therefore do not seem to provide any windows for incorporation of SEA.
- **Whether (and if so how) SER and SEA could be made compatible?** Given the above incompatibilities of SER and SEA good practice, should the SER system be dismantled and give way to a more 'modern' EA system? Or can SER be reformed to accommodate SEA principles? If so how? What would be the role of the renewed SER in SEA?
- **What is the best approach to strengthen SEA capacities in the EECCA countries?** This is a question of priorities. Where should key capacity-building measures be applied: to legal reform, training, guidance, awareness-raising, formation of networks or support centres?

Review of SEA SWOT in the EECCA region

Based on the discussion at the Prague SEA conference, a SWOT analysis of SEA systems in EECCA is presented in this section (see Table 7.1).

Strengths of SEA systems

The existing strengths of SEA systems in the region include enabling legal requirements for conducting environmental assessment of strategic activities.

Table 7.1 *SWOT analysis of SEA systems in the EECCA region*

Strengths	Opportunities
Legal requirements for EA (SER) of strategic documents. Established practice and some capacity for project-level EIAs. Established planning systems. Availability of technical environmental expertise.	Commitment to harmonize the EA systems with various international standards, especially the Kiev SEA Protocol.* Economic recovery and increasing attention to strategic planning. Mounting pressures for 'better governance'.
Weaknesses	Threats
Technocratic character of existing SER provisions (focus on 'environmental standards'). Dominant role of environmental authorities in SERs. 'Mandatory resolution' is seen as the main outcome of SER. Planning practice is largely obsolete and inefficient; capacity for strategic planning is lacking.	Declining interest in environmental matters. Authoritarian trends in governance hindering public participation and independent discussions. Declining scientific expertise due to brain drain and diminishing funding for research and education.

* The SEA Protocol to the Espoo Convention has been signed by Armenia, Georgia, Moldova and Ukraine

The project-level EIA systems have been in operation for 10–20 years, depending upon a particular country or jurisdiction, and have resulted in awareness, knowledge and skills regarding impact assessment principles and approaches. EIA, in the form of SER/OVOS, is a widely accepted and adopted practice, albeit with many shortcomings. In addition to SER and environmental protection laws, there is also rather developed planning regulation, especially concerning urban planning that often indirectly provides for SEA-type – or 'para-SEA', in the words of Dalal-Clayton and Sadler (2005) – instruments. Moreover, technical expertise for undertaking environmental studies is often available in the EECCA countries, particularly in larger university centres. These strengths, naturally, vary from country to country with SEA capacity larger in more economically developed EECCA countries.

Weaknesses of SEA systems

Key weaknesses of SEA systems in the EECCA region include their continuing basis in SER/OVOS systems that may be ill-suited to accommodate many of the current SEA approaches. The deficiencies of the SER/OVOS system, with respect to its focus, scope, analytical approaches, capacities for integration and participation, were outlined in the previous section. In addition, as discussed at the Prague conference, general planning and strategy-making practice in most of the region is far from meeting international standards. Planning processes are often neither formal and rational nor participatory with few 'windows' or possibilities for integrating SEA. For example, in one of case studies tabled at Prague, a draft of the programme undergoing a pilot SEA was made officially available for comments and consultations only a couple of days before it was formally adopted. Naturally, SEA could not be completed within such a timeline and had to rely on an earlier released 'unofficial' draft (Tchoulba, 2005).

These weaknesses vary across the region with some countries (for example, Russia) undertaking comprehensive reforms of their strategic planning systems, which in certain cases provide more opportunities for integrating sustainability considerations. Less democratic countries usually face larger problems with implementing SEA requirements. The difficulty of incorporating SEA in existing planning systems due to their limited openness was also noted as a key issue of concern in all pilot countries of the EECCA region (Dusik et al, 2006).

In addition, there is a low level of awareness of SEA benefits among all groups of stakeholders. Even the promoters of SEA in environmental authorities often see it as an extension of project-level SER, merely as an environmental permitting tool. Such a perspective not only prevents the design of effective SEA systems, but also 'scares away' developers of strategic initiatives who tend to see SEA as yet another bureaucratic control instrument. The academic community generally lacks an understanding of or experience in the SEA process. When involved in SEA pilots they often look for a universal 'SEA method' rather than trying to design approaches suitable for the specific situation as international good practice dictates. Finally, the general public and special interest groups often lack capacities and interest to participate meaningfully in SEA processes. Public consultation often fails due to poorly designed processes and prejudice among experts and planners regarding the public's interest in issues.

Opportunities for reform of SEA systems

Despite the above weaknesses, there are significant opportunities for reforming SEA systems in the EECCA region. Some of these opportunities arise from external pressures for complying with international legislation, most notably the Kiev SEA Protocol, but also the European 'SEA' Directive 2001/42/EC – especially relevant in Moldova and Ukraine, which have ambitions for European Union (EU) accession, and also in Georgia. For example, the Ukraine EU Action Plan provided the stimulus and framework for initiating the pilot project to implement SEA for regional planning in the Dnepropetrovsk region (Schmidt and Palekhov, 2005).

Other driving forces are internal and connected with economic recovery of the recent years, which has shifted attention from solving immediate short-term problems to developing longer-term plans. In the 1990s, longer-term planning in the region was largely absent, now it is increasingly practised at both national and regional levels. These emerging longer-term plans are often prepared with new, internationally recognized planning approaches rather than with old Soviet-style, centralized planning tools.

Such approaches allow better integration of SEA and similar tools. For example, the integrated assessment of the Tomsk Oblast regional socio-economic development programme (2005–2020) (Ecoline and REC, 2006; TACIS and UNEP, 2006) was relatively well-received and integrated in the strategy formulation process. SEA of the management programme for the lowering of the water level in the Krasnodarskoye Reservoir in 1991 is also an encouraging example since it had significant impact on the programme development (Kovalev, 2005).

Non-governmental organizations (NGOs) can play an important role in pressing for more effective SEA systems, especially if they operate in an international context. For example, in a recent Greenpeace Finland report, several Finnish timber producing companies were accused of procuring wood from Russian Karelia despite the fact that no SEA for the Regional Forest Management Plan had been conducted. As a result, the company started a dialogue with the regional authority on a need to conduct such an assessment.

Finally, the opportunity for SEA may also result from efforts for introducing better governance. Such efforts are most prominent in those countries that are responsive to strong external pressures for better governance, most notably in Georgia, Ukraine and Moldova. All in all, SEA awareness and knowledge are increasing, as are the number of its supporters especially among NGOs and academia, but also in government bodies.

Threats to further progress in developing SEA systems

On the other hand, the introduction of effective SEA systems proceeds relatively slowly due to many unsupportive trends and threats, including authoritarian trends in governance that hinder transparency, participation and public discussions, declining interest in environmental matters and low and decreasing external support for SEA development. For example, in the case of pilot SEA of the Yerevan City Master Plan, the proponent claimed the right to keep some parts of the documentation secret, which 'hindered studying the document subject to

SEA, understanding of the details of the Master Plan and making more informed judgments on its environmental impacts' (Ayvazyan, 2005). The systemic capacity to undertake SEA also may be declining due to a brain drain and diminishing funding for scientific research. As with other aspects of our analysis, the threats differ between the countries of the region and are most profound in more authoritarian, isolationist and economically unsuccessful states.

Strengthening SEA capacity in the EECCA region

SEA promotion in the EECCA region faces largely unfavourable conditions, which are not necessarily improving with the passage of time. This situation requires significant creativity in interpretation and application of generic SEA principles. Any efforts to develop the capacity for SEA in the region should be strategic and take into account the lessons of strengthening EA systems in the region. These lessons indicate that stimulating expansion and strengthening of EA policy networks – involving practitioners, academics, NGOs, developers and regulators and sharing broad goals of improving EA systems – is central to capacity-building (von Ritter and Tsirkunov, 2002; Cherp and Golubeva, 2004; Khusnutdinova, 2004). At the moment, such networks are nearly absent due to: (a) the lack of interest in developing effective SEA systems; and (b) poor interaction between promoters of SEA from various sectors.

In particular, the key obstacle to SEA development in the region has been the lack of interest from key stakeholders. Political leaders do not see how SEA could ensure broader support for their policies. Proponents of strategic initiatives – sectoral ministries, municipal administrations, and so on – do not believe that SEA can improve their plans or programmes, rather they view it as another bureaucratic obstacle that the Ministry of Environment seeks to impose to expand its control and constrain others' initiatives. Ministries of environment, in turn, are often confused by the 'soft' nature of SEA and not sure whether and how it can be smoothly integrated with SER, OVOS and other tools that they are familiar with. The example of the SEA report of the Yerevan City Master Plan being used in the SER process by the state environmental authority indicates a shift in perception of SEA. Experts and practitioners from the region are often scared by the perceived 'complexity' of SEA processes. Politicians, the general public and media see little connection between strategic initiatives and the day-to-day concerns of ordinary citizens. Finally, NGOs and public interest groups – who are often among the strongest proponents of SEA – are typically too weak to be heard in the present circumstances.

Ideally, this situation should be overcome by reversing perspectives of all these stakeholders so that:

- Policy-makers start perceiving SEA as an integral part of 'better governance' agenda.
- Proponents start seeing SEA as a guarantee of sustainability of their strategic initiatives.
- Ministries of environment find ways of integrating SEA with SER and OVOS.

- Experts and practitioners understand that SEA does not need to be very complex even if it is applied to large-scale strategic initiatives.
- The public and the media appreciate the value of 'deliberative democracy' when strategic decisions are objectively and transparently justified with reference to SEA and similar tools.

In addition, all of these groups of stakeholders should be collaborating or at least communicating with each other to build mutual trust which is a precondition for successful application of SEA.

Unfortunately, not all capacity-building initiatives are designed to contribute to this agenda. Many focus on producing 'training' or 'guidance' that at best are seen as irrelevant to the pressing issues and, at worst, aggravate rather than allay existing fears. For example, disseminating complex SEA

Box 7.1 *Findings of SEA capacity needs analysis in the EECCA region*

A recent capacity needs analysis for certain EECCA countries, undertaken by the UNDP and REC, pointed to the following needs and challenges in the area of SEA capacity-building:

- **Development of clear SEA related terminology:** Clear definition of terms 'plan, programme and policy' is crucial for further SEA system development.
- **Development of the legal framework for SEA** by either developing new laws or amending the existing ones.
- **Development of SEA national guidance, methodologies and training materials** for different SEA process stages. Guidelines are needed for screening, scoping, evaluation methods, assessment of cumulative impact, terms of reference for SEA preparation, monitoring, consultation and public participation, and so on.
- **Training** in forms of seminars and workshops structured around individual SEA related issues/topics and prepared in a way to reach different stakeholders: representatives of government and public authorities at different level, experts, trainers, NGO representatives, journalists, students, as well as the broader public.
- **Demonstration of SEA application in practice by implementing SEA pilot projects.**
- **Development of procedural schemes for different types of strategic documents** by presenting examples and lessons learned from other countries.
- **Creation of EIA/SEA national centres** (Armenia and Georgia) responsible for conducting seminars, training, developing educational and methodological documents, advertising campaigns, full training of specialists for the environmental assessment, licensing, networking, and so on. Those centres could also serve as the national EIA/SEA quality control bodies.
- **Development of accreditation system** for certifying the experts eligible to perform SEA.

Source: Jurkeviciute, Dusik and Martonakova (2006)

approaches used in developed countries or international organizations – which are clearly incompatible with the SER/OVOS and planning systems in EECCA countries – does little to persuade any of the key stakeholders of the potential utility of SEA. Calls for 'legal reform', which often implies dismantling or radically reforming the SER/OVOS system, are usually negatively received not only by 'conservative' officials, but also by environmentalists who feel that this system is the last of the remaining safeguards against unchecked environmental destruction in their countries. Capacity needs analysis in the region has pointed to the need for diverse, broad-based effort to build SEA capacities (Box 7.1).

'Smart' capacity-building efforts should facilitate the creation of 'adaptive EA policy systems' (Cherp and Antypas 2003), which are capable not only of copying someone else's approaches, but also of self-reflection and developing effective sustainable solutions to problems. Thus, successful capacity development efforts could use traditional approaches such as pilot studies but focus them on the strategic goals arising from this analysis. An example is given in Table 7.2. Finally, as noted by participants at the Prague conference, there is a need for enhanced regional cooperation and networking, taking into account the commonalities of the current EA system which are very specific to the region.

Table 7.2 *Focusing typical capacity-building tools on the overarching goals of promoting SEA in the EECCA region*

Capacity development tools	Focus on priority goals
Awareness-raising and advocacy	Invite both 'friends' and 'adversaries' of SEA with a focus on the key stakeholders listed above. Involve effective communicators who would be able to explain benefits of SEA to media, political leaders and the public.
Support to legal and regulatory reforms	Involve legislators or policy-makers on par with technical experts. Ensure that proposals for legal changes take into account the interests of key stakeholders otherwise it is unlikely they will be implemented.
Training	Make sure that training is demand rather than supply-driven. Focus on creating an in-country community of SEA educators (for example, in universities) that has a stake in an effective SEA system.
Pilot SEA projects	Focus on 'buy-in' of key participants. SEA may be 'packaged' as sustainability assessment and credibly linked to key policy concerns such as security, poverty and economic development. Set realistic expectations. Emphasize the learning nature of pilot projects. Establish mechanisms by which positive and negative lessons can be captured, discussed and disseminated. Provide seed support to networks emerging during the pilot projects.
Production of guidance and other materials	As much as possible, this should be used as an opportunity to reflect on the existing system with its advantages and disadvantages rather than on 'ideal' systems that 'should be' applied.

Note

1 The EECCA regional session of the SEA Prague conference was facilitated by Aleh Cherp (Central European University, Budapest) and Henrietta Martonakova, UNDP Regional Centre for Europe and the CIS, Bratislava. Contributed papers were: Chulba, I., 'SEA of National Tourism Development Programme in Belarus'; Schmidt, M. and Palhekov, D., 'Pilot Project on Implementation of Strategic Environmental Assessment on a Regional Level in Ukraine'; Kovalev, N., 'Examples of SEA in Russia'; Ayvazyan, S., 'Public participation in the SEA of Master Plan of Yerevan City in Armenia'; Jurkeviciute, A., Dusik J. and Martonakova, H., 'Capacity Building Needs Assessment for Implementing the UNECE SEA Protocol in Selected EECCA countries'; Borysova, O. and Varyvoda, Y., 'Ukrainian SEA System Development: Key Issues, Needs and Drawbacks'; Agakhanyants, P., 'Adopting New Regional SEA Legislation in Russia'.

References

Ayvazyan, S. (2005) 'UNDP/REC pilot project: Strategic environmental assessment (SEA) of the Yerevan master plan as the capacity building tool for SEA protocol implementation in Armenia', project report, www.unece.org/env/sea/eecca_capacity. htm

Cherp, A. (1999) *Environmental Assessment in Countries in Transition*, PhD thesis, School of Planning and Landscape, University of Manchester, Manchester

Cherp, A. (2001) 'Environmental assessment legislation and practice in Eastern Europe and the former USSR', *EIA Review*, vol 21, pp335–361

Cherp, A. (2003) 'Dealing with continuous reform: Towards adaptive EA policy systems in countries in transition', *Journal of Environmental Assessment, Policy and Management*, vol 5, no 4, pp455–476

Cherp, A. and Golubeva, S. (2004) 'Environmental assessment in the Russian Federation: Evolution through capacity building', *Impact Assessment and Project Appraisal*, vol 22, pp121–130

Cherp, A. and Lee, N. (1997) 'Evolution of SER and OVOS in the Soviet Union and Russia (1985–1996)', *EIA Review*, vol 17, pp177–204

Dalal-Clayton, B. and Sadler, B. (2005) *Strategic Environmental Assessment: A Sourcebook and Reference Guide to International Experience*, Earthscan, London

Dusik, J., Cherp, A., Jurkeviciute, A., Martonakova, H. and Bonvoisin, N. (2006) 'SEA protocol – Initial capacity development in selected countries of the former Soviet Union', UNDP, REC, UNECE

Ecoline and REC (Regional Environmental Centre) (2006) 'Integrated assessment of the Tomsk Oblast development strategy', Ecoline, Moscow, www.unep.ch/etb/areas/ IAPcountryProject.php

Jurkeviciute, A., Dusik, J. and Martonakova, H. (2006) 'Capacity development needs for implementation of the UNECE SEA Protocol: Sub-regional overview of Armenia, Belarus, Georgia, Republic of Moldova and Ukraine', www.unece.org/env/sea/ eecca_capacity.htm

Khusnutdinova, G. (2004) 'Environmental impact assessment in Uzbekistan', *Impact Assessment and Project Appraisal*, vol 22, pp125–129

Kovalev, N. (2005) 'Examples of SEA in Russia', paper presented at the SEA Conference, Prague

OECD (Organisation for Economic Co-operation and Development) (2003) *Linkages between Environmental Assessment and Environmental Permitting in the Context of the Regulatory Reform in EECCA Countries*, issue paper CCNM/ENV/EAP(2003)26, OECD, Paris

Schmidt, M. and Palekhov, D. (2005) 'Pilot project on implementation of SEA for regional planning in Ukraine', paper presented at the SEA Conference, Prague

TACIS and UNEP (2006) 'Integrated assessment of Tomsk Oblast development strategy till 2020 and Tomsk Oblast program of socio-economic development from 2006–2010', www.tacis.eac-ecoline.ru/pilots/tom/index-eng.html

Tchoulba, I. (2005) 'Pilot SEA of the National Programme for Tourism Development in Belarus', paper presented at the SEA Conference, Prague

von Ritter, K. and Tsirkunov, V. (2002) *How Well is Environmental Assessment Working in Russia?* World Bank, Washington, DC

8
SEA in the European Union

Barry Sadler and Ausra Jurkeviciute

Introduction

This chapter gives an overview of strategic environmental assessment (SEA) systems of member states of the European Union (EU), particularly those established pursuant to Directive 2001/42/EC on the environmental assessment of certain plans and programmes (also the SEA Directive). As a framework law, the SEA Directive lays down a minimum procedure and requirements for SEA of certain plans and programmes that must be given effect across all EU member states. However, to date, progress with national transposition and application of the Directive has been variable. Member states have moved at different speeds in introducing SEA and bringing existing systems into operational compliance. National arrangements and activities are diverse and, in some countries, also include SEA processes that are unrelated to the requirements of Directive 2001/42/EC. In both contexts, much about the status and scope of SEA practice across the EU still remains unclear.

Nevertheless, a general profile can be drawn of emerging aspects of SEA experience under the European Directive. Key features and characteristics are discussed in this chapter, together with reference to SEA systems in member states that address policy and legislative proposals. The discussion is organized into three main parts:

1   Background on the adoption and requirements of the SEA Directive and their relationship to other SEA legal and policy frameworks.
2   Review of the transposition and implementation of the SEA Directive in EU member states.
3   Analysis of the current state and quality of practice in the EU generally and in selected countries.

Background on the Directive and its adoption

Within the EU, the SEA Directive represents a major advance in SEA process development and practice. It is primarily procedural in nature and lays down the elements of approach that will form the basis of the SEA systems of all member states including those that previously had made little or no provision for this process. The SEA Directive is modelled along the lines of the environmental impact assessment (EIA) Directive (85/337/EEC, as amended by 97/11/EC) and applies similar requirements for certain plans and programmes, particularly those which set the framework for future development consent of projects. As the recitals to both directives attest, environmental assessment (EA) is positioned as a major instrument for giving effect to the evolving EU environment and sustainable development policy agenda (Sheate et al, 2005). However, much is assumed in relation to *how* the SEA Directive will achieve its stated objectives (see below). Moreover, the provisions of the SEA Directive were hard fought, long in coming and, inevitably, represent the residual product of much bargaining and compromise among member states and European institutions – which some consider to represent the lowest common denominator of acceptance (for example, Glasson and Gosling, 2001).

The making of the Directive

Like much EU legislation, the negotiation and adoption of Directive 2001/42/EC was a lengthy process that dates back by some accounts to early discussion of whether to include policies and plans in the EIA Directive (for example, Wathern, 1988). As a separate instrument, an initial proposal for a SEA Directive was released in 1990 by the European Commission (EC-Directorate General XI), based on commissioned research (Wood and Djeddour, 1989). Over the next five years, this proposal was discussed extensively, notably in relation to the types of strategic actions to be covered (Thérivel, 2004, p21), and revised in a series of drafts leading eventually to the adoption of an official proposal (COM (96) 511 final). In this process, Jones et al (2004, p16) consider the fifth environmental action programme (1993–2000) to have been an important policy driver to the development of a SEA Directive, despite resistance by many member states, 'not least the UK' (Reynolds, 1998, p241).

Five years elapsed before EC proposal (COM (96) 511 final) became Directive 2001/42/EC (see Feldmann et al (2001) for a review of this phase). Based on Opinions on the proposal by three EC committees and a First Reading in the European Parliament (1998), an amended proposal (COM (99) 73 final) was discussed by the (then 15) member states at the Council and common position was adopted in March 2000. Following negotiation under the co-decision procedure of the Parliament and Council, the text of a jointly adopted Directive was published in the Official Journal (L197 of 21 July 2001, p30). This culminated a decade-long process from initial draft to final conclusion of the SEA Directive, much longer if earlier discussions around the EIA Directive are accepted as the starting point and further extended if the three-year implementation period is taken into account. Given its protracted history, Thérivel (2004, p32) considers that the SEA Directive is 'much better than it could have been' and 'a great improvement on earlier versions'.

In retrospect, many may be inclined to agree with this sober summation of the result of what, after all, is a complex, entrenched process of European law-making. Of course, there is room for other interpretations or further qualification; for example, by those who question the scope of coverage of strategic actions in the SEA Directive or the reliance on EIA-based procedure (for example, Sadler, 2001a). Such issues were much discussed in commentaries and comparisons of the earlier drafts (for example, Feldmann, 1998; von Seht and Wood, 1998) and the SEA Directive in Article 12(3) provides for further review including consideration by the Commission of 'the possibility of extending the scope of this Directive to other areas/sectors and other types of plans and programmes'. They continue to be replayed today in the literature of the field, including recent EC-commissioned research as discussed below. As far as the historical record goes, however, Thérivel's (2004) comparative judgement stands up as well as any.

The requirements of the Directive

The SEA Directive is the subject of considerable review in the scholarly literature. It has been dissected individually and analysed comparatively in relation to other SEA legal instruments, notably the EIA Directive, on which it is modelled but differs in certain respects, and the SEA Protocol to the United Nations Economic Commission for Europe (UNECE) Espoo Convention on EIA in a Transboundary Context, which it has heavily influenced (Marsden, 2008). A thorough explanation of the key provisions of the SEA Directive is available in a number of sources including Commission and member state guidance documents (for example, CEC, 2003; ODPM, 2005a, b). Only a brief review of the main requirements of the SEA Directive will be given here, followed by short description of their relationship to other legal and policy frameworks that provide for or relate to SEA at the European or member state level.

In structure and content, the SEA Directive is a reasonably straightforward document, perhaps deceptively so for a closer reading of the language suggests a number of ambiguities and possible inconsistencies (discussed below). The anatomy of the Directive has been variously classified (for example, Thérivel, 2004). For present purposes, the fundamentals of the SEA Directive may be said to rest on three cornerstones: (a) rationale and objective; (b) coverage and scope; and (c) procedural requirements for undertaking assessment (Sadler, 2001b; Dalal-Clayton and Sadler, 2005). Brief commentary on their respective characteristics and issues is given below

Rationale and purpose

The rationale and purpose of the SEA Directive are described in the recital, primarily in relation to the principle of environmental integration. Substantively, paragraphs 1–3 refer to relevant international and EU environmental legal and policy documents (Articles 174 and 6 of the Treaty, the Fifth Environment Action Programme and the Convention on Biological Diversity) and Article specifies the objective of the Directive as being 'to provide for a high level of protection of the environment and to contribute to the integration of environmental considerations into the preparation and adoption of plans and programmes with a view to promoting sustainable development'. Procedurally, other paragraphs of the recital (particularly 4–6) underline the importance of establishing a common framework and requirements to ensure that SEA contributes to this objective across all member states.

In relying on due procedure to deliver its stated aim, the SEA Directive corresponds to internationally accepted practice. On coming into force, many saw it as giving a 'much-needed boost to environmental integration' (Sheate, 2003, 2004), although due procedure, while a prerequisite, provides for only a relatively weak level of environmental integration as a stand-alone provision. This has led some analysts to argue for the inclusion of more specific environmental safeguards such as 'duty of care' obligation safeguards to reinforce a presumption for a 'high level of environmental protection' in applying the provisions of the SEA Directive or other similar instruments (Sadler, 2001b).

Coverage and scope
The coverage and scope of the SEA Directive are described, respectively, in Articles 2 and 3. The 'certain plans and programmes' referred to in its formal title are defined as those 'which are subject to preparation and/or adoption by an authority at national, regional or local level' and 'are required by legislative, regulatory or administrative provisions' (Article 2(a)) and 'are likely to have significant environmental effects' (Article 3(1)). The scope of application is delimited further in Article 3.2 to plans and programmes which are prepared for defined sectors and actions 'and which set the framework for future development of projects listed in Annexes I and II to [EIA] Directive 85/337/EEC, or which, in view of the likely effects on sites, have been determined to require an assessment pursuant to Article 6 or 7 of [Habitat] Directive 92/43/EEC'. In Articles 3(3)–3(7), obligations are imposed on member states to determine whether the Directive applies: (a) to specified plans or programmes that undergo minor modifications or determine the use of small, local areas; or (b) to other types of plans or programmes, not referred to above. Articles 3(8) and 3(9) identify plans and programmes that do not require SEA, excluding those that address financial or budgetary matters or are solely for national defence and civil emergency purposes, or are co-financed for structural funds or rural development under the then current programming period (to 2006).

On balance, the scope of the Directive may be considered as reasonably all-encompassing. It includes many of the types of plans and programmes that are likely to be environmentally significant but excludes any that neither set a framework for projects nor affect a protected site. In addition, there are and remain areas of uncertainty about the strategic actions that are subject to the requirements of the Directive and questions continue to surface about how this provision has been and is being interpreted in different member states. These issues are the subject of an increasing literature (for example, Dalal-Clayton and Sadler, 2005; Jones et al, 2005a; Schmidt et al, 2005) and, almost certainly, the subject of future interpretation by the European Court of Justice (Marsden, 2008).

Procedural requirements
Procedural requirements for undertaking environmental assessment, defined in Article 2 as 'the preparation of an environmental report, the carrying out of consultations, the taking into account of the environmental report

and the results of the consultations in decision-making and the provision of information on the decision', comprise the main body of text. Key features comprise:

- Article 4 describes general obligations regarding timing of the assessment (notably during plan or programme and before its adoption or submission), integration of the requirements of the Directive (either into existing or newly designed procedures) and avoiding duplication where plans and programmes form part of a hierarchy.
- Article 5, supplemented by Annex 1, describes the information to be included in the preparation of an environmental report to analyse the likely significant effects of implementing a plan or programme and its reasonable alternatives, the considerations to be taken into account, such as 'reasonable alternatives' (5(1)) and 'current knowledge and methods of assessment' (5(2)), and the obligation to consult with designated authorities when deciding on the scope and level of detail.
- Article 6 describes the obligations to make the environmental report available to designated authorities and the public (6(1)) and to provide an 'early and effective' opportunity for them to comment (6(2)) and for member states to identify relevant authorities and the public and make detailed arrangements related to information and consultation (6(4)).
- Article 7 describes requirements related to transboundary consultations (subsequently overtaken by the adoption and pending ratification of the SEA Protocol).
- Articles 8 and 9 relate to decision-making and, respectively, describe the obligation to take account of the information and inputs from consultation during plan or programme preparation, and the information to be made available on the how these considerations have been integrated and the reasons for decisions.
- Article 10 requires member states to monitor the significant environmental effects of implementation of plans and programmes 'in order, inter alia, to identify at an early stage unforeseen adverse effects, and to be able to undertake appropriate remedial action'.
- Article 11 prescribes the relationship with other Community legislation. It requires an SEA to be undertaken 'without prejudice' to other legal requirements (11(1)) and gives member states the discretion 'to provide for coordinated or joint procedures' to avoid duplication of assessment arising from simultaneous obligations under different laws (11(2)), for example, Wild Birds Directive (79/409/EEC), Habitats Directive (92/43/EEC) and Water Framework Directive (2000/60/EC) are cited in Recital 19 of the SEA Directive.
- Article 12 concerns information, reporting and review and specifically requires member states to 'ensure that environmental reports are of a sufficient quality to meet the requirements of this Directive' (12(2)) and the 'Commission to report on the application and effectiveness of this Directive' before 21 July 2006 (12(3)).

The above articles lay down the procedural cornerstones for undertaking SEA of plans and programmes in the EU. In combination, they reflect many of the basic principles of good practice that are widely cited in the literature, albeit communicated in the legalese of the Brussels commissariat. Despite the prescriptive language, a number of legal commentaries have indicated that the wording of the Directive lacks clarity on a number of procedural matters including those relating to scoping, consultation and monitoring (Marsden, 2008), for example, what constitutes 'reasonable alternatives' (5(1)) or an 'early and effective' opportunity for public comment (6(2)) and does the requirement to 'monitor the significant environmental effects of the implementation of plans and programmes' (11(1)) apply individually or generally? In these and other cases, much has been left to the discretion of member states in transposing and implementing the Directive and many questions remain outstanding.

Relationship to other legal instruments
The relationship of the SEA Directive with other relevant instruments has become a matter of some consideration particularly in respect of areas of potential overlap. Guidance on this matter has been provided by the Commission with regard to implementation obligations under Article 11 (above) and the linkages among SEA of plans and programmes required under several directives (CEC, 2003, pp47–56). For example, specific reference is made to the Water Framework Directive (2000/60/EC), which is complementary in providing for a similar process for assessment of plans to the SEA Directive, and the Habitats Directive (92/43/EEC), which applies cumulatively with the SEA Directive for plans or programmes that potentially affect designated protected sites. Any joint assessment has to meet the procedural requirements of the SEA Directive and the substantive test of the Habitats Directive, namely certification that a plan does not adversely affect the integrity of a protected site (CEC, 2003, 51). Unlike the SEA Directive, the longer standing obligations under the Habitats Directive are the subject of a body of jurisprudence that also will bear upon joint assessment (Marsden, 2008).

In principle, the SEA and EIA Directives are complementary and vertically linked or tiered notably in respect of those plans and programmes that set the framework for development consent of projects listed in Annex I and II of the EIA Directive. However, a recent Commission study identified a number of areas of possible overlap that could be the source of confusion and may lead to non-compliance with the requirements of both Directives (Sheate et al, 2005). Examples include plans and programmes subject to SEA that, when adopted or amended, establish binding criteria for subsequent (and conforming) and large or complex projects that may be subject to both SEA and EIA requirements. In that case, Sheate et al (2005) argue that there could be scope for parallel or joint procedures that satisfy both sets of requirements and provide non-prescriptive guidance on how these might be undertaken and illustrate a range of approaches that may help member states to decide whether EIA or SEA or both might apply in different overlap situations. However, the practical extent of these discrepancies across member states is unclear and case law on the EIA

Directive has addressed such issues only indirectly and recently (for a UK example, see Tromans, 2008).[1]

Within the EU and at an international and pan-European level, there is a material relationship between the SEA Directive and the UNECE (Kiev) SEA Protocol (2003, now ratified) and, by implication, the UNECE (Aarhus) Convention on Access to Information, Public Participation in Decision-Making and Access to Justice in Environmental Matters (1998, came into force 2001). On adoption, the SEA Protocol was signed by the European Community and all member states, although, to date, only a few have ratified it (www.unece.org/env/eia/protocol_status.html). On coming into force, the SEA Protocol will create additional legal obligations on the parties. Assuming these include the European Community, this may require amending the SEA Directive or possibly the Public Participation Directive (2003/35/EC), which implements certain provisions of the Aarhus Convention with respect to plans and programmes. Although the Directive and Protocol are broadly similar in scope of coverage and procedural requirements, they also differ in certain respects; for example, the Protocol includes additional requirements for public participation (reflecting the Aarhus Convention) and a body of rules relating to the responsibilities of the Parties and to amending, ratification and acceptance (see Chapter 10 for further details).

Finally, although of singular importance, the regime established by the EC Directive and the transposing legislation of member states represent only one form of SEA provision within the EU. For example, the European Commission has developed an internalized procedure for impact assessment of the potential economic, social and environmental effects of policy and legislative proposals that is intended to support the implementation of the European Strategy for Sustainable Development (COM (2002) 276 final, also COM (2005) 97 final). A number of member states have broadly comparable forms of regulatory impact assessment (RIA) or have SEA-specific procedures that apply to policy and/or legislation. These will be mentioned and exemplified at other points in the following text; for a typology and review of their application, see Dalal-Clayton and Sadler (2005, pp44–102).

Transposition and implementation of the Directive in member states

This section provides a brief review of the SEA frameworks and legal measures adopted by member states and progress with their implementation. It draws on a number of sources of information including: the presentation at the Prague workshop by Soveri (2005); review of selected EU member states by Dalal-Clayton and Sadler (2005); relevant chapters on EU countries in Jones et al (2005a), Sadler (2005) and Schmidt et al (2005); the evaluation of the quality of national transposition and application by the European Environmental Bureau (EEB, 2005); and the survey of EU transposition and practice by Fischer (2007). More recent, country-specific information on national legislation was obtained as available on the EUR-LEX website (http://eur-lex.europa.eu), supplemented by ongoing work of the Regional Environmental Centre on Central and Eastern European member states (www.rec.org).

However, there are many gaps with regard to the particulars of implementation across and within member states. Specifically, there is considerable uncertainty surrounding basic facts, such as the number of SEAs undertaken or completed. Most member states do not appear to keep statistics on this subject and the information that is available on this subject is variable and often unclear or contradictory. It is thus difficult to piece together and come to a reliable judgement regarding the pattern of SEA implementation under the regime established by Directive 2001/42/EC. Accordingly, estimates of SEA application for each member state made in this section represent only a 'best guess' of their likely range.

Initial perspectives and comparisons

The requirements of the SEA Directive are considered by some analysts to be non-restrictive, leaving 'ample room for creativity, flexibility and adaptability to suit each member state's context' (Risse et al, 2003, p467). Such a wide level of discretion can be a double-edged sword, opening up differences and uncertainties in how certain procedural requirements might be interpreted (Marsden, 2008) and thus jeopardizing the European Commission's objective of ensuring consistency of SEA application across member states (CEC, 2003). Despite the common framework of European law, member states differ, in some cases markedly, in their mode of environmental governance, legal and policy frameworks and administrative systems and practices, all of which have exerted an influence on transposition of the SEA Directive (Soveri, 2005).

In this context, there is an acknowledged north-south divide in planning cultures, environmental attitudes and approach to EIA and SEA (Gazzola, 2008). Some analysts have interpreted such differences as a reflection of underlying processes and elements of 'ecological modernization' (Elling, 2007), recognizing the particular role of 'policy trendsetters' from the northern tier of EU countries (Janicke, 2005). Other mediating factors that may be expected to influence the timing and quality of transposition and the extent of implementation of the SEA Directive in that regard include evident variations in institutional capacity, particularly between smaller and larger countries, older and newer member states[2] and those with and without previous SEA experience.

SEA practice pre-Directive

Broadly understood, the current state and quality of SEA practice in EU member states can be expected to reflect their territorial size and prior record of experience. As indicated above, countries were at very different stages of SEA prior to the Directive coming into force. For summary purposes, they can be grouped into three broad categories:[3]

1   SEA practice developed already and predating the adoption of Directive 2001/42/EC (for example, Finland, France, Germany, Netherlands, Germany, Sweden and the UK).
2   SEA practice at a relatively early or interim stage of development and introduced in response to the requirements of the Directive (majority of countries).

3   SEA practice limited or non-existent with take-up only following the transposition of the Directive (for example, Cyprus, Greece and Portugal).

The type and relevance of SEA practice at the time of the adoption of Directive 2001/42/EC is also important, particularly in member states that had more than one form of SEA provision. For example, Finland and the Netherlands applied EIA-type processes to plan and programme proposals and appraisal-type processes to draft policies or legislation. In these cases, the two bodies of SEA practice are distinct and, respectively, directly and indirectly related to the requirements of the SEA Directive. Hildén (2005) has described these relationships in terms of Finnish practice and particularly the correspondence of SEA experience with plans and programmes to key features of the SEA Directive (also Hildén and Jalonen, 2005). A comparison of UK practice pre-Directive brings out similar differences. In this case, however, the two systems were based on different forms of environmental appraisal and the SEA regime for planning differed more substantially from the requirements of the Directive, although subsequently elements were merged with them (Sadler, 2005, also below).

Typically in member states that introduced SEA practice in response to the Directive, the start-up phase was through a series of pilot studies that were designed to integrate its requirements into the planning systems of individual countries. For example, Scott (2005) describes the value of the Irish experience in highlighting the key challenges that would be encountered in formal implementation. On an EU-wide basis, there were two distinct types of approach. In the EU-15, the pre-2004 member states, SEA pilots were largely informal, *ad hoc* and country-specific. In then accession countries, SEA pilots were more formalized, externally-driven within the framework of EU structural funds and, among Central and Eastern European countries, the subject of regional exchanges of experience under the Sofia Initiative on EIA. This regional process is acknowledged as playing an important role in building capacity to undertake SEA in accordance with the requirements of the Directive, and SEA experience of certain then accession countries, notably Poland, Estonia, Czech Republic and Slovakia, was likely in advance of a number of the EU-15 (Dusik and Sadler, 2004).

Time frame for transposition

Article 13(1) of the Directive required member states to be in compliance with its provisions before 21 July 2004. Only nine member states reportedly had given effect to the provisions of the Directive by this date and at that time 12 were sent a 'reasoned opinion' or warning about their failure to comply (EEB, 2005).[4] Despite this notice, transposition extended over the next three years, although there may have been extenuating circumstances in the case of federal states where the SEA Directive had to be transposed into regional as well as national law (for example, Austria, Germany and Italy). By most standards, however, this represents a pedestrian pace particularly bearing in mind the experience with the EIA Directive on which it was modelled. This slow progress had a number of implications, for example, rendering moot the 21 July 2006 timeline for the Commission to report to the European Parliament on the application and effectiveness of the SEA Directive (as required by Article 12(3)).[5] In fact, it was mid-2008 before all member states had 'brought into force the laws, regulations and administrative provisions necessary to comply with the SEA Directive' – to use the language of Article 13(1).

Conformity with the Directive

The fact of the transposition of the Directive into national legislation by member states is not necessarily the same thing as conforming to its requirements (Fischer, 2007; Marsden, 2008). As described below, the member states have used different legal measures for this purpose: most amended existing EIA or umbrella environmental laws (for example, respectively); others introduced new SEA-specific acts or, in one case, integrated the requirements of the SEA directive as part of a radical overall of planning legislation (for example, the UK with respect to land-use plans only). One initial look at the quality of transposition noted 'significant legal gaps' in some of the countries surveyed (EEB, 2005); another noted that, in many cases, it was 'unclear ... whether the Directive has been fully or only partly transposed' (Fischer, 2007). These have been the subject of ongoing review by the EC, which, as of October 2008, had opened 14 infringement procedures related to incomplete or incorrect transposition of the SEA Directive (Novakova, 2008). At least some of these are likely to be settled through a pilot process of conflict resolution; but others may end up before the European Court of Justice (ECJ).

SEA application

If transposition of and conformity with the SEA Directive are not necessarily the same thing, its implementation across member states is another matter and the quality and effectiveness of SEA practice are different issues again. The variable pace of transposition has strongly influenced the initial pattern of SEA application. As Table 8.1 indicates, some member states already have relatively high levels of SEA activity with hundreds of applications completed already or underway annually. Others are still at a relatively early stage of the implementation phase. Most fall within an intermediate range. This picture is highly incomplete (see note to Table 8.1) and subject to continuing change. However, for present purposes, it is the overall pattern that is important and this is likely to hold for the near future.

Several issues of SEA implementation have been raised already, for example with regard to exemption of plans and programmes as a result of inadequate screening procedure (EEB, 2005). Recently, the EC-funded study of the application and effectiveness of the SEA Directive (COWI, 2009) and the subsequent report of the Commission (COM (2009) 469 final) has shed further light on key trends and issues and preliminary perspectives on the state of practice and how well the SEA process works in different member states.[6] Much awaited by SEA scholars and practitioners, particularly with respect to any proposed amendments that might be included, the study and report represent an EU-wide review of progress in implementing the Directive. This information, together with other sources, has been used to update the following sections of this chapter.

Table 8.1 *Application of the SEA Directive in EU member states (as of mid-2008)*

Category/range of activity	Member states
Low (less than 10)	Cyprus, Italy, Luxembourg, Malta, Portugal
Low/moderate (10–50)	Belgium, Greece, Ireland, Lithuania, Slovakia, Spain
Moderate/high (50–150)	Austria, Bulgaria, the Czech Republic, Denmark, Estonia, Hungary, Latvia, the Netherlands, Poland, Romania, Slovenia
High (more than 150)	Finland, France, Germany, Sweden, the UK

Note: This is a highly approximate categorization of the level of applications per annum in implementing the SEA Directive in member states to mid-2008. Given data limitations, estimated process transactions in member states are given only within a broad range to give a relative measure of SEA implementation across the EU. Even within these band widths, in many cases the grouping of countries is arbitrary, particularly in the intermediate ranges and to a lesser degree in the upper and lower range of activity.
Sources: Updated from Fischer (2007) and COWI (2009); initial survey carried out by Jurkeviciute (Regional Environmental Centre for Prague SEA Conference)

Profile of individual countries' SEA arrangements and implementation

This section provides a brief summary of the status of SEA legislation and implementation in the individual member states. Neither the study nor the Commission's report address the application of the Directive on a country-by-country basis, although the former provides an annotated summary of national legislation (COWI, 2009, pp23–29) and also describes the experience of selected countries based on information supplied by contact points for member states and local consultants. Initial work for this section was undertaken by Jurkeviciute for the Prague SEA conference and updated from Fischer (2007) and COWI (2009). All estimates of the level of SEA activity are relative and keyed to categories in Table 8.1.

Austria
The SEA Directive was transposed at the federal and provincial ('länder') levels through numerous amendments to integrate its requirements into existing legislation and new statutory enactments (totalling more than 30 by 2008). At the federal level, for example, these include several acts that relate to competencies in waste management, transport, environmental noise, air quality and water management (for example, the Federal Act on Strategic Assessment into the Transport Sector) and amendment of the EIA Act (I 2/2008). Similar processes of legal reform have characterized the provincial level, where the requirements of the SEA Directive have been integrated into spatial planning as well as sector competencies (for example, the Tyrolean Spatial Planning Act, the Salzburg Waste Management Act). Guidance on screening and other steps in the SEA process has been issued by the federal Ministry of Environment and on the conduct of SEA within local land-use planning by certain provincial governments. Under these frameworks, a moderate to high number of assessments have been undertaken in Austria, particularly for spatial and local plans.

Belgium

The SEA Directive was transposed at the federal level in three pieces of legislation in 2006 and 2007, the most recent being the Royal Decree of 5 June 2007, on assessment of plans and programmes in a transboundary context. Separate legal measures apply in the Flanders, Walloon and Brussels Capital regions. In Flanders, the SEA Directive was transposed in 2003, based on the EIA and SEA Decree of 2002, and guidance issued on how to carry out SEA. In the Walloon region, the requirements of the SEA Directive were transposed through amendments to various decrees that distinguish land-use from other types of plans (for example, the Code for Spatial, Urban and Heritage Planning 2005) and through rules included in the Code of Environment (2005). A similar process has been followed in the Brussels Capital Region (for example, through the repeal of town planning ordinances and creation of the Code for Spatial and Urban Planning). The level of SEA application in Belgium is estimated to be moderate to low.

Bulgaria

The SEA Directive was transposed in the Environmental Protection Act (2002, numerous amendments to 2007) and Decree No 139 of the Council of Ministers (2004, amended 2006) also referred to as the SEA regulation. Bulgaria thus completed the legal measures necessary to bring the provisions of the Directive into force prior to its accession to the EU. Initially, it was thought that the integration of requirements of the SEA Directive with existing procedures for planning in Bulgaria might be problematic. However, this does not appear to be the case as more than 100 proposals have reportedly been subject to SEA, mainly urban plans and mostly included through a screening procedure.

Cyprus

The Directive was transposed in facsimile in the law on assessment of impacts on the environment from certain plans and programmes (102(I)/2005). The Environment Service has issued an information circular for the relevant authorities, consultancies and other interested parties. So far only a handful of SEAs have been undertaken in Cyprus.

The Czech Republic

In large part, the SEA Directive was transposed in a new Czech EIA Act (100/2004, amending 244/1992), which applies to policies and strategies as well as to plans and programmes as required under Article 3 of the SEA Directive. Article 10 of the Act lays down procedural requirements that apply to plans and programmes with certain exceptions, notably for land-use plans. These are addressed in the Building Code (183/2006) and are pending further revision in a proposed amendment to the Law on Construction and Land-Use Planning. Guidance on SEA was issued in 2004 and updated in mid-2006 and new guidance on land-use plans is in preparation. SEA application in the Czech Republic is estimated to be at a moderate to high level and includes a range of types of plans and programmes.

Denmark

Under an administrative order (Prime Minister's Office, 1993, as amended), provision for SEA bills and other governmental proposals to be approved or considered by the Parliament has been in place for more than 15 years, making this one of the earliest purpose-specific SEA systems in the EU. The SEA Directive was transposed by the Act on Environmental Assessment of Plans and Programmes (316/2004, amended by 1398/2007). Guidance was drafted in 2005 and issued in 2006, and there are supplementary materials on examples of SEA application. Prior to the SEA Directive coming into force, SEA was undertaken on an experimental basis at the regional level and to a lesser extent at the municipal level in Denmark (Elling, 2005a). The level of SEA application is estimated to be moderate to high.

Estonia

The SEA Directive was transposed by the Environmental Impact Assessment and Environmental Management System Act (2005), which is a framework law that is supplemented by regulations to give force to SEA requirements as stipulated in the Directive. However, the scope of Estonian legislation is much broader in coverage. SEA applies to all 'strategies' and the environmental report has to cover all aspects of the potential environmental impact, not only those 'likely to have significant effect'. No national guidelines have been issued, although authorities and stakeholders are asked to consult with the Ministry of Environment as necessary. The level of SEA application is estimated to be moderate.

Finland

Pre-Directive SEA systems were in place for legislative proposals (administrative order) and for certain policies, plans and programmes (Act on EIA Procedure, 1994) and for specific land-use plans under the Building and Planning Act (132/1998) and Decree (1998). The procedural requirements of the SEA Directive were largely transposed by the SEA Act (200/2005) and Decree (347/2005) on Assessment of the Impact of Authorities' Plans, Programmes and Policies on the Environment. In addition, the Building and Planning Act and Decree and to the Water Management Act were also amended. Guidance on the content and process of SEA in accordance with the Directive has been issued; it is complemented by earlier guidelines on how to assess social, biodiversity and Natura site impacts in land-use planning. Section 3 of the SEA Act is very broad (similar to the repealed Section 24 of the EIA Act) and encompasses a potentially extensive range of plans and programmes (Hildén, 2005). This is reflected in the high level of assessments particularly of local land-use plans undertaken in Finland.

France

The SEA Directive was transposed by a legislative framework established by a special Ordinance (489/2004) and series of regulatory decrees that define the rules of assessment and implementing measures for spatial planning and other types of plans and programmes. Specifically, Decree 608/2005 modified the French Land-Use Code and the French Code of Territorial and Local Authorities (relating to spatial planning) and Decree 613/2005 modified the French

Environmental Code (relating to other plans and programmes). In addition, Decree 454/2006 amended the French Forest Code. There are also different sets of SEA guidelines (Circulaires), respectively, for transport planning (2004), town and country planning, environment and waste management (all issued in 2006) and more recently for land-use plans at the regional level. The number of assessments undertaken in France is estimated to be high, in the area of several hundred annually.

Germany

The SEA Directive was transposed into federal law by amending the EIA Act (in 2005) with respect to general provisions and by amending the Federal Building Code (in 2004) with respect to specific provisions for urban and regional land-use planning. The Federal Building Code also includes regulations permit environmental assessment as a joint procedure to fulfil the provisions the EIA, SEA and Habitats Directives. At the regional level, the states or Bundesländer enacted separate SEA legislation for spatial and other plans and programmes (largely completed by 2006). Under these frameworks, various guidance documents have been released; for example, for transport planning, spatial and land-use planning under the Federal Construction Act, implementation of the SEA Directive through the länder, and to responsible authorities on SEA practice. The level of SEA application in Germany is estimated to be high.

Greece

The SEA Directive was transposed by Joint Ministerial Decision (2006/107017) on the assessment of the effects of certain plans and programmes on the environment. At the time of writing, only sketchy details were available on legislation, guidance and application. The level of SEA application is estimated to be low but an increase is expected under current EU co-financed programming for 2007–2013.

Hungary

The SEA Directive was transposed by an amendment of the Environment Act (53/1995, amended 2004) and by Decree 2/2005 on the Environmental Assessment of Certain Plans and Programmes in 2005. As amended, Article 44 of the Environment Act describes the SEA procedure and repealed the very general provisions for SEA that were previously in place and little used. Guidance documents on SEA include 'methodological questions of socio-economic and environmental impact assessments associated with regional development programmes', issued by the Hungarian Agency for Regional Development and Country Planning (2003). The level of SEA application is estimated to be moderate to high.

Ireland

The SEA Directive was transposed through two sets of regulations. Planning and Development (SEA) Regulations (436/2004) address specific land-use plans and European Communities (Environmental Assessment of Certain Plans and Programmes) Regulations (435/2004) address other types of plans and programmes that lie outside the scope of the Planning and Development Act (2000). Guidelines for regional and local (land-use) planning authorities on implementation of the provisions of the SEA Directive was issued in 2004 by the Department of the Environment, Heritage and Local Government and guidance on SEA methodologies was released in 2003 by the Environment Protection Agency. The level of SEA application is estimated to be moderate.

Italy
The SEA Directive was initially transposed in the Environment Code (152/2006) but its entry into force was postponed pending resolution of discrepancies with EC requirements – now addressed in Decree 4/2008, which separately prescribes the procedure for SEA and EIA. Not all Italian regions and autonomous provinces had transposed the Directive into legislation as of October 2008. A number of guidance documents are available including on the application of the SEA Directive to the EU Structural Funds for the 2007–2013 programming period (issued by the Ministry of the Environment, the Italian Environmental Authorities Network, and the Ministry of Economic Development). The level of SEA application is estimated to be low.

Latvia
The SEA Directive was transposed by amendment of the EIA Act (1998) and by the introduction of Regulations on Procedures for Strategic Environmental Assessment (157/2004). SEA application to specific sectors is extended beyond those listed in Article 3(2) of the Directive to include planning documents that are prepared for regional development, extraction of mineral resources and harbour development plans. Guidance documents include a guide to the SEA process (2005) and a Manual on SEA practice (2007). The level of SEA application is estimated to be moderate to high.

Lithuania
Pre-Directive, the Law on Spatial Planning (1-1120/1995) required a 'thorough assessment' of master and general plans (using EIA procedure). The SEA Directive was transposed by amending general provisions in two umbrella statutes: the Law on Environmental Protection (1992, amended by 36-1179/2004) and the Law on Territorial Planning (1995, amended by 21-617/2004). Specific requirements are regulated through several regulations on SEA (Government Decision 967/2004), on public participation (Order of Minister of Environment 455/2004), on screening procedure (Order of Minister of Environment 456/2004); and on determination of significance in Natura areas (Order of Minister of Environment 255/2006). guidance documents include a SEA Manual. The level of SEA application in is estimated to be low to moderate.

Luxembourg
The law of 30 April 2008, transposes the SEA Directive essentially verbatim. Little or no guidance or and implementation activity had occurred as of October 2008.

Malta
The SEA Directive was transposed by the SEA Regulations (418/2005). Draft guidance has been issued. The level of SEA application is estimated to be low.

The Netherlands

The SEA Directive was transposed by amending the Environmental Management Act (1987, 1994, amended 2006) and the relevant regulatory provisions of the EIA Decree (1987, 1994, amended 2006). Under this Decree, there was a mandatory application to certain plans and programmes, particularly those that fixed the location of projects. Despite this experience, Dutch transposing legislation only enshrines the minimum procedural requirements of the Directive. It makes no provision for mandatory independent review other than for plans and programmes with potential impacts on protected areas. A number of guidance documents on SEA have been issued (for example, by the Ministry of Transport, Water Management and Public Works). The level of SEA application is estimated to be moderate to high.

Poland

SEA provision was made initially through the Law on Access to Information on the Environment and its Protection and on Assessment of Environmental Impacts (2000), which applies to policies, as well as plans and programmes (pursuant to the then draft SEA Directive (COM/99/73)). The SEA Directive was transposed in several other statutes, namely the Environmental Protection Act (2001), the Spatial Planning and Management Act (2003), National Development Plan Act (2004), and Development Policy Principles Act of 2006. Also relevant is the Order of the Minister of Environmental Protection (2002) which details criteria for the environmental impact for local land-use plans. Guidance has been issued on SEA methodology for spatial plans and for plans and programmes (strategic documents), respectively. The level of SEA application is estimated to be moderate to high.

Portugal

The SEA Directive was transposed generally in Decree 232/2007 and in Decree 316/2007 (amending Decree 380/99) in respect of integrating SEA into the process of land-use planning. Subsequently, guidance on SEA methodology was issued by the Portuguese Environment Agency, supplementing earlier guidelines on strategic assessment for spatial/land and resource use plans (issued in 2003 by the Directorate General for Land-Use and Urban Planning). The level of SEA application is estimated to be low.

Romania

The SEA Directive was transposed prior to Romania joining the EU in Government Decision (1076/2004), which establishes the procedure that conforms to EC requirements as earlier enacted (707/2004). Guidance on applying the procedure was issued by the Ministry of the Environment and Water Management and the Environmental Protection Agency of Romania (2006). The level of SEA applications is estimated to be moderate to high.

Slovakia

SEA provision was initially made through the EIA Act (127/1994), which covers policy and legislative proposals in environmentally important sectors, as well as territorial or spatial plans (although, in practice, legislation is addressed through regulatory impact assessment). The SEA Directive was transposed by amending the EIA Act (24/2006) particularly at Part II which addresses scope of application to development 'concepts and strategies'. Under this amendment, SEA covers land-use/spatial planning, and any 'substantial development policy' in the sectors and areas prescribed in Article 3.2 of the Directive (which broadly correspond to those originally listed in the 1994 EIA Act). The level of SEA application is estimated to be low to moderate, although a number of major national development strategies have been subject to review.

Slovenia
SEA provision was initially made through the requirement for EIA of physical plans in the Environmental Protection Act (808/1998), which must be based on an environmental vulnerability study (pursuant to Article 51). The SEA Directive was transposed by amending this Act (57/2006) and by implementing regulations on the environmental report and on the detailed procedure to be followed. The level of SEA application is estimated to be moderate to high with a relatively large number of national strategies and local spatial plans processed by a small country.

Spain
Prior to 2000, a number of the autonomous regions of Spain had made provision for SEA in EIA, environmental protection or planning laws. The SEA Directive was transposed at the national level in the SEA Law (9/2006) and at the regional level by introducing new legislation or amending existing statutes. No guidance reportedly has been issued at the national level but there are various regional documents (for example, for Basque Country) and case materials (for example, relating to Andalucía, Baleares and Cataluña). The level of SEA application is estimated to be low to moderate (based on the limited number of cases at national level).

Sweden
In the 1990s, SEA provision was variously introduced for some sectors (for example, road transport) and for land-use plans (through revisions to Planning and Building Act (1992) as further amended in 1197/1995). The SEA Directive was transposed largely by amendments to the consolidated Environmental Code (808/1998) in 2004 and later in Law 57/2006. Related amendments were also made to the Ordinance on Environmental Impact Statements (905/1998). A number of guidance documents have been issued on SEA, both for general application by the Environmental Protection Agency and with specific reference to land-use planning by the National Board of Housing, Building and Planning. The level of SEA application in Sweden is estimated to be high.

The UK
Prior to 2001, non-statutory provision for SEA was made through guidance on policy appraisal (1991, for central government agencies) and environmental appraisal of development plans (1994, for local authorities). Given the devolved system of territorial administration in the UK, the SEA Directive was transposed

through several regulations and contemporaneously with a major reform of the land-use planning framework (the Planning and Compulsory Purchase Act, 2004). An umbrella regulation applies to plans and programmes that apply only to England or to England and any other part of the UK (1633/2004). Separate regulations apply, respectively, to Northern Ireland (280/2004), Scotland (258/2004, amended 2005) and Wales (1656/2004).[7] For land-use plans, the regulatory regime provides for an integrated process of SEA and sustainability appraisal (reflecting elements of approach from the earlier system of planning appraisal). A large body of guidance on SEA implementation, individually and subsumed into sustainability appraisal, has been issued by the responsible government bodies jointly and separately. The level of SEA application is estimated to be high.

State and quality of SEA practice

As the above profiles illustrate, the implementation of the SEA Directive is now underway in all EU member states, although to date their progress is very uneven. In this section, the focus is on the emerging state and quality of SEA practice, which represents the real test of the intent and requirements of the European Directive. Such features are difficult to evaluate and piece together into a coherent picture at this relatively early phase, when the body of SEA work is fluid and still evolving. The emphasis here is on emerging trends and issues of SEA practice including concerns that were anticipated in analyses of the transposition of the SEA Directive (Soveri, 2005) and in preliminary information and insights on the state and quality of SEA practice from a number of sources including papers and discussion at the Prague workshop on SEA in Europe, which were used as a baseline reference.[8] Subsequently, a more in-depth understanding of recent experience has been gained from the Commission study and report on the application and effectiveness of the SEA Directive (COWI, 2009; COM (2009) 469). However, it is probably still too early to reach informed judgements of effectiveness.

Areas and aspects of application

In its full scope, the body of SEA practice in the EU extends well beyond the experience gained through implementation of the requirements of Directive 2001/42/EC. As noted previously, some member states apply separate appraisal-based or RIA-type procedures in policy and law-making. Examples of the former include the Danish system for SEA of draft bills (Elling, 2005b) and the Netherlands environmental test (van Dreumel, 2005). The European Commission uses an RIA-type procedure for impact assessment of the environmental, social and economic effects of major new initiatives included in the Annual Policy Strategy or in the annual Legislative Work Programme. Although intended to be comprehensive and integrative, this procedure operates within 'somewhat tighter walls of cost-benefit analysis' (Renda, 2006). This is also the case in the UK, where an earlier process of environmental appraisal of policy was subsumed first into a framework for integrated policy appraisal (IPA) and then into a more formalized RIA procedure (Sadler, 2005).

As transposed in the legislation of many countries, the scope and elements of SEA practice also extend beyond the minimum requirements of the SEA Directive. Some member states (such as Poland and the Czech Republic) and sub-national jurisdictions (such as Scotland) apply SEA at the level of policies and strategies. In particular, Czech experience with SEA of major policies ('development concepts') predates the transposition of the Directive by several years and, under the new EIA Act, still applies to this level across a range of environmentally important sectors, such as energy, transport and regional development (Smutny et al, 2005). By many standards, the most significant innovation in the scope of SEA practice has taken place in the UK, where a new generation of Directive-compliant sustainability appraisals of land-use plans take account of social and economic as well as environmental effects. A large body of work has been rolled out already, comprising several hundred cases each year based on official estimates and covering regional spatial strategies, unitary development plans, local plans, structure plans and minerals and waste local plans (ODPM, 2005a). This area of SEA practice has been the subject of much attention (for example, Jones et al, 2005b; Sadler, 2005; Thérivel and Walsh, 2006).

The type and diversity of plans and programmes subject to SEA under Directive-based systems vary across member states, in some cases significantly between countries in the low and upper range of process applications (Table 8.1). In several countries, SEA applies to a broader scope of plans and programmes than specified in the Directive as illustrated by Finnish practice, which is grounded in particular experience with detailed local plans. Within the scope of plans and programmes listed in Article 3(2) of the Directive, SEA is most widely applied to land-use and spatial plans, predominantly at the local level, and there is now a wealth of experience in this area (Fischer, 2007). For sector plans and programmes, transport appears to stand out as an area of major application. Otherwise, from the limited information available, experience seems mixed and inconsistent across member states. As might be expected, in addition to transport, a range of sectors (for example, water, energy and waste) are represented in countries in the upper range of SEA transactions (such as France and the UK). The sectoral challenges and opportunities of implementing the SEA Directive have been discussed by Sheate et al (2004).

Community supported plans and programmes are now subject to the requirements of the SEA Directive and represent a rapidly emerging area of practice. Initially exempt under Article 3(9), structural and development funds for the programming cycle to 2006 were subject to a separate assessment procedure. Under the current framework of the Cohesion Policy (2007–2013), an estimated 350 Operational Programmes underwent SEA in 2007 and this number is projected to increase (Parker, 2008). This area of practice represents an important opportunity for ramping up low or low-moderate levels of SEA activity among new member states and in Greece and Portugal, which qualify as Cohesion Policy beneficiaries as the least developed countries of the EU-15, and also possibly in Italy through the 'statistical effect' of the Mezzogiorno, where gross domestic product (GDP) per capita is less than 75 per cent of the average for the EU-15. There is much riding environmentally on this so-called convergence objective, which has a budget allocation of €250 billion for growth and job creation (Regulations 1083(2006) and 1084(2006)).

Quality of practice – emerging issues and challenges

As discussed here, the quality of practice refers generally to how well (or badly) an SEA is carried out procedurally and analytically and specifically to whether or not the initial crop of applications are consistent with the requirements and purpose(s) of the Directive (contribute to environmental integration *and* protection). SEA experience to date, although still limited in many member states, indicates a number of emerging developments and issues related to the quality of practice. These are briefly discussed below and also annotated in the summary statement at the end of this paper.

Enabling conditions

A number of factors other than the prior level of experience (a proxy of capacity) support and shape the quality of SEA practice and input to decision-making. These include:

- **Provision of adequate procedural and methodological guidance:** A large body of SEA guidance on implementing the Directive has been issued including by the CEC (2003). Its availability and adequacy varies markedly across member states and as yet there is limited information on its use in and relevance for good practice (on drafting guidance, see Thérivel et al, 2004). The scope and detail of UK guidance is unparalleled. Key generic documents cover SEA of all plans and programmes in the UK and SEA/sustainability appraisal of land-use and spatial plans (ODPM, 2005a, b). Other guidance is specific to Scotland, Northern Ireland or Wales or to a particular sector (such as transport) or issue (such as climate change). This body of advice is comprehensive and somewhat daunting in its entirety and SEA practitioners would be expected to refer only to those parts that apply to the task at hand.
- **Nature and scope of public consultation:** Although public consultation is widely understood as an important component of SEA procedure, the Commission reports that the level of engagement in a number of member states 'was not as high as it might have been' largely because of the tight timeframes adopted (COM (2009) 469). In the detailed arrangements for public consultation, left to member states under Article 6(5), the emphasis has been largely on specifying the minimum conditions specified in Articles 6(1)–6(4) rather than going much beyond them. These arrangements include defining an 'appropriate time frame' for the public to express an opinion on the draft SEA (for example, 30 days in Germany, six weeks in the Netherlands) and the environmental authorities to be consulted when deciding on the scope of information to be included in a report. Since few countries provide for public consultation at this stage, the role of 'designated authorities' ('statutory consultees') is particularly important to ensuring SEA quality as exemplified by UK experience (Susani, 2005).
- **Role of environmental and independent review bodies:** In most member states, the authority responsible for a plan or programme also has the

responsibility for undertaking an SEA (COWI, 2009). This arrangement leans heavily on procedural checks and balances for quality assurance (see below) and particularly on the intervention of statutory consultees and the interested and affected public (see above). In some countries, the environmental agency has a direct role in overseeing or determining the quality of the SEA (such as in Spain, where the environmental agency prepares the draft scoping report). Only limited provision is made for independent review of SEA. In the Netherlands, for example, SEA of plans or programmes that potentially affect protected areas and sites are subject to mandatory review by the independent EIA Commission and, in France, an independent commissioner monitors the quality of public participation.

SEA practice at key stages

Experience with SEA application indicates that there are number of issues emerging in relation to key stages in the process (although much remains to be verified). These are summarized here in three main categories which have a particular relationship to quality of practice:

- *Screening and scoping*: Although screening procedure and practice do not appear to be issues of much concern, determining if the Directive applies raises interpretive issues for a few member states centring around what is meant by the terms 'setting the framework for future development consents' and 'administrative provisions' (COWI, 2009). Scoping is left to the procedural discretion of member states and according to the Commission (COM (2009) 469) does not appear to be problematic. It is undertaken on a case-by-case basis using different methods including consultation with designated authorities. Some countries also consult routinely, or in particular cases, with the public on the scope of the assessment. Key issues that have their origins in scoping include difficulties in interpreting 'significant effects' and identifying 'reasonable alternatives'.
- **Identification of reasonable alternatives:** This stage of the SEA process has important implications for the quality of the environmental report and subsequent decision-making on managing adverse effects while meeting plan or programme objectives. In the Commission's opinion, it is 'one of the few issues that have given rise to problems in Member States' (COM (2009) 469). Most of the member states have not considered how alternatives should be identified and selected, leaving it to case-by-case assessment (COWI, 2009). Earlier discussions at Prague suggested that the consideration of alternatives is a *pro forma* analysis, undertaken during report preparation to meet requirements rather than as a creative exercise in environmentally sound planning (see also Fischer, 2007).
- **Environmental report:** The quality of information in the environmental report was identified as an area of weakness at the Prague workshop, possibly reflecting the early stage of SEA implementation and the then limited capacities of many countries. More worrisome perhaps were the perceived deficiencies of environmental reporting, particularly an over-emphasis on technical, descriptive material that copies the information

listed in Annex 1 of the SEA Directive (which makes no reference to public consultation) and insufficient attention to its integration into plan or programme preparation and implementation. If this critique holds, the environmental report should also be written as a strategic, analytical tool for communicating with decision-makers and stakeholders and include a statement of the information gathered through public consultation process (consistent with the Aarhus Convention).

• **Monitoring and review:** Not much seems to be known about practice in monitoring environmental effects of implementing plans and programmes (Article 10(1)) or reviewing environmental reports to ensure they are of 'sufficient quality to meet the requirements of this Directive' (Article 12(2)) – both of which are critical to gaining a firmer understanding of SEA effectiveness. EC guidance describes general obligations related to monitoring and practical steps and measures that may be taken (CEC, 2003, respectively, at pp43–46 and 57–61) and similar discussions can be found in the national guidance issued by some member states such as the UK (ODPM, 2005b, pp86–89). Yet it is not clear whether member states undertake effects monitoring systematically, selectively or occasionally, what types of information is gathered and how it is used (for example, to take appropriate remedial actions if unforeseen adverse effects are identified). Similar questions apply to the review of the quality of environmental reports, although this is the subject of research as part of broader evaluations of SEA effectiveness (for example, RSPB, 2007).

Environmental integration

The basic tests of SEA effectiveness are whether and to what extent the SEA process: (a) integrates environmental considerations into decision-making (such as green plans and programmes); and (b) helps to deliver good outcomes. In the absence of review and monitoring information (as discussed above), provisional indications may be gained from other dimensions of integration including:

• **Type and significance of the issues and impacts addressed:** One indication of this relationship is the consideration of cumulative effects and the large-scale changes in SEA of plans or programmes and particularly in relation to protected and conservation areas. Despite its acknowledged potential to address these issues, in practice, SEA falls short as tool for identifying and managing cumulative effects both generally (see Chapter 24) and in many member states (as identified at the Prague workshop). Similar reservations apply to the use of SEA to integrate climate warming and biodiversity concerns and priorities into plans and programmes. In most countries, these aspects were either not included or information was not available in the initial crop of SEAs, although some progress had been made (EEB, 2005). For example, specialized guidance on SEA as a tool to take account of biodiversity and climate change has been issued and applied in certain cases in the UK (RSPB, 2007) and attention is given to both in SEA of plans and programmes in the Netherlands, although shortcomings in including ecological impacts remain the most visible deficiency in most environmental reports (NCEA, 2007).

- **SEA application to plans and programmes:** Environmental integration is reflected in the steps taken to integrate the SEA and planning processes (as opposed to undertaking SEA as a separate, parallel procedure). In principle, SEA application would be expected to follow the first model; in practice, it likely varies among member states and there will be different degrees of relative integration (or separation). Experience with SEA of land-use plans suggests generally that integration can be more readily accommodated within structured, hierarchical planning systems (Jones et al, 2005a) such as those in place in Ireland (Scott, 2005) and the Netherlands (Thissen and van der Heijden, 2005). However, numerous other factors shape the integration of SEA and planning processes and in some cases innovative approaches have been tried. For example, in Austria, integration was facilitated by the experimental use of round tables (such as in SEA of the Vienna waste management plan) and resulted in a series of specific benefits including better quality of planning, reconciliation of different interests, facilitation of plan implementation and contribution to environmental problem-solving (Arbter, 2005).
- **Benefits delivered and transaction costs:** If replicated on a larger scale, nationally or EU-wide, the above list of benefits could be taken as indicators of success in achieving the objective of the SEA Directive. Such benefits are numerous when aggregated from sources cited in this chapter and include both procedural (for example, transparency) and substantive (for example, environmentally sound plans) accruals. But they are unevenly distributed among member states and within an individual country on a case-by-case basis. For example, a survey of SEA quality in the UK identified a number of processes that illustrated aspects of good practice (checked against ODPM (2005a) guidance) that should ensure an environmentally sound plan (RSPB, 2007). To date, little or no information is available on the interrelationship of SEA quality, benefits delivered and transaction costs (fiscal and processing), which would be material to coming to firmer appreciation of the effectiveness of SEA.

Conclusions

A composite profile of experience with SEA in the EU has two main parts: Much of the attention in the literature and in this chapter is focused on the SEA Directive and the legal frameworks and operational systems that are in place in member states. In some countries, however, there is a parallel body of SEA processes that are applied particularly to policy and legislation. This adds up to an extensive and diversified picture of SEA within the EU and in some cases nationally, as in the UK, which applies multiple forms of SEA including sustainability appraisal of land-use plans within a devolved system of administration.

Internationally, the SEA Directive represents an important legal and procedural benchmark, establishing basic standards that now apply in 27 member states and have wider European reference, most notably in accession countries in the Balkan region. The influence as opposed to the remit of the Directive is more extensive, reflected in the comparable provisions included in the SEA Protocol which is potentially open to signatory countries from the UNECE and other regions. However, the singular imprint of the Directive is within the EU, notably when compared to what was there before in terms of SEA provision and practice. This comparative advance is particularly evident in the introduction of SEA in member states that had little or no previous experience in this field but it is also reflected in the strengthening the pre-existing SEA systems of certain countries. A notable example is the UK, where the SEA Directive, among other things, precipitated both a wholesale reform of land-use planning and a unique system of SEA-based sustainability appraisal.

Despite much progress, both the evolving regime and the state of current practice under the SEA Directive have been the subject of much concern and critical commentary. Key trends and issues identified in the analysis undertaken in this chapter:

- The making and adoption of the Directive (1985–2001) was long in coming and the product of much bargaining and many compromises (such as the stuff of European governance). As the residue of protracted negotiation, the Directive was not as good as some hoped for but better than many feared. It laid down the cornerstones of due procedure for SEA of specified plans and programmes but also has left a hangover of legal questions regarding the wording and interpretation of the Directive.
- The transposition of the Directive (2001–2008) into national legislation by member states was uneven and slow. The majority did not make the 21 July 2004 deadline and some took another three years to do so. As noted, transposition of the Directive is not the same as compliance with its requirements and a number of infringement procedures are now underway, some of which are likely to be the subject of European Court of Justice rulings.
- The implementation of the SEA Directive (ongoing since 2004) has proceeded at very different speeds in member states, reflecting the timeliness of transposition and degree of prior experience with SEA practice. There are significant differences in the level of SEA activity. In some countries, hundreds of applications are completed or underway annually; in others only a handful of processes have been initiated so far. Much is incomplete or likely to change with regard to this picture, although the progress of member states with a low level of SEA processing is open to question.
- The state and quality of SEA practice also vary markedly among member states, reflecting particularly the level of prior experience but also influenced by the provisions made for guidance, public consultation and independent review. Specific difficulties encountered at key stages of the SEA process include establishing the scope of an assessment and the alternatives to be considered, quality of environmental reports and monitoring the effects of plan implementation. At the Prague workshop, the perceived state and quality of SEA practice was found wanting in a number of respects and improving its effectiveness was identified as the core priority in moving forward (see Table 8.2)

Table 8.2 *SEA in the EU*

Main trends and issues	The development of the SEA Directive has gone through three main phases: EU adoption, transposition and implementation in member states and review of initial experience. After a lengthy transposition, the level of SEA implementation in member states varies significantly. Questions continue to surface regarding how the Directive is being interpreted in different countries, and now attention is turning to compliance and the quality of SEA practice.
Main perspectives	The spectrum of SEA application ranges from several hundred transactions each year in some countries to less than a handful in others. On an EU-wide basis, this spread reflects territorial size and the level of prior experience with SEA, as well as certain north-south and east-west differentials in capacity and culture of decision-making. These dimensions also help explain many other aspects of the variable geography of national performance in SEA.
	Emerging challenges of SEA application identified at the Prague workshop included screening, scoping, particularly related to interpreting significance of effects, tiering and the relationship of SEA and EIA and public consultation (which as a discretionary procedure varies widely in scope and form among member states). Much awaited is a mandatory review and report on these and other aspects of SEA practice by the Commission, although whether it will 'consider the possibility of extending the scope of this Directive' (as called for in Article 12(3)) is a matter of debate.
	The quality of SEA reports is also coming under scrutiny, particularly in member states where a large number have been completed already. In other countries, where experience is still limited, the focus is on the capacity for SEA practice and requirements for training. This aspect will need to be systematically addressed if there is to be a reasonably comparable standard across member states as called for by the European Commission in its SEA guidance.
	At the EU level, there are infringement procedures underway, reservations about the clarity of certain provisions and questions regarding the relationship of the SEA Directive to the requirements of other EC directives, the UNECE (Aarhus) Convention and when eventually ratified to the SEA Protocol.
Key lessons	Although narrower in scope than many wanted, the Directive represents an important advance; it lays down a minimum, EU-wide procedure for SEA of specified plans and programmes.
	Many questions remain about the extent of compliance with its requirements and almost certainly some of these will only be resolved only through jurisprudence (eventually building a similar body of SEA case law to that in EIA).
	In certain member states, low levels of SEA application suggest progress has been halting to date and needs to be improved.
	Quality of SEA practice, reported to be uneven and wanting at key stages of the SEA process at Prague, does not appear to have significantly improved since then, although some countries likely exceed minimum standards.

(continued)

Table 8.2 (*continued*)

Future directions	If the above observations hold, core priorities (strongly supported at Prague) were to strengthen quality and effectiveness of SEA, making it more consequential for decision-making, and to extend the scope of the Directive to policies and legislation and strengthen its procedures in areas of perceived weakness such as scoping and monitoring and follow-up. Other areas that need work include methodologies for analysing cumulative impacts and integration of health considerations into SEA. There was less agreement on the extent to which SEA should evolve from an environmental to a sustainability instrument.

Looking ahead, the Commission's long-awaited report to the European Parliament and to the Council on SEA application and effectiveness has now been received and has brought the analysis of experience up to date. Under Article 12(3), the Commission is mandated to bring forward proposals for amending the SEA Directive and particularly to 'consider the possibility of extending the scope of this Directive to other areas/sectors and other types of plans and programmes'. It now looks as if it will not do so. This was a topic of discussion among participants at a Prague round table in response to de Boer's (2005) presentation (see Table 8.2). In Prague, there was support for applying the Directive to the policy level including laws as well as strategies and legislation, for expanding the formal requirements for public and stakeholder consultation and for addressing the challenge of integrating SEA and health impact assessment. Finally, there was considerable discussion about the pros and cons of SEA as a basis for sustainability assessment: although most leaned in that direction, others were more sceptical about the advisability or practicality or doing so – mirroring a wider debate in the literature.

Notes

1 Tromans (2008) has reviewed the amendment made to EIA Regulations (2093/2008) regarding two-stage assessment (and found it lacking in clarity and likely to impact adversely on unwary planning authorities). He also cites work in which he examined the decisions of the European Court of Justice of 4 May 2006 on two linked cases (C-290/03, C-508/04). These related to UK rules for outline planning permission and subsequent approval of reserved matters, and focused on the obligation of the competent authority to carry out an assessment only at the initial stage (even though all aspects of the project may not be assessed). In both cases, the Court found that the rules were wanting in terms of compliance with the EIA Directive and the UK had not fully transposed Articles 2(1) and 4(2) into national law.

2 The distinction between older and newer member states is drawn here with reference to the expansion that occurred on 1 May 2004, when the then EU-15 became the EU-25 with the accession of eight Central and European and two Mediterranean countries, and subsequently the EU-27 with the accession of Bulgaria and Romania on 1 January 2007. In terms of transposition of the SEA Directive, the statutes of accession countries were substantially aligned with the European legal code, reflecting several years of EC-funded SEA capacity-building (see also note 3).

3 Not all countries fit readily into these categories. For example, it is difficult to classify the para-SEA processes that were applied as part of land-use planning in a number of Central and Eastern European countries in the 1990s, well before the adoption of the Directive and their accession to the EU. In this case, a distinction is made between these *ad hoc*, internally-driven reforms and the systemic, externally driven reforms to respond to the requirements SEA Directive (Dusik and Sadler, 2004).

4 The member states which received a final written warning (the last procedural step before referral to the European Court of Justice) to transpose the SEA Directive were Austria, Belgium, Cyprus, Luxembourg, Greece, Italy, Malta, the Netherlands, Portugal, Spain, Slovakia and Finland (only in respect of the autonomous province of Aland). Subsequently, five member states were condemned by the European Court of Justice (ECJ) for failing to transpose the Directive (COM (2009) 469 final)

5 The text of Article 12(3) reads as follows: 'Before 21 July 2006 the Commission shall send a first report on the application and effectiveness of this Directive to the European Parliament and to the Council. With a view further to integrating environmental protection requirements, in accordance with Article 6 of the Treaty, and taking into account the experience acquired in the application of this Directive in the Member States, such a report will be accompanied by proposals for amendment of this Directive, if appropriate. In particular, the Commission will consider the possibility of extending the scope of this Directive to other areas/sectors and other types of plans and programmes.'

6 This study and the report from the Commission to the Council, the European Parliament, the European Economic and Social Committee and the Committee of the Regions on 'the application and effectiveness of this Directive to the European Parliament and to the Council' (COM (2009) 469 final) meets the requirement of Article 12(3) (note 5 above), albeit three years after the date cited therein. In Section 2 of its report, the Commission explains that this delay was because the information available on 21 July 2006 was 'not sufficient to produce a report as planned' as a result of 'delays in transposing the Directive in many Member States (MS) and to the limited experience of its application'. Moreover, it noted that 'this first report had to take into account the experience of the new MS that acceded in 2004 and 2007'.

7 As formally titled, the relevant SEA legal framework in the UK comprises: the Environmental Assessment of Plans and Programmes Regulations 2004 (applies to England or to England and any other part of the UK); Environmental Assessment of Plans and Programmes (Northern Ireland) Regulations 2004; Environmental Assessment (Scotland) Act 2005 (came into force in 2006 and largely repealed the Environmental Assessment of Plans and Programmes (Scotland) Regulations 2004); and Environmental Assessment of Plans and Programmes (Wales) Regulations 2004. The Regulations for Northern Ireland and Wales are similar to those for England; the regulations for Scotland differ more notably in their application to all public sector strategies, including policies as well as plans and programmes.

8 This workshop was convened and chaired by David Aspinwall (then with the European Commission) and Ursula Platzer (Austrian Federal Ministry of Agriculture, Forestry, Environment and Water Management) with presentations from Ulla-Rita Soveri (Finland), Kerstin Arbter (Austria), Jan-Jaap de Boer (Netherlands), Lucia Susani (UK) and Ann Akerskog (Sweden). The authors of this chapter gratefully acknowledge their contribution and the inputs of participants to the discussion.

References

Akerskog, A. (2005) 'How is environmental assessment dealt with since new rules of SEA were introduced in comprehensive planning in Sweden?', presentation to the IAIA SEA Conference, Prague

Arbter, K. (2005) 'Testing SEA in practice: Two practical examples', presentation to the IAIA SEA Conference, Prague

CEC (Commission of the European Communities) (2003) 'SEA Guidance on the Implementation of Directive 2004/42/EC on the assessment of effects of certain plans and programmes on the environment', European Commission, Brussels

Dalal-Clayton, B. and Sadler, B. (2005) *Strategic Environmental Assessment: A Sourcebook and Reference Guide to International Experience*, Earthscan, London

de Boer, J-J. (2005) 'Future of SEA in Europe', presentation to the IAIA SEA Conference, Prague

Dusik, J. and Sadler, B. (2004) 'Reforming strategic environmental assessment systems: Lessons from Central and Eastern Europe', *Impact Assessment and Project Appraisal*, vol 22, pp89–97

EEB (European Environmental Bureau) (2005) *Biodiversity in Strategic Environmental Assessment, Quality of National Transposition and Application of the Strategic Environmental Assessment (SEA) Directive*, EEB Publication Number 2005/011, Brussels

Elling, B. (2005a) 'Denmark', in Jones, C., Baker, M., Carter, J., Jay, S., Short, M. and Wood, C. (eds) *Strategic Environmental Assessment and Land Use Planning: An International Evaluation*, Earthscan, London

Elling, B. (2005b) 'SEA of Bills and other government proposals in Denmark', in Sadler, B. (ed) *Recent Progress with Strategic Environmental Assessment at the Policy Level*, Czech Ministry of the Environment for UNECE, Prague

Elling, B. (2007) *Rationality and the Environment: Decision-making in Environmental Politics and Assessment*, Earthscan, London

Feldmann, L. (1998) 'The European Commission's proposal for a strategic environmental assessment directive: expanding the scope of environmental impact assessment in Europe', *Environmental Impact Assessment Review*, vol 18, pp4–15

Feldmann, L., Vanderhaegen, M. and Pirotte, C. (2001) 'The future directive on strategic environmental assessment of certain plans and programmes on the environment; state of the art and how this new instrument will link to integration and sustainable development', *Environmental Impact Assessment Review*, vol 21, pp203–222

Fischer, T. B. (2007) *Theory and Practice of Strategic Environmental Assessment*, Earthscan, London

Gazzola, P. (2008) 'What appears to make SEA effective in different planning systems', *Journal of Environmental Assessment Policy and Management*, vol 10, pp1–24

Glasson, J. and Gosling, J. (2001) 'SEA and Regional Planning – Overcoming the Institutional Constraints: Some Lessons from the EU', *European Environment*, vol 11, pp89–102

Hildén, M. (2005) 'SEA Experience in Finland', in Sadler, B. (ed) *Recent Progress with Strategic Environmental Assessment at the Policy Level*, Czech Ministry of the Environment for UNECE, Prague

Hildén, M. and Jalonen, P. (2005) 'Implementing SEA in Finland: Further development of existing practice', in Schmidt, M., João, E. and Albrecht, E. (eds) *Implementing Strategic Environmental Assessment*, Springer-Verlag, Berlin

Janicke, M. (2005) 'Trendsetters in environmental policy: The character and role of pioneer countries', *European Environment*, vol 15, pp129–142

Jones, C., Baker, M., Carter, J., Jay, S., Short, M. and Wood, C. (eds) (2005a) *Strategic Environmental Assessment and Land Use Planning: An International Evaluation*, Earthscan, London

Jones, C., Baker, M., Carter, J., Jay, S., Short, M. and Wood, C. (2005b) 'United Kingdom', in Jones, C., Baker, M., Carter, J., Jay, S., Short, M. and Wood, C. (eds) *Strategic Environmental Assessment and Land Use Planning: An International Evaluation*, Earthscan, London

Marsden, S. (2008) *Strategic Environmental Assessment in International and European Law: A Practitioner's Guide*, Earthscan, London

NCEA (Netherlands Commission for Environmental Assessment) (2007) *Annual Report 2007*, NCEA, Utrecht

Novakova, M. (2008) *Legal issues on EIA/SEA: Infringement cases and ECJ judgements*, European Commission, (Env.D.3, p16). Paris

ODPM (Office of the Deputy Prime Minister) (2005a) *Sustainability Appraisal of Regional Spatial Strategies and Local Development Documents*, ODPM, London

ODPM (2005b) *A Practical Guide to the Strategic Environmental Assessment Directive*, Scottish Executive, Welsh Assembly Government, Department of the Environment, Northern Ireland, ODPM, London

Parker, J. (2008) 'SEA Directive (2001/42/EC): Preliminary Evaluation of the Experiences, with a focus on the Structural Funds Programmes', report for DG XI (Environment), European Commission, Brussels

Renda, A. (2006) *Impact Assessment in the EU: The State of the Art and the Art of the State*, Centre for European Policy Studies, Brussels

Reynolds, F. (1998) 'Environmental planning', in Lowe S. and Ward, P. (eds) *British Environmental Policy and Europe*, Routledge, London

Risse, N., Crowley, M., Vincke, P. and Waaub, J-P. (2003) 'Implementing the European SEA Directive: The member states' margin of discretion', *Environmental Impact Assessment Review*, vol 23, pp453–470

RSPB (Royal Society for the Protection of Birds) (2007) *Strategic Environmental Assessment – Learning from Practice*, RSPB, Sandy, UK

Sadler, B. (2001a) 'A framework approach to strategic environmental assessment: Aims, principles and elements of good practice', in Dusik, J. (ed) *Proceeedings of the International Workshop on Public Participation and Health Aspects in Strategic Environmental Assessment*, Regional Environmental Centre (REC), UNECE, WHO/Euro, Szentendre, Hungary

Sadler, B. (2001b) 'Strategic environmental assessment: An aide memoir to drafting a SEA Protocol to the Espoo Convention', in Dusik, J. (ed) *Proceedings of International Workshops on Public Participation and Health Assessment in Strategic Environmental Assessment*, REC, UNECE, WHO/Euro, Szentendre, Hungary

Sadler, B. (2005) 'SEA developments in the United Kingdom', in Sadler, B. (ed) *Progress with Strategic Environmental Assessment at the Policy Level*, Czech Ministry of the Environment for UNECE, Prague

Schmidt, M., João, E. and Albrecht, E. (eds) (2005), *Implementing Strategic Environmental Assessment*, Springer-Verlag, Berlin

Scott, P. (2005) 'Ireland', in Jones, C., Baker, M., Carter, J., Jay, S., Short, M. and Wood, C. (eds) *Strategic Environmental Assessment and Land Use Planning: An International Evaluation*, Earthscan, London

Sheate, W. R. (2003) 'The EC Directive on strategic environmental assessment: A much-needed boost for environmental integration', *European Environmental Law Review*, vol 12, pp333–347

Sheate, W. R. (2004) 'The SEA Directive 2004/42/EC: Reinvigorating environmental integration', *Environmental Law and Management*, vol 16, pp115–120

Sheate, W. R., Byron, H. and Smith, S. (2004) 'Implementing the SEA Directive: Challenges and opportunities for the UK and EU', *European Environment*, vol 14, pp3–93

Sheate, W., Byron, H., Dagg, S. and Cooper, L. (2005) 'The relationship between the EIA and SEA Directives', final report to the European Commission, Contract No ENV.G.4./ETU/2004/0020r, Imperial College London Consultants, London

Smutny, M., Dusik, J. and Kosikova, S. (2005) 'SEA of development concepts in the Czech Republic', in Sadler, B. (ed) *Recent Progress with Strategic Environmental Assessment at the Policy Level*, Czech Ministry of the Environment for UNECE, Prague

Soveri, U-R. (2005) 'Overview of the Implementation of the SEA Directive', presentation to the IAIA SEA Conference, Prague

Susani, L. (2005) 'The role of the consultee in shaping the SEA process', presentation to the IAIA SEA Conference, Prague

Thérivel, R. (2004) *Strategic Environmental Assessment in Action*, Earthscan, London

Thérivel, R., Caratti, P., Partidário, M., Theodorsdottir, A. and Tydesley, D. (2004) 'Writing strategic environmental assessment guidance', *Impact Assessment and Project Appraisal*, vol 22, no 4, pp259–270

Thissen, W. and van der Heijden, R. (2005) 'The Netherlands', in Jones, C., Baker, M., Carter, J., Jay, S., Short, M. and Wood, C. (eds) *Strategic Environmental Assessment and Land Use Planning: An International Evaluation*, Earthscan, London

Thérivel, R. and Walsh, F. (2006) 'The strategic environmental assessment directive in the UK: One year on', *Environmental Impact Assessment Review*, vol 26, no 7, pp663–675

Tromans, S. (2008) 'The impact of the two-stage assessment', *The Environmentalist*, no 66, pp26

van Dreumel, M. (2005) 'Netherlands E-test', in Sadler, B. (ed) *Recent Progress with Strategic Environmental Assessment at the Policy Level*, Czech Ministry of the Environment for UNECE, Prague

von Seht, H. and Wood, C. (1998) 'The proposed European Directive on environmental assessment: Evolution and evaluation', *Environmental Policy and Law*, vol 28, pp242–249

Wathern, P. (1988) 'The EIA Directive of the European Community', in Wathern, P. (ed) *Environmental Impact Assessment: Theory and Practice*, Unwin Hyman, London

Wood, C. and Djeddour, M. (1989) *The Environmental Assessment of Policies, Plans and Programmes and preparation of a Vade Mecum*, vol 1, interim report to the European Commission, EIA Centre, University of Manchester

9
SEA in Southern Africa

Michelle Audouin, Paul Lochner and Peter Tarr

Introduction

On a continent where the livelihoods of the majority of Africans are closely linked to the health of the natural environment, and where poverty and land degradation has increased in recent decades, there is a critical need for sustainable management of the resource base and the ecosystem services that this provides. Most southern African countries already have environmental assessment and management policies and legislation in place and specific provision for strategic environmental assessment (SEA) exists in a number of them. Despite these trends, however, the opportunities that SEA can offer to facilitate sustainable development are not being realized.

In this chapter, we describe the emergence of SEA in the post-colonial, democratic context of southern Africa, provide an overview of the recent developments and argue that there is considerable scope for SEA to have a greater impact on sustainable development than it does at present. The metaphor used is that current practice of SEA is but 'the ear of the hippo'... there is huge potential beneath the surface.

African context of SEA

Placing SEA in the context of its potential application in southern Africa, requires understanding: firstly, of the intimate relationship of Africans to their predominantly rural environmental setting and the direct access to local natural resources that sustain them; and, secondly, of the socio-political context that has shaped the emergence of environmentalism and environmental assessment in post-colonial Africa.

Africa's dependency on natural resources

The well-being of African people is intricately linked to the health of the continent's natural resources (MEA, 2005). Most communities in Africa are particularly vulnerable to environmental and resource degradation as a consequence of their relatively immediate economic and social dependency on these resources. These factors make it exceptionally difficult for many African communities to adapt to deterioration in the state of their natural resource base, caused, for example, by natural phenomena such as droughts and floods (UNEP, 2002b). The connection to impoverishment of affected communities becomes obvious as the persistence of human demands compromises the capacity for essential ecosystem services to be provided on a sustained basis. This situation is well documented in the African Union's Action Plan of the Environment Initiative (NEPAD, 2003), which stated: 'At the beginning of the new millennium, Africa is characterized by two interrelated features – rising poverty levels and deepening environmental degradation.'

Both the formal and informal economies of most African countries are based on natural resources and activities such as agriculture, mining, logging and pastoralism (IPCC, 2001). Regarding the agriculture sector, the Intergovernment Panel on Climate Change (IPCC) reports that more than half of Africa's population is rural and directly dependent on locally grown crops or on locally harvested food. This renders Africans vulnerable from impacts on food security, for example, as a result of soil nutrient depletion and changes in rainfall, which is particularly important in the light of the future warming across Africa (IPCC, 2001).

Africa's dependence on natural resources is clearly illustrated in southern Africa, where the economies of all countries are heavily reliant on the agriculture (such as Tanzania, Malawi and Mozambique) or mining sectors (such as Zambia and Angola), or in several countries, a mixture of agriculture and mining (such as Botswana) (World Bank, 2006). The agricultural sector mostly uses traditional methods and employs more than 60 per cent of the labour force in the southern African region (SAIEA, 2003). In Malawi, for example, agriculture contributes to more than 45 per cent of gross domestic product (GDP) and supports 90 per cent of the population, while in Mozambique about 8 per cent of the estimated labour force of 8.8 million is employed in the agricultural sector (World Bank, 2006). Agricultural potential in the region, much like in many other parts of Africa, is negatively affected by land degradation caused by human-induced stresses, such as unsustainable farming practices, as well as natural factors, such as variable rainfall and fragile soils (SAIEA, 2003). Mining, much of it practised at an artisanal scale, is an important source of income in several countries in southern Africa, contributing up to 5 per cent of GDP (MMSD Southern Africa, 2002).

The unsustainable management of natural resources, leading, for example, to land degradation, desertification, decreasing water quality and quantity, decreasing biodiversity and increasing health risks, among other impacts, is a major constraint to the achievement of sustainable development (Regional Round Table for Africa, 2001). A significant proportion of Africa's biodiversity is either endangered or under threat of extinction, with some 2018 animal and 1771 plant species currently threatened with extinction (NEPAD, 2003). The status of the continent's forest resources are in overall decline and aquatic ecosystems are increasingly coming under stress due to altered hydrological processes attributable to catchment degradation, pollution, invasive aquatic species, urbanization and climate change, among several other factors (NEPAD, 2003).

Rapid urbanization and the associated deterioration of urban infrastructure compounds Africa's sustainability challenges (NEPAD, 2003). In particular, these are manifest as human health impacts as population concentrations result in the breakdown of services and supplies of essential resources such as potable water.

The vulnerability of African communities to environmental degradation is increased by a number of social factors, of which poverty is one of the most significant. The greatest hardships associated with resource depletion and deterioration are experienced by poor people (UNEP, 2002b). In a cyclical process, poverty is exacerbated by environmental change such as land degradation and deforestation (UNEP, 2002a).

Africa contains 34 of the 48 least-developed countries in the world (Regional Round Table for Africa, 2001), with 50 per cent of the population living on less than $1 per day (NEPAD, 2003). The amount of food produced per person in Africa has, contrary to global trends, decreased in the last two decades, leading to malnutrition and a greater reliance on aid, among other factors (IPCC, 2001). The African Round Table Report to the 2002 World Summit on Sustainable Development (Section II, 2, (21)) stated that: 'Poverty is projected to increase in Africa, and within two decades some 60 per cent of the population could live in abject poverty.'

Human vulnerability in Africa is also compromised by the pattern of external trade, which reflects low local levels of industrial beneficiation, in particular, of minerals (IPCC, 2001). This leaves many countries highly vulnerable to changes in the global market for raw materials. Wars and civil unrest are other key factors that increase the vulnerability of African communities, through the disruption of societies and the destruction of infrastructure (Regional Round Table for Africa, 2001).

This strong, close link between the current and future well-being of Africans and the natural resources of the continent highlights the critical need for effective environmental management at a strategic level. There are a number of policies, strategies and other initiatives, such as the New Partnership for Africa's Development (NEPAD), that articulate an African-derived plan for the sustainable development of the continent. The realization of these initiatives and the social development priorities that they promote will be achieved only through sustained access to ecosystem services. SEA, as a tool for integrating sustainability objectives into planning and policy-making, can perform a valuable role in this respect. However, to understand this role, it is necessary to first understand the context and factors influencing the emergence of environmental assessment in post-colonial Africa.

Environmental assessment in post-colonial southern Africa

The process of decolonization of southern Africa has revealed a fascinating, if not fully appreciated, coalition of parties eager to establish a sustainable new democratic order in many countries in the region. A common experience of colonial repression explains much of this phenomenon. Colonial rule inevitably led to well-documented liberation struggles in many southern African countries. The forced exile of indigenous leaders resulted in an interesting mix of political ideologies in the respective liberation movements that later became powerful political parties.

In this regard, the 'East' was important as it reinforced the desire among Africans for social justice, centralized planning and top-down rule. This contrasted with the ideologies espoused by a smaller number of exiled leaders who graduated from universities in the 'West' where they mostly studied law, politics, philosophy, education and the economics of capitalism. Thus, it was that diametrically opposing ideologues laid new platforms for governance in most countries in the region. Political leaders who had returned from exile, the private sector that had benefited from the colonial era, academics, trade unionists and human rights activists, suddenly found themselves around the same table, contemplating the best way to ensure a sustainable future for their country.

New constitutions, policies, laws and practices soon emerged in order to accommodate the vastly different perspectives from outside and within. Moreover, the citizenry in the respective countries increasingly demanded services and rights that were generally denied them during colonialism or apartheid, in the case of South Africa and Namibia. Balancing these demands with the political hype of liberation wars was (and continues to be) a tricky business. It was the need to meet these demands that forced the merging of seemingly antagonistic ingredients that in some cases was nothing short of a miracle.

In this context of political change, it is apparent that environmental assessment, as a new planning tool, had no currency in the powerful political and economic streams of influence that shaped the new post-colonial governments of southern Africa. Instead, the introduction of environmentalism within the region was predominantly externally imposed through donor funding, international lending institutions and other Western influences.

Surprisingly, the small number of local non-governmental organizations (NGOs) and environmentalists in early post-colonial Africa were often able to exert a disproportionate influence in promoting their environmental agendas in their countries. Emerging NGOs were successful in mobilizing resources from overseas and their relatively well-educated staff and volunteers could articulate coherent policies and mission statements for local application. They became useful partners for Western governments that needed to ensure that their development assistance programmes included environmental safeguards. Growing access to the internet enabled like-minded individuals to network at previously unprecedented levels.

Environmental management policy development in Africa was helped by the 1992 Rio Earth Summit and the international conventions that were developed at that time. Newly formed governments were quick to sign Multinational Environmental Agreements – perhaps in the expectation that they would boost their international profile and result in a fresh wave of donor support. In turn, regional economic organizations such as the Southern African Development Community (SADC) strengthened the environmental aspects of their own treaties or protocols, or created new ones.

In spite of the rapid emergence of environmental governance, the general reluctance of the political and economic stream of influence to actually embrace concepts such as sustainable development and environmental assessment (EA) is completely understandable under the circumstances. However, the limited appreciation among many politicians of the importance of ecosystem services for the development and maintenance of economies and livelihoods remains a cause of great concern for environmentalists.

To date, the environment has not featured prominently in the manifesto of any liberation movement or ruling party. Environmentalism remains on the fringe of mainstream thinking – kept alive mostly by small citizen interest groups, universities and NGOs. This explains why so many SADC countries look good on paper in terms of environmental assessment legislation and policies but their institutions remain severely underfunded, understaffed and politically weak. This is somewhat paradoxical given the entrenched and clearly appreciated human-environment relationships that exist in Africa.

Currently, however, there is an emerging realization within African governance structures that health and safety in the workplace, livelihoods and general quality of life can be promoted through the application of environmental assessment in development planning. Also, many communities are becoming concerned that industrial, mining and agricultural projects potentially cause impacts that compromise their well-being and development options for future generations. The environmental agenda is gradually becoming relevant to the general public and it can be argued that it is only a matter of time before it also becomes a mainstream political priority. Environmental assessment will then no longer be regarded as a green handbrake imposed by the West, but as an essential development planning tool. This change in mindset is emerging in some recent examples of policy and legislative developments concerning environmental assessment and management in the region. These are described in the section that follows.

Legislative and policy context of environmental assessment and management in southern Africa

Promotion of environmental assessment and management within SADC

SADC, which was established in 1992, is a key institution through which developmental challenges can be addressed on a regional scale and within member countries. The forerunner of SADC was the Southern African Development Coordination Conference, which was established in the late 1970s. The current members of SADC are Angola, Botswana, Congo, Lesotho, Madagascar, Malawi, Mauritius, Mozambique, Namibia, South Africa, Swaziland, Tanzania, Zambia and Zimbabwe (www.sadc.int/english/about/profile/index.php).

The principles according to which SADC and its members are expected to act are articulated in Chapter 3, Article 3 of the Treaty of the Southern African Development Community (SADC, 1992) as follows:

- Sovereign equality of all member states.
- Solidarity, peace and security.
- Human rights, democracy and the rule of law.

- Equity, balance and mutual benefit.
- Peaceful settlement of disputes.

SADC has developed a number of policies and protocols that have been ratified by member states and generally have influence on the way that development projects are implemented (Brownlie et al, 2006). With regard to the environment, these include protocols concerning shared watercourses, forestry, mining, fisheries, energy and wildlife conservation (www.iss.co.za/af/RegOrg/unity_to_union/SADC.html). In 2004, SADC approved a Regional Indicative Strategic Development Plan (RISDP) to provide clear strategic direction for future SADC policies and programmes (SADC, 2004). Twelve priority intervention areas were listed for which key strategies and broad targets were identified. Section 4.7 of the Plan relates to the environment and sustainable development. It includes a commitment by SADC to integrated and sustainable development and a recognition that 'encouraging progress' has been made in environmental management, but also notes that the SADC region still experiences high rates of land degradation, loss of biodiversity, pollution and other environment problems which undermine the sustainability of socio-economic development in the region (Section 4.7.1).

Brownlie et al (2006) identify SADC policy for the environment and sustainable development as notably enlightened. Through this policy, SADC aims to, among other things, accelerate economic growth with greater equity and self-reliance, improve the living conditions of the poor, ensure the equitable and sustainable use of the environment for current and future generations, improve the use of tools such as impact assessment and ensure a governance system that secures effective stakeholder participation in decision-making (SADC in Brownlie et al, 2006). Despite this commitment, SADC has not made significant progress in raising the level of environmental consciousness in the region and in the view of Brownlie et al (2006) the policy seems to have been a 'flash in the pan', as evidenced by very limited follow-up and little mention in subsequent SADC policies and strategies.

A related development is the SADC Regional Biodiversity Strategy (2006), which aims to provide a framework for regional cooperation in biodiversity issues that transcend national boundaries, and to stimulate the combined and synergistic efforts by the SADC member states and their communities in biodiversity conservation and its sustainable use (SADC, 2006). Despite the commitments to the conservation of biodiversity presented in this strategy, Brownlie et al (2006) state that it is weak in the sense that it does not provide an argument showing that biodiversity will underpin future economic growth. In addition, the strategy does not explicitly warn decision-makers that alternative ways of stimulating growth need to be found, rather than relying so heavily on natural resources.

Provision for SEA within SADC countries

Legal provision for SEA is made in a surprising number of countries within southern Africa. In several cases, however, this general provision is not supported by detailed regulations stipulating how an SEA should be undertaken (such as in South Africa and Swaziland). A brief summary of the general policy and legislative requirements for SEA within southern African countries is provided in Table 9.1.

Table 9.1 *Overview of policy and legal requirements for SEA in selected southern African countries*

Country	Legislation
Botswana	The Environmental Impact Assessment (EIA) Act (No 6 of 2005) makes provision for authorities to require the assessment of proposed projects, programmes and policies. The legislation also requires that the development of policies and programmes is accompanied by an SEA (Section 6(1)(b)). The process of undertaking SEAs as well as their content is currently being elaborated through Regulations for the Act.
Lesotho	The Environment Act (2008) requires an SEA to be undertaken for any governmental bill, regulation, policy, programme or plan that could have a significant effect on the environment. The specific processes that need to be undertaken within an SEA and requirements for its content are not presented in the Act.
Malawi	The Environmental Management Act (No 23 of 1996) requires environmental assessment of 'major policy reforms'. A revised National Environmental Policy was published in June 2004 by the Ministry of Natural Resources and Environmental Affairs, replacing the previous such policy of 1996. The key objective of this revised policy is to integrate environmental considerations into Malawi's social and economic development programmes thereby promoting sustainable development. Although the latest policy does not specifically mention SEA, it does mandate the authorities or anyone undertaking major development work to undertake a strategic assessment of the potential impacts, thus including elements of an SEA process (Kambewa, 2006).
Mozambique	The Environment Law (No 20/97 of 1997) is the foundation for a set of legal instruments for enabling the preservation of the environment. The Regulations (Decree No 45 of 2004) promulgated in terms of Article 16(2) of the Act, list activities for which an environmental assessment is required, some of which can be seen as programme-level activities.
Namibia	In terms of the Environmental Management Act (No 7 of 2007), government agencies are required to appoint a professional environmental assessment practitioner to determine whether a policy, plan or programme is likely to have a significant effect on the environment and an SEA is therefore required. The procedure for undertaking an SEA is outlined in draft regulations.
South Africa	Chapter 5 of the National Environmental Management Act (NEMA) No 107 of 1998 makes provision for the development of procedures for the assessment of the impact of policies, plans and programmes. No such procedures have been developed yet. The Municipal Planning and Performance Regulations (Ch2, s2(4)(f)) promulgated in 2001, in terms of the Municipal Systems Act No 32 of 2000, state that a strategic assessment is required of the spatial development framework contained in the municipality's integrated development plan. Requirements for Environmental Management Frameworks (EMFs), which fulfil many of the objectives of an SEA, are outlined in the EMF regulations (No 33306) promulgated in June 2010.

(continued)

Table 9.1 (*continued*)

Country	Legislation
Swaziland	Section 31 of the Environmental Management Act (No 5 of 2002) makes provision for the strategic environmental assessment of parliamentary bills, regulations, policies, plans and programmes, which may have a significant negative impact on the environment, or on the sustainable management of resources.
Tanzania	SEA is required in terms of Part VII of the Environmental Management Act of 2004. In this Act the type of information that must be included in an SEA is listed.
Zambia	The Environmental Protection and Pollution Control Act (1990) enables the Environmental Council of Zambia to identify plans and policies for which an environmental assessment is required. This can only be brought into effect through regulations, however, these have not been drafted as yet and therefore SEA is not formally enforced.
Zimbabwe	No formal requirements for SEA.

Source: Dalal-Clayton and Sadler (2005); DBSA and SAIEA (2009)

Current and emerging SEA practice in southern Africa

This section provides an overview of recent and emerging examples of SEA practice in southern Africa. It is not intended to repeat information provided in recent publications, but rather to supplement this information. For valuable reference material on SEA in southern Africa, the reader is referred to Dalal-Clayton and Sadler (2005), as well as DBSA and SAIEA (2009).

Countries within the SADC region are starting to experiment with SEA. There is a growing body of examples of SEA-type processes that have aimed to incorporate sustainability into the early stages of preparing policies, plans and programmes. There are various forms of SEA emerging, although such studies are not always given the title of SEA. Rather, these studies reflect certain principles of SEA and often aim to set strategic management objectives. Many of the studies undertaken in the region adopt a sustainability-led approach to SEA, rather than an EIA-based approach. This is possibly due, in part, to the sustainability-led approach to SEA advocated in the SEA Guidelines prepared for South Africa (DEAT, 2000) and a similar approach advocated by SEACAM (Audouin et al, 2003). Some examples of processes broadly reflecting the principles of SEA are provided in Box 9.1. These examples show that SEA tends to be undertaken as part of other processes, such as integrated land-use planning in South Africa, conservation planning, or resource management programmes (for example, fisheries management under the Benguela Current Large Marine Ecosystem (BCLME) Programme).

In general, little research on – or critical analysis of – SEA practice has been conducted within the SADC region. However, a review of 50 SEAs conducted in South Africa between 1997 and 2003 (Retief et al, 2006) was undertaken 'to evaluate the performance of SEA practice in South Africa in order to gain a better understanding of how SEA functions within a developing country context

Box 9.1 *Examples of SEA-type processes in southern Africa*

Management plan for the Okavango Delta

Several SEA processes have been undertaken in Botswana since the early 1990s. Most of these were for the water sector and include the development of the National Water Master Plan as well as management plans for the Okavango basin and delta. Others were done as part of the district development planning process (Keatimilwe and Kgabung, 2005).

A recent example of an SEA-type process is the development of the management plan for the Okavango Delta. The plan was prepared because of the need to resolve competing regional water demands through integrated management of the Delta's resources. Such planning is aimed at ensuring long-term conservation of the Delta, particularly in light of concerns regarding the importance of its ecological functioning, including threats to some species that live in it. The management plan (completed at the end of 2006) encompasses:

- A long-term vision for the Okavango Delta that includes development options and management scenarios.
- An integrated, dynamic management plan, providing the overarching framework and contextual guidelines for specific strategies and plans.
- Determination of levels of use in order to ensure sustainability and protection of the natural resources.
- Development options for the management of the entire basin (Okavango Delta Management Plan Project, 2005).

SEA and conservation planning

The philosophy of providing high-level plans that set the overall vision, objectives and targets (strategic framework) for subsequent more-detailed projects has been incorporated into several conservation planning projects in southern Africa. The Cape Action Plan for People and the Environment (CAPE) was an early example of SEA thinking framing the overall planning process (Lochner et al, 2003). The CAPE process included: a situation assessment to understand regional opportunities and constraints for conservation of biodiversity; a strategy phase to develop the overall vision and objectives for conserving biodiversity in a manner that delivered sustainable socio-economics benefits; and an implementation programme phase that developed actions plans for realizing the strategic objectives. Other subsequent examples of SEA being used to inform conservation planning are the SEA for the creation of the Greater Addo Elephant National Park in South Africa and the SEA for the Wildcoast region of South Africa.

This experience has generated valuable lessons on how to improve strategic processes, centred on two particular needs:

1 The need to improve the **usability** of the results, particularly by decision-makers (authorities, policy implementing agencies), for example, when identifying critical biodiversity areas, clear management guidelines must be provided as to what activities are appropriate in those areas and what should be avoided;

2 The need to provide clear **links to implementation**, for example though identifying who will implement the elements of the SEA (the 'institutional champion'), under what mandate, with what funding, and in terms of what existing statutory requirements/legal mechanisms.

Benguela Current Large Marine Ecosystem (BCLME) Programme

BCLME is one of the most productive marine ecosystems on Earth and is a globally important centre of biodiversity concentration, commercial fisheries, marine diamond mining and offshore oil and gas production. Critical transboundary issues exist, such as the migration or straddling of valuable fish stocks across national boundaries, the introduction of invasive alien species via the ballast water discharged from ships moving through the region, and impacts of pollutants or harmful algal blooms that can move from the territorial waters of one country into another. These issues led to the initiation of the BCLME Programme, a joint initiative by the governments of Angola, Namibia and South Africa to manage and utilize the resources of the ecosystem in an integrated and sustainable manner (Hempel, 2008). The programme was designed to improve the structures and capacities of these countries to deal with environmental problems that occur across their boundaries, in order that the ecosystem may be managed as a whole.

The principles, objectives and actions for the BCLME Programme were embodied in the Strategic Action Plan, with the actions including, for example (Hempel, 2008):

- Developing an improved understanding of the ecosystem and monitoring priorities.
- Building capacity and institutional structures for ongoing management.
- Sustainable resource management (for example, coordinated management of fish catches among the three countries).
- Harmonizing of policy and legislation relating to human activities in the BCLME.
- Modelling of cumulative effects of these activities on the ecosystem.

with a voluntary SEA system' (Retief et al, 2006, p1). Although specific to SEA practice in South Africa, the findings of this study could be considered to have wider relevance in southern Africa.

From their research, Retief et al conclude that SEA is well-established in South Africa and they expect it to continue growing, in particular as a result of potential new legislation requiring SEA as an input to planning and decision-making processes (SEA would be implicit in this legislation, without explicit requirements). They also noted a diversity of forms of SEAs – for different sectors, different policy, planning or programme levels and from transboundary to local scales. Although there is reference to SEA in existing policies and legislation (see to Table 9.1), detailed and explicit requirements for SEA have not been promulgated in the form of regulations.

A strong consultancy sector in South Africa has, in the past, driven SEA practice, a feature that may be unique among developing countries. However, when analysing the performance of SEA using selected case studies,

Retief et al found that SEA was largely ineffective in influencing decision-making. This indicates that, while a strong consultancy sector can facilitate SEA practice, it cannot ensure effective implementation and the outcomes are likely to be ineffective without support from the public sector (Retief et al, 2006).

Further analysis by Retief et al identified three key features in the application of SEA in South Africa. They are shown in Table 9.2 with further responses provided by the authors of this chapter.

It is the impression of the authors, that since the study undertaken by Retief et al (2006), the number of SEAs conducted per year is, in fact, declining in some countries. A notable exception is Namibia, where four major SEAs were undertaken in the past five years.[1] A likely contributing factor for the decline in the number of SEAs in South Africa is the introduction, within legislation, of Environmental Management Frameworks (EMFs), which fulfil many of the typical requirements of an SEA. Regulations (No 33306, 2010) promulgated under the

Table 9.2 *Key features from recent analysis of the application of SEA in South Africa*

Features of SEA in South Africa, as identified by Retief et al (2006)	Responses
Lack of focus: The SEAs tended to be too extensive with an unmanageable number of issues and objectives, and lacked a formal scoping process.	This is a reflection of the challenges in grappling with the concept of sustainability and the broad understanding of the term 'environment' used in South Africa (including the biophysical, social and economic spheres). These SEAs were usually done in the absence of higher level strategies or plans (for example, the National Sustainable Development Strategy, the National Biodiversity Strategy and Action Plan, and so on), which have been developed subsequently and would assist in focusing SEAs on recognized priorities.
Lack of integration with decision-making: The SEAs were overloaded with information (often in the form of 'hard science'), but weak in creating the link to how that information could be used effectively in the more subjective value-driven political realm of strategic decision-making.	A critical area for improvement in SEA is to ensure that the outcomes dovetail with existing decision-making processes and implementation programmes, wherever possible; and give more consideration to how value systems and opinions will influence the effectiveness of the SEA.
Lack of 'assessment': The SEAs were closer to planning and frequently did not include a formal 'assessment' of the policy, plan or programme. The more proactive the SEA, the more it moved towards planning.	This could be because the SEAs adopted a 'sustainability-led' approach rather than the 'EIA-based' model, in order to be more proactive. Using the former model, SEA provides a framework for planning and decision-making, rather than a formal 'assessment'. Both forms of SEA are useful, depending on the stage in the life cycle of the policy, plan or programme at which the SEA is being initiated.

National Environmental Management Act (NEMA) (No 107 of 1998) enable the national or provincial Environmental Minister to initiate the compilation of an EMF, which aims to promote sustainability and cooperative governance and ensure environmental protection (DWEA, 2010, chapter 2, section 3 (a−c)). The process of compiling an EMF must be a participatory one that includes an analysis of the environmental attributes of a particular geographical area, as well as a description of the desired state of the environment and the way in which such a state will be reached (DWEA, 2010, chapter 3, section 3(b−d)). This information is then used to inform environmental management in the area in general, as well as to inform decisions concerning applications for environmental authorizations in particular (DWEA, 2010, chapter 2 (1)(b and c)).

Future of SEA in southern Africa

Existing experience with SEA-type processes in southern Africa are, to use an African metaphor, just the 'ear of the hippo', meaning just the beginning, with huge potential beneath the surface. There are lots of opportunities for SEA-type studies and they are much needed. Several factors point to an increased use of SEA philosophy and process, for example:

- A growing pool of strategic-level plans that identify development priorities at various scales. These plans provide a crucial reference point in scoping and sourcing information for SEA applications, thus making the SEA process more efficient and focused. For example, for conservation planning in South Africa, there is now a national spatial biodiversity assessment, which is supported by equivalent sub-national assessments (either provincial or biome scales) and local scale assessments. A selling point for SEA is that it is intended to speed up subsequent project-level decisions and having these spatial assessments available to support this process enables this benefit of SEA to be realized more readily.
- The promulgation of regulations, in June 2010, specifically related to EMFs.
- Increasing intergovernmental cooperation, as indicated in the case study on the BCLME Programme.
- Results of SEA-type processes are becoming more usable, as experience enables the gap between 'science' and 'politics' to be narrowed through both parties moving closer together, as indicated in the conservation planning examples.

Conclusion

Africa's natural resources are vulnerable and need to be managed holistically. There is a good policy and legislative framework in place – both political and technical (such as laws) to manage these resources. However, the SADC and NEPAD development protocols have weak environmental components. Consequently, the southern Africa region is missing the opportunity to apply

SEA effectively and thereby enjoy the benefits that such processes can provide. There is an abundance of opportunities for SEA-type studies and the examples to date only hint at the full potential of SEA to assist in growing the socio-ecological capital of the region in a sustainable manner, particularly at a transboundary scale. To start realizing the full potential of SEA, vision and commitment is needed to promote and apply SEA effectively in southern Africa.

Note

1 The recent SEAs in Namibia are: SEA for the Coast, SEA for the Millennium Development Challenge Rural Development Programme, SEA for the central Namib Uranium Rush and SEA of the Karas Land Use Plan.

References

Audouin, M., Govender, K. and Ramasar, V. (2003) *Guidelines for the Strategic Environmental Assessment*, prepared by the Council for Scientific and Industrial Research (CSIR) for The Secretariat for Eastern African Coastal Area Management (SEACAM), SEACAM, Maputo

Brownlie, S., Walmsley, B. and Tarr, P. (2006) 'Southern African situation assessment', report to IAIA Capacity Building for Biodiversity and Impact Assessment (CBBIA) Project, Southern African Institute for Environmental Assessment, Windhoek

Dalal-Clayton, B. and Sadler, B. (2005) *Strategic Environmental Assessment: A Sourcebook and Reference Guide to International Experience*, Earthscan, London

DBSA (Development Bank of Southern Africa) and SAIEA (Southern African Institute for Environmental Assessment) (2009) *Handbook on Environmental Legislation in the SADC Region*, available at www.saiea.com, accessed 24 September 2010

DEAT (Department of Environmental Affairs and Tourism) (2000) *Strategic Environmental Assessment in South Africa*, DEAT, Pretoria

DWEA (Department of Water and Environment Affairs) (2010) *Environmental Management Framework Regulations*, Government Gazette, 18 June 2010, no 33306, Pretoria

Hempel, G., O'Toole, M. and Sweijd, N. (eds) Benguela-Current of Plenty, Benguela Current Large Marine Ecosystem Programme (BCLME), Benguela Current Commission, Cape Town

IPCC (Intergovernmental Panel on Climate Change) (2001) *IPCC Third Assessment Report – Climate Change 2001, Chapter 10: Africa, Intergovernmental Panel on Climate Change*, www.grida.no/climate/ipcc_tar/wg2/pdf/wg2TARchap10.pdf, accessed 24 April 2006.

Kambewa, E. (2006) personal communication

Keatimilwe, K. and Kgabung, B. (2005) 'SEA experience in developing countries – Botswana', in Dalal-Clayton, B. and Sadler, B. (eds) *Strategic Environmental Assessment: A Sourcebook and Reference Guide to International Experience*, Earthscan, London

Lochner, P., Weaver, A., Gelderblom, C., Peart, R., Sandwith, T. and Fowkes, S. (2003) 'Aligning the diverse: The development of a biodiversity conservation strategy for the Cape Floristic region', *Biological Conservation*, vol 112, pp29–43

MEA (Millennium Ecosystem Assessment) (2005) *Ecosystems and Human Well-being: Synthesis*, Island Press, Washington, DC

MMSD Southern Africa (2002) *Mining, Minerals and Sustainable Development in southern Africa*. Report of the Regional MMSD (Mining, Minerals and Sustainable Development) Process, MMSD Southern Africa, University of the Witwatersrand, Johannesburg

NEPAD (New Partnership for Africa's Development) (2003) *Action Plan of the Environment Initiative of the New Partnership for Africa's Development*, NEPAD, www.environment-directory.org/nepad/documents/action, accessed 5 May 2006

Okavango Delta Management Plan Project (2005) *Final Inception Report: Volume 1 – Main Report*, Okavango Delta Management Plan Secretariat, Maun, Botswana

Regional Round Table for Africa (2001) *Regional Round Table for Africa: 2002 World Summit on Sustainable Development Report*. Cairo, Egypt, 25–27 June 2001, www.un.org/jsummit/html/prep_process/africa/africa_roundtable_report.htm, accessed 24 April 2006

Retief, F., Jones, C. and Jay, S. (2006) 'The Emperor's New Clothes – Reflections on SEA Practice in South Africa', paper presented at the IAIA conference in Norway

SADC (South African Development Community) (1992) *Treaty of the Southern African Development Community*, www.iss.co.za/af/RegOrg/unity_to_union/pdfs/sadc/sadctreatynew.pdf, accessed 4 May 2006

SADC (2004) *SADC Regional Indicative Strategic Development Plan (RISDP)*. Gaborone, www.sadc.int/english/documents/risdp/index, accessed 3 May 2006

SADC (2006) 'SADC Biodiversity Support Programme (BSP) website', SADC Biodiversity Support Programme, www.sabsp.org/strategy/index.html, accessed 5 May 2006

SAIEA (Southern African Institute for Environmental Assessment) (2003) *Environmental Impact Assessment in Southern Africa*, Southern African Institute for Environmental Assessment, Windhoek

UNEP (United Nations Environment Programme) (2002a) *Africa Environment Outlook: Past, Present and Future Perspectives*, UNEP, www.grida.no/aeo/019.htm, accessed 6 April 2006

UNEP (2002b) *Global Environment Outlook 3, Chapter 3: Human Vulnerability to Environmental Change*, UNEP, www.cgner.nies.go.jp/geo/geo3/pdfs/chapter3 vulnerability.pdf, accessed 24 April 2006

World Bank (2006) 'Country Briefs for Angola, Botswana, Malawi, Mozambique, Namibia, Tanzania, Zambia', http://web.worldbank.org/WBSITE/EXTERNAL/COUNTRIES/AFRICAEXT, accessed 2 May 2006

10
The SEA Protocol

Nick Bonvoisin[1]

Introduction

This chapter provides an introduction to the Protocol on Strategic Environmental Assessment (SEA), negotiated and adopted by member states of the United Nations Economic Commission for Europe (UNECE) in Kiev, 2003 (see www.unece.org). The chapter describes the background to the Protocol, its negotiation, essential characteristics, differences to Directive 2001/42/EC, and potential opportunities to evolve as a global legal framework for SEA.

The SEA Protocol was developed to supplement the UNECE Convention on Environmental Impact Assessment (EIA) in a Transboundary Context (adopted in Espoo (Finland) on 25 February 1991 and commonly referred to as the Espoo Convention). Before introducing the Protocol in detail, it may be useful first to correct two misunderstandings about the Protocol, as explained in detail later in this chapter. Firstly, although negotiated by UNECE member states, the SEA Protocol is not limited to the UNECE region and, through wider ratification, may evolve into a global treaty on SEA. Secondly, although a Protocol to the Espoo Convention, it applies to all relevant plans and programmes and, to the extent appropriate, policies and legislation, irrespective of whether or not these have a transboundary context.

Negotiation of the Protocol began in 2001, just as the European Parliament and Council of the European Union (EU) adopted Directive 2001/42/EC on the assessment of the effects of certain plans and programmes on the environment (SEA or EU Directive). The EU Directive greatly influenced the negotiation of the Protocol. However, there are a number of important differences between the two legal instruments, including the geographical scope and the consideration and integration of environmental concerns in the preparation of policies and legislation. These are as discussed in the analysis and review section below.

Background on the Protocol

Protocol negotiations concluded in January 2003, and an extraordinary meeting of the Parties to the Espoo Convention adopted the Protocol on 21 May 2003, in Kiev (Ukraine), during the 'Environment for Europe' Ministerial Conference. This section provides information on the procedural rules relating to the Protocol, the negotiation process, international institutional arrangements and international activities to support implementation of the Protocol.

Signatories and ratification procedure

Thirty-six states and the EU signed the Protocol comprising: all EU member states (except Malta); all seven southeast European states (Montenegro later became independent of Serbia); Norway; two Eastern European states (Republic of Moldova and Ukraine) and two Caucasus states (Armenia and Georgia).

Signature is only the first stage of the treaty procedure. Sixteen UNECE member states needed to ratify, accept, approve or accede to the Protocol for it to enter into force, after a further delay of 90 days. The Protocol entered into force on 11 July 2010 and by the end of July 2010 had as parties the EU plus 18 states: Albania, Austria, Bulgaria, Croatia, Czech Republic, Estonia, Finland, Germany, Luxembourg, Montenegro, Netherlands, Norway, Romania, Serbia, Slovakia, Spain and Sweden. In this chapter, ratification is taken to include the different means by which a state consents to be bound by a treaty, which means acceptance, approval and accession as well as ratification. The UN *Treaty Handbook* provides an explanation of these terms (UN, 2001).

By signing a treaty, a state does not express 'its consent to be bound by the treaty until it ratifies ... it. [However, it] is obliged to refrain, in good faith, from acts that would defeat the object and purpose of the treaty. Signature alone does not impose on the State obligations under the treaty' (UN, 2001).

The Protocol (UNECE, 2003) is open for ratification by the signatory states or for accession by any of the other UNECE member states. To find out the latest status of the Protocol, see www.unece.org/env/sea.

In addition, any UN member state may accede to it upon approval. This means that a state that is not a member state of the UNECE must first obtain the approval of the Meeting of the Parties to the Protocol (strictly the 'Meeting of the Parties to the Espoo Convention serving as the Meeting of the Parties to the Protocol', Article 23, paragraph 3).

If, as expected, the parties to the Protocol adopt rules of procedure similar to those adopted by the parties to the Espoo Convention, approval would require a three quarters majority vote of those present and voting at a session of the Meeting of the Parties. If the parties so choose, and in accordance with the Cavtat Declaration by the Meeting of the Parties to the Convention (UNECE, 2004), the Protocol may thus evolve into a global treaty on SEA.

Negotiation of the Protocol on SEA

The UNECE is a regional commission of the United Nations Economic and Social Council. The 56 UNECE member states are the countries of Europe, the Caucasus, Central Asia, as well as Canada, Israel and the US. As part of its mission to promote sustainable economic growth across the region, the UNECE assists in negotiating international legal instruments addressing the environment.

The senior advisers to UNECE Governments on Environmental and Water Problems developed the Espoo Convention on EIA in a Transboundary Context (1991). Twenty-nine states and the EC signed the Convention. It entered into force on 10 September 1997, once 16 states had ratified it. By mid-2010, 43 states and the EU had ratified and become Parties to the Convention – for its current status, see www.unece.org/env/eia.

In 1995, the third 'Environment for Europe' Ministerial Conference, held in Sofia (Bulgaria), welcomed the Sofia Initiative on Application of Environmental Impact Assessment (Sofia EIA Initiative) (UNECE, 1995). Following up on the Sofia EIA Initiative, recommendations were made to the fourth 'Environment for Europe' Ministerial Conference, held in Aarhus (Denmark) in 1998, on the use of SEA in Central and Eastern Europe and in Newly Independent States (Croatia and REC, 1998). The Conference invited countries to introduce or carry out SEAs (UNECE, 1998). The Convention on Access to Information, Public Participation in Decision-Making and Access to Justice in Environmental Matters was also adopted at the Conference and is generally referred to as the Aarhus Convention.

In 2000, a background paper on options for developing a legally binding UNECE instrument on SEA was discussed at sessions of the Committee on Environmental Policy (Seventh Session), the Meeting of the Signatories to the Aarhus Convention and the Espoo Convention's Working Group on EIA (UNECE, 2000). The Working Group on EIA decided in principle to proceed with negotiation of a Protocol on SEA.

This decision was supported in 2001 when the Meeting of the Parties to the Espoo Convention decided to start negotiations on a protocol to the Convention addressing SEA (UNECE, 2001a). The UNECE member states, with the exception of Canada and the US, then negotiated a draft Protocol on SEA at a series of eight meetings, beginning in May 2001 and lasting until January 2003 (www.unece.org/env/eia). The provisions of the Espoo and Aarhus Conventions and the EU Directives on EIA and SEA influenced those negotiations. The Protocol is now open for ratification, as described in the introduction to this chapter.

International institutional arrangements

Pending its entry into force, the Meeting of the Signatories to the Protocol was the decision-making body for the Protocol. The first session of the Meeting of the Signatories was held in Cavtat (Croatia) in 2004, during the Espoo Convention's third session of the Meeting of the Parties (MOP), and endorsed decision III/12 of the Espoo MOP on preparations for entry into force of the Protocol (UNECE, 2004). The Espoo MOP also adopted a work plan, including activities supporting implementation of the Protocol, as discussed later in this section.

A second session of the Meeting of the Signatories was held in 2005, and a third is expected in November 2010 to make the final preparations for the first meeting of the Protocol's governing body. The governing body will be the MOP to the Convention serving as the MOP to the Protocol (the 'MOP/MOP'), which is required to meet first within 12 months of the Protocol's entry into force; the first session is planned for June 2011. At its first meeting, the MOP/MOP 'shall consider and adopt the modalities for applying the procedure for the review of compliance with the Convention to this Protocol' (Article 14, paragraph 6). It is anticipated that the mandate of the Espoo Convention's Implementation Committee will be expanded to address issues of compliance with the Protocol. Information on the Espoo Convention's Implementation Committee is available at www.unece.org/env/eia/. In addition, a Working Group on SEA is likely to be established.

The Executive Secretary of the UNECE provides the secretariat functions for both the Espoo Convention (Article 13 of the Convention) and SEA Protocol (Article 17 of the Protocol).

International activities to support implementation

A Resource Manual to support Application of the Protocol on SEA was developed as decided by the first session of the Meeting of the Signatories to the Protocol in June 2004. The Manual does not constitute formal legal or other professional advice, but instead provides guidance to those applying the Protocol or supporting others in doing so. The Manual is available at www.unece.org/env/sea/.

The Meeting of the Signatories also initiated a capacity-development process in five States in Eastern Europe, the Caucasus and Central Asia (EECCA), four being Signatories (Armenia, Georgia, Republic of Moldova and Ukraine) and the fifth being Belarus. This process has been interwoven with a United Nations Development Programme (UNDP) project with similar aims in the same countries, and involving the Regional Environmental Centre (REC) for Central and Eastern Europe, so that in total:

- Capacity-building needs analyses were undertaken in the five states and a subregional overview prepared.
- Pilot projects were undertaken in Armenia (Yerevan City Master Plan) and Belarus (National Tourism Development Plan).
- Capacity-development materials were produced in Georgia, Republic of Moldova and Ukraine.
- Capacity-development strategies and plans were developed in four of the countries (Georgia had already developed such a strategy with the assistance of the Dutch EIA Commission) and a series of subregional initiatives prepared.

For information on these activities see www.unece.org/env/sea/. This process is also described in a bulletin (Dusik et al, 2006). An initiative on SEA, proposed by Armenia, Belarus and the Republic of Moldova at the Belgrade Ministerial Conference 'Environment for Europe' (10–12 October 2007), subsequently continued supporting countries of Eastern Europe and the Caucasus (UNECE, 2007).

Analysis and review

Provisions of the Protocol

The text of the SEA Protocol may be considered in four parts:

1 The preamble, giving the context for the provisions that follow.
2 The operative provisions, essentially saying how environmental, including health, concerns are to taken into account in strategic decision-making under the Protocol.
3 The final provisions, relating to the Protocol as a legal instrument such as meetings, secretariat, signature, ratification and withdrawal.
4 The annexes, providing details for the operative provisions.

This discussion focuses on the operative provisions. These may be further divided:

- Objectives, definitions, general provisions (Articles 1–3, respectively).
- SEA of plans and programmes, comprising field of application, screening, scoping, environmental report, public participation, consultation with environmental and health authorities, transboundary consultations, decision and monitoring (Articles 4–12, respectively).
- Policies and legislation (Article 13).

Article 1 defines the **objective** of the Protocol – to provide for a high level of protection of the environment, including health – and lists five means by which it is to be achieved:

1 Ensuring that environmental, including health, considerations are thoroughly taken into account in the development of plans and programmes.
2 Contributing to the consideration of environmental, including health, concerns in the preparation of policies and legislation.
3 Establishing clear, transparent and effective procedures for strategic environmental assessment.
4 Providing for public participation in strategic environmental assessment.
5 Integrating by these means environmental, including health, concerns into measures and instruments designed to further sustainable development.

Each of these means provides an introduction to provisions elsewhere in the Protocol.

The Protocol's objective is broadly similar to that of the SEA Directive (2001/42/EC).

The core process of SEA of plans and programmes (set out in Articles 4–12) is straightforward, and broadly similar to that set out in the SEA Directive. Differences between the Protocol and the Directive are discussed below.

Articles 4 (**field of application**) and 5 (**screening**) determine whether SEA is required under the Protocol for a given plan or programme. The main SEA elements that follow in the Protocol for plans and programmes are:

- The first element (following screening to determine that a plan or programme is to be subject to SEA) is to determine the **scope** of the environmental report (Article 6). Determining the scope of the report also implies defining the scope of the analyses that will lead to the preparation of the report. Scoping provides an opportunity to focus the report on the important issues to maximize its usefulness to the public, authorities and decision-makers. It does not preclude changes in the scope of the report if the need for them becomes apparent at a later stage. Environmental and health authorities have to be consulted in scoping, and the public may be provided with opportunities to participate.
- The second element is the preparation of the **environmental report** in line with the scope to provide the public and the authorities consulted with information on the environmental, including health, effects of the plan or programme (Article 7). The environmental report is subject to public participation and to consultation with environmental and health authorities.
- The third element is the **participation of the public** (Article 8). This may have begun already during scoping or even during the determination of whether SEA is required under the Protocol for a plan or programme. The public concerned must be allowed the opportunity to express its opinion on the draft plan or programme and the environmental report.
- The fourth element is the **consultation of the environmental and health authorities** (Article 9). Consultation occurs subsequent to the preparation of the environmental report when authorities must be allowed the opportunity to express their opinion on the draft plan or programme and the environmental report. Consultation and public participation may occur at the same time.
- If it appears that the plan or programme may have significant transboundary effects (on another party to the Protocol), or if a potentially 'affected party' so requests, the affected party or parties should be notified and invited to enter into consultations (Article 10). Those **transboundary consultations** – the fifth element in the SEA process – must lead to an opportunity for the concerned public and the authorities in the affected party to express their opinion on the draft plan or programme and the environmental report.
- The sixth element is the **decision** on the adoption of a plan or programme (Article 11). This decision has to take into account the environmental report and the opinions expressed by the public and the authorities, both domestic and of any affected party. The decision-maker has to produce a statement summarizing how that information was taken into account and why the plan or programme is being adopted in the light of other reasonable alternatives. The adopted plan or programme, the decision and the justification must be made publicly available.

- The final element is **monitoring** (Article 12). SEA does not stop with the decision to adopt a plan or programme. The significant environmental, including health, effects have to be monitored to, among other things, identify unforeseen adverse effects and enable appropriate remedial action to be taken. Monitoring results have to be made available to the authorities and to the public.

The reader is referred to the extensive Resource Manual to Support Application of the Protocol on SEA, mentioned above, which provides a detailed examination of the practical application of this SEA process.

Finally, Article 13 relates to **policies and legislation**, requiring that parties endeavour to consider and integrate environmental, including health, concerns in the preparation of policies and legislation. This provision is important as it provides a framework for extending the consideration of the environment higher up the decision-making tree, and so furthering sustainable development.

The initial elements for the Protocol (UNECE, 2001b) foresaw the application of SEA to 'strategic decisions at plan, programme, policy, regulatory and legislative level[s]'. During the negotiation of the Protocol, this changed substantially to bring the mandatory provision in line with the Directive, so that the mandatory requirement is for the SEA of relevant plans and programmes only. However, Article 13 of the Protocol requires that parties 'endeavour to ensure that environmental, including health, concerns are considered and integrated to the extent appropriate in the preparation of its proposals for policies and legislation that are likely to have significant effects on the environment, including health'. In addition, the appropriate principles and elements of the Protocol should be considered when doing so and practical arrangements should take into account the need for transparency in decision-making. Furthermore, the protocol requires that parties report on their application of Article 13.

Though this does not represent a mandatory requirement to undertake SEA or a similar process for policies and legislation, it does provide the framework for integration of the environment into higher levels of decision-making. Mandatory reporting backs it up.

Differences between the Protocol and the Directive

As noted in the introduction, there are a number of important differences between the SEA Directive and the Protocol on SEA.

The first difference concerns the states that are subject to the Directive or party to the Protocol. The Directive is strictly applicable only to the 27 EU member states, together with Iceland, Liechtenstein and Norway, which entered into the Agreement on the European Economic Area in 1992. In addition, the EU candidate states (Croatia, Iceland, the former Yugoslav Republic of Macedonia and Turkey) have to implement the Directive before accession to the EU, and other aspiring candidates are doing so on a voluntary basis. In addition to the above-named states, the member states of the UNECE include the following:

- Other states in southeast Europe – Albania, Bosnia and Herzegovina, Montenegro and Serbia.

- EECCA states – Armenia, Azerbaijan, Belarus, Georgia, Kazakhstan, Kyrgyzstan, Republic of Moldova, Russian Federation, Tajikistan, Turkmenistan, Ukraine and Uzbekistan.
- Other States in Western Europe – Andorra, Monaco, San Marino and Switzerland.
- Israel.
- Canada and the US (neither of which took part in the negotiation of the Protocol).

Also, as explained earlier, the Protocol, through its procedures, may evolve into a global treaty on SEA. Specifically, any UNECE member state may ratify the Protocol and any UN member state may accede to the Protocol upon approval by the parties to the Protocol.

The second key difference relates to policies and legislation, as discussed earlier in this section.

In addition, there are numerous other ways in which the Protocol differs from the SEA Directive and that may strengthen the application of SEA to relevant plans and programmes, such as:

- Mandatory consultation of health authorities.
- Optional public participation in the screening of plans and programmes (significance determination) and when determining the relevant information to be included in the environmental report (scoping).
- Inclusion in the environmental report of a description of any likely significant transboundary effects.

Conclusion

The Protocol provides a similar legal framework to the SEA Directive, but is not limited to the EU. It thus provides a potentially global legal framework and consistent standard for SEA.

Within the EU, the Protocol should strengthen the application of SEA to plans and programmes, complementing the Directive, and its transboundary provisions will assist EU member states in their consultations with states outside the EU.

Finally, the Protocol provides a non-mandatory framework for the consideration and integration of environmental, including health, concerns in the preparation of policies and legislation, extending SEA-like processes up the decision-making tree.

Future directions for implementation of the Protocol include; supporting its application to plans and programmes; encouraging ratification by the signatories and accession by states outside the UNECE; supporting legal implementation; and developing experience in the application of Article 13 (policies and legislation).

Note

1 The opinions, interpretations and conclusions expressed in this paper are those of the author and do not necessarily represent the views of the UN or of its member states.

References

Croatia and REC (Regional Environmental Centre) (1998) *Sofia Initiative: Environmental Impact Assessment – Policy Recommendations on the Use of Strategic Environmental Assessment in Central and Eastern Europe and in Newly Independent States*, Fourth Ministerial Conference, Environment for Europe, Århus, Denmark, 23–25 June 1998, www.rec.org/REC/Programs/EnvironmentalAssessment/pdf/AarhusSEAno17.pdf, accessed June 2006

Dusik, J., Cherp, A., Jurkeviciute, A., Martonakova, H. and Bonvoisin, N. (2006) 'SEA Protocol – Initial Capacity Development in Selected Countries of the Former Soviet Union', UNDP, REC, UNECE

UN (United Nations) (2001) *Treaty Handbook*, Treaty Section of the Office of Legal Affairs, United Nations, http://treaties.un.org/doc/source/publications/THB/English.pdf, accessed July 2010

UNECE (United Nations Economic Commission for Europe) (1995) *Environmental Programme for Europe*, Third Ministerial Conference, Environment for Europe, www.unece.org/env/europe/Epe.htm, accessed June 2006

UNECE (1998) *Ministerial Declaration*, Fourth Ministerial Conference, Environment for Europe, www.unece.org/env/efe/history%20of%20EfE/Aarhus.E.pdf, accessed July 2010

UNECE (2000) *Background Document on Options for Developing a Legally Binding UNECE Instrument on Strategic Environmental Assessment*, Seventh Session of the Committee on Environmental Policy, Second Meeting of the Signatories to the Aarhus Convention and the Working Group on EIA, www.unece.org/env/documents/2000/eia/mp.eia.wg.1.2000.16.e.pdf, accessed June 2006

UNECE (2001a) 'Decision II/9 in Annex IX', *Report of the Second Meeting*, Meeting of the Parties to the Convention on EIA in a Transboundary Context, www.unece.org/env/documents/2001/eia/ece.mp.eia.4.e.pdf, accessed June 2006

UNECE (2001b) *Draft Elements for a Protocol on SEA*, *ad hoc* Working Group on the Protocol on SEA, Meeting of the Parties to the Convention on EIA in a Transboundary Context, www.unece.org/env/documents/2001/eia/ac1/mp.eia.ac.1.2001.3.e.pdf, accessed June 2006

UNECE (2003) *Protocol on Strategic Environmental Assessment to the Convention on EIA in a Transboundary Context*, UN, New York and Geneva, www.unece.org/env/eia/documents/legaltexts/protocolenglish.pdf, accessed July 2010

UNECE (2004) *Report of the Third Meeting*, Meeting of the Parties to the Convention on EIA in a Transboundary Context, www.unece.org/env/documents/2004/eia/ece.mp.eia.6.e.pdf, accessed July 2010

UNECE (2007) 'Initiative on Strategic Environmental Assessment, submitted by Armenia, Belarus and Moldova to the Sixth Ministerial Conference "Environment for Europe"', Belgrade, 10–12 October 2007, www.unece.org/env/documents/2007/ece/ece.belgrade.conf.2007.18.e.pdf, accessed August 2010

Part II

SEA Application

11
SEA and Transport Planning

Paul Tomlinson

Introduction

This chapter describes the relationship of strategic environmental assessment (SEA) and transport planning, a sector where process integration has gone further than in many others. The discussion is organized in four main sections. First, the changing policy context of transport planning is outlined with particular reference to the forces that are driving a new, multi-modal approach to transport planning. Second, reflecting these changes, key trends in the application of SEA to transport planning are described. Third, the agenda of issues of SEA practice in transport planning are reviewed, drawing on the discussion of this theme at the International Association for Impact Assessment (IAIA) Prague conference of 2005. Finally, the conclusion focuses on the measures that are needed to fully integrate SEA into transport planning and the methodological, procedural, technical and cultural issues that merit particular attention.

The changing context of transport planning

Across many countries, economic and demographic changes, broadening public policy goals, increased emphasis on accountability, consumer demand and technological innovation are changing the approach to transport. Transport projects are, on occasion, being delayed or rejected by the public due to an absence of support. It is also increasingly recognized that a wide array of travel options is needed to sustain economic growth and that highway solutions do not guarantee economic growth or equality of access to opportunities and services within urban and rural communities. Furthermore, national planning is increasingly recognizing that it is impossible to cater for ever more private vehicle use and that innovation is needed regarding the way transport planning meets widely shared community goals.

In some countries, the provision of new highway infrastructure dominates the transport agenda, such as the more than doubling of expressway and other roads in South Korea over the next 15 years. Here the issue is how to manage the effects of such provision particularly when adverse public reactions begin to appear.

Transport planning has also been changing as a result of similar forces across some countries that include:

- Increased competition for public funding at all levels of government.
- Fragmented responsibilities among transport authorities, infrastructure and service providers.
- Societal trends that reduce the attractiveness and relevance of traditional public transport services.
- Difficulties to reconcile competing or contradictory transport goals and objectives, for example, between support for economic growth versus environmental protection versus cost control.
- Vehicle miles of travel increasing faster than population or economic growth.
- Urban sprawl and diffuse travel patterns that impede service by traditional public transport.
- Limited incentives for innovation or risk-taking.
- Increasing participation of women in the labour force and increasing home working.
- Growth in the elderly population, single parents and single-adult households.
- Change in business structures with increasing outsourcing and just-in-time logistics.
- Increasing contribution made by transport to global warming.
- New vehicle and traffic management technologies.
- Increased public involvement in decision-making (TRB, 1999).

Reflecting upon these trends, the policy framework within which transport planning operates is also subject to numerous competing forces operating within the following domains: transport policy; environmental policy; energy policy; taxation policy; land-use policy; and other policies such as health.

Where transport networks are well-established, transport planning is tending to move towards the management of the networks rather than the provision of new infrastructure. Consequently, the rationale for increasing capacity is increasingly seen as only 'buying time', or that it is impossible to build a way out of congestion even if it were affordable in environmental or economic terms. As a result, new investments are being judged by their network-wide effects rather than as individual projects. Also, as management of a network rather than new build begins to dominate transport planning, so the environmental impacts associated with land take become subservient to both physical and social impacts associated with movement.

These trends suggest an increasingly integrated approach to transport planning in which transport serves to meet community objectives (growth, equity, employment, protecting health and the environment), rather than its own self-serving objectives. After all, transport is a means to an end and not an end in itself. This means that transport plans and projects should be assessed by their contribution towards sustainable development (jobs, communities, and so on) instead of growth in mobility or reductions in congestion.

As transport planning becomes focused upon the needs of the users rather than those of the infrastructure or service providers, so the accessibility and impacts upon all social groups and transport's contribution to wider societal objectives become important considerations to monitor. Under this new paradigm new measures of efficiency become not only multi-modal with a focus upon the entire transport system, but also more focused on social and environmental needs.

Across Europe and North America there has been an increased attention given to multi-modal studies that set the context within which transport measures (demand management, traffic management and new infrastructure) are conceived. However, this is not the case across all countries. For example, in Germany the Federal Transport Infrastructure Plan (FTIP) has the task of choosing between approximately 2000 infrastructure measures proposed from lower tier plans. While at the state level, a transport plan has to deal with approximately 500 projects. The German bottom-up approach to planning perhaps inhibits integrated and sustainable transport. Top-down approaches, however, such as in Spain, experience difficulties in cascading new policy directions into the plans and direction of projects of the highway authorities.

The main objective of SEA is to provide a robust analysis of the contribution that transport policy and proposals make to each of the main relevant goals of government, highlighting outcomes, conflicts and trade-offs. Assessments need to illuminate the issues and propose ways forward, providing a mechanism for delivering consensus among stakeholders on the nature of the problem, the alternatives available and the preferred solution. This is no easy task, but one in which transport planning may be more capable of addressing than perhaps some of the other development sectors such as land-use planning, given its tradition in dealing with alternatives.

At the Prague Council of the European Conference of Ministers of Transport in 2000, the Ministers agreed to a common approach to developing sustainable transport policies (ECMT, 2000) that highlighted the need for improved support for decision-making on transport projects and policies. The importance of good cost benefit analysis and effective SEA was stressed and guidance sought on developing better procedures and tools for presenting the results to decision-makers. Improved decision-making was seen as being key to integrating transport and environment policies (ECMT, 2004).

Trends in SEA application to transport planning

Given the context into which SEA is being integrated, the following trends can be identified in the application of SEA to transport planning: context for SEA; legislative frameworks; and process or methodological integration into transport planning.

Context for SEA

In addressing the new paradigm, transport has responded with an array of strategic multi-modal studies and policy studies on issues such as road user pricing. These have required transport planners to consider criteria such as justice and equity alongside economics, safety and soft and hard transport responses. In response, multi-criteria approaches that recognize these wider considerations have emerged. This has provided a suitable context within which SEA can function. As a result, we have seen the voluntary adoption of SEA type approaches across Europe and in North America (ECMT, 2004). In addition, countries that are expanding their transport networks such as South Korea have seen the value of strategic assessments, in reducing delay and conflict (Lee, 2005). For these countries, better transport planning and SEA can provide a means by which questions not addressed in environmental impact assessment (EIA) could be answered.

Given the different reasons for strategic transport planning and assessment, it is not surprising that SEA processes differ between those countries with fully development transport networks and countries where core networks are still being established. In countries with mature transport systems, the management of capacity calls for a multi-modal approach and clearer links with spatial planning. Successful assessments are likely to emerge with recognition of the complex relationships that need to be harnessed to manage transport demand and deliver community objectives. Where countries are establishing transport networks, SEA should help test the transport objectives of the proposed projects and define alternatives. It should also be open, or be a vehicle, to debate the provision of new transport infrastructure where such an opportunity has not previously existed. In both contexts, SEA should help expose some of the traditional transport – jobs/economic objectives to greater public critique and the generation of alternatives beyond the remits of individual transport infrastructure and service providers.

Legislative frameworks

As noted earlier, legislation has not been a driver for strategic studies and countries such as Switzerland have adopted sustainability appraisal or other studies to support transport planning (Hilty, 2005). However, within the European Union (EU), transport is identified as a sector formally requiring SEA.

England was the first country to undertake widespread delivery against the regulations implementing the SEA directive for more than 70 local transport plans and environmental reports produced before July 2006. These SEAs were undertaken for metropolitan authorities, urban authorities and rural counties comprising several lower level authorities. As a result, there will be considerable variation in the transport problems and planning contexts in which the SEA is to be undertaken, albeit in accordance with the same legislation and government guidance. An interesting issue will be to judge the extent to which the SEAs diverge in their approaches – whether they reflect local context or strictly observe the legislation/guidance to minimize fears of legal challenge.

Process or methodological integration into transport planning

A central thread in the SEA Directive is that duplication of assessment should be avoided. Hence transport planning and environmental assessment should be fully integrated in multi-modal transport studies and transport plans. There is, however, a cautionary note. The disadvantages of cost benefit analysis – a favoured tool in transport planning – and multi-criteria analysis methods is that they all too often give the appearance of producing precise results and focusing the decisions of politicians upon a number. As a result, they tend to ignore uncertainties and assumptions that underlie such methods.

Balancing of issues is the task of the politicians, not the authority nor the consultants. Unfortunately, some assessment tools lead to a degree of integration that masks the real conflicts that should be explored in the decision-making process. The techniques reduce the array of issues to a single or small number of values to be reported, using aggregation methods that are often at best opaque and sometimes ignored.

While SEA must be integrated into the process of transport planning, it should strive to make these conflicts visible and to show the consequences of any decision rather than be subsumed within a highly numerical approach to the analysis.

Issues for SEA to address

The following issues have been identified for SEA practitioners to consider in dealing with transport planning: tiering; assessment tools; participative processes; objectives setting, relationship of objectives-led and evidence-based approaches; consideration of alternatives; significance criteria; strategic mitigation; monitoring significant effects; linking SEA to EIA; independence or integration of assessment; and integration of SEA with economic appraisal.

Tiering

Tiering, in which topics are assessed in different plans, is promoted as a solution to the complexity of assessment at higher planning levels. It requires that topics are only considered that are appropriate to the planning tier and the levels of uncertainty that are acceptable to the decision-making process. (Further discussion of tiering can be found in Chapter 26.)

Transport planning may comprise national plans, regional and local plans as well as projects, some subject to EIA, others not. Transport plans are also key components in other plans such as spatial or land-use development plans. Consequently, SEAs prepared for transport planning should be effectively linked with those undertaken at different levels in transport planning and with those prepared for spatial planning and other sectors. With different administrations, devolved responsibilities and different spatial scales, the task of providing effective integration is challenging. Apart from creating links across administrative boundaries and topics, the allocation of issues to an appropriate tier in the plan and project planning processes is also a challenge if duplication of effort is not to result.

The transfer of issues from one assessment to another must be undertaken in a transparent manner, as there is a risk that some plan assessments will abdicate responsibility for particular issues, instead passing them to other plans. There is also the question of how to deal with the impacts from a transport plan on say a river basin management plan, where the transport interventions may give rise to only a slight impact individually, but cumulatively they could cause major problems. Is it appropriate that such potential issues are handed over without the transport assessment having some recognition of the potential consequences? Clearly there is a danger in a lack of overall transparency and accountability in the tiering of plans and assessments.

Assessment tools

Aside from the procedural and administrative aspects of incorporating SEA into transport planning, the assessment tools need to be fit for purpose. Some guidance has sought to apply project-level assessment tools to strategic studies with mixed results, while others tend to be broad-brush providing little meaningful assistance to the plan-making processes. While expert opinion is of increased importance in SEA, statistical analysis should not be neglected. Expert opinion should be supported by evidence that can be defended at public hearings.

Transport planning is frequently a highly numerical process placing reliance upon transport models and cost benefit analysis. While quantification is generally a desirable activity, in the context of SEA, it can distort assessments as numbers often hide the fact that they are based upon value judgements that have not been subject to external review and numerical values can give rise to a perception of accuracy that can be misplaced. This tends to devalue qualitative assessments given that monetary valuation techniques often only capture a fraction of the issues associated with an environmental impact. For example, the monetization of noise based on its effect on house prices assigns zero value on noise levels in those places where no one lives.

Motivated by this criticism, Borken (2005a) presented a flexible multiple criteria approach that explicitly accounts for uncertainties and diversity of stakeholder opinions. This outranking approach seems particularly suited to lead stakeholder involvement and to identify compromise in the light of diverging values. All issues that are considered relevant by the stakeholders can be taken up, be it in quantitative or qualitative terms.

Also evident in some countries is the reliance of geographic information systems (GISs) to drive SEA of transport plans. Essentially, GIS functions as a modern day overlay map from the popular hand-drafted technique of the late 1970s. However, behind the GIS manipulation are issues associated with the rules for adding together different mapped constraints. Such techniques adopt weights for each layer corresponding to a different mapped constraint to enable aggregation to define a 'preferred' route. As a result, these techniques produce the 'least worst' option rather than the best option.

As qualitative aspects are missing from GIS methods, so uncertainty and risk management practices are omitted as well as non-mapped information. Consequently, the solutions fail to consider the ease with which adverse effects can be resolved and the contribution that enhancements can make to select the preferred option.

An alternative method that is amenable to both qualitative and quantitative approaches is that of causal links analysis or system maps. This approach was used in the Spanish Strategic Infrastructure and Transport Plan as described by Jiliberto (2005), who stressed the power of qualitative system models in exploring the structural underpinning of the environmental profile of the transport plan and allowing an appreciation of the relative intensity of the relationship between action and effect.

Participative processes

To be effective, SEA should be embedded in the transport planning process. In that regard, several steps and measures are important including:

- Officers responsible for plan-making are actively involved in the SEA in a timely and constructive manner.
- Stakeholders should be involved in agreeing the environmental objectives.
- The public should be given adequate opportunity to contribute to key stages of the assessment in a seamless manner corresponding to the opportunities that plan formulation provides.
- SEA professionals should not constrain reporting to the scoping and environmental report stage but should also identify the elements in the transport plan-making processes in which contributions can be made.

When dealing with the public, several questions arise as noted by Borken (2005b):

- How to move from passive to active involvement?
- How to maintain participation?
- Who are 'the public'?
- Should all members of the public/stakeholders be involved in all phases of SEA?
- Do the public need to be organized by representatives?
- How to manage diverging opinions in participation?
- How to deal with interest groups?
- How to deal with planning blight?
- How to establish 'truth'?

These are not so much SEA issues as wider issues of public engagement in democratic planning systems. Nevertheless, assessment professionals need to be familiar with the questions and possible strategies to be promoted. Furthermore, assessment professionals need to adopt good practice and deliver on the following (Alton and Underwood, 2005):

- Transparency of the process.
- Accountability: You need to know, which intervention was taken up where?
- Demonstrate take-up and link with decision.
- Equal role and voice of participants.
- Participation should go along with empowerment of the participants.
- Develop criteria on how to derive conclusions, what to accept as a conclusion/decision and when to summarize or to continue the process.

Objective setting

Establishing the regional economic development, environmental and community objectives that transport schemes are intended to achieve at an early plan-making stage is critical if risks of delays and revisions are to be minimized. To achieve this, political decision-makers should play an integral part in the process of defining problems and community objectives that the plan is to address. Transparent mechanisms that integrate wider economic, social and environmental issues into the plan and project formulation processes are therefore needed.

Objectives-led or evidence-based approaches

SEA has been seen to be either data-led – demanding large databases – or objectives-led – where reliance is based upon predefined indicators offering consistency of approach. An alternative may be termed evidence-based, in which knowledge is to be used to identify significant impacts. These different approaches are academic models rather than practical realities. Nevertheless, they do set the context for procedural, technical and cultural issues associated with SEA.

At the centre of this aspect is whether the objectives are defined in advance of an exploration of the potential environmental impacts associated with a plan. Where the plan is dominated by policies rather than projects, then using objectives set in higher level or associated plans is generally an appropriate approach. However, where there is a higher project content, an objectives-led approach is not guaranteed to identify all significant effects, particularly when the objectives and associated indicators are required to be in conformity with other plans.

An evidence-based approach relies upon an exploration of the potential impacts of both policies and projects before defining the objectives and potential indicators. However, it is critical that this exploration does not descend to EIA levels of detail. Where plans contain some project content, such projects are often founded in some level of prior assessment that the SEA can exploit. Through this approach, the SEA aggregates knowledge on the likely environmental consequences of the projects with the assessment of the policies and is thus more likely to report the significant environmental effects in a more robust manner than objective-led approaches.

Consideration of alternatives

SEAs face the challenge of delivering an appropriate amount of information on the environmental performance of alternative transport strategies being considered in the plan. Unfortunately, plans do not commence as a blank piece of paper. There is often a series of constraining factors imposed by:

- Higher level plans.
- Government regulations/guidance on the plan being assessed.
- Previous plans for the locality.
- Earlier studies such as multi-modal studies, prepared to inform the plan being assessed.

- Decisions and interests of the elected members.
- Other sectoral plans.
- Major transport and other projects in the planning process.

It thus seems spurious for the SEA to generate new alternatives for decisions that have previously been taken. Nevertheless, alternatives may exist in relation to the range of policies if not the broad transport strategies, in scheduling of transport projects, such as delivering public transport measures ahead of new road projects and in the location of infrastructure proposals.

This transition period before SEA becomes fully embedded may result in superficial assessments that are 'add-ons' to the transport planning process that do not adequately deal with alternatives. Apart from failing to add value, such assessments also bring the process into disrepute and create opportunities for legal challenge.

Significance criteria

The process of identifying significant environmental impacts, particularly cumulative impacts, is the key to both the scoping of the assessment and the importance attached to the impacts that are identified. It appears that, in order to avoid legal challenges, assessments are not being subject to meaningful scoping exercises. Indeed the topics, and the way they are being addressed, are not being defined in a way that provides a focus to the assessment. Furthermore, the desire to 'cover all the bases' results in assessments that report any impact whether or not it is significant. This 'bottom-fishing' then generates excessively long reports that risk failing to communicate to the decision-makers the key assessment findings.

How significance criteria are developed for individual impacts and the mechanisms by which the individual impacts are aggregated to provide scores across the alternative strategies, also merit attention (see Tomlinson, 2004). This also raises issues of quantification and monetization techniques. For example, where multiple areas of ecological interest are affected, what is the basis on which a slight or moderate adverse significance is assigned to the overall effects? Are all affected ecological sites of equivalent worth? Can adverse impacts in one area be 'traded' with beneficial impacts in others? These issues need to be explicitly considered in the Environmental Reports if SEA is to be seen to be rigorous and robust.

Strategic mitigation

SEA provides new opportunities for mitigation in that measures need no longer be conceived as a 'bolt-on' to the project design. Instead, longer-term mitigation can be undertaken, perhaps with mitigation remote to the project being both more financially and environmentally beneficial than the delivery of measures local to the project. For example, mitigation banking may be regarded as a more financially and environmentally efficient approach. Also, SEA creates opportunities for organizational or institutional change or advanced data assembly offering new means of avoiding or minimizing significant impacts.

Monitoring significant effects

The SEA Directive makes it a requirement to monitor significant environmental effects resulting from plans or programmes. This raises issues of what to monitor, how to detect trends and attribute effects to specific causes given natural and induced environmental variability. Then there are the organizational aspects of data assembly and management not just for single plans, but coordinated across all plans operating in an area that need to be considered.

Often plans have annual monitoring programmes to meet the reporting requirements of government. Such annual progress reports may be using standardized indicators and reporting metrics dictated by government in order to deliver comparability across the plans. The challenge will be to extend these indicators with those that track significant environmental effects both predicted and unforeseen.

Linking SEA to project EIA

How SEA interacts with EIA is a key aspect if the burden of assessment is to be lightened and if the environmental benefits of SEA are to be realized (Tomlinson and Fry, 2002). For transport planning, this could mean that certain types of project no longer require an EIA if an SEA establishes that no significant effects are likely. To lighten the burden of the project, EIA would require national regulations to recognize the role of SEA, as well as project-specific thresholds or lists, as a means of screening the need for EIA.

Also in the spirit of lightening the burden, SEA could better define the scope of the EIA so that they may be undertaken more efficiently. Here, the environmental report could contribute to the EIA scoping activity by identifying key issues to be addressed as well as those that should be confirmed as needing only a less detailed level of assessment.

One of the reasons for undertaking SEA is to consider the cumulative effects of all transport interventions and, as a result, SEA should consider EIA and non-EIA projects. It is therefore appropriate for the SEA process to assist in the specification of non-EIA projects.

Perhaps the greatest benefit would be the delivery of a clear set of environmental design objectives within which specific transport projects must conform. Having such a set of specific objectives defined in advanced could help to replace the mitigation culture with one of impact avoidance and delivery of enhancements.

Independence or integration of assessment

Linked with communication is the task of safeguarding the independence of assessments where the plan-making authority is also responsible for the SEA. This is a situation that does not normally arise with EIA. In France, credible independent institutions are able to act as arbiters (ECMT, 2004), while in the Netherlands, separation of stakeholder consultation from expert appraisal is viewed as important. A key issue is how to ensure the objectivity of the assessment and avoid similar failures to those of early EIAs. The need for independent advisors in Switzerland was highlighted in a presentation by Hilty (2005).

Integration of SEA with economic appraisal

It is becoming recognized that a single measure of economic efficiency as a means of making decisions is flawed and many countries are undertaking multi-criteria analysis of transport plans and projects. This is particularly important, as a focus on economic efficiency does not assist in fully understanding the distribution of the costs and benefits. Options that are equally economically efficient may result in a very different distribution of costs and benefits. As a result of SEA, it should be less likely that scarce financial resources are wasted, allowing more cost-effective delivery of objectives. Questions as to how to integrate environmental and economic appraisal activities throughout the transport planning process will undoubtedly continue to arise.

Conclusions

The introduction of SEA to transport planning is envisaged to be somewhat easier than in other sectors given its tradition of evaluation of alternatives. Nevertheless, efforts are needed to fully embed SEA into transport planning and to ensure SEA is not regarded as a waste of time or as an administrative hurdle to be jumped. It is also important to recognize that the additional resources being spent on SEA represent an additional overhead to transport authorities. As a result, it should deliver what is intended, namely an increased likelihood of sustainable development. Failure to deliver a real benefit would result in an overloading of the system and a waste of public resources that perhaps would be better spent on downstream environmental enhancement and mitigation or on health promotion.

It is vital that the assessment community recognizes its role in delivering tangible benefits for the resources being allocated to SEA. To achieve this, it can be beneficial to link the procedure up with health, social and possibly also economic assessments.

While tiering is a nice concept, the chapter by Arts, Tomlinson and Voogd (Chapter 26) indicates that practice is somewhat divergent from theory, often because of discontinuities in assessment procedure and subject, personal and administrative responsibility, timing and spatial frame of the process, non-aligned planning, and so on.

In seeking integration with the transport plan-making processes, the assessment professional must recognize the existing culture and pressures upon the plan-making professions. In the context of transport planning, it is the belief in numbers, difficulties in reopening old ground in which alternatives have been foreclosed and establishing meaningful integration that present the main challenges. In particular, the following methodological, procedural, technical and cultural issues merit particular attention:

* **Devising and assessing alternative strategies in transport plans:** How are strategies devised, what level of detail, who is involved, how are the boundaries with other plans and jurisdictions handled?

- **Integrating SEA into other assessment activities:** How to bring economic, social, health and environmental assessments together at the same plan level and provide integration between SEA and project EIA?
- **Stakeholder involvement in defining the problem and objectives:** How to engage the public when they tend only to become involved in transport planning when projects directly affect their interests? How to manage bias, conflicts and interventions from pressure groups?
- **Assessment tools for SEA:** Are we properly equipped with tools and techniques for SEA? How to ensure GIS is used correctly? Are more appropriate tools needed for integrated assessment or should the process not merit closer attention? At what stage of the process are qualitative procedures best, at what stage quantitative? How to aggregate impacts for strategies with multiple transport measures? Can environmental capacity be defined?
- **Communicating the assessment:** How to keep the assessments meaningful for the different audiences yet technically robust? What is the best way to communicate inherent uncertainties?
- **Quality control in SEA:** Is it an issue when the plan-maker is also judging the SEA and its mitigation/monitoring requirements? What rules are needed for significance criteria?
- **Changes to transport planning:** How will SEA change the culture of transport planning, will the US model be followed? Can SEA only be successfully implemented when current planners and decision-makers have fundamentally opened up their routines and thereby changed the planning culture?

While transport is perhaps better placed to accommodate SEA than other sectors, the key task remains to deliver the change in the culture of transport planning so that problems are better understood and sustainable transport is delivered. Key to this will be more effective and open mechanisms for involving the public, a willingness among transport planners to accept the legitimacy of the views of others and the need to address objectives beyond those of road safety and reducing congestion and eventually also accepting limits, for example, the environmental carrying capacity.

References

Alton, C. and Underwood, B. (2005) 'Successful tiering of policy-level SEA to project-level environmental impact assessments', paper presented at the IAIA SEA Conference, Prague

Borken, J. (2005a) 'Strategic environmental indicators for transport and their evaluation – qualitative decision aiding for SEA', paper presented at the IAIA SEA Conference, Prague

Borken, J. (2005b) personal communication

ECMT (European Conference of Ministers of Transport) (2000) *Sustainable Transport Policies*, ECMT, Paris

ECMT (2004) *Assessment and Decision Making for Sustainable Transport*, ECMT, Paris

Hilty, N. (2005) 'Transport sectoral plan – Switzerland', paper presented at the IAIA SEA Conference, Prague

Jiliberto, R. (2005) 'System model for SEA of transport', paper presented at the IAIA SEA Conference, Prague

Lee, M. (2005) 'Strategic environmental assessment of road construction', paper presented at the IAIA SEA Conference, Prague

Tomlinson, P. (2004) 'The role of significance criteria in SEA', conclusions of an informal workshop on significance criteria, IAIA Annual Meeting, Vancouver

Tomlinson, P. and Fry, C. (2002) 'Improving EIA effectiveness through SEA', paper presented at the IAIA Annual Meeting, The Hague

TRB (Transport Research Board) (1999) 'New paradigms for local public transportation organizations', TCRP Report 53, TRB, National Research Council, National Academy Press, Washington, DC

12
SEA and Water Management

Sibout Nooteboom, Patrick Huntjens and Roel Slootweg

Introduction

Water management is one the world's most pressing issues. Major regions and subcontinents have serious problems of water shortage, flooding and pollution that present serious risks to people and wetland ecosystems that provide invaluable services. Technical solutions to water management are often difficult to implement cost-effectively for many reasons, including the scale and inter-jurisdictional complexity of water systems and their multiple uses, many of which conflict, impeding cooperation and cost-sharing. In some cases, there is also skewed interdependency, for example, where upstream jurisdictions control the water on which downstream jurisdictions depend or undertake major developments that have adverse downstream impacts.

Against this background, many efforts have been made to improve the way communities deal with water issues. International agencies such as the World Bank and intergovernmental and supranational organizations such as the European Union (EU) can assist in getting to grips with cooperative water management and joint decision-making in support of sustainable development. A particular concern is to create transparency and participation in the planning process using assessment to produce sound and publicly available information for decision-making. By experimenting with such approaches, a more or less standardized practice or institutionalized system may evolve. These are variously named and here referred to as systems of strategic environmental assessment (SEA).

This chapter describes some recent trends and developments in SEA for water management and draws lessons from practical cases presented in the 2005 International Association for Impact Assessment (IAIA) SEA conference in Prague. These developments encompass different stages of institutionalization, from legal systems and derived practices in the EU to experimental cases such as those undertaken by the World Bank, in part following from its internal procedures. After a general review of recent literature on participative water management planning, we undertake case reviews, asking the following questions:

- How are the water system and its problems structured?
- What is the system of governance in relation to these problems?

- How is transparency and participation created?
- What is the outcome of this process?
- What are the success factors?

The cases reviewed vary in several respects, for example, whether or not there is a tradition of detailed joint planning. In some cases, there is some form of centralized government that to some degree can be held responsible for common problems, in others there is not. In some cases, policies are primarily aimed at safety or avoiding damage to property; in others, the aim is to protect ecosystems. This variety may be expected to lead to different outcomes and different types of adequate systems of SEA.

Background: The urgency of sound water management

Global importance of water

Water is a critical, but often overlooked, element in sustainable development. This was a theme of the 2002 World Summit on Sustainable Development (WSSD). In commenting on its outcomes, the then Executive-Director of the United Nations Environment Programme (UNEP) stated that:

> The WSSD highlighted that water is not only the most basic of needs but is also at the centre of sustainable development and is essential for poverty eradication. Water is intimately linked to health, agriculture, energy and biodiversity. Without progress on water, reaching the other Millennium Development Goals will be difficult, if not impossible. (Toepfer, 2003)

The facts are staggering. According to the 2003 United Nations World Water Development Report, between 1991 and 2000, more than 665,000 people died in 2557 natural disasters – 90 per cent of which were water-related and 97 per cent of the victims were from developing countries (UNWWAP, 2003). The recorded annual economic losses associated with these disasters have grown from US$30 billion in 1990 to US$70 billion in 1999. Health problems related to water are estimated to have similar costs. Water problems are as much a product of the social, economic and institutional context as they are of the biophysical and technical factors governing local hydrological conditions (Gleick, 2003). Many water-related challenges are related to socio-economic distribution and access, especially in developing regions. For people who can afford to pay or who belong to elite social groups, water is often not scarce, even in situations where the supply is extremely limited. Since water is the cornerstone of most economic activity, equitable distribution of supplies under changing conditions is often more of a challenge than absolute limitations on the available resource (Pahl-Wostl et al, 2005).

Evolving approach to water management

Communities all over the world, affected by water problems, have long tried to address them. In this context, thinking about water as a physical system has become popular since the 1970s when a 'command and control' approach to water management and river basin management was predominant. Later, this approach was extended to other physical systems and to the social system. Now, terms such as integrated water resources management (IWRM), adaptive water management and water governance are used to describe practices that have emerged worldwide (Pahl-Wostl and Sendzimir, 2005). This thinking has also led to interest in engaging and institutionalizing social processes, giving a central place to participation, transparency and information, the three pillars of impact assessment.

The Global Water Partnership (GWP), an international think tank, defines IWRM as 'a process which promotes the coordinated development and management of water, land and related resources in order to maximize the resultant economic and social welfare in an equitable manner without compromising the sustainability of vital ecosystems' (GWP-TAC, 2000). Figure 12.1 schematically illustrates the three pillars of IWRM, identifying assessment and information as major management instruments. Figure 12.2 summarizes the steps in the IWRM cycle and how they can be performed. Adaptive water management is used to deal with fundamental uncertainties in IWRM, stressing a process of continuous social learning to adapt to changing circumstances and creating adaptive regimes (Pahl-Wostl and Sendzimir, 2005). These uncertainties relate more to the social development (governance structure, governance agendas that affect water) than to the physical system (Gunderson et al, 1995). The implication is that the cycle in Figure 12.2 has to constantly be redone, involving elements of transparency, information and participation in most steps.

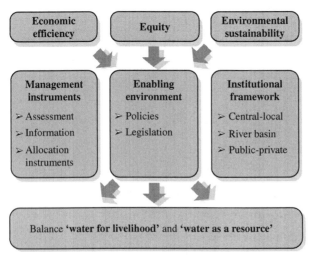

Source: GWP-TAC (2004)

Figure 12.1 *The 'three pillars' of IWRM*

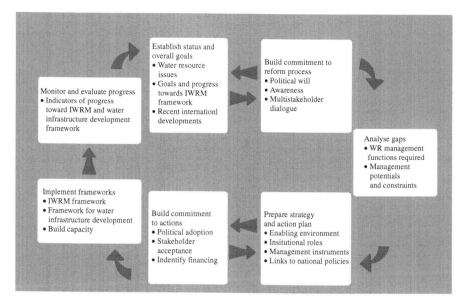

Source: GWP-TAC (2005)

Figure 12.2 *Steps in the IWRM cycle*

Institutional approaches

Like assessment practices, formal systems of water management continue to evolve. For example, the World Bank provides institutional and technical assistance for their borrowing countries and the EU has established framework legislation. Worldwide, environmental assessment is formally applied to water management plans and to other plans that create an impact on water. Both the World Bank and the EU adhere to the principle of subsidiarity: decentralization of responsibilities where possible, centralization where required.

This principle is enshrined in the EU Water Framework Directive (2000/60/EC), which requires that water planning and management should consider river basins as comprehensive units and that member countries should set water quality objectives for them in addition to EU-wide minimum quality standards. The main pillars of the Directive are public participation, basin-wide water management and policy planning and monitoring, all at member state level. Elsewhere, this principle has been promulgated extensively over the past 15 years, leading to the creation of many river basin management organizations structured around a broader participation of stakeholders from different user groups and sectors in order to achieve more integrated water resources management.

Based on experience with World Bank-financed projects, Kemper et al (2006) have concluded that decentralization works best in the context of a sufficiently strong central government that can support this process over time, including financially (see also World Bank, 2003). Specifically, this should lead to a comprehensive set of centralized policies that explicitly address water management and treat water as an economic good. Policies should be combined with decentralized management and delivery structures and fuller participation by stakeholders.

Successful decentralization, according to Kemper et al (2006), depends on the regions or districts concerned having a sufficient revenue base to undertake activities. It requires the existence of clearly defined property and water rights among potential stakeholders (for effective negotiation and commitment to operations and maintenance); socio-political preconditions for participation and resistance of elite capture (for example, unstratified social structures); and transparency, including clear roles and responsibilities with legal authority and good quality information. This also makes clear that institutionalized responsibilities cannot be the full answer to water problems and water governance. That also depends on a culture of cooperation between different stakeholder groups and governments, which share an interest in water management. This cooperation cannot be enforced through legislation that only creates transparency or some form of compulsory participation.

Based on experience with World Bank-financed projects worldwide (Kemper et al, 2006) it seems to be comparatively easy to translate the concept of management at the lowest appropriate level into laws and regulations. Yet its application often encounters obstacles due to the varying interests of different stakeholder groups, including those that would have to promote the decentralization. In practice, this means that projects and policies based around integrated water resources management principles may not fully achieve their potential benefits.

Even with good cooperation, the sheer complexity of physical and social systems imposes limits on 'rational' water management. There is increasing worldwide recognition that individual projects and policies that affect water also have implications for other water users within the river basin, both upstream and downstream, and for the health or quality of the environment generally. Increased development pressures are placing stresses on the natural resource base of river basins and leading to degradation that is felt well beyond the immediate area of a particular project. The degree to which stakeholders will share costs and benefits has great consequences for the appropriate design of a water and land management system. By showing stakeholders the consequences of their negotiation activities on welfare they can make better-founded decisions. Integrated river basin management has been the primary mechanism to addressing these issues and impacts (World Bank, 2006).

Future challenges

All rivers create some degree of tension among the societies that they bind. The cooperative or non-cooperative responses that are elicited can reach far 'beyond the river'. Recognizing that water bodies are key natural resources for future prosperity and security, it is important to identify mechanisms and instruments to support the use of water as a catalyst for regional cooperation rather than a source of potential conflict. Cooperatively managing and developing these rivers requires great skill, robust institutions, significant investment, and strong cooperation across jurisdictions (World Bank, 2006).

The following key areas require scientific breakthroughs and transfer into practical applications (from Pahl-Wostl et al, 2005):

- Governance in water management (methods to arrive at polycentric, horizontal and broad stakeholder participation in IWRM).
- Sector integration (integration of IWRM and spatial planning, integration with climate change adaptation strategies, cross-sectoral optimization and cost-benefit analysis).
- Scales of analysis in IWRM (methods to resolve resource use conflicts; transboundary issues).
- Information management (for example, multi-stakeholder dialogue; multi-agent systems modelling; role of games in decision-making; novel monitoring systems; community decision support systems).
- Infrastructure (innovative methods for using river basin buffering capacity; role of storage in adaptation to climate variability and climate extremes).
- Finances and risk mitigation strategies in water management (new instruments, role of public-private arrangements in risk-sharing).
- Stakeholder participation, promoting new ways of bridging between science, policy and implementation.

Participation, transparency and reliable information, the key elements of SEA, remain at the heart of this learning process. However, little information is available about the role of formalized procedures for SEA, in addition to other procedures related to water management, which also create transparency, participation and information. For example, in the EU, water management plans often require an SEA under either the Water Framework Directive or the SEA Directive.

World Bank experience

In developing countries, the World Bank and other international lending and aid agencies have had an important role in improving water management systems. Several cases discussed at the Prague workshop illustrate the use of SEA for this purpose in India, Pakistan, Egypt, Argentina and Colombia (Panneer-Selvan and Harshadeep, 2005; Slootweg et al, 2007; Sanchez-Triana and Enriquez, 2005). These are reviewed against the checklist of questions cited earlier.

How are the water system and its problems structured?

One thing the above five countries have in common is that even basic water services are not available to a significant part of the population, and water is first and foremost an economic and social priority. Many people have no access to healthy drinking water, sanitation or water supply for agriculture. All of these cases were similarly aimed at addressing structural causes of water shortage, flooding and pollution but they differed in terms of their solutions. In India, the planning and SEA processes focused on the whole Palar river basin $(18,000 \text{ km}^2)$ where serious water resource issues (scarcity, competition across sectors and regions, sustainability) are inextricably intertwined with environmental (industrial and domestic pollution and natural resources management) issues. In Egypt and Pakistan, the emphasis was on irrigation and drainage interventions but also extended to their implications for other water services and the affect on stakeholders beyond the agricultural sector. In Argentina and Columbia, the planning and assessment process focused directly on institutional reforms.

What is the system of governance in relation to these problems?

The social complexity of the planning and assessment process was often reduced by focusing on a major problem area or aspect, building on existing governance structures and cooperation cultures. In India, in keeping with basin-wide focus, stakeholders were engaged through representatives of cities, industries and farmers. In Egypt and Pakistan, the process focused primarily on the governance of the irrigation and drainage system. In Argentina and Colombia, previous social processes had created a wide awareness that the governance system had flaws and created less than optimal outcomes.

How is transparency and participation created?

In India, SEA was used as a tool to analyse the problem and identify interventions at policy and project levels to contribute to overall economic, environmental and social improvement. In Egypt and Pakistan, a comparable analytical tool served to create more transparency and joint thinking about interventions in the irrigation and drainage system, identifying and involving affected groups. In Argentina and Colombia, much like in India, the focus was on a social learning process building on a wider consensus regarding sustainable scenarios for water management that had been achieved already. The learning process therefore was aimed at developing a transparent and participative institutional system with adequate powers and responsibilities for implementation of agreed scenarios.

What is the outcome of this process?

In India, SEA internalized environmental aspects in a basin planning framework. A combination of analytical and participatory approaches helped in developing a common vision for the Palar Basin among different stakeholders – including government, farmers, industry associations, academia, research institutions and non-governmental organizations (NGOs). Through a structured consultative process, basin stakeholders identified supporting objectives, strategies and tactics and finally a set of tasks or actions that are essential to realize the common vision. These interventions include both software (knowledge management, training and research) and investment elements.

In Egypt and Pakistan, the application of the drainage integrated analytical framework (dubbed Drainframe) proved to be effective to assess irrigation and drainage interventions from an integrated natural resources management perspective (Abdel-Dayem et al, 2004). The framework provides for discussion and negotiation of trade-offs related to the different functions and values of natural resources influenced by water resources management interventions. It is therefore applicable to natural resources management in general rather than to drainage only. It is a tool for integrated analysis and assessment, embedded in a participatory planning process. The instrument has been field-tested in integrated strategic assessments in irrigation improvement in Egypt, in the Pakistan national drainage master plan, and a planned public-private partnership project for surface water supply to the West Delta region of Egypt.[1]

In Argentina and Colombia, the institutional reforms identified created more optimism that water management would be solved in a sustainable way.

What are success factors?

In India, the World Bank focused on a combination of providing tools for information analysis and providing moderators who had the skill to convince the involved groups of the pressing need to address common issues. The initial focus was on developing a common view on the structure of the problem. From that process, solutions started to emerge. This process benefits from an existing social structure that facilitates influential representatives of several groups to participate in developing solutions for the common good of a whole river basin. Over a period of several years, the World Bank invested in fostering this structure to develop greater involvement, trust and common understanding among core representatives, which allowed them to communicate with their supporter groups and facilitated a wider process of social learning. A crucial success factor was the subtle way in which the World Bank representatives could moderate a process by jointly looking with recipients for allies in different stakeholder groups to address long-term issues. That small-scale and little structured social process was needed to find acceptable options for large-scale social interventions, which would create the support for joint interventions in the water system. The major success factor was therefore the combination of, first, long-term involvement of the World Bank as a strategic actor in the river basin, with no specific local interests of itself, moderating a process behind the scenes, and, second, the provision of tools to develop widely accepted information bases regarding current situation and possible futures.

In Argentina and Colombia, the situation was more advanced in the sense that social capital (wide agreement on the nature of problems and directions for solutions) had emerged already, and the World Bank could assist directly with institutional reforms that would create a national context for improved water management. In similar situations, international agencies may stimulate such social learning processes by assisting working groups of different stakeholders to address a shared problem, through identification of their priorities and perspectives including the most vulnerable groups and of joint perceptions of desirable sustainable water management strategies and required policies and institutions.

In Egypt and Pakistan, the assessments resulted in a better perception of the multiple services provided by the water system. By identifying the stakeholders linked to these services, it was possible to provide better insight into the social and economic consequences of irrigation and drainage interventions. Invitation of all stakeholders, both beneficiaries as well as those potentially harmed by proposed plans, created a transparent process of plan formulation. An important lesson, well-known already to the impact assessment community, is that SEA becomes more effective when it starts as early as possible in the planning process. The cases clearly showed that each additional step in the planning process makes it more difficult for SEA to influence the process, for example, in generating meaningful alternatives. A progressing planning process (because of the time and energy invested) increases sectoral interests within both the country and the World Bank. When planning is well advanced, there is very little room to change the course of the process.

In summary, SEA and related processes undertaken by international agencies can be a positive outside force to bring groups together and help them to address and serve their own needs in developing effective water management systems. Nonetheless, much depends on the willingness of actors from different backgrounds in a river basin to seek common objectives and take their supporter groups along in this process. World Bank effectiveness depends on its ability to engage such people and create national competencies by stimulating large-scale social learning. Since that process can be slow, sustained effort is necessary, with a focus on identifying opportunities and small successes at a social level, which can be interpreted as good practices to achieve long-term aims.

Flood management in northwest Europe

Two trends point to an increase of flood risk in Europe in the coming decades. Firstly, the magnitude and frequency of floods are likely to increase in the future as a result of climate change (higher intensity of rainfall as well as rising sea levels). Secondly, there has been a marked increase in the number of people and economic assets located in flood risk zones. The challenge is to anticipate these changes now and to protect society and the environment from the negative effects of floods. SEA has been used extensively for this purpose in northwestern Europe to move from a piecemeal to a more coherent, area-wide approach. UK experience in applying SEA to flood management strategies was particularly well represented in the cases discussed at Prague (Ashby-Crane, 2005; Collyer and Marshall, 2005; Slater et al, 2005). Key aspects are summarized in Box 12.1. In this section, we place this approach in the wider context of governance systems and social processes that are critical to develop long-term resolutions of complex issues. This discussion is based on a comparative study of flood management in England, Belgium, France, Germany and the Netherlands (DHV and RIZA, 2005). Since there is no European policy on flood control, all these countries have national and decentralized systems. Although the EU is developing a Floods Directive, in order to reduce the risks of floods to people, property and environment, this Directive has not been legally enforced at the time of writing. Its implementation is underway.

How are the water system and its problems structured?

In northwest Europe, major international rivers such as the Rhine and Meuse make flood management a transboundary as well as basin-wide issue. However, there are few, if any, international policies since it is difficult enough to agree on

---

Box 12.1 *UK experience with SEA for flood risk management plans*

The Environment Agency of England and Wales is the regulator of the water sector and acts as a responsible authority, a consultation body and a proponent in the undertaking of SEA for water management plans. In the preparation of its flood risk management plans and programmes, the agency has developed a particular approach to SEA based on an objective-led approach and the relationship with EIA of subsequent projects. Key challenges in implementing this approach include: (a) objective setting in SEA – managing stakeholder expectations in SEA through effective consultation; and (b) tiering of SEA and EIA down the plan, programme and project hierarchy.

SEA applications also reflect the regional issues addressed in flood risk management plans as in the industrial northeast of England, which has an extensive network of ageing flood and water infrastructure, a high concentration of designated protected sites and high population demands (Slater et al, 2005). In the Fluvial Trent Flood Risk Management Strategy, SEA focused on a 200 km stretch of river covering 27 identified flood risk locations and a wide range of environmental issues and often conflicting public interests and used best practice guidance available at the time (Collyer and Marshall, 2005). The Humber Estuary Flood Risk Management Strategy (HEFRMS) is a long-term (100-year) plan, initiated to replace an earlier approach of piecemeal repairs and improvements to deteriorating flood defences and to respond to new legal requirements under the Habitats Directive. SEA was used to inform all phases of strategy development of a range of flood defence measures that attempt to reconcile the needs of floodplain residents, industry and infrastructure and nature conservation; it included appraisal of 'strategic' impacts and identification of the relationship of environmental risks and opportunities (Ashby-Crane, 2005).

---

flood management at the national level. There are considerable differences in approach across EU member states. For example, in the Netherlands and parts of the UK, flood damage is mainly to property and consequently an economic issue, whereas in France and Germany, floods have resulted in loss of life and are safety issues.

In the Netherlands, one third of the country lies below sea-level and flood protection has a high profile. However, sea and river defences are assumed to be secure and human safety is a lesser national political issue. Other interests have to accommodate the main river dykes, which are often relocated inland to broaden riverbeds to deal with higher peak-levels when zones of collection and inundation overlap in low-lying terrain. Flood protection here is primarily a local issue, covering the area of several municipalities which are affected by national defence measures.

In other Western European countries, policy objectives have to address major differences between upstream drainage areas and downstream flooding areas. A common challenge in assessing the impact of flooding is how to reflect the gradual change in baseline represented by the intensification of farming and urban land-use patterns, which accelerates run-off and flood accumulation. The planning solutions are well understood: upper watershed protection (retaining natural vegetation for water retention), riparian buffers to slow run-off and restrictions on building in flood hazard zones, supplemented by limitations of liability for damage compensation. SEA in a non-perfect world.

What is the system of governance in relation to these problems?

All of these countries have well-developed systems of governance for implementing these flood protection measures. Without exception, these include transparent and participative procedures for land-use planning and an explicit requirement to assess the plans and projects that have a potentially significant impact on the environment. Dutch legislation, for example, provides for tiers of environmental assessment in dyke location and development. In terms of safety, for example, main dykes must be sufficient to withstand a once in every 10,000 years flood. However, there are no norms for damage protection. Each decision has to be based on a customized trade-off and it is difficult to assess flooding effects, since there is a long delay between incremental changes of land-use and their contribution to future floods. When building in flood prone places, it is hard for investors to estimate the increase in future risk or accept any responsibility for preventing faster run-off upstream even though no one else may be either.

In response to flood calamities, European countries have adjusted their systems of governance for water management. In all countries, governmental agencies responsible for flood management and the maintenance of dykes and infrastructure participate in spatial planning processes but have no power to make land-use decisions, since that requires a trade-off between different interests. It is widely recognized that flood protection has been given insufficient consideration in land-use trade-offs in the past. There have been different solutions to this issue in different countries. For example, in France, a national fund for damage compensation has acted almost as an incentive to continue land-use developments. In contrast, the government of the Netherlands have communicated to local authorities that they will no longer have state coverage for future damages caused by current spatial decisions. A 'water test' of the impacts of land-use plans also has been introduced. UK policies focus on preventive measures for flood protection, mainly dykes, based on a centralized social cost benefit analysis. Local actors have no influence on the use of these budgets and bear the full risk of any spatial or development decisions that increase flood risk.

How is transparency and participation created?

It has become clear that the improvement of flood management involves far more than the improvement of impact assessment or planning procedures that apply to major dykes and other infrastructure. The real difficulty is the large number of groups affected by small decisions with incremental, cumulative and ultimately large-scale downstream impacts and the reliance on a government to either take preventive action or compensate damage. Traditions of damage compensation after major losses do not foster taking local or personal responsibility and spatial developments still do not take account of the impact in other jurisdictions or in the long-term into consideration.

Several countries have understood that social complexity is the main barrier, which cannot be addressed by procedures alone. Instead, they are experimenting with mass communication regarding the risks (and future risks) of building in flood prone areas and the responsibility to insure against flood damage. Given the continuing process of urbanization in these areas, there is agreement among experts that this dynamic creates tremendous risks, which do not consider the very long term.

In parts of Germany and the Netherlands, governments are using social learning processes to address this issue. These processes involve the establishment of formal and informal social networks 'downstream and upstream', to search for acceptable solutions, such as the use of land for double purposes (for example, water retention and some other benefits). Since the solutions are yet unknown and require the participation of many, these groups develop their own dynamics and information bases. Depending on the type of outcome, they can make more adequate interventions. However, these processes are still limited to small areas, covering a number of municipalities.

What is the outcome of this process?

Proactive assessment of flood risks in spatial developments probably has its positive impacts, but these are difficult to establish. Nonetheless, retention areas are increasing and, in principle, urban developments do take flood risk into consideration. An evaluation therefore depends on the view of insiders who can tell whether process transparency and participation has led to a change of perceptions of planners about desirable courses of action. In the Netherlands, at least, preliminary reviews indicate that social learning competencies are improving in part but outcomes are still limited to less expensive solutions or solutions which do not require significant exchange of resources between different actors (in terms of 'I take measures to protect you, you take measures to protect me'; or 'I will make much higher costs that I would since it is my responsibility to protect you').

What are success factors?

In the situation where the responsibilities for water management and land-use planning and environmental assessment are well-developed, as are EU countries, the low-hanging fruit is picked already. After that, progress becomes slow because of the social complexity of the issues: there are too many groups involved in a single package of related policies. Urban and agricultural developments also have their own internal dynamic, which is not controlled by procedures. It is therefore likely that land-use decisions will continue to reflect short-term needs, therefore increasing flood risks. The answer from several countries is first to make completely clear that damage will not be compensated by the government if the victim has not insured himself against flood risk, second to ensure full transparency of such risks in planning and assessment processes, and to use the concerns created by greater risk awareness to initiate a social learning process that also creates awareness of possible solutions. This will, at the same time, foster support for the associated interventions.

EU procedures for water quality

Within EU, SEA has emerged as a crucial instrument for water planning and decision-making as a result of the coincident implementation of the SEA and Water Framework directives. Under the SEA Directive, member states have the discretion 'to provide for coordinated or joint procedures' to avoid duplication of assessment arising from simultaneous obligations under different laws (Article 11(2)) and this would certainly include the Water Framework Directive (WFD, see Chapter 8). The links between the two directives were explored at Prague in general and with particular reference to the potential contribution that SEA could make towards a sustainable planning and management of water resources (Gullón, 2005). In this section, we examine the WFD from that perspective.

How are the water system and its problems structured?
The purpose of the EU WFD (2000) is 'to establish a framework for the protection of inland surface waters, transitional waters, coastal waters and groundwater'. It requires – among other things – the preparation of river basin management plans and programmes of measures to safeguard water quality. These action plans involve setting water quality goals for water bodies that fit their function and linking water basin management to land-use planning and environmental planning. Implementation in national law and in river basin plans is ongoing.

What is the system of governance in relation to these problems?
The Directive's approach is based on river basins. It also has to be implemented by countries that often share river basins, where some level of international cooperation is required, at least implicitly. Formally, countries should develop a six-yearly river basin management plan for each river basin, with a programme of pollution control measures, based on the 'polluter pays' principle. Procedures related to physical planning, environmental management and other EU-directives (for example, SEA and EIA) should be aligned.

The EU SEA Directive entered into force in 2004 and adds to WFD requirements that a wider report regarding environmental impacts and alternatives is provided before decision-making about the water management plans. How countries implement their mandate under the WFD is a national matter. There is no jurisdiction at international river basin level, although at sub-national level this might be the case. National systems of water governance are decentralized in different degrees. In most EU countries, water management authorities have different geographic coverage than land-use planning and pollution control authorities.

Water quality ambitions downstream affect polluting activities upstream and vice versa. Trade-offs are required with respect to functions of water bodies. The implication is that functions of water bodies have to be determined in relation to land-use in general, and with coherence over large areas. For example, in the Netherlands, water management boards traditionally have high ambitions for the ecosystem quality of many water bodies. However, achieving these ambitions is costly, for example, because they cannot be combined with the economic system that has developed in the area (mainly agriculture). If ambitions are not lowered, the programme of measures may be tantamount to changing the function of land in the area from agriculture to other uses.

A previous water-related EU Directive on Nitrates has had the effect of reducing the profitability of pig farms and the sector is disappearing due to environmental regulations. With the WFD, similar trade-offs are needed, which creates political dilemmas that are not easily solved, for example, in the Dutch system of governance. While the Netherlands has not substantially changed its water management procedures in response to the WFD, Spain, for example, has moved substantially toward and improvement of its system for water quality protection and water pricing (Gullón, 2005).

How is transparency and participation created?

The WFD requires ensuring information supply and consultation and encourages the active involvement of all water users and stakeholders in the river basin planning. In cases where the SEA Directive applies, the required scope is widened. The WFD also requires reporting to the European Commission about the public participation process, indicating its effects on the river basin.

What is the outcome of this process?

It is difficult to speculate on the impact of the WFD and the associated transparency and participative procedures on the functions of water or the environment in general. Earlier water-related EU legislation had less transparent procedures. Also, the central issue in water quality management is the spatial decision-making function of the water bodies. Spatial planning procedures are not regulated at EU level, but SEA is required for spatial plans if they are mandatory and set a framework for projects that require an EIA. With the SEA Directive, the WFD has significant impacts on the way water function decisions are made in EU member states. Its procedures lead to extremely complex trade-offs between spatial functions and between upstream and downstream areas. The involved authorities need to make that complexity manageable if they are to prepare plans that can be realistically implemented.

The issues are country-specific and in some cases may be unique, for example, the reduction of pig farming in the Netherlands. Another interesting question is how public participation in the case of river basin plans should be related to the public participation in the case of land-use plans or environmental plans. The WFD indicates that these procedures should be aligned, but this may not be so simple. Issues for spatial decision-making may not coincide with issues of water management. The planning process and procedures may have to follow different rhythms. It is not yet clear how countries deal with such complexity, and how such alignment can even be achieved between different countries sharing river basins. This will have implications for SEA.

What are success factors?

We believe that the WFD requirements, and the EU SEA requirements for spatial plans and associated river basin plans, are invaluable incentives for better cooperation and more rational water use planning. As of now, this is mainly a belief based on preliminary and scattered observations at the Prague workshop. But the fact that implementation meets resistance could mean that polluters are now confronted with public authorities and stakeholders that are aware of the trade-offs associated with a choice to clean up their water, for example, possibly at short-term expense of specific economic interests. Transparency and the pressure from the European Commission, which can sanction countries with a malfunctioning system, should be enough to get the authorities to act but not so much that complexity of governance interdependencies becomes discouraging.

Conclusion

Transparency, participation and high-quality information (as resources for decision-making) have the attention of governments in many parts of the world. International organizations such as the World Bank and the European Commission act in subtle processes to encourage lower scale jurisdictions to improve their system of water management and to apply elements of SEA. The World Bank builds a long-standing relationship with national and local actors, building trust that attractive loans will be given if countries try hard enough to improve their process. The World Bank subsequently assists countries to do that using international experts to describe examples or suggest approaches that might work under local circumstances. The European Commission mandates national planning systems that include requirements for participation and reporting and requires the sound implementation of action plans to achieve water quality targets. EU directives create a new game of water governance, where real pressure seems to be imposed on polluters to adjust their practices according to water functions that are in the general interest.

In Western European countries, similar approaches are taken in flood management. Several countries implement transparent procedures to ensure that planners and investors become aware of the flood risks caused by their decisions and that the state will not compensate for any damages that result from such decision. That awareness plus transparent and participative procedures are a stimulus for more rational planning at the lower level. In addition, in the UK there is a strong system of tiered planning and associated SEA applied to the flood management and governance system that clarifies the responsibilities of different layers and levels of government. As elements of SEA are increasingly used, they should create an incentive for the better cooperation between interdependent actors who are jointly involved in water management. These elements are not just formally instituted under SEA or water sector legislation but may be voluntarily applied through the soft pressure of influential agencies such as the World Bank.

Since the Prague IAIA meeting, key developments have been the linkage of water management SEA to climate change and to the assessment of institutions. In most parts of the world, climate change is expected to have considerable impact on water-related interests, such as flood protection, ecosystems and food supply. Against this emerging background, SEA is considered a useful instrument to insert principles of integrated water resources management into wider decision-making (Slootweg, 2010). Where IWRM provides the necessary water-sector experience and 'contents' for an assessment, SEA provides the internationally accepted procedural instrument to provide information for decision-making, guaranteeing a minimal level of transparency and public involvement. The advantage of using SEA for the advancement of IWRM principles is that SEA is known and accepted outside the water sector. The cause of water and climate-change related water issues can thus be promoted in plans originating from other sectors.

Simultaneously, it is increasingly recognized that sustainable water management, also in relation to climate change, depends on adequate institutions. To this and wider ends, the World Bank have summarized general methods for SEA of sectoral reform (World Bank, 2010). A specific method, termed 'Adaptive Capacity Wheel' (Gupta et al, 2010a), has been applied to the institutional capacities in The Netherlands to adapt the water system to climate change. Preliminary outcomes (personal communication, C. Termeer) indicate that formal powers and responsibilities for adaptation of water management and water-related land use to climate change are scattered over many interdependent governments, and therefore development and implementation of adaptive measures depends highly on informal leadership networks. Cases show that such networks might emerge more easily 'under the shadow of hierarchy' if a law on climate change adaptation were to be introduced. Among other weaknesses are the ability to mobilize creativity in society, and the capability to deal with inequalities created by adaptations to land use (Gupta et al, 2010b).

Acknowledgements

The authors thank Ernesto Sanchez-Triana for his review of a draft of this chapter.

Note

1 Further information on Drainframe analysis in the three cases discussed here (Egypt West Delta Water Conservation and Irrigation Rehabilitation project, Pakistan Master Drainage Plan and Egypt Integrated Irrigation Improvement and Management project) is available from R. Slootweg (email: sevs@sevs.nl).

References

Abdel-Dayem, S., Hoevenaars, J., Mollinga, P., Scheumann, W., Slootweg, R. and van Steenbergen, F. (2004) 'Reclaiming drainage: Toward an integrated approach', Agriculture and Rural Development Department, Report No 1, Inter-American Bank for Reconstruction and Development, Washington, DC

Ashby-Crane, R. (2005) 'Has SEA influenced the development of the Humber Estuary flood risk management strategy (UK)?', paper presented at the IAIA SEA Conference, Prague

Collyer, E. and Marshall, R. (2005) 'SEA of water management: Issues identified and lessons learnt luring the Fluvial Trent Strategy', paper presented at the IAIA SEA Conference, Prague

DHV and RIZA (2005) 'Europlano II Comparison of the Approach to Flood Management in Western European Countries', consultant report

Gleick, P. (2003) 'Global freshwater resources: Soft-path solutions for the 21st century', *Science*, vol 302, pp1524–1528

Gullón, N. (2005) 'SEA and hydrological planning: Two synergetic European Directives', paper presented at the IAIA SEA Conference, Prague

Gunderson, L., Holling, C. and Light, S. (eds) (1995) *Barriers and Bridges to the Renewal of Ecosystems and Institutions*, Columbia University Press, New York

Gupta, J. C., Termeer, C., Klostermann, J., Meijerink, S., van den Brink, M., Jong, P., Nooteboom, S. and Bergsma, E. (2010a) 'The adaptive capacity wheel: A method to assess the inherent characteristics of institutions to enable the adaptive capacity of society', *Environmental Science and Policy*, vol 13, pp459–471

Gupta, J. C., Termeer, C., Bergsma, E., Biesbroek, R., van den Brink, M., Jong, P., Klostermann, J., Meijerink, S. and Nooteboom, S. (2010b) 'Assessing the ability of Dutch institutions for stimulating the adaptive capacity of society (Project IC-12)', IVM report

GWP-TAC (Global Water Partnership Technical Advisory Committee) (2000) 'Integrated water resources management', Technical Advisory Committee Background Paper No 4, GWP, Stockholm

GWP-TAC (2004) Technical Advisory Committee Background Paper No 10, Global Water Partnership, Stockholm

GWP-TAC (2005) *Catalyzing Change: A Handbook for Developing Integrated Water Resources Management (IWRM) and Water Efficiency Strategies*, GWP-TAC, Stockholm

Kemper, K., Dinar, A. and Blomquist W. (eds) (2006) 'Institutional and policy analysis of river basin management decentralization: The principle of managing water resources at the lowest appropriate level – when and why does it (not) work in practice?', research paper, World Bank, Washington, DC

Pahl-Wostl, C. and Sendzimir, J. (2005) 'The relationship between IWRM and adaptive management', NeWater Working Paper 3, Institute of Environmental Systems Research, University of Osnabrück

Pahl-Wostl, C., Downing, T., Kabat, P., Magnuszewski, P., Meigh, J., Schlueter, M., Sendzimir, J. and Werners, S. (2005) 'Transition to adaptive water management', NeWater Working Paper 10, Institute of Environmental Systems Research, University of Osnabrück

Panneer-Selvam, L. and Harshadeep, N. (2005) 'SEA in basin planning in India', paper presented at the IAIA SEA Conference, Prague

Sanchez-Triana, E. and Enriquez, S. (2005) 'Using strategic environmental assessments for environmental mainstreaming in the water and sanitation sector: The cases of Argentina and Colombia', paper presented at the IAIA SEA Conference, Prague

Slater, M., Murphy, J. and Empson, B. (2005) 'Implementing SEA for flood risk management plans: The experience of the UK's Environment Agency', paper presented at the IAIA SEA Conference, Prague

Slootweg, R. (2010) 'Integrated water resources management and strategic environmental assessment: Joining forces for climate proofing', *Perspectives on Water and Climate Change Adaptation*, vol 16, Co-operative Programme on Water and Climate (CPWC), the International Water Association (IWA), IUCN and the World Water Council

Slootweg, R., Hoevenaars, J. and Abdel-Dayem, S. (2007) 'Drainframe as a tool for integrated strategic environmental assessment: Lessons from practice', *Irrigation and Drainage Management*, vol 56, ppS191–S203

Toepfer, K. (2003) 'Balancing competing water uses – a necessity for sustainable development', *Water Science and Technology*, vol 47, no 6, pp11–16

UNWWAP (United Nations World Water Assessment Programme) (2003) *UN World Water Development Report: Water for People, Water for Life* United Nations Educational, Scientific and Cultural Organization (UNESCO) and Berghahn Books, Paris, New York and Oxford

World Bank (2003) *World Resources Sector Strategy*, World Bank, Washington DC

World Bank (2006) 'The Water Resources Management Group', www.worldbank.org

World Bank (2010) 'Policy SEA: Conceptual model and operational guidance for applying strategic environmental assessment in sector reform', www-wds.worldbank.org/external/default/WDSContentServer/WDSP/IB/2010/06/29/000333038_20100629002611/Rendered/PDF/553280REPLACEM1EA1Final0Report12010.pdf

13
Regional Sectoral Assessment and Extractive Industries

Jill Baker and Friederike Kirstein

Introduction

Early and regional consideration is increasingly being given to the impacts of extractive industries prior to the development of new areas. These broad-scale assessments can be employed to achieve a number of objectives. For example, they can be used to determine if a given area is appropriate for the development of a particular industry taking into account sustainability criteria. In addition, they can be used as a tool to canvas public perspectives and to facilitate their consideration in decision-making.

This chapter summarizes the current state of regional sectoral assessment (RSA) with specific focus on experience with its application to extractive industries.[1] The discussion will: (a) highlight some experiences with RSA; (b) discuss select benefits and challenges of RSA; (c) reflect on innovative practice and lessons learned; and (d) identify some future challenges including consideration of how RSA can contribute to planning and sustainable outcomes.

Background: Definitions, objectives and cases

Terms and definitions

RSA is an inclusive term to describe the assessment of extractive industries beyond the individual project level. As implied by its name, this form of strategic assessment is focused on the development of specific industrial sectors in a defined area (for example, gold-mining in a specific region). The process may be used in evaluating the area-wide environmental and socio-economic effects of a sector policy, plan or programme (PPP), and to determine the conditions under which development scenarios could be deemed appropriate.

The term RSA is employed here rather than strategic environmental assessment (SEA), recognizing that certain criteria for SEA (for example, as defined by IAIA, 2002) are unlikely to be met by most RSA applications. For example, unlike SEA, RSA may not take into account alternatives to the

---

Box 13.1 *Terminology used in EIA which partially overlaps with RSA*

Cumulative effects assessment: An assessment of the incremental effects of an action on the environment when the effects are combined with those from other past, existing and future actions (Hegmann et al, 1999).

Ex ante evaluation: Refers to forward-looking assessment of the likely future effects of new policies or proposals (EEA, 2001).

Ex post evaluation: Refers to backward-looking assessment of the effects of introduced policies or proposals (EEA, 2001).

Regional environmental assessment: Examines issues and impacts associated with a particular strategy, policy, plan, programme, or a series of projects for a particular region (FAO, 1999).

SEA: A process of defining goals, visions and objectives, proposing alternative possibilities to achieve them, and selecting the preferred approach.

Sectoral environmental assessment: Used to assess environmental issues and impacts associated with a sector-specific strategy, policy, programme, or series of projects, providing a basis to identify the necessary measures to strengthen environmental management in the sector (FAO, 1999).

---

development of the industry sector involved. Specifically, an RSA might examine the appropriateness of metal mining in a given area, but not consider the larger, strategic questions of whether there are preferential alternatives to mining (for example, increased recycling or development of alternative sectors) as would be discussed in an SEA (Noble, 2000). Nonetheless, RSA can play an important role in facilitating the consideration of environmental and socio-economic factors in the planning process.

Although distinctive, RSA also shares characteristics with SEA and other environmental impact assessment (EIA) processes described in the literature (Box 13.1). However, existing terminology does not fully describe key elements of RSA (such as the assessment of a specific sector on a regional scale resulting in the development of recommendations to guide future development). Thus, the term RSA is proposed as an addition to the lexicon.

Objectives of RSA

Key objectives of RSA include the following:

- To determine how much of an area, if any, is appropriate for the development of a specific industrial sector, taking into account sustainability criteria, and the conditions under which development scenarios could be deemed appropriate.
- To understand and set thresholds for acceptable impact levels and to provide direction on necessary mitigation or monitoring (such as upfront identification of the conditions for future development).

- To provide the best available basis for decision-making and management strategies, including a forum to consider strategic decisions or area-wide planning that may take into account sustainability goals.
- To obtain a holistic understanding of the cumulative effects of a particular sectoral development in a given area (to examine the effects of multiple projects).
- To obtain a baseline of environmental conditions in an area as required to support an impact analysis and that can be used for comparative purposes in future years.
- To provide an understanding of data needs and to develop strategies to collect data over time.
- To canvas public and stakeholder opinions to influence decision-making.
- To integrate environmental, social and economic factors into planning processes.
- To improve and simplify future project-specific assessment work through the factors described above.

RSA case experience

This chapter draws from experiences in Mali, Peru, Norway and the Barents Sea. Each case study provides a slightly different approach to RSA, although all have the common element of evaluating a sector (or sectors) within a defined region. The difference between these case studies is the timing of assessment in relation to development – the RSA may be an ex post evaluation, an ex ante evaluation, or a combination of both. In the Norwegian offshore petroleum development case study, regional environmental impact assessment (REIA) is used in advance of a large-scale development in the seas bordering Norway (ex ante). The Peru mining case study is an ex post evaluation that followed the World Bank environmental impact report, building on social and environmental impact predictions. The Mali mining case study, although described as an SEA, examined past mining projects and their effects in an effort to learn from these experiences to prepare for anticipated future development. As such, it is better described as an ex post evaluation conducted for an ex ante purpose. The Barents Sea Integrated Management approach takes RSA one step further by assessing the potential effects of multiple activities and sectors on the ecosystem (Government of Norway, 2002).

Current experience and state of RSA

In general, the practice of RSA remains somewhat limited, although several processes are now well-established and continue to evolve. For example, the offshore oil and gas industry has considerable and increasing experience with RSA including as a variant of SEA (for example, in Brazil and the UK), programmatic review (the US) and regional environmental impact assessment (Norway). The environmental implications of this activity are considered at the regional level, in some cases before areas are 'opened' to development (Kirstein and Jeffrey, 2004). For other industries, assessments with similarities to RSA may be conducted, although not formally labelled as such (for example, 20-year forestry management plans conducted by the province of Saskatchewan, Canada, as discussed by Noble, 2004). It is likely that the EU SEA legislation (for example, Directive 2001/42/EC) and recognition of the merits of broad-scale, sectoral assessments (World Bank, 1996) will result in increasing experience with RSA.

There are a number of potential catalysts to RSA process development. For example, a regional approach may be considered necessary to address the cumulative effects of an industry in a region. Alternatively, an RSA may be developed in response to inefficiencies and frustration with project-specific EIA, if the same type of project is being assessed repeatedly and issues would better be accommodated at a regional level. Efficiencies may be realized if RSA results in specific recommendations to guide future EIA of projects (for example, tiering). In some cases, the public or industry could advocate for the development of an RSA process in response to the situations listed above. RSA may also be employed as a forum in which strategic questions regarding regional development can be discussed (issues that are typically outside the scope of a project-EIA). Finally, an RSA process may be necessary to meet legislative requirements.

As RSA of extractive industries becomes more common, questions regarding the quality and effectiveness of current experience follow. Advantages and challenges of SEA have been documented over the years (for example, Dalal-Clayton and Sadler, 1999; UNDP and REC, 2003) but they merit further consideration and ground-truthing with respect to RSA. Of course, as with any assessment process, RSA must be 'fit for purpose' (have the quality needed for the decision to be taken) in order to realize potential benefits. Elements of RSA are presented below in conjunction with examples of current practice.

Experience of RSA in facilitating stakeholder involvement

Public participation has been identified as a fundamental principal of SEA (IAIA, 2002). Given the regional implications of RSA outcomes, providing thorough and meaningful opportunities for participation will be important to the development of any process. Specifically, an RSA should typically: (a) involve stakeholders throughout the process; (b) explicitly address stakeholder's inputs and concerns in documentation and decisions; (c) have clear, easily understood information requirements; and (d) ensure easy access to relevant information. Early stakeholder intervention should help ensure that key issues of concern are understood and considered in RSA. Likewise, opportunities for stakeholders to be heard and ultimately influence regional development should help legitimize this process and the acceptability of associated outcomes. At the same time, local knowledge may be necessary to allow a comprehensive understanding of key systems. According to Gibson (2004), incentives for stakeholder participation include clear process definition and an understanding of how stakeholder input will be used.

It appears that the role and definition of stakeholder engagement currently varies within RSA and may need to be further developed, with lessons learned from similar processes. SEAs conducted for offshore petroleum activities in the UK exemplify a process that places an emphasis on public participation. This process is led by a multi-stakeholder steering committee and includes an SEA website, workshops and multiple opportunities for public input (Hartley, 2004). The RSA conducted for the mining sector in Peru resulted in a number of lessons on the benefits of stakeholder involvement, as well as recommendations respecting elements that were thought necessary for success (Zarzar, 2005). Specifically, this case study highlighted that RSA: (a) raises public awareness in general, and specifically that of government, investors and the affected communities; (b) contributes to stakeholder communications both on a policy and technical level; (c) can have a significant impact in the decision-making process; and (d) can improve social outcomes and sustainability of investments. It emphasized that to be successful, RSA: ought to be timely; must involve all the main stakeholders in the consultation process; requires a champion in the government's sector in order to facilitate its development and align it with the concerns and requirements of the sector authorities; and must rely on a pool of experienced local experts for the field research.

Benefits of RSA for environmental protection

The potential benefits of RSA for environmental protection are numerous. Intuitively, RSA should be the ideal tool for the analysis of cumulative environmental effects, which are often neglected or cannot be adequately accommodated in project-specific EIA. RSA allows stakeholders to step back from specific projects and examine the development of an extractive industry in a region as a whole. A comprehensive approach to RSA would assess the benefits and impacts of various development alternatives or a maximum foreseeable level of sectoral activity in a given area (in combination with other environmental pressures from other industries and activities). This holistic approach presents several opportunities. For example, it may be used to identify impact thresholds for environmental components affected by proposed development and can thereby be used to ensure that the total activity within a region does not impose unacceptable levels of damage.

RSA also may be employed to identify sensitive, representative or cultural areas in a given region. Again, this is facilitated by examination of the region as a whole. An assessment of impacts on special areas can be used to determine conditions under which future activity could be permitted while protecting environmental values. In other words, an RSA can be used to identify those parts of a region that are best suited to industrial development and to specify whether activities in special areas should be limited, require special management or should be prohibited altogether, depending on the nature of the interaction.

RSA also may reveal gaps in environmental data for a study area and point to the types of baseline data that need to be collected to support impact analysis. In this case, the RSA may assist the development of regional data or monitoring programmes, whereby information is collected so that it can be used by multiple proponents. The quality of the data generated and the overall acceptability of a regional approach will be enhanced if it is developed in collaboration with respected scientists, researchers and regulatory authorities. In theory, the establishment of a collaborative database, which is updated continuously from monitoring results and lessons, should improve impact predictions, future EIA applications and consequently also improve the information upon which decisions are made.

It is perhaps most important that an RSA results not only in information about potential outcomes but also in recommendations to guide future industrial development in an area. As described above, this could include recommendations related to the type and level of industrial activity that is appropriate in an area based on environmental (and socio-economic) considerations. Other types of management provisions (for example, pertaining to technology, timing, spatial scale, no development zones and monitoring needs) also may be prescribed based on impact analysis, public perspectives or other factors.

Like SEA, RSA can lead to heightened awareness of the environmental consequences of regional development. This awareness may encourage environmental considerations being given the same weight as social and economic considerations in policy and planning discussions. Ideally, these discussions would consider both the positive and negative effects of development – an RSA also could consider the contribution of regional development scenarios to sustainability (as discussed by Gibson et al, 2005). RSA also has the potential to contribute to the development of sector-specific policies. For example, a recent RSA of the metal mining sector in Mali led to specific recommendations with respect to the integration of the mining development plans into the national policies on energy, water and land use (Bouchard and Keita, 2005).

Benefits of RSA for proponents

RSA can provide significant benefits for industry. For example, early identification of special areas and associated management expectations can provide valuable information about investment opportunities in a region. Investment certainty comes with obvious benefits – most notably, it may prevent a proponent from investing in a particular area, only to determine at the EIA stage that the region is too sensitive for the type and level development as proposed. A related advantage of RSA may stem from management provisions that are developed to guide activity in a region. These provisions can provide clarity for proponents on requirements and expectations (for example, regarding mitigation or monitoring) associated with sector development in a particular region. Detailed analysis as part of an RSA may also serve to decrease the subsequent level of effort required when specific projects are proposed and subject to EIA. This type of tiering, and resulting efficiencies in the EIA process may result in considerable time and cost-savings (as in the Norwegian REIA process for offshore petroleum activities, for example, which has resulted in certain activities being exempted altogether from project-specific EIA (Kinn, 2004)).

Baseline data collection, the mitigation of project-specific impacts and related follow-up are components of most project-EIAs. By taking a regional approach to the management of an industry, efficiencies for proponents may be realized through agreement on fair share approaches to data collection and the management of cumulative effects (Kirstein and Jeffrey, 2004). Net savings for

---

Box 13.2 *Norwegian REIA – benefits and challenges for proponents*

The key benefits of the Norwegian REIA system are:

- Increased efficiencies in the EIA process, including a simplified and transparent process.
- Improved EIAs that are based on a better understanding of the regional environmental impacts of petroleum activities.
- Avoidance of duplication of effort and conflicting assessments of impacts of different project-specific activities within the same region.
- Substantial cost-efficiencies for project specific EIAs.
- Improved communications between stakeholders.
- Provide a basis for common industry objectives, plans and commitments.
- Integrated and cooperative regional monitoring programmes, which allow for improved future predictions of impacts and information for use in future environmental audits.

Although these advantages of the REIA approach are most evident for proponents, improvements to the quality, efficiency, transparency of EIA process will benefit all participants.

Key challenges of the REIA system are:

- Staying focused, as REIAs cannot deal with every regional impact; they need to be focused on the main regional issues relevant for the approval of new projects.
- Developing a common environmental strategy for many operators in the same region.
- Agreeing upon the distribution of responsibility, both for delivery and quality assurance of the data.
- Ensuring continuous improvements to the methods and models for predicting impacts.

Source: Kinn (2005)

---

proponents may stem from: (a) the early understanding of regulator expectations (such as for data collection or mitigation); (b) efficiencies related to the collective management of key interactions; and (c) the availability of baseline data for a region.

Challenges and future directions

Contribution to sustainability

International Association for Impact Assessment (IAIA) criteria indicate that SEAs should be sustainability-led, defined as the 'identification of development options and alternative proposals that are more sustainable' (IAIA, 2002).

Although strategic decisions about alternatives (such as recycling versus mining) are not typically considered in an RSA, the process still presents several opportunities to take sustainability into account.

An RSA may be conducted in accordance with regional sustainability goals for environmental protection (such as biodiversity conservation) and socio-economic development (such as employment targets). In this case, sustainability goals should be clearly defined prior to commencing an RSA, so that the corresponding impact analysis can be conducted with these outcomes in mind. Advantages of conducting an RSA according to predefined sustainability goals include creating incentives for industry to ensure that development meets stated objectives.

A more comprehensive way of integrating sustainability into RSA may be to base the process on sustainability assessment principles (for example, Pope et al, 2004; Gibson et al, 2005). Sustainability assessment requires a shift in the focus of impact assessment from the mitigation of negative effects to ensuring that development makes a positive overall contribution to sustainability (durable net gains are demonstrated). It also requires the integration of economic, social and ecological factors, and a consideration of the long-term implications of development. This approach can be used to provide stakeholders with clear information about the benefits and consequences of developing an extractive industry in a given region. The process can be used to weigh the trade-offs associated with regional development and determine whether these can be justified in achieving sustainability in the long-term (Gibson et al, 2005).

The integration of sustainability assessment principles into an RSA can help promote development that provides greater net benefit for the region as a whole. For example, the upfront recognition of specific sustainability goals could provoke industry groups or government to taking collective action toward their advancement. Specifically, development could be planned in a manner that creates the optimum type or scale of employment. Ultimately, an RSA could recommend that a percentage of profits from a non-sustainable extractive industry be directed toward the development of more sustainable alternatives in accordance with the theory of sustainability defined by El Serafy (2003a, b) whereby the depletion of non-renewable resources should drive the development of renewable substitutes.

Gibson (2004) suggests that, in integrating sustainability assessment principles into RSA, an explicit commitment to do so would be required upfront, along with an acceptance that the process would vary from a conventional regional study. The process would be about public choice – enabling a selection of potential futures and desired trade-offs. To date, we are not aware of a RSA that has incorporated sustainability assessment principles in this way.

Integrated assessments – the way of the future?

Another future challenge for RSA is to move towards integrated assessments, whereby multiple sectors are considered in the evaluation instead of assessing the benefits and impacts of only a single industry in isolation. The Barents Sea Integrated Plan is an innovative and challenging evaluation process, which, while promising, will likely be challenged in moving the process from theory to practice.

Box 13.3 *Lessons learned from the Barents Sea Integrated Management Plan*

- Sectoral plus integrated assessment is a good approach if there is sufficient time, but the process must be planned and coordinated first.
- Ensure there is sufficient expertise on methodology (SEA/EIA and stakeholder involvement).
- Spend time on getting a mutual understanding of the approach in the beginning.
- Traditional methods of stakeholder involvement are not effective if the ambition is to achieve 'consensus' (dialogue becomes paramount).
- Need to break down sectoral barriers.
- Scenarios are a good method of developing strategic alternatives, particularly if balanced with traditional approaches for impact assessment.
- Cumulative effects on an ecosystem are hard to assess when we hardly know the impact of specific pressures.
- Fill knowledge gaps as soon as they are recognized.
- Establish clear rules for how to treat uncertainty (recognizing that stakeholders – including experts – tend to use this strategically).
- Develop specific methodologies for integrated assessments, which is different from EIA.

Source: Sandar (2005)

The Regional Environmental Study for the Great Sand Hills in Saskatchewan, Canada, is an example of a process that integrated social, economic and ecological considerations into regional development. This initiative involved land-use planning for multiple sectors including oil and gas, ranching, recreation and tourism. The appropriateness of key areas for development or protection was considered through the examination of alternative development scenarios. Its recommendations will be used to guide future activities in a manner that allows economic benefits to be realized while protecting ecological integrity (Saskatchewan Environment, undated). The Great Sand Hills initiative will be worth watching for outcomes and lessons that can be applied to other regions and industries, particularly with respect to its success in integrating multiple industries and interests.

Conclusion

This paper has described RSA as the assessment of industrial sectors in defined geographic areas or regions. RSA may be used to determine the type and scale of development appropriate for a region based on ecological and socio-economic objectives. Associated benefits include the potential to manage a sector with full consideration of cumulative effects and local environmental thresholds. Early assessment of an area and articulation of conditions for development may also provide investment certainty and future efficiencies for proponents. As with any impact analysis, RSA must be fit for purpose (have the scope and quality needed for decisions to be taken) in order to realize potential benefits.

Future directions for RSA include a focus on integration – the incorporation of multiple sectors and activities within a single assessment process. Integration can provide a forum for the assessment of cumulative effects, while enabling various sectors to be considered in relation to common environmental and socio-economic goals. Integration may be complemented in RSA with the incorporation of sustainability principles. The consideration of sustainability can help ensure that, at a minimum, regional development meets predefined societal objectives. Ultimately, it should be used to facilitate development in a manner that optimizes environmental and socio-economic outcomes, ensuring that activities result in net gains.

While the overall experience with RSA is limited, it is becoming more established in certain sectors, such as oil and gas, and appears to be gaining attention in others. Some lessons that can be learned from the outcomes of past processes are summarized in this chapter; while integration and sustainability assessment are highlighted as areas for future research and action. As these concepts are furthered both in the literature and practice, their application and fit with RSA may ultimately define them as essential elements of any RSA process. Ongoing experiments to watch include RSAs currently being conducted for the Barents Sea (Norway) and the Great Sand Hills (Canada).

Acknowledgements

The authors would like to thank all participants of the IAIA 2005 Prague Conference, particularly those who made presentations in the RSA workshop and whose work this paper is based upon: Michel Bouchard, Sigurd Juel Kinn, Gunnar Sander, Clive Wicks, and Alonso Zarzar. Thanks to William Verkamp for his assistance as co-chair for this session in Prague and to Barry Jeffrey and Jayne Roma for comments on an early version of this chapter.

Note

1 This paper is based in part upon presentations made at the IAIA SEA Conference in Prague. In addition, the findings are based on key case studies identified by the authors. This paper does not attempt to summarize all experiences and case studies on the topic.

References

Bouchard, M. and Keita, S. (2005) 'SEA of the mining sector in Mali', paper presented at the IAIA SEA Conference, Prague
Dalal-Clayton, B. and Sadler, B. (1999) 'Strategic environmental assessment: A rapidly evolving approach', *IIED Environmental Planning Issues*, no 18, www.nssd.net/pdf/IIED02.pdf, accessed October 2010
Dalal-Clayton, B. and Sadler, B. (2004) 'Strategic environmental assessment: An international review, with a special focus on developing countries and countries in

transition', final draft, www.iied.org/pubs/pdfs/G02207.pdf, accessed October 2010

EEA (European Environment Agency) (2001) 'Reporting on environmental measures: Are we being effective?', *Environmental Issue Report No 25*, EEA, Copenhagen

El Serafy, S. (2003a) 'Structural adjustment in retrospect: Some critical reflections', in Goodland, R. (ed) *Strategic Environmental Assessment and the World Bank Group*, www.eireview.org

El Serafy, S. (2003b) 'Serafian quasi-sustainability for non-renewables', in Goodland, R. (ed) *Strategic Environmental Assessment and the World Bank Group*, www.eireview. org

FAO (Food and Agriculture Organization of the United Nations) (1999) Environmental Impact Guidelines, FAO Investment Centre, Rome

Gibson, R. B. (2004) 'Sustainability assessment and implications for regional effects assessment', in Kirstein, F. and Jeffrey, B. (eds) *Proceedings of the Information Session: Learning about Regional and Strategic Environmental Assessments, 22–23 May 2003, Halifax, Canada*, Environment Canada, Dartmouth

Gibson, R. B., Hassan, S., Holtz, S., Tansey, J. and Whitelaw, G. (2005) *Sustainability Assessment: Criteria, Processes and Applications*, Earthscan, London

Government of Norway (2002) 'White Paper', no 12 (2001–2002), Rent og Rikt Hav, (Clean and Rich Seas), Oslo

Hartley, J. (2004) 'SEA for UK offshore oil and gas licensing', in Kirstein, F. and Jeffrey, B. (eds) *Proceedings of the Information Session: Learning about Regional and Strategic Environmental Assessments, 22–23 May 2003, Halifax, Canada*, Environment Canada, Dartmouth

Hegmann, G., Cocklin, C., Creasey, R., Dupuis, S., Kennedy, A., Kingsley, L., Ross, W., Spaling, H. and Stalker, D. (1999) *Cumulative Effects Assessment Practitioners Guide*, Cumulative Effects Assessment Working Group and AXYS Environmental Consulting Ltd, prepared for Canadian Environmental Assessment Agency, Ottawa

IAIA (International Association for Impact Assessment) (2002) *Strategic Environmental Assessment Performance Criteria*, Special Publication Series No 1, IAIA, Fargo, ND

Kinn, S. J. (2004) 'The Norwegian experience with regional environmental impact assessment', in Kirstein, F. and Jeffrey, B. (eds) *Proceedings of the Information Session: Learning about Regional and Strategic Environmental Assessments, 22–23 May 2003, Halifax, Canada*, Environment Canada, Dartmouth

Kinn, S. J. (2005) 'Regional-sectoral assessments in the Norwegian offshore petroleum industry', paper presented at the IAIA SEA Conference, Prague

Kirstein, F. and Jeffrey, B. (eds) (2004). *Proceedings of the Information Session: Learning about Regional and Strategic Environmental Assessments, 22–23 May 2003, Halifax, Canada*, Environment Canada, Dartmouth

Noble, B. (2000) 'Strategic environmental assessment: What is it and what makes it strategic?', *Journal of Environmental Assessment Policy and Management*, vol 2, no 2, pp203–224

Noble, B. (2004) 'Environmental, regional and strategic assessment: Canadian perspective', in Kirstein, F. and Jeffrey, B. (eds) *Proceedings of the Information Session: Learning about Regional and Strategic Environmental Assessments, 22–23 May 2003, Halifax, Canada*, Environment Canada, Dartmouth

Pope, J., Annandale, D. and Morrison-Saunders, A. (2004) 'Conceptualising sustainability assessment', *Environmental Impact Assessment Review*, vol 24, pp595–616

Sandar, G. (2005) 'Integrated management plan for the Norwegian part of the Barents Sea', paper presented at the IAIA SEA Conference, Prague

Saskatchewan Environment (undated) 'The Great Sand Hills Regional Environmental Study', www.environment.gov.sk.ca/2007-104GreatSandHillsEnvironmentalStudy, accessed April 2006

UNDP and REC (United Nations Development Programme and Regional Environmenal Centre) (2003) *Benefits of a Strategic Environmental Assessment*, prepared by J. Dusik, T. Fischer and B. Sadler with further input from A. Steiner and N. Bonvoisin for UNDP and RCE for Central and Eastern Europe, http://archive.rec.org/REC/Programs/EnvironmentalAssessment/pdf/BenefitsofSEAeng.pdf, accessed October 2010

Wicks, C. (2005) 'WWF and SEAs', paper presented at the IAIA SEA Conference, Prague

World Bank (1996) 'Regional environmental assessment', *in Environmental Assessment Sourcebook Update, No 15*, Environment Department, World Bank, Washington, DC

Zarzar, A. (2005) 'A social assessment of the mining sector in Peru: Issues and recommendations', paper presented at the IAIA SEA Conference, Prague

14
SEA and Coastal Zone Management

Kogi Govender and Ivica Trumbic

Introduction

In coastal countries, half of the population are estimated to live in coastal zones, with two thirds of the world's largest cities located on the coast (Reports of the Conference Working Groups, 2001). In many of these countries, large parts of the coastal zone are negatively affected by anthropogenic impacts. These include pollution from local or upland sources, population increase resulting in habitat degradation, multiple resource use conflicts and over-exploitation of resources (Norse, 1993). If these areas are to be restored, enhanced or maintained then management intervention is necessary. To that end, the system of integrated coastal zone management (ICZM) was promoted as the approach best suited to addressing this problem. The purpose of ICZM is to ensure that the process of setting objectives, planning and implementation involves as broad a spectrum of interest groups as possible, so that the best possible compromise between different interests is found and a balance is achieved in the overall use of a coastal area (Post and Lundin, 1996).

Strategic environmental assessment (SEA) of policies, plans and programmes (PPPs) is another key tool that has been used to integrate environmental management considerations into the decision-making process above the project level. The application of SEA in various sectors is well developed generally, and experience in transport and land-use planning is particularly extensive (Dalal-Clayton and Sadler, 2005). To date, despite its potential, limited use appears to be made of SEA in support of ICZM. Specifically, SEA can enhance the process of coastal zone management by identifying environmental opportunities and constraints on development activities, thereby providing a strategic framework for sustainable development of this zone including port planning.

The purpose of this chapter is to provide an introduction to the relationship of SEA and ICZM. It describes the potential that SEA holds for coastal zone management in general, and port planning in particular. Finally, case examples are cited to illustrate the use of SEA for coastal management, to highlight aspects of best practices, and to identify some of the challenges faced.

Background: The coastal zone

The coastal zone contains some of the planet's most productive ecosystems and areas of rich biodiversity; it also supports the majority of the world's human population. Broadly defined, the coastal zone includes both the area of land subject to marine influences and the area of the sea subject to land influences. The coastal zone is divided in three main components (UNEP, 2001):

1   The marine zone extending from the low water mark seaward.
2   The land-sea interface extending from the low water mark to the seaward edge of coastal vegetation.
3   The adjoining coastal land zone extending for some distance from the end of the interface zone (its definition may vary according from country to country).

The three components described above interact in many ways and the boundaries between them fluctuate. Furthermore, the coastal zone is not an isolated system but a complex, highly productive environment. Chua (1993) described the coastal zone as a special geographical area with productive and natural defence functions that are intimately linked to environmental and socio-economic conditions far beyond its physical boundary. In addition, it is estimated that coastal zones create a large number of products (oil, gas, shipping, tourism, fisheries, and so on) and services (gas control, disturbance control, waste treatment and nutrient circulation) of extremely high value for the population. The above definition encompasses the sustainable development philosophy that the biophysical environment cannot be separated from the socio-economic environment and recognizes that the coastal zone contains diverse and productive habitats that are important for human settlements, development and subsistence.

Integrated coastal zone management (ICZM)

In the middle of the 20th century, the management of human activities along the coastal zone was brought together under the term ICZM (Haag, 2002). In recent years, ICZM has become the umbrella term for the various names and acronyms including: coastal zone management (CZM), integrated coastal zone planning, integrated coastal management, integrated coastal area management, coastal area planning and/or management and integrated coastal resources planning and/or management (Hildebrand, 2002).

Most of the theory on ICZM today takes as its starting point Chapter 17(A) of Agenda 21, titled *Protection of the Oceans, all kinds of Seas, including Enclosed and Semi-enclosed Seas and Coastal Areas and the Protection, Rational Use and Development of their Living Resources*. Agenda 21 concludes that the 'marine environment – including the oceans and all seas and adjacent coastal areas forms an integrated whole that is an essential component of global life-support systems and a positive asset that presents opportunities for sustainable development'. In view of the interrelationships between coastal resources and their users, coastal states at the Rio Summit committed themselves to the integrated management and sustainable development of coastal areas and the marine environment under their national jurisdiction (UN, 1992).

The idea of sustainable development is encapsulated in the ICZM concept, which can be defined as a continuous and dynamic process by which decisions are taken for the sustainable use, development and protection of coastal and marine areas and resources (Cicin-Sain and Knecht, 1998). Fundamental to ICZM is the understanding of the relationships between coastal resources, their uses and the mutual impacts of development on the economy and the environment. As coastal resources are used simultaneously by the different economic and social sectors, ICZM can only be accomplished when all these uses, users and relationships are clearly known (UNEP, 1995).

The main principles of ICZM include (UNEP, 1995):

- The coastal area is a unique resource system that requires special management and planning approaches.
- The land-water interface is an integrating force in coastal resource systems.
- Land and sea uses, and their particular characteristics and requirements, should be planned and managed in combination.
- Coastal management and planning boundaries should be issue-based and adaptive.
- Institutional responsibilities for coastal planning and management should involve all levels of government.
- Economic and social benefit evaluation and public participation form important components of coastal area management.
- Conservation is an important goal in sustainable coastal development.
- Multi-sectoral approaches are essential to the sustainable use of resources as they involve multi-sectoral interactions.

Although the ICZM process needs to be adaptive in order to be capable of responding to local conditions and needs, there is widespread agreement that the process generally consists of the four main steps. These are outlined in Box 14.1.

One of the key factors for successful ICZM is to have the necessary strategic tools in place to include extensive stakeholder participation, to identify and understand the range of issues affecting the marine and coastal environment, and to know what management issues should be put in place (Audouin et al, 2003). 'Classical' environmental impact assessment (EIA), which has been in use for a long time, could not fully respond to the above needs. Even a series of EIAs with a strategic dimension (for example, in the case of large infrastructure development or large marinas) could not uncover, for example, the cumulative impacts of a string of strategic projects, because each EIA is being implemented

---

Box 14.1 *Steps in ICZM*

Identification and assessment of issues

- The collection of baseline data and understanding the current state of resources.
- Compiling, integrating, analysing and prioritizing information.
- Use of remote sensing techniques and a geographical information system (GIS).

Development of policies, plans and programmes

- Identification of management goals and objectives.
- Preparation of an alternative management strategy and the selection of the most appropriate one.
- Producing a framework to guide decision-makers in the current and future allocation of scarce or threatened resources (such as land, fish and water) to support human needs within the coastal zone.

Implementation

- Strategic action plan for ICZM.
- Responsibilities assigned for the practical realization of programmes, strategies and projects developed in the planning phase.
- Capacity-building and assessment.
- Development of programmes for public awareness.

Monitoring and evaluation

- Testing whether ICZM is achieving its objective and to recommend improvements where needed.

Source: Audouin et al (2003); ICZM Basics (2003); Gerges (2002); Dalal-Clayton and Sadler (2005)

---

in relative isolation. SEA is more appropriate to respond to the above needs. It could be considered as an environmental assessment for policies, plans or programmes but could also be considered as a planning tool on its own (Kay and Alder, 1999).

SEA for ICZM

There is no coast-specific SEA legislation or guidance. However, national and international legislation (for example, the European Directive and United Nations Economic Commission for Europe (UNECE) Protocol on SEA) regulating the use of SEA is generic enough to be applied to ICZM, particularly if supplemented by guidelines for the application of SEA in a specific coastal context. To this end, guidelines for SEA for coastal management were developed by the Secretariat for Eastern African Coastal Area Management (SEACAM) for the countries of eastern Africa and the Western Indian Ocean Island States. These guidelines call for SEA to be applied as an integrated part of the ICZM process. Ideally, SEA principles and tools would be integrated into the ICZM process so that the planning and management of the coastal area are viewed in a holistic manner. Specifically, the application of SEA should ensure that important coastal concerns are identified and addressed, facilitate the consultation process among stakeholders and consider the environmental implications of the various activities within the context of sustainable development (Audouin et al, 2003).

The aim of applying SEA within this context is not to replace the ICZM process but rather to inform and strengthen existing procedures. As indicated in Box 14.1, the ICZM and SEA processes have much in common with each other and with principles of good planning (Dalal-Clayton and Sadler, 2005). SEA steps and tools can be used throughout the ICZM process to provide appropriate information at the appropriate stage, to integrate the concept of sustainability into planning and to increase the value and validity of its outputs. For example, in step one of the ICZM process – the identification and assessment of issues – the following tools (usually applied within SEA) can be used to strengthen as well as provide information for this phase: situational analysis; state of the environment reporting; inputs from stakeholder interaction; analysis of existing PPPs; GIS-based suitability analysis; and sensitivity mapping.

A key strength in SEA lies in its robustness, flexibility and adaptation to different circumstances (Kjörven and Lindhjem, 2002). SEA can be used to integrate economic, biophysical and social issues in coastal area planning in order to facilitate sustainable development in the coastal zone. There are various approaches to SEA. The 'objectives-led' or 'sustainability-led' model (after Sadler, 1996; Thérivel and Partidário, 1996; DEAT, 2000) appears to be a suitable approach that can be adapted to suit the context, needs and issues of an individual country.

This model involves the development of a sustainability framework including environmental parameters to facilitate decision-making with regard to specific ICZM issues. Such a framework can make the ICZM process more effective and efficient. It also provides the basis against which existing ICZM PPPs can be assessed. In setting environmental parameters for ICZM, the sustainability framework performs the proactive function of integrating the principles of sustainability into decision-making, for example, with regard to future coastal developments, exploitation of coastal resources, and the management of coastal use issues. Where initiatives currently exist, a more reactive SEA approach can be used to assess their effects and implications within the sustainability framework.

To date, few case studies of SEA application for CZM are available. Several examples of recent experience were presented and discussed at the International Association for Impact Assessment (IAIA) SEA conference as described below and in the following section on port planning.

The Fuka Matrouh Project, Egypt

The need for SEA was recognized in the Fuka Matrouh pilot project in Egypt, funded by the Mediterranean Action Plan's Coastal Area Management Programme (CAMP). The purpose of this project was to prepare an integrated management plan for sustainable development through the establishment of a system of integrated planning for the Fuka Matrouh coastal area in response to tourism development trends. SEA of the integrated management plan of the Fuka Matrouh area was undertaken to assess the cumulative, secondary, long-term and delayed impacts on the entire coastal segment (Abul-Azm et al, 2003).

The matrix method was used in predicting the magnitude and significance of impacts for six major sectors of activities proposed in the management plan, namely transportation, urbanization and services, industry, agriculture, tourism and complementary activities. The proposed development of the area includes the development of five new tourist clusters with the total capacity of 100,000 beds. The local population is planned to increase to 480,000 from the current 100,000 inhabitants. Such growth will generate huge impacts on natural resources of the area as well as conflicts with the local, mainly Bedouin, population.

SEA focused on the major resource management problems and impacts of the planned development. It proposed a number of mitigation measures to combat air, freshwater, marine and noise pollution, to protect biodiversity, to reduce the negative impacts of soil erosion and contamination, to reduce negative impacts on the fragile social environment and to maintain traditional community values. Since this SEA was one of the first prepared in Egypt, and in the coastal region in particular, a number of difficulties were encountered during its preparation. At the time, the EIA Law (1994) had no specific provisions for SEA. In the absence of a legal requirement, local authorities did not consider it their duty to participate actively in the process. As a result, it was difficult to obtain information such as maps to serve as the basis for a proposed GIS-based analysis. Despite these problems, SEA was able to identify potential cumulative impacts of the proposed development of the coastal area.

SEA and coastal shrimp farming, Thailand

Farmed shrimp is an export-oriented seafood product that is primarily raised in coastal regions of tropical and semi-tropical developing nations, often accompanied by a range of environmental impacts. Thailand is the world's largest producer of farmed shrimp. Generic SEA principles and procedures were adapted to assess the environmental effects of shrimp farming in Bangpakong River Basin. This SEA used regional impact scenario modelling supported by GIS to evaluate cumulative effects in situations where development activities were not conducted in a uniform matter (Szuster and Flaherty, 2002; Szuster, 2005).

Water supply, water quality and agricultural use were chosen as valuable ecosystem components for the study. The selection was based on a detailed review of the Bangpakong River Basin and the environmental issues commonly associated with shrimp farming. Using these variables, data were collected and an assessment undertaken to identify the cumulative effects of shrimp farming in the basin.

A limited amount of SEA research has focused on aquaculture. Previous research into the environmental effects of shrimp farming adopted an issue or project-specific focus, but this narrow approach overlooked the broader implications of aquaculture development on regional environmental quality. The study of the Bangpakong River Basin showed that introducing SEA techniques in a developing country context presented numerous challenges, many of which related to data availability and quality. For the SEA to be successful, a substantial amount of baseline information on environmental systems and the development context was required to assess cumulative effects. Much of this information was unavailable and, where detailed data sets were available, data quality was an issue. Regardless of these constraints, SEA in this case proved to be a useful management to address environmental issues related to aquaculture and other economic activities.

SEA in the Atlantic Canadian coastal zone

This case example illustrates the application of SEA in relation to coastal planning and community development and survival (Collins and Wilkie, 2005). Climate change, both mitigation and adaptation, was integrated into the analytical process. An SEA of a 16,123 km² area off northeast Nova Scotia was conducted by the Canada–Nova Scotia Offshore Petroleum Board (CNSOPB) to determine if exploration for oil and gas should be allowed, and if so, under what conditions.

The SEA received support from two government departments under whose authority the CNSOPB operates. It was conducted pursuant to the requirements of the Government of Canada Cabinet Directive on SEA that apply to federal departments and agencies and consistent with the Province of Nova Scotia's Energy Strategy. The SEA did not consider social issues and benefits, which are dealt with under a separate regulatory system.

The aim of the SEA was to identify knowledge and data gaps, highlight issues of concern and make recommendations for mitigation and planning. In this case, the SEA reports were information rather than decision-making documents. They were intended to assist the CNSOPB in determining whether exploration rights should be offered for the whole or part of the area, to identify appropriate regulatory or mitigation measures that should be considered for exploration activities and to build knowledge and understanding of regional environmental effects. Overall, SEA was found to be a useful tool to clarify issues of concern and provide guidance.

SEA and port planning

Port construction and operations change or disrupt the ecological functioning of coastal habitat. The value of SEA as a tool that promotes sustainable development planning is increasingly recognized by ports throughout the world. Three case examples are discussed briefly below to show how elements of SEA can be used to support port planning, operations and management.

SEA for the ports of Richards Bay and Cape Town, South Africa

As defined in South African guidelines, SEA is a process of integrating the concept of sustainability into strategic decision-making. The merits of SEA for port planning, operations and management is recognized nationally in the White Paper on National Ports Policy (2002), which recommends that SEA should be used for the proactive integration of biophysical and socio-economic issues at the policy and planning level. This policy is implemented by the National Ports Authority of South Africa (the 'landlord' of the ports) as exemplified in commissioning SEA for the development of the ports of Richards Bay and Cape Town (Govender et al, 2005).

In both cases, the SEA process broadly followed that outlined in South African SEA guidelines, comprising three distinct phases of scoping, situation assessment and the development of a sustainability framework. During scoping, a vision for sustainable port development and strategic issues for detailed investigation were identified through stakeholder participation. Examples of issues identified included ecosystem and habitat maintenance, marine archaeology, shoreline stability, access to the port, urban spatial planning, socio-economics, economics and institutional arrangements.

In the assessment phase, the strategic issues identified during scoping were investigated in detail. Specialist studies were undertaken to: describe the existing state of the environment and relevant trends; identify sustainability objectives, indicators and targets; analyse environmental opportunities and constraints on future port development; develop guidelines to overcome the constraints and enhance the opportunities; and recommend a monitoring programme using key sustainability indicators. In the final report, the findings of these studies were integrated into a 'sustainability framework' that included guidelines and actions for port development, management and monitoring. Various departments within the two ports will be responsible for implementing these.

Several lessons can be drawn from experience with these SEA processes. For SEA and its outcomes to be successful, it is critical to obtain commitment to the process from the outset. Specialists need to understand the purpose of the SEA to avoid looking at issues through an 'EIA' lens so that their focus is on opportunities and constraints to future development rather than on conventional impact assessment. Finally, prioritization of plans and programmes is essential and detailed guidance must be provided for implementation plans; for example, development options that may occur in 25 years may need to be informed by monitoring programmes that begin now.

SEA of the Port Plan, China

The Chinese EIA law of 2003 establishes requirements for the assessment of certain types of government plans including master plans of ports. Pursuant to this law, the State Environmental Protection Agency has enacted four ordinances and guidance on its implementation. Under the 'Scope of Plans to prepare Environmental Impact Statements (EISs)', the EIS procedure must include: a plan analysis; environmental status analysis; identification of environmental impacts and establishment of environmental targets and evaluation indicators; forecasting, analysis and evaluation of environmental impacts; proposed measures to mitigate adverse environmental effects; public participation; monitoring and follow-up assessment; and preparation of SEA documentation.

In accordance with these requirements, a SEA was carried out for the master plan for Yingkou Port, which is a major port for foreign trade in Northeast China (Lili et al, 2005). Environmental issues were analysed in relation to five main aspects: port location; plan objectives; comparability with the relevant plan; general layout and land-use zones; and environmental infrastructure. Various methods and techniques were used in the analysis including matrices, mathematical models, scenario analysis, statistical analysis and analogous cases. Data from these sources were integrated using GIS technology to forecast the environmental impacts of development trends and inform decision-making.

As in many developing and rapidly industrializing counties, the collection of appropriate data was one of the greatest challenges. In this study, data were limited and some of the indicators required in the assessment process had never been monitored. Furthermore, the SEA timeframe was extremely short and further constrained data collection and analysis. Despite these very real difficulties, the SEA reportedly still provided useful inputs into port master planning.

SEA of port development in the Vung Tau area, South Vietnam

The Vung Tau area, near the Thi Vai River downstream of Ho Chi Minh City and Vung Tau City in the south of Vietnam is one of the fastest growing and developing areas of the country. Many ports and port-related industry have been developed or are planned for the near future. This has major consequences for land use in the area as many of these ports will be located within sensitive ecosystem habitats, for example, mangrove forests. The SEA focused on the following issues: water; noise and vibrations; air and light; socio-economics; health and safety; fauna and flora; soil archaeology and cultural history. The SEA also addressed cumulative effects within these aspects (Rutten et al, 2005).

Topographic maps and spot images were used to interrogate the images and classify land use into forests, aquaculture, rivers, canals, settlements, bare land and humid land. Ground truth checks with GPS and questionnaires were performed to validate the data. Land-use changes were noted for the last five years, which show an increase in urbanization of these areas, especially near the national road that connects to many of the port developments. With the changes noted within the last few years, it is expected that the new port master plan will take into account the decrease in resources such as the decline in the mangrove forests. This information proved to be useful in predicting future changes and hence recommend management measures.

Conclusion

SEA has become a major focus for the international impact assessment community. Recent discussions on SEA have centred around the potential achievements of SEA rather than capitalizing on practical experiences, resulting in unnecessary pressures on this tool to respond to increasingly diverse demands (Govender, 2005). However, of more concern is a pronounced lack of experience in implementing SEA in general, especially in relation to issues of CZM. This is particularly clear when SEA practice is compared to implementation of EIA, which has become a standard tool in many countries. The discrepancy between expectations of SEA and its practical application is a key issue for future research.

Another issue of concern is a lack of standard methodology as well as a typology of SEA. While general principles and basic steps of SEA procedure are reasonably well-known, there is much less agreement on the tools that should be used and the final outputs of SEA that should be sought. Often there is some confusion on whether an assessment should be considered as EIA or SEA. The recent EIA of an oil pipeline with potentially profound effects on the Adriatic Sea is a case in point; it could easily be considered as an SEA bearing in mind the strategic and region-wide implications of this development.

Key outcomes of the discussions of SEA and ICZM at Prague included:

- Some SEAs can be largely knowledge generation exercises and do not influence decision-making.
- An SEA is only effective if it has institutional support; obtaining political buy-in and support for the process is critical.
- SEA typically focuses on the local coastal environment and does not consider global issues such as the impact of climate change or sea level rise; guidance on how these issues can be addressed within SEA is needed given the far-reaching effect of such changes.
- For SEA to be effective for decision-makers, findings and recommendations must be linked to an economic framework, for example, the monetary costs of ecological impacts. However, this is not easily done and further work is required on how to apply environmental and resource economics within SEA.
- Although the value of SEA for coastal zone management is recognized, many countries lack planning structures and tools and further work is needed on how to integrate these processes and avoid duplication.
- In most cases, SEA stops once a report is written; it should included ongoing monitoring and evaluation based on simple indicators and data collection that do not require specific skills and expensive tools and so on.
- Many SEAs do not engage the people who live in impact areas; local knowledge and capacity-building are essential components of this approach.
- SEA needs to consider appropriate public participation techniques that suit the context within which it is applied.

In summary, SEA is a tool that can be applied in various contexts for various purposes including CZM. In order to be successful and to ensure implementation, there are critical factors that must be considered including institutional support; practical cost effective recommendations; monitoring and improvement systems and effective public participation techniques.

References

Abul-Azm, A., Abdel-Gelil, I. and Trumbic, I. (2003) 'Integrated coastal zone management in Egypt: The Fuka-Matrouch project', *Journal of Coastal Conservation*, vol 9, pp5–12

Audouin, M., Govender, K. and Ramasar, V. (2003) *Guidelines for Strategic Environmental Assessment*, Secretariat for Eastern African Coastal Area Management (SEACAM), Maputo, Mozambique

Chua, T. (1993) 'Essential elements of integrated coastal zone management', *Ocean and Coastal Management*, vol 21, pp81–108

Cicin-Sain, B. and Knecht, R. (1998) *Integrated Coastal and Ocean Management: Concepts and Practices*, Island Press, Washington, DC

Collins, N. and Wilkie, A. (2005) 'SEA in the Atlantic Canadian coastal zone', paper presented at the IAIA SEA Conference, Prague

Dalal-Clayton, B. and Sadler, B. (2005) *Strategic Environmental Assessment: A Sourcebook and Reference Guide to International Experience*, Earthscan, London

DEAT (Department of Environmental Affairs and Tourism) (2000) *Guideline Document: Strategic Environmental Assessment in South Africa*, DEAT, Pretoria

Gerges, M. (2002) 'Integrated coastal zone management: Environmental vision or national necessity?', in Al-Sarawi M. and Al-Obaid E. (eds) *The International Conference on Coastal Management and Development*, Kuwait

Govender, K. (2005) 'The integration of strategic environmental assessment with integrated development planning: A case study of the uMhlathuze Municipality', unpublished master's dissertation, University of KwaZulu-Natal, South Africa

Govender, K., Heather-Clark, S., Nkomo, B. and Ndema, F. (2005) 'Strategic environmental assessment: The key to incorporating the ethos of sustainable development into port planning, operations and management', *International Navigation Association – On Course PIANC magazine*, vol 21, pp35–43

Haag, F. (2002) 'A remote sensing based approach to environmental security studies in the coastal zone: A study from Eastern Pondoland, South Africa', unpublished document

Hildebrand, L. (2002) *Integrated Coastal Management: Lessons Learned and Challenges Ahead*, discussion document for Managing Shared Water/Coastal Zone International Conference, Hamilton Ontario, Canada

ICZM Basics (2003) 'Integrated coastal management functions', www.icm.noaa.gov/story/icm_funct.html, accessed 5 March 2003

Kay, R. and Alder, J. (1999) *Coastal Planning and Management*, E. & F. N. Spon, London

Kjörven, O. and Lindhjem, H. (2002) *Strategic Environmental Assessment in World Bank Operations*, Environment Strategy Paper No 4, World Bank, Washington, DC

Lili, T., Xu, H., Jing, W. and Jun, Z. (2005) 'Strategic environmental assessment of port plan in China', paper presented at the IAIA SEA Conference, Prague

Norse, E. (1993) *Global Marine Biological Diversity*, Island Press, Washington, DC

Post, J. and Lundin, G. (eds) (1996) *Guidelines for Integrated Coastal Zone Management*, Environmentally Sustainable Development Series and Monograph Series No 9, World Bank, Washington, DC

Reports of the Conference Working Groups (2001) *Toward the 2002 World Summit on Sustainable Development*, Working Group 5: Integrated Coastal and Ocean Management, Global Conference on Oceans and Coast, 3–7 December 2001, UNESCO, Paris

Rutten, C., Binh, D. and Hens, L. (2005) 'Land cover changes in SEA of port development in the Vung Tau area (South Vietnam)', paper presented at the IAIA SEA Conference, Prague

Sadler, B. (1996) *Environmental Assessment in a Changing World: Evaluating Practice to Improve Performance*, International Study of the Effectiveness of Environmental Assessment, final report, IAIA and Canadian Environmental Assessment Agency, Ottawa

Szuster, B. (2005) 'Strategic environmental assessment and coastal shrimp farming in Thailand', paper presented at the IAIA SEA Conference, Prague

Szuster, B. and Flaherty, M. (2002) 'Cumulative environmental effects of low salinity shrimp farming in Thailand', *Impact Assessment and Project Appraisal*, vol 20, pp1–12

Thérivel, R. and Partidário, M. (1996) *The Practice of Strategic Environmental Assessment*, Earthscan, London

UN (United Nations) (1992) 'Agenda 21 Report', www.un.org/sustdev/agenda21chapter40.htm, accessed 7 March 2003

UNEP (United Nations Environment Programme) (1995) *Guidelines for Integrated Management of Coastal and Marine Areas with Special Reference to the Mediterranean Basin*, Regional Seas Reports and Studies No 161, UNEP, Split, Croatia

PART III

SEA LINKAGE TO OTHER INSTRUMENTS

15
Thematic Overview of Linkages between SEA and Other Instruments

Thomas B. Fischer

Introduction

This chapter provides a thematic overview of the linkages between strategic environmental assessment (SEA) and other instruments, elaborated on in the next few chapters. It focuses on policy, plan and programme (PPP) instruments that are related to SEA and that can be used to address specific issues within the SEA process or that have potential to complement or support this process. The instruments discussed here aim to raise the status of issues that tend to be underrepresented in PPP processes and comprise environmental planning and management, landscape planning, conservation and sustainable use of biodiversity, and poverty reduction strategies. Spatial planning is also addressed as a mechanism by which information regarding spatial aspects of many relevant issues can be fed into the SEA process to ensure a balanced view is achieved overall.

The subsequent chapters in environmental planning and management and landscape planning are written from the standpoint of developed countries, whereas those on conservation and sustainable use of biodiversity and poverty reduction strategies take a developing countries' perspective. The chapter on spatial planning is based on both developed and developing perspectives. The main difference is that, when applied in a developed country context, SEA is normally expected to work within a well-established planning system and needs to be carefully adapted and fitted into existing structures. On the other hand, when applied in a less structured planning system, as is frequently found in developing countries, SEA may actually provide for an overall decision-making and planning framework. Common to both types of application is that SEA may promote the better consideration of environmental aspects which would normally be underrepresented or ignored.

The instruments in perspective

Environmental planning and management tools

In Chapter 16, Sheate focuses on the possible linkages of SEA and different environmental planning and management tools, particularly environmental management systems (EMS). In order to be able to establish potential benefits of linking EMS and SEA, he first discusses what makes SEA effective, noting that evaluating effectiveness of any decision-making support instrument is difficult as it is normally impossible to decide on what would happen in the absence of the instrument. Furthermore, Sheate suggests that, if there are existing decision support instruments that already work well, integration with these instruments is vital and will increase the likelihood of SEA to actually have an impact. In this context, the need to adapt SEA in order to fit into existing structures is underlined. Currently, Sheate emphasizes there is no need for new instruments or tools and that those that have been introduced over the past decade tend to only repeat what is already in place.

Sheate also points out that the participants of the Prague workshop on environmental planning and management tools suggested that the focus on tools may be too narrow. More importantly, he considers that closer attention should be paid to the institutional capacity and the cultural context within which SEA is applied. This is critical for an effective integration of SEA with EMS tools and for the ability to influence decision-making processes. An insufficient consideration of existing decision-making processes would normally mean environmental planning and management tools cannot be applied effectively. Regarding the extent of integration, Sheate suggests that, from an environmental planner's perspective, linking different tools may be more important than full integration, as this may hide the trade-offs made between different aspects. This may be problematic, particularly for environmental aspects that tend to be underrepresented.

Reflecting on various case studies, the author suggests that an important benefit of linking environmental planning and management tools and SEA is improved transparency and accountability. This is shown by the example of a strategic management plan of nuclear submarine decommissioning in Russia. Another important aspect is the ability of SEA to encourage more baseline-led thinking in environmental planning and management.

Overall, although linking tools is desirable, in practice there may be problems, particularly because different instruments may work at different geographical and temporal scales. Furthermore, while SEA is now frequently legally required, other instruments are often voluntarily applied; therefore, there may not be any clear incentives for actors to link them. A country where connections between EMS and SEA have been made and have shown to be beneficial is Sweden, where both are applied at municipal levels. Making a clear connection with established EMS practice means that here, resistance to SEA has been limited. However, and positively, as EMS experiences do not stem from strategic levels of decision-making, SEA has brought in a new perspective.

As Sheate points out, interdisciplinary research is needed, showing that links are beneficial, but it may be difficult to secure funding for this, due to a tradition of a single academic disciplinary focus. Furthermore, a lack of inter-disciplinary thinking also stands in the way of achieving a better understanding of how the concept of sustainable development can serve as the main overall aim of environmental planning and management tools. In this context, working across sectoral boundaries and overcoming mutual antipathy, for example, of practitioners of economic valuation on the one hand and environmental assessment on the other, is of great importance.

Landscape planning and SEA

In Chapter 17, Hanusch and Fischer reflect on landscape planning instruments in four countries: Germany (landscape planning), Canada (landscape management models, LMM), Ireland (landscape heritage assessment, LHA) and Sweden (ecological landscape plans, ELP). Only German landscape planning is based on legal requirements and extensively applied; the other instruments are currently used only occasionally.

The authors start with an overview of the evolution of the terms 'landscape' and 'landscape planning'. This is important as the use of certain words can either trigger or prevent an interest in an instrument. A comprehensive review of German landscape planning is undertaken to raise the status of landscapes and a range of other environmental aspects, as well. Hanusch and Fischer suggest that this instrument would probably have raised more interest internationally, had it been translated as 'environmental and landscape planning and management'. In the English-speaking world, the term 'landscape' is normally understood in terms of a visual entity; in Germany, it is perceived to inherently include the biophysical environment.

The German landscape planning system was introduced in 1976 by the Federal Nature Conservation Act. Since then, landscape plans and programmes have been prepared at all main levels of PPP-making, serving as comprehensive state of the environment reports and establishing overall environmental goals and objectives. Furthermore, they identify measures for developing and enhancing the biophysical environment. This is particularly useful when looking for mitigation and compensation measures. Methods and techniques used in landscape planning, such as overlay mapping, can also be readily used in SEA.

In Canada, LMM have been used in areas of potential conflict among land-use and management objectives. These include, for example, areas of population growth, economic or agricultural development, conservation initiatives and watershed management. LMMs are quantitative projective tools for examining how ecological and socio-economic features of an area are likely to change, considering different policy and management decisions. They are advertised as being particularly useful for assessing alternatives within participatory planning processes. In this context, they can contribute effectively to SEA.

Irish LHA uses a geographical information systems' (GIS) approach based on a pressure-state-response framework and comprising inventory, analytical and communication functions. Ultimately, LHA aims at achieving better landscape management and also contributing to a basic landscape characterization of Ireland. The main contribution of LHA to SEA is seen in its capability to provide for baseline data and monitoring.

Swedish ELPs are supposed to fulfil a similar purpose to that of German landscape plans and programmes. Within this context, a characterization of open green urban areas has recently been developed at the Swedish University of Agricultural Sciences. This characterization has been used as the basis for mapping and assessing the existing status of health aspects connected with landscape values.

Overall, it is concluded that landscape planning instruments from all four countries can effectively support SEA application, particularly regarding the following aspects:

- The generation and evaluation of landscape and environmental baseline data.
- The generation of landscape and environmental aims and objectives.
- The identification of conflicts and impacts connected with anticipated land-use.
- The establishment of landscape and environmental protection and management measures.

Conservation and sustainable use and management of biodiversity

In Chapter 18, Treweek et al discuss the role of SEA as a tool for conservation and sustainable use of biodiversity, which has been the focus of the International Association for Impact Assessment (IAIA) capacity-building for biodiversity and impact assessment programme (CBBIA). SEA is seen as an important mechanism for supporting participation and stakeholder involvement with respect to biodiversity issues; for example, between governments, business partners and the general public.

The UN Millennium Development Goals (MDGs, www.un.org/ millenniumgoals) are presented as a key point of departure for development that is compatible with the conservation of biodiversity and the sustained delivery of ecosystem services in developing countries. MDG7 on environmental sustainability is of particular relevance. In this context, SEA is seen as a potential tool for internalizing the costs associated with biodiversity degradation and loss and for mainstreaming biodiversity as a key planning issue. Proposed economic development PPPs frequently lead to decisions that are harmful to biodiversity, but the loss of ecosystem services is rarely given sufficient consideration. Although monetization of ecosystems' services is difficult, it is essential that the role of ecosystem services in supporting livelihoods should be better recognized.

Due to ongoing degradation and loss of biodiversity, the consideration of cumulative effects is of increasing importance and requires a strategic approach. Treweek et al stress that, ultimately, a failure to conserve and use biological diversity sustainably will perpetuate poverty. In this context, it is important to clearly show the risks as well as the opportunities of proposed action for biodiversity. Increasing economic pressures (for example, raw material extraction) raise important questions of whether SEA can help to resolve tensions and act as a balancing tool, indicating necessary trade-offs and making their implications explicit.

Particularly challenging are those activities that are not regulated and that do not require development consent. Agriculture is mentioned in this context: it has increasingly pervasive effects across a broad spectrum of intensity but involves land-use changes which are largely unregulated at a farm scale. SEA offers some potential for considering the close interlinkages between agricultural policy and biodiversity at an appropriate scale.

Based on experience in various developing countries, the authors stress the importance of communication and partnership in the effective application of SEA. In this context, they suggest that SEA can be particularly useful to achieve improved partnership management.

National development strategies with particular emphasis on poverty reduction strategies and SEA

In Chapter 19, Ghanimé, Risse, Levine and Sahou discuss the relationship of development strategies and SEA against the frame of various international declarations and agreements that support application of SEA. The Paris Declaration on Aid Effectiveness commits donors and their partner countries to 'develop and apply common approaches for Strategic Environmental Assessment'. As a response, the Organisation for Economic Co-operation and Development (OECD) Development Assistance Committee (DAC) established a task team on SEA under the auspices of the DAC Network on Environment Co-operation. Complementing this work, the United Nations Development Programme (UNDP) is engaged in SEA in the context of supporting national development and poverty reduction strategies.

The authors identify Poverty Reduction Strategy Papers (PRSP) as offering an effective framework to manage development aid with a social equity agenda. To date, the full application of SEA to such macro-development policy instruments is limited but there are increasing efforts to build capacity to support the integration of SEAs into PRSP development and implementation processes. The importance of MDGs for effective application of SEA in developing countries is stressed. In particular, only a few poverty reduction strategies have targets aligned with the MDG7 on environment sustainability and SEA may help to improve the current situation.

Ghanimé et al identify means of enhancing the role of SEA based on lessons from their analysis of the application of SEA to PRSPs in four African countries. They state that proper resourcing is important, with regard to the budgetary and human aspects and to the creation of information and data systems. In addition, SEA workshops can be highly beneficial provided they are adequately designed and the right people are involved. In line with wider experiences in SEA literature, the authors state that SEA needs to be applied at the start of the plan-making process in order to be effective. In this context, SEA should support the problem formulation process, it should be used before any concrete suggestions for action are made. Currently, there is widespread concern that SEA is narrowly understood as a tool that serves only to assess the impacts of a proposal. Therefore, Ghanimé et al suggest that SEA should be based on a more comprehensive and upstreaming approach for defining the environmental content of the relevant PPP.

Finally, the authors point out that SEA is still often understood as a document-focused exercise and that further effort is needed in order to develop an understanding of how SEA is effective as a systematic and participative process. In this context, they suggest that the instrument will only be effective if it is properly institutionalized. This also means achieving effective participation, developing a true dialogue between the various stakeholders and ensuring that economic and financial analysis are part of the process in order to have a complete needs assessment.

Spatial planning and SEA

In Chapter 20, Nelson explores the linkages between SEA and spatial planning. He explains that, although spatial planning can be understood and interpreted in different ways, it has evolved in different parts of the world around two conceptual models; one driven by socialist theory and the other one by free market economics. The former is more rationalistic and works a top-down manner while the latter allows for great flexibility. As such, they 'represent the ends of a continuum, neither of which can be seen as a preferred model'.

The author describes possible relationships between spatial planning and SEA, focusing on the evolution of SEA concepts, systems and approaches in spatial planning, the various types of SEA applied for spatial plans and the evidence provided by nine case studies tabled at the Prague workshop on this theme. Importantly, he observes two principle approaches of spatial plan SEA, namely 'environmental impact assessment (EIA)-based' and 'plan-based'. The former is more scientific with a heavy demand for data; the latter relies more on qualitative interpretation of issues and options. EIA-based systems are found, for example, in the US, the Netherlands, Italy, South Africa, California, Germany, the Balkans and countries of the former Soviet Union. 'Plan-based' approaches are found in Canada, New Zealand, the UK and the Scandinavian countries.

Nine spatial planning SEA case studies are described in terms of the spatial plan status, SEA legal status, the contents and key issues raised. Case studies include experience from the Azores (Portugal), Mura River (Croatia), Sao Paulo (Brazil), the Dutch Polder (Netherlands), Ekurhuleni Municipality (South Africa) and Valjevo Municipality (Serbia), as well as more general reviews of Chinese, UK and transnational (Germany, Poland and Czech Republic) developments. An important conclusion is that there is no simple 'one size fits all' approach to SEA in spatial planning and that any SEA requires adaptation to a specific system.

What separates spatial planning and SEA? Nelson observes that the latter can potentially provide a framework for addressing two main shortcomings of spatial planning, namely a 'lack of transparency' and an 'absence of any genuine exploration of alternative choices of action'. Although the debate on whether SEA should evolve as a largely unstructured and creative process for testing planning concepts or be more procedural and tied to specific targets and outputs is still largely unresolved, there appears to be some broad agreement that 'the development of indicators and creation of better frameworks for monitoring the outcome of SEAs and related plans is an important area for research'. Also, while the extent to which SEA should also consider social and economic aspects is still undefined, 'over recent years there has been increased recognition of the need to link SEA for spatial plans with other forms of sustainability appraisal'. Finally, public participation was found to be a key element that SEA can add to spatial planning.

A broad consensus was reached at the Prague meeting regarding the question of what constitutes a successful SEA for spatial planning. In this context, important elements include an early application and an agreement at the outset between interested parties regarding scope, content and outputs of SEA. Furthermore, SEA should challenge and test assumptions on spatial concepts and alternatives. Public consultation for both, spatial planning and SEA should be done in parallel and should receive sufficient time. Finally, decision-makers should be encouraged to participate in SEA and should be required to indicate how they have taken account of SEA when reaching a decision.

Conclusions

The chapters that follow explore some of the many potential linkages that SEA may have with other instruments and tools. All of them ask a common core question of how the different instruments can support effective SEA application and the other way around

Despite the very different nature of these instruments, SEA tends to fulfil a very similar purpose for all of them. First and foremost, this includes raising the status of those aspects that tend to be underrepresented in decision-making and serving as an advocacy tool for an improved consideration of environmental aspects. Based on the evidence provided, and in line with the wider literature, it is suggested that, in order to be able to effectively link instruments with SEA, the cultural context and the institutional capacity need to be taken into account. Only then can decision-making processes be effectively influenced.

It is clear that linking SEA with existing instruments can be highly beneficial. SEA has a particularly important role to play in improving transparency and accountability. Furthermore, it may increase baseline-led thinking. This is most easily achieved in the presence of an area-wide environmental management system, such as landscape planning. Various authors have suggested that no new instruments are currently needed and the practice of 'inventing' new decision-making support and assessment tools, which are in effect only old wines in new bottles, has created some unnecessary confusion among practitioners. In this context, Sheate remarked that 'if it looks, sounds and feels like an elephant, it probably is one'.

Particularly in developing countries, the MDGs play an important role of identifying overall objectives and providing for an important value framework. In this context, SEA has proven to be a suitable instrument for managing and ultimately enhancing biodiversity as well as for poverty reduction strategies.

Furthermore, the possibility of using SEA to enhance communication and partnership has been stressed. In this context, people from different disciplines may be brought together and dialogue between different stakeholders may be enhanced. However, in order to work effectively, meetings and workshops need to be adequately designed and engage the right people.

At least in theory, spatial planning has the potential to replace SEA, as it aims at achieving a balanced view of the various planning aspects. However, in reality, there are problems with this, particularly in the presence of aspects in decision-making that are weaker than others and potential problems of transparency. Currently, therefore, SEA can also play an important role in achieving a more balanced approach in spatial planning, particularly through encouraging communication and evidence-based thinking.

16
SEA and Environmental Planning and Management Tools

William R. Sheate

Introduction

This chapter draws on a 2005 workshop session at the International Association for Impact Assessment (IAIA) Conference in Prague on strategic environmental assessment (SEA) and environmental planning and management tools, but also reflects a wider developing trend in understanding the linkages and overlaps between such tools. The workshop papers and discussions provide a stepping stone for a wider analysis, drawing on a developing, though limited, literature on linking SEA (and its variations) and strategic environmental planning and management tools.

The aim of the chapter is to highlight the importance of maximizing the benefits of using existing tools and approaches effectively and to suggest an agenda for action which will help facilitate making better linkages in future. A more secondary aim perhaps is to provide a counter argument to the seemingly constant desire to 'develop' new tools (or if being less generous, the constant effort to rename or reinvent the wheel). While a personal view, it is nevertheless one that also reflects a widespread frustration among many practitioners, academics and students at the plethora of names and acronyms that increasingly infest the assessment and management field. Often these arise merely from the renaming of the application of some variation on an environmental assessment or management tool as a shiny new tool that will somehow make a difference. If it looks, sounds and feels like an elephant, it probably is one. So why not call it an elephant?

The basic premise of this chapter, therefore, is that there is considerable scope for better use, adaptation and linking of existing environmental assessment and management tools, and that the best use possible of these tools should be sought rather than assume that entirely new tools are needed to address new contexts and problems. Some new tools may be needed, but such a need will be better identified if the existing ones have been used to their full potential first.

Four key questions were posed for the Prague workshop, and these form the focus for the chapter:

1 What are the benefits of making linkages between tools?
2 Do we need new tools or can we make existing tools work better together?
3 How do SEA and other tools working together fit with decision-making processes?
4 If there are benefits to linking tools, what needs to be done to facilitate this working in practice?

The chapter is therefore structured broadly around these questions, with the last of these providing the springboard for suggestions for how to take this whole field forward.

Four papers were presented in the Prague workshop, covering a diverse range of topics from SEA/environmental management systems(EMS)/systems flow analysis in Swedish local authorities (Emilsson and Tyskeng, 2005), strategic environmental analysis (SEAN) in Nicaragua (Castillo et al, 2005), SEA and strategic master planning (SMP) in nuclear decommissioning of Russian submarines (Blank and Smith, 2005) to use of a sustainable reference baseline using geographical information systems (GIS) in Brazil (Oliveira et al, 2005). While diverse, they nevertheless each highlighted important issues for this debate on exploring linkages between tools, in particular:

- The nature of the tools.
- The nature of the decision-making and institutional context.
- The nature of data used by tools.
- The extent of wider public engagement with the tools.
- The degree of transparency in decision-making.

The following discussion focuses particularly on SEA and EMS, though many of the issues raised are equally pertinent to other tools such as life cycle analysis (LCA), substance flow analysis (SFA) or cost benefit analysis (CBA). It also draws on previous similar workshops convened by the author at IAIA in Glasgow (1999), The Hague, Netherlands (2002) and Marrakech (2003) – see for example papers such as those by Ridgway (1999), Sheate (2002) and Vanclay (2004). These workshops have served as a useful forum for bringing experiences in this field together.

Background – what makes effective SEA?

Before considering the potential benefits of linking SEA and other environmental assessment and management tools, it is important to reflect briefly on the issue of effectiveness. If linking tools is to bring benefits then in some way it will be also necessary to improve the 'effectiveness' of one or more of the tools being brought into closer liaison. Evaluating effectiveness of tools is notoriously difficult, since it is unlikely that a control is available against which to compare the implementation of the tool, it is not possible to judge what would have happened in the absence of the tool. It is therefore very difficult, if not impossible, to separate out the effect of using the tool from the effect of many of the other variables affecting decision-making. The tool, for example, SEA, will have been just one factor exerting some degree of influence.

There have, however, been plenty of attempts at evaluating or promoting effectiveness in SEA and environmental integration (see, for example, Sadler and Verheem, 1996; Fergusson et al, 2001; Sheate et al, 2001, 2003; IAIA, 2002; Fischer, 2005; Fischer and Gazzola, 2006; Emmelin, 2006; Retief, 2007). IAIA has published SEA performance criteria (IAIA, 2002) which aim:

> To provide general guidance on how to build effective new SEA processes and evaluate the effectiveness of existing SEA processes.

These criteria include the need for SEA to be integrated, sustainability-led, focused, accountable, participative and iterative. Implicit in this is that if such elements are in place this is likely to lead to effective SEA processes. Fischer (2005) defines SEA effectiveness more succinctly as the ability of SEA to influence the decision-making process and also the mindset of the actors involved.

A simple understanding of effectiveness more generally, therefore, may be that for a tool to be effective it needs to be able at least to meet its own objectives. In the case of SEA, this will be to ensure that environmental considerations inform and influence the decision-making process regarding whether a plan or programme will be adopted or approved, ensuring that the environment is integrated into decision-making. This influence may occur at various stages throughout the planning process: early on in influencing the options considered, and at later stages to inform mitigation and monitoring. Arguably it is at the earliest stages where SEA can be most effective in influencing the overall direction and objectives of the plan, programme or strategy under consideration. As Noble (2000, 2002) suggests, a truly strategic consideration of alternatives requires the assessment of *alternative options*, alternatives for meeting the objectives set, such as alternative modes of transport. This is in contrast to a consideration of *option alternatives*, such as alternative locations or routes that might occur in an environmental impact assessment (EIA) of a road scheme where the option of a road has already been decided. In the European Union (EU), the SEA Directive requires the evaluation of reasonable alternatives and is creating an important lever in ensuring that alternatives are properly considered.

SEA itself can of course exist in many guises, including as part of a wider sustainability assessment addressing economic and social parameters as well as environmental (Dalal-Clayton and Sadler, 2005; Gibson et al, 2005). Verheem and Tonk (2000) recognize there are several approaches to SEA that have been developed that differ in openness, scope, intensity and duration. They suggest that differences originate from the specific context in which they are used and that although design for purpose helps effectiveness, the sheer variety of approaches can be confusing and impede the take up of SEA. Kørnøv and Thissen (2000) also recognize the duality of SEA, identifying SEA as either having an advocacy role, where its primary purpose is to raise the profile of the environment, or an integrative role where environmental, social and economic considerations are combined in a more objective way.

SEA, then, should take detailed information from different aspects of the environment and bring it together in an accessible form for the decision-maker (Sheate et al, 2003). How effectively SEA can do this will depend on a number of factors, for example, the policy context, such as whether there is multiple or single actor decision-making (Kørnøv and Thissen, 2000), and the nature of the SEA. One of the key benefits of SEA is that it can provide a framework within which more strategic participation of the public and stakeholders can take place. The stages of SEA provide excellent opportunities for the inclusion of participation, in order to better inform options (for example, at the scoping stage) and the assessment of options.

Various conditions are therefore needed to allow SEA to work and so influence decision-making. Since the decision-making context clearly makes a difference to how well SEA is able to operate, can that context be influenced by other tools, for example, if a local authority has a strong environmental policy framework created by an EMS, does that influence the way in which SEA is implemented? And therefore could linking SEA to other tools make SEA more effective? And could linking SEA with other tools bring benefits or enhancements to those tools as well?

Benefits of linking tools

The starting point is invariably the question, 'what are the benefits of making linkages between tools?' Linkages between SEA and other 'tools' such as LCA, SFA and EMS are not very well-developed, though this is improving with some advances in the literature over recent years (for example, Baumann and Cowell, 1999; van der Vorst et al, 1999; Emilsson et al, 2004; Vanclay, 2004; Cherp et al, 2006). EMS is most often associated with project and site-level decisions so experience of applying EMS at strategic levels is limited. Sweden, however, is one country where there is experience of EMS at municipality level (Burström, 1999; Cherp et al, 2006), but it is not necessarily always applied in a very strategic way (Emilsson et al, 2004). Experience of integrating SEA (or forms of SEA) into planning processes is now widespread (for example, in the EU following the implementation of the SEA Directive 2001/42/EC since 2004), but context clearly is important. For example, it may be that the simplified SEA represented by SEAN[1] – the form of SEA developed in the Netherlands for use in overseas development aid – may enable linkages into less well-developed planning processes better than SEA, where a more structured planning process is most beneficial (Castillo et al, 2005).

SEA needs to be flexible so it can be adapted to context-specific circumstances (Nitz and Brown, 2001; Nilsson and Dalkmann, 2001; Partidário, 2000; Thérivel and Minas, 2002), compared to EIA which is perhaps more standardized. In the case of nuclear submarine decommissioning presented at the workshop (Blank and Smith, 2005), it was not necessarily the technical value but its transparency and accountability aspects that were most important from applying SEA, linked to the SMP being promoted. This experience is not uncommon where SEA is applied, either in a formal process or in a more voluntary, informal or *ad hoc* way, as recognized in a number of cases in research undertaken for the European Commission on SEA and its integration in strategic decision-making (Sheate et al, 2001, 2003). One example of this from the UK was the first formal application of SEA by a government department – the application of SEA to the Strategic Defence Review by the Ministry of Defence (MoD), specifically by the Defence Estates agency in 2000. In this case the SEA was rather an ex post affair, but it set in train a much broader development of SEA and the application of sustainable development principles throughout Defence Estates and the rest of the MoD, including the training of new staff.

A baseline and a clear understanding of environmental capacity thresholds and constraints can provide a means of encouraging participation, enabling people to think more strategically if a suitable visual tool, such as GIS, is used to establish a clear baseline (Oliveira et al, 2005). Generic baseline can only go so far; there is a clear need to have specific and context relevant baseline for each specific SEA situation. The use of baseline as a 'tool' in its own right was valuable in the Brazilian case study presented in Prague (Oliveira et al, 2005) as a precursor to SEA and as a means of engaging the public in considering alternative options relating to potential landfill sites. Baseline studies can, therefore, provide a useful focus and precursor to full SEA as a means of engaging communities in understanding the values and qualities of their environment, aiding transparency and later engagement. In the context of linking tools, it is baseline data that provides a crucial means by which SEA can connect to EMS, through monitoring, follow-up and continuous improvement in environmental performance. A clear benefit from making such links, therefore, will be in the efficiency and effectiveness of monitoring programmes and data gathering for both SEA and EMS purposes.

New tools or use of existing tools – working together

Do we need new tools or can we make existing tools work better together? There was no sense from the discussions in the Prague workshop that new tools were really needed. Indeed, one of the conclusions that received widespread support (Emilsson and Tyskeng, 2005) was perhaps that we focus far too much on the tools themselves rather than the institutional capacity and cultural context in which they are used. Linked to this was a clear sense in the workshop that SEA needed to be flexible and responsive to context requirements, and that links to other tools and/or decision-making/planning processes will only happen where there is institutional capacity to facilitate beneficial outcome. This will include mechanisms that encourage different departments within an authority or agency, for example, not just to talk to each other, but to engage actively together on a common cause.

The common frustration with the creation of 'new' tools that are usually just variations on the theme of an existing tool was also widely shared among participants in the workshop. There is an important difference to recognize, too, between linking tools and integration of tools or integrated tools. The workshop was encouraging the linking of tools rather than necessarily their integration, which may be too rigid or formalized. Integration itself, in any case, is not a panacea, since it can mean very different things to different people and may not inherently provide greatest benefit to the environment (Scrase and Sheate, 2002).

Tools and decision-making

How do SEA and other tools working together fit with decision-making processes? Key trends identified at the workshop, which support much of the literature discussed above, included:

- The important role of SEA in creating transparency and accountability.
- The significance of context and that SEA needs to be integrated into existing planning processes, or else appropriate processes need to be created.
- The importance of SEA making the most of existing processes so, for example, if there is an existing strategic EMS context then SEA can engage with it. The corollary of this, of course, is that it is difficult if not.
- SEA may need to be reinforced by legislation, to ensure SEA happens by making it a requirement.
- Institutional capacity can prove to be particularly limiting to the ability of practitioners, decision-makers and stakeholders to integrate SEA with other tools and/or with planning and management processes, and institutional capacity building is critical (for example, Oliveira et al, 2005) in offering accessibility to decision-making processes from the bottom up.
- SEA has encouraged better thinking about baseline, for example, the need to establish thresholds and context-specific data for each SEA, and increasingly the power of GIS for use in strategic policy and decision-making is being recognized (CEP, 2007).

Scale provides another dimension to context (João, 2002) since, if different tools are operating at different geographical or temporal scales, linkages will be made difficult if not impossible. Different geographical scales, for example, of SEA and EMS, will mean that different levels of detail and types of data are involved, which adds a further difficulty for tools such SEA and LCA or EMS to overcome. Temporally, SEA and EMS for example can be sequential, where EMS also provides a monitoring mechanism to SEA, so providing a basis for subsequent review and updating of the plan or programme to which SEA is being applied.

Linking tools in practice

If there are benefits to linking tools, what needs to be done to facilitate this working in practice? There is a question as to how much we should seek to standardize SEA and its linkage to other tools through the use of principles or frameworks when it fundamentally needs to be responsive to context. Broad principles may be fine, but not rigid frameworks. Adapting SEA to fit the existing processes may be sufficient or using SEA to adapt the processes. In the UK, for example, the offshore oil, gas and wind power licensing rounds were made subject to SEA, which itself helped to create a planning process that previously was missing (Sheate et al, 2004).

From the experience of those participating in the Prague workshop, as well as previous such IAIA workshops, it is clear that SEA needs to be integrated in an institutional strengthening process to ensure the actors involved are able fully to take it on board. To link SEA with other tools, such as EMS, becomes more difficult if there are no real mechanisms or incentives for actors to make those links. For example, in local authorities, even if they have a municipal-wide EMS, most probably it will be dealt with by different people from those who deal with SEA of land-use plans. Even if there are benefits in terms of information sharing and flows and broader environmental efficiencies, it is unlikely to happen without the institutional capacity or communication routes to facilitate it.

Research

To move linkages among tools ahead needs targeted research focused on organizational and institutional capacity to link tools rather than merely focusing on the tools themselves (Emilsson and Tyskeng, 2005). In other words, the past focus on methodological aspects of SEA or on creating new tools perhaps needs to move on to examine more closely the way in which SEA and other tools are used together, who they are used by and in what ways, and the capacity to use them. Capacity-building among practitioners, decision-makers and stakeholders is critical, since often those skilled in SEA have little experience or expertise in EMS or LCA, or vice versa. Building multidisciplinary and interdisciplinary teams is essential. Many existing networks, including IAIA, by their nature tend to reinforce disciplinary (or at least specialist) boundaries, even while there are diverse interests represented. Individuals also often stick with the same sets of comfortable and friendly networks, rather than breaking out into new networks, making new contacts and sharing different experiences among a wider group of people.

Perhaps the greatest challenge lies within the academic preoccupation with published outputs in well-established and internationally recognized journals (for which read high impact factor, because of large constituency); a preoccupation that is fundamentally biased toward long-established single academic disciplinary rather than applied interdisciplinary research, which is often working at the interface between research and practice. Only recognition of the fundamental misuse of impact factors as indicators of individual academic performance (Amin and Mabe, 2000) and a change in the way research funding is allocated will allow and encourage researchers to engage more in interdisciplinary research and communicate across boundaries and through publications in each others' journals.

Legislation

Legislation can help provide the impetus to making linkages between tools, if common requirements are embedded in the law. So, for example, the EU Water Framework Directive (WFD) 2000/60/EC establishes a requirement for extensive public consultation on River Basin Management Plans (RBMPs) created under the WFD (Article 13). Such plans themselves are new and, generally for most EU member states, there is no existing planning process through which this requirement can be delivered. A new process is therefore required. RBMPs are likely to trigger the criteria of the SEA Directive 2001/42/EC, and therefore SEA is likely to be required. Here the SEA process can facilitate the delivery of the planning and consultation process (Sheate and Bennett, 2007; Carter and Howe, 2005).

Both the EIA and the SEA Directives make provision for common or joint procedures, for example with Integrated Pollution Prevention and Control (IPPC), though this is not an extensively used provision by member states. (Denmark is one example where this provision has been taken up) (Sheate et al, 2005). But such a provision makes an explicit link between tools, and could be used as a lever for ensuring such links are delivered in practice. In reality, of course, land-use and spatial planning processes are often quite separate from pollution regulation and licensing processes in EU member states, and so the potential links between these tools are not facilitated, since different national legislation, different agencies and different people are likely to be involved in implementation of the different regimes.

Links between SEA and EMS are not helped either when SEA is legally mandated, for example, in the EU through the SEA Directive, and EMS is a voluntary instrument, albeit supported in the EU in the form of the Eco-Management and Audit Scheme (EMAS) by the Council Regulation (EEC) No 1836/93 (revised and updated as Regulation (EC) No 1221/2009), and elsewhere by the ISO140001 standard. But the decision as to whether to apply EMS is a voluntary one, unlike SEA where a plan or programme either meets the SEA Directive criteria or it does not (notwithstanding ambiguity and legal interpretation). In such a case, there will need to be alternative reasons as to why there should be linkage and cooperation between the tools – the law will not require it.

Communication and participation

New processes and communication routes may need to be established to facilitate linkages being made between tools. Linkages are unlikely to happen without proactive encouragement. Sometimes creating mechanisms or research activities that force different interests into collaboration are needed for these things to actually take place. Increasingly we may find mutual tools or techniques need to be used that help to link together diverse processes. Particularly at strategic levels, communication processes may become more relevant and effective than technical methodologies (Sheate et al, 2003; Vicente and Partidário, 2006). Using scenarios or foresight studies[2] to link tools, for example (Audsley et al, 2006; van Latesteijen and Scoonenboom, 1996; DTI, 2002; CEC, 2006; Keough and Blahna, 2006; Sheate et al, 2008), may provide just such a mechanism, exploring how different tools may respond under different future conditions. Scenarios also offer a useful communication medium, through story telling – the 'what if...?' situation – around which discourse and knowledge brokerage can occur (Sheate and Partidário, 2010).

Given the importance of alternatives to SEA (Noble, 2000), discussion around alternative scenarios can create a suitable forum for engaging the public and other stakeholders. Importantly – for consideration regarding linking tools – this creative domain could be extended to other tools, such as EMS:

- What happens after a decision has been made and an option chosen?
- How should business respond under different pressures or regulatory regimes?

Or LCA may be used to inform an understanding about and assessment of the various options available under each scenario, or to inform the EMS. The benefit here is that the scenario provides a 'meeting place' where the tools and actors can interact with a common purpose, rather than trying – perhaps artificially – to make links between elements of the tools themselves, when the prevailing institutional and cultural context is not supportive. Rather than trying to change the institutional or cultural context – which may be too big a challenge – the creation of a common space may be easier and more effective in creating opportunities for dialogue between the tools. In turn, this may help build institutional capacity to recognize and develop the value of linking tools, and the sharing and exchange of knowledge.

Public and stakeholder participation may be another common currency through which linkages can be better explored, particularly in the land-use and spatial planning sphere, where public engagement often is already formalized. So while it may be second nature for a public authority (for example, a local authority) to engage the public in spatial planning and SEA, this may not be the case for the same authority in undertaking EMS or LCA. If the public participation mechanisms were used as the basis for linkage research, for example, through transdisciplinary approaches, engaging stakeholders actively in research (Wiek and Binder, 2005; Scholtz et al, 2005, 2006), between say SEA, EMS and LCA, that may facilitate a much better understanding of where the linkages might occur and how.

Sustainability

Another important avenue to explore in enhancing opportunities for linkages may lie within our understanding of sustainable development and sustainability, as individuals and as organizations (Faber et al, 2005; Jan Kiewert and Vos, 2007) and approaches to assessment (for example, Pope, 2006), as well as in different ways of interpreting these. The traditional approach – of balancing environmental, economic and social elements – has tended to result, inevitably, in setting one or more of these three elements against the other(s) and consequently with varying degrees of trade-offs ensuing (Gibson, 2006; Sheate, 2003). This seems rather counter-productive and does not help to facilitate a common understanding of sustainability (Vanclay, 2004), nor a sharing of expertise or linking between, for example, environmental and social impact assessment (SIA) tools, triple bottom line thinking and economic CBA and valuation tools. If anything, there is much continuing mutual antipathy among impact assessment specialists and economic valuation specialists.

An alternative approach to conceptualizing sustainability (for example, as suggested by Gibson et al, 2005, and Gibson, 2006) may offer some hope here, approaching sustainability from the point of using criteria or objectives that cross the boundaries of economic, social and environmental. This could challenge traditional triple bottom line thinking and therefore provide a possible meeting place for engaging EIA, SEA and SIA experts with EMS and corporate social responsibility (CSR) experts on organizational and capacity issues rather than focus on the tools themselves. Other techniques, such as the use of ecosystem services (MEA, 2005) also offer ways of considering and evaluating sustainability in the context of land use and spatial planning (CEP, 2007). Ecosystem services – including provisioning, regulating, cultural and supporting services – are, as an assessment technique, much favoured by economists who can see ways in which one can value such services. However, they also may provide opportunities for enhancing win-win opportunities rather than encouraging trade-offs, and may be particularly well-suited to spatial planning contexts. Such alternative ways of approaching sustainability may encourage more collaborative working among the interested disciplines and therefore help build capacity to engage in truly interdisciplinary research that exchanges knowledge and experience across the boundaries of the tools used by specialists within and across disciplines. This would certainly help facilitate working together among specialists in EIA, SIA, SEA, EMS, CSR, LCA, CBA, health impact assessment (HIA), triple bottom line, planning and so on, and the development of more common language and understanding.

Conclusions

For SEA to be effective it needs to be integrated into existing planning or decision-making processes – or other decision-making processes need to be adapted. This creates challenges for linking with other tools if no explicit planning or decision-making process already exists between tools, such as SEA and EMS, to facilitate such linkages being established. With the rapid expansion of SEA application, however, comes the opportunity and indeed an urgency to make links to EMS in particular, to facilitate follow-up. But the links still will not happen if the institutional and cultural capacity is not in place. This points to the need for institutional strengthening, less focus on the actual tools and more on identifying the organizational and cultural prerequisites for developing processes that seek to build on the benefits of linking tools. This, in itself, is difficult since it may mean departing from an organization's usual reality and existing structures and routines. Active mechanisms, such as the use of scenarios, foresight studies, public participation or debates about sustainability, among others, may provide opportunities for linkages to be made by providing common 'meeting places'. But to succeed there will need to be benefits of linking tools and these will need to be mutual, not one way, if linking is to be actively encouraged.

A priority, therefore, must be to provide many more case study examples of tangible benefits that linking tools can provide, and across a range of tools. In practice, there will need to be individual champions within organizations (public and private) who have the vision and drive to make the links happen, and to create imaginative opportunities through which links between tools can be delivered. What is clear from the Prague workshop, the preceding IAIA workshops and the literature is that links will not happen by themselves – there are too many institutional and procedural hurdles created by the disparate evolutionary histories of each of the separate tools. But that does not mean there is not value in trying to deliver practical benefits beyond the theoretical synergies that already can be clearly recognized.

Notes

1 SEAN is a method with practical tools and guidelines for a systematic analysis of the environmental potentials for and constraints on human development. The analysis itself, including priority setting and making strategic choices, is steered by social and economic development criteria mainly. See www.seanplatform.org for a fuller explanation of SEAN.
2 For foresight studies, see European Commission and UK government websites, http://ec.europa.eu/research/foresight/11/home_en.html and www.foresight.gov.uk.

References

Amin, M. and Mabe, M. (2000) 'Impact factors: Use and abuse', *Perspectives in Publishing*, no 1, Elsevier Science, www.elsevier.com/framework_editors/pdfs/Perspectives1.pdf, accessed 29 March 2007

Audsley, E., Pearn, K. R., Simota, C., Cojacaru, G., Kousidou, E., Rounsevell, M. D. A., Trinka, M. and Alexandrov, V. (2006) 'What can scenario modeling tell us about future European scale land use, and what not?', *Environmental Science and Policy*, vol 9, pp148–162

Baumann, H. and Cowell, S. J. (1999) 'An evaluative framework for environmental management approaches', *Greener Management International*, vol 26, pp109–122

Blank, L. and Smith, E. (2005) 'The challenge of nuclear decommissioning: The role of SEA in the planning process', paper presented to the IAIA SEA Conference, Prague

Burström, F. (1999) 'Material accounting and environmental management in municipalities', *Journal of Environmental Assessment Policy and Management*, vol 1, no 3, pp297–327

Carter, J. and Howe, J. (2005) 'The Water Framework Directive and the Strategic Environmental Assessment Directive: Exploring the linkages', *Environmental Impact Assessment Review*, vol 26, no 3, pp287–300

Castillo, P., van der Zee Arias, A. and Klein, M. (2005) 'Incorporating strategic environmental analysis (SEDAN) in local development planning and enhancing decentralized environmental management: Current effort in Nicaragua', paper presented to the IAIA SEA Conference, Prague

CEC (Commission of the European Communities) (2006) 'Using foresight to improve the science-policy relationship', report for CEC by Rand Europe/NL, March 2006, http://ec.europa.eu/research/foresight/pdf/21967.pdf, accessed 29 March 2007

CEP (Collingwood Environmental Planning) (2007) 'Thames Gateway ecosystem services assessment using green grids and decision support tools for sustainability (THESAURUS): Literature review, for DEFRA Natural Environment Programme (NEP) Phase II Project NR0109: Case study to develop tools and methodologies to deliver an ecosystem-based approach', CEP with GeoData Institute, www.cep.co.uk/thesaurus.htm, accessed 12 August 2010

Cherp, A., Emilsson, S. and Hjelm, O. (2006) 'Strategic environmental assessment and management in local authorities in Sweden', in Emmelin, L. (ed) *Effective Environmental Assessment Tools: Critical Reflection on Concepts and Practice*, Blekinge Institute of Technology, Sweden, Research Report No 2006:03

Dalal-Clayton, B. and Sadler, B. (2005) *Strategic Environmental Assessment: A Sourcebook and Reference Guide to International Experience*, Earthscan, London

DTI (Department of Trade and Industry) (2002) *Foresight Futures 2020: Revised scenarios and guidance*, DTI, London

Emmelin, L. (ed) (2006) *Effective Environmental Assessment Tools: Critical Reflection on Concepts and Practice*, Blekinge Institute of Technology, Sweden, Research Report No 2006:03

Emilsson, S. and Tyskeng, S. (2005) 'Potential benefits of combining different environmental management tools', paper presented to the IAIA SEA Conference, Prague

Emilsson, S., Tyskeng, S. and Carlsson, A. (2004) 'Potential benefits of combining environmental management tools in a local authority context', *Journal of Environmental Assessment Policy and Management*, vol 6, no 6, pp131–151

Faber, N., Jorna, R. and van Engelen, J. (2005) 'The sustainability of "sustainability" – a study into the conceptual foundations of the notion of "sustainability"', *Journal of Environmental Assessment Policy and Management*, vol 7, no 1, pp1–33

Fergusson, M., Coffey, C., Wilkinson, D., Baldock, D., Farmer, A., Kramer, R. A. and Mazurek, A. G. (2001) 'The effectiveness of EU council integration strategies and options for carrying forward the "Cardiff Process"', IEEP/Ecologic, March 2001

Fischer, T. B. (2005) 'Having an impact? Context elements for effective SEA application in transport policy, plan and programme making', *Journal of Environmental Assessment Policy and Management*, vol 7, no 3, pp407–432

Fischer, T. B. and Gazzola, P. (2006) 'SEA effectiveness criteria – equally valid in all countries? The case of Italy', *Environmental Impact Assessment Review*, vol 26, pp396–409

Gibson, R. B. (2006) 'Beyond the pillars: Sustainability assessment as a framework for effective integration of social, economic and ecological consideration in significant decision-making', *Journal of Environmental Assessment Policy and Management*, vol 8, no 3, pp259–280

Gibson, R. B., Hassan, S., Holtz, S., Tansey, J. and Whitelaw, G. (2005) *Sustainability Assessment: Criteria, Processes and Applications*, Earthscan, London

IAIA (International Association for Impact Assessment) (2002) *Strategic Environmental Assessment Performance Criteria*, Special Publication Series No 1, IAIA, Fargo, ND

Jan Kiewert, D. and Vos, J. (2007) 'Organisational sustainability: A case for formulating a tailor-made definition', *Journal of Environmental 2Assessment Policy and Management*, vol 9, no 1, pp1–20

João, E. (2002) 'How scale affects environmental impact assessment', *Environmental Impact Assessment Review*, vol 22, no 4, pp289–310

Keough, H. L. and Blahna, D. J. (2006) 'Achieving integrative, collaborative ecosystem management', *Conservation Biology*, vol 20, no 5, pp1373–1382

Kørnøv, L. and Thissen, W. A. H. (2000) 'Rationality in decision and policy-making: implications for strategic environmental assessment', *Impact Assessment and Project Appraisal*, vol 18, no 3, pp91–200

MEA (Millenium Ecosystem Assessment) (2005) 'Guide to the Millennium Assessment Reports', www.maweb.org/en/index.aspx, accessed 29 March 2007

Nilsson, M. and Dalkman, H. (2001) 'Decision making and strategic environmental assessment', *Journal of Environmental Assessment Policy and Management*, vol 3, no 3, pp305–327

Nitz, T. and Brown, A. L. (2001) 'SEA must learn how policy making works', *Journal of Environmental Assessment Policy and Management*, vol 3, no 3, pp329–342

Noble, B. (2000) 'Strategic environmental assessment: What is it and what makes it strategic?', *Journal of Environmental Assessment Policy and Management*, vol 2, no 2, pp203–224

Noble, B. (2002) 'The Canadian experience with SEA and sustainability', *Environmental Impact Assessment Review*, vol 22, pp3–16

Oliveira, I. S. D., de Souza, M. and Montano, M. (2005) 'Contributions of baseline sustainable zoning for SEA', paper presented at the IAIA SEA Conference, Prague

Partidário, M. R. (2000) 'Elements of an SEA framework: Improving the added-value of SEA', *Environmental Impact Assessment Review*, vol 20, pp647–663

Pope, J. (2006) 'What's so special about sustainability assessment?', Guest editorial, *Journal of Environmental Assessment Policy and Management*, vol 8, no 3, ppv–x

Retief, F. (2007) 'A performance evaluation of strategic environmental assessment (SEA) processes within the South African context', *Environmental Impact Assessment Review*, vol 27, pp84–100

Ridgway, B. (1999) 'The project cycle and the role of EIA and EMS', *Journal of Environmental Assessment Policy and Management*, vol 1, no 4, pp393–405

Sadler, B. and Verheem, R. (1996) *Strategic Environmental Assessment: Status, Challenges and Future Directions*, Ministry of Housing, Spatial Planning and the Environment, The Hague

Scholtz, R. W., Lang, D., Wiek, A., Walter, A. and Stauffacher, M. (2005) 'Transdisciplinary case studies as a means of sustainability learning: Historical framework and theory', in Wiek, A., Walter, A., Lang, D. and Scholtz, R. W. (eds) *Proceedings from Transdisciplinary Case Study Research for Sustainable Development*

Scholtz, R. W., Lang, D., Wiek, A., Walter, A. and Stauffacher, M. (2006) 'Transdisciplinary case studies as a means of sustainability learning: Historical framework and theory', *International Journal of Sustainability in Higher Education*, vol 7, no 3, pp226–251

Scrase, J. I. and Sheate, W. R. (2002) 'Integration and integrated approaches to assessment: What do they mean for the environment?', *Journal of Environmental Policy and Planning*, vol 4, no 4, pp275–294

Sheate, W. R. (2002) 'Conference report: Workshop on Linking Environmental Assessment and Management Tools', *Journal of Environmental Assessment Policy and Management*, vol 4, no 4, pp465–474

Sheate, W. R. (2003) 'Changing conceptions and potential for conflict in environmental assessment: Environmental integration and sustainable development', *Environmental Policy and Law*, vol 33, no 5, pp219–230

Sheate, W. R., Byron, H. and Smith, S. (2004) 'Implementing the SEA Directive: sectoral challenges and opportunities for the UK and EU', *European Environment*, vol 14, pp73–93

Sheate, W. R., Byron, H., Dagg, S. and Cooper, L. M. (2005) 'The relationship between the EIA and SEA Directives', final report to the European Commission, Contract NoENV.G.4./ETU/2004/0020r, Imperial College London Consultants, London, http://ec.europa.eu/environment/eia/pdf/final_report_0508.pdf, accessed 12 August 2010

Sheate, W. and Bennett, S. (2007) 'The Water Framework Directive, assessment, participation and protected areas: What are the relationships?', ERTDI Report 67,

Synthesis Report to the Environmental Protection Agency, Republic of Ireland, www.epa.ie/downloads/pubs/research/water/name,23575,en.html

Sheate, W. R. and Partidário, M. R. (2010) 'Strategic approaches and assessment techniques – potential for knowledge brokerage towards sustainability', *Environmental Impact Assessment Review*, vol 30, pp278–288

Sheate, W. R., Dagg, S., Richardson, J., Aschemann, R., Palerm, J. and Steen, U. (2001) *SEA and Integration of the Environment into Strategic Decision-Making* (three volumes), Final Report to the European Commission, DG XI, Contract No B4-3040/99/136634/MAR/B4, http://ec.europa.eu/environment/eia/sea-support.htm, accessed 12 August 2010

Sheate, W. R., Dagg, S., Richardson, J., Aschemann, R., Palerm, J. and Steen, U. (2003) 'Integrating the environment into strategic decision-making: Conceptualizing policy SEA', *European Environment*, vol 13, no 1, pp1–18

Sheate, W. R., Partidário, M. R., Byron, H., Bina, O. and Dagg, S. (2008) 'Sustainability assessment of future scenarios: Methodology and application to mountain areas of Europe', *Environmental Management*, vol 41, no 2, pp282–299

Thérivel, R. and Minas, P. (2002) 'Ensuring effective sustainability appraisal', *Impact Assessment and Project Appraisal*, vol 20, no 2, pp81–91

Vanclay, F. (2004) 'The triple bottom line and impact assessment: How do TBL, EIA, SIA, SEA and EMS relate to each other?', *Journal of Environmental Assessment Policy and Management*, vol 6, no 3, pp265–288

van der Vorst, R., Grafé-Buckens, A. and Sheate, W. R. (1999) 'A systemic framework for environmental decision-making', *Journal of Environmental Assessment Policy and Management*, vol 1, no 1, pp1–26

Verheem, R. A. A. and Tonk, J. A. M. N. (2000) 'Strategic environmental assessment: One concept, multiple forms', *Impact Assessment and Project Appraisal*, vol 18, no 3, pp177–182

Vicente, G. and Partidário, M. R. (2006) 'SEA – enhancing communication for better environmental decisions', *Environmental Impact Assessment Review*, vol 26, pp696–706

van Latesteijen, H. and Scoonenboom, J. (eds) (1996). *Policy Scenarios for Sustainable Development: Environmental Policy in an International Context 3*, Arnold, London

Westhoek, H. J., van den Berg, M. and Bakkes, J. A. (2006) 'Scenario development to explore the future of Europe's rural areas', *Agriculture, Ecosystems and Environment*, vol 114, pp7–20

Wiek, A. and Binder, C. (2005) 'Solution spaces for decision-making: A sustainability assessment tool for city-regions', *Environmental Impact Assessment Review*, vol 25, no 6, pp589–608

17
SEA and Landscape Planning

Marie Hanusch and Thomas B. Fischer

Introduction

Most strategic environmental assessment (SEA) systems have one thing in common; the quest for effective ways to support the application of SEA. In this context, integration with existing environmental planning and management instruments is seen to be of particular importance. There are currently a range of instruments internationally that offer valuable support for applying SEA (Thérivel and Wood, 2004). These include, for example, environmental impact assessment (EIA) in the Netherlands, sustainability appraisal in the UK and environmental management systems (EMS) in Sweden. In addition, landscape planning instruments exist in a number of countries (Herberg, 2000).

These instruments are normally baseline-led instruments that aim to outline, evaluate and assess the existing and anticipated status of the landscape, and frequently also of the biophysical environment for a certain planning area. Frequently, anticipated conflicts and impacts connected with future potential land use are also identified. Landscape planning instruments, therefore, can contribute to a sound database, the lack of which has been identified as one of the biggest problems of SEA application in many countries. For example, João (2004, p694) concluded that the 'lack of right data' is a major SEA barrier and Sheate et al (2004, p89) highlighted 'data' as 'key issue confronting all future SEA practice'.

This chapter introduces and reviews landscape planning instruments in four countries – Germany, Canada, Ireland and Sweden. In this context, the main focus is on possible linkages with SEA. Particular emphasis is put on practice in Germany, which has currently the only formalized and most comprehensive landscape planning system in place anywhere in the world. Two main questions are at the heart of this chapter:

1 What are the main linkages of SEA and landscape planning instruments?
2 How can existing landscape planning instruments be beneficial for SEA?

The chapter is divided into four parts. This introduction is followed by a section that describes the evolution of the terms 'landscape' and 'landscape planning' and establishes the potential connections of landscape planning and SEA. Subsequently, how landscape planning instruments in Germany, Canada, Ireland and Sweden can contribute to SEA is explored. In this context, the main focus is on objectives, substantive focus, methods and procedures. Finally, conclusions are drawn and recommendations made on further research and action.

Background: Landscape planning and potential relationships with SEA

A number of landscape planning instruments exist worldwide. These differ in terms of focus and contents, reflecting different understandings of the terms 'landscape' and 'landscape planning' in different countries and their historical, political and cultural contexts. In this context, Antrop (2006, p187) suggested that: 'As landscape changes, also its meaning and significance changes and consequently its management.'

The oldest written reference to the term 'landscape' has been said to be the Old High German term 'lantscaft', dating back to roughly 830 AD (Tress and Tress, 2001). Since then, the term 'landscape' has been subject to many changes. These are related to, for example, the specific region, territory, countryside, scenery, nature, environment, administrative organization, social structure, physical form, ecological system, cultural unit and political system within which the term is used. In the academic literature, the term 'landscape' has been discussed and interpreted in a range of different ways by different disciplines, revolving around historical, ecological, interdisciplinary and sustainable approaches (Forman and Gordon, 1986; Haase, 1991; Naveh, 1995; Hard, 2001; Nohl, 2001; Tress et al, 2001; von Haaren, 2004; Marsh, 2005; Musacchio et al, 2005; Jensen, 2006; Antrop, 2006).

According to European Directive 2001/42/EC (the SEA Directive) and the United Nations Economic Commission for Europe (UNECE) Protocol on SEA, 'landscape' is one out of a range of factors that jointly compose 'the environment'. Other factors include human health, biodiversity, fauna, flora, soil, water, air and cultural heritage. While a distinction of the different environmental factors within SEA can help to make its application easier, looking at factors in isolation means that the manifold overlaps between them are ignored. For example, biodiversity has overlaps with most other environmental factors, including flora and fauna, soil, water, climate and landscape. In European Union (EU) member states, under the SEA Directive, it is now a legal requirement to consider the interactions between all environmental factors.

There is currently no definition regarding what aspects have to be assessed when considering landscape impacts within SEA and there is only an emerging academic debate on this question (see, for example, Jessel, 2006). However, there is some consensus that: (a) visual landscape as perceived by people; and (b) landscape character are important aspects to be considered within SEA. Within the session on landscape planning at the International Association for Impact Assessment (IAIA) SEA conference in Prague in 2005, the definition of the European Landscape Convention was taken as a workable approach to develop a joint understanding of 'landscape' in the context of SEA.

> *Landscape means an area as perceived by people, whose character is the result of the action and interaction of natural and/or human factors. (Council of Europe, 2000a, Article 1)*

The European Landscape Convention definition is also followed in the work of Tress et al (2006) on landscape research and landscape planning. On the one hand, this definition is broad enough to reflect different meanings of landscape; on the other, it is narrow enough to allow for the development of a joint understanding. What is important within the context of SEA is that landscape refers to a specific, spatially designated area. The notion of the 'character' being 'the result of the action and interaction of natural and/or human factors' reflects the idea that landscapes have evolved over time, and that they are the outcome of natural and human forces. It also reflects the idea that a landscape forms a whole, the natural and cultural components of which have to be considered together, and not separately (Council of Europe, 2000b).

'Landscape' in the context of landscape planning normally has a broad meaning – similar to 'nature' or 'environment'. While landscape planning has different roots and meanings in different countries, a common driving force for its recent development has been the environmental crisis of the 1960s and 1970s. Landscape planning can therefore be seen to be embedded in the philosophy of environmentalism, the movement of the protection and preservation of the environment. 'Environment' was taken by this movement to mean all things of natural origin in the landscape (Marsh, 2005). Therefore, in all landscape planning instruments, there is normally a causal relationship between 'landscape', 'nature' and 'environment'. In the US and Canada, for example, landscape planning covers the macro environment of land-use and planning activity, dealing with landscape features, processes and systems (Marsh, 2005). In Germany, following the Federal Nature Conservation Act (2004, last amended in March 2010), both, nature conservation and landscape management are the subjects of landscape planning.

The overall task of landscape planning instruments in most systems is to take stock of and assess the status of the landscape in a certain planning area, normally including aspects of nature and the environment. Furthermore, landscape planning normally deals with the establishment of compensation measures for identified impacts of policies, plans and programmes (PPPs). In Europe, various landscape planning instruments are used in Austria, France, Germany, Ireland, Italy, Luxembourg, the Netherlands, Spain, Sweden and Switzerland. In these countries, instruments are designed differently, for example in terms of objectives, legal status and scope of application (Herberg, 2000). Landscape planning instruments are also in use in Canada, the US (Marsh, 2005) and Russia (Meißner and Köppel, 2003). To date, only in Germany is landscape planning a formal instrument, covering all major scales of planning with an over 30-year track record of practice.

Linkages between landscape planning instruments and SEA

In this section, potential linkages of SEA and landscape planning instruments are discussed with reference to four countries. The main focus is on Germany, the only country worldwide where landscape plans and programmes are formally required in an area-wide manner for all main levels of public planning. In addition, landscape planning instruments from Canada, Ireland and Sweden are discussed.

Landscape planning in Germany

The roots of landscape planning in Germany go back to the early 20th century and formal requirements for the preparation of landscape plans and programmes were introduced more than 30 years ago by the Federal Nature Conservation Act 1976. The 2004 revision of the Act states that 'the contents of landscape planning shall be taken into consideration in environmental assessments' (Federal Nature Conservation Act 2004, Article 14(2)). Landscape plans and programmes serve as state of the environment reports that proactively set objectives for environmentally sustainable land use.

They include information on:

- The existing and anticipated status of nature and landscape.
- The objectives and principles of nature conservation and landscape management.
- The assessment and evaluation of the existing and anticipated status of nature and landscape on the basis of overall aims and principles, including any possible conflicts.
- The anticipated measures for avoiding, reducing or eliminating adverse effects on nature and landscape, and protecting, managing and developing certain parts or components of nature and landscapes, among which the European ecological network Natura 2000 (Federal Ministry for Environment, 2002).

Subsequently, objectives, contents and methods used in landscape plan and programme-making in Germany are described, mirroring it with the requirements of the SEA Directive.

Objectives

Both landscape plans/programmes and SEA act as advocate instruments for the environment. The former focuses on aspects revolving around nature, biodiversity and landscape. Under Directive 2001/42/EC, SEA focuses on all types of environmental factors from human health, through biodiversity to landscape and material/cultural assets, Whereas the SEA Directive calls for a promotion of sustainable development, German landscape planning provisions require the 'sustained availability of the natural resources for human use' (Federal Nature Conservation Act 2004, Article 1(2)). Furthermore, through landscape planning, 'non-regenerating natural resources shall be used in a sustainable manner' (Federal Nature Conservation Act 2004, Article 2(1)).

Both, SEA and landscape planning aim at integrating considerations of the environment, nature, biodiversity and landscape into decision-making and planning. In this context, while SEA aims at integrating environmental considerations into the preparation and adoption of certain plans and programmes, landscape plans and programmes provide for aims and principles of nature conservation and landscape management for other planning and administrative procedures. In addition, landscape planning is supposed to fulfil implementation tasks, such as the formulation of measures to protect, manage and develop nature and landscapes (Bruns, 2003). Table 17.1 compares objectives of SEA and landscape planning in Germany.

Contents

Landscape plans and programmes prepared at different levels of decision-making are supposed to address different issues. In order to be able to better appreciate the potential contributions of different landscape plans and programmes, see Table 17.2, which compares the contents of an environmental report, prepared according to the SEA Directive (Annex I) with those of: (a) a regional landscape framework plan, which contributes to regional plan preparation; and (b) a local landscape plan, which contributes to local land-use plan preparation.

Table 17.1 *Comparison of objectives of SEA and landscape planning in Germany*

Themes	Objectives of SEA (according to the European SEA Directive 2001/42/EC)	Objectives of German landscape planning (according to the Federal Nature Conservation Act 2004)
Environmental protection and sustainable development	Provide for a high level of **protection of the environment** and promote **sustainable development** (Article 1)	Provide for an effective and **sustained functioning of nature and landscapes** (Sections 1 and 2 in combination with Section 13(1))
Integration with other planning instruments	Contribute to the **integration of environmental considerations** into the preparation and adoption of **certain plans and programmes** (Article 1)	Provide for the **integration of considerations of nature and landscape** into decision-making, especially in terms of **spatial planning** (Sections 13(1) and 14(2))
Setting of objectives and implementation	–	**Conceptual** and **implementation tasks,** such as the definition of objectives of nature and landscapes and the formulation of requirements and measures to protect, manage and develop nature and landscapes (Section 14(1))

Table 17.2 *Comparison of contents of SEA and landscape planning*

Contents of SEA (as required for the environmental report, Annex I, EC SEA Directive)	Contents of a landscape framework plan (LFP) (as contribution to a regional plan) and of a local landscape plan (LP) (as contribution to local land-use plan)	Overlaps LFP/LP and SEA
(a) An outline of the contents, main objectives of the plan or programme and relationship with other relevant plans and programmes.	Outline of the environmental objectives of the regional/local plan (for example, priority areas for certain land uses designated in the plan). No outline of the other objectives of the plan.	☺
(b) The relevant aspects of the current state of the environment and the likely evolution thereof without implementation of the plan or programme.	Baseline information on the current state of nature and landscape and prognosis of its likely evolution without implementation of the plan.	☺
(c) The environmental characteristics of areas likely to be significantly affected.	Assessment of the environmental sensitivity of areas likely to be significantly affected.	☺
(d) Any existing environmental problems that are relevant to the plan or programme including, in particular, those relating to any areas of a particular environmental importance, such as areas designated pursuant to Directives 79/409/EEC and 92/43/EEC.	Analysis of the existing environmental problems that are relevant to the regional/local plan, including those relating to areas designated pursuant to Directives 79/409/EEC and 92/43/EEC.	☺
(e) The environmental protection objectives, established at international, community or member state level, which are relevant to the plan or programme and the way those objectives and any environmental considerations have been taken into account during its preparation.	Objectives and guidance principals of nature conservation and landscape management, including designated spatial target zones (for example, areas for conservation, development, and redevelopment).	☺
(f) The likely significant effects on the environment, including issues such as biodiversity, population, human health, fauna, flora, soil, water, air, climatic factors, material assets, cultural heritage including architectural and archaeological heritage, landscape and the interrelationship between the above factors.	Assessment of the likely significant effects of anticipated developments laid down among others in the regional/local plan, regarding the aspects soil, water, air/climate, fauna/ flora, natural scenery and cultural assets and interrelationship between the above factors.	☺

(continued)

Table 17.2 (*continued*)

(g) The measures envisaged to prevent, reduce and as fully as possible offset any significant adverse effects on the environment of implementing the plan or programme.	Compensation concept for nature and landscape, including measures for protection, management and development.	😐
(h) An outline of the reasons for selecting the alternatives dealt with, and a description of how the assessment was undertaken including any difficulties (such as technical deficiencies or lack of know-how) encountered in compiling the required information.	Development and comparison of site alternatives including the considerations for or against a selected site alternative.	😐
(i) A description of the measures envisaged concerning monitoring in accordance with Art 10.	Periodic revision of the LFP/LP providing information about the development of nature and landscape.	😐
(j) A non-technical summary of the information provided under the above headings.	Documentation of main problems/ solutions, but no non-technical summary.	😟

😊 = requirements basically the same; 😐 = some differences in requirements; 😟 = different requirements

As Table 17.2 shows, there are many overlaps regarding the contents of an SEA environment report and regional and local landscape plans, particularly regarding (see also Scholles and von Haaren, 2005):

- The collection of environmental baseline data (see aspects (b), (c) and (d)).
- The outline of environmental objectives (see aspect e).
- The assessment of the likely significant effects of the regional/local land-use plan on the environment (see aspect f).

Existing landscape plans and programmes can therefore contribute significantly to SEA, potentially simplifying it. Currently, however, landscape plans and programmes do not cover all environmental factors that need to be considered within SEA, including population, human health, and material assets, although there is no reason for why these factors could not be included in the future.

Landscape planning also contributes to the development of mitigation measures (see aspect g). In this context, it is important that landscape plans and programmes normally identify measures envisaged to mitigate or compensate significant adverse effects on nature and landscape of those actions proposed in spatial plans. Landscape plans and programmes thus provide for suitable baseline data, enabling the comparison of spatial alternatives (aspect h). Landscape plans frequently provide for conflict maps (see next section on methods), facilitating better informed decisions on site alternatives. Finally, landscape planning can contribute to the description of the measures envisaged for monitoring (aspect i), as periodic revisions of landscape plans and programmes provide information on the development of nature, biodiversity and landscape (Hanusch et al, 2005). This is of particular importance, as 'existing monitoring arrangements may be used if appropriate' (EC SEA Detective, Article 10(2)). However, in order to contribute optimally to SEA monitoring, other aspects will have to be included in the future, such as material and cultural assets and health.

Methods

Methods currently used in landscape planning are all useful for SEA as well (Fischer, 2007). These particularly include baseline data collection, identification of aims and objectives and evaluation of potential conflicts. The first step in the preparation of a landscape plan is the collection and recording of baseline information on the current state of biodiversity, nature and the environment. Baseline information is taken from existing sources that are provided by environmental authorities, nature conservation organizations, individuals and others. Additional data is collected through specific surveys. Data are provided in text format and maps are extensively used (see Figure 17.1).

Landscape plans and programmes provide for an evaluation of data, based on predefined criteria, such as degree of diversity, presence of rare species or degree of negative impacts arising from land-use plans. By comparing the outcome with information produced through other planning processes, areas with conflicting land-use claims are identified. In order to resolve conflicts, scenarios for site alternatives are developed, for example, regarding residential developments. At times, technical alternatives are also described and recommendations are given on how and when to act.

Following evaluation, objectives and guidance principles of nature conservation and landscape management are developed (see Figure 17.2). A compensation concept needs to be set up in order to mitigate the conflicts identified earlier as well as measures for the protection, management, and development of nature and landscape. Figures 17.1 and 17.2 illustrate sections of the local landscape plan Rothenburg-Hänichen for environmental baseline data and environmental objectives. Within a pilot study on SEA and land-use planning, this landscape plan was found to be greatly beneficial for SEA (Reinke, 2005).

Procedure

In addition to substantive overlaps and the application of mutually beneficial methods, there are a range of procedural linkages between landscape plans and programmes and SEA. In this context, it is important that, at every level of decision-making, landscape plans and programmes are prepared in parallel to spatial plans and programmes, on the same scale, and by the same authority in an area wide manner (see Figure 17.3).

However, administrative boundaries may not always be the same and several landscape framework plans may be relevant for one regional plan. This is why parallel timing of planning procedures should always be secured (Schmidt, 2004). Currently, public participation only takes place indirectly through the spatial/land-use plan-making process. Furthermore, alternatives are normally only considered indirectly, through land suitability mapping. Finally, monitoring is currently also only happening indirectly through updates of

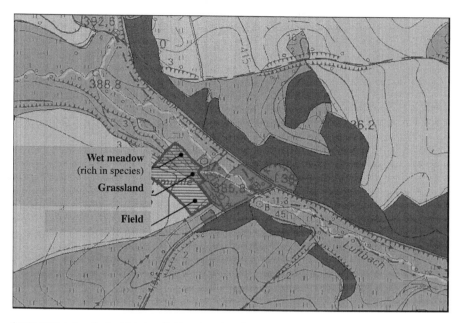

Source: Sächsisches Staatsministerium für Umwelt und Landwirtschaft (2004)

Figure 17.1 *Section of the landscape plan Rothenburg-Hänichen showing environmental baseline data, such as biotope types in a planned settlement extension*

landscape plans (Fischer, 2005; Jessel et al, 2003; Siemoneit and Fischer, 2001). However, both public participation and monitoring can be easily aligned with landscape plans. In this context, new technologies, for example, interactive, web-based landscape plans can be particularly helpful (see von Haaren and Warren-Kretzschmar, 2006).

Landscape planning instruments in other countries

This section reviews landscape planning instruments from three other countries; Canada, Ireland and Sweden. Although all of them can potentially contribute significantly to SEA, none of them are currently formally required and applied in an area wide manner similar to German landscape plan and programme making.

Canada: Integrated landscape management (ILM)

In Canada, ILM models have been used in areas that potentially have conflicting land-use and management objectives. These particularly include areas characterized by population growth, economic or agricultural development, conservation initiatives and watershed management (Government of Canada, 2005a). ILM comprises a range of quantitative, projective tools for examining how ecological and socio-economic features of an area are likely to change as a result of different policy and management decisions. To date, the scale and

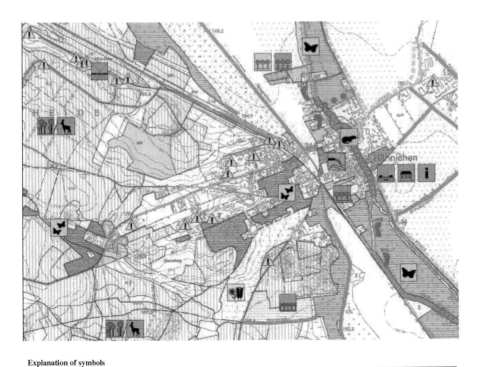

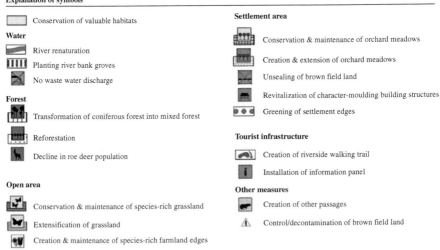

Explanation of symbols

Conservation of valuable habitats

Water

River renaturation

Planting river bank groves

No waste water discharge

Forest

Transformation of coniferous forest into mixed forest

Reforestation

Decline in roe deer population

Open area

Conservation & maintenance of species-rich grassland

Extensification of grassland

Creation & maintenance of species-rich farmland edges

Settlement area

Conservation & maintenance of orchard meadows

Creation & extension of orchard meadows

Unsealing of brown field land

Revitalization of character-moulding building structures

Greening of settlement edges

Tourist infrastructure

Creation of riverside walking trail

Installation of information panel

Other measures

Creation of other passages

Control/decontamination of brown field land

Source: Sächsisches Staatsministerium für Umwelt und Landwirtschaft (2004)

Figure 17.2 *Section of landscape plan Rothenburg-Hänichen showing environmental objectives*

application of existing ILM applications have varied widely, depending on individual objectives. ILM models are increasingly used for sustainable transportation planning, urban growth planning and, to a lesser extent, for cumulative impact assessments at municipal and regional scales.

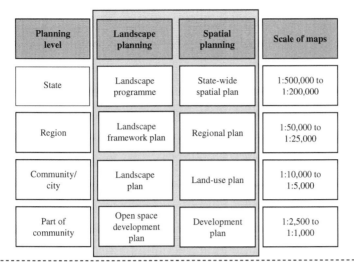

Planning level	Landscape planning	Spatial planning	Scale of maps
State	Landscape programme	State-wide spatial plan	1:500,000 to 1:200,000
Region	Landscape framework plan	Regional plan	1:50,000 to 1:25,000
Community/ city	Landscape plan	Land-use plan	1:10,000 to 1:5,000
Part of community	Open space development plan	Development plan	1:2,500 to 1:1,000

Has partly been covered by existing EIA requirements before the SEA Directive was introduced

Source: Adapted from Federal Ministry for Environment (1998)

Figure 17.3 *The system of landscape planning and spatial planning in Germany*

A basic principle of an ILM model is to involve the public and stakeholder groups in the development and evaluation of strategies for integrating socio-economic objectives and environmental protection. Once set up, the integrated approach of ILM allows for a sophisticated assessment of alternatives within a participatory planning process and the identification of the most sustainable alternative. ILM models are therefore considered suitable tools for supporting SEA, aiming at identifying complex interactions and cumulative effects of multiple land-uses. Furthermore, they provide for opportunities early in the decision-making process, exploring ways to mitigate negative effects on the environment, society, and the economy (Government of Canada, 2005b). In this context, the Policy Research Initiative (2005) suggested that a national strategy is required to expand the application of ILM modelling systems to larger scales, capable of evaluating the implications of cross-sectoral activities.

Ireland: Landscape heritage assessment (LHA)

In Ireland, LHA has been brought forward by the Heritage Council. It works with landscape indicators that are based on a pressure-state-response framework, and is applied within geographical information systems (GISs). LHA is intended to fulfil inventory, analytical and communication tasks. Its main aim is to come up with a digital database, based on which assessment allows for the identification of critical areas, and the visualization of the results for use in potential management regimes. The key challenge of LHA has been said to be the choice of appropriate data and information to be collected and the derivation of suitable indicators.

The instrument was first applied in County Clare in Western Ireland, based on a pilot study on Landscape Characterization for the County (Environmental Resources Management and ERA-Maptec Ltd, 2000). At the same time, consultation draft Guidelines on Landscape and Landscape Assessment were issued by the Department of the Environment and Local Government (2000). The pilot study also aimed at exploring the feasibility of establishing a basic landscape characterization for Ireland as a whole.

The pilot study underlined the potential benefits of a national system of landscape characterization that could be used as a reference point in PPP formulation, SEA, EIA, and also for monitoring countryside change (Julie Martin Associates, 2006). Building on the findings of the pilot study, the Heritage Council (2002) published a *Policy Paper on Ireland's Landscapes and the National Heritage*. This paper stressed that decisions on landscape can only be taken from an informed and up-to-date basis, encouraging improvement of landscape information and access to such information. LHA is a reaction to that suggestion for establishing of a sound database and appropriate assessment benchmarks. Based on the experiences of the instrument in County Clare, further development of LHA is foreseen. It is anticipated that LHA may support SEA particularly in providing for baseline data and monitoring. In this context, a GIS-based indicator set may be designed for the purpose of systematic monitoring.

Sweden: Ecological landscape plans and other approaches

In Sweden, use is made of a number of different landscape planning instruments and, recently, a method has been developed to specifically address health aspects. These approaches include ecological landscape plans, which are supposed to fulfil a similar purpose to that of German landscape plans and programmes. However, Swedish ecological landscape plans are not required by law and, therefore, they are less frequently prepared.

At the Department of Landscape Planning of the Swedish University of Agricultural Sciences, a group of researchers have developed eight characteristics of open green urban areas that are of great importance for people's preferences and well-being. These comprise: 'the serene', 'the spacious', 'the wild', 'the lush', 'the festive', 'the common', 'the pleasure garden' and 'the cultural' (Grahn and Stigsdotter, 2003; Grahn et al, 2005). Research on these eight characteristics was initially conducted in the fields of environmental perception and environmental psychology. The framework is being implemented in planning projects for different purposes and on different scales in the Interreg project Landscape as a resource for health and development in the Öresund Sound region. Using the eight characteristics, the existing status of health aspects connected with landscape values have been mapped and assessed. This has resulted particularly in recommendations for mitigation and compensation in order to promote creativity and development. So far, the method has been perceived to be suitable for implementing health aspects in physical planning, landscape and spatial planning as well as in SEA (Skärbäck, 2005).

Possible contribution of the different landscape planning instruments to SEA

Extensive time and resource requirements have been said to be a limitation to effective SEA application (Thérivel, 2004). In this context, landscape planning instruments can function as a comprehensive information source for SEA, potentially helping to save time and resources and reducing the efforts connected with producing an SEA. The greatest potential of landscape planning instruments lies in the collection and evaluation of environmental baseline data, as well as the setting up of environmental objectives. Furthermore, the methods used within landscape planning can also be used within SEA. Based on the information provided by the landscape planning case studies presented at the Prague conference, the main contributions of landscape planning from the four countries to selected elements of SEA are summarized in Table 17.3.

Table 17.3 shows that landscape planning instruments introduced in this chapter can contribute to varying extents to a number of SEA elements. It indicates that each instrument has different strengths and weaknesses. German landscape planning has particular strengths in the provision of baseline data, helping to overcome data constraints within SEA. It can also contribute significantly to impact assessment and the preparation of compensation measures. Indirect contributions are made to alternatives assessment, public participation and monitoring.

The Canadian instrument of ILM has particular strengths in the assessment of alternatives, the identification of impacts and public participation. However, it is currently applied only occasionally and therefore currently only of limited benefit. It has the potential, though, to develop into a more beneficial and widely used decision-making support tool.

Besides providing for baseline data and supporting impact analysis, the Irish instrument of LHA has particular strengths regarding monitoring and public participation. However, LHA reportedly will only be able to work effectively in the future if the challenge of gathering and processing relevant data is met, requiring some substantive investment first. Moreover, the political

Table 17.3 *Contributions of current landscape planning instruments to selected elements of SEA*

Elements of SEA	Contributions of landscape planning from			
	Germany[1]	Canada	Ireland	Sweden[2]
Environmental baseline information	■	■	■	■
Impact assessment	■	■	■	■
Alternatives assessment	■	■	■	■
Compensation measures	■	■	□	■
Public participation	■	■	■	■
Monitoring	■	□	■	□

■ = major contribution; ■ = some/indirect contribution; □ = minor contribution
1 Formalized instrument, prepared at all major planning levels in an area wide manner.
2 The Swedish approach presented at the IAIA conference in Prague, 2005, is strictly focused on health aspects of landscape planning.

backing of the instrument needs to be reinforced to promote its advancement and scope of application.

Swedish ecological landscape plans, finally, also have the potential to contribute significantly to SEA. Their limiting factor is currently a rather narrow understanding of landscape planning. At the moment, particular emphasis is only put on health aspects.

Conclusions

The chapter has described and reviewed existing and potential linkages between SEA and landscape planning instruments from four countries: Germany, Canada, Ireland and Sweden. The main focus has been on Germany, where landscape planning has been required by law for all main planning levels in an area wide fashion since the late 1970s. This chapter has shown that there are substantial potential linkages between SEA and landscape planning and the examples presented above show that landscape planning instruments can contribute significantly to SEA. As a consequence, time and resource requirements for SEA might be reduced significantly.

The main strength of all landscape planning instruments is the capability to provide for some comprehensive environmental baseline data for SEA. Furthermore, all instruments can contribute extensively to impact analysis and evaluation. Landscape planning can also contribute to the assessment of alternatives, the identification of compensation measures, public participation and monitoring (see Table 17.3).

There are two main challenges of all four landscape planning instruments introduced in this chapter:

1 The consideration of environmental impacts is normally more limited than what is required by SEA.
2 Integration with the underlying plan and programme-making process is not always fully addressed.

However, the first challenge is not difficult to overcome; it simply requires an extension of the aspects to be covered. Regarding the second challenge, as stated above, there are positive examples showing that a smooth integration into decision-making is possible.

The European SEA Directive explicitly calls for the use of existing sources of baseline data and suitable methods for impact assessment. This is also one of the core tasks of all landscape planning instruments. In those countries where landscape planning instruments are applied in a non-formalized manner, SEA can contribute to the wider application and further development of these instruments.

As a word of caution, it should be added that landscape planning is susceptible to the same general limitations and challenges of SEA. These particularly include lacking political will, limited financial and personal capacities, as well as technical and logistical constraints. However, the positive German experience with formally required and area wide landscape plans and programmes shows that the instrument can be highly beneficial.

In order to meet the challenges identified and to enhance the beneficial linkages between SEA and landscape planning, the following are key priorities for future research and action:

- Transfer of knowledge of different landscape planning approaches via:
  - ○ Circulation of good practice case studies where landscape planning contributes to SEA.
  - ○ Expert exchange (institutionalized or case-specific).
  - ○ Preparation of guidance documents on landscape planning (in English).
- Enhancement of the scope of landscape planning in order to improve the support of SEA.
- Promotion of a better integration and coordination of strategic action, landscape planning and SEA.
- Testing the practical application of contents and methods of landscape planning within SEA in form of pilot projects.
- Awareness-raising of the strength of landscape planning in order to overcome the missing political will and to promote formalized landscape planning approaches.

Acknowledgements

The authors wish to thank Stefan Lütkes (Federal Ministry for the Environment, Germany), Maren Regener (Leibniz Institute of Ecological and Regional Development, Germany), Markus Reinke (Weihenstephan University of Applied Sciences, Germany), Erik Skärbäck (Department of Landscape Planning, SLU, Alnarp, Sweden), Ebbe Adolffson (Environmental Protection Agency, Sweden), Linda d'Auria (University College Dublin, Ireland) and Ruth Waldick (Habitat Division, National Wildlife Research Centre, Canada) for their contributions at the IAIA conference in Prague, 2005.

References

Antrop, M. (2006) 'Sustainable landscapes: Contradiction, fiction or utopia?', *Landscape and Urban Planning*, vol 75, pp187–197
Bruns, D. (2003) 'Was kann Landschaftsplanung leisten?', *Naturschutz und Land-schaftsplanung*, vol 4, pp114–118
Council of Europe (2000a) *European Landscape Convention*, European Treaty Series No 176, Florence, 20 October 2000, http://conventions.coe.int/treaty/en/Treaties/Html/176.htm
Council of Europe (2000b) *Explanatory Report on the European Landscape Convention*, Florence, 20 October 2000, http://conventions.coe.int/treaty/en/Reports/Html/176.htm
Department of the Environment and Local Government (2000) *Landscape and Landscape Assessment: Consultation Draft of Guidelines for Planning Authorities*, Dublin, Ireland
Environmental Resources Management and ERA-Maptec Ltd (2000) *Pilot Study on Landscape Characterization in County Clare*, Report to the Heritage Council, Kilkenny

Federal Ministry for Environment (1998) *Landscape Planning – Contents and Procedures*, Bonn

Federal Ministry for Environment (2002) *Landscape Planning for Sustainable Municipal Development*, Bonn

Fischer, T. B. (2005) 'SEA in Germany', in Jones, C., Baker, M., Carter, J., Jay, S., Short, M. and Wood, C. (eds) *Strategic Environmental Assessment and Land Use Planning: An International Evaluation*, Earthscan, London, pp79–96

Fischer, T. B. (2007) *Theory and Practice of Strategic Environmental Assessment*, Earthscan, London

Forman, R. T. T. and Gordon, M. (1986) *Landscape Ecology*, Wiley, New York

Government of Canada (2005a) 'Integrated landscape management models for sustainable development policy making', briefing note, January 2005, Policy Research Initiative, http://policyresearch.gc.ca/doclib/SD_BN_IntLandscape_E.pdf

Government of Canada (2005b) 'Towards a national capacity for integrated landscape management modelling', briefing note, May 2005, Policy Research Initiative, http://policyresearch.gc.ca/doclib/ILMM2_Briefing_Note_E.pdf

Grahn, P. and Stigsdotter, U. (2003) 'Landscape planning and stress', *Urban Forestry & Urban Greening*, vol 2, pp1–18

Grahn, P., Stigsdotter, U. and Berggren-Bärring, A.-M. (2005) 'A planning tool for designing sustainable and healthy cities: The importance of experienced characteristics in urban green open spaces for people's health and well-being', conference proceedings of Quality and Significance of Green Urban Areas, 14–15 April 2005, Van Hall Larenstein University of Professional Education, Netherlands

Haase, G. (1991) 'Theoretisch-methodologische Schlußfolgerungen zur Landschaftsforschung', *Nova acta Leopoldina*, vol 64, no 276, pp173–186

Hanusch, M., Köppel, J. and Weiland, U. (2005) 'Monitoring-Verpflichtungen aus EU-Richtlinien und ihre Umsetzbarkeit durch die Landschaftsplanung', *UVP-report*, vol 3–4, pp159–165

Hard, G. (2001) 'Der Begriff Landschaft: Mythos, Geschichte, Bedeutung', in Konold, W., Böcker, R. and Hampicke, U. (eds) *Handbuch Naturschutz und Landschaftspflege, Landsberg*, Loseblattsammlung, Teil

Herberg, A. (2000) 'Umwelt und Landschaftsplanung in den Ländern der EU und der Schweiz', *Arbeitsmaterialien zur Landschaftsplanung, Issue 15* (CD-Rom), Technical University of Berlin

Heritage Council (2002) *Policy Paper on Ireland's Landscapes and the National Heritage*, Heritage Council, Kilkenny

Jensen, L.-H. (2006) 'Changing conceptualization of landscape in English landscape assessment methods', in Tress, B., Tress, G., Fry, G. and Opdam, P. (eds) *From Landscape Research to Landscape Planning: Aspects of Integration, Education and Application*, Springer, Dordrechtpp161–171

Jessel, B. (2006) 'Elements, characteristics and character: Information functions of landscapes in terms of indicators', *Ecological Indicators*, vol 6, pp153–167

Jessel, B., Müller-Pfannenstil, K. and Rößling, H. (2003) 'Die künftige Stellung der Landschaftsplanung zur Strategischen Umweltprüfung (SUP)', *Naturschutz und Landschaftsplanung*, vol 11, pp332–338

João, E. (2004) 'SEA outlook: Future challenges and possibilities', in Schmidt, M., João, E. and Albrecht, E. (eds) *Implementing Strategic Environmental Assessment*, Springer, Berlin, pp691–700

Julie Martin Associates (2006) *Landscape Character Assessment in Ireland: Baseline Audit and Evaluation*, final report to the Heritage Council, March 2006

Marsh, W. M. (2005) *Landscape Planning: Environmental Applications*, Wiley, New York

Meißner, C. and Köppel, J. (2003) 'Umwelt- und Naturschutz in Russland – Recht und Umsetzung im Transformationsprozess', *Natur und Landschaft*, vol 78, no 11, pp468–475

Musacchio, M., Ozdenerol, E., Bryant, M. and Evans, T. (2005) 'Changing landscapes, changing disciplines: Seeking to understand interdisciplinary in landscape ecological research', *Landscape and Urban Planning*, vol 73, pp326–338

Naveh, Z. (1995) 'Interactions of landscapes and culture', *Landscape and Urban Planning*, vol 32, pp43–54

Nohl, W. (2001) 'Sustainable landscape use and aesthetic perception: Preliminary reflections on future landscape aesthetics', *Landscape and Urban Planning*, vol 54, pp223–237

Policy Research Initiative (2005) 'Integrated landscape management modelling', workshop report, Ottawa

Reinke, M. (2005) 'Pilotvorhaben für eine Strategische Umweltprüfung zur Flächennut-zungsplanung, 2 Zwischenbericht', IOER, Stuttgart

Sächsisches Staatsministerium für Umwelt und Landwirtschaft (2004) 'Landschaftsplan Rothenburg/O.L.-Hähnichen', Dresden

Schmidt, C. (2004) *Die Strategische Umweltprüfung in der Regionalplanung*, Forschungsprojekt im Auftrag des Bundesministeriums für Bildung und Forschung, Erfurt

Scholles, F. and von Haaren, C. (2005) 'Co-ordination of SEA and landscape planning', in Schmidt, M., João, E. and Albrecht, E. (eds) *Implementing Strategic Environmental Assessment*, Springer, Berlin, pp557–570

Sheate, W. R., Byron, H. J. and Smith, S. P. (2004) 'Implementing the SEA Directive: Sectoral challenges and opportunities for the UK and EU', *European Environment*, vol 14, pp73–93

Siemoneit, D. and Fischer, T. B. (2001) 'Die Strategische Umweltprüfung – das Beispiel des Regionalplans Lausitz-Spreewald in Brandenburg', *UVP-report*, vol 5, pp253–258

Skärbäck, E. (2005) 'Mental health consideration in planning', paper presented at the IAIA SEA Conference, Prague

Thérivel, R. (2004) *Strategic Environmental Assessment in Action*, Earthscan, London

Thérivel, R. and Partidário, M. R. (1996) *The Practice of Strategic Environmental Assessment*, Earthscan, London

Thérivel, R. and Wood, G. (2004) 'Tools for SEA', in Schmidt, M., João, E. and Albrecht, E. (eds) *Implementing Strategic Environmental Assessment*, Springer, Berlin, pp349–363

Tress, B. and Tress, G. (2001) 'Theorie und System der Landschaft', *Naturschutz und Landschaftsplanung*, vol 33, pp52–58

Tress, B., Tress, G., Décamps, H. and d'Hauteserre, A.-M. (2001) 'Bridging human and natural sciences in landscape research', *Landscape and Urban Planning*, vol 57, pp137–141

Tress, B., Tress, G., Fry, G. and Opdam, P. (2006) *From Landscape Research to Landscape Planning: Aspects of Integration, Education and Application*, Springer, Dordrecht

von Haaren, C. (2004) *Landschaftsplanung*, UTB, Stuttgart

von Haaren, C. and Warren-Kretzschmar, B. (2006) 'The interactive landscape plan: Use and benefits of new technologies in landscape planning, including initial results of the interactive Landscape plan Koenigslutter am Elm, Germany', *Landscape Research*, vol 31, no 1, pp83–105

18
SEA as a Tool for the Conservation and Sustainable Use of Biodiversity in Developing Countries[1]

Jo Treweek (ed), Susie Brownlie, Helen Byron, Thea Jordan, Katia Garcia, Juan Carlos Garcia de Brigard, Tarita Holm, David le Maitre, Vinod Mathur, Susana Muhamad, Elsabeth Olivier, Asha Rajvanshi, Jan Peter Schemmel, Martin Slater and Kaveh Zahedi

Introduction

This chapter explores the use of strategic environmental assessment (SEA) as a tool for the conservation and sustainable use of biodiversity and draws on international experience to outline some of the issues that need to be addressed to make this application effective. Firstly, it makes the case for biodiversity as a cross-cutting issue, which should always be included in strategic assessment and decision-making because it is fundamental to the sustained provision of ecosystem services. Drawing on practical cases, this chapter sets out to establish whether SEA can be successful in promoting biodiversity as a fundamental objective of decision-making and planning and whether it does in fact deliver better outcomes for biodiversity. The chapter then reviews some of the requirements for effective SEA with respect to biodiversity. It presents some examples from South Africa, where outputs of systematic biodiversity conservation planning have been used to support a strategic planning approach. The chapter goes on to consider the roles of some of the different stakeholders in the process and presents some examples of effective stakeholder participation in India to ensure that local community needs for biodiversity are recognized and provided for. Finally, the role of SEA as a tool for engaging government and business partners is considered.

Background: Why consider biodiversity in SEA?

Ecosystems directly support many livelihoods and provide essential goods and services to millions of people (for example, Daily, 1997; Chapin et al, 2000; Brooks and Kennedy, 2004; UNEP, 2005) but they are also being damaged by human activity at an unprecedented rate. The Millennium Ecosystem Assessment (MEA, 2003) report *Ecosystems and Human Well-Being: A Framework for Assessment* concluded that economic development has led to ecosystems being degraded more rapidly and extensively during the past 50 years than at any previous period in history, with some 60 per cent of ecosystem services (for example, pollution control by wetlands, production of fish by coral reefs; absorption of CO_2 by forests) examined in the assessment being used unsustainably. The consequences and costs of this degradation are generally not accounted for in development planning, because most the services (for example, clean water, harvestable crops, fuel wood supply) are considered to be public goods. The fact that there is no market value associated with them means they are typically underpriced or not priced at all (Costanza et al, 1997).

Ecosystems are exposed to cumulative stresses from a wide variety of sources and these are universally increasing, resulting in fragmentation of forests, progressive pollution of surface and groundwater supplies and a general loss of biodiversity at all levels. Human activities are the main threat to biodiversity globally and all available evidence suggests that their impacts on ecosystems will continue to increase as a result of global population growth. Cumulative effects on biodiversity are best anticipated at a strategic level by applying the principles of the ecosystem approach to consider both the full range of activities affecting the ecosystem services which support human well-being (CBD, 2005) and the measures needed to maintain the integrity and resilience of the ecosystems that provide these services (Kremen, 2005).

The MEA (2005) report also emphasizes that the international community needs to make environmental protection a top priority if it wants to meet the Millennium Development Goals (MDGs). Although it receives little direct mention, biodiversity is fundamental to achievement of most of the MDGs because (WRI, 2005):

- Only MDG7 (environmental sustainability) explicitly targets the environment but achieving each of the other MDGs requires functioning ecosystems.
- Failure to conserve and use biological diversity sustainably will perpetuate poverty.
- Biodiversity underpins ecosystem services on which the poor are directly dependant.
- Biodiversity and ecosystem-based 'environmental income' is a major constituent of the household incomes of the rural poor.

In sum, progressive reduction in the diversity of life has direct consequences for human well-being, livelihoods and even conventional economic activity (Le Maitre, 2005; Zahedi, 2005).

Improved planning and management of human activity is vital if biodiversity is to be sustained as the basis for essential ecosystem services. However, the benefits of biodiversity are often unacknowledged in development planning, as are the costs of substituting associated ecosystem services (Treweek et al, 2005a). For example, if all environmental costs and benefits are taken into account, intact mangrove forests have a significantly greater economic value than areas cleared for other uses. Yet mangrove conversion continues at unprecedented rates as the intact resource is less profitable in conventional economic terms of harvestable products (not taking account of the costs of environmental damage). A study in Thailand (MEA, 2005) estimated the value of services provided by intact mangroves to be nearly US$4000 per hectare, double that provided by land converted for shrimp farming (see Figure 18.1).

Although biodiversity resources and services can be valued to help strengthen the case for conservation, many governments rely on other resources to generate inward investment, for example, availability of cheap land or infrastructure. The question of how inward investment opportunities based on biodiversity can be developed and promoted therefore needs to be addressed. This can be achieved only by giving biodiversity prominence throughout the planning and decision-making process so that biodiversity-based alternatives can be developed: simply attaching economic values to biodiversity that will be lost does not necessarily result in better outcomes.

Economic valuation of proposed development plans also can result in highly skewed or partial assessments of the true impacts if the values of the services themselves are not brought into the decision-making process. This is an issue that is being addressed but, ultimately, society and its decision-makers are

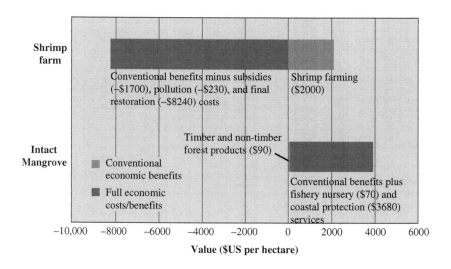

Source: MEA (2005); Sathirathai and Barbier (2001)

Figure 18.1 *The cost of mangrove conversion in southern Thailand*

going to have to deal with the fact that the value of many of the services, notably cultural services, cannot be converted into monetary terms but may be essential to a cultural group's well-being (Daily, 1997). This type of problem has to be included in the decision-making process, perhaps through multi-criteria or other approaches to dealing with these difficult problems. In addition, the role of species-level biodiversity in sustaining most ecosystem services is poorly understood, as are the links to human well-being (for example, Turner et al, 2003; Hooper et al, 2005). These gaps are being addressed and ways need to be found to rapidly integrate new research findings into planning and decision-making processes such as SEA.

Use of SEA as a tool for the conservation and sustainable use of biodiversity

Both environmental impact assessment (EIA) and SEA are recognized in the United Nations Convention on Biological Diversity (CBD) and in other biodiversity-related conventions as important tools for identifying, avoiding, minimizing and mitigating adverse impacts on biodiversity (see, for example, CBD, 1998, 2000, 2002, 2003, 2006; CMS, 2002; Pritchard, 2005; Ramsar Convention on Wetlands, 2002; Ramsar Convention Secretariat, 2004).

EIA has well-documented limitations with respect to effective assessment of impacts on biodiversity (see Box 18.1 and Byron and Treweek, 2005a, b). Within the timeframes and geographic limits normally associated with project-EIA, it is

---

Box 18.1 *Some limitations of project-level EA*

- Project-level EIA cannot adequately address cumulative impacts or impacts at landscape scale: these impacts are frequently neglected as each development proposal is seen in isolation. SEA can help address these impacts within a framework of resource sustainability.
- Project-level EIA seldom addresses impacts on ecological processes and tends to take a 'static view'.
- Project-level EIA is weak in addressing the wider context for development, tending to focus largely on 'on-site' impacts, except where water resources, air quality and (sometimes) landscape aesthetics are involved. It rarely addresses the impacts of site-specific development in terms of the biodiversity and ecosystem functioning of adjacent areas. SEA takes a wider view and looks at the 'bigger picture' landscape processes.
- EIA approaches are concerned with minimizing current impacts (once choices are made) rather then being forward-looking.
- EIA approaches are rarely strategic because they are focused only on single development proposals. SEA can inform sound land-use planning at a landscape scale, allocating land for the most appropriate use and avoiding areas that are a priority for ensuring the persistence of biodiversity. Such planning cannot happen on a piecemeal EIA basis.

difficult to set up biodiversity studies that 'capture' or explain the ecosystem processes and interactions that drive responses to change or to identify the full range of cumulative threats and pressures acting on biodiversity resources (Treweek, 1999). There are also a great many threats to biodiversity associated with developments and activities that are not regulated and that do not require development consent on a case-by-case basis. An example of this is agricultural land use, which is one of the major influences on biodiversity worldwide (Donald, 2004).

SEA is seen as a way to overcome many limitations of project-level EIA (see Box 18.1) by providing opportunities to ensure that the conservation and sustainable use of biodiversity is pursued as a fundamental objective of strategic decision-making and not just as one specialist topic to be considered (Byron and Treweek, 2005b). It does this by providing opportunities to:

- Build biodiversity objectives into land-use, urban or sectoral policies, plans and programmes at international, national, provincial (county or state) or local level.
- Identify biodiversity-friendly alternatives that are compatible with sustained delivery of ecosystem services.
- Identify and manage cumulative threats that might appear insignificant if assessed in isolation.
- Plan effective mitigation strategies to ensure that biodiversity and ecosystem services are sustained.
- Put in place monitoring programmes to provide necessary biodiversity information.
- Strengthen biodiversity partnerships and information networks.
- Create an opportunity for biodiversity specialists to engage with planners and decision-makers.
- Create opportunities for people who need and use biodiversity to influence strategic decisions that might affect their biodiversity resources and access to them.
- Integrate biodiversity into a range of activities that affect the way environmental resources are dealt with, including agriculture, agro-forestry and minerals from central government level downwards.

The move away from isolated case-by-case assessment towards more strategic assessment should facilitate the incorporation of biodiversity-based ecological planning principles aimed at reducing the ongoing fragmentation of landscapes that is characteristic of human development (Pautasso, 2007). Conventional planning philosophies need to be updated to include principles aimed at maximizing connectivity and functional integrity of our remaining natural ecosystems and to ensure they continue to deliver the services our society requires to sustain human well-being. A strategic approach is also required to deliver many biodiversity benefits due to long lead times and the need to secure land, management resources and community support.

The need to consider biodiversity risks and opportunities earlier in the planning of development is well-documented, whether the proponent is a government or a business (Selvam Panneer, 2005; Mandelik et al, 2005; IEEM,

2006). Mathur and Rajvanshi (2005) refer to limitations of EIA carried out for proposed irrigation project in central India, where lack of knowledge and inadequate stakeholder consultation made it impossible to address biodiversity issues effectively and a more strategic approach was ultimately found to be necessary and useful (see Box 18.2). The need to consider biodiversity risks and opportunities earlier in the planning of development is well-documented. SEA is one way to achieve earlier consideration of biodiversity risks and opportunities, so long as it is developed *with* plans and not applied retrospectively, such as when biodiversity constraints and opportunities are considered and incorporated only after key decisions about alternatives have already been made. If SEA is integrated into the planning process, biodiversity-based alternatives can be developed that may carry cost savings and result in more sustainable outcomes in the longer term. Ideally, SEA should be integrated throughout the development process of a policy, plan or programme (PPP), starting as early as possible with an input into development of alternatives and continuing to play a meaningful role in implementation and follow-up, for example, to decide on necessary mitigating actions.

In practical terms, SEA provides an opportunity to look at the 'big picture' and plan practical, viable and long-term solutions for biodiversity based on ecological units (for example, a watershed or catchment). It can also be preemptive in identifying which areas should be developed or conserved and

---

Box 18.2 *SEA for irrigation projects in Central India*

The Human River Irrigation Project in Maharashtra State, India, was discussed in the early 1980s and was granted initial site clearance under EIA Notification in 1994. However, conservation organizations and other stakeholders questioned the ecological viability of the project, as the EIA report had not taken into consideration the close proximity of the proposed location to a tiger reserve. Development consent was ultimately withheld due to the fact that biodiversity conservation concerns (in particular possible impacts on the tiger, its habitat and its movement corridors) had been inadequately addressed in the EIA report.

A 'biodiversity-driven' SEA of a plan for harnessing irrigation benefits for Maharashtra was then conducted by a team from the Wildlife Institute of India, to mainstream biodiversity concerns and facilitate decision-making. The SEA:

- Helped to overcome inconsistencies and uncertainties that had constrained decision-making at the project level.
- Played a meaningful role in addressing biodiversity concerns and thereby facilitating decision-making.
- Played an important role in engaging stakeholders.
- Was effective both as a process for mainstreaming biodiversity in development planning and as a decision-making tool.

Source: Mathur and Rajvanshi (2005)

ensuring that the results of any systematic biodiversity planning – for example, National Biodiversity Strategy Action Plans (NBSAPs) – can be integrated during the development of new strategic proposals.

The challenge to SEA in relation to biodiversity is to go beyond the limits of statutory protection and to increase the emphasis given to biodiversity in economic development planning for different development sectors and in unprotected areas. Even in global hotspots, such as the Cape Floristic Region of South Africa, the protected area network is inadequate to conserve a representative sample of biodiversity and supporting processes (Cowling et al, 2003; Pressey et al, 2003; Retief et al, 2007). As emphasized by the CBD, it is essential to 'mainstream' biodiversity in development sectors and activities taking place outside Protected Areas (IAIA, 2004, 2005; O'Riordan and Stoll-Kleemann, 2002).

Although it is important to minimize loss and mitigate for damage, it is also important to use SEA to create circumstances in which biodiversity is promoted as an integral element of a PPP or indeed as a strategy in itself to ensure that the requirements for sustained delivery of ecosystem services are met (Gelderblom et al, 2002). In other words, SEA should be used as a proactive instrument to identify biodiversity-based development objectives. The motivation for this often comes directly from stakeholders. Because much SEA legislation includes a requirement for explicit, formal (and often documented) involvement of stakeholders, it provides opportunities for people who need and use biodiversity to influence planning decisions and make sure that their needs and aspirations for biodiversity are recognized and taken into consideration (Treweek et al, 2005a). This can make SEA an effective tool for bringing stakeholders 'on-board' and raising the profile of biodiversity issues.

SEA should have an advocacy role, where its primary purpose is to raise the profile of the environment, and an integrative role, where the focus is on combining environmental, social and economic considerations, to assist in the implementation of sustainable development into the planning process (Olivier, 2005).

On the other hand, SEA may be seen as an extra hurdle to negotiate during the development of plans. Biodiversity may have low priority and there may be pressure to carry out rapid assessments at a surface level, which in reality means that biodiversity concerns are 'glossed over'.

SEA as a tool to align biodiversity and development priorities

Regardless of legal requirements for SEA (now in place in about 35 countries), the need for SEA is increasing in more and more countries. For example, in Asia, strategic-level assessments have been carried out for forest plans in Nepal (Khadka et al, 1996), hydropower projects in Nepal (Ahmed, 2006; Uprety, 2005), development of water and drainage infrastructure in Pakistan, for eco-tourism in Sri Lanka (Ahmed, 2006) and for protected areas in India (Rajvanshi, 2005) and in Vietnam for environment-development planning (Schemmel, 2005, see Box 18.3). SEA is also seen as a useful tool for aligning

---

Box 18.3 *SEA for planning of activities in the Tam Dao National Park, Vietnam*

The purpose of the SEA was to provide guidance, for incorporation into the Dai Tu district draft Strategic Environmental Development Plan (SEDP), on the way in which activities can be carried out in the Tam Dao National Park in Vietnam and its buffer zone to: (a) achieve the development objectives set by Dai Tu district, while (b) maintaining sustainability of valued biodiversity.

The SEA was successful in securing commitment from the planning authority to integrate environmental considerations in the SEDP and to revise the plan accordingly. It also secured stakeholder agreement on the need for collaborative management of resources and on the use of community-level Resource Use Plans as a basis for planning

Source: Schemmel (2005)

---

sustainable development strategies with biodiversity objectives, for example in Mauritius (see Box 18.4).

SEA is potentially a good tool for aligning biodiversity and development priorities, but its effectiveness depends strongly on the availability of reliable and up-to-date information regarding biodiversity and its values and uses. SEA both needs information on biodiversity and provides opportunities to collect new information. Different approaches may be required depending on the capacity available in a country to collect and organize biodiversity information.

Relatively few countries in the world benefit from rigorous, systematic spatial planning for biodiversity (Knight et al, 2006) and where it does take place (for example, in the Netherlands and Germany), the resulting outputs are not always communicated effectively to decision-makers. Even in countries where a considerable amount of information is available, it can be difficult to decide how much information should be included in an SEA and what should be done about any information gaps. We therefore need to consider whether different approaches to SEA are required in information-rich or information-poor situations.

A review of the extent to which decision-makers understand the concept of biodiversity in South Africa was carried out through the International Association for Impact Assessment (IAIA) 'Capacity Building for Biodiversity and Impact Assessment' (CBBIA) Project in 2006 (www.iaia.org, Southern Africa Situation Assessment). In South Africa, a lot of effort has been invested in spatial planning for biodiversity, with a primary focus on identifying land that should be prioritized for protection. Despite the availability of reliable information regarding the status of biodiversity in the country, the review revealed a general lack of understanding among planners and decision-makers about the importance of biodiversity and a failure of impact assessment professionals to communicate this effectively. It also strongly reinforced the

Box 18.4 *SEA as a tool to align National Sustainable Development Strategies in Small Island Developing States with biodiversity policies and objectives*

Agenda 21, the Johannesburg Plan of Implementation (JPOI) and the Mauritius Strategy for the Further Implementation of the Programme of Action for the Sustainable Development of Small Island Developing States call upon countries to develop national sustainable development strategies (NSDSs). Strategy development is not a simple, one-off activity: it is a cyclical process that ranges from national vision through formulation, implementation, monitoring and evaluation and needs to engage a broad range of stakeholders. NSDSs integrate and link the three pillars of sustainable development (economic, social and environmental) and should provide guidance to the development of goals that are specific and measurable and conducive to supporting lifestyles of Small Island Developing States.

Most Small Island Developing States rely heavily on biodiversity and natural resources to support semi-subsistence lifestyles and also rapidly expanding eco-tourism. The maintenance of the structure and functioning of ecosystems and the provisioning, regulating and cultural services they provide is critical to sustainable development. SEA can provide a useful framework and approach to strategy development, enabling stakeholders to discuss priorities and agree to development plans that are compatible with biodiversity.

As stated by one of Palau's leading biologists: 'Natural systems have some resilience and are able to recover or adapt to damage as long as that damage does not exceed the tolerance levels of the system. Natural systems have the potential to be seriously damaged if development proceeds without proper environmental consideration. We know very little about the tolerance levels of island ecosystems and are not likely to know when we've gone too far until it is too late. On large continents, mistakes can sometimes be overcome by moving or borrowing resources from another area. On small islands, however, mistakes have much greater consequences. In general, we have only one chance to do things right.'

Source: Holm and Ucherbelau (personal communication)

need for outputs of systematic planning for biodiversity conservation to be presented to planners and decision-makers in a clear and straightforward way (Brownlie et al, 2005).

The outputs of systematic conservation planning therefore should be 'packaged' to suit their application. This might include identification of relative levels of sensitivity to different types of activity so that land-uses can be appropriately zoned. Zoning of development might also be carried out in order to ensure that critical ecosystem services or biodiversity values can be sustained (see Box 18.5). An adaptive and responsive system is also necessary in light of rapidly changing threats to biodiversity. Planners need to be able to readily detect when the condition or status of biodiversity is becoming critical. In countries where there is no systematic planning, a participatory approach is essential to

---

Box 18.5 *SEA helps identify and value ecosystem services provided by urban open space in a rapidly expanding South African city*

Cities are important 'sites' of national development. As urbanization increases, so the demand for cities to perform in a sustainable and efficient manner escalates. It is imperative that cities are planned and managed to enable a balanced utilization of resources and the opportunity for improved quality of life.

In many cases, however, the demand for environmental services exceeds supply, resulting in:

- More frequent flooding with damage to roads, homes and storm water infrastructure, air pollution and communities opposed to new industrial developments.
- Sedimentation of estuaries with less capability to produce fish.
- Poor water quality in rivers and the sea with costs to health, food production and tourism.
- Less resources for the poor, who often rely on environmental services for their livelihoods.

If human systems and natural systems are not aligned, conflict between 'economics' and 'ecology' is prevalent and costs are generated that somebody or a community in the region must bear.

When the uMhlathuze Municipality in South Africa undertook to extend its municipal open space system into the new and expanding municipal area, it attempted to move beyond merely identifying the open space 'footprint' and towards recognition of the status of open space as a vital and valuable physical, social and economic asset. In order to identify, value and protect this asset, a proactive strategic assessment of the services provided by the environment in the uMhlathuze area was undertaken. The study identified the boundaries of areas that should be protected, ecological linkages between them and the value of the ecosystem services provided. The study also identified the planning and management controls that needed to be implemented to protect open spaces within the city. It is estimated that the environmental services or assets within the city of uMhlathuze were worth approximately US$0.24 billion.

Source: Jordan et al (2005)

---

understand local dependencies on biodiversity and ensure that these are recognized in the planning process. SEA can be a very useful tool to enable this.

Key characteristics of biodiversity information to make it useful for application in SEA are that it should be objective and outcome-driven, include 'significance thresholds', be useful for land-use zoning, provide clear triggers for further investigation including those based on ecosystem services, include an implementation strategy that stakeholders can identify with and have 'buy in' from stakeholders.

SEA can also help generate biodiversity information when this is deficient or lacking. One of the reasons why EIA was ineffective as a tool to plan the Indian Human River Irrigation Project referred to in Box 18.2, was the lack of knowledge and understanding regarding biodiversity distribution and behaviour. In particular, movement patterns of tiger populations in the area were poorly understood. An SEA for a larger geographic area, based on ecosystem boundaries, was able to generate necessary information on critical habitat requirements and possible designs for protected areas that would allow development compatible with conservation of tigers in the area (Mathur and Rajvanshi, 2005). If SEA had been applied previously to plan irrigation at a more strategic level, project design and assessment would have been facilitated. The same applies to integrating biodiversity planning principles into, for example, local government development planning processes at an early stage to ensure that the requirements for sustaining biodiversity and ecosystem services are addressed (Gelderblom et al, 2002).

SEA as a means of engaging stakeholders in strategic planning for biodiversity and development

Much existing legislation for SEA includes a requirement for active involvement of stakeholders. SEA can be an effective means of engaging stakeholders in assessment and planning, not only allowing them to express and document concerns but also to make biodiversity uses and values explicit (see Box 18.6).

Getting business on board

Partnerships between government and business are central to a great deal of development. For sectoral development activities, the need to carry standard operational risk assessments to a more strategic level (for example, to manage down biodiversity risk at earlier stages in planning) is increasingly recognized. SEA can help to move companies and governments from damage limitation to strategic avoidance of risks, positive management and enhancement of biodiversity.

Advantages of SEA to a company and partner country government include the ability to set conditions for development and to agree on trade-offs (for example, renegotiation of protected area boundaries, planting of new forests to compensate for loss of forest area or creation of new protected areas to compensate for disturbance of existing ones). Use of SEA for this purpose has been explored by some companies in the oil and gas sector and is increasingly being pursued by governments wishing to let concessions for oil exploration or production.

Rising world energy demand is placing increasing pressure on non-renewable resources, including oil and gas reserves. Oil exploration and production is becoming more common in sensitive environments, including areas of high biodiversity importance. This generates a need for effective techniques to assess and manage risks to biodiversity. For the oil and gas sector, SEA offers a potential tool to complement the EIA and environmental

---

Box 18.6 *SEA of the India Eco-Development Project*

SEA of the India Eco-Development Project was a catalyst for new thinking regarding the benefits of biodiversity and access to biodiversity resources so that impacts on protected areas could be better managed. Indigenous communities living in and around protected areas exerted intense pressure for extraction of fuel, fodder, timber and non-wood forest products, grazing of livestock and encroachment for cultivation and public thoroughfares. These were identified as the most significant threats common to all of the protected areas. The core objective of the SEA was to strengthen biodiversity conservation through community involvement, with the support of and collaboration among donors, implementing agencies, protected area authorities and various stakeholders. The SEA acted as a 'sounding board' to prevent or mitigate significant potential impact where possible and facilitate continuous improvement in overall project performance by providing guidance on options for improved protected area management and effective strategies for maximizing the intended conservation and community benefits.

Involvement of local communities was the key factor, especially during the design and planning of the SEA process. It was through the involvement of local people that the values of ecosystem services could be clarified and alternatives developed to ensure that these would be sustained.

An important lesson was that the use of SEA in the earliest phases of planning can serve as a diagnostic tool for improving the prospects for biodiversity. It can produce proposals based on clear understanding of community perceptions of wellbeing and on community 'ownership' of key eco-development activities.

Source: Rajvanshi (2005)

---

risk procedures already carried out by most companies for their exploration and production projects. It can help to plan activities so that damage to biodiversity can be avoided at an earlier stage, for example, when deciding whether to acquire or operate concessions within a country (see Box 18.7). SEA also may help to identify opportunities to benefit biodiversity in association with sensitively designed operations, for example, by clarifying trade-offs and requirements early (providing a streamlining role). This facilitates more focus on enhancement and less on fire-fighting and damage limitation.

Corporate policies and standards, backed by 'biodiversity champions', can help deliver enhancement through strategic planning (see Box 18.8). There are some very good examples of corporate tools (Shell Biodiversity Standard and Biodiversity Base Map) which could support a strategic approach (Muhamad, 2005). A common barrier is a lack of robust regulatory frameworks within which effective SEA can be developed. It is not unusual for corporate policies and standards to demand higher standards of environmental assessment than those prescribed by government.

Box 18.7 *Use of SEA to help build partnerships between business and government in Brazil: Identifying biodiversity sensitivities*

Oil and gas companies planning activities in new locations need to understand the sensitivity of the environment in which they will be operating, so that they can implement effective management systems and ensure that their operations are appropriately designed and managed.

At the same time, governments need to ensure that their plans for development of energy reserves are compatible with the maintenance of important biodiversity values and ecosystem services. It cannot be assumed that important biodiversity will be readily identifiable from maps or existing databases or included in protected areas. Obtaining reliable information about biodiversity is a challenging and important task for both companies and governments, which benefits from a formal, shared process of assessment at strategic level. SEA helps companies to choose exploration areas with acceptable biodiversity risks and to select technologies appropriate to the types of risk. It helps governments to ensure that the integrity of biodiversity resources can be sustained by avoiding sensitive areas

Source: Garcia (2005)

Box 18.8 *Shell's view of SEA benefits*

SEA is considered to be beneficial because:

- Conditions for development have been set in advance. Trade-offs are agreed.
- Regional planning frameworks provide a better context for implementation of biodiversity strategy and the company is able to play its role and contribute within a broader framework.
- Dos and don'ts are identified at a policy level before development starts.
- Strategic and sustainable social investments are possible to support sustained provision of ecosystem services.
- EIAs can be more efficient.
- Cumulative impacts are taken into account.

Source: Muhamad (2005)

Conclusions

Strategic planning is essential if biodiversity is to be sustained as the basis for critical ecosystem services. Even where systematic spatial planning for biodiversity is carried out, however, the results are not always recognized or taken into consideration in the planning process: there remains a major challenge of 'mainstreaming' biodiversity as an issue and convincing decision-makers of its value and importance. SEA is a potential means of incorporating results of spatial planning for biodiversity into development planning. Although there is little consensus regarding the merits of formalizing SEA for this purpose, there is general agreement that an SEA-type mechanism is required to ensure that biodiversity and associated ecosystem services receive due prominence in the planning and decision-making process. Recent guidance issued by the CBD (2006) reinforces this and provides some general guidance on possible approaches to SEA that could be adopted to encourage more emphasis on biodiversity and ecosystem services. This stresses the need to identify key trends and pressures already affecting biodiversity and then to focus on the main drivers of change associated with a policy or plan, with the aim of addressing the factors driving the trends and reducing the pressures on biodiversity and the ecosystem services it provides.

Note

1 IAIA Capacity Building for Biodiversity and Impact Assessment (CBBIA) Project

References

Ahmed, K. (2006) *Good Practices in Strategic Environmental Assessment: A Review of a Sample of World Bank Activities 1993–2002*, Environmental Department, World Bank, Washington, DC

Brooks, T. and Kennedy, E. (2004) 'The Red List Index as a basis for measuring rate of species loss', *Nature*, vol 431, p1046

Brownlie, S., de Villiers, C., Driver, A., Job, N., von Hase, A. and Maze, K. (2005) 'Systematic conservation planning in the cape floristic region and succulent karoo, South Africa: Enabling sound spatial planning and improved environmental assessment', *Journal of Environmental Assessment and Planning*, vol 7, no 2, p201

Byron, H. and Treweek, J. (eds) (2005a) 'Special issue on biodiversity and impact assessment', *Impact Assessment and Project Appraisal*, vol 23, no 1

Byron, H. and Treweek, J. (eds) (2005b) 'Special issue on strategic environmental assessment and biodiversity', *Journal of Environmental Assessment Planning and Management*, vol 7, no 2

CBD (Convention on Biological Diversity) (1998) 'Decision IV/10 Measures for implementing the Convention on Biological Diversity: C. Impact assessment and minimizing adverse effects: Consideration of measures for the implementation of Article 14', www.biodiv.org/decisions/default.aspx?dec=IV/10

CBD (2000) 'Decision V/18 Impact assessment, liability and redress: I. Impact Assessment', www.biodiv.org/decisions/default.aspx?dec=V/18

CBD (2002) 'Decision VI/7 Further development of guidelines for incorporating biodiversity-related issues into environmental-impact-assessment legislation or processes and in strategic impact assessment', www.biodiv.org/decisions/default.asp?lg=0&dec=VI/7

CBD (2003) 'Proposals for further development and refinement of the guidelines for incorporating biodiversity-related issues into environmental impact assessment legislation or procedures and in strategic impact assessment: Report on ongoing work', www.biodiv.org/doc/meetings/sbstta/sbstta-09/information/sbstta-09-inf-18-en.pdf

CBD (2006) 'COP decision VIII/28 (adopted March 2006) Impact assessment: Voluntary guidelines on biodiversity-inclusive impact assessment', www.biodiv.org/decisions/default.aspx?m=COP-08&id=11042&lg=0

Chapin, F. S., Zaveleta, E. S., Eviners, V. T., Naylor, R. L., Vitousek, P. M., Reynolds, H. L., Hooper, D. U., Lavorel, S., Sala, O. E., Hobbie, S. E., Mack, M. C. and Diaz, S. (2000) 'Consequences of changing biodiversity', *Nature*, vol 405, pp234–242

CMS (2002) 'Resolution 7.2 Impact Assessment and Migratory Species', www.wcmc.org.uk/cms/COP/cop7/proceedings/pdf/en/part_I/Res_Rec/RES_7_02_Impact_Assessment.pdf

Constanza, R., d'Arge, R., de Groot, R., Farber, S., Grasso, M., Hannon, B., Limburg, K., Naeem, S., O'Neill, R. V., Paruelo, J., Raskin, R. G., Sutton, P. and van den Belt, M. (1997) 'The value of the world's ecosystem services and natural capital', *Nature*, vol 387, pp253–260

Cowling, R. M., Pressey, R. L., Rouget, M. and Lombard, A. T. (2003) 'A conservation plan for a global biodiversity hotspot – the Cape Floristic Region, South Africa', *Biological Conservation*, vol 112, pp191–216

Daily, G. C. (ed) (1997). *Nature's Services: Societal Dependence on Natural Ecosystems*, Island Press, Washington, DC

Donald, P. F. (2004) 'Biodiversity impacts of some agricultural commodity production systems', *Conservation Biology*, vol 18, pp17–38

Garcia, K. C. (2005) 'Inclusion of environmental risk assessment within strategic environmental assessment (SEA) as a way to ensure the biodiversity conservation in Brazilian oil and gas exploration and production (E&P) offshore areas', paper presented at the IAIA SEA Conference, Prague

Gelderblom, C. M., Krüger, D., Cedras, L., Sandwith, T. and Audouin, M. (2002) 'Incorporating conservation priorities into planning guidelines for the Western Cape', in Pierce, S. M., Cowling, R. M., Sandwith, T. and MacKinnon, K. (eds) *Mainstreaming Biodiversity in Development: Case Studies from South Africa*, Environment Department, World Bank, Washington, DC, pp117–127

Hooper, D. U., Chapin, F. S., Ewel, J. J., Hector, A., Inchausti, P., Lavorel, S., Lawton, J. H., Lodge, D. M., Loreau, M., Naeem, S., Schmid, B., Setälä, H., Symstad, A. J., Vandermeer, J. and Wardle, D. A. (2005) 'Effects of biodiversity on ecosystem functioning: A consensus of current knowledge', *Ecological Monographs*, vol 75, pp3–35

IAIA (2004) *Best Practice Principles for Biodiversity and Impact Assessment*, IAIA, Fargo, ND

IAIA (2005) *Strategic Environmental Assessment and Biodiversity Guidance*, draft report, IAIA, Fargo, ND

IEEM (Institute of Ecology and Environmental Management) (2006) *Guidelines for Ecological Impact Assessment in the United Kingdom*, IEEM, UK, www.ieem.net/ecia

Jordan, T., Diederichs, N., Mander, M., Markewicz, T. and O'Connor, T. (2005) 'Integrating biodiversity in strategic environmental assessment and spatial planning: A case study of the Umlathuze Municipality, Richards Bay, South Africa', paper presented at the IAIA SEA Conference, Prague

Khadka, R., McEachern, J., Rautianen, O. and Shrestha, U. S. (1996) 'SEA of the Bara Forest Management Plan, Nepal', in Thérivel, R. and Partidário, M. R. (eds) *The Practice of Strategic Environmental Assessment*, Earthscan, London

Knight, A. T., Driver, A., Cowling, R. M., Maze, K., Desmet, P. G., Lombard, A. T., Rouget, M., Botha, M. A., Boshoff, A. F., Castley, J. G., Goodman, P. S., Mackinnon, K., Pierce, S. M., Sims-Castley, R., Stewart, W. I. and Von Hase, A. (2006) 'Designing systematic conservation assessments that promote effective implementation: Best practice from South Africa', *Conservation Biology*, vol 20, pp739–750

Kremen, C. (2005) 'Managing ecosystem services: what do we need to know about their ecology?', *Ecology Letters*, vol 8, pp468–479

Le Maitre, D. (2005) 'Biodiversity and the Millennium Development Goals', paper presented at the IAIA SEA Conference, Prague

Mandelik, Y., Dayan, T. and Feitelson, E. (2005) 'Planning for biodiversity: The role of ecological impact assessment', *Conservation Biology*, vol 19, no 4, pp1254–1261

Mathur, V. B. and Rajvanshi, A. (2005) 'Integrating biodiversity considerations in SEA of an irrigation project in Central India', paper presented at the IAIA SEA Conference, Prague

MEA (Millennium Ecosystem Assessment) (2003) *Ecosystems and Human Well-Being: A Framework for Assessment*, Island Press, Washington, DC

MEA (2005) *Synthesis Report*, Island Press, Washington, DC

Muhamad, S. (2005) 'SEA and implementation of the Shell Biodiversity Strategy: Opportunities and challenges', paper presented at the IAIA SEA Conference, Prague

Olivier, E. (2005) 'Possible methods of entrenching biodiversity principles into all aspects of the Erkuhuleni Integrated Development Plan', paper presented at the IAIA SEA Conference, Prague

O'Riordan, T., Stoll-Kleemann, S. (eds) (2002) *Biodiversity, Sustainability and Human Communities: Protecting Beyond the Protected*, Cambridge University Press, Cambridge

Pautasso, M. (2007) 'Scale dependence of the correlation between human population presence and vertebrate and plant species richness', *Ecology Letters*, vol 10, pp16–24

Pressey, R. L., Cowling, R. M. and Rouget, M. (2003) 'Formulating conservation targets for biodiversity pattern and process in the Cape Floristic Region, South Africa', *Biological Conservation*, vol 112, pp99–127

Pritchard, D. (2005) 'International biodiversity-related treaties and impact assessment – how can they help each other?', *Impact Assessment and Project Appraisal*, vol 23, no 1, pp7–17

Rajvanshi, A. (2005) 'Strengthening biodiversity conservation through community-oriented development projects: Environmental review of the India Eco-Development Project', *Journal of Environmental Assessment Policy and Management*, vol 7, no 2, pp299–325

Ramsar Convention on Wetlands (2002) 'Resolution VIII.9 Guidelines for incorporating biodiversity-related issues into environmental impact assessment legislation and/or processes and in strategic environmental assessment adopted by the Convention on Biological Diversity (CBD), and their relevance to the Ramsar Convention', www.ramsar.org

Ramsar Convention Secretariat (2004) *Ramsar Handbooks for the Wise Use of Wetlands*, Volume 11 Impact Assessment, 2nd Edition, Ramsar Convention Secretariat, Gland, Switzerland

Retief, F., Jones, C. and Jay, S. (2007) 'The status and extent of strategic environmental assessment (SEA) practice in South Africa 1996–2003', *South African Geographical Journal*, vol 89, no 1, pp44–54

Sathirathai, S. and Barbier, E. B. (2001) 'Valuing mangrove conservation in Southern Thailand, contemporary economic policy', *Western Economic Association International*, vol 19, no 2, pp109–122

Schemmel, J. P. (2005) 'SEA of the Tam Dao National Park Buffer Zone in Dai Tu District, Vietnam', paper presented at the IAIA SEA Conference, Prague

Selvam Panneer, L. (2005) 'SEA in basin planning in India', paper presented at the IAIA SEA Conference, Prague

Treweek, J. (1999) *Ecological Impact Assessment*, Blackwell Science, Oxford

Treweek, J., Byron, H. and Le Maitre, D. (2005a) 'SEA practice and biodiversity', position paper for the IAIA SEA Conference, Prague

Treweek, J., Thérivel, R., Thompson, S. and Slater, M. (2005b) 'Principles for the use of strategic environmental assessment as a tool for promoting the conservation and sustainable use of biodiversity', *Journal of Environmental Assessment Policy and Management*, vol 7, no 2, pp173–199

Turner, R. K., Paavola, J., Cooper, P., Farber, S., Jessamy, V. and Georgiou, S. (2003) 'Valuing nature: Lessons learned and future research directions', *Ecological Economics*, vol 46, pp493–510

UNEP (United Nations Environment Programme) (2005) 'Multilateral environmental agreements and pro-poor markets for ecosystem services', discussion paper, High-Level Brainstorming Workshop (10–12 October 2005), London, organized by UNEP, Division of Environmental Conventions in conjunction with the London School of Economics, www.unep.org/dec/support/mdg_meeting_lon.htm

Uprety, B. K. (2005) 'Biodiversity considerations in strategic environmental assessment: A case study of the Nepal Water Plan', *Journal of Environmental Planning and Management*, vol 7, no 2, p247

WRI (World Resources Institute) (2005) *The Wealth of the Poor: Managing Ecosystems to Fight Poverty*, WRI, Washington, DC

Zahedi, K. (2005) 'SEA practice and biodiversity', paper presented at the IAIA SEA Conference, Prague

19
Using SEA to Enhance Poverty Reduction Strategies

Linda Ghanimé, Nathalie Risse, Tamara Levine and Jean-Jacob Sahou

Introduction

The sustainable use of natural resources, recognizing and maintaining ecosystem services and natural capital, is central to economic growth and pro-poor development. Many high-income countries have relied heavily on their natural assets to achieve sustainable economic growth and development, for example, Canada (wood and grain), Australia and New Zealand (agricultural land, products and livestock). In addition, a small number of resource-rich developing countries, notably Botswana, Indonesia and Malaysia, have converted natural wealth into sustained rapid economic growth. Other developing countries, from Bhutan to Kenya, rely on their natural landscapes and diversity of wildlife to develop a significant eco-tourism industry. Yet developing countries with a rich environmental resource base have grown more slowly than others. Often, this is a result of underestimating the value of natural capital for economic and human development, and the mismanagement of environmental resources with the entrenchment of unequal power relationships in the use and management of those resources.

In short, development choices too often fall short of sustainable use. The associated environmental damage is having substantial effects on health and welfare, hindering global capacity to achieve the Millennium Development Goals (MDGs) – the results framework of the Millennium Declaration agreed upon by 191 United Nations (UN) members in 2000, which highlights global priorities for bridging gaps in human health, growing inequalities and environmental sustainability. Poverty Reduction Strategy Papers (PRSPs) were introduced as an instrument to assist countries to strategically examine current and planned macro-economic structural policies and programmes and to specifically identify opportunities to promote long-term growth, reduce poverty and achieve the MDGs. In principle, they provide an opportunity for countries to set specific targets, to reconcile global frameworks and local action, to bring coherence, balance and sustainability to the national development agenda and to take òn the MDG challenge. The same aspiration was behind the launch of National Strategies for Sustainable Development (NSSDs) and Agenda 21 following the Rio Declaration, but the PRSP process offers better hopes of financing assistance.

The first generation of PRSPs have, for the most part, poorly integrated environment-development linkages and the goal of environmental sustainability (Bojö and Reddy, 2003a). However, more recent iterations of PRSPs offer better promise for moving towards country-owned and driven human development processes that give due considerations to social equity, health and environmental sustainability. The application of SEA to the PRSP process is an opportunity to move beyond analysis of the adverse ecological impacts of certain forms of development and towards ex ante upstream analysis for the direct purpose of improved development planning. A more 'upstream' approach to SEA is proactively aimed at the identification of human development opportunities through effective and efficient use of natural resources and environmentally friendly innovation in the choice and design of policies, plans and programmes (PPPs). SEA is also a valuable approach to achieve social benefits and broader cooperative stakeholder participation in policy-making.

This chapter analyses selected experiences in the application of SEA to PRSP processes. After describing the context of the analysis, it exemplifies SEA approaches and experiences in Bénin, Ghana, Rwanda and Tanzania, highlights their main results and draws lessons learned in the form of recommendations for improvement.

PRSP: An important stepping stone instrument for improved national development planning

PRSPs were introduced in 1999 by the World Bank and the International Monetary Fund (IMF) as a precondition for low-income countries to access debt relief and concessional financing from both organizations (World Bank and IMF, 2005). Designed to be renewed every three years, this instrument catalysed international interest in national plans for poverty reduction and has been an impetus for renewed and coordinated assistance to the developing world for social development. It was intended as a participatory process to articulate a comprehensive country-owned strategy for poverty reduction linked to the MDGs. By the end of 2006, 64 countries were engaged in the PRSP process (World Bank, 2006a).

Many have questioned the country ownership of PRSPs and the extent to which these instruments have facilitated nationally driven human development processes fitted to the specific context. For example, the World Bank's Operations Evaluation Department has recommended that the World Bank 'reduce or eliminate uniform requirements and foster better customization' of PRSPs to country circumstances (World Bank, 2004, pxiii). It has also noted a lack of country ownership, maintaining that the World Bank Executive Board's review of a PRSP appears redundant to a country's ongoing planning processes with a potential distorting effect of attenuating ownership in the eyes of most stakeholders' (World Bank, 2004, pxvii).

Over time, however, there appears to have been a successful shift from bank and donor-driven PRSPs to country leadership in setting strategic priorities and driving the process. This has, in many cases, started with a PRSP established under a national process such as the Comprehensive Poverty Reduction and Growth Strategy (CPRGS) in Vietnam, the Action Plan for the Reduction of Absolute Poverty (PARPA) in Mozambique or the National Strategy for Growth and Reduction Poverty (NSGRP) in Tanzania. Moreover, in several cases MDG-based national strategic frameworks for development superseded PRSPs and broadened the social and environment base of national development strategies. Such umbrella strategies comprise a set of coordinated mechanisms and participatory processes to develop vision, long-term goals and targets for development, to coordinate implementation and to review progress and effectiveness in an iterative learning system.

MDGs offer a powerful framework for linking environment and development

The integration of environmental considerations into development processes is called for in Target 9 of MDG7 on environmental sustainability, which stresses the need to: 'Integrate the principles of sustainable development into Country policies and programmes and to reverse the loss of environmental resources.'

A United Nations Development Programme (UNDP, 2006a) evaluation of more than 150 MDG country experiences (based largely on the examination of the country MDG Reports) notes that countries continue to face challenges to achieving progress on MDG7. This is due to various factors, such as a lack of political will, pressure on environmental resources from high use and natural disasters, insufficient governance and planning policies, social unrest and a lack of financial resources. The conclusions of the UNDP analysis is consistent with earlier evaluation reports of PRSPs, which concluded that, despite some country successes and some improvement from the interim to the full version, overall integration of environment into PRSP processes remained low (Bojö and Reddy, 2003a; Bojö et al, 2004).

Evaluations and reviews have shown that most PRSPs lack adequate considerations of environmental sustainability. In their study of the alignment of PRSP with the MDG7 goal of environmental sustainability, Bojö and Reddy (2003b) showed that only 12 of the 28 full PRSPs presented some baseline and targets aligned with MDG7 and attention centred almost exclusively on water and sanitation. They concluded that a major effort was needed to raise the level of attention to environmental sustainability, consistent with MDG7, in the PRSPs.

A further study funded under the Poverty Environment Partnership examined the integration of environment into the PRSP of four countries: Ghana, Honduras, Vietnam and Uganda (Waldman, 2005). It argued that, where environmental concerns had been integrated into PRSPs, the emphasis was on technical solutions and the political aspects of environmental management were ignored. These solutions, while they often met the basic criteria of environmental sustainability, did not contribute to poverty alleviation, livelihood development and the resolution of ingrained power inequalities that will inevitably augment poverty and environmental degradation in the long-term (PEP, 2005).

More recent efforts to integrate environmental sustainability in PRSPs appear more promising. However, their scale and depth are not yet commensurate with the level needed to make significant progress toward environmental sustainability and to meet MDG 2015 targets.

SEA in the context of development cooperation

The role of SEA in development cooperation has been recognized by the Paris Declaration on Aid Effectiveness, adopted in 2005, where both donors and development country partners made a commitment to 'develop and apply common approaches for strategic environmental assessment at the sector and national levels' (OECD, 2005, p7). In response to this commitment, the Organisation for Economic Co-operation and Development (OECD) Development Assistance Committee (DAC) established a Task Team on SEA, co-chaired by the UK Department for International Development (DfID) and UNDP, under the auspices of the OECD DAC Network on Environment and Development Co-operation.

The task team developed guidance on *Applying Strategic Environmental Assessment: Good Practice Guidance for Development Co-operation* (hereafter OECD DAC guidance on SEA). This guidance provides a commonly-agreed and shared model for developing appropriate, fit to purpose applications of SEA in diverse areas relevant to donor agencies and their partners. It defines SEA as: 'Analytical and participatory approaches that aim to integrate environmental considerations into policies, plans and programmes and evaluate the inter linkages with economic and social considerations' (OECD, 2006, pp24–25). Here, SEA is not portrayed as a single, fixed and prescriptive approach used mainly to predict the impacts of PPPs on the environment but as an umbrella approach that uses a basket of tools that is:

- Principles-based.
- Continuous, iterative and adaptive.
- Applied throughout the entire decision-making process.
- Focused on strengthening institutions and governance.
- Adaptive and tailor-made.

The OECD DAC guidance on SEA identifies 12 entry points for process application within three types of PPP:

- **Strategic planning processes led by a developing country:** These include national overarching strategies, programmes and plans; national policy reforms and budget support programmes; sectoral PPPs; infrastructure investments plans and programmes; national and sub-national spatial development plans and programmes and transnational plans and programmes.

- **Development agencies' own processes:** These include donors' country assistance strategies and plans; partnership agreements with other agencies; donors' sector-specific policies; donor-supported public-private infrastructure support facilities and programmes.
- **Other related circumstances:** These include independent review commissions and major private sector-led projects and plans.

In order to enhance the use of SEA and test the effectiveness of the guidance, task team member agencies are undertaking initiatives to better institutionalize the practice of SEA within their organizations. For example, UNDP has developed a Strategic Environmental Assessment Implementation Plan that identifies a series of interventions to systematize SEA application within the agency. This plan also addresses interventions to support countries in the process of developing and implementing MDG-based national development strategies, including PRSPs. To date, although UNDP has successfully assisted countries in SEA application, most often this has been on an *ad hoc* basis. The following section outlines some of these experiences.

The use of SEA to integrate environmental considerations into PRSP: Selected experiences[1]

Additional work needs to be undertaken to integrate environmental and related social concerns into macro-development frameworks and to address long-term sustainability. Reinvigorating the application of SEA in the preparation and implementation of PRSP process is a helpful pathway towards progress on environmental sustainability. SEA systematically examines the relevant environmental issues, and monitors and evaluates implementation processes and successes. SEA that leads to a well-considered PRSP can provide the foundation for improved sectoral and sub-national strategies, plans and programmes.

To date, the full application of SEA to macro-development policy instruments such as PRSPs has been limited. There is, however, a growing body of experience and increasing efforts by donors to build capacity to support the integration of SEA into PRSP development and implementation processes. For example, countries such as Bénin, Ghana, Rwanda and Tanzania have carried out an SEA of their PRSPs and an analysis of their experiences provides lessons and insights on practice in this area.

SEA context and approaches

SEA of the Bénin PRSP 2007–2009
Source: République du Bénin (2006a, b); LIFAD and ABPEE (2006); UNDP (2006c)
Bénin's first PRSP covered the period 2003–2005. It comprised quantitative economic and social objectives until 2015 including, for example, increase in gross domestic product (GDP), increase in the real income per inhabitant, reduction of the incidence of urban and rural poverty and increase in life expectancy at birth.

In 2005, an ex post SEA of this PRSP was carried out by national consultants, under the guidance of a support committee composed of the Bénin Agency for the Environment, the German Technical Cooperation (GTZ) and UNDP. This SEA aimed, among other things, to: synthesize existing information on the state of the environment in Bénin; analyse the ways in which the first PRSP took into account environmental factors related to poverty; and identify relevant effects of the first PRSP on prior environmental objectives in order to better prepare SEA of the second PRSP for the period 2007–2009.

The SEA covered critical issues of poverty reduction and environmental management, mainly in a descriptive manner. It concluded that the basis on which environmental strategies are to be used as strategies to reduce poverty was not well-defined, nor were indicators of effect and impact and targets and actions needed to reach the MDGs. It also showed that there was insufficient integration of environmental considerations in the majority of the agency planning and implementation processes that were reviewed; weak consideration of the Poverty Reduction Strategy by certain agencies; and the absence of a functional framework to facilitate the integration of the environment in different sectors.

Taking into account lessons learned from the SEA of the first PRSP and experience from other African countries, the second PRSP – called Stratégie de Croissance et de Réduction de la Pauvreté (SCRP) – aimed to define a policy of sustainable economic growth and poverty reduction compatible with the MDGs. One of its specific aims is to ensure 'greening' of the PRSP by a better integration of environmental aspects and by improving the relations between environment and poverty through an integrated approach to SEA.

The SCRP was prepared by the Permanent Secretariat of the National Commission for Development and the Fight against Poverty. Nine thematic groups were in charge of the formulation of different policies that formed the basis of the Strategy (for example, social sectors and basic infrastructures; good governance, decentralization and capacity-building; private sector and employment). One of these groups, called Environment and Quality of Life, was responsible for preparing the environmental dimensions, covering both the probable impacts and externalities of other sector policies and identifying the responses to these externalities, as well as 'stand alone' environmental proposals. Both are essential to environmental mainstreaming and progress on environmental sustainability.

The policies developed by the thematic groups were consolidated in the first draft of the SCRP. A workshop held in November 2006 aimed to: (a) analyse the coherence and consistency between policies prepared by different groups; (b) analyse the extent to which they respond to priority national needs; and (c) propose options deriving from SEA.

Various actors have been involved in the environmental mainstreaming process, such as the Environmental Protection Agency and the National Commission to fight poverty. The media – mainly press representatives – were also engaged to ensure communication between local elected representatives and their constituent communities. Meetings with departmental representatives, public administration and civil society in Bénin were organized to receive their comments on the first draft of the SCRP and to encourage them to take it into account in their local planning policies. In addition, training of local elected people was organized to sensitize them to the SCRP greening process and its benefits. Economic and financial costs of the greening process are to be evaluated.

SEA of the Ghana's PRSP 2003–2005

Source: Dalal-Clayton and Sadler (2005); OECD (2006); IAIA (2005); UNDP (2006b); NDPC and EPA (2004a, b); EPA Ghana (2006); Republic of Ghana (2005)

Ghana was one of the first countries to make use of SEA as a vehicle for reviewing and refining a PRSP. In February 2002, the government of Ghana published a first draft of the Ghanian Poverty Reduction Strategy (GPRS), which was intended to be the overarching policy framework to set the focus and tone of all other government policies. After review, this first draft was modified and reissued for the period 2003–2005.

An SEA of the GPRS 2003–2005 was initiated in response to the following weaknesses of the first draft: (a) the environment was treated as a sectoral or 'add-on' issue rather than a cross-cutting one so the environmental impacts of the policies and strategies for delivering growth and poverty reduction were not adequately addressed; and (b) the potential for sustainable development of key resources (land, forests and water) needed further analysis to drive pro-poor economic growth. It took place within a collaborating framework involving ministries, departments and agencies, district assemblies, civil society organizations and non-governmental organizations (NGOs). It was supported financially by the government of the Netherlands.

SEA was applied to all themes and sectors of the GPRS, covered national, regional and district levels. The approach involved establishing an evaluation framework for reviewing the sectoral dimensions of the GPRS that:

- Assesses the extent to which environment has been integrated in discussion and analysis of policies.
- Examines the environmental opportunities and risks presented by individual policies.
- Identifies and strengthens priority policy actions that benefit the poor and the environment.
- Increases understanding of the spatial dimensions of policies at international, national, regional and district levels.
- Analyses the effectiveness of policies in terms of their ease of implementation, timescale, costs and ability to bring benefits to the poor and the environment.

It also involved:

- Conducting sustainability appraisal (SEA) of the District Medium Term Development Plans.
- Developing methods for assessing PPPs (such as matrices and checklists).

- Creating individual products such as handbooks, training manuals, guidelines and reports.
- Articulating planning concepts and frameworks to support PPP preparation, implementation and monitoring.
- Building capacity with training sessions, workshops and meetings.
- Developing proposals for institutional strengthening and support for good governance.

Different tools (matrices, sustainability tests, baseline reviews and geographic information systems) were used and a wide range of stakeholders was involved in the SEA process as evidenced by the endorsement of the process by 27 ministries, departments and agencies, 108 district assemblies (out of 110), parliamentary representatives, civil society, NGOs, the Bank of Ghana and business associations. In total, more than 600 individuals were involved in the work over a nine-month period.

SEA of the Rwanda Economic Development and Poverty Reduction Strategy

Source: UNDP (2005, 2006b); World Bank (2006b); Rwanda Development Partners (2006); Evans et al (2006); Opio-Odongo (2006)

Rwanda first developed a PRSP in 2002. The next version (Rwanda's Poverty Reduction Strategy 2002–2005) emphasized the need for reconciliation, regional cooperation and good governance but insufficiently dealt with environment as a cross-cutting issue. As stressed by a final independent evaluation of this process (Evans et al, 2006), environmental considerations were not integrated systematically into the different areas of government policy and the analysis of linkages between environment, land-use policies and reduction of poverty were insufficient.

Recognizing these shortcomings, the government of Rwanda decided that poverty-environment concerns must be better integrated in the revised PRSP, titled the Economic Development and Poverty Reduction Strategy (EDPRS). This strategy represents a comprehensive development agenda considered as an operational tool, which is supported by detailed sector strategic plans.

To contribute to the integration of environment into the EDPRS, the Minister of State for Environment endorsed the establishment of a National Task Team (NTT). The NTT, supported by the Poverty Environment Initiative (PEI) and the Decentralized Environment Management Project (DEMP)[2] applied a strategy based on SEA basic principles to facilitate the integration of environment into the EDPRS. (This strategy aims particularly to UNDP, 2006b, pp6–7):

- Generate well-packaged information and knowledge materials that stakeholders can use in evidence-based lobbying and advocacy to ensure effective embedding of environment in the EDPRS.
- Influence indicator development and survey instruments in order to ensure adequate incorporation of poverty-environment indicators in the EDPRS monitoring and evaluation framework.

- Support targeted analysis of why environment matters and the wisdom of increasing investment in environment and natural resources.
- Enable stakeholders to acquire the knowledge and tools for mainstreaming environment so that they can animate and influence practical mainstreaming at the sector and district levels.
- Ensure that environmental stakeholders were ... represented in the various committees of the national coordination structures, including the EDPRS drafting committee.
- Ensure that stakeholders at the district levels were abreast of and attuned to environmental mainstreaming efforts in the country.
- Draw upon experiences with environmental mainstreaming in the Africa region.

In the framework of this strategy, the NTT carried out a training workshop on the application of SEA at the district level. The main outcomes of the training comprised: (a) exposing district planners and environment officers to some of SEA tools relevant to district development planning; (b) extracting concrete recommendations based on learning experience that the NTT could use for promoting effective mainstreaming of natural resource and environment issues in the EDPRS; and (c) proposing strategies for a possible scaling up of SEA during phase II of the PEI, focusing on capacity development.

Moreover, consistent with the Vision 2020 Strategy (the government's long-term strategy for national transformation), the promotion of SEA was intended to strengthen Rwanda's institutional capacity to consider environmental issues when developing or revising national, sector and district development strategies and plans.

Various factors were identified for supporting SEA application in Rwanda, namely: (a) the political visibility of environmental agenda (recognizing, among other things, the level and scope of environmental degradation and the insufficient attention given so far to the management of environmental resources); (b) progress with policy, legal and institutional frameworks for promoting sustainable development and for integrating planning with budgeting; (c) a commitment to the promotion of democratic governance with a strong decentralization policy that is enhancing a people-driven sustainable development process; (d) an impressive beginning to integrated policy-making through application of the sector-wide approach and thematic cluster; and (e) a demonstrated commitment to undertaking environmental assessment of development programmes.

SEA of the Tanzania National Strategy for Growth and Reduction of Poverty

Source: OECD (2006); IAIA (2005); United Republic of Tanzania Vice-President's Office (2004); UNDP (2006b); Ceche (2006); Lyatuu (2006)

Tanzania developed its first PRSP (2000–2003) in response to the National Poverty Eradication Strategy and the Heavily-Indebted Poor Countries initiative. This PRSP identified six priority sectors for poverty reduction, namely primary education, rural roads, water and sanitation, judiciary, health and agriculture. In October 2003, the government launched a one-year review of the PRSP. The review aimed at: (a) updating the PRSP by making it more comprehensive and pro-poor; (b) identifying gaps or areas for improvement; and (c) strengthening awareness and national ownership of the strategy document. The consultations organized during the review process highlighted various needs, including mainstreaming priority cross-cutting issues, such as governance, HIV/Aids and environment, and revising PRSP indicators and targets especially for environment, governance and agriculture.

This review process led to the second generation PRSP – called National Strategy for Growth and Reduction of Poverty (NSGRP) 2005–2010. The new strategy changed from priority sectors to a focus on development clusters, and adopted an outcome approach, which counts on the contribution of all sectors to deliver specific outcomes. The clusters are: growth and reduction of income poverty; improved quality of life and social well-being; and good governance and accountability. In order to ensure proper monitoring of performance, the use of indicators was strongly emphasized and an integrated approach incorporating key SEA elements was adopted (for example, systematic and integrated assessment to incorporate environment in sector policies and in the national budget).

Within the framework of the NSGRP, an SEA was also applied to the second Poverty Reduction Support Credit (PRSC), an instrument introduced by the World Bank to support countries that are eligible for International Development Credits to support policy and institutional forms necessary for poverty reduction. This SEA aimed to assess the cumulative environmental and socio-economic impacts of the PPPs supported by the NSGRP, and to propose appropriate measures related to mitigation, monitoring and capacity strengthening. Initiated by the government of Tanzania and supported by the World Bank, it focused on reform of the Crop Boards, the development of a strategic plan to operationalize implementation of the Land Act and Village Land Act, the introduction of a Road Act to support the maintenance and rehabilitation of district roads, and a new business licensing system. It also took into account of the capacity for environmental management and assessment, and looked at the objectives, methods used, barriers, outcomes achieved and the remaining challenges.

Key results

The analysis of the Bénin, Ghana, Rwanda and Tanzania experiences illustrates key results from the application of SEA to PRSP:

- Useful for mainstreaming environment and sustainability into macro-development frameworks such as PRSPs.
- Gave guidance and recommendations for the formulation of next generations of national development plans.
- Helped to structure and define the environmental content.
- Increased opportunities for resources mobilization.
- Opened political space to test policies and strategies through project recommendations emanating from the 'greened' PRSPs.
- Raised awareness of environmental issues in macro-policy and planning.
- Helped to build capacity for environmental mainstreaming, and increased cooperation and collaboration between groups (for example, planning and environmental agencies).

- Provided the context for refining sector and district level plans and programmes.
- Helped to balance competing concerns relating to natural resources and economic conditions.
- Raised issues on what is needed for effective mainstreaming of environment action (for example, data needed, support from sector and district leaders, and so on).
- Assisted with refining priority and target setting for reaching the MDGs.
- Supported improved reporting on MDG progress.

The above results of SEA go well beyond the integration of the environment in the planning process, and include good governance, awareness-raising, multi-sectoral planning and reporting aspects. These experiences also confirm the added value of SEA in the preparation of macro-level overarching strategies such as PRSP and highlight SEA contributions in terms of helping countries to reach the MDGs, in particular MDG7 on environmental sustainability.

In Bénin for example, ex post assessment of the first PRSP led to a better identification of the environmental needs of the second PRSP. In the second PRSP, SEA was applied throughout the development process and in a cross-cutting manner; this helped to structure and define the environmental content of the PRSP. It increased opportunities for mobilizing resources in environment and opened political space to test policies and strategies through project recommendations from the 'greened' PRSP. Also, it helped, to raise awareness on environmental issues and to promote partnerships and inter-agency cooperation (between, for example, the Ministry in charge of the Environment and the National Commission to fight poverty).

In Ghana, SEA of the GPRS led to the development of environmental policies, legislation and regulations that will prevent or mitigate future environmental and poverty impacts of economic growth measures. It provided the context for refining sector policies through highlighting conflicting objectives where a closer look at appropriate policy measures was needed: for example, it showed that the health policy to eradicate malaria had the potential to conflict with the Ministry of Food and Agriculture's policy to encourage irrigation through construction of small dams (NDPC and EPA, 2004a). It also provided clear findings and recommendations that contributed to the update of the subsequent GPRS, 2006–2009, which has additional environmental focus and policies. These findings and recommendations included key environmental concerns (soil degradation, loss of biodiversity, forest cover, and so on) and sources of data for establishing baselines on these concerns in GPRS 2006–2009 relevant to the MDGs.

The key success of the SEA of the GPRS was that it raised awareness about environmental issues and considerations in policy and planning: it put the environment on the development policy agenda (at national, sectoral and district level) and enabled policy and planning stakeholders to understand the wider impacts of certain PPPs on the environment, economic growth and poverty reduction (NDPC and EPA, 2004b). In addition, SEA led to improved relations between the National Development Planning Commission (NDPC) and environmental agencies such as the Environmental Protection Agency

(EPA). The oversights that were rectified by the SEA strengthened relations between Ministers and District Assemblies and the centralized core group that produced the GPRS. Finally, SEA identified lack of attention to natural resources and the environment as a major contributory factor in weakening macro-economic performance and led to a changing attitude of officials responsible for planning and budgeting toward recognizing the opportunities in integrating environment into other PPPs. For example, the Ministry of Lands and Forestry adopted a novel plan of marketing rattan and bamboo after having been influenced by the SEA and struggling to reduce pressure on natural forest resources.

In Rwanda, the workshop on SEA raised important issues related to data needed for effective environmental mainstreaming, requisite support from sector and district leaders and decision-makers, adequate timeframe for training and follow-up and need for a trainer of trainers prior to scaling up.

Finally, in Tanzania, the integrated approach used to incorporate environment in the NSGRP helped to set specific quantitative goals and targets for the environment against an established baseline, which facilitated good planning and accountability for delivering results and monitoring progress in concrete terms. Examples of targets set in the Tanzanian NSGRP include (Ceche, 2006):

- Increased proportion of rural population with access to clean and safe water from 53 per cent in 2003 to 65 per cent in 2010 within 30 minutes time spent on collection of water.
- Increased urban population with access to clean and safe water from 73 per cent in 2003 to 90 per cent by 2010.
- Increased access to improved sewerage facilities from 17 per cent in 2003 to 30 per cent in 2010 in respective urban areas.
- 100 per cent of schools to have adequate sanitary facilities by 2010.
- Reduced water related environmental pollution levels from 20 per cent in 2003 to 10 per cent in 2010.

The more recent reviews (UNDP, 2010) of MDG progress in Tanzania shows that while there has been good progress on access to clean water many of these targets need further attention.

The integrated environmental approach also allowed development of a set of poverty-environment indicators as part of the national poverty monitoring system that will be used to assist reporting on the MDGs (OECD, 2006).

Key challenges

Still a new evolving practice, SEA application to PRSP faces a number of challenges including political, organizational, institutional and methodological concerns. In order to improve good practice, the following SEA components need to be reinforced:

- **Properly resource the process – including financial means – to ensure implementation of SEA recommendations:** In Bénin, for example, progress in applying SEA to the SCRP was sometimes hard, due to lack of political support and inadequate financial and human resources capacity. The greening process was also characterized by a lack of time (due to too tight an agenda for performing the process), weak capacity for prioritization and weak mainstreaming of gender issues (which have a close link to environmental considerations). In addition, the SEA results were weakened at national level as the costing of the SCRP had not foreseen the required resources to face environmental risks.

- **Reinforce the information and data systems:** In Ghana, experience indicated that the level of detail of information and data for the SEA was low, for example, information concerning some aspects of the GPRS (for example, spatial location of schools, health clinics, distribution of natural resources) was poor and few districts possessed digital maps or the capacity to produce maps in computer generated reports. There were also problems concerning the collation and storage, in easily accessible form, of data, at national level (NDPC and EPA, 2004a).

- **Adequately design and prepare workshops, and get the right people involved:** In Rwanda the absence of sector staff from the Ministry of Local Government was of concern at the training workshop on SEA organized during the elaboration of the EDPRS. Therefore, the district planners at the training workshop questioned the levels of support they could count on from local government representatives in applying the skills acquired from the training workshop to their regular work. In addition, although this training was welcomed by workshop participants, some were not proficient in both French and Kinyarwanda (the local language). This made animated learning difficult to achieve (UNDP, 2006b).

- **Improve the application of SEA as a planning and decision-making process:** The biggest challenge in Rwanda was the perception of SEA as a narrow environmental assessment (EA) tool, rather than a more comprehensive and upstream mainstreaming approach (the model for SEA application defined in the OECD DAC guidance on SEA). This led to misunderstandings between the donors and the government agency on what an SEA process could offer to mainstream environment in the PRSP process.

- **Build capacity in SEA and decentralize national environmental mainstreaming experiences at sub-national government levels:** In Tanzania, the SEA of the NSGRP showed that many PPPs could potentially improve environmental sustainability but there was limited capacity to implement, enforce and monitor them. This was a major obstacle. Limited experience with the use of SEA also constrained the development of appropriate regulations and guidelines. There is also a limited grasp of SEA and what it can offer among stakeholders; only now are many starting to learn about the use of EIA. Moreover, experience in Tanzania highlighted difficulties in replicating national-level success in planning at the district and village levels and in linking the country's multilateral commitments to its national plan (Ceche, 2006).

Looking ahead

Experience with the application of SEA to PRSPs confirm that each application of SEA is its own unique case, that there is no single right approach to adopt and that the benefits and challenges of implementing SEA are diverse. Based on our analysis of practice, a number of lessons to improve the effectiveness of SEA as an environmental mainstreaming approach can be identified. These are listed below in the form of recommendations for enhancing PRSPs:

- **Identify key entry points, and recognize and effectively use windows of opportunity:** Finding the right time to introduce SEA into a macro-development planning process such as the PRSP, as well as the right entry points, can significantly increase the willingness of local actors to engage. In the Bénin experience, for example, implementing SEA at the beginning of the PRSP process, elaborating SEA concomitantly to the PRSP and integrating environment in a cross-cutting manner to other sectors have led to good environmental mainstreaming results.
- **Problem formulation:** Defining problems in such a way as to overcome different ideologies of development, as well as conflicting material and political interests, facilitates engagement. Defining issues in terms of 'livelihoods', 'health' and 'vulnerability' –the framework for poverty and environment links – have helped overcome traditional fears of SEA as an environment-focused process that fails to address participant concerns.
- **Stop stand-alone environmental assessment writing exercises** and avoid considering SEA as only a document but rather as a process integrated within the broader strategic national development planning process.
- **Institutionalize the practice:** SEA is not something you do and finish. It is a matter of institutionalization. Governments are the key players and have their own policies: SEA has to fit to these as well as to a country's circumstances and capacities. It has to be accompanied by capacity-building actions and support material. In Bénin, the environmental desks have been well involved in the SEA process and are now being trained for the implementation phases. Also, in the four countries analysed, the development of guidelines on environmental mainstreaming was useful in supporting the process of integrating the environment into the PRSP.
- **Broad and effective participation** of all key stakeholders is necessary for local ownership, resolution of conflict and innovation in the SEA process. SEA endeavours to promote equitable access to information and ensure representation of issues, accountability and legitimacy of government and civil society organizations engaged in the process. In Ghana, the wide range of national, sectoral and district level stakeholders involved in the GPRS process was crucial not only to raise awareness on environmental issues, opportunities and constraints but also to ensure its ownership. In Bénin, involving departmental representatives in the greening process and assisting local authorities in implementing the SEA recommendations through pilot demonstration projects was also useful for a better appropriation of the process.

- **Reliable evidence** is essential to convince decision-makers of the benefit and value added by SEA. Therefore, the quality of analytical work and the adequate articulation of poverty-environmental linkages in terms that are meaningful to decision-makers (particularly economic information) will critically affect the value and applicability of SEA results. Evidence, however, must be based not only on remote technical information but rather incorporate local understanding and studies.
- **Develop dialogue:** The extent of coherence, cooperation and collaboration between the stakeholders is essential for ensuring good SEA outcomes. In Bénin, for example, all the donors active in environment meet as a group on a monthly basis. Partners who are supporting the SEA process of the SCRP (UNDP and GTZ) have developed and shared widely information within the group. This has helped to build a common vision around some key concepts such as environmental costs and environmental assessments, and has increased the awareness of donor group members on the importance of mainstreaming environmental issues in policies and strategies. This will surely facilitate resources allocation for the implementation of projects and programmes emanating from the SEA process.
- **Ensure economic and financial analysis is part of the process:** It is important that SEA integrates economic and financial analysis for a complete needs assessment. An SEA will recognize economic cost and benefits of recommendations for proposals to be considered by finance agencies. Developing countries need to estimate the cost and benefits of policy measures and cost the proposed interventions as part of the PRSP.
- **Innovative solutions:** There has been a tendency for SEA of PRSPs to focus on technical solutions and to exclude the issues that draw attention to politicized aspects of the environment. SEA must seek to move beyond traditional discourses related to environment and development linkages to assess complex relationships and harness citizen innovation and creativity to find solutions best for all.
- **Good packaging of SEA:** How SEA is packaged for decision-makers is critical for its success. In Ghana, for example, success of SEA was related, among other things, to the fact that SEA consisted of an executive summary (for decision-makers), a process report, a contents report, an SEA manual for national and district level, advisory notes and a CD-Rom. There was also a leaflet on SEA in pictures and capacity-building for high-level representatives. In Bénin, a SEA manual is being elaborated to facilitate the decision-making process. Finally, in Rwanda, some of the principles that informed SEA application involved keeping it simple and practical, as well as concentrating on aspects that would enable participants to appreciate the relevance and merits of SEA application to the mainstreaming agenda.
- **Process convergence:** Poverty and social impact assessment (PSIA) is the main diagnostic tool used to assess the results of poverty reduction strategies. While PSIA does take account of some long-term distributional environmental impacts, environment and poverty linkages are not explicitly addressed. This suggests a need to bring together the best of both practices to advance the common objective of support to human development.

Conclusion

Endorsed by 191 UN member states to tackle poverty and promote human development, the MDGs stress the need to improve environmental sustainability integration in country development strategies. As argued in this chapter, SEA is a critical means of doing so. It is a complete environmental mainstreaming approach which serves as a framework for: formulating next generations of national development plans; helping to structure and define the environmental content; refining sector and district-level plans and programmes; assisting with refining priority and target-setting for reaching the MDGs; and supporting improved reporting on MDG progress. SEA also contributes to: increased opportunities for resources mobilization; 'opening political space' to test policies and strategies through project recommendations from 'greened' PRSPs; raising awareness of environmental issues in macro-policy and planning; building capacity for environmental mainstreaming and increasing cooperation and collaboration between groups; balancing competing concerns relating to

---

Lessons learned from the application of SEA to PRSP

- Identify key entry points, and recognize and effectively use windows of opportunity to increase the willingness of local actors to engage.
- Formulate problems in such a way as to facilitate engagement and overcome traditional fears of SEA as a narrow environment-focused process.
- Stop stand-alone environmental assessment writing exercises and avoid considering SEA only as a document but rather as a process integrated within the broader strategic national development planning process.
- Institutionalize SEA practice.
- Encourage broad and effective participation in order to contribute to local ownership, resolution of conflict and innovation in the SEA process.
- Improve SEA reliability by ensuring quality of analytical work and the adequate articulation of poverty-environmental linkages – in language meaningful to decision-makers.
- Develop dialogue to build a common vision on key environmental components, to align donor group members on priority to be mainstreamed in policies and strategies and to facilitate resources allocation for programmes emanating from the SEA process.
- Ensure economic and financial analysis are part of the SEA process.
- Focus on innovative solutions by drawing attention to not only technical but also political aspects, and by assessing complex relationships and harness citizen creativity to find solutions best for all.
- Package SEA for successful engagement of stakeholders and decision-makers.
- Increase cooperation between SEA and PSIA practitioners in the integration of environmental considerations into PRSPs and ensure they bring together the best of both processes to the common objective of support to human development.

natural resources and economic conditions; and raising issues on what is needed for efficiently mainstreaming environment.

Additional efforts are needed to: properly resource the process including financial means to ensure implementation of SEA recommendations; reinforce the information and data systems for carrying out the SEA; adequately design and prepare SEA workshops and get the right people involved; improve the application of SEA as a planning and decision-making process; build capacity on SEA and decentralize national environmental mainstreaming experiences at sub-national government levels.

The lessons of experience are growing as is the number of case studies. Accordingly, results from the application of SEA to overarching national development strategies such as PRSP need to be documented more systematically in the future with a common evaluation framework. Further experience and documentation of the added value and benefits of applying a broad scope SEA approach to macro-development levels should lead to recognition of the value of SEA as a means of mainstreaming the environment as a pathway for human development, thereby contributing to global knowledge and to helping countries shift to their own learning systems of development.

Acknowledgements

This work benefited from discussions and exchanges with several people participating in the application of SEA to Poverty Reduction Strategies, PRSPs and National Development Strategies. We thank Gertrude Lyatuu (UNDP, Tanzania), Joseph-Opio-Odongo (UNDP, Regional Service Centre for Eastern and Southern Africa, Nairobi), and Jean-Paul Penrose (Consultant) for their useful contribution. We are also grateful to the panel members of the SEA Prague Conference session on SEA and Poverty Reduction Strategies held in 2005, namely Evans Darko-Mensah (Consultant, Environmental Protection Agency, Ghana), John Horberry (Consultant), Ineke Steinhauer (Netherlands Commission for Environmental Impact Assessment) and Laura Tlaiye (World Bank, Environment Department), and to all the participants who attended this session.

Notes

1 This section is based on the summary paper of session B1 'Strategic Environmental Assessment in Poverty Reduction Strategies' prepared by Ghanimé (2005) after the IAIA SEA Conference, Prague.
2 Project funded by the Swedish International Development Cooperation Agency (SIDA) and UNDP.

References

Bojö, J. and Reddy, R. C. (2003a) *Status and Evolution of Environmental Priorities in the Poverty Reduction Strategies: An Assessment of Fifty Poverty Reduction Strategy*

Papers, Environmental Economic Series, paper no 93, World Bank Environment Department, Washington, DC

Bojö, J. and Reddy, R. C. (2003b) *Poverty Reduction Strategies and the Millenium Development Goal on Environmental Sustainability: Opportunities for Alignment*, Environmental Economic Series, paper no 92, World Bank Environment Department, Washington, DC

Bojö, J., Green, K., Kishore, S., Pilapitiya, S. and Reddy, R. C. (2004) *Environment in Poverty Reduction Strategies and Poverty Reduction Support Credits*, paper no 102, World Bank Environment Department, Washington, DC, www.basel.int/industry/wkshop-071206/3.%20Additional%20materials/Bojo%20paper%20on%20env%20in%20PRSPs.pdf

Ceche, B. (2006) 'Summary of the presentation entitled: "Ecosystem services in National Development and Poverty Reduction Strategies: The Tanzanian Experience"', *Biodiversity in European Development Cooperation Conference*, Paris, 19–21 September 2006

Dalal-Clayton, B. and Sadler, B. (2005) *Strategic Environmental Assessment: A Sourcebook and Reference Guide to International Experience*, Earthscan, London

EPA Ghana (Environmental Protection Agency) (2006) 'Hands-on strategic environmental assessment training workshop for district planners in Rwanda', report, EPA Ghana, Accra

Evans, A., Piron, L. H., Curran, Z. and Driscoll, R. (2006) *Independent Evaluation of Rwanda's Poverty Reduction Strategy 2002–2005 (PRSP1)*, Overseas Development Institute and Institute of Development Studies, UK

Ghanimé, L. (2005) 'International experience and perspectives in SEA: Global Conference on strategic environmental assessment', *Summary of the session B1: Strategic Environmental Assessment in Poverty Reduction Strategies*, Prague

IAIA (International Association for Impact Assessment) (2005) 'International Experience and Perspectives in SEA: Conference on Strategic Environmental Assessment', final programme, Prague, 26–30 September 2005

LIFAD and ABPEE (2006) *Etude initiale des impacts environnementaux du premier DSRP dans le cadre d'une évaluation environnementale stratégique (EES) au Bénin*, supported by UNDP, the Bénin Ministry of the Environment, Habitat and Urban Planning and the Federal Ministry for Economic Cooperation and Development

Lyatuu, G. (2006) personal communication, UNDP, Tanzania

NDPC and EPA (National Development Planning Commission and Environmental Protection Agency Ghana) (2004a) 'Draft report of the SEA of the GPRS', NDPC and EPA, Accra, Ghana

NDPC and EPA (2004b) 'Report of the SEA of the GPRS', executive summary, NDPC and EPA, Accra, Ghana

OECD (Organisation for Economic Co-operation and Development) (2005) 'Paris Declaration on aid effectiveness: Ownership, harmonization, alignment, results and mutual accountability', high-level forum, Paris, 18 February–2 March 2005, www.oecd.org/document/18/0,2340,en_2649_3236398_35401554_1_1_1_1,00.html

OECD (2006) *DAC Guidelines and Reference Series: Applying Strategic Environmental Assessment: Good Practice Guidance for Development Co-operation*, OECD, Paris

Opio-Odongo, J. (2006) personal communication, UNDP, Regional Service Centre for Eastern and Southern Africa

PEP (Poverty-Environment Partnership) (2005) *Sustaining the Environment to Fight Poverty and Achieve the MDGs: The Economic Case and Priorities for Action*, UNDP, New York

Republic of Ghana (2005) 'Growth and Poverty Reduction Strategy (GPRS II) (2006–2009)', National Development Planning Commission, Ghana

République du Bénin (2006a) 'Termes de références: Elaboration de la Deuxième Génération du Document de Stratégie de Réduction de la Pauvreté (DSRPII) du Bénin', Ministère du Développement de l'Economie et des Finances, Commission Nationale pour le Développement et la Lutte contre la Pauvreté et Secrétariat Permanent, Bénin

République du Bénin (2006b) 'Atelier sur l'intégration de l'environnement dans le DSRPII', Ministère de l'Environnement et de Protection de la Nature et Agence Béninoise pour l'Environnement, Bénin

Rwanda Development Partners (2006) 'Economic Development and Poverty Reduction Strategy', Development Partners Coordination Group, Rwanda, www.devpartners.gov.rw

UNDP (United Nations Development Programme) (2005) 'Mainstreaming environment into poverty reduction strategies: Lessons for Rwanda', MINITERE/UNDP/UNEP workshop, Kivu Sun, Rwanda, 15–17 February 2005

UNDP (2006a) *Making Progress on Environmental Sustainability: Lessons and Recommendations from a Review of Over 150 MDG Country Experiences*, UNDP, New York

UNDP (2006b) 'Capacity development in SEA application in Rwanda: Lessons learnt and implications for economic development and poverty reduction strategy (EDRS) process', internal report, UNDP, New York

UNDP (2006c) 'Standard progress report', UNDP, Bénin

UNDP (2010) 'MDG report midway evaluation 2000–2008', www.tz.undp.org/mdgs_progress.html

United Republic of Tanzania Vice-President's Office (2004) 'Guide and action plan to mainstreaming environment into the poverty reduction strategy review', draft report, Tanzania

Waldman, L. (2005) *Environment, Politics, and Poverty: Lessons from a Review of PRSP Stakeholder Perspectives*, Institute of Development Studies, Brighton, www.ids.ac.uk/ids/KNOTS/PDFs/Synthesis_Review_%20EN.pdf

World Bank (2004) *The Poverty Reduction Strategy Initiative: An Independent Evaluation of the World Bank's Support Through 2003*, World Bank, Operations Evaluation Department, Washington, DC, www.worldbank.org/ieg/prsp

World Bank (2006a) 'Completed PRS documents', World Bank, Washington, DC, http://web.worldbank.org/WBSITE/EXTERNAL/TOPICS/EXTPOVERTY/EXTPRS/0,menuPK:384207~pagePK:149018 ~ piPK:149093 ~ theSitePK:384201,00.html

World Bank (2006b) 'Country Brief', World Bank, Washington, DC, http://web.worldbank.org/WBSITE/EXTERNAL/COUNTRIES/AFRICAEXT/RWANDAEXTN/0,menuPK:368714 ~ pagePK:141132 ~ piPK:141107 ~ theSitePK:368651,00.html

World Bank and IMF (International Monetary Fund) (2005) *Synthesis 2005 Review of the PRS Approach: Balancing Accountabilities and Scaling Up Results*, World Bank and IMF, Washington, DC

20
SEA and Spatial Planning

Peter Nelson

Introduction

Spatial planning – also referred to as land-use planning – shares many elements of the strategic environmental assessment (SEA) process and is one of the areas to which SEA has been extensively applied over the past two decades. This chapter provides an overview of the state of art in this field based on the international literature, the author's own experience, papers contributed to the International Association for Impact Assessment (IAIA) SEA Conference in Prague and subsequent discussion. It also describes the 'added value' and benefits of linking SEA with spatial/land-use planning. An early draft of the chapter was prepared by Dr Ingrid Belcakova, Co-Chair of the Prague debate. Her contribution in analysing the history of SEA in Spatial Planning and undertaking the literature review is gratefully acknowledged.

The chapter is organized into three main parts. First, the nature and characteristics of spatial planning are summarized. Second, the linkages between SEA and spatial/land-use planning are described. A discussion of best practices and experience follows. This is based on case studies that were presented and discussed among participants at the Prague conference.

The nature of spatial planning

Different definitions and models exist for both spatial planning and SEA. Superficially, the meaning of the term 'spatial planning' is easily understood but, in practice, it can take different forms and have different meanings throughout the world. In a European context various definitions have been employed:

> *Regional/spatial planning gives geographical expression to the economic, social, cultural and ecological policies of society. It is at the same time a scientific discipline, an administrative technique and a policy developed as an interdisciplinary and comprehensive approach directed towards a balanced regional development and the physical coordination of space according to an overall strategy. (Council of Europe, 1983)*

Spatial planning refers to the methods used largely by the public sector to influence the future distribution of activities in space. It is undertaken with the aim of producing a more rational organization of activities in space, including the linkages between them; and to balance development with the need to protect the environment. (European Commission, 1997)

Although the last definition includes environmental protection as a principal objective, this is not the case with all spatial planning systems and there are many examples of sectoral plans (for example, in infrastructure development for water, energy transmission and transport) which do not have protection of the environment as a primary focus.

Spatial and land-use planning has evolved in different parts of the world around two conceptual models: one is driven by socialist theory, in which the main decisions are taken by the state; the other focuses on free market economics where there is greater flexibility for developers to determine the content of a plan (Nelson, 2005). These two extremes represent the ends of a continuum, neither of which can be seen as a preferred model. International experience has shown that both can result in severe adverse social, environmental and local economic impacts. Two examples illustrate this premise. Desiccation of the Aral Sea between Kazakhstan and Uzbekistan was a direct consequence of decisions by Soviet planners to divert the Amu-darya and Sir-darya rivers to irrigate cotton (Glantz, 1999). In a free market economy, the effects of over-intensification of agriculture in the US midwest, coupled with the economic slump and prolonged drought, resulted in the US dustbowl of the 1930s. (Cunfer, 2005) Many other examples of past mistakes can be found ranging from the unforeseen impacts of the Three Gorges Dam on the Yangtze River to the evidence of past mistakes displayed in current plans to demolish dams on rivers in the Pacific Northwest to save the Pacific salmon.

Under centrally controlled economies, such as that of the former USSR, environmental issues have tended to be assessed on strictly 'scientific' grounds using State Environmental Review (SER) supported by ecological assessment. In free market economies, social and local economic factors have tended to be given more weight within assessments with the emphasis moving increasingly towards 'sustainability' appraisal. Figures 20.1 and 20.2 illustrate the way in which the form of environmental assessment may differ when applied to spatial plans in different contexts. The aim is not to suggest that there is necessarily a 'right' or 'wrong' application but to emphasis that SEA process design should have regard to the context in which both the SEA and spatial plan are being prepared.

Critical factors which should be considered when designing a SEA of a spatial plan include:

- The scale of the application (international, national, regional or local).
- The political economy and institutional context within which the plan is to be adopted.
- The timescale over which the plan is expected to be effective.

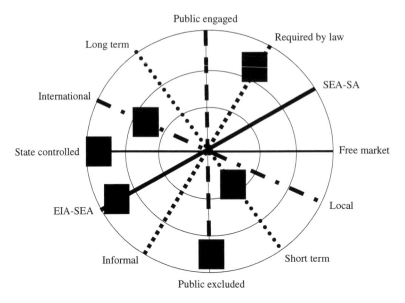

Source: Nelson (2005)

Figure 20.1 *National development plan – socialist economy*

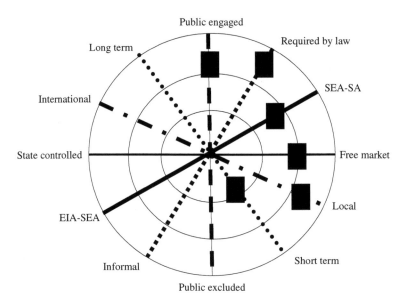

Source: Nelson (2005)

Figure 20.2 *District development plan – free market economy*

- The legal status of the SEA (mandatory or voluntary).
- The degree of public participation.

Spatial plans are usually tiered and may be applied at any level from national, through regional to local. Where tiering of plans occurs, it is usual for the higher level plan to set the policy context for subordinate plans. Figure 20.3 describes a typical sequence for developing a spatial plan with the same sequence alongside it for introducing SEA (Nelson, 2005). It is important to bear in mind that the formal definition of spatial planning in any particular country may differ from actual practice within that country; aspirations often run ahead of reality.

Relationships between spatial planning AND SEA

Most discussions on the role of SEA highlight its application to higher tiers of decision-making. In this respect, spatial planning is one of the most appropriate contexts for the use of SEA since it invariably combines policy formulation, planning and programming in a single operation. Spatial planning has been undertaken in most parts of the world since the mid-20th century and, as noted by Wood (1992), spatial/land-use planning is one of the easiest subject areas to which all types of SEA can be applied. However, just as there are different models and applications of spatial planning, so there are different views of the role of SEA within spatial planning. This fact was clearly reflected in the different presentations and points of discussion raised in the Prague workshop (see Boxes 20.1–20.9).

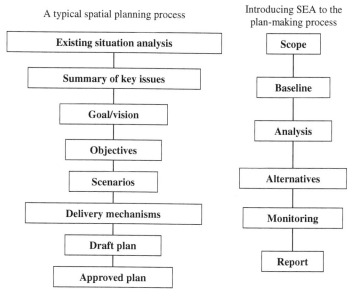

Source: Nelson (2005)

Figure 20.3 *Comparison of spatial planning and SEA processes*

Box 20.1 *SEA in the Autonomous Region of the Azores, Portugal*

Status of spatial plan: All plans in Portugal are subject to approval by central government, although in the Autonomous Regions, including the Azores, some powers are delegated to the Azorean government. Planning legislation introduced in 1999 and 2003 has given increased emphasis to public participation, which was given little attention until the mid-1990s.

Legal status of SEA: As a member of the EU, Portugal and the Azores are obliged to implement the SEA Directive (2001/42/EC). While legislation was still being formulated for this purpose in 2004/2005, specific guidance on implementing SEA had been produced (SEA for Spatial Planning – methodological guidance for application in Portugal, 2003). Transposition of the SEA Directive into Portuguese law was completed in 2007.

Description: The coastline of the Azores is under heavy development pressure. Standard EIA procedures and Local Plans have failed to control inappropriate development. Coastal Zone Management Plans (CZMPs) have been introduced and are regarded as a very important spatial planning implement for linking national, regional and local planning measures but they tend to be governed by environmental protection objectives. CZMPs are binding on lower tier plans but in many cases these Municipal Master Plans are non-existent or, where they do exist, they ignore environmental concerns.

SEA has been trialled on the San Miguel CZMP produced in 2002 and approved by the Environment Secretary. The review by the research team concluded that the CZMP would satisfy SEA Directive requirements by:

- Analysing alternative development scenarios.
- Including production of an environmental report and non-technical summary.
- Involving public participation at different stages in the planning process.
- Establishing specific procedures for ongoing and ex post evaluations to be implemented.

In these respects the San Miguel CZMP was substantially ahead of other CZMPs in the Azores and on the mainland, which fail to establish a monitoring framework.

Key issues:

- At the time of writing, Portugal had not transposed the SEA Directive into national law.
- Lack of know-how and the low level of public awareness is hindering introduction of SEA methods to the Azores planning system.
- SEA can bring an increased complexity to spatial planning but it also helps to ensure preparation of more sustainable plans.

Source: Calado et al (2005)

Box 20.2 *Transnationally approved indicator set: The core module in SEA for regional planning*

Status of spatial plan: Different planning regimes operate in the Czech Republic, Germany and Poland, three adjacent countries that are cooperating on building a joint transnational set of indicators.

Legal status of SEA: SEA legislation in all three countries follows the SEA Directive framework.

Description: The paper outlined the experience of a pilot project on SEA at regional planning level co-financed by the Interreg IIIa programme of the European Union (EU). The aim of the pilot was to develop a framework and procedures for introducing a common set of environmental indicators within a region spanning Germany, Poland and the Czech Republic.

A total of 34 indicators were selected to provide the regional planning authorities with critical information on the environmental baseline, critical environmental thresholds for development, environmental objectives for setting policy, and the capacity to undertake environmental impact assessments (EIAs) on individual projects without resorting to further data-gathering.

One challenge of the study has been to identify the range of likely future development scenarios in order to determine the choice of indicators. A major component of the study has been to apply established methods and techniques used in German landscape planning, spatial potential analysis and EIA and ecological risk assessment.

Indicators cover soil, ground water, water bodies, air and climate, landscape and recreation, flora, fauna and biodiversity, human health and cultural and other material assets.

The mapped data is analysed in relation to potential risks from individual developments and spatial zoning is introduced to show areas that lie outside any potential conflict with sensitive environments, areas of medium conflict and areas which would incur high levels of conflict. The result is a development potentials map.

Key issues:

- The strength of this strategic indicator set lies in its transferability to other regions, and the fact that it offers an initial sieve and strategic direction for spatial planning.
- Potential weakness lies in the demanding nature of the data and the time required in assembling and processing it.
- Choice of indicators, which rely on expert consultations and scoping meetings, could also be expanded, and the classification of potential conflicts could require modification in the future.

Source: Helbron et al (2005)

Box 20.3 *Environmental vulnerability analysis as a tool for SEA of spatial plans*

Status of spatial plan: The 1997 National Strategy of Physical Planning of the Republic of Croatia and the 1999 Programme of Physical Planning set the framework for lower tier plans. The case analysis is based on a University research project for the region of the Mura River, Croatia.

Legal status of SEA: SEA was not formally adopted in Croatia in 2005, but harmonization of the country's legislation through implementing regulations has subsequently been put in place.

Description: In Croatia, plans still focus primarily on physical siting of development with little harmonization of spatial, social and economic objectives. There is no uniform system of criteria and indicators to assist in the review and control of spatial development objectives.

This project was designed to demonstrate alternative approaches to spatial planning and assessment using geographical information systems (GIS). It explores five different scenarios for development in the Mura Region of Croatia against a background of different levels of environmental vulnerability, using 23 different development activities, including tourism and waste disposal. The GIS model generates a sophisticated series of vulnerability maps with the level of risk from different types of development scored on a scale of 0–5 (0 being the lowest and 5 the highest impact). The information base was developed over the period 2001–2004 using ArcView, IDRISI and ProVal software.

Five groups of students each developed their own vision for development of the region based on nature protection, environmental protection, development of natural resources, tourism and recreation and regional identity. Each group prepared maps of the likely environmental impact of the 23 different activities and assessed the vulnerability of different areas from the standpoint of their own visionary theme.

Key issues:

- Most plans still focus primarily on physical siting of development with little harmonization of spatial, social and economic objectives.
- The use of an interactive GIS-based SEA provides a framework for encouraging stakeholder involvement in planning.
- Public participation in spatial planning is increasing but it is focused mainly at endorsing the final plan and the public have little opportunity to participate in plan preparation.

Source: Miocic-Stosic and Butula (2005)

Box 20.4 *Strategic environmental analyses in the urban planning of Sao Paulo Municipality, Brazil*

Status of spatial plan: 2002 Sao Paulo City Strategic Master Plan.

Legal status of SEA: Application of principles but no formal SEA.

Description: Report of a study into ways of improving the sustainability of the Strategic Master Plan for one of the largest conurbations in the world. Existing legislation is considered to provide an adequate framework for decision-making and for taking the output of SEAs and EIAs into account, but the major problem lies in ensuring that the responsible agency will actually undertake strategic assessment in parallel with plan or policy-making, rather than using it only as a mitigation tool once key decisions have been taken.

Key issues:

- Existing EIA regulations deal only with development projects and cannot address the broad strategic choices for the city on energy, transport, water supply, and so on.
- EIA is used only to secure mitigation.
- Public participation has been substantially increased.

Recommendations: SEA should:

- Not be linked formally to the permitting and licensing systems that lead to excessive bureaucracy.
- Include an accepted list of sustainability indicators.
- Introduce indices for controlling annual expansion rates, transformation of rural land, minimization of the loss of natural vegetation, urban density and available resources.
- Include formal indicators for measuring and monitoring air pollution.
- Be applied simultaneously with the plan production.
- Be prepared by an independent team of consultants working with the plan-makers.
- Include extensive public participation in selecting and evaluating alternatives.
- Result in a separate, impartial published report.
- Be included in a review of the effectiveness of the City Code 2001 and other planning legislation to deliver sustainability goals.
- Increase the empowerment of community representatives.

Source: Maglio et al (2005)

Box 20.5 *Integrating strategic assessment and spatial planning: Experiences from the 'Dutch Polder'*

Status of spatial plan: In the Netherlands, a clear hierarchical structure of spatial plans is produced in accordance with the Spatial Planning Act (1965).

Legal status of SEA: In 2005, the SEA Directive was in the process of being transposed into Dutch law to accommodate the comprehensive strategic assessment processes for plans and programmes that had been in place since 1987 under existing EIA law and regulations. Reconciliation of the Directive and Dutch legislation was completed shortly after.

Description: The paper provides information on procedures, costs and practical issues in undertaking strategic assessment of spatial plans in the Netherlands. Higher level plans set out strategic direction but the local land-use plan is the only document which is legally binding on building and land-use proposals A characteristic of former Dutch planning was a strong emphasis on consensus building (the Polders approach). However, the changing nature of society now requires a more formalized planning system that is robust enough to withstand legal challenges and disputes within government at different levels and between authorities and the public. Seven spatial plans at different levels (regional, sectoral and subregional structure plans) formed the basis for this analysis.

Within the spatial planning framework, there are some exemption procedures that allow municipalities to promote or permit individual projects that may be in conflict with national or provincial policies. Use of such exemptions can be controversial.

Key issues and recommendations:

- SEAs tend to go into too much detail in relation to provincial plans. They should seek to focus on strategic level decisions, within a clear framework and a balanced set of assessment criteria using concise factsheets.
- Assessors should avoid using personal judgements and prejudices and rely on evaluating the spatial plan against existing policies and accepted goals of environmental sustainability.
- It is normally beneficial to carry out an SEA even if there is no formal legal requirement because this has benefits for the plan process, avoids possible procedural challenges at a later date and saves money.
- SEA should follow the lead set by the plan-makers and not seek to take over the planning role. It can make an effective input both in plan creation and plan validation.
- Decisions on the role of the SEA should be taken before either the spatial planning or SEA process begins.
- Clarify exactly what the SEA will cover in terms of subject matter, and what can be left until later stages in the spatial planning process.
- Identify what follows the SEA in terms of work on mitigation and further design and development.
- Introduce the findings and results of the SEA into the political process.

- Seek harmonization of the legislation (applies particularly to the Netherland) but also relevant in most other countries.
- Aim to record and report not only the SEA findings but also the views of stakeholders and the public.

Source: Nuesink (2005)

Box 20.6 *SEA in South African spatial development frameworks: The Ekurhuleni experience*

Status of spatial plan: An environmental management framework linked to municipal integrated development plans and spatial development frameworks (SDFs).

Legal status of SEA: SEA formally required under the South African Municipal Systems Act (2000).

Description: Detailed account of the spatial planning system and related SEA processes for municipalities in South Africa with a case study of Ekurhuleni municipality.

In 2002, the Ekurhuleni Environment and Tourism Department was established. This body prepared a State of the Environment Report in 2004 accompanied by a comprehensive SEA (the first in Ekurhuleni) to prepare an Environmental Management Framework (EMF) for the Northern Service Delivery Region of the Municipality (950km^2, including Johannesburg International Airport – the busiest in Africa). The work was undertaken as a collaborative exercise with Gauteng provincial department.

The SEA involved use of layered environmental information bases contained within a GIS. Interrogation of the database, using policy analysis and stakeholder discussions, led to the definition of Environmental Constraint Zones and Environmental Control Zones. The output is a Strategic Environmental Management Plan (SEMP) which can be used to guide development to environmentally suitable areas, and avoid areas of constraint.

Key issues: Early versions of the SDF were based on disjointed and incomplete environmental information collected from different sources. Accuracy of data was not verified, and much of the information related to large-scale maps with little detail.

The SEMP is now being used to reassess development guidelines in the SDF. It should ensure that future editions of the SDF are prepared on the basis of sound environmental information, rather than applying SEA as a retrospective tool.

Preparation of the SEA was undertaken partially to enhance the environmental knowledge of all stakeholders and to widen understanding. Although undertaken as a collaborative project between the municipality and province, the experience revealed very different levels of competencies and conflicting mandates. This created a situation in which the ultimate development goals could not be established and a process of negotiation was required to resolve the issues.

Source: Olivier (2005)

Box 20.7 *Application of EIA/SEA system in land-use planning:
Experience from Serbia*

Status of spatial plan: A complex set of overlapping spatial and sector plans within the Valjevo municipality in Serbia.

Legal status of SEA: New EIA and SEA laws were introduced in 2004, which comply with EU Directives 97/11/EC and 2001/42/EC in order to address weaknesses of the former two stage EIA process and prepare the ground for possible accession to the EU.

Description: Academic review of shortcomings in former systems of assessment and the prospects for improvement under new legislation.

Key issues: Under the Spatial Planning Law (1995), the former EIA process was carried out in two stages involving a preliminary EIA (as part of the spatial planning process) and detailed EIA in relation to individual projects and detailed plans. In practice, the integration of environmental considerations into strategic plans was invariably treated as an appendage, focusing on the need for environmental remediation after the economic priorities had been determined.

The main problems in EIA implementation were found to be inconsistency in the ways in which planning regulations were treated by different tiers of government and different authorities, marked shortcomings in the level of institutional cooperation, unsatisfactory quality of environmental impact statements (EISs), and lack of public participation. A particular area of uncertainty in Serbia is the use of screening processes to determine what plans and programmes should be subject to SEA. This highlights a lack of coordination between responsible institutions, a basic misunderstanding and misuse of the hierarchy of planning decisions and the risks of duplicate assessments where several plans cover different parts of the same territory.

The essential conclusion is the need to establish a clearer understanding of the role of SEA in spatial planning, and to ensure that EIA procedures are coordinated and aligned with the hierarchy and structure of spatial plans.

Source: Stojanovic (2005)

Evolution of SEA concepts, systems and approaches in spatial/land-use planning

Environmental assessment (EA) was first introduced as a mandatory requirement within public decision-making in accordance with the 1969 US National Environmental Policy Act (NEPA). This act did not differentiate between SEA and EIA procedures but required environmental assessment for any major public decisions on new regulations, plans, programmes or projects (Jones et al, 2005). The term 'major public decision' was defined more precisely

Box 20.8 *SEA and land-use planning in China*

Status of spatial plan: In China, land-use planning is practised as 'master planning', 'specialized planning' and 'detailed planning'. Five tiers exist from the national level, through provincial, municipal and town to village level.

Legal status of SEA: Under the Environmental Impact Assessment Law of the People's Republic of China (2002, effective from 1 September 2003), plan environmental impact assessment (PEIA) is required for land-use master plans. Technical guidelines have been published to assist municipal and provincial governments in PEIA preparation.

Description: Discussion on the application of PEIA to policies, plans and programmes (PPPs) at all levels in China.

Key issues: The advantages of PEIA lie in the fact that environmental issues are explored much earlier in the planning process. In addition, strategic decisions on the plan can help to lead and shape the nature of individual projects (rather than simply providing a framework to accommodate projects after their approval). Other benefits include incorporating a review of cumulative and synergistic effects, facilitating public participation – at least in theory – and strengthening understanding of environmental issues within plan-making authorities.
  Weaknesses arise primarily because PEIA is still a new process:

- In practice, it can be difficult to align timescales for land-use planning processes and the procedures for integrating the findings of PEIA/SEA into decision-making.
- There is lack of knowledge and experience of which environmental factors to consider, what potential effects may occur and how to predict and evaluate these impacts at the plan level.
- Mechanisms for public participation are not well-established, public involvement in decision-making is limited and communications between government agencies can be minimal and ineffective.
- Alternatives are seldom proposed and considered. In practice, PEIA is often started after the draft land-use plans have been prepared and in spite of hard work, it can be difficult to influence the results of decision-making.
- Baseline information is not always available due to time and financial constraints.

Scope for improvement: Despite the limitations cited above, implementation of SEA is seen as vitally important in China. Specific recommendations for improvement include:

- Organizing training programmes to educate and familiarize decision-makers and PEIA administrators.
- Preparing case studies for developing appropriate assessment methods at plan level, including checklists, matrices, scenario analysis, GIS technologies, and so on.

- Increasing public participation and strengthening both vertical and horizontal communication within relevant authorities.
- Comparing and reviewing China's approach to SEA with international experience.

Source: Tang et al (2005)

Box 20.9 *Dealing with alternatives in spatial planning: Experiences from the UK*

Status of spatial plan: The UK has adopted new spatial planning legislation covering regional and district/municipal levels (Town Planning and Compensation Act 2004).

Legal status of SEA: SEA is a formal requirement in accordance with the European Directive. The UK has also introduced a legal requirement for Sustainability Appraisal of plans and programmes and the two processes are undertaken jointly.

Description: Three case studies are used to illustrate different approaches being taken towards the identification and evaluation of alternatives within local authority spatial plans. One example considered proposals for different levels of housing development within the plan period ranging from 30,000–80,000 new homes; a second case study addressed policy 'options' for promoting healthy environments and healthy lifestyles and the third examined policies in a Local Transport Plan.

Key issues:

- Most UK planning authorities are struggling to produce genuine options for assessment in accordance with the SEA Directive.
- Many local plans are focused primarily on the issue of housing supply and demand and do not really represent choice of alternatives in spatial terms.
- Policies for promoting healthy environments (and many other planning objectives) invariably list a range of 'options' which are mutually self-supporting and therefore not true alternatives.
- In the case study on transport, levels of growth in road traffic (due primarily to use of private cars) were found to be unsustainable – but the proposed solutions in the plan were not capable of tackling this strategic issue.

Conclusions: These examples suggest the need for further guidance on what is meant by the adoption of 'reasonable' alternatives with greater emphasis being given to the likely outcomes of policies and plans on the environment, rather than focusing on the issues of need and demand.

Source: Venn (2005)

in relation to the area of spatial/land-use planning in the 1978 Council on Environmental Quality (CEQ) Regulations.

In NEPA implementation, the US pioneered an approach to strategic scale environmental assessment referred to as 'programmatic EIA' and EISs for spatial plans (elsewhere these models are often referred to as 'regional', 'cumulative' or 'generic' EISs). Over the next decade, a number of countries followed the US example, including Canada (1973), Australia (1974), West Germany (1975) and France (1976). However, none of these process used what would now be regarded as systematic SEA processes (Belcakova and Finka, 2000).

Further evolution in the use of SEA-type processes in relation to spatial/land-use planning in the EU occurred during the 1990s when the fifth environmental action programme was approved and various draft versions of formal SEA frameworks were elaborated. During this period there were substantial differences in the way in which EIA/SEA was applied in individual countries reflecting the following characteristics (see Lee and Walsh, 1992; Sadler and Verheem, 1996; Thérivel and Partidário, 1996; Commission of the European Communities DGXI, 1998; Elling, 2000; Kleinschmidt and Wagner, 1998; Platzer, 2000; ICON, 2001; Sadler, 1996, 2001b):

- Legislative framework of the SEA process.
- The extent of SEA application in individual areas including physical and spatial plans.
- The form of recording SEA.
- The types of information necessary for the EIS.
- Formal requirements for public participation and the process of collecting comments.
- Measures for integration of the results of environmental assessment of policies, plans and programmes into the decision-making and approval processes.

In the EU, formal SEA procedure, based heavily on EIA, was eventually introduced by Directive 2001/42/EC on the assessment of the effects of certain plans and programmes on the environment (the SEA Directive) (Lee and Hughes, 1995). Countries seeking accession to the EU were also required to undertake SEA pilot projects in relation to regional development programmes in order to obtain resources from structural funds (for example, Poland, Hungary, Czech Republic, Slovakia, Slovenia, Estonia, Latvia and Lithuania).

Countries in other parts of the world adopted their own formal requirements for environmental assessment of spatial/land-use plans during the 1980s. The latter half of the 1980s saw a dramatic expansion in application of environmental assessment into planning (Wood and Djeddour, 1992). Spatial/land-use planning systems in California, Western Australia, New Zealand, Canada, South Africa, the Netherlands, Italy, Germany, Finland and the UK, all had their unique administrative actions, decision-making levels, and formal requirements for SEA coverage (Verheem, 1992; Fischer, 2007).

The European Directive does not use the term 'SEA' explicitly. It requires EA to be undertaken for a wide range of spatial/land-use plans that establish a framework for future development consent of projects. These plans are developed under more detailed planning regulations operated by each member state. The SEA Directive emphasizes the need to consider the relevance of other plans and programmes, recognizes the concept of tiering, establishes procedural steps such as scoping, consideration of alternatives, consultation and public participation, environmental report preparation, consideration of assessment results in decision-making, monitoring, follow-up, consultation and participation, and requires monitoring and consideration of cumulative, synergistic and secondary impacts (Jones et al, 2005).

Types of SEA for spatial plans

The demand for new tools for applying EA to policies, plans and programmes (PPPs) has generated two principle approaches, referred to in the literature as 'EIA-based' and 'plan-based'. EIA-based approaches incorporate scientific appraisal techniques with a heavy emphasis on data and baseline information which can be input into geographical information systems (GISs) or other models to replicate the planning environment. Plan-based approaches also require evidence from surveys but rely more on qualitative interpretation of issues and options which reflect the forward-looking and uncertain nature of spatial/land-use planning (for example, Lee and Walsh, 1992; Thérivel et al, 1992; Wood and Djeddour, 1992; Sadler and Verheem, 1996; Thérivel and Partidário, 1996; Partidário and Clark, 2000; Partidário, 2004).

The EIA-based model is applied widely in the US, the Netherlands, Italy, South Africa, Germany, the Balkans and countries which were formerly part of the USSR, while countries such as Canada, New Zealand, the UK and the Scandinavian countries prefer the strategic approach (Verheem, 1992). In addition to differences in methodological approaches there are also differences in terminology. For example a wide range of expressions are used to describe environmental assessment of spatial/land-use plans including 'regional EIA', 'strategic environmental assessment analysis,' 'environmental appraisal of development plans', 'sustainability appraisal of regional planning', 'strategic EIA', and 'programmatic environmental assessment' (Partidário, 2004).

Other forms of strategic assessment have been introduced by countries seeking to apply formal requirements for SEA to spatial/land-use planning including Korea, Norway and the Newly Independent State (NIS) countries. This latter group (NIS countries include Russia, Belarus, Ukraine, Kazakhstan, Turkmenistan, Armenia, Georgia, Moldova, Azerbaijan, Kyrgyzstan, Tajikistan and Uzbekistan) use SEA-type frameworks based on the system of the SER. Among these countries, only Ukraine shows a high compatibility with internationally accepted standards (Cherp, 2001; Klees et al, 2002; Fischer, 2007). In the case of NIS countries, the driving forces behind establishment of SEA procedures has been mainly international donors, the World Bank and international initiatives such as the Sofia Initiative (Dusik and Sadler, 2004).

Dalal-Clayton and Sadler (2005) remark that the European SEA Directive is probably the best known SEA framework law, and together with the 2003 SEA

Protocol to the United Nations Economic Commission for Europe (UNECE) Espoo Convention, it will likely influence not only the EU countries but also stand as a 'reference point' internationally (see also Sadler, 2001a). But these authors also query its practical applicability and value, particularly for many developing countries. While the influence of European practice has been very strong in terms of the spread and adoption of SEA frameworks, the evidence of widely different spatial planning models throughout the world suggests that there are dangers in seeking to apply a standardized solution in all circumstances.

Experience of SEA and spatial plans: Evidence from the Prague case studies

The group of papers presented at the Prague SEA Conference provided a cross-section of current international experience of SEA and spatial plans and illustrate issues that are relevant and need to be addressed in the coming years. It is important to note that the background of the participants and their own knowledge and experience of SEA and spatial planning in practice varied considerably. It is against this background and qualifications that the following summary has been made. Summary extracts from the papers appear in Boxes 20.1–20.9.

Authors were asked to structure their papers around common themes to assist in making comparisons and to anticipate a debate based on the following key issues:

- What separates spatial planning and SEA practice?
- What specific skills are required to undertake the SEA of spatial plans?
- Should SEA be allowed to evolve as a largely unstructured and creative process for testing planning concepts or should it be more procedural and tied to specific targets and outputs?
- What consitutes effective public participation in SEA of spatial plans, as opposed to public involvement in plan-making?
- What sort of objectives and indicators should be employed in SEAs of spatial plans?
- Can the experience of particular countries provide role models for wider application?
- What are the essential components of a successful SEA linked with spatial planning?
- How far should SEA focus on the environmental dimensions of plans and programmes compared to its role in integrating broader social and economic objectives?
- How can the standards and performance of spatial planning SEA be measured?

Nature of spatial planning and SEA systems

It is important to stress at the outset of this review that political, legislative and social and economic conditions have been changing rapidly in many of the countries included in the sample. In each country, the form of strategic assessment (whether modelled on EIA or SEA) has had to be adapted to national and local circumstances. The Prague debate confirms an important and established conclusion – that there is no simple 'one size fits all' solution, rather the principles of planning, SEA and sustainable development need to be moulded together to satisfy national, regional and local needs.

Although all nine countries included in the sample either have, or are in the process of adopting, free market economies, three continue to exhibit some elements of centrally controlled economies. These include China and Serbia and Croatia, formerly part of the socialist Republic of Yugoslavia. In the case of China, the recently adopted (2003) planning and SEA framework is closely modelled on international and European experience, but as Tang et al (2005) note, planning at national and regional (provincial) level is largely a bureaucratic process with little real involvement of communities and the public at large in the use of SEA.

Croatia has a strong democracy and a fast-growing market economy but some areas of development continue to be controlled by the state. According to Miocic-Stosis and Butala (2005) this limits the scope for public participation. Stojanovic (2005) reaches the same conclusion in relation to the EIA/SEA system in Serbia and notes that a high degree of state control continues to exist over infrastructure development.

Political and legislative constraints over the introduction of new approaches to SEA for spatial planning are not restricted to countries with strong state control over planning decisions. In the EU, both the Netherlands (Nuesink, 2005) and Portugal (Calado et al, 2005) experienced difficulty in transposing the European SEA Directive into national law. In the Netherlands, the existence of well-established assessment procedures for plans and programmes was seen by many professionals as being prejudiced by the introduction of a more generic form of assessment required by the Directive. Both of these member states (and others) were also confronted by the demands of national governments to reduce rather than increase the burden of environmental regulation.

Other country case studies exposed different dimensions of the political, social and economic context within which strategic assessment needs to be carried out. Maglio et al (2005) highlighted the need for reform of urban planning, SEA and sustainability appraisal within one of the world's largest metropolis, Sao Paulo in Brazil where the sheer scale of development and disparities between rich and poor present an enormous challenge. In South Africa (which is also undergoing a rapid transformation), Olivier (2005) pointed to practical difficulties in combining different forms of environmental assessment under separate legislative procedures and of ensuring effective cooperation between higher and lower tier authorities. Helbron et al (2005) discussed the application of SEA indicators across national boundaries between Germany, Poland and the Czech Republic. While some of the complexities were only hinted at in this paper, it is easy to see why difficulties arise in applying a common SEA framework to plans and programmes which fall under different national jurisdiction.

The conclusion that can be drawn from this review is that it is essential to have a clear understanding of the national context within which any SEA and spatial planning system operates, before seeking to make judgements on the relevance and effectiveness of the process.

What separates spatial planning and SEA practice?

Spatial planning has been enshrined in most countries' legislation for much longer than SEA and it has invariably included some form of EA. Spatial planning has also included a requirement for public participation in a number of democracies since the 1960s. However, even in countries with a strong tradition for both EA and public participation, the tendency for the 'competent' or 'promoting' authority to be both the author of a plan or programme and the decision-maker on its adoption has often led to criticism regarding lack of transparency and the absence of any genuine exploration of alternative choices of action.

SEA offers a framework for tackling both of these concerns. As Nuesink (2005) clearly illustrated, SEA, if undertaken from the outset of the planning process, can test alternative solutions before political views become entrenched and can stimulate more open debate than would be the case otherwise. It can also be used to 'proof' a plan and ensure, at least in theory, that environmental mitigation measures are identified and, more importantly, implemented.

There is a continuing debate as to who should undertake the SEA of spatial plans. If it is the plan proponent, this has the merit of ensuring that any issues can be identified and potentially resolved within the drafting stages – but it also runs the risk that the SEA may become a mere formality and 'rubber stamping' exercise. The temptation for the plan proponent to understate or overlook inconvenient issues can be high. Alternatively, SEA may be conducted by independent entities (consultants, universities or staff from other departments). This approach has the benefit of ensuring that the SEA is produced at arm's length (which is not always a guarantee of independence if the cost of the SEA is paid for by the promoting authority) but it can also result in the findings being disowned by the client – or not taken to heart and acted on. Other solutions seek to combine these two approaches by creating joint teams from the proponent and consultancies, or by appointing an independent reviewer to comment on the work at different stages.

Spatial planning and SEA share similar techniques and processes in preparing baseline information, developing scenarios, testing these through public consultation and presenting a final plan or report. However, the key distinction between the two processes is seen to lie in the fact that an SEA has an obligation to identify potentially significant adverse environmental (and under some systems social and economic) impacts, to quantify the nature, scale and magnitude of the likely effects and to explore the scope for avoiding, reducing and where necessary mitigating any adverse effects. This information, when published for public consultation in a separate report prior to any decision on the plan, is a powerful additional tool.

What specific skills are required to undertake the SEA of spatial plans?

SEA practitioners come with a wide range of specialist skills including geography, biology and other Earth sciences, engineering, landscape management and design, GIS, politics, economics, sociology anthropology and planning. Many have more than one qualification. Some individuals may choose to specialize in individual tasks (for example, development of pollution indicators and monitoring, or the application of GIS databases). However, evidence presented from the case studies and discussion suggests that, in order to undertake SEA in spatial planning, it is essential that the team leader and core team should have a through grounding in the planning processes to which the particular SEA is being applied and should be fully aware of the political, social and economic context for decision-making on the plan content. There is, invariably, a real tension between some of the development objectives of a plan and programme and the environmental goals for the locality or region. The SEA team must be capable of carrying out a through and objective evaluation of the likely environmental impacts and of representing the different views within the community on how these issues should be resolved. This requires excellent report writing skills and a capacity to give both a qualitative and quantitative response,

Should SEA be a largely unstructured and creative process for testing planning concepts or should it be more procedural and tied to specific targets and outputs?

Opinions were strongly divided between participants in terms of the degree of flexibility or formality required for SEA of spatial plans. This goes to the heart of the debate between proponents of EIA or plan-based SEA. By its very nature, spatial planning tends to be strongly regulated by law and procedures. This is essential given the power of the resulting plans to control development and constrain the freedom of individuals to do what they want with land.

The regulatory nature of planning encouraged some SEA practitioners to argue for clearly defined stages in the SEA of spatial plans with binding technical manuals and guidelines for completing different types of land-use plan. Others argue that a more flexible approach is required and that one of the strengths of an SEA is its capacity to see around the corners of potential obstacles and come up with new solutions. This freedom to examine issues from new perspectives could be lost if a rigid structure for conduct of the SEA is imposed.

While the debate is unresolved, there was broad agreement that the development of indicators and creation of better frameworks for monitoring the outcome of SEAs and related plans is an important area for research. This was reinforced by the research undertaken by Maglio et al (2005) and Helbron et al (2005).

What constitutes effective public participation in SEA of spatial plans, as opposed to public involvement in plan-making?

Discussion on this topic was limited at Prague, but there is a body of practical experience on this question, which can be drawn on together with the findings of Venn's (2005) case study on reasonable alternatives.

When presenting the findings of a scoping study or a draft SEA report, it is a real challenge to get stakeholders and members of the general public to distinguish between the role of the SEA and the content of the spatial plan. Many people with fixed views on the issues and choices represented in a draft plan will only want to focus on these basic concerns (for example, opposition to incineration as a means of waste disposal or allocation of environmental sensitive sites for new housing). This response is understandable and provides useful feedback on the strength of public opinion, but it can be much harder to get stakeholders to leave aside their personal interests and prejudices and engage in a full dialogue about the merits of alternatives.

Another harsh reality about many planning systems is that planners (guided by their decision-makers) often have preconceived ideas about what the solutions to particular problems should be (for example, in relation to the number of houses that should be planned for, or acceptable methods and sites for waste disposal). Under these circumstances, there is a conscious or unconscious desire on the part of the planners to steer public debate towards the same conclusion. This often leads to the 'preferred solution' being placed between two extreme 'options' that cannot really be regarded as reasonable alternatives. As Venn (2005) pointed out, it is also the case that many 'alternatives' presented in policy statements in municipal plans are either mutually supportive of each other or contain internally conflicting objectives. Faced with a long list of complex policy options, it is not surprisingly that many people fail to see the value in participating in such SEA reviews. For the comparison of alternative courses of action to be a worthwhile exercise, it is essential that real choices are offered and the public debate takes place early enough in the planning process to influence the outcome.

What sort of objectives and indicators should be employed in SEAs of spatial plans?

This question raises interesting methodological issues and goes to the heart of what is meant by SEA of spatial plans and the distinctions between the process of preparing spatial plans and carrying out a strategic environmental assessment of these plans.

Three of the case studies presented valuable background information on this issue. Olivier (2005) discussed the range of objectives and indicators considered appropriate within an EMF for the northern area of Ekurhuleni in South Africa. The EMF is itself a form of spatial planning and is indirectly linked to preparation of a SDF and an integrated development plan (IDP). The focus of an EMF is on the protection of sensitive environmental areas and the indicators used included presence and distribution of red data species, water quality, geotechnical constraints, agricultural land and noise levels. This SEA process shared similarities with the development of transnational SEA indicators in Saxony discussed by Helbron et al (2005), both being based on largely physical parameters contained within a GIS.

Maglio et al (2005), discussing the city-region of Sao Paulo, emphasize not only physical parameters (for example, air and water quality) but also social and economic factors including indicators of the rate of urban growth (conversion of farmland to built development), housing density, growth in traffic and numbers of vehicles, and changes in land value. Their work emphasizes that the role of SEA within spatial plans should be based on sustainability objectives as well as physical parameters.

The transnational SEA (involving Germany, Poland and the Czech Republic) generated a list of 34 indicators based primarily on physical determinants, although measures are included for land consumption and land-use change and subjective values for visual impact. This work on indicators by Helbron et al (2005) is described as the 'core module' of the SEA and is recognized as the first step in setting up an overall SEA system.

As noted elsewhere in this book, the term SEA is seen by some as synonymous with preparation of landscape framework plans (as in Germany) Others suggest that the generation of objectives, criteria and indicators within a GIS or similar database forms part of the baseline and creates a framework for analysing competing or alternative development proposals but is not an SEA in the full sense of the word. For an SEA to have been completed, it is argued that alternative forms of development and the preferred solution incorporated within the spatial plan need to be tested using SEA methods and the results published in a SEA report for public discussion before the spatial plan is adopted.

Leaving aside this broader question, it is interesting to note the difference in emphasis on the type of indicator to be included within SEAs of spatial plans. Where countries have adopted SEA procedures modelled largely on existing EIA frameworks the tendency is to focus largely on the physical environmental impacts of plans and programmes. Countries with plan-led SEA systems are more likely to include elements of sustainability appraisal (for example the UK) (Curran et al, 1998). In the latter case, it is necessary to include a much wider range of social and economic indicators as part of the SEA.

What are the essential components of a successful SEA linked with spatial planning?

A broad consensus was reached in Prague about what constitutes a successful SEA for spatial planning:

- The process should begin as early as possible in the planning process.
- Agreement should be reached at the outset between interested parties on the scope, content and outputs of the SEA.
- The plan should lead the development of spatial concepts and alternatives, but the SEA should challenge and test those assumptions and where necessary propose further variants.
- Public consultation on the content of the spatial plan and the SEA should be carried out in parallel to avoid wasted time and effort.
- Sufficient time should be allowed for genuine consultation with stakeholders and the public, and for the results to be fed back into the SEA and spatial plan before both documents are completed.
- Decision-makers should be encouraged to participate in the SEA.
- Decision-makers should be required to indicate how they have taken account of the SEA when discussing the final adoption of the spatial plan.

How far should SEA focus on the environmental dimensions of plans and programmes, given its role in integrating broader social and economic objectives?

As noted earlier, the answer to this question clearly depends on individual countries and contexts. However, it is interesting to note the different responses of industrialized and developing countries. In industrialized countries, the focus of SEA is often on protection of remaining semi-natural vegetation and associated ecosystems. In developing countries, the 'environment' (however impoverished) for most people is the basis of their livelihoods and conditions their health and welfare; and social and economic issues cannot be divorced from environmental ones under these conditions. In recent years, there has been increased recognition of the need to link SEA for spatial plans with other forms of sustainability appraisal, especially in terms of developing responses to climate change.

How can the standards and performance of spatial planning SEAs be measured?

Very few countries have set standards or requirements for the output of SEAs on spatial plans. In the UK, both spatial plans and their accompanying SEAs are subjected to examination in public conducted by a inspector from the government's planning inspectorate. The plan and SEA are tested for 'soundness' based on nine criteria and if either is found lacking, the plan may be rejected outright or may require modification. The Republic of Montenegro is another country that sets out mandatory standards for SEA performance. Other countries, notably the Netherlands and Canada, have formal review procedures.

Two fundamental questions need to be addressed in any review of the standards of a SEA of a spatial plan. The first relates to conformance with the regulations of the country. It is a relatively simple exercise to test whether certain outputs (for example, final report, inclusion of non technical summary, proposals for monitoring) have been delivered or not. However, the second question is more complex – has the SEA successfully identified the range of likely significant impacts emanating from the plan proposals and have realistic alternative solutions been explored and debated objectively in a public forum before a decision to adopt the plan is taken?

Concluding remarks

This review of SEA and spatial planning, based largely on the IAIA SEA Conference in Prague, has revealed a number of problems and issues that are encountered across different countries despite the range of approaches being followed. These included: the invariable gap between what theories say and what happens in practice; legislation that is seldom up-to-date; frequently changing political influences and economic fluctuations that have major effects on policy; and constantly expanding pressures on the environment. Despite these constraints, based on the evidence at Prague and discussions since, many practitioners seem confident that SEA is bringing greater objectivity and transparency to plan-making. There was and remains still enormous value in bringing case studies together from different countries in order to gain a wider understanding of potential solutions.

References

Belčáková, I. and Finka, M. (2000) 'Strategic environmental assessment of land use/spatial plans in EU and SR', in Gal, P. and Belčáková, I. (eds) *Current Legislation and Standards of Spatial Planning in Social Transformation and European Integration*, FA STU, Bratislava

Calado, H., Cadete, J. and Porteiro, J. (2005) 'SEA in the Autonomous Region of the Azores, Portugal', paper presented at the IAIA SEA Conference, Prague

Cherp, A. (2001) 'SEA in Newly Independent States', in Dusik, J. (ed) *Proceedings of International Workshop on Public Participation and Health Aspects in Strategic Environmental Assessment*, Regional Environmental Centre for Central and Eastern Europe, Szentendre

Commission of the European Communities DGXI (1998) 'Case studies on SEA', Brussels

Council of Europe (1983) 'Recommendation (84)2: European Regional Spatial Planning Charter', 6th Session of the European Ministers responsible for regional/spatial planning (CEMAT), Torremolinos, Spain

Cunfer, G. (2005) *On the Great Plains: Agriculture and Environment*, A&M University Press, Texas

Curran, J. M., Wood, C. M. and Hilton, M. (1998) 'Environmental appraisal of UK Development Plans: Current practice and future directions', *Environmental and Planning B: Planning and Design*, vol 25, pp411–433

Dalal-Clayton, B. and Sadler, B. (2005) *Strategic Environmental Assessment: A Sourcebook and Reference Guide to International Experience*, Earthscan, London

Dusik, J. and Sadler, B. (2004) 'Reforming strategic environmental assessment systems: Lessons from Central and Eastern Europe', *Impact Assessment and Project Appraisal*, vol 22, pp89–97

Elling, B. (2000) 'Integration of strategic environmental assessment into regional spatial planning', *Project Appraisal*, vol 18, pp233–243

European Commission (1997) 'Compendium of European planning systems', *Regional Development Studies Report 28*, Office for Official Publications of the European Communities, Luxembourg

Fischer, T. B. (2007) *Theory and Practice of Strategic Environmental Assessment*, Earthscan, London

Glantz, M. H. (ed) (1999) *Creeping Environmental Problems and Sustainable Development in the Aral Sea Basin*, Cambridge University Press, Cambridge

Helbron, H., Schmidt, M. and Storch, H. (2005) 'Transnationally approved indicator set: The core module in SEA for regional planning', paper presented at the IAIA SEA Conference, Prague

ICON (IC Consultants Ltd) (2001) *SEA and Integration of the Environment into Strategic Decision-Making*, European Commission, Brussels

Jones, C., Baker, M., Carter, J., Jay, S., Short, M. and Wood, C. (eds) (2005) *Strategic Environmental Assessment and Land Use Planning*, Earthscan, London

Klees, R., Capcelea, A. and Barannik, A. (2002) *Environmental Impact Assessment (EIA) Systems in Europe and Central Asia Countries*, World Bank, Washington, DC

Kleinschmidt, V. and Wagner, D. (eds) (1998) *Strategic Environmental Assessment in Europe*, Kluwe Academic Publisher, Germany

Lee, N. and Hughes, J. (1995) 'Strategic environmental assessment, legislation and procedures in the community', final report to European Commission, EIA Centre, University of Manchester

Lee, N. and Walsh, F. (1992) 'Strategic environmental assessment: An overview', *Project Appraisal*, vol 7, pp126–136

Maglio, I. C., Philippi, A. and Malheiros, T. F. (2005) 'Strategic environmental analyses in the urban planning of Sao Paulo municipality, Brazil', paper presented at the IAIA SEA Conference, Prague

Miocic-Stosic, V. and Butula, S. (2005) 'Environmental vulnerability analysis as a tool for SEA of spatial plans', paper presented at the IAIA SEA Conference, Prague

Nelson, P. J. (2005) 'The application of SEA/SA to spatial planning at regional and local level in England and Wales', 4th Plannet Seminar on SEA of Urbanism Plans and Programs, http://plannet.difu.de/2005/proceedings/2005_plannet-proceedings.pdf

Nuesink, J. (2005) 'Integrating strategic assessment and spatial planning: Experiences from the "Dutch Polder"', paper presented at the IAIA SEA conference, Prague

Olivier, E. (2005) 'SEA in South African spatial development frameworks: The Ekurhuleni experience', paper presented at the IAIA SEA conference, Prague

Papoulias, F. and Nelson, P. (1996) 'Cost-effectiveness of European EIA directive', paper presented at the 16th Meeting of the International Association for Impact Assessent, 17–23 June, Estoril

Partidário, M. R. (2004) 'The contribution of strategic impact assessment to planning evaluation', in Miller, D. and Patassini, D. (eds) *Accounting for Non-Market Values in Planning Evaluation*, Ashgate, Aldershot

Partidário, M. R. and Clark, R. (eds) (2000) *Perspectives on Strategic Environmental Assessment*, Lewis, Boca Raton, FL

Platzer, U. (2000) 'Strategic environmental assessment', report of the workshop in Semering, Austria, October 1998

Sadler, B. (1996) *Environmental Assessment in a Changing World: Evaluating Practice to Improve Performance*, final report, International Study of the Effectiveness of Environmental Assessment, Canadian Environmental Assessment Agency, Ottawa

Sadler, B. (2001a) 'Strategic environmental assessment: An aide memoire to drafting a SEA Protocol to the Espoo Convention', in Dusik, J. (ed) *Proceedings of International Workshop on Public Participation and Health Aspects in Strategic Environmental Assessment*, Regional Environmental Centre for Central and Eastern Europe, Szentendre

Sadler, B. (2001b) 'A framework approach to strategic environmental assessment: Aims, principles and elements of good practice', in Dusik, J. (ed) *Proceedings of International Workshop on Public Participation and Health Aspects in Strategic Environmental Assessment*, Regional Environmental Centre for Central and Eastern Europe, Szentendre

Sadler, B. and Verheem, R. (1996) *Strategic Environmental Assesment: Status, Challenges and Future Directions*, Ministry of Housing, Spatial Planning and the Environment, The Hague

Stojanovic, B. (2005) 'Application of EIA/SEA system in land use planning: Experience from Serbia', paper presented at the IAIA SEA Conference, Prague

Tang, T., Zhu, T. and Xu, H. (2005) 'SEA and land use planning in China', paper presented at the IAIA SEA Conference, Prague

Thérivel, R. (2004) *Strategic Environmental Assessment in Action*, Earthscan, London

Thérivel, R. and Partidário, M. R. (eds) (1996) *The Practice of Strategic Environmental Assessment*, Earthscan, London

Thérivel, R., Wilson, E., Thompson, S., Heany, D. and Pritchard, D. (1992) *Strategic Enviornmental Assessment*, Earthscan, London

Venn, O. (2005) 'Dealing with alternatives in spatial planning: Experiences from the United Kingdom', paper presented at the IAIA SEA Conference, Prague

Verheem, R. (1992) 'Environmental assessment at strategic levels in the Netherlands', *Project Appraisal*, vol 7, pp150–156

Wood, C. M. (2002) *Environmental Impact Assessment: A Comparative Review*, 2nd edition, Prentice Hall, Harlow

Wood, C. M. and Djeddour, M. (1989) 'The environmental assessment of policies, plans and programmes', vol 1, Interim Report to the European Commission on *Environmental Assessment of Policies, Plans and Programmes and Preparation of a VadeMecum*, EIA Centre, University of Manchester

Wood, C. M. and Djeddour, M. (1992) 'Strategic environmental assessment: EA of policies, plans and programmes', *Impact Assessment Bulletin*, vol 10, pp3–22

PART IV

CROSS-CUTTING ISSUES IN SEA

21
Development and Application of Environmental Indicators in SEA

Alison Donnelly and Tadhg O'Mahony

Introduction

An indicator is used to show that a change has occurred, for example, in chemistry, litmus paper turns red under acidic conditions. If we want to know whether or not the wind is blowing we can look to see if the plants are swaying. This is a good indicator of the wind. But what this tells us depends on who we are and what we want to know. It may mean it is a good day for sailing or that the weather is about to change. But it will never tell us why the wind is blowing or what complex environmental changes are occurring to cause the wind to blow. Indicators can tell us that conditions are changing, but it is up to us to discover why and what we should do about it.

By verifying that change is occurring, indicators can demonstrate progress when things go right and provide an early warning when things go wrong (UNDP, undated). The continuous monitoring of indicators also facilitates effective evaluation. The fundamental challenge with indicators is to meaningfully capture key changes. It is important to carefully consider the type of indicator to use. If the wrong aspect is measured or if it is measured in the wrong way, the evaluation may be misleading and the quality of subsequent decisions could be affected. The selection of indicators is an iterative process, building on consultations between expert judgements, stakeholders and end-users. The process of selecting indicators takes several steps, including brainstorming ideas, assessing each one, narrowing the list (using criteria) and, finally, making an indicator monitoring plan. This suggests that an indicator is an important factor but so is finding, recording and presenting the data.

Because of their multifunctional nature, the development and selection of environmental indicators has become a relatively complex process (Kurtz et al, 2001). They are expected to reflect a variety of environmental issues, track or predict change, identify stressors or stressed systems and inform management and policy decisions. Therefore, time and effort, by as many stakeholders as possible, should be put into the selection of environmental indicators to ensure effective strategic environmental assessment (SEA) process.

There remains little published material on the successful use of environmental indicators in SEA, which partly reflects the challenges surrounding identifying suitable indicators and the lack of long-term established SEA monitoring programmes to date. Therefore, much of the work on environmental indicators remains in the theoretical stage. However, our aims are to demonstrate: (a) the vital role that environmental indicators can play in ensuring effective SEA; (b) how well-chosen indicators will help maximize existing resources, focus the monitoring system and therefore reduce costs associated with the implementation phase of SEA; and, finally, (c) a methodology to develop plan or programme-specific environmental indicators.

Background

In brief, SEA ensures that the environmental consequences of plans and programmes are identified and analysed during the plan-making process and before the adoption of the plan or programme. SEA should be carried out in tandem with the development of a plan to inform the planning process of possible alternatives to the proposed plan, raise awareness of both positive and negative environmental impacts of the plan and facilitate monitoring of the implementation of the plan through the inclusion of measurable targets and indicators (DOEHLG, 2004).

Having conducted several literature searches both on the internet and in various journals, it became apparent that there was very little published information pertaining to environmental indicators used in SEA. Consequently, in order to ensure no important literature was overlooked in the search, it was decided to contact SEA experts in various locations who may have knowledge of any guidance that may be available locally but not necessarily at an international level. Of the countries and regions contacted – Africa, Asia, Australia, Canada, the European Union (EU), Latin America, Newly Independent States (NISs), New Zealand, the US and the UK – only the UK was able to provide official guidance on the use of environmental indicators in SEA and provide examples for each environmental receptor.

The Environment Agency, UK, provides good practice principles, which include:

- Integrating environmental objectives from stakeholders.
- Using a limited number of objectives and indicators to ensure monitoring is manageable and strategic.
- Agreeing objectives and indicators with stakeholders as early as possible.
- Objectives that should reflect ends not means.
- Promoting creative strategic thinking.
- Indicators that should be simple, measurable and allow for unforeseen effects to be identified.
- Targets that should be associated with objectives and ideally should be quantified.

In addition, the Office of the Deputy Prime Minister (ODPM, 2005) provides a comprehensive list of potential social, environmental and economic objectives, targets and indicators for use in sustainability appraisal of regional spatial strategies and local development documents which are useful for SEA.

Role of environmental indicators in the SEA process

There is growing recognition for the need to establish appropriate environmental indicators to allow decision-makers to make informed judgements regarding protection of the environment in developing policies, programmes, plans and projects (Cloquell-Ballester et al, 2006). According to Bockstaller and Girardin (2003), in order for an environmental indicator to be considered valid, it should be scientifically designed, provide relevant information and be useful to the end-user. Currently, environmental indicators in SEA are the principal tool through which the impacts of plans and programmes on the environment are demonstrated. Therefore, they are pivotal to a successful, comprehensive and rigorous SEA process. They are used to describe and monitor the baseline data and together with objectives and targets are used for predictions of future environmental impacts (Figure 21.1) (Thérivel, 2004). Environmental indicators should not be developed in isolation but should be closely associated with objectives and targets. In order to demonstrate the achievement of SEA objectives, environmental indicators require a baseline (the situation before the activity begins) and a target (the expected situation at the end of the activity). SEA objectives are broad overarching principles (Thérivel, 2004) positioned at the apex of a hierarchy which goes from a general statement – such as 'improve air quality' – to more detailed targets – such as the percentage of commuters to move from road to rail by a given date (Figure 21.2) (Donnelly et al, 2006a). Guidelines for the implementation of SEA in EU member states often suggest objectives that may be used in the SEA process; however, these objectives need to be carefully tailored to meet local circumstances. SEA targets may be taken from legislation already in existence, such as pollution standards or conservation targets. In addition, corresponding indicators should be developed to suit

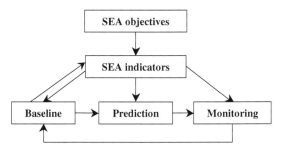

Source: Thérivel (2004)

Figure 21.1 *Links between indicators and other aspects of SEA*

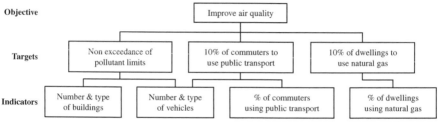

Figure 21.2 *Hierarchy of objectives, targets and indicators for use in SEA*

specific plans or programmes. However, there are often circumstances where a generic set of indicators can be broadly applicable across a series of similar sectors.

Development of objectives, targets and indicators for SEA – team approach

Objectives, targets and indicators are widely used in the SEA process to determine the environmental impact of proposed plans. In a SEA Indicator workshop, Donnelly et al (2006a) considered them to be a useful tool for this purpose, provided care and attention was paid to the way in which they were developed. Assessment of lists of indicators in Ireland available at the time of the workshop revealed that they were of limited use to SEA unless possibly for national plans or for plans at higher levels (for example, European). These lists were originally designed for something other than SEA and did not cover all requirements of the SEA Directive.

Having examined four environmental receptors (biodiversity, water, air and climatic factors) of the 12 (biodiversity, population, human health, fauna, flora, soil, water, air, climatic factors, material assets, cultural heritage – including architectural and archaeological heritage – and landscape) included in the SEA Directive, it became clear during the workshop that identifying objectives, targets and indicators for each receptor presented its own challenges. The main difficulty with biodiversity was considered to be a lack of available data especially at the lower levels of planning. The opposite was true for water, where a lot of data existed at all planning levels in relation to the EU Water Framework Directive (WFD). However, the question of their suitability for SEA reporting was raised. As regards air and climatic factors, direct measurements of components of these factors were considered to be of limited use to SEA, due to the difficulties in isolating a plan-specific contribution, although proxy data was considered to be a more accurate and reliable alternative worth exploring.

The types of objectives, targets and indicators developed during the workshop could be divided into two broad groups: those pertaining to proposed plans in general and those relating specifically to a particular plan. Table 21.1 gives examples of potential environmental objectives, targets and indicators developed for climatic factors for a national waste management plan, a regional

Table 21.1 *Proposed SEA objectives, targets and indicators for climatic factors for a national waste management plan, a regional development plan and a local area plan*

Objectives	General targets	General indicators
Reduce greenhouse gas (GHG) emissions	Meet regional targets for the waste sector for emissions of CO_2 and CH_4	Waste arising per capita (kg) Number of tonnes of waste going to landfill per capita Number of tonnes of waste combusted per capita Number of tonnes of waste digested per capita Number of tonnes of waste recycled per capita Number of km travelled per tonne of waste per year Amount of energy converted from waste
	Meet national targets for the agricultural sector for emissions of CO_2, CH_4 and N_2O	Number of Live Stock Units per type and per hectare Tonnes of fertilizer (artificial nitrogen) applied ha^{-1} Percentage of land area receiving fertilizer (artificial nitrogen)
	Meet national targets for the forestry sector for emissions of CO_2	Percentage of increase in land area devoted to forestry Age of plantation and type Percentage of selected species (for example, deciduous versus coniferous) in forest
	Meet national targets for transport for emissions of CO_2	Number of vehicle kms travelled, by mode
	Meet national targets for the housing sector for emissions of CO_2	Number of new dwellings Number of existing dwellings Average energy rating of new houses Average energy rating of existing houses
	Switching to lower carbon fuels	Carbon emissions per person
	5% of energy to come from biofuels by 2010 and 10% by 2020	Area of land planted under biocrops 2010, 2015 and 2020 Percentage of energy supplied by alternatives to fossil fuels
	Specific targets Limit commercial peat extraction to 1990 levels by 2010 and 50% of that by 2020	*Specific indicators* Number of tonnes of commercial peat extracted in 2010, 2015 and 2020

(continued)

Table 21.1 (*continued*)

Objectives	General targets	General indicators
	10% of all new dwellings to be constructed from wood by 2015 and 30% by 2020	Percentage of dwellings constructed from different materials by 2015 and 2020
	Energy supply from renewable forms X% by 20XX and Y% by 20YY	Percentage of energy supply per house that is renewable 20XX and 20YY
	No air conditioning units installed	Number of houses with air conditioning units installed per year
	No air conditioning units sold	Number of air conditioning units of X capacity sold in the region per year
Reduce impact of climate change	*General targets* Provide flood management plan where necessary	*General indicators* Insurance claims due to flooding
	Specific targets Suggestion to impose land-scaping into planning con-ditions	*Specific indicators* Percentage of increase in green space
	Maintain hedgerows	Length and type of hedgerows

Source: Donnelly et al (2006a)

development plan and a local area plan, that may be potentially used in SEA. For all four environmental receptors and three scales of plans addressed in the workshop the same SEA objective(s) could be used at most levels of planning due to their inherent overarching and broad thematic nature (Donnelly et al, 2006a). But it was considered that SEA targets and indicators were best divided into general and specific groups. General targets and indicators could be applied to a range of plans, whereas specific and more focused targets and indicators were necessary to describe, monitor and help make predictions of environmental impacts of specific plans. Figures 21.3 and 21.4 illustrate a question-based methodology that has been developed to help guide SEA practitioners in choosing plan specific objectives, targets and indicators (Donnelly et al, 2006b).

The authors concluded that, to ensure a successful SEA process: (a) carefully chosen objectives, targets and indicators were a useful tool for determining the environmental impact of plans at different levels; (b) objectives, targets and indicators, if developed correctly, should help maximize existing resources, focus the monitoring system and therefore reduce associated costs; (c) proxy data were considered, in some instances, to be more readily available and suitable than directly measurable data; and (d) objectives, targets and indicators should not be considered in isolation for a particular environmental receptor due to the potential influence of environmental receptors on each other.

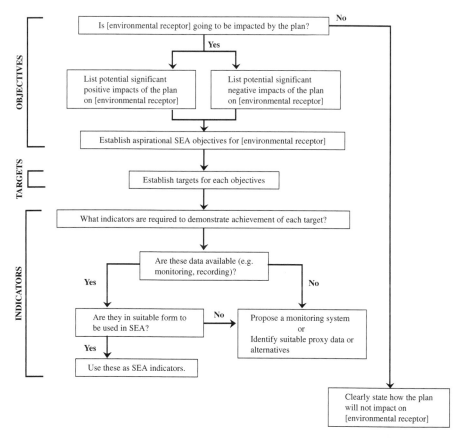

Source: Donnelly et al (2006b)

Figure 21.3 *Decision support framework for establishing objectives, targets and indicators for use in SEA*

Development of objectives, targets and indicators for SEA – methodological framework

Figure 21.3 presents a simple and logical methodology for developing objectives, targets and indicators for a specific plan (Donnelly et al, 2006b). It was designed for practitioners with limited experience in SEA and with the task of developing a monitoring programme. The following is an account of how it works.

Putting the framework into practice

In order to test the framework, a hypothetical Local Area Plan was developed that predicted an increase in the number of satellite towns in an area, an increase in the number of 'one-off' houses and an improvement in the transportation infrastructure. Air, biodiversity, water and climatic factors were chosen as working examples (Donnelly et al, 2006b) although the framework may be applied to all environmental receptors listed in the SEA Directive. Having

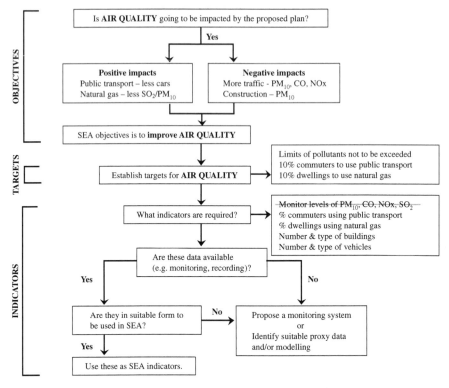

Note: Abbreviations: PM_{10} (particulate matter with a diameter less than or equal to ten microns), CO (carbon monoxide), NO_x (nitrogen oxides) and SO_2 (sulphur dioxide)
Source: Donnelly et al (2006b)

Figure 21.4 *Decision support framework for establishing objectives, targets and indicators for air quality in SEA*

decided that the proposed plan was going to impact on these environmental receptors examples of both significant positive and negative impacts were proposed for each (the questions posed in Figure 21.3 are considered for air quality in Figure 21.4). The significant positive impacts were based on encouraging the use of public transport over private transport, which may lead to a reduction in atmospheric concentrations of particulate matter with a diameter less than or equal to ten microns (PM_{10}), carbon monoxide (CO) and nitrogen oxides (NO_x). Whereas encouraging the use of natural gas as a primary source of energy in place of coal and oil may lead to a reduction in emissions of sulphur dioxide (SO_2) and PM_{10}. Significant negative impacts were related primarily to increasing the population in the area, which may lead to an increase in traffic volumes and a greater degree of construction. These activities were predicted to result in an increase in PM_{10} during construction and an increase in CO, CO_2 (carbon dioxide) and NO_x due to higher traffic volumes. The overall SEA objective decided upon was to improve air quality in the area of the proposed plan (Figure 21.4).

In order to meet the requirements of the SEA objective, a set of targets proposed for the environmental receptor (Figures 21.3 and 21.4) was based on the parameters used to determine the impact (positive and negative) of the proposed plan on the particular receptor. In this case, the targets for air included non-exceedence of limits for certain pollutants, including SO_2, PM_{10}, CO and NO_x (Figure 21.4), established in the EU Air Quality Directive. In addition, threshold values were assigned to the percentage of commuters using public transport and the percentage of dwellings using natural gas (Figure 21.4). It was considered that these targets were sufficient to address the SEA objective for air quality for the hypothetical plan.

The next step in the process was to establish indicators associated with the chosen targets and to identify data sets to support the indicators. Initially, the indicators for air quality comprised: (a) monitoring the atmospheric concentration of the pollutants listed above; (b) transportation mode of commuters; and (c) primary energy source of dwellings (Figure 21.4). With regard to the monitoring of air pollutants, the data were not available and it was necessary to either consider establishing a monitoring system or using proxy data coupled with predictive modelling. Establishing a monitoring system was considered to be expensive and to require a high degree of technical expertise. In addition, the atmospheric concentration of these pollutants would not be exclusive to the plan and therefore the data was considered to be unsuitable for SEA purposes. This would also be the case if these data were being collected by a local authority or some other such body.

Therefore, in the case of air quality, it was necessary to explore alternatives to direct atmospheric measurements of these pollutants, such as using proxy data to estimate the concentration of pollutants being generated specifically by the plan. This could be achieved using transportation models to estimate the number and type of kilometres travelled, by different modes of transport together with their emissions profile to give a plan-specific estimate of pollutant loads generated. In addition, the duration of the construction phase and number and type of buildings could be used to estimate PM_{10} generated by construction. Consequently, the number and type of vehicles and the number and type of buildings were considered more appropriate and accurate indicators than concentrations of pollutants in the atmosphere. These data were also considered to be more readily available at low cost. It was considered that, the percentage of commuters using different modes of transport and the percentage of dwellings with natural gas as the primary energy source were straightforward data requests and would be available from local authorities.

The framework should help the SEA practitioner to concentrate on relevant and significant (positive and negative) environmental issues. In turn, this will ensure that only appropriate data are collected and the monitoring system will be optimized as irrelevant and inappropriate data would have been identified early on, avoiding valuable resources being spent on their collection and analysis. Just because data are available or easily acquired is not a sufficient reason to use them. The data should be scrutinized to determine their applicability to the SEA process. Where appropriate data do not exist, it is essential to explore the possibility of using proxies, alternatives and modelling techniques to fill the gaps before developing sophisticated and often expensive monitoring systems. This approach will maximize the use of resources, both in terms of time and expertise, and ultimately reduce costs associated with the implementation phase of SEA.

Selecting environmental indicators

Donnelly et al (2006a) reviewed several sets of indicators, available in Ireland, that have been used to determine the environmental impact of the transport sector, the impact of climate change on the environment and key environmental indicators used for reporting the state of the environment. The authors concluded that, whereas these documents provided a valuable source of environmental indicators, they did not cover all sectors or all environmental receptors required under the SEA Directive, principally because the criteria did not fit SEA purposes. Therefore, it may not always be feasible and straightforward to simply transfer currently available processed data to SEA. This suggests the need to develop SEA process-specific environmental indicators. These should be informed by an associated set of documented criteria to ensure the indicators are fit for the purpose for which they are intended.

Criteria for selecting environmental indicators for SEA

Table 21.2 presents a list of criteria for selecting environmental indicators for SEA (Donnelly et al, 2007). Continuing evaluation of the indicators against these criteria will be an important basis for future quality assurance of the indicator selection process. The following is a brief explanation of the list of criteria to help identify environmental indicators that will ensure a rigorous and robust SEA. This will also inform the development of fit-for-purpose SEA-related monitoring programmes.

Table 21.2 *List of criteria for SEA indicator selection*

Criteria	Brief description
Policy-relevant	Consistent with significant legislation already in existence
Cover a range of environmental receptors	The data gathered should provide information that extends beyond that which is being measured
Relevant to the plan	Plan specific environmental impacts should be detectable
Shows trends	Responsive to change, measurable, capable of being updated regularly, demonstrates progress towards a target
Understandable	Ability to communicate information to a level appropriate for making policy decisions and to the general public
Well-founded in technical and scientific terms	Data should be supported by sound collection methodologies, clearly defined, easily reproduced and cost-effective
Prioritize key issues and provide early warning	Identifies areas most at risk of damage. Provide early warning of potential problems before it is too late
Adaptable	Emphasis can change at different stages of the plan
Identify conflict	With plan objectives in order that alternatives may be explored

1. Policy-relevant

This criterion ensures that the indicator is consistent with significant environmental policy goals/standards/commitments already established at different levels of planning such as WFD, the Convention on Biological Diversity (CBD) and Biodiversity Action Plans (BAPs). The indicator(s) chosen should inform decision-making to allow action to occur and, where appropriate, should provide opportunities for policy change.

2. Cover a range of environmental receptors

The indicator should be broadly applicable to different stressors and situations. Where possible, the indicator should be reflective of a wider system, for example, the presence or absence of key invertebrate species in waterways gives an indication of the quality of the water and the biodiversity of the system. Therefore, by gathering data for a particular issue the significance of the information collected extends beyond what is actually measured to a larger phenomenon of interest.

3. Relevant to the plan in question

The indicator should be relevant to the plan and and capable of reflecting specific changes imposed by the plan in question. For example, it would be pointless to use 'GHG concentrations in the atmosphere' or 'the number of vehicles on a particular stretch of roadway' as environmental indicators of a development plan if it was not possible to isolate the contribution of the plan to these indicators.

4. Show trends

This criterion ensures the data for the indicator has been collected over a sufficient period of time to allow trends to be detected and analysed. The indicator should be responsive to change and measurable. In addition, it should be capable of being updated regularly (ideally be part of an existing monitoring network) and should demonstrate progress towards a target. The indicator should also show trends on an appropriate geographic and temporal scale consistent with the environmental objective to be detected/analysed and should be reproducible, within defined and acceptable limits for data collection over time and space.

5. Easily understandable to decision-makers and the public

The indicator should have the ability to convey information to a level appropriate for making policy decisions and for the general public. For example, a water quality index may comprise several chemical and biological parameters, but what is important to the decision-maker or the general public is whether the water in question is suitable for drinking or bathing or whether or not it can sustain a population of fish. It is not necessary to know the technical detail behind the indicator, just whether the quality is good or bad and whether the trend is improving or getting worse over time. The indicator should be simple, clear and sufficiently non-technical to be understandable with brief specific explanations. It should also lend itself to effective display and presentation.

6. Well-founded in technical and scientific terms

The data supporting the indicators should be adequately backed up by sound collection methodologies, data management systems and quality assurance procedures to ensure the indicator is accurately represented. The data should be clearly defined, verifiable, scientifically acceptable and easy to reproduce. Scientific validity ensures data can be compared with reference conditions or other sites. In addition to being scientifically valid, the indicator's application should be practical (cost-effective and not technically complex). Practical issues that require consideration include monitoring costs, availability of experienced personnel, the practical application of the technology and the environmental impact of the monitoring system used.

7. Prioritize key issues and provide early warning

Indicators are useful tools for prioritizing which environmental information is most useful to inform decision-making. Tracking the progress of a suite of relevant environmental indicators should highlight the areas at greatest risk of damage, thereby identifying priority environmental issues that may require a greater amount of management or intervention. For example, a regional forestry plan may have a significant detrimental impact on soils (due to the use of heavy machinery at planting and logging) and surface waters (due to lowering of the water-table and excess suspended solids in run-off during certain operations). But there may be no significant adverse effect on human health or climate. Therefore, more resources should be put into selecting and monitoring suitable indicators for soil and water impacts compared to other environmental receptors. In addition, indicators can provide an early warning of potential problems, such as a change in environmental condition; for example, a decrease in water quality due to increased development may indicate that a higher level of wastewater treatment is needed. Providing an early warning mechanism allows time for appropriate remedial action to be undertaken before irreparable damage occurs.

8. Adaptable

The initial list of indicators selected should be monitored to ensure it is measuring what it is intended to measure or achieving what it is intended to achieve. At different stages of a plan the same indicator may be paramount or may become redundant; for example, in the case of air quality, dust particles (PM_{10}) may be an important measure of environmental impact during the construction phase of a roads programme but once this phase is finished, traffic may become the most important contributor of emissions to air. The list of indicators will need to be updated to reflect this change indicating the iterative nature of the process.

9. Identify conflict between plan objectives and SEA objectives

Inevitably, there will be some conflict between development and environmental protection unless the plan in question targets conservation such as a BAP. Environmental indicators in the SEA process should be able to identify this conflict at an early stage so that a compromise may be reached before it is too late. For example, if a proposed transport plan is predicted to impact negatively on an area designated for conservation by developing a new road, an indicator could be developed that allows a certain amount of land to be used that would not significantly impact on the designated area. However, if the plan would breach this threshold, an alternative route would have to be considered. In this instance, the environmental indicator would suggest that the plan objective would have to be amended to avoid significant damage to the designated site and alternatives should be explored.

These criteria were established to ensure the environmental indicators would meet the needs of SEA. In addition, by standardizing the selection criteria the indicator development process should be more streamlined, costs should be reduced, duplication of effort should be minimized and consistency ensured, thereby increasing the potential for cross SEA comparison (ITFM, 1994).

Evaluation of indicators against criteria

In order to evaluate the SEA indicators against the established criteria, a matrix format can be employed. Table 21.3 presents an example of potential environmental indicators for biodiversity, air, water and climatic factors. The environmental indicators are listed on the vertical axis and the criteria on the horizontal axis. Information is recorded in the cells relating to each indicator and each criterion. This allows the SEA practitioner to evaluate, at a glance, which criteria are covered by particular indicators thus enabling any gaps to be quickly identified. If an indicator fails to meet the majority of the criteria it may be discarded but only after some consideration to identify why the indicator was chosen in the first place. For example, an indicator may only meet the criterion 'relevant to the plan' and, depending on the importance of the indicator (to the SEA), this may be enough to ensure its continued inclusion in the list. These examples highlight the importance of local knowledge of the plan in evaluating environmental indicators.

In order to reduce the amount of information required in the matrix, each criterion is designated a set of abbreviations that must be clearly defined in the legend of the table. These abbreviations should be adapted to suit each set of SEA indicators for a particular plan or programme. The matrix should be kept as simple as possible while still remaining useful. The level of detail will depend on the type of SEA in question. The list below gives examples of potential abbreviations which could be tailored to a proposed plan or programme (see also Table 21.3).

1 Policy relevant: Y = yes; N = no.
2 Range of environmental receptors: Y = yes; N = no.
3 Relevant to the plan: Y = yes; N = no.
4 Show trends: S = short-term effect; L = long-term effect; C = continuous; W = weekly; 2W = every two weeks; M = monthly; 6M = six monthly; A = annually; 2A = every two years; 3A, 4A, etc; L = local; R = regional; N = national; TA = has target(s) associated with it; TN = does not have associated target(s).
5 Understandable: E = easily understandable: D = easy to display.

Table 21.3 *Indicators versus criteria matrix with examples from biodiversity, air, water and climatic factors*

	Indicator	Policy relevant	Range of environmental receptors	Relevant to the plan	Show trends	Understandable	Well-founded	Provide early warning	Adaptable	Identify potential conflict
1	*Biodiversity*									
	Number of sites with habitat enhancement	Y	Y	Y	L; R; N; TN; ST; LT	E; D	Y; A	Y	Y	Y
2	*Air*									
	Number of exceedences of air quality limits	Y	Y	Y	L; R; N; TA; ST; LT	E; D	Y; A	Y	Y	Y
3	*Water*									
	Minimize culverting of watercourses	Y	Y	Y	L; LT; TN;	E; D	Y; A	Y	Y	Y
4	*Climatic factors*									
	Insurance claims due to flooding	N	N	Y	L; TN; ST; LT	E; D	Y; A	N	Y	N

6　Well-founded in technical and scientific terms: Y = data and underlying methodology is quality assured; N = data and underlying methodology is not quality; A = data available at reasonable cost; NA = data not available at reasonable cost;

7　Prioritize key issues: Y = yes, can potentially provide an early warning; N = no, cannot potentially provide an early warning;

8　Adaptable: Y = yes; N = no.

9　Identify conflict: Y = yes; N = no.

The set of criteria presented here was based on criteria widely used elsewhere, both nationally and internationally, while at the same time accommodating SEA needs and requirements. As expected, it was not possible to use a set of criteria already in existence to select environmental indicators for SEA purposes due to the fact that they were not developed specifically for SEA. Evaluating the indicators against the criteria using a matrix format proved useful to ensure all criteria were accounted for in the list of indicators.

Limitations of environmental indicators

Although environmental indicators are widely used in many different environmental contexts, they should not be seen to be the only way to measure environmental impact in an SEA. They are certainly a very useful tool but are fraught with uncertainty and misinterpretation. Table 21.4 presents some examples of advantages and disadvantages of environmental indicators in an SEA context. Environmental indicators do not provide an explanation of why change is occurring, rather they provide evidence of change. They should be seen as part of a toolkit for demonstrating the environmental impact of proposed plans and programmes. Careful consideration and attention should be given to their identification, selection and interpretation to ensure they are fit for purpose, that is, they are capable of assessing what they are intended to assess. Finding successful plan-specific environmental indicators can be a challenging exercise due to the potential impacts from external plans and unrelated factors. However, there is a growing wealth of guidance and expertise available that can help overcome these difficulties. Supporting data may not always be available for the chosen environmental indicators and very often SEA practitioners report data gaps. Where data is unavailable or inaccessible, a request to the relevant authorities may be made to extend the monitoring programme to cover these gaps, may be one solution.

Table 21.4 *Advantages and disadvantages of environmental indicators in SEA*

Advantages	Disadvantages
Simplify	Can be difficult to select
Focus monitoring	Appropriate data may not be available
Reduce costs	May be affected by external factors
Maximize resources	Require continual updating
Reduce workload	

Application of indicators within the Irish SEA system

Approximately 16 SEAs were carried out in Ireland in the two to three-year period following the transposition of the Directive 2001/42/EC in July 2004. These focused to a large extent on land-use plans but also included plans for water management, waste management, flood risk management and energy. In order to assess the quality and effectiveness of SEA, it is necessary to review the environmental report to ensure it is in compliance with its stated objectives. The quality assessment of SEA is a requirement under Article 12 of Directive 2001/42/EC in which EU member states must ensure that environmental reports are of sufficient quality to meet its demands. However, the Directive does not provide guidance on how to ensure quality.

The quality of the SEA process is paramount (João, 2005). To date, a number of quality review checklists have been proposed (ODPM, 2004; IAIA, 2002; IEMA, 2004; EPA, 2001). In general these checklists are intended to help test whether the requirements of the SEA Directive are met, identify any problems in the Environmental Report and show how effectively the SEA has integrated environmental considerations into the plan making process. According to the IAIA (2002), a good quality SEA is considered to be one that is integrated, sustainability led, focused, accountable, participative and iterative.

In both Poland (Maćkowiak-Pandera and Jessel, 2005) and the Czech Republic (Václavíková and Jendrike, 2005), the quality of an environmental report is based on the proven skills and track record of experts employed to carry out the process. In addition to this, Powell (2005) argues that expert judgement can be overrated and the value of local parties and stakeholders should not be underestimated. Given these observations, an analysis of the composition of the team carrying out the SEA may be a good indication of quality. In Ireland, an assessment of the usefulness of environmental indicators in the quality review process is currently being undertaken. Given that carefully chosen objectives, targets and indicators will help lead to an unbiased SEA process, analysis of the indicators could potentially be a useful tool in quality review.

Lessons learned from the use of environmental indicators
Experience gained from devising a monitoring programme for the Dublin Docklands SEA (Prendergast and Donnelly, 2006) may be of benefit to SEA practitioners and local/regional authority staff engaged in carrying out similar exercises. The following were considered important lessons learned during the development of objectives, targets and indicators for the Dublin Docklands SEA:

- The Docklands Master Plan SEA was the first SEA conducted in Ireland under the terms of the Directive, and the SEA objectives represented a 'first attempt' at devising appropriate objectives. The objectives were drawn up by the SEA team, which comprised one consultant and two in-house members of the Docklands Authority. In hindsight, some of the objectives were ambiguous and vague in their wording. In the case of the Docklands Master Plan SEA, an example of imprecise wording occurred in relation to one of the objectives for water, which initially read 'to ensure adequate good quality water supply'. However, as the responsibility for supplying water to the area falls to Dublin City Council, it is outside the remit of the Docklands Master Plan. The authority does have a responsibility to provide a water supply *network*, in particular on the lands it owns in the area. The objective has been amended to include the term network: 'To provide an efficient water supply network in the Docklands Area.' The simple rewording of the objective has lead to greater clarity and focus.

- It was considered that a multidisciplinary team was required to devise the monitoring programme, with a particular need for input from both planners and environmental scientists. Some of the environmental impacts of the plan may be outside the scope of expertise of many planners, and this needs to be recognized in the process and the relevant scientific expertise included. Without that expertise, inappropriate objectives, indicators and targets may be devised that may add to monitoring costs and lead to a biased SEA. Having the relevant scientific expertise as part of the team enables a more focused monitoring programme to be developed.

- A current issue in SEA is whether the SEA process should be employed to monitor not only environmental, but other impacts of a plan or programme, for example, socio-economic impacts. In addition, planning authorities are now required to carry out Housing and Retail Strategies. The team concluded that SEA should not be combined with any other form of assessment; this could lead to confusion and the blurring of what the environmental impacts of the plan are.

Conclusions

In conclusion, the choice of successful environmental indicators is vital to ensure a robust SEA process. If the environmental indicators are inaccurate, they may give misleading information that may result in flawed decision-making. It is also important not to overestimate the role of environmental indicators. They should focus on key changes and indicate that change is occurring. However, it is up to the end-user to correctly interpret why the change has taken place.

The more stakeholders that are involved in the initial development of environmental indicators for SEA the better, so as to ensure as many aspects and viewpoints as possible are considered in the process. In turn, this will ensure validation of the indicators by consensus of experts and end-users. All the examples and criteria in the world cannot substitute for local knowledge of the environmental issues related to the plan.

Finally, it is worth spending time and resources in the initial stages of SEA and plan development to establish successful environmental indicators. This will maximize resources, minimize duplication of effort and costs and result in a successful monitoring programme.

References

Bockstaller, C. and Girardin, P. (2003) 'How to validate environmental indicators', *Agricultural Systems*, vol 76, pp639–653

Cloquell-Ballester, V-A., Monterde-Diaz, R. and Santamarina-Siurana, M-C. (2006) 'Indicators validation for the improvement of environmental and social impact quantitative assessment', *Environmental Impact Assessment Review*, vol 26, pp79–105

DOEHLG (Department of Environment Heritage and Local Government) (2004) 'Implementation of SEA Directive (2001/42/EC): Assessment of the effects of certain plans and programmes on the environment', guidelines for regional authorities and planning authorities, DOEHLG, Dublin

Donnelly, A., Jennings, E., Finnan, J., Mooney, P., Lynn, D., Jones, M., O'Mahony, T., Thérivel, R. and Byrne, G. (2006a) 'Workshop approach to developing objectives, targets and indicators for use in strategic environmental assessment (SEA)', *Journal of Environmental Assessment Policy and Management*, vol 8, pp135–156

Donnelly, A., Jones, M., O'Mahony, T. and Byrne, G. (2006b) 'Decision support framework for establishing objectives, targets and indicators for use in SEA', *Impact Assessment and Project Appraisal*, vol 24, pp151–157

Donnelly, A., Jones, M., O'Mahony, T. and Byrne, G. (2007) 'Selecting environmental indicators for use in strategic environmental assessment (SEA)', *Environmental Impact Assessment Review*, vol 27, pp161–175

EPA (Environmental Protection Agency) (2001) *Development of Strategic Environmental Assessment (SEA) methodologies for plans and programmes in Ireland*, EPA, Wexford, ERTDI Programme

IAIA (International Association for Impact Assessment) (2002) 'Strategic environmental assessment performance criteria', *Special Publications Series*, No 1, IAIA, Fargo, ND

IEMA (Institute of Environmental Management and Assessment) (2004) *IEMA Strategic Environmental Assessment (SEA) Environmental Report (ER) Review Criteria*, IEMA, Lincoln

ITFM (Intergovernmental Task Force on Monitoring) (1994) 'Water-quality monitoring in the United States', ITFM, http://acwi.gov/overview.html

João, E. (2005) 'SEA outlook: Future challenges and possibilities', in Schmidt, M., João, E. and Abbrecht, E. (eds) *Implementing Strategic Environmental Assessment*, Springer-Verlag, Berlin

Kurtz, J., Jackson, L. and Fisher, W. (2001) 'Strategies for evaluating indicators based on guidelines from the Environmental Protection Agency's Office of Research and Development', *Ecological Indicators*, vol 1, pp49–60

Maćkowiak-Pandera, J. and Jessel, B. (2005) 'Development of SEA in Poland', in Schmidt, M., João, E. and Abbrecht, E. (eds) *Implementing Strategic Environmental Assessment*, Springer-Verlag, Berlin

ODPM (Office of the Deputy Prime Minister) (2004) *A Draft Practical Guide to the Strategic Environmental Assessment Directive*, ODPM, London

ODPM (2005) *Sustainability Appraisal of Regional Spatial Strategies and Local Development Documents, Guidance for Regional Planning Bodies and Local Development Authorities*, ODPM, London

Powell, N. (2005) 'SEA in Canada', in Schmidt, M., João, E. and Abbrecht, E. (eds) *Implementing Strategic Environmental Assessment*, Springer-Verlag, Berlin

Prendergast, T. and Donnelly, A. (2006) 'Reconciling planning with environmental issues in the SEA process – Dublin Docklands: A case study', *Pleanáil* (Journal of the Irish Planning Institute), vol 17, pp101–118

Thérivel, R. (2004) *Strategic Environmental Assessment in Action*, Earthscan, London
UNDP (United Nations Development Programme) (undated) 'Signposts of development', www.undp.org/eo/documents/methodology/rbm/Indicators-Paperl.doc
Václavíková, L. and Jendrike, H. (2005) 'National strategy for the implementation of SEA in the Czech Republic', in Schmidt, M., João, E. and Abbrecht, E. (eds) *Implementing Strategic Environmental Assessment*, Springer-Verlag, Berlin

22
Some Wider Reflections on the Challenge of Public Participation in SEA

Bo Elling

Introduction

Debates about public participation in environmental assessment (EA) often concern when participation should take place, how it can be practised and who should participate. In recent years, discussions have focused also on its efficiency and outcomes in general. This chapter focuses on why public participation is essential for strategic environmental assessment (SEA). It will be argued that public participation faces many challenges that still have to be met or dealt with more appropriately than has hitherto been the case in SEA research and development. The argument is based on the author's theoretical research on the subject of SEA and case studies carried out over many years. It also incorporates presentations and discussions that took place at the sessions on public participation at the 2005 International Association for Impact Assessment (IAIA) SEA Conference in Prague. The intent in this chapter is not to provide detailed recommendations about how public participation in SEA should take place, rather it contains reflections on the different challenges of public participation in the SEA process and the principal matters that must be taken into account in the conduct of SEA. These matters have core aspects in common although they must be applied in practice in each individual case.

Background

If public participation is going to be improved, three essential aspects need attention:

- Firstly, the increasing use of legal provision for SEA that can be observed worldwide.
- Secondly, the strategic and abstract character of SEA in general.

- Thirdly, the issue of ownership and responsibility for final decisions, which exists when wider use of public participation becomes a reality.

Implications of legal requirement for SEA

In coming years, SEA practice will develop from being conducted on a case-by-case basis to become a more systematically utilized process conducted in accordance with certain rules and principles. In recent years, there has been an enormous rise in the number of SEAs. This has been the result of legislated requirements, for example in European Union (EU) member states where SEA is obligatory for certain plans and programmes, and in some countries and cases also for policies (see Sadler, 2005; Dalal-Clayton and Sadler, 2005). Undoubtedly, this will lead to the development of standardized methods of assessment and to efforts to improve the effectiveness and efficiency of SEA application. Such tendencies may compromise public participation in many ways. However, this situation will also favour those concerned, especially among politicians and decision-makers, to make public participation procedures work better and bring them to the stage where major inputs to the whole process come from the broader public and not solely from stakeholders with strong economic or political interests in the plan or programme in question. The reasons for this are closely linked to the strategic and abstract character of SEA, which we shall return to later.

In Directive 2001/42/EC, there is a legal obligation to undertake SEA monitoring (Article 10). The rationale for monitoring must be seen in connection to the strategic character of SEA, which makes it very different from project environmental impact assessment (EIA). Policies, plans and programmes (PPPs) can be changed or revised without complicated technical and economic interventions if they do not work as intended. But one cannot remove an airport or a highway from one day to another because the impacts turn out to be somewhat different from what was assessed or predicted. Strategic decisions that create a framework for future developments can be modified and changed overnight and thus their actual or real implications for the environment are of great interest. In this way, monitoring can play a central role in the continual process of planning and programming. This raises several questions, namely: What role can or should public participation play in monitoring? Why is it of vital interest and how can it be designed? These issues are new and must be addressed when dealing with public participation in SEA in monitoring. Specifically, as argued below, public participation in monitoring can prove to be a vital renewal of the field and moreover give public involvement a new dimension.

Strategic character and abstract nature of SEA

The strategic character of SEA also reinforces the role of public participation and the need to conduct it differently than public involvement in EIA. Strategic planning is first and foremost about values and priorities for future developments. Values and priorities are the crucial basis for any plan or programme, and not just something that should be reflected in or added to technical or economic design of an action. Such values and priorities cannot be produced solely by planners or decision-makers. They also must be drawn from the process of consultation with the ordinary public and reflect the values and priorities that exist amongst citizens and different interest groups. At least, this is the case when the planning and programming process is part of a democratic decision-making process or that is conducted by democratically elected bodies, which is normally the situation when dealing with SEA.

These characteristics make public involvement not only desirable but necessary, however, they are also the reason why it is rather difficult to involve the public. The character of SEA that deals with mainly planning frameworks or matters of an abstract and general nature complicates such involvement, which is restricted to objectives and values that lie behind planning or programming steps. At this level of decision-making, it is much more difficult to motivate and encourage public input to strategic actions than if more concrete actions are at stake. Case studies in California clearly demonstrated that the public experienced difficulties in grasping and staying involved with abstract and long planning processes (Schaffer and Ortolano, 2005). Thus, in undertaking SEA, it is a major challenge to motivate public involvement and to an extent that makes the process fulfil democratic standards and expectations (Croal, 2005).

Ownership and responsibility for final decisions

Finally, the issue of ownership of and responsibility for final decisions has been a major challenge when dealing with public involvement in SEA. If public involvement and participation is intensified and widened, especially to strategic topics and issues of basic or essential character, then questions arise regarding who owns the final decisions and consequently who is to be held responsible for them. In a representative democratic system, decision-makers must be able to legitimize their choices on the bases of political criteria. They should not be able to legitimize decisions simply by saying, for instance, these are the outcome of public involvement and contributions.

In such a case, capabilities to and possibilities for involvement should be the same for all citizens and fully democratic as in the representative political system itself. But this is not the situation. Furthermore, it is an open question as to whether or not such a situation would be desirable. Public involvement and participation should be a supplementing (rather then competing) process to representative democracy, helping this system to take better decisions and helping citizens to act in conjunction with democratic decisions instead of reacting according to narrow self-interest (for example, the 'not in my backyard' (NIMBY) syndrome).

If the above argument holds, it points to a need to make major changes in how SEA is practised to ensure public participation will play a core role. At this time, the discussion should not be about whether or not public participation should be part of SEA. Moreover, there is little doubt that public involvement must take place at the earliest possible stage and at all other relevant stages during the entire SEA process. Discussions regarding public participation, to a much greater extent, should be linked to the actual design of an SEA including how this process gives space for public participation, what type of participation is needed, and what should come out of it.

Wider analysis and review

A wider analysis of the issues outlined above and challenges to public participation in SEA shows that substantively they are closely linked. There is no good reason *not* to believe that a massive application of SEA to certain planning and programming processes in accordance with supra-national or international standards will lead to various efforts to make the conduct of an SEA in specific cases more efficient and to improve its effectiveness in affecting final decisions. Such efforts have been observed in the developments in EIA that have taken place since its application to projects from the beginning of the 1970s and onwards throughout the 1980s and 1990s until today (Sadler, 1996). The application of SEA in itself is part of this trend (Sadler and Verheem, 1996; Thérivel and Partidário, 1996), recognizing that it can provide a framework for improving the effectiveness of EIA or even make some EIA applications superfluous (Lee and Walsh, 1992). Concern has been expressed that such developments will compromise public participation in the case of EIA given the development of standard methods and procedures and the claims for efficiency are necessarily linked to attempts by governing authorities to control the process and its outcome (Elling, 2008). This includes attempts to control the identification of substantive issues, to control the subjects for public participation, balancing effects during the assessment, and to limit the process to instrumental matters of efficiency.

On the other hand, the claim that the application of SEA will support the need for public involvement and participation might seem a contradiction at first sight. But it should be taken as evidence of a complex situation in that developments cannot be expected to follow one-sided or prejudiced positions. This is also why the analysis offered here looks at a wider utilization of SEA reflective of its strategic and abstract character. This characteristic demands a high level of public participation in all steps of the SEA process, however, the often abstract and highly general content of strategic proposals makes it difficult to engage and motivate citizens to become involved in and contribute to SEA. Obviously, this is a challenge that cannot be ignored; it is also obvious that no single action or effort can meet it. A range of different actions and steps is needed.

The issues to be taken into account include:

- Should the assessment be integrated into the planning/programming process or not?
- Where or when are information technology and internet facilities useable?
- Can the process of SEA be oriented towards certain objectives, aims or goals?
- Which type of rationality should be applied or be made a criterion for good SEA practice and how can rationality be applied?

- Should public participation in monitoring be obligatory?
- Who has the ownership and responsibility for final decisions?

Integration of the SEA

Without taking account of the serious barriers to public involvement outlined above, it is still widely suggested that the integrative approach to SEA – integrating it into PPP processes rather than applying to a final proposal – is the most effective way the assessment can influence the final decision (for example, Eggenberger and Partidário, 2000). Moreover, it is a common view that more knowledge brought into the assessment leads to better planning decisions (for example, Kørnøv and Thissen, 2000).

Immediately one could ask: effective for whom, effective in relation to which aims or interests? Which type of knowledge is needed in relation to what purpose? Is planning about taking account of as much knowledge as possible or should it be directed instead towards dialogue and deliberative debates among the different interests involved or concerned?

Moreover, very few people have focused on the concern that the integrative approach can be counterproductive in relation to two other major aims of SEA: (a) to create transparency in the process of decision-making; and (b) to open up the possibility for public participation. Integrating SEA into PPP processes means that environmental priorities and balance of effects become less visible in relation to other aims and interests and that it becomes more difficult for citizens and other outside reviewers to be involved in the assessment. For example, it can be much more complicated to be aware of when citizens can be involved, and on the basis of which subjects, issues or priorities.

At the least, discourse on the integrative approach should address these issues. Furthermore, it should address issues such as: how are public proposals recorded during the process of planning and assessment and made available to decision-makers? How can citizens' proposals be made available and useful for other citizens – immediately or at a later stage of the process? Such issues add to the complicated fact of substantive planning processes and make it difficult for citizens to be involved.

The right answer to this issue may not be the counterfactual of not integrating SEA into the process of planning or programming. But those difficulties and barriers that the integrative approach implies should not be ignored. If public participation is to play a major role in SEA, such difficulties and barriers should be explicitly addressed with conscious and appropriate steps and efforts.

Information technology and the internet

Digital technologies have proved to be powerful and creative tools for communication. They can promote and enhance communication, dissemination and updating of information, in this case on the stage and substance of the planning and assessment process. For citizens and the general public, it makes access to that information and submission of comments and proposals so much easier. It can promote reciprocal communication between the competent authority and the general public at all stages of the SEA process. A study carried out by Gonzales et al (2005) demonstrates such possibilities and illustrates how information technology (IT) can be applied to knowledge processing and monitoring.

Although IT may facilitate the SEA process in many ways, it may also change the direction and control of the process in favour of outside reviewers and commentators. What will happen if such developments take place more widely and how would it change the process of planning and SEA? Will it, for example, result in an SEA process of a more deliberative and dialogical character? Yet capitalizing on new opportunities to employ IT might lead to a digital divide between citizens, since not all people have access to IT and the internet. Such concern will therefore be part of the discussion on how to utilize new digital instruments.

Orientation of SEA

The pressure to make SEA more efficient and to include public participation in these efforts is consistent with the thesis that public involvement is necessary to ensure public institutions fulfil their tasks (Fischer, 2000). The justification of this discourse is that reality is complicated and manifold and without the representation of various local interests, planning institutions will not function efficiently. However, this view only represents the instrumental side of public planning and programming. Some fear that such an approach will leave SEA as an exercise in formalism at an abstract level instead of a means to achieve environmental protection and enhancement. In a much wider view, it is the very strategic character of SEA that makes public participation desirable and necessary, providing decisive inputs on the objectives and the underlying values of planning.

This could point to a divide between citizens with such motivation and citizens with the skills to gain an overview and address abstract matters, leading consequently to more formalized practise of public participation (for example, formal hearings on certain matters). But it could also be taken as evidence that these challenges should be met with a variety of different efforts. Moreover, experience from specific cases, trial runs and research projects indicate that such challenges appear at all levels and steps of conducting SEA as a part of strategic planning and not only at specific phases for public involvement (Croal, 2005).

Another issue that complicates strategic planning and programming is how to take account of different considerations with counteractive implications. One response is to orient the process towards specific goals that are defined beforehand. In the case of SEA, it is often suggested that the process should be guided by sustainability criteria (Sadler, 1996; Partidário and Clark, 1999; Hilding-Rydevik and Theodórsdóttir, 2004). Orienting SEA towards specifically defined sustainability criteria or balancing environmental and socio-economic objectives helps address the abstract and general character of SEA.

If the SEA process is directed towards such specific goals, it could open up the possibility for *early* public participation, for example, in the identification of the objectives for the proposal in question and in defining the scope of the assessment. This would also open the process to specific criteria for balancing effects and to submission of balanced proposals to decision-makers. But first and foremost, the assessment would have to rely on involving experts and officers from different spheres of interest. Thus having an SEA guided by sustainability criteria could open up the possibility for early public involvement, but it could also result in more balancing and priority setting, for example between environmental and economic values or concerns. Such attempts could compromise or constrain public involvement.

An alternative approach may be to orient the assessment towards reaching an understanding of all likely environmental effects and interests linked to different policy, planning or programming options and then let the politicians/decision-makers make the priorities afterwards (Elling, 2008). This may also open the possibility for early public participation and for introducing different dimensions of rationality into the process through involving citizens. These dimensions would include ethical and aesthetical rationality and not just the cognitive-instrumental rationality related to efficiency in obtaining specific goals (aspects explained in more detail below).

Notions of rationality

As suggested already, the two orientations of SEA involve two very different notions of rationality. The orientation of SEA to specific goals – as in the case of sustainability – involves cognitive-instrumental rationality, referred to here as instrumental rationality. Being rational or acting rationally in this case will mean to act in a way that fulfils the defined objectives or goals to the highest possible degree. This is the purpose of the action. The criterion for rationality (in this sense of the term) is efficiency.

If SEA is oriented towards reaching an understanding of all likely environmental effects, it involves not only cognitive-instrumental rationality (understanding the impacts cognitively) but also ethical and aesthetic rationality. Understanding impacts does not involve only cognition, but understanding can depend on certain norms of what is good or bad. This is the ethical side of being rational. If an action corresponds with norms related to it then the action is ethically rationally. The criterion of rationality in this sense is thus rightness; obviously something that is very different from efficiency.

Furthermore, understanding can depend on concepts of what is beautiful. This is the aesthetic-expressive side of being rational in this sense. In this case, the criterion for rationality is whether or not the action is meant as stated or expressed – also called truthfulness.

So, in summary, the criteria of being rational and acting rationally in all three SEA orientations is effectiveness, rightness and truthfulness; as a unity, not just in terms of only one aspect. In the matter of rationality, we urgently need to comprehend that modern societal norms regarding what is good or bad or what is beautiful or ugly do not have their origin solely in tradition, habits and culture – as it is the case in pre-modern societies – but are linked to mutual understanding among ordinary people and different groups in everyday life (Elling, 2008). What is ethical and aesthetic can thus be highly fluid and dependent on ordinary people's views and feelings. It cannot be predefined by certain technical or economic standards but must rely on the specific context, time and the people involved.

Deontological or teleological views

As mentioned above, SEA can be oriented towards either specific goals defined beforehand or all likely effects. In that context, note that an SEA is related to a specific plan or programme, which can be called the original action in the sense that it triggers actions to assess its potential environmental impact. Also, this original action can be oriented either to goals or mutual understanding. So now we have two actions – the original action and the SEA action – and both can be oriented either toward specific goals or mutual understanding.

The risk of conflict exists. If we want to employ all three types of rationality in the assessment process, they must be oriented towards mutual understanding. An SEA that is oriented towards understanding can be integrated into a planning process that is oriented towards specific goals. But this will probably not be done without contradictions. On the other hand, we cannot always expect the original action to be oriented towards understanding.

Further complicating this situation, there are three principal acting parties – the developer, the authorities and the public or citizens – who cannot be presupposed to all have the same views on what should be the orientation of these two actions. They can have very different views on what is at stake, especially when it comes to normative statements, which we call teleological when they are oriented towards predefined objectives/goals and deontological when they are oriented towards understanding.

The assessment is a reflection on different options and their implications for the environment. But as argued in detail in Elling (2008), it should be expected that both the developer and the administration reflect purposively or in a goal-oriented way, whereas the citizens can be predicted to reflect with an orientation towards reaching understanding. Thus, the reflexive process may be doomed from the outset. Not only because the problem may preclude a consensus, but also because it eliminates, in fact, the chance of even conducting reflexive processes in a dialogue between the actors. This problem may be illustrated on the basis of the points of departure expected from each of the acting parties.

Three acting parties and their specific points of departure

The developer starts from a given objective and supports the realization of his original proposal in a relationship between means and ends. Developers also use arguments concerning the consequences of implementing their proposal, for example, of a technical nature, concerning the economic effects, moral values and interests in the proposal, such as benefits to the environment. They deploy teleological arguments for the realization of the proposal.

The administration must look into the likely environmental consequences of the proposal and does so in the light of the means to realize the objective pursued by the developer. In this context, note that Directive 2001/42/EC (like Directive 85/337/EEC and Directive 97/11/EC) does not at any stage mention the aim of the proposal at hand as relevant to the assessment of its environmental impact. Accordingly, the administration will argue in favour of the least possible harm and the highest possible benefits, it will champion environmental values as a means of realizing the objective. Such arguments also will be teleological.

Conversely, citizens as a body will not consider the proposal in the means-to-an-end dimension, but will question both its objective and the means for its realization, including the potential consequences. As far as citizens are concerned, the environmental values being affected feature as an end, and not as a means. Their argumentation will be geared towards enhancing environmental values, and takes a critical approach to any weakening of these. It will seek out possible improvements to the environment, unfettered by the developer's objective behind the proposal. As a result, citizens argue in a manner that subordinates the developer's proposal to environmental values, and not vice versa. This means that their arguments are deontological.

For a chance of a consensus to be present beforehand, it must be possible to argue with teleological or with deontological primacy. If primacy is given to teleological argumentation, the process will be reduced to instrumental thinking, and hence in actual fact this gives the developer or the administration the option of controlling the contents and aim of the process in line with the given relation between means and end. Conversely, deontological primacy will enable us to escape from such a relation between means and ends, freeing the diversity of communicative rationality.

Deontological primacy is not tantamount to preventing the developer and the administration from tabling teleological arguments. But it does mean that they cannot *a priori* set the terms or preconditions for the dialogue. Nor is it desirable to veto such arguments from the developer or administration, because they need to be presented before they can be responded to.

In addition, if teleological arguments are not stated at this stage, they could be deployed and become decisive in the subsequent decision-making process. For example, it could be asserted that, although the assessment shows that a series of environmental considerations would be beneficial, these should be set aside to some degree in view of the actual objective. Deontological primacy thus only refers to instrumental reason not being in control from the outset. Of course, this is not brought about merely be stating its desirability, but must, in the real world, be advanced through various means. These means are outlined in Elling (2008), who also exemplifies the highly different outcomes from a deontological versus a teleological optimization of environmental concern.

Rational or post-rational

The task of a reflexive SEA must be to optimize concern for the environment in a form that sets or seeks out the objective, meaning not just stating what the objective is but also how it may be fulfilled in the situation at hand. In this manner, the assessment aims to 'set reason free' in connection with the proposed action to the greatest extent possible, so that environmental optimization encompasses cognitive-instrumental facts, normative values and interests, aesthetic and visual conditions, as well as self-expressive factors. We do not need to carry this argument further since it fully illustrates the three core issues for public involvement in SEA, in particular with reference to the issue of rationality.

It is public participation that brings the ethical and aesthetic dimensions into assessment. This provides a major reason to orient the SEA process towards understanding and not towards objectives or goals defined beforehand, for example, as in certain criteria for sustainability. Public participation that involves all three aspects of rationality is essential to SEA; without it the process loses its spirit.

Discussion about a rational or a post-rational approach to SEA often becomes derailed (Bina et al, 2005; Fischer, 2003). The term post-rational is confusing, leading to misunderstanding. Of course the SEA must be based on rationality – what else should it be based on? Tradition is not a possibility as there is none in these cases or matters and nor will an appropriate one be developed for assessments. Power is not acceptable, since SEA must be based on scientific and lay knowledge and assessments of impacts from a given action.

Instead the discussion on rationality should be focused on which type of rationality should be adopted (Elling, 2008). Instrumental rationality is solely a matter of efficiency either of the process or of the effect of the process on the final decision. A wider concept of rationality includes ethical and aesthetic rationality and brings together all three sides of the concept (cognitive-instrumental, ethical and aesthetic). Public participation at all levels, in the identification of objectives for a specific PPP process and in the EA, will prevent developers from steering or controlling the process and avoid narrow instrumentalism.

The ownership and responsibility for final decisions

The key issue of ownership of the final decision has to do with political responsibility. If public involvement in the assessment of likely impacts leads to a dilution of the political responsibility for decision-making, it has failed in its aim. Public participation should contest the legitimacy that decision-makers claim for their decisions by bringing into the process the widest knowledge and rationalities other than those of the decision-makers. These conditions mean the political decision-makers are persuaded by knowledge.

Combined with the issue of rationality, this issue demonstrates that good decisions are not just dependent on the amount of knowledge they can be based on but on which type of information that is available and from where or whom this information is gained.

Openness is not just a matter of letting different groups and stakeholders participate in the assessment but also of allowing them to submit their views and knowledge to other stakeholders and those interested in the assessment and, finally, to present all of this material to decision-makers. If such openness and access to participation by the public, citizens and individual stakeholders are to be maintained, certain procedural requirements for the SEA process need to be considered. In the case of an integrated approach, this means ensuring that the SEA process is oriented towards understanding all likely impacts, that the findings of the assessment in their full extent are submitted to the final decision-makers on the proposal in question, and that the latter assume full responsibility for their selection. This will include the abandonment of balancing effects and self-serving solutions.

Such an approach will contribute to a deontological optimization of environmental concern. This means that assessment takes advantage of public participation that is dialogical and applies a notion of rationality that includes cognitive, ethical and aesthetical aspects; and that political ownership and responsibility for the final decision-making can be clearly identified and pursued.

Public participation in monitoring

The European Directive on SEA demands an obligatory monitoring of environmental effects after the implementation of a plan or programme. In the context of this chapter, it is appropriate to ask if public participation should be applied to such monitoring. If monitoring is left to the authorities alone, the fear is that what is monitored will be biased toward favouring their final decision. This constrains the whole idea of monitoring actual effects and raises the issue of whether public participation in monitoring might have a qualifying effect, broadening it to issues identified in the assessment process. In turn, this raises the question of whether mandatory provision should be made for public participation in monitoring including, for example, obligatory monitoring of subjects proposed by the public or individual citizens. On the other hand, more informal modes of participation in monitoring could stimulate public involvement efforts and activities in the other stages of the SEA process.

Finally, public involvement in monitoring should be seen in relation to the issue of ownership of final decisions already outlined. Monitoring, first of all, can be seen as follow-up measure that identifies what is the real impact of actions that have taken place and how these effects are connected to other activities and impacts from other actions. But it also should be viewed as a quality control on the SEA process, applied in order to inform the decision-makers. Without going more thoroughly into the issue here, it can be said that it underlines the importance of defining ownership of final decisions. At present the issue has not been addressed properly in SEA research.

Conclusion

The intention of this chapter was to point to some challenges to public participation in the development of SEA, to outline some ways of addressing them and to analyse their pros and cons. It was not intended to give an account of how public participation should be practised in all cases. General experience and some of the analysis here have clearly demonstrated that the form of public participation and how it can take place is always dependent on the context. Some approaches will be generally applicable, others only in certain situations.

What these reflections indicate is that, if the involvement of the public and single citizens is taken seriously, with the aim of having an effect on final decision-making to the benefit of the environment, it will change the planning process and the role of planners in that process. The planning process will change from being expert-ruled to one of dialogue between all parties involved. Ideally, SEA will be integrated into that process and strengthen the need for reporting and submission of information to all involved parties at each stage of the process. IT and the internet will be indispensable tools in this process and might create barriers for involvement of some of the interested public. This issue must be addressed appropriately.

If the planning process and the EA are to have a dialogical character, it will not only involve all interested parties, it will also affect the orientation of the SEA process and the notion of rationality on which it should be based. The assessment process must be oriented towards understanding and highlighting all likely effects and interests in relation to the various alternatives. It should not balance effects and create 'best solutions'. The aim of public participation is not to create consensus and balance pros and cons but to ensure that people have understood the impacts of various options and are able to comment on them and register their views and priorities. Final decisions must take such views and priorities into account to be politically legitimate.

Rationality in the process is not about being effective – whether effectiveness of assessment is seen in relation to carrying out the process or as the degree to which it affects the final PPP. Rationality is about taking cognitive, ethical and aesthetic aspects into account as a whole and realizing that this cannot happen without public involvement and contributions from individual citizens.

The role of the planners is not to create a best solution to be submitted to the public for comments, possibly disregarding them, and then presenting the results for decision-makers. On the contrary, their role is to facilitate and guide public dialogue and be a 'dialogue partner' for individual citizens and the general public. Planners' expert knowledge is not something that should overrule common and public views, rather it qualifies and facilitates their appearance in the process.

In this way, public participation becomes more than just a matter of creating democratic decision-making – it becomes a matter of supporting rationality so that it includes not only technical and environmental data and knowledge effectively but also includes the ethical and aesthetic aspects and values of various alternatives in furtherance of the optimization of environmental concerns.

Acknowledgements

The author would like to thank all participants at the sessions on public participation at the IAIA SEA Conference in Prague for their contributions to discussions and especially those giving presentations. My thanks also go to the editors of this book, in particular to Ralf Aschemann and Barry Sadler for their reviews.

References

Bina, O., Wallington, T. and Thissen, W. (2005) 'SEA Theory and Research: An Analysis of the Discourse', Chapter 28 in this volume
Croal, P. (2005) 'Calabash Program: Increasing capacity of civil society in the SACD region to participate in environmental decision-making', project summary of conclusion of two-year contract period, Southern African Institute for Environmental Assessment, Windhoek, Namibia
Dalal-Clayton, B. and Sadler, B. (2005) *Strategic Environmental Assessment: A Sourcebook and Reference Guide to International Experience*, Earthscan, London

Eggenberger, M. and Partidário, M. R. (2000) 'Development of a framework to assist the integration of environmental, social and economic issues in spatial planning', *Impact Assessment and Project Appraisal*, vol 18, no 3, pp201–207

Elling, B. (2008) *Rationality and the Environment*, Earthscan, London

Fischer, F. (2000) *Citizens, Experts, and the Environment: The Politics of Local Knowledge*, Duke University Press, Durham, NC

Fischer, T. B. (2003) 'Strategic environmental assessment in post-modern times', *EIA Review*, vol 23, no 2, pp155–170

Gonzales, A., Gilmer, A., Foley, R., Sweeney, J. and Fry, J. (2005) 'New technologies promoting public involvement: An interactive tool to assist SEA', paper presented at the IAIA SEA Conference, Prague

Hilding-Rydevik, T. and Theodórsdóttir, Á. H. (eds) (2004) *Planning for Sustainable Development: The Practice and Potential of Environmental Assessment*, Nordregio, Stockholm

Kørnøv, L. and Thissen, W. (2000) 'Rationality in decision and policy-making: Implications for strategic environmental assessment', *Impact Assessment and Project Appraisal*, vol 18, no 3, pp191–200

Lee, N. and Walsh, F. (1992) 'Strategic environmental assessment: An overview', *Project Appraisal*, vol 7, no 3, pp126–136

Partidário, M. R. and Clark, R. (1999) *Perspectives on Strategic Environmental Assessment*, Lewis Publishers, Boca Raton, FL

Sadler, B. (1996) *Environmental Assessment in a Changing World: Evaluating Practice to Improve Performance*, International Study of the Effectiveness of Environmental Assessment, final report, Canadian Environmental Assessment Agency, Canada

Sadler, B. (ed) (2005) *Strategic Environmental Assessment at the Policy Level*, Czech Ministry of the Environment for UNECE, Prague

Sadler, B. and Verheem, R. (1996) *Strategic Environmental Assessment: Status, Challenges and Future Directions*, Ministry of Housing, Spatial Planning and the Environment, The Hague

Schaffer, H. and Ortolano, L. (2005) 'Do impact assessments have impact? Influence of SEA on consultation in California land-use plans', paper presented at the IAIA SEA Conference, Prague

Thérivel, R. and Partidário, M. R. (eds) (1996) *The Practice of Strategic Environmental Assessment*, Earthscan, London

23
Addressing Health Impacts in SEA

Alan Bond, Ben Cave, Marco Martuzzi and
Suphakij Nuntavorakarn

Introduction

This chapter addresses the options for addressing health impacts in strategic environmental assessment (SEA). It sets the background for the consideration of health in decision-making, starting with recognition of the potential implications on health and well-being of public policies in general, not just those aiming at health improvements; explains the drivers for the consideration of health in decision-making, including policy and regulatory influences; and examines the tensions between developing a separate health impact assessment (HIA) process at the strategic level to inform decision-making as compared to integrating health issues into an all-encompassing SEA process.

The chapter is written against a background of limited practical experience of considering health in strategic decision-making, although the evolving experience is included. It is also the case that in different countries and even regions, cultures and administrative contexts vary a great deal. As such, no attempt is made to dictate any particular approach for addressing health in SEA; it is recognized that different solutions will suit the different contexts. From the background described, a number of key questions are outlined that formed the basis for discussion at the 2005 International Association for Impact Assessment (IAIA) SEA Conference in Prague. This analysis of these questions is based on papers presented in Prague along with additional evidence gathered by the authors. On this basis, we identify key lessons emerging from the developing practice and suggest areas for future effort, particularly in relation to capacity-building.

Background

In 1974, the Canadian *Lalonde Report* focused on the potential influences that public policies can have on health (Ritsatakis, 2004). In 1986, the World Health Organization (WHO) Ottawa Charter, adopted at the First International Conference on Health Promotion, stated that: 'Health promotion goes beyond health care. It puts health on the agenda of policy makers in all sectors and at all levels' (WHO, 1986). Consequently, healthy public policy has been a main goal of health development and also a driver for the development of HIA in many countries, for example, the Netherlands, Canada and Thailand (Banken, 2003; den Broeder et al, 2003; Phoolcharoen et al, 2003).

Some driving forces can be identified towards this end. WHO has been influential in promoting the integration of health issues into strategic-level thinking and cross-sectoral action is part of its corporate strategy (Ritsatakis, 2004). The Third European Conference on Environment and Health held in London (16–18 June 1999) was attended by more than 70 ministers of health, environment and transport from 54 countries. One agreed action from this meeting was to 'invite countries to introduce and/or carry out strategic assessments of the environment and health impacts of proposed policies, plans, programmes and general rules' (WHO, 1999, p4).

In a legal context at a European level, Hart (2004) argues that the European Convention on Human Rights places obligations on public authorities to prevent the infringement of citizens' rights to life, and this might mean any court may expect some form of assessment to have taken place beforehand. Where the infringement is health-related, the courts may well expect some form of HIA to have been undertaken.

In the European Union (EU), the SEA Directive was adopted in 2001 and came into force on 21 July 2004, now binding 27 member states. This requires specific consideration of 'the likely significant effects on the environment, including on issues such as ... human health' (European Parliament and the Council of the EU, 2001). Furthermore, the United Nations Economic Commission for Europe (UNECE) have supplemented the Espoo Convention (UNECE, 1991) with the SEA Protocol (UNECE, 2003) which came into force on 11 July 2010. The Protocol implements the political commitments made at the Third European Conference on Environment and Health and uses the term 'environment and health' throughout. It indicates that health authorities should be consulted at the different stages of the process (Dora, 2004) and so goes further than the SEA Directive. On 15 July 2004, the European Commissioner for Health and Consumer Protection, David Byrne, launched a reflection process on EU health policy to help shape the future EU health strategy with a paper that stressed the importance of putting health at the centre of EU policy-making (Byrne, 2004).

Thus, there is clearly momentum for addressing health at the strategic level, sometimes driven by existing practice, sometimes driving that practice. For example, HIA is taking place at policy level in the following jurisdictions: Québec, Canada, and also by Health Canada of trade policies (Banken, 2004); the Netherlands (Roscam Abbing, 2004); and Wales (Breeze and Kemm, 2000).

So, although we can see evidence of action in some countries, it is clear that consideration of health at strategic levels in other sectors is far from widespread. The way in which health is addressed also differs considerably. For example, in Australia, HIA is a component of environmental impact assessment (EIA)/SEA procedures (Wright, 2004) while in some German

Bundesländer, HIA is a separate process at strategic levels (Fehr et al, 2004). The provision for HIA also differs: in Québec, HIA is based on a statutory requirement; in England, it is undertaken as a voluntary procedure (Kemm, 2004) mainly at project level, although some local authorities have begun to formalize its requirement as part of development control policies.

Health is often defined as 'a state of complete physical, mental and social well-being and not merely the absence of disease and infirmity' (WHO, 1946). In this context, sustainability and health are inextricably linked: public policies which promote long-term sustainability also promote health.

There is a clear need for a strong interface between health and other sectors, including spatial and land-use planning, education, employment, social affairs, justice, agriculture, and so on. However, there is evidence that health remains out of touch with other sectors (for example, in relation to health and planning, see Fitzpatrick, 1978). This suggests that the cross-sectoral application of health has not yet been achieved.

Banken considered the institutionalization of HIA and suggested that there may be a 'policy window for implementing HIA in decision-making for non-health sectors' (Banken, 2001, p15). Many countries are just beginning to institutionalize SEA and it is clear that there is currently pressure for addressing health in SEA. Does this present an opportunity for integration?

There are many threats to such a development, including the failure of the health sector to engage with SEA. In England and Wales, the National Health Service (NHS) turned down the opportunity to be listed as a statutory consultee for review and comment on SEA applications: to be so listed would involve allocation of considerable resources and it was feared that the health sector would not have the capacity to support the full assessment of health. It should be noted that obligations imposed by the UNECE SEA Protocol, now ratified, are likely to require the NHS to be a statutory consultee in the future. Also, Bond (2004) points out that screening on environmental grounds can remove the need for an EIA that, if health was integrated, might preclude its consideration even though significant health outcomes were possible.

A key threat is that health will be inadequately addressed in SEA as is currently the case in EIA (Arquiaga et al, 1994; BMA, 1998). Vanclay (2004, p276) argues that WHO promotes 'a social definition of health' which makes HIA no different to social impact assessment (SIA). Of concern here is that existing evidence suggests that social issues are considered to be poor relations in EIA (Glasson and Heaney, 1993; Chadwick, 2002). However, health is determined by both physical and social factors, indicating that environmental, social and health issues all need to be given appropriate consideration in an assessment. A key to enhancing the evidence base for HIA is good practice standards for review (Mindell et al, 2004a); such standards have already been proposed for SEA (see, for example, Bonde and Cherp, 2000). But are they good enough to consider the health issues? This means that quality criteria may need to be developed covering, among others, the quality of evidence, methods, participation, transparency, and equity.

In addition to the strong link between health and sustainability, the main goals of healthy public policy are comparable to those of sustainable development.

Indeed, Principle 1 of the Rio Declaration on Environment and Development states:

> *Human beings are at the centre of concerns for sustainable development. They are entitled to a healthy and productive life in harmony with nature. (UNCED, 1992, p11)*

A number of key questions can be drawn from this background, which provides the basis for the following analysis and review:

- How is it possible to strengthen the cross-sectoral application of health in SEA?
- What are the opportunities and approaches for integrating HIA and SEA?
- How can the engagement of health professionals in SEA be improved?
- Are there case examples of the consideration of health in SEA where real benefits can be identified?
- Is integration of HIA and SEA desirable?

Analysis and review

Instead of considering HIA and SEA as two separate tools and trying to integrate them, the experiences of HIA at the strategic level and the experiences of SEA that have included health issues should be shared, critically examined and used to advance understanding.

How is it possible to strengthen the cross-sectoral application of health in SEA?

Although there is recognition that health professionals need to understand and engage with SEA processes, this must be placed in the context of an overall need for the improvement of the consideration of health in environmental decision-making in general. Studies are beginning to report an increasing appreciation of the need to incorporate health issues into transport planning (Tiwari, 2003; Davis, 2005; Coyle et al, 2009), into land-use planning (Jackson, 2003; France, 2004; Cave et al, 2005; Kidd, 2007, Burns and Bond, 2008) and into SEA (Kørnøv, 2009). It also clear that in these fields, as a general rule, engagement with health professionals is either not examined (for example, Davis, 2005) or is not practised (for example, France, 2004, Fischer et al, 2010).

Experience from the Netherlands demonstrates that cross-sectoral consideration of health is possible, although the model used is that of HIA applied to the policy level by the Ministry of Health working with the Netherlands School of Public Health (Put et al, 2000). The disadvantage of this approach is that the Ministry of Health remains responsible for assessing the health implications of policies in non-health sectors. Interestingly, the study indicated that the policies of all ministries investigated had the potential to affect one or more determinants of health (Put et al, 2000).

What are the opportunities and approaches for integrating HIA and SEA?

Nuntavorakarn et al (2005) categorize different approaches to SEA that are evolving within Thailand into four types: SEA-EIA school; SEA area base; SEA policy options; and SEA development direction. At the same time, they categorize different ways of considering health at the strategic level into four approaches: EIA approaches; ecosystem approaches; healthy public policy approaches; and health inequalities approaches. The feasibility of addressing health through these different approaches is cross-referenced in Table 23.1.

It is clear that both the nature of the SEA and the approach to gathering the evidence base for HIA have consequences for the feasibility of integration of health issues into SEA. Furthermore, research has shown that where HIA is carried out at the strategic level (as opposed to being integrated into SEA), decision-makers can view its conclusions and dissemination as a threat to be managed (Bekker et al, 2005); it is not clear whether an integrated HIA/SEA process would have the same problems.

Table 23.1 *Conceptual map indicating the feasibility of addressing health in different SEA approaches*

	EIA approach to health	Ecosystem approach	Healthy public policy approach	Health inequalities approach
SEA-EIA school	Compatible and directly addresses health	Compatible only for scientific and quantitative economic and social data	Not compatible – cannot address health	Not compatible – cannot address health
SEA area base	May be compatible if this approach has a narrow scope of the environment only	Compatible	Can address only factors in the study area – needs to link with other SEA approaches	Can address only factors in the study area – needs to link with other SEA approaches
SEA policy options	Not compatible – health already addressed beyond the scope of EIA approach	Compatible	Compatible and directly addresses health	Compatible and directly addresses health
SEA development direction	Not compatible – health already addressed beyond the scope of EIA approach	Compatible	Compatible but depends on the competence of the stakeholders involved	Compatible but depends on the competence of the stakeholders involved

Source: Nuntavorakarn et al (2005)

How can the engagement of health professionals in SEA be improved?

There is much evidence of the application of strategic level HIA, for example, on the effect of accession to the EU on agriculture and food policy in Slovenia (Lock et al, 2004), of policy in Canada (Banken, 2004) and of policies/strategies in Wales and in London, respectively, (Breeze and Kemm, 2000; Mindell et al, 2004b). This evidence predominantly refers to the mechanism for the consideration of health rather than, specifically, to the engagement of health professionals. We also see that increasing political will, exemplified in SEA Directives and Protocols at the European level and wider, is promoting a position of greater consideration of health within SEA (Dora, 2004) although, beyond the requirement in the Kiev SEA Protocol to consult with health authorities (UNECE, 2003), these do not promote, or provide advice on techniques for, engagement *per se*.

However, studies have indicated that health professionals need to be better engaged in sectoral decision-making, particularly for land-use planning (Cave and Molyneux, 2004; Cave et al, 2005). These studies indicate that there are a number of barriers to appropriate engagement, primary among them being a lack of good understanding of the workings of the other sector (for example, land-use planners have little understanding of the health system and health issues and health professionals have little understanding of the planning system or its influences on health). A key finding from these and other studies (for example, Griffiths, 2004) is that capacity has to be built both in the health sector and other sectors. From the basis of better understanding, more progress can be made through engagement in the SEA process.

Are there case examples of the consideration of health in SEA where real benefits can be identified?

A critical issue is that real benefits due to impact assessment are hard to identify. Much literature has looked at the effectiveness of impact assessment and has concluded that many studies look at procedural compliance rather than real benefits in terms of outcomes (Bond et al, 2005), a significant issue being that, at strategy level, it is hard to demonstrate what has led to any benefits. For example, if a health assessment of a government policy on energy might have health repercussions because of increased air pollution, and that policy were changed, it would be difficult to prove later on that the absence of more disease was due to this policy in the light of all others influencing the same outcome, for example transport policy. As such, it is not unexpected that case studies of the consideration of health in SEA leading to real benefits are, as yet, hard to find in the literature.

In contrast, evidence of SEA identifying the potential for real benefits or of HIA applied at strategic levels identifying the potential for real benefits is plentiful (see, for example, Lock et al, 2003). The emphasis with SEA is very much on effective assessment being defined as affecting the decisions made, rather than on any health outcomes (for example, Fischer et al, 2010), thus efforts are not made to identify health outcomes and to verify any predictions made in the SEA. It is clear that more research is needed on this subject in order to be able to prove that health issues identified in SEAs are leading to real benefits.

Is integration of HIA and SEA desirable?

Birley (2003) argued for the integration of health, social and environmental impact assessment; but is this the right solution at the strategic level? In order to move forward to properly integrate health in SEA, there is a need to build on existing success stories, where they can be found to exist. In particular, the following questions are asked:

- Is there case study evidence of the consideration of health in SEA or at the strategic level of public policy processes?
- Is there case study evidence of HIA that works at the strategic level of public policy processes?
- How can the appropriate health expertise become involved in the SEA process?
- Does the current momentum mean that this policy window for integration is open?
- What models are available for integration?

Assuming that integration is desirable (at least in some cases), a further issue is whether capacity exists to integrate health into SEA and, if not, how it can be best built. The discussion may be able to learn from examples of capacity-building (see, for example, Griffiths, 2004). As for EIA, there is current debate about whether SEA should be more integrated into decision-making rather than simply providing information (see, for example, Dalkmann et al, 2004). This debate also needs to consider whether HIA (with or without SEA) should be a decision-support tool or a decision-making tool and whether the objectives of the SEA are likely to deliver suitable health goals.

Conclusions

It is clear that all decision-making has the potential to impact human health and well-being, and that the consideration of the implications at strategic levels could have significant benefits in the long-term, leading to a consensus that health should be integrated into SEA.

Table 23.2 provides a summary of the state of practice in strategic health assessment, based on the discussion at Prague and subsequent evidence from the academic literature. This indicates that consideration of the need to integrate health and well-being into SEA can lead to more significant issues being identified that need addressing by national governments. In particular, if health infrastructure is primarily aimed at health protection, it may be time to reconsider, strategically, the institutions that exist and their remits. The health profession needs to have the right organizations to engage in SEA, ones that can help in terms of health promotion. A note of caution here is that examples of good practice do exist, whereby engagement between health, SEA and land-use planning professionals is excellent, but frequent reorganization of the health sector, or of the sectors with which health professionals engage, threatens the relationships that have built up.

- In the short-term, there is a need to improve the consideration of health in guidance for implementing SEA. Progress is already being made in some countries (for example, Williams and Fisher, 2007) and WHO has published guidance to help governments understand what they need to do to improve the consideration of health in SEA (Nowacki et al, 2010).
- In the medium-term, there is a need to continue to gather and disseminate case study and capacity-building experience. This needs to build on the evidence that researchers have already started to compile (for example, Kørnøv, 2009; Fischer et al, 2010; Nowacki et al, 2010).
- In the medium to longer-term, development of understanding among all stakeholders of the critical linkages between health and other aspects of sustainability is a key requirement. A particular challenge is to establish the evidence base to demonstrate that consideration of health in SEA leads to real improvements in health outcomes.

Table 23.2 *State of practice in strategic health assessment*

Main trends and issues	HIA has been driven by the need for healthy public policy since the 1970s – as a parallel, rather than integrated, requirement. Momentum has developed for addressing health at the strategic level.
	Some evidence of practice of the consideration of health at the strategic level in some countries, although it was clear that the consideration of health at strategic levels is not yet widespread.
	Experience to date indicates that HIA may be carried out as a statutory requirement or on a voluntary basis; also, it may be carried out as part of EIA/SEA or as a self-standing assessment. There is no common model.
	Sustainability and health are inextricably linked – so health needs a strong interface with other sectors.
Important aspects or challenges for SEA	There may be a window of opportunity for institutionalization of HIA – either as a self-standing assessment process recognized as important in its own right or integrated into SEA, which is undergoing rapid institutionalization.
	The health sector often fails to engage with SEA and, where it does, often has an inadequate view of the scope of 'health' such that the engagement is directed at improving health infrastructure rather than helping to design sustainable developments/communities.
	Concern that health is, and will be, inadequately addressed by SEA mainly because of the limited engagement with health professionals. This is not a problem unique to health and well-being, for example, there are equivalent issues with cultural heritage impacts. The overall challenge for SEA is to properly address all impacts.
Key findings and lessons	Unanimous consensus was achieved on the need to integrate health into SEA.
	There is a need to build capacity in:
	<ul><li>the community so that members of the public can better engage in the SEA process in relation to land-use, sectoral, environmental and health issues.</li><li>methods/knowledge used for consideration of health and well-being within SEA.</li><li>institutions of state to deliver heath promotion not just health protection.</li><li>all sectors to consider health, including within university curricula.</li></ul>

References

Arquiaga, M. C., Canter, L. W. and Nelson, D. I. (1994) 'Integration of health impact considerations in environmental impact studies', *Impact Assessment*, vol 12, no 2, pp175–197

Banken, R. (2001) 'Strategies for institutionalising HIA, ECHP Health Impact Assessment Discussion Papers, Number 1', www.nice.org.uk/media/hiadocs/19_echp_strategies_for_institutinalising_hia.pdf, accessed 27 July 2010

Banken, R. (2003) 'Health impact assessment: How to start the process and make it last', *Bulletin of the World Health Organization*, vol 81, no 6, p389

Banken, R. (2004) 'HIA of policy in Canada', in Kemm, J., Parry, J. and Palmer, S. (eds) in *Health Impact Assessment*, Oxford University Press, Oxford, pp165–175

Bekker, M. P. M., Putters, K. and van der Grinten, T. E. D. (2005) 'Evaluating the impact of HIA on urban reconstruction decision-making: Who manages whose risks?', *Environmental Impact Assessment Review*, vol 25, no 7–8, pp758–771

Birley, M. H. (2003) 'Health impact assessment, integration and critical appraisal', *Impact Assessment and Project Appraisal*, vol 21, no 4, pp313–321

BMA (British Medical Association) (1998) *Health and Environmental Impact Assessment: An Integrated Approach*, Earthscan, London

Bond, A. (2004) 'Lessons from EIA', in Kemm, J., Parry, J. and Palmer, S. (eds) *Health Impact Assessment*, Oxford University Press, Oxford, pp131–142

Bond, A., Cashmore, M., Cobb, D., Lovell, A. and Taylor, L. (2005) *Evaluation in Impact Assessment Areas Other than HIA*, National Institute for Health and Clinical Excellence, London

Bonde, J. and Cherp, A. (2000) 'Quality review package for strategic environmental assessments of land-use plans', *Impact Assessment and Project Appraisal*, vol 18, no 2, pp99–110

Breeze, C. and Kemm, J. (2000) *The Health Potential of the Objective 1 Programme for West Wales and the Valleys: A Preliminary Health Impact Assessment*, Health Promotion Division, National Assembly for Wales, Cardiff.

Burns, J. and Bond, A. (2008) 'The consideration of health in land use planning: barriers and opportunities', *Environmental Impact Assessment Review*, vol 28, no 2–3, pp184–197

Byrne, D. (2004) 'Enabling good health for all: A reflection process for a new EU health strategy', http://ec.europa.eu/health/archive/ph_overview/documents/pub_good_health_en.pdf, accessed 27 July 2010

Cave, B. and Molyneux, P. (2004) *Healthy Sustainable Communities: A Spatial Planning Checklist*, Milton Keynes and South Midlands Health and Social Care Group, Milton Keynes

Cave, B., Bond, A., Molyneux, P. and Walls, V. (2005) *Reuniting Health and Planning: A Training Needs Analysis*, East of England Public Health Group, Cambridge

Chadwick, A. (2002) 'Socio-economic impacts: Are they still the poor relations in UK environmental statements?', *Journal of Environmental Planning and Management*, vol 45, no 1, pp3–24

Coyle, E., Huws, D., Monaghan, S., Roddy, G., Seery, B., Staats, P., Thunhurst, C., Walker, P. and Fleming, P. (2009) 'Transport and health – a five-country perspective', *Public Health*, vol 123, no 1, ppe21–e23

Dalkmann, H., Herrera, R. J. and Bongardt, D. (2004) 'Analytical strategic environment assessment (ANSEA): Developing a new approach to SEA', *Environmental Impact Assessment Review*, vol 24, no 4, pp385–402

Davis, A. (2005) 'Transport and health: What is the connection? An exploration of concepts of health held by highways committee chairs in England', *Transport Policy*, vol 12, pp324–333

den Broeder, L., Penris, M. and Put, G. V. (2003) 'Soft data, hard effects: Strategies for effective policy on health impact assessment – an example from the Netherlands', *Bulletin of the World Health Organization*, vol 81, no 6, pp404–407

Dora, C. (2004) 'HIA in SEA and its application to policy in Europe', in Kemm, J., Parry, J. and Palmer, S. (eds) *Health Impact Assessment*, Oxford University Press, Oxford, pp403–410

European Parliament and the Council of the EU (2001) 'Directive 2001/42/EC of the European Parliament and of the Council of 27 June 2001 on the assessment of the effects of certain plans and programmes on the environment', *Official Journal of the European Communities*, L197, pp30–37.

Fehr, R., Mekel, O. and Welteke, R. (2004) 'HIA: The German perspective', in Kemm, J., Parry, J. and Palmer, S. (eds) *Health Impact Assessment*, Oxford University Press, Oxford, pp253–264

Fischer, T. B., Martuzzi, M. and Nowacki, J. (2010) 'The consideration of health in strategic environmental assessment (SEA)', *Environmental Impact Assessment Review*, vol 30, no 3, pp200–210

Fitzpatrick, M. (1978) *Environmental Health Planning*, Ballinger, Cambridge

France, C. (2004) 'Health contribution to local government planning', *Environmental Impact Assessment Review*, vol 24, no 2, pp189–198

Glasson, J. and Heaney, D. (1993) 'Socio-economic impacts: The poor relations in British environmental impact statements', *Journal of Environmental Planning and Management*, vol 36, no 3, pp335–343

Griffiths, R. (2004) 'Health impact assessment in the West Midlands: A managerial view', *Environmental Impact Assessment Review*, vol 24, no 2, pp135–138

Hart, D. (2004) 'Health impact assessment: Where does the law come in?', *Environmental Impact Assessment Review*, vol 24, no 2, pp161–168

Jackson, R. J. (2003) 'The impact of the built environment on health: An emerging field', *American Journal of Public Health*, vol 93, no 9, pp1382–1384

Kemm, J. (2004) 'What is health impact assessment and what can it learn from EIA?', *Environmental Impact Assessment Review*, vol 24, no 2, pp131–134

Kidd, S. (2007) 'Towards a framework of integration in spatial planning: An exploration from a health perspective', *Planning Theory & Practice*, vol 8, no 2, pp161–181

Kørnøv, L. (2009) 'Strategic Environmental Assessment as catalyst of healthier spatial planning: The Danish guidance and practice', *Environmental Impact Assessment Review*, vol 29, no 1, pp60–65

Lock, K., Gabrijelcic-Blenkus, M., Martuzzi, M., Otorepec, P., Kuhar, A., Robertson, A., Wallace, P., Dora, C. and Zakotnic, J. M. (2003) 'Health impact assessment of agriculture and food policies: Lessons learnt from the Republic of Slovenia', *Bulletin of the World Health Organization*, vol 81, no 6, pp391–398

Lock, K., Gabrijelcic-Blenkus, M., Martuzzi, M., Otorepec, P., Kuhar, A., Robertson, A., Wallace, P., Dora, C. and Zakotnic, J. M. (2004) 'Conducting an HIA of the effect of accession to the European Union on national agriculture and food policy in Slovenia', *Environmental Impact Assessment Review*, vol 24, no 2, pp177–188

Mindell, J., Boaz, A., Joffe, M., Curtis, S. and Birley, M. H. (2004a) 'Enhancing the evidence base for health impact assessment', *Journal of Epidemiology and Community Health*, vol 58, pp546–551

Mindell, J., Sheridan, L., Joffe, M., Samson-Barry, H. and Atkinson, S. (2004b) 'Health impact assessment as an agency of policy change: improving the health impacts of the mayor of London's draft transport strategy', *Journal of Epidemiology and Community Health*, vol 58, pp169–174

Nowacki, J., Martuzzi, M. and Fischer, T. B. (2010) 'Health and strategic environmental assessment WHO consultation meeting, Rome, Italy, 8–9 June 2009: Background information and report', www.euro.who.int/__data/assets/pdf_file/0006/112749/E93878.pdf, accessed 30 July 2010

Nuntavorakarn, S., Sabrum, N. and Sukkumnoed, D. (2005) 'Addressing health in SEA for healthy public policy: A contribution from SEA development in Thailand', paper presented at the IAIA SEA Conference, Prague

Phoolcharoen, W., Sukkumnoed, D. and Kessomboon, P. (2003) 'Development of health impact assessment in Thailand: Recent experiences and challenges', *Bulletin of the World Health Organization*, vol 81, no 6, pp465–467

Put, G. V., den Broeder, L. and Abbing, E. R. (2000) 'Health impact assessment and intersectoral policy at a national level in the Netherlands', International Workshop on Public Participation and Health Aspects in Strategic Environmental Assessment, Regional Environmental Centre for Central and Eastern Europe, Szentendre, Hungary

Ritsatakis, A. (2004) 'HIA at the international policy-making level', in Kemm, J., Parry, J. and Palmer, S. (eds) *Health Impact Assessment*, Oxford University Press, Oxford, pp153–164

Roscam Abbing, E. W. (2004) 'HIA and national policy in the Netherlands', in Kemm, J., Parry, J. and Palmer, S. (eds) *Health Impact Assessment*, Oxford University Press, Oxford, pp177–189

Tiwari, G. (2003) 'Transport and land-use policies in Delhi', *Bulletin of the World Health Organization*, vol 81, no 6, pp444–450

UNCED (United Nations Conference on Environment and Development) (1992) *Earth Summit '92*, Regency Press, London

UNECE (United Nations Economic Commission for Europe) (1991) *Convention on Environmental Impact Assessment in a Transboundary Context*, UNECE, Geneva

UNECE (2003) *Protocol on Strategic Environmental Assessment to the Convention on Environmental Impact Assessment in a Transboundary Context*, UNECE, Geneva

Vanclay, F. (2004) 'The triple bottom line and impact assessment: How do TBL, EIA, SIA, SEA and EMS relate to each other?', *Journal of Environmental Assessment Policy and Management*, vol 6, no 3, pp265–288

WHO (World Health Organization) (1946) *Constitution*, WHO, Geneva

WHO (1986) 'Ottawa Charter for Health Promotion: First International Conference on Health Promotion Ottawa, 21 November 1986 – WHO/HPR/HEP/95.1', www.who.int/hpr/NPH/docs/ottawa_charter_hp.pdf, accessed 14 October 2004

WHO (1999) 'Declaration: Third Ministerial Conference on Environment and Health, London, 16–18 June 1999', WHO Regional Office for Europe, www.euro.who.int/__data/assets/pdf_file/0007/88585/E69046.pdf, accessed 27 July 2010

Williams, C. and Fisher, P. (2007) *Draft Guidance on Health in Strategic Environmental Assessment*, Department of Health, London

Wright, J. S. F. (2004) 'HIA in Australia', in Kemm, J., Parry, J. and Palmer, S. (eds) *Health Impact Assessment*, Oxford University Press, Oxford, pp223–233

24
Managing Cumulative Impacts: Making It Happen

Jennifer Dixon and Riki Thérivel

Introduction

Cumulative impact assessment (CIA) is the flip side of strategic environmental assessment (SEA): it focuses on the resource rather than on the plan. It thus acts as a useful counterpoint and cross-check to SEA. In this way, it helps to ensure that multiple activities (including the plan in question), each of which having perhaps only limited impacts on a resource, do not cumulatively have a markedly significant impact.

Although an analysis of cumulative impacts is a component of much SEA legislation (for example, the European SEA Directive, the SEA Protocol, Canada's Cabinet Directive on SEA), it would seem that CIA is currently being carried out half-heartedly and sporadically at best. CIA techniques are in their infancy. Authorities are still struggling with basic SEA requirements and, in some cases, CIA is perceived as a luxurious add-on to an already complex and expensive process. However, unless we deal quickly with some significant cumulative impacts, such as climate change, biodiversity loss, plummeting fish stocks and water demand outstripping supply, we may not have much to pass on to future generations.

Early experience with CIA suggests that the hardest stage is the last one: managing cumulative impacts (Thérivel and Ross, 2006). Avoiding, reducing and compensating, where necessary, for cumulative impacts, typically involves multiple actors with different remits, interests and spatial jurisdictions. If the impact management stage of CIA is not carried out well, the previous stages will have been in vain.

This chapter focuses on managing cumulative impacts. In part, this can be done through technological measures but mostly it involves behavioural change. As such, this chapter focuses on mechanisms for influencing behaviour. It starts with a brief explanation of the CIA process and the role of impact management in it. It considers which tools for impact management have worked in practice and which have not, and what common themes link the effective tools. It then discusses the institutional context and factors needed for such tools to be applied effectively. The chapter focuses, in particular, on governance and capacity-building as critical areas for targeting how we might improve the management of cumulative impacts. Where possible, it suggests how practitioners might act at key points in policy-making processes and outlines examples of capacity-building initiatives that can be taken.

CIA and management of cumulative impacts

CIA focuses on the receiving environment. It considers all of the impacts on a given receptor, including those of the plan or project that triggered the CIA in the first place. Examples of cumulative impacts include habitat fragmentation, reductions in biodiversity, water shortages, climate change and urbanization. Cumulative impacts are sometimes caused by individual projects or plans. Creasey and Ross (2005) cite examples of cumulative impacts caused by several mines or projects. However, most cumulative impacts are caused by a wide range of factors, including people's choices about where to live and travel, government policies (such as for energy and transport), international trade agreements, price and subsidy structures, and similar choices and activities.

The main steps of CIA are:

- Identify the affected receptors (scoping).
- Determine what past, present and future human activities have affected or will affect these receptors, and what has led to these activities (context).
- Predict the impacts on the receptors of the project/plan being assessed, in combination with the impacts of other human activities, and determine the significance of the impacts.
- Suggest how to manage the cumulative impacts.

The ultimate test of CIA is whether it helps to protect and improve the quality of the receiving environment. In part, this will be accomplished through changes to the plan that triggers the CIA, but much will be through changes in people's behaviour and changes to the policy and political context within which the plan operates.

Yet a range of factors make achieving such changes difficult. First, many cumulative problems are caused by a multitude of small impacts rather than a few big ones. Many have accumulated over years or even centuries: we are having to cope with our grandparents' impacts in terms of long-lasting industrial pollutants, the extinction of some high-profile species (auk, carrier pigeon) and change from wooded to agricultural landscapes. And of course we are contributing to similar impacts that will affect our grandchildren. Often, cumulative problems can be solved only by equally cumulative means: it requires the collaboration of multiple stakeholders. Yet it is all too easy for actors to claim that they contribute only minimally to the problem (or not at all where the problems are historical), and so should contribute only minimally to the solution. Many measures to manage cumulative impacts will be outside the remit of the plan-making authority, and as such cumulative impacts are often felt to be someone else's remit.

Thérivel and Ross (2006) identify a number of factors that support effective management of cumulative impacts. These include strong legal requirements for cumulative impact management; informed and proactive decision-makers; support for inter-authority working; the development of management measures that are within the plan-maker's remit; and a consistent approach to all development that provides certainty for all participants. In addition, practical measures that are not self-defeating (in terms of encouraging counter-productive behaviour), a proactive approach that does not constrain people's behaviour once they have made decisions, and follow-up studies linked to management to ensure that measures work as planned, are similarly important. Some of these factors are explored below.

Effective management of cumulative impacts

Measures to manage cumulative impacts do not have to arise as a result of a formal CIA; people put such measures in place for many different reasons, notably to deal with insupportable cumulative problems. Approaches that have been effective include:

- Charging to tackle increasing traffic congestion, as in London: after introduction of a congestion charge of £5 per day (now £8 per day) for any vehicles entering central London, traffic in that area dropped by 18 per cent and congestion was reduced by 30 per cent. Traffic levels remained low five years after the charge was introduced, although congestion returned to pre-charge levels as a result of changes to the road network that reduced overall road capacity. Transport for London estimates that, without the charge, congestion would be 30 per cent worse in the central London zone (House of Commons Transport Committee, 2009).
- Parking restrictions in Vienna: restricting on-street parking to 1.5 or 2 hours maximum duration and requiring a parking fee were first introduced in one pilot area in 1993. By 1995, car traffic volume had been reduced by 10 per cent (by 15 per cent during peak hours) and parking space use had fallen by a third. Although residents initially protested against this measure, it soon became widely accepted, with 89 per cent positive reaction in later surveys. The city government later rolled out parking restrictions to all inner city districts (EAUE, 2001).
- 'Individualized marketing' in Perth to tackle traffic growth: 8000 households were contacted and offered advice about the journeys they make. Car use fell by 14 per cent as a result, with a shift to public transport and cycling (Government of Western Australia, 2005).
- Water metering in Canadian households to help reduce water use: where meters were fitted, water use dropped sharply, to less than 60 per cent of that of households who continued to pay a static fee independent of water use (Infrastructure Canada, 2005). Similarly, compulsory water metering in the UK in the 1980s showed an average reduction in domestic consumption of 11 per cent in homes with meters (BBC, 2006). Compulsory water meters

are currently (2010) being rolled out in other parts of the UK, with the aim of reducing people's water use.

- Education to help reduce water use: a Danish survey indicated that consumer education explained 60 per cent of changes in water use patterns, and pricing 40 per cent (Policy Research Initiative, 2005).
- Regulations that make hunting of endangered species illegal: a 2005 study (Taylor et al, 2005) showed that, the longer a species was listed as threatened or endangered under the United States Endangered Species Act 1973, the more likely it was to have an improving population trend.
- Increased security at red kite nest sites to prevent robberies, consultation with farmers about how they manage their land, and reintroduction of red kites, led to a recovery in red kite populations in the UK.

In contrast, approaches that have not been effective include:

- Rules on net fisheries loss in Canada: under the Canadian Fisheries Act, project proponents must demonstrate how they will achieve no net loss of fish habitat and must compensate two for one for any habitat loss. However, in practice, actual alterations to habitats have often been much larger and compensation areas smaller than those agreed (Quigley and Harper, 2004).
- A laissez-faire approach to urban design in an effects-based approach to city planning in Auckland, New Zealand, led to widespread calls for tighter controls (Dixon, 2005) and more recently to the establishment of a Technical Advisory Group to recommend changes to the Resource Management Act to improve urban form (New Zealand Government, 2009).
- More fuel efficient cars pre-recession: prior to the economic recession in the UK, technical improvements in vehicles to make them more fuel efficient were being counterbalanced by a trend towards greater car use (Defra, 2004) and larger cars (which comprised one in seven new cars bought in London – an urban area in a country with mild weather).
- Improved energy efficiency in UK homes has been counterbalanced by higher internal temperatures, higher levels of central heating and the heating of larger parts of the home and a much greater number of energy-using appliances, so that energy consumption per household has remained roughly stable. The growth in the number of households (for example, through divorce, more people living alone) has meant that total domestic energy demand for space heating rose by 25 per cent between 1970 and 2008 (DECC, 2010).

What works and what does not work?

These examples suggest common themes for what is and is not effective as a management measure for cumulative impacts. First, sticks work. Fiscal sticks, such as congestion charges and water meters, make people more aware of the value of the resource, and allow people to get personal benefits (lower bills) from helping to maintain it. Legal sticks, such as making hunting illegal, also work.

Second, because sticks tend to be unpopular, they are often only put in place as a measure of last resort. For instance, compulsory water metering is being required in England in response to the drought of 2004–2006 and subsequent concern about water security, but would not have been put in place without the drought. This is not the way to proactively manage cumulative impacts. But, in the absence of outside imperatives, difficult decisions typically need to be made, and often only charismatic individuals are willing to make them. For instance, London's congestion charge was only imposed because of the personal intervention of its then mayor, Ken Livingstone. On the other hand, government departments may be willing to make such decisions on the basis of pilot studies that bear positive results. Some measures take time to accept. Increasing choice and reducing prices is always popular, but often works against sustainability.

Targeted education works. Individualized marketing and one-on-one discussion provides individuals with information that is specifically suited to their needs, and so most likely to change their behaviour. Individuals are probably most receptive to educational measures at key decision-making times. For instance, if parents are provided with information about public transport, walking and cycling access to their children's school shortly before their children start school, this is much more likely to change behaviour than if the information is provided during the school term, when the parents and children have already settled into a transport pattern (Levett-Therivel, 2005).

Technical fixes do not work. Although they are publicly acceptable and have short-term benefits, in the long run, people tend to change their behaviour to take advantage of the new technology: they buy more appliances, keep their houses warmer (or cooler) and drive bigger vehicles further. They become used to living behind levees and, over time, build more intensively in the floodplain. So, if fiscal sticks, regulation, charismatic individuals and education work, what kind of political and policy context is needed to support these and how might it be supported through capacity-building?

Governance: A framework for managing cumulative impacts

There are, broadly, two types of environmental regime in operation with different approaches to managing development. One is more prescriptive and includes development control systems that set out clearly where, what and how activities might occur. This regime can be referred to as conformance-based (Laurian et al, 2010). The second regime is more laissez-faire and less prescriptive, setting out a performance-based framework within which development can occur, focused on management of effects, rather than specifying activities.

The approach to economic management underpinning governance can be important in ensuring how well cumulative impacts are identified and addressed. For example, a laissez-faire approach to dealing with natural hazards that relies on education as the main means of informing communities about the dangers of locating in a floodplain might lead to some mixed outcomes and painful lessons for homeowners when a major flood occurs (May et al, 1996). Alternatively, a more prescriptive approach could prevent homeowners from locating in floodplains in the first place, but may exclude some flexibility in respect of development options for the floodplain and is unlikely to lead to more informed residents who could then be discriminating about where they choose to live in the future.

In order to accommodate the need for both flexibility and certainty, most systems of governance use a mix of policy tools. Some are prescriptive (they stipulate the type and range of activities that can be established in particular locations); others are non-mandatory and voluntary (such as the adoption of codes of practice by developers and land-users and the promotion of education). Some carrots (such as incentives to influence project design resulting in benefits for the wider community) and sticks (such as fines for breaches of conditions) will also be present. Whatever the mix, however, the nature and form of governance is influential in shaping the way in which cumulative impacts are managed. In the next section we identify and discuss several issues in respect of governance that are pertinent for practitioners engaged in the practice of CIA.

Understanding governance

Governance is highly significant for the management of cumulative impacts. Understanding governance assists practitioners to manage cumulative impacts more effectively. A simple definition of governance is that it comprises the cooperative processes of governing, policy-making and decision-making (van Bueren and ten Heuvelhof, 2005). It incorporates a myriad of interactions between government and community groups at different scales (local through to international).

The complex nature of many cumulative environmental problems means that many government and stakeholder groups often need to be engaged in their resolution. This is particularly important in a context where responsibilities for environmental management are spread across a number of agencies with different agendas and constituencies, often cutting across local, regional, national and sometimes international boundaries. Tackling issues such as traffic congestion, climate change and sustainable urban development can easily seem overwhelming in the face of institutional complexities.

Governance often has an inherently 'messy character' (Lane and McDonald, 2005). Various alliances and partnerships between government, business and community groups can form and reform around particular issues at different scales. As the complexities of governance increase, so too does the multiplicity of planning and policy instruments designed to address environmental issues and development impacts. Some of these instruments will be formally required by legislation. Other non-statutory initiatives will be produced in response to particular needs. Examples include strategies for regional growth management or managing sectors such as housing, or the development of integrated catchment management plans to inform structure planning. Yet others may be prepared by non-government groups, such as indigenous peoples, as a way of both managing resources under their control and influencing statutory plans prepared by government agencies. The proliferation of planning instruments being produced at different levels of government, and by different agencies is creating complex environmental regimes that practitioners sometimes find hard to navigate their way around. However, there are some useful steps that practitioners can take to tackle the management of cumulative impacts, among them making sense of the planning system in place.

Making sense of plans and influencing policy development

A key means of making sense of an environmental regime and its ability to address cumulative impacts is to become familiar with its system of plans and policies. We have a number of suggestions to make here. Typically, a statutory plan will guide development and could be expected to address cumulative impacts at both policy and practical levels, especially if the plan is based upon a conformance-based model with stated planning outcomes (Beattie, 2010; Laurian et al, 2010). In addition, there may be other relevant plans, both statutory and non-statutory, in one or several agencies that exercise some influence in regard to cumulative impacts. Reviewing the plans will also identify the remits and interests of the agencies that may be involved in the management of cumulative impacts.

Second, it is important to identify which plans have statutory weight or are especially relevant and therefore worthy of close scrutiny. This issue is critical particularly if there is conflict between the plans. The statutory plan will always take precedence in legal proceedings over a non-statutory plan (Beattie, 2010). Identifying these conflicts will assist practitioners to focus their attention on where they may achieve best results in changing policies and practices. Relevant documents, such as design guidelines and codes of practice, may also influence decisions and be used to determine development conditions.

Third, the extent to which the various layers of plans are aligned both within and across agencies may indicate whether coordinated approaches might be taken by these agencies in dealing with cumulative environmental problems. Of key importance here, too, is to identify key individuals who may act as champions in respect of managing the resolution of issues and whose support may be crucial in determining where and how best to intervene in the process.

Fourth, while it is easy to get enmeshed in the detail, it is critical to keep the bigger cumulative picture in mind and seize opportunities to influence policy development at early stages. These moments may arise infrequently, but can be pivotal in influencing the way in which an agency decides to tackle particular issues within its remit. Choosing not to participate at strategic levels of policy-making may make it much more difficult later to redress cumulative impacts, particularly if appropriate policies are not in place.

The gap between policy and implementation

The gap between policies and their implementation is where difficulties in management of cumulative impacts can be compounded. Environmental outcomes often do not conform to the prescriptions of institutional arrangements (Lane and McDonald, 2005). But this recognition at least enables some action to be taken. Here we identify some factors that account for the gap between policy and implementation and point to how they might be addressed.

Time lags between policy-making and policy implementation can often extend several years, if not decades. In addition, some plans take so long to resolve, they are out of date by the time they commence. Often, too, those involved in administration of policies are not engaged in their development, creating a situation where the plan administrators may not have any real ownership or in-depth understanding of the plan's desired outcomes (Beattie, 2010). The current preoccupation in many countries with process and consultation, given enhanced requirements for civic participation, has tended to focus on policy development at the expense of implementation and outcomes (for example, Ericksen et al, 2004 in the New Zealand context).

This situation can be compounded by frequent changes to legislation and requirements for new planning instruments to be developed. It can mean that agencies are focused on creating a new round of plans rather than on promoting, implementing and monitoring recently-formed policies. Statutory changes, when undertaken too frequently or in an uncoordinated way, can also mean that plans get prepared out of sequence, particularly where more than one statute or agency is involved. It may not be until that the second or third generation of plans is reached that policies and proposed actions across and within agencies are properly aligned, both spatially and territorially.

The quality of implementation will also depend on the adequacy of funding by the relevant agencies, not just for implementation but monitoring as well. In addition, the organizational cultures and practices that surround the implementation of plans and their policies, both within and across agencies, will be influential. The calibre of administrative teams, for example, will contribute to how effectively policies are implemented. The skills and experience of staff, the commitment to mentoring new graduates, the speed of staff turnover and the size of workloads will all influence policy implementation (Beattie, 2010; Dixon, 2005).

These issues are mostly beyond the capacity of individual practitioners to address. Nonetheless, small incremental changes can be effective. Identifying key people to advise how best to proceed when seeking resolution can be crucial. Highlighting and publicizing problems of implementation can lead to change at the political level. For example, highlighting underfunding can lead to increased funding for plan evaluation monitoring. Advocating for well-resourced policy implementation can also assist in supporting inter-organizational connections critical for managing cumulative impacts. Many issues have to be tackled systematically through various capacity-building initiatives within organizations.

The following example aptly demonstrates difficulties with time lags between identifying, investigating and responding to an environmental issue. It also highlights the gaps between policy-making and implementation and the need for strong capacity to support implementation efforts. In North Shore City, New Zealand, increasing urbanization of a particular catchment and the incidence of zinc and copper in estuarine sediments is increasing despite a long-standing planning system in place designed to minimize or reduce adverse environmental effects of land-use change. The publication dates of land-use plans reveal sharply the time lags between the growing awareness by scientists of the consequences of urbanization on estuarine sediments, the time it took for research findings to confirm their concerns, and relevant policies to be developed to address the issues. It took 20 years for responsive policies to grapple adequately with the relationships between urbanization and its environmental impacts. Because of this delay, despite more robust measures now in place for new developments, ongoing degradation will continue for many years (Dixon and van Roon, 2005; van Roon, 2010).

Tackling a problem such as this requires greater interdisciplinary skills on the part of practitioners; a planning system that is more responsive to new knowledge; a stronger alignment of policies and plans within and across agencies (and possibly fewer plans overall); and long-term monitoring. It also requires connections with other sectors such as transport and building, where changes to building materials and infrastructure can make a significant difference in preventing pollutants from entering receiving environments.

Capacity-building for managing cumulative impacts

Much can be done to support the implementation of policies as well as advocating for change. However, changing stakeholder behaviour and planning instruments can be 'like turning a supertanker around' (Dixon, 2005, p82). This section briefly explores several examples of capacity-building that can enhance the management of cumulative impacts, ranging from the provision of training to what it takes to achieve organizational change.

Capacity-building to assist the implementation of policies, along with the willing commitment of those engaged in its delivery, are critical for reducing cumulative impacts. Education in both enhancing the skills of practitioners, as well as encouraging stakeholders to adopt more sustainable behaviours in their day-to-day practices, is also important. Capacity-building can be used to fill in 'deficits', for example, the existing skills base of practitioners, or 'empower' individuals to act in some way. But the broader institutional context can also be important for determining how readily new ideas can be taken up (Brown, 2004) and facilitate more radical transformations (Heslop, 2010). Hence, increasing attention is being paid to the way organizations manage the change process (Feeney et al, 2005; Heslop and Dixon, 2008).

A typical approach in building capacity is to identify gaps in the expertise of practitioners that arise, for example, as a consequence of a newly introduced requirement, such as the SEA Directive, and then to equip them with the skills and knowledge required to work effectively. Indeed, requirements for members of professional bodies, such as planning and engineering institutes, to regularly undertake continuing professional development are common. Often, however, these initiatives relate to improving practice in discrete disciplines, rather than addressing how practitioners might work together across a range of disciplines.

The very nature of cumulative impacts requires practitioners to work not just in multidisciplinary teams but also in interdisciplinary ways to solve seemingly intractable problems. However, there are barriers to the achievement of effective interdisciplinary outcomes (Dixon and Sharp, 2006). These relate to issues such as the capacity, experience and willingness of practitioners to work with those from other disciplines, whether organizational structures facilitate interdisciplinary collaboration through the provision of sufficient time and resources, and whether the tertiary education that practitioners have received exposes them to other disciplinary perspectives (Heslop et al, 2010).

Practitioners can readily follow up at least two avenues. First, they can seek out training programmes that assist participants from a range of disciplines to learn new ways of working together that will facilitate constructive problem-solving. Second, organizations can be encouraged to provide more support for staff to work in ways that foster collaborative approaches to solving problems, breaking down the 'silos' that often exist in internal structures (Heslop, 2006).

Training can also be provided to assist decision-makers, typically elected politicians, who make decisions that may have significant implications for the management of cumulative impacts. For example, a training scheme in New Zealand has had significant buy-in from elected councillors and is probably the most advanced of its kind to date in local government. The Making Good Decisions Programme is a training and certification package (Leggett, 2006) that has been developed for councillors and others who determine the outcome of formally notified applications for resource consents (such as planning permission). These applications are lodged under the Resource Management Act (RMA) 1991, the main environmental statute in New Zealand. Launched in 2004, more than 1200 people have received certification to date (Ministry for the Environment, 2010). Certification has been recognized as a means of statutory accreditation through amendments to the RMA in 2005.

This programme goes further than the typical training packages that simply inform newly elected councillors on their responsibilities, as the participants are formally tested and assessed. In return for successfully completing a two-day workshop and assignments, both before and after the workshop, participants receive a certificate valid for three years (the term of the electoral cycle). Already there is some evidence that practice in running hearing processes has improved. However, assessing whether the quality of deliberations has improved is harder to ascertain (Leggett, 2006). Course content has undergone significant improvements and is now focusing more closely on areas such as questioning, and the testing and weighing of evidence.

Ongoing education of general stakeholders is perhaps most important for achieving the behavioural change needed to tackle most cumulative problems. Central and local governments invest to varying degrees in a range of measures designed to encourage communities to act in more sustainable ways. However, more intense and focused learning in multi-stakeholder groups can be particularly effective. This approach rests on the principle that the participants engage in both technical and conceptual learning to resolve an issue (World Bank, 2005; van Roon et al, 2006).

For instance, a six-year research programme in New Zealand fostered this approach to learning with stakeholders to encourage a shift away from conventional land development practices toward more sustainable, low impact urban design and development practices. It brought together councils, developers, community groups and researchers to collaborate on greenfield and brownfield projects at varying spatial scales (Eason et al, 2009). A strong driver has been the need to enhance the sustainability of the built environment and improve the quality of receiving environments through an integrated approach to urban design and development (van Roon, 2005).

The researchers adopted a collaborative learning approach (Trotman, 2009) and worked with stakeholders to explore a variety of topics, such as how household rain tanks perform as a stormwater management device, as well as an additional source of household water. The group examining the performance of rain tanks, for instance, unpacked a range of assumptions about and attitudes towards the use of rain tanks. A key challenge was to ensure that different disciplinary perspectives could be respected and accommodated in order to proceed (van Roon et al, 2006). The group determined that people from different backgrounds with expertise in working across disciplines would be invited to manage the process from that point.

Ultimately, to secure radical change, it may be necessary to undertake major reforms of governance, but this is a huge task that is not undertaken lightly, or very frequently, by governments. Our final example reports on what it takes to achieve major organizational change in order to implement more sustainable practices. A major study undertaken in Australia surveyed 166 councils in New South Wales – along with surveys and interviews with 150 local government officers and stakeholders – to explore what factors generated capacity in local government to facilitate integrated urban water management and what were important characteristics for improving implementation performance (Brown, 2004). The research identified five key phases of organizational development: 'project', 'outsider', 'growth', 'insider' and 'integrated', encompassing councils that could be classified as low, variable or high performing. Each phase was characterized by factors that related to issues such as the knowledge and skills of staff, level of funding, presence of key champions to promote change, coherence of policies, quality of external relations with research and environmental agencies, strength of community relations, relations between internal council units and commitment to innovation.

The research concluded that three dimensions of capacity-building are important for mobilizing change:

- Directive reform that promotes interactions across and within organizations, regulates and monitors organizational capacity, and fosters political and community support.
- Organizational strengthening that includes internally consistent policies, sufficient resources, active stakeholder networks, good working relationships within and across agencies, and access for community participation.
- Human resource development that encourages the acquisition of specific knowledge along with skills in facilitation and negotiation, relationship-building and change management (Brown, 2004, p13).

Making difficult decisions

Good democratic governance, good policy implementation and good education can only go so far. In some cases, managing cumulative impacts requires constraints on people's behaviour that can only be achieved through tough regulations and financial sticks, such as requirements for water meters, preventing cars from entering certain areas, energy and water prices that rise with increasing use, and so on. Although these may end up being well-accepted in time (such as the Viennese parking restrictions), in the short-term they are likely to encounter opposition.

Improving people's choice – of schools, cars, mobile phone providers, hospitals, and so on – is often popular in the short-term but can easily lead to unsustainable behaviour (such as longer journeys to school and increasing disparities in the quality of schools; larger and more polluting cars that demonstrate people's purchasing power). Constraints on choice, instead, feel as if they reduce people's quality of life, even where they allow the base standards of all schools, hospitals and cars to be improved.

It is correspondingly difficult to put measures in place that constrain people's behaviour. Short electoral cycles encourage short-term decisions by politicians who want to be (or remain) elected, for instance: 'Democrats focus on fuel... 54 per cent of [US] respondents said they trusted Democrats to tackle gas prices, while 23 per cent favored Republicans' (Murray, 2006). In the absence of national legislation, local or regional authorities that try to impose unilateral measures to reduce cumulative impacts can be accused of being *ultra vires* and of 'gold-plating' their policies. For example, an SEA for an UK region noted:

> It is not realistic or reasonable to include a requirement to exceed national building standards due to legal problems (i.e. [the regional authority] could be held to be ultra vires in setting requirements that are addressed through other legislation other than Planning Act powers), economic problems (i.e. developers would find it less profitable to build in the region, thereby reducing the number of homes built in region) and social problems (i.e. a lower number of house completions could result in fewer affordable homes being built). (Levett-Therivel and EDAW, 2005)

The trend towards increasing public consultation can lead to submission fatigue, public cynicism and small-scale, incremental, populist decisions that may not get close to the scale of change needed to deal with cumulative impacts. NIMBY attitudes can prevent developments that help to counter cumulative impacts, such as wind turbines or new cycle lanes. Many planning decisions can descend into a legal quagmire.

At times, only tough decisions made by tough people will be strong enough to manage cumulative impacts. Yet if elected politicians make unpopular decisions, they risk losing office. Achieving behavioural change may mean one government department giving up some funding or passing some of its remit to another department. Systems of governance that support these kinds of decisions – such as trial periods for new management measures, hypothecation of revenue to support sustainable activities (for example, congestion funds supporting better bus services), 'young leaders' programmes, local referenda – may not directly engender such decisions, but can help to set the framework within which they can be made.

Conclusions

This chapter has reviewed the CIA process and the role of impact management, identified a raft of tools that have worked in practice and given examples of those that have not. In contrast to the other steps in CIA – scoping, context-setting and impact prediction – the final step, managing cumulative impacts, is not a technical problem: it is an institutional and behavioural one. It requires a good system of governance, good implementation of plans and policies and, most importantly, good education.

The chapter also identifies the need to know your plan, to know what other plans give the most leverage, to identify key players and to participate at strategic levels. It has highlighted the gap between policies and implementation, identified typical problems that frequently undermine the management of cumulative impacts, and recommended identifying key players. Strong inter-organizational linkages can help. Some examples of capacity-building are given on a continuum ranging from information through to transformation. These include building knowledge and skills of practitioners and politicians, learning new ways of working together, and what it takes to achieve major organizational change. At times unpopular decisions need to be made, but this, too, requires enhanced organizational and professional capacity, along with the strong commitment and support of various constituencies.

The need to manage cumulative impacts is a multi-institutional, multidimensional, multidisciplinary and interdisciplinary task. Often their recognition and resolution is buried within layers of governance and planning instruments of variously performing organizations at different spatial levels. Consequently, management of cumulative impacts is difficult. This explains why our progress so far has been limited. In order to make progress in overcoming these difficulties, the attention of the CIA community needs to focus much more intentionally on issues of governance and capacity-building.

References

BBC (British Broadcasting Corporation) (2006) 'Homes forced to get water meters', 1 March, http://news.bbc.co.uk/1/hi/england/4759960.stm

Beattie, L. (2010) 'Changing urban governance in the Auckland region: Prospects for land use planning', paper presented to the Conference of the Association of European Schools of Planning, Helsinki, Finland, 7–10 July

Brown, R. (2004) 'Local institutional development and organisational change for advancing sustainable urban water futures', paper presented at the International Water Sensitive Urban Design Conference, Adelaide, 21–25 November

Creasey, R. and Ross, W. (2005) 'The Cheviot Mining Project: Cumulative effects assessment lessons for professional practice', in Hanna, K. (ed) *Environmental Impact Assessment: Practice and Participation*, Oxford University Press, Oxford

DECC (Department of Energy and Climate Change) (2010) *Energy Consumption in the United Kingdom*, www.decc.gov.uk/en/content/cms/statistics/publications/ecuk/ecuk.aspx

Defra (Department for Environment, Food and Rural Affairs) (2004) *Indicators of Sustainable Development*, London, www.sustainable-development.gov.uk/sustainable/quality04/maind/04d15.htm

Dixon, J. (2005) 'Enacting and reacting: Local government frameworks for economic development', in Rowe, J. (ed) *Economic Development in New Zealand*, Ashgate, Aldershot, pp69–86

Dixon, J. and Sharp, E. (2006) 'Collaborative research in sustainable water management: Issues of interdisciplinarity', paper presented at the World Conference on Accelerating Excellence in the Built Environment, Birmingham, 2–4 October

Dixon, J. and van Roon, M. (2005) 'Coming on heavy: The need for strategic management of cumulative environmental effects', paper presented at the IAIA SEA Conference, Prague

Eason, C., Dixon, J. and van Roon, M. (2009) 'A transdisciplinary research approach providing a platform for improved urban design, quality of life and biodiverse urban ecosystems', in McDonnell, M., Breuste, J. and Hahs, A. K. (eds) *The Ecology of Cities and Towns: A Comparative Approach*, Cambridge University Press, Cambridge, pp470–483

EAUE (European Academy of the Urban Environment) (2001) 'Vienna: The new concept for transport and city planning', extract from the database 'SURBAN: Good practice in urban development', www.eaue.de/winuwd/89.htm

Ericksen, N. J., Berke, P. R., Crawford, J. L. and Dixon, J. E. (2004) *Plan-making for Sustainability: The New Zealand Experience*, Ashgate, Aldershot

Feeney, C., Heslop, V. and Lynsar, P. (2005) 'LIUDD change management: Easing the transition to sustainability', internal report prepared with and for the University of Auckland

Government of Western Australia (2005) *Household – Individualised Marketing*, Department for Planning and Infrastructure, Perth

Heslop, V. (2006) 'Towards a better understanding of the institutional development and change required to improve the uptake of low impact urban design and development', paper published in Proceedings of 7th Urban Drainage Modelling and 4th Water Sensitive Urban Design Conference, Melbourne, 2–6 April

Heslop, V. (2010) *Sustaining Capacity: Building Institutional Capacity for Sustainable Development*, unpublished doctoral thesis, University of Auckland, New Zealand

Heslop, V. and Dixon, J. (2008) 'Challenging the norm: The capacity of local government to implement "low impact" design practices', paper presented at the 11th International Conference on Urban Drainage, Edinburgh, Scotland, 1–5 September

Heslop, V., Dixon, J. and Trotman, R. (2010) 'Valuing learning networks in enhancing sustainable practice', paper presented to the 30th Annual Meeting of the International Association for Impact Assessment, Geneva, 6–11 April

House of Commons Transport Committee (2009) 'Taxes and charges on road users', Sixth Report of Session 2008–09, www.publications.parliament.uk/pa/cm200809/cmselect/cmtran/103/103.pdf

Infrastructure Canada (2005) *The Importance of Water Metering and Its Uses in Canada*, www.infc.gc.ca/altformats/pdf/rn-nr-2005-06-eng.pdf

Lane, M. B. and McDonald, G. (2005) 'Community-based environmental planning: Operational dilemmas, planning principles and possible remedies', *Journal of Environmental Planning and Management*, vol 48, no 5, pp709–731

Laurian, L., Crawford, J., Day, M., Kouwenhoven, P., Mason, G., Ericksen, N. and Beattie, L. (2010) 'Evaluating the outcomes of plans: Theory, practice, and methodology', *Environment and Planning B: Planning and Design*, vol 37, no 4, pp740–757

Leggett, M. (2006) 'Training the decision makers: The Making Good Decisions Programme', paper presented at the Second Joint Congress of the New Zealand Planning Institute and the Planning Institute of Australia, Gold Coast, Queensland, 2–5 April

Levett-Therivel (2005) 'Decisions, decisions: Lifestyles, behaviour and energy demand', report for the Department of Trade and Industry, London

Levett-Therivel and EDAW (2005) 'Sustainability appraisal (integrating strategic environmental assessment) of the Yorkshire and Humber draft RSS', report for the Yorkshire and Humber Assembly, Wakefield

May, P., Burby, R. J., Ericksen, N. J., Handmer, J., Dixon, J. E., Michaels, S. and Smith, D. I. (1996) *Environmental Management and Governance: Intergovernmental Approaches to Hazards and Sustainability*, Routledge, London

Ministry for the Environment (2010) *Making Good Decisions: A Training, Assessment and Certification Programme for RMA Decision-makers*, www.mfe.govt.nz/rma/practitioners/good-decisions/index.html#certificate

Murray, S. (2006) 'Democrats to focus on fuel', *Washington Post*, 20 May, www.washingtonpost.com/wp-dyn/content/article/2006/05/19/AR2006051901626.html

New Zealand Government (2009) 'Progress of Phase Two of the resource management reforms', Cabinet Minute CAB Min (09) 34/6A, www.mfe.govt.nz/cabinet-papers/cab-min-09-34-6a.html

Policy Research Initiative (2005) *Market-based Instruments for Water Demand Management 1: The Use of Pricing and Taxes*, sustainable development briefing note, Ottawa

Quigley, J. and Harper, D. (2004) 'Compliance with Fisheries Act Section 35(2) Authorisations: A field audit of habitat compensation projects in Canada', paper presented at the IAIA Annual Meeting, Vancouver, www.iaia.org/Non_Members/Conference/IAIA04/Publications/04%20abstracts%20volume%205-70.pdf

Taylor, M. F. J., Suckling, K. F. and Rachlinski, J. J. (2005) 'The effectiveness of the Endangered Species Act: A quantitative analysis', *BioScience*, vol 55, no 4, April, pp360–367

Thérivel, R. and Ross, W. (2006) 'Cumulative effects assessment: Does scale matter?', *Environmental Impact Assessment Review*, vol 27, no 5, pp365–385

Trotman, R. (2009) 'Valuing learning networks: A review of the Low Impact Urban Design and Development National Task Force', a report for The University of Auckland as part of the Low Impact Urban Design and Development research programme

van Bueren, E. and ten Heuvelhof, E. (2005) 'Improving governance arrangements in support of sustainable cities', *Environment and Planning B: Planning and Design*, vol 32, pp47–66

van Roon, M. R. (2005) 'Emerging approaches to urban ecosystem management: The potential of low impact urban design and development principles', *Journal of Environmental Assessment, Policy and Management*, vol 7, no 1, pp1–24

van Roon, M. (2010) *Low Impact Urban Design and Development: Ecological Efficacy as a Basis for Strategic Planning and its Implementation*, unpublished doctoral thesis, The University of Auckland, New Zealand

van Roon, M., Greenaway, A., Dixon, J. and Eason, C. (2006) 'New Zealand low impact urban design and development programme: Scope, founding principles and collaborative learning', paper published in proceedings of 7th Urban Drainage Modelling and 4th Water Sensitive Urban Design Conference, Melbourne, 2–6 April

World Bank (2005) *Integrating Environmental Considerations in Policy Formulation: Lessons from Policy-Based SEA Experience*, Report no 32783, World Bank, Washington, DC

25
Transboundary Issues in SEA

Nick Bonvoisin[1]

Introduction

This chapter provides a discussion of transboundary issues in strategic environmental assessment (SEA), drawing on presentations and discussions at the International Association for Impact Assessment (IAIA) Conference on SEA held in September 2005 in Prague and on other reported activities. As a result, the examples cited pre-date that conference. More recent examples have been described in papers such as that by Brecht (2007).

The discussion focuses on two rather distinct situations, both of which might be termed 'transboundary SEA':

1   SEA of national plans (with 'plans' being taken to include programmes and possibly policies and legislation) proposed in one country (the country of origin) but considered likely to have significant environmental effects on the territory of another (the affected country).
2   SEA of transboundary plans that extend over more than one country.

These two situations have invoked different approaches to undertaking SEA, though these approaches share many features and they encounter similar problems.

This chapter is divided into the following sections:

*   A background review of frameworks for considering transboundary issues in SEA and focusing on two international legal instruments – the United Nations Economic Commission for Europe (UNECE) Protocol on SEA and the European Union (EU) Directive on SEA.
*   An analytical review of examples from the two situations mentioned above, highlighting common issues and difficulties.
*   A conclusion, providing ideas on how to approach transboundary issues in SEA.

Background

Legal frameworks for considering transboundary issues in SEA are provided in both the UNECE Protocol on SEA (UNECE, 2003) and the EU Directive on SEA (2001/42/EC) (see Boxes 25.1 and 25.2). The two instruments require that transboundary consultations take place if either party (the country of origin or the affected country) considers that the implementation of a plan or programme is likely to have significant transboundary environmental effects. Similar, or weaker, provisions may be found in other bilateral and multilateral agreements, for example:

Box 25.1 *Provision for transboundary consultations in the Protocol on SEA*

Article 10 – Transboundary Consultations

1 Where a Party of origin considers that the implementation of a plan or programme is likely to have significant transboundary environmental, including health, effects or where a Party likely to be significantly affected so requests, the Party of origin shall as early as possible before the adoption of the plan or programme notify the affected Party.
2 This notification shall contain, *inter alia*:
   (a) The draft plan or programme and the environmental report including information on its possible transboundary environmental, including health, effects; and
   (b) Information regarding the decision-making procedure, including an indication of a reasonable time schedule for the transmission of comments.
3 The affected Party shall, within the time specified in the notification, indicate to the Party of origin whether it wishes to enter into consultations before the adoption of the plan or programme and, if it so indicates, the Parties concerned shall enter into consultations concerning the likely transboundary environmental, including health, effects of implementing the plan or programme and the measures envisaged to prevent, reduce or mitigate adverse effects.
4 Where such consultations take place, the Parties concerned shall agree on detailed arrangements to ensure that the public concerned and the authorities referred to in article 9, paragraph 1, in the affected Party are informed and given an opportunity to forward their opinion on the draft plan or programme and the environmental report within a reasonable time frame.

Note: There are further provisions relating to transboundary consultations in the Protocol's preamble, in Articles 2.3 and 2.4 (in 'definitions') and 11 ('decision'), in Annexes III, IV (item 10) and V.

Source: UNECE (2003)

Box 25.2 *Provision for transboundary consultations in the SEA Directive*

Article 7 – Transboundary Consultations

1   Where a Member State considers that the implementation of a plan or programme being prepared in relation to its territory is likely to have significant effects on the environment in another Member State, or where a Member State likely to be significantly affected so requests, the Member State in whose territory the plan or programme is being prepared shall, before its adoption or submission to the legislative procedure, forward a copy of the draft plan or programme and the relevant environmental report to the other Member State.

2   Where a Member State is sent a copy of a draft plan or programme and an environmental report under paragraph 1, it shall indicate to the other Member State whether it wishes to enter into consultations before the adoption of the plan or programme or its submission to the legislative procedure and, if it so indicates, the Member States concerned shall enter into consultations concerning the likely transboundary environmental effects of implementing the plan or programme and the measures envisaged to reduce or eliminate such effects.

   Where such consultations take place, the Member States concerned shall agree on detailed arrangements to ensure that the authorities referred to in Article 6(3) and the public referred to in Article 6(4) in the Member State likely to be significantly affected are informed and given an opportunity to forward their opinion within a reasonable time-frame.

3   Where Member States are required under this Article to enter into consultations, they shall agree, at the beginning of such consultations, on a reasonable time-frame for the duration of the consultations.

Note: There are further provisions relating to transboundary consultation in the Directive's preamble, in Articles 2(b), 8 and 9(1) and in Annex II (item 2).

Source: EU (2001)

- The Kiev Framework Convention on the Protection and Sustainable Development of the Carpathians (2003), Article 12, paragraph 1.
- The Bonn Convention on the Conservation of Migratory Species of Wild Animals (1979), Resolution 7.2, paragraph 2.

Under both the Protocol and the Directive, the transboundary consultations proceed approximately as follows. Before adopting or submitting to the legislative procedure a proposed plan (or programme), the country of origin notifies potentially affected countries. Similarly, if a country considers it likely that it will be significantly affected by a proposal in another country, it may request notification. The notification includes the following elements:

- The draft plan.
- The environmental report, including information on the possible transboundary environmental effects of the plan.
- Information regarding the decision-making procedure, including an indication of a reasonable time schedule for the transmission of comments.

The affected country then indicates, within the time specified in the notification, whether it wishes to be consulted. If so, the two countries consult each other concerning the likely transboundary environmental effects of implementing the plan and the measures envisaged to prevent, reduce or mitigate adverse effects. The two countries also need to agree on detailed arrangements to ensure that the authorities and the public concerned in the affected country are informed and given an opportunity to forward their opinion on the draft plan and on the environmental report within a reasonable time frame.

This procedure is similar to that defined for environmental impact assessment (EIA) in a transboundary context as provided for in the EU Directive on EIA (85/337/EC) and in the UNECE Convention on EIA in a Transboundary Context (the Espoo Convention) (UNECE, 1991).

This procedure is particularly appropriate in addressing the first situation described in the introduction to this chapter, the national plan with transboundary effects. However, as with transboundary EIA, it may also be used for reciprocal consultation in the second situation – transboundary plans extending over more than one country.

As well as these legal bases for transboundary SEA, there are relevant SEA guidelines and procedures. For example, the World Bank lending is subject to an environmental assessment (EA) policy that states that 'EA takes into account ... transboundary and global environmental aspects' (World Bank, 1999). However, the World Bank's more detailed *Environmental Assessment Sourcebook* makes only passing reference to transboundary issues (World Bank, 1991). The policy also states that 'when the project is likely to have sectoral or regional impacts, sectoral or regional EA is required'. However, there is no suggestion that such a regional EA cover a 'region' extending across more than one country or that it address transboundary issues (World Bank, 1996).

Analysis and review

There is limited experience with transboundary SEA, particularly for consulting foreign stakeholders on a domestic plan having transboundary effect. There is a little more experience where a plan is being implemented across borders and there is some form of institutional framework for intergovernmental cooperation. This section looks at some examples of transboundary SEA cases and the difficulties encountered, and of SEA procedures and the solutions they propose, with details provided in a series of boxes.

Transboundary consultations on domestic plans

Within the EU, it is becoming more common to consult neighbouring EU member states on domestic plans and programmes, including land-use or spatial plans. Early examples include:

- SEA of spatial plans in Germany with notification of the Czech Republic (Czech Republic, 2005) and Poland (Box 25.3).
- SEA of spatial plans in Poland with notification of Germany (Box 25.3).
- EU ('INTERREG III A') co-financed research project on SEA for regional planning with development of a transboundary assessment and practice concept for Saxony (Germany), Poland and the Czech Republic (Leibniz Institute of Ecological and Regional Development, 2006).
- SEA of energy (oil, gas and wind) licensing offshore of the UK, with notification of several other EU member states and others (Box 25.4).

Box 25.3 *Transboundary consultations between Germany and Poland*

- A questionnaire was completed by 59 of the 207 municipalities in Brandenburg in Germany, May–July 2005 – 26 municipalities had experience of SEA (whether completed or underway).
- The questionnaire revealed very little experience in transboundary consultations, with only two respondents indicating transboundary consultation and neither were from municipalities on the border or for SEAs that had been completed. The two municipalities concerned (Mühlberg/Elbe and Rietz-Neuendorf) reported 'good' experiences in transboundary consultations. The lack of transboundary consultations by municipalities on the German-Polish border was considered suspect.
- The questionnaire was also completed by 13 of the 83 municipalities in Lubuskie Woivodeship (province) in Poland, August–September 2005 – all 13 had completed SEAs.
- Polish law amended to include transboundary consultations in SEA only in July 2005.
- Six municipalities reported transboundary consultations, with their experiences reported as very good (one municipality), good (three), bad (one), very bad (one). Difficulties reported included language problems and institutional arrangements.
- The questionnaire also provided interesting information on quality of decisions, costs, public participation, consultation of authorities (in general, not specifically transboundary SEA).

Source: Albrecht (2005)

Box 25.5 provides an example of a North America case where the US did not initially notify Canada, although this may have changed as a result of a subsequent court case.

Box 25.4 *SEA of energy (oil, gas and wind) licensing offshore of the UK*

The UK Department of Trade and Industry (DTI) undertook a series of SEAs of offshore energy licensing (www.offshore-sea.org.uk). For certain SEAs, it notified all states bordering the North Sea via the OSPAR Commission (www.ospar.org) under the Convention for the Protection of the Marine Environment of the North-East Atlantic (1992), providing copies of consultation documents. The DTI stated that it would consider all feedback received in decisions relating to the licensing round (although the documentation reviewed by this author did not reveal any transboundary consultation as such).

Regarding transboundary effects from oil and gas development, documents typically state:

> *Sources of potentially significant environmental effects, with the additional potential for transboundary effects, are underwater noise, marine discharges ('produced water' and drilling discharges), atmospheric emissions and accidental events (oil spills). All of these aspects may be able to be detected ... in adjacent state territories, particularly from activities undertaken in areas close to the international boundary. The scale and consequences of environmental effects in adjacent state territories will be comparable to those in UK territorial waters. There are no identified transboundary effects in which environmental consequences in a neighbouring state are overwhelmingly due to activities resulting from the proposed licensing.*

Source: DTI (2001, 2002)

Box 25.5 *Transboundary watershed management on the border between Canada and the US*

Background

- Two water diversion projects in Missouri River Basin, North Dakota, US, with potential significant transboundary environmental effects on Hudson Bay Basin, Province of Manitoba, Canada: Garrison Diversion for domestic and irrigation water supply; Devils Lake Diversion for flood control.

- Projects approved without EIA or SEA.
- No use of the Boundary Waters Treaty (1909) (www.ijc.org/rel/agree/water.html) or of its International Joint Commission (www.ijc.org).
- In October 2002, the Province of Manitoba filed a legal challenge against the Garrison Diversion in the US District Court in Washington, DC, to compel the US Department of the Interior to complete an environmental impact statement (EIS) on the project. A Court Order on 3 February 2005 remanded the case to the Bureau of Reclamation for completion of additional environmental analysis. In March 2006, the Bureau of Reclamation gave notice of intent to prepare an EIS under the National Environmental Policy Act (EPA, 2006).
- Numerous policy decisions before plan and project decisions prevented effective bilateral cooperation, denying opportunities for joint impact mitigation and ensured potential for environmental impacts to occur.
- These policy decisions were critical to both projects, but are not now typically the subject of SEA.

How to improve the process

- Need to ensure equity of concerned countries by: (a) honouring transboundary bilateral agreements, where they exist; and (b) ensuring equivalent knowledge is available on both sides of the border: foster joint research and monitoring to ensure information is both comparable, sufficient, and available to address the issue.
- Need for transparent policy decisions:
  o Make more transparent programme and plan decisions.
  o If politicization of decisions is unavoidable, then exercise extreme diligence to ensure transparency of these decisions and earlier examination of decision consequences.
  o Countries must establish joint communications and information-sharing protocols and permanent bilateral structures to accomplish protocol goals.
  o Information registries can make a difference if comprehensive, and contain critical information (even if confidential).
  o Ensure equivalent knowledge is available on both sides of border and ensure data is available early enough.
- Need to ensure due process:
  o Willingness of countries to cooperate or honour relevant bilateral agreements and domestic requirements.
  o Have a common goal actively to avoid litigation – ensures process is cooperative, information-based.
  o Actively encourage development of non-governmental organization (NGO) linkages so information exchange and coordination of participation is ensured.
  o Adopt common standard of environmental care and stewardship – common definitions.
  o Ensure that bilateral arrangements to prevent transboundary impacts provide formal, science-based mechanisms for challenge of policy or plan decisions by individual private citizens of the other country.

> ○ Government should support environmental NGOs to remove bottlenecks from their communications capacities.
>
> *Source:* Phare (2005)

Box 25.6 *Nile River Basin transboundary environmental analysis (TEA)*

'[The TEA] was undertaken as part of the Nile Basin Initiative that was launched formally in February 1999 as a cooperative effort of the ten riparian countries. The Initiative (www.nilebasin.org) has a "shared vision ... to achieve sustainable socio-economic development through the equitable utilization of, and benefit from, the common Nile Basin resources". The TEA aimed at identifying priority transboundary environmental issues to be tackled, and defined elements of an Agenda for Environmental Action.

'The TEA report describes the key environmental issues and threats (land degradation, wetlands, lake degradation and biodiversity loss, water quality degradation, and natural disasters and refugees). The root causes of these threats can be found in widespread poverty, inappropriate macro and sectoral policies, inadequate regulatory systems, institutional constraints, lack of proper land-use planning, limited awareness and information, population growth, climatic vulnerability and urbanization.

'The elements of the Agenda for Environmental Action prepared in response to this analysis have been grouped into six components: political commitment, outreach activities, preventive and curative measures, resources management programmes and monitoring of environmental changes. All these components are being implemented. Of particular relevance to the [World Bank's] SEA Structured Learning Program is the preparation of a Sectoral and Strategic Environmental Assessment of the Power Sector in three countries of the Basin... required to look into the longer-term effects of several key planning decisions that require rapid decision ...'

Source: Mercier (2003); Nile Basin Initiative et al (2001)

Consultations on transboundary plans

Early examples of SEA cases or procedures for multilateral plans, undertaken or planned, include:

- TEA of the Nile River Basin (Box 25.6), which is a situation assessment rather than an impact assessment.
- Mekong River Commission arrangements for transboundary assessment and management of the Mekong River Basin (Box 25.7).
- SEA Transport Manual for EU trans-European transport networks (Box 25.8) – should facilitate SEA of whole transport networks and should help

discourage the practice of 'salami slicing' (chopping up of large plans into small chunks that are perceived as being easier to get approval for, but that prevent proper consideration of alternatives and of cumulative effects).

- United States Agency for International Development (USAID) Eastern and Southern Africa Strategy: Environmental Threats and Opportunities Assessment, with Special Focus on Biological Diversity and Tropical Forestry (Moore and Knausenberger, 2000).
- Regional guidelines for EA (EIA and SEA) of shared ecosystems within the East African Community (African Centre for Technology Studies, 2002).
- Flood management in the Scheldt Estuary between Flanders (Belgium) and the Netherlands (Box 25.9).
- North America, tri-countries (Canada, Mexico, US) Commission for Environmental Cooperation (Box 25.10).

Box 25.7 *Transboundary environmental assessment in the Mekong River Basin*

The Mekong River Commission (MRC, see www.mrcmekong.org) was established under the Agreement on the Cooperation for the Sustainable Development of the Mekong River Basin (1995) concluded by Thailand, the Lao People's Democratic Republic, Cambodia and Vietnam. The remit includes optimizing the use and mutual benefits of all MRC member countries and minimizing harmful effects that may results from natural occurrences and man-made activities. In 2002, MRC recommended that member countries hold formal discussions on a transboundary process for both EIA and SEA. It was considered such a process would be a 'major step forward' in promoting sustainable development of navigation across the Mekong basin (MRC, 2004).

Adoption of a transboundary EA agreement in the Lower Mekong Basin met with resistance and nervousness for the following reasons:

- Implications of identifying transboundary impacts, possibly leading to claims for compensation.
- Infringement of sovereignty and the 'right' to develop national resources.
- Internal politics around development aspirations versus sustainability.
- Weak national institutional structures for law enforcement and environmental protection.
- Limited national capacity to undertake EIA.
- Limited knowledge and understanding of river system and impacts.

Some key lessons from a study tour:

- Practical experience in carrying out a transboundary EIA is crucial when developing bilateral agreements.
- Differences in legal and institutional structures necessitate broad regional framework and detailed bilateral agreements.

- Crucial that each country fully understands each party's transboundary EIA process.
- Clear lines of communication must be established, widely disseminated and enforced.

Need good practice to:

- Ensure comparable standards in impact assessment.
- Give credibility to research and impact assessment results.
- Promote transparency in decision-making.
- Forge understanding and trust between countries.

MRC is attempting to develop a standard level of good practice across its member countries in:

- EIA, SEA and country environmental analysis (for example, good practice guidelines in environmental assessment in a transboundary context)
- Scientific research on the river basin and its dynamics (for example, through core programmes).
- Data collection and interpretation methods for each member country.

Concluding remarks:

- MRC eager to learn from others' experiences on the development and implementation of transboundary EIA processes – need to overcome nervousness.
- Also recognizes the opportunity afforded by SEA and country environmental analysis-type approaches – great potential for such tools but very little capacity or understanding in the MRC member countries.
- Sharing and development of good practice is therefore key to future environmental management of the Mekong River Basin.

Source: Horberry (2004)

Box 25.8 *Handling transboundary issues in transport SEA – trans-European transport networks*

The European Commission's Building Environmental Assessment Consensus (BEACON) project has developed an SEA Transport Manual and supporting factsheets, from which the following is drawn.

An **institutional basis** will be needed for cooperation in handling transboundary issues between politicians, the public, planners, environmentalists and other groups of experts. A **common perception** and understanding of objectives, issues and policies with the view to establish transboundary sustainable management by the participating countries will be a desired output from transboundary cooperation in an SEA process.

An important element is to describe the process of handling transboundary issues and establish a **holistic approach** on an international level. What is it that the investment aims to accomplish? Will all the affected countries get the same output? What about impacts, direct and indirect? The output of such cooperation on transboundary issues will probably be a set of indicators, objectives and measures to enable a desired development and output of the investment on an environmental as well as economical and social level in the affected countries. Another important outcome is to highlight and enable a common understanding of the visions and goals behind the planning process.

A **joint working group** should be formed and if necessary also sub-groups for sub-topics of the process. The working group should involve representatives from national, regional and/or local governments. The group should also consist of the different expertises needed and should foster mutual understanding of the aims, goals and impacts of different developing strategies can be achieved. The key objective of the working group is to enable and stimulate the exchange of experience and expertise.

Procedures for **consensus building** and conflict management are central to successful handling of transboundary issues. Conflicts can occur for many reasons, including: differences in organizational status and influence; incompatible objectives and methods; differences in behavioural style; differences in information; distortions in communications and unequal power or authority.

Just as in all aspects connected with SEA and infrastructure planning, the final conclusion is that the transboundary goals, impacts and effects of different scenarios need to be discussed and handled at a very **early stage** in the planning process. Only when this is achieved can a fair discussion of the visions and goals behind the discussed investments become a reality.

It is of vital importance to ensure that the **public** in the affected countries involved in the creation and discussion of long- and short-term visions that the discussed strategies and investments are based on. Arrangements need to be made to ensure an exchange of information so that the decision-makers are fully aware of the views expressed by the public on the other side of the border.

The **availability of adequate information** about the proposed activity, its likely effects on environmental, social and economic levels and the measures proposed to mitigate negative effects is a key issue in **effective public participation** in a transboundary SEA process. Specific arrangements should be made to ensure that members of the public have access to relevant information about the effects of the whole of the planned development strategy, its investments and the impact on environmental, economical and social level. A good and timely **translation of documentation** into the relevant languages will greatly facilitate meaningful involvement in the SEA procedure of the authorities and members of the public in the affected countries. On the other hand, a poor translation may impede the process.

Technical issues

- **Coupling of scenarios/alternatives:** Transboundary plans have to be coupled to form a reasonable network, in space and time, tracks have to be linked and are fully effective only after they connect with each other.
- **Consolidation of the indicator sets and weighting:** In a transboundary approach, different cultures are facing each other. Before commencing, it is useful to define a common evaluation framework. If this does not seem to be possible, tools might be used to use different weights to determine the stability of results ('sensitivity analysis'). This might save time that would have been spent on mediation before having real results as basis for discussion.
- **Common objective functions and exposure thresholds:** Starting with environmental targets the objective functions define the relationship between the effects and the final indicators. Exposure thresholds reflect the national legislation but may rely on World Health Organization (WHO) or European limits. Mediation may be necessary if special protection is given to parts of the population or cultural heritage.
- **Transboundary data merging and preparation:** Transboundary plans or programmes may be assessed only once by the two or more parties to save money but all of them should provide national data in an appropriate format.
- **Coupling of national simulation models:** Transboundary infrastructure eases problems in transboundary transport and iterates the demand in the supranational network. If there are more connecting points and modes involved the national models should be coupled.
- Also, the scales for the indicators and the objective function in general may be on the agenda for transboundary projects. Relative biodiversity, for example, should be defined for different ecosystems.

Source: European Commission, Directorate-General for Energy and Transport (2005a, b)

Box 25.9 *SEA for the Scheldt Estuary Development Plan 2010 – Flanders (Belgium) and the Netherlands*

The SEA reflected a preliminary study 'Long-Term Vision' signed in 2001 by the governments of Flanders and the Netherlands.
Problem definition, issues included:

- Accessibility of harbours (particularly Antwerp).
- Decrease of biotopes of international significance (Dutch and Flemish problem).
- Flood safety (mainly a Flemish problem).

Legal context for transboundary SEA includes the Espoo Convention and its Protocol on SEA, Scheldt Treaty (2003) and a draft bilateral agreement between the Netherlands and Flanders (Belgium) supporting implementation of the Espoo

Convention. Key issues were:

- Need to establish a procedure acceptable to both countries.
- Problems of differences in legislation:
  - Who is competent authority in a joint procedure?
  - Identical guidelines for the environmental report.
  - Differences in timing between legislation.
- Opportunities for public participation at beginning of the SEA procedure (starting notice) and in review of the environmental report.

Source: de Groote (2005)

Box 25.10 *Commission for Environmental Cooperation in North America and the Draft North American Agreement on Transboundary EIA*

The North American Agreement on Environmental Cooperation (NAAEC) is a side-agreement to the North American Free-Trade Agreement (NAFTA) signed by the governments of Canada, Mexico and the US (1993). It 'promotes strengthened cooperation between the three countries regarding the conservation, protection and enhancement of the environment'.

Article 10: Council Functions (paragraph 7) provides:

'Recognizing the significant bilateral nature of many transboundary environmental issues, the Council [the three countries' ministers for the environment] shall, with a view to agreement between the Parties pursuant to this Article within three years on obligations, consider and develop recommendations with respect to:

(a) assessing the environmental impact of proposed projects subject to decisions by a competent government authority and likely to cause significant adverse transboundary effects, including a full evaluation of comments provided by other Parties and persons of other Parties;
(b) notification, provision of relevant information and consultation between Parties with respect to such projects; and
(c) mitigation of the potential adverse effects of such projects.

'The objectives of the proposed transboundary [EIA] agreement would be to provide decision-makers with timely information on the transboundary environmental consequences of proposed projects to ensure that decisions on such projects take into account such consequences and to provide a mechanism for potentially affected people and governments to participate in the process leading to a decision on the project.'

In 1997, 'the Council considered recommendations of a group of experts for an agreement on transboundary [EIA]. As a result, the Council decided that the parties would complete a legally binding agreement' by 15 April 1998. The group of experts then developed a draft agreement, but negotiations on this draft came to an impasse on the issue of the scope of application.

In April 2006, at a meeting under the Espoo Convention, the delegation of Canada provided contextual information on the 1997 draft agreement. Canada, the US and Mexico were once again pursuing a trilateral agreement on transboundary environmental impacts, this time not under the NAFTA/NAAEC but further to a commitment in the Security and Prosperity Partnership that the leaders of the three countries signed in 2005. The goal was to have an agreement in place by June 2007. However, no agreement was reached.

Source: Commission for Environmental Cooperation (1997); UNECE (2006)

Transboundary SEA difficulties

Given the similarities to the transboundary EIA procedure, similar issues are likely to need to be addressed in transboundary SEA (Bonvoisin and Horberry, 2005a):

- Identification of points of contact – who to contact for different types of plans, in different sectors and at different levels of government. This may become more complex for more decentralized governments.
- Lack of response – if the affected country does not respond to the notification, it is not clear whether this means that it does not wish to be consulted. The question then arises of whether to continue sending information.
- Language – translation of documents and interpretation during meetings. How much of the documentation has to be translated, into which languages, by whom (plan proponent, central government, the affected country, and so on) and who pays?
- Public access to documents in an affected country – beware of over-reliance on the internet and excluding disadvantaged groups.
- Access to public hearings if only held in the country of origin – costs of travel, border restrictions, need for interpretation, and so on.
- Willingness of the public to participate, recognizing a plan in another country may not attract much public interest as it may not appear concrete and may be too remote.
- Equity – whether equal opportunities to participate are sought for the public in the country of origin and in the affected country. If so, how this may be achieved.
- Timing of notification – when to notify? At the latest, transboundary effects might be identified during preparation of the environmental report, but if identified earlier then informal notification would best be initiated earlier as well, during scoping; doing so may reduce delays in reaching the decision stage.

- Delays in implementing the plan – a transboundary consultation process may significantly lengthen the plan-making because of delays in notification, having to wait for a response from a potentially affected country, translation of documentation, additional consultation and public participation, and so on.
- Need to work within institutional arrangements for transboundary plans to identify entry point for SEA.
- Compatibility of national systems for environmental assessment and public participation, and so on, including time allowed for different stages, public participation in scoping. Incompatibility may lead to practical difficulties, including delays, and to problems of equity.
- Covering of costs incurred by or in the affected country, including the costs of public hearings and of review of documentation by government.

The cases outlined above also illustrate the following issues:

- Failure to carry out transboundary consultations.
- Numerous policy decisions may have already been taken before the plan is developed, thus limiting consideration of alternatives (though this is not a problem unique to transboundary SEA but common to SEA of plans and programmes).
- Problems with working within inappropriate cross-border institutions.
- Differing requirements in national legislation for the content of the environmental report.
- Differing national methodologies and available information.
- Unequal power relationships between bodies on either side of the border.
- Need for agreement on the identity of the competent authority for transboundary plans.

Conclusion

Transboundary notification and consultations may be arranged purely case-by-case. However, with EIA in a transboundary context (under the Espoo Convention, for example) it has been found that the process can be accelerated and simplified through developing bilateral or multilateral agreements that provide a framework for transboundary consultations. Specific parameters include: contact points, a joint body, language considerations including translation arrangements, assigning costs, criteria for determining the significance of effects, public participation arrangements and dispute settlement procedures. Bilateral and multilateral agreements that have been established in the framework of the Espoo Convention or for transboundary EIA, when suitably modified to cover plans and programmes, may provide a pattern for transboundary SEA arrangements.

Regional and subregional agreements may provide a broad framework for transboundary SEA, taking into account the wide diversity of national legal and institutional arrangements, but bilateral (and more local multilateral) agreements are needed to provide details. Such agreements must be honoured. The development of such agreements will probably be facilitated by first gaining experience in transboundary SEA through pilot projects. Pilot projects can help overcome teething problems, including the practical issues identified in the previous section, as well as nervousness about embarking on transboundary SEA. The sharing and development of good practice will help in building understanding of other countries' SEA processes, as well as broader understanding and trust. Sharing good practice might also lead to common standards of assessment. The SEA Transport Manual (Box 25.8) provides many practical suggestions for carrying out SEA of transboundary plans.

The application of bilateral agreements can be facilitated through joint bodies, either standing bodies or established for each SEA case (*ad hoc*). Permanent bodies have certain benefits, such as their members gaining a better understanding of each other's legislation, procedures, approaches and concerns, although the mandate and membership of an *ad hoc* body might better reflect the specific needs of the individual case. Whichever approach is taken, clear lines of communication need to be set up, widely disseminated and consistently used.

The key role of joint bodies should be to promote dialogue, consensus and a common understanding of plans, including their vision, goals, objectives and issues, among politicians, the public, planners, environmentalists and other groups of experts, with appropriate representation from local and national levels. It is therefore of great importance to begin consultations as early as possible; if not, it will be difficult to arrive at a consensus on plans and their vision, goals and objectives.

The policy setting of plans is often the subject of public comments and objections. It might not be appropriate to subject the relevant policies to SEA, but it might be possible to arrive at a common cross-border vision or objectives for a plan by involving the different stakeholders. A common vision is likely to help avoid conflicts.

Permanent bodies can promote ongoing dialogue and transboundary research that can facilitate transboundary SEA as a basis for cooperative and information-based decision-making, reducing the potential for conflict. Transboundary research and monitoring can promote the availability of similar information for assessment and decision-making on both sides of a border. Joint bodies, whether permanent or *ad hoc*, can also promote sustainable management linked to the implementation of the plan.

The public and NGOs may play an important role in identifying issues and finding solutions. Effective means of communicating their views between countries are therefore essential, as is an ethic of transparency and of promoting public involvement. Cross-border NGO linkages can also be important in facilitating public participation in the SEA. Bilateral agreements might also facilitate the public challenge of decisions.

Table 25.1 summarizes the transboundary SEA issues identified at the Prague Conference.

Table 25.1 *Profile of transboundary issues in SEA*

Main trends and issues	Absence of SEA was identified as a problem at Prague.
	Potential solutions depend on clear agreements between countries at the appropriate political level.
	Effective application also requires established cooperation mechanisms at regional level.
	Public involvement is crucial for identifying and addressing key issues – often the driver for raising issues to decision-making level.
	Transboundary environmental issues at project level generally stem from upstream policy decisions.
Main perspectives	Key issues that may influence SEA effectiveness or impact in a transboundary context include:
	• Clear agreement on level of government at which decision-making and communication responsibilities are located.
	• Recognition of existing international agreements.
	• Open recognition of conflicts of interest at government level.
	• Avoidance of 'hidden' policy decisions that shape future transboundary projects.
	• Joint data collection.
	• Enabling NGOs to access assessment data.
Key lessons	Achieving transboundary SEA at policy level is a significant challenge; but also has significant consequences downstream that are hard to remedy through transboundary EIA.
	Major barrier seems to be at political level – unwillingness to enter into transboundary agreements and difficulty of coordinating central and regional government level responsibilities.
Future directions	Priority lies in developing effective agreements (bilateral or multilateral) to ensure that SEA can be considered in relation to upstream policy decisions.

Source: Bonvoisin and Horberry (2005b)

Note

[1] The opinions, interpretations and conclusions expressed in this paper are those of the author and do not necessarily represent the views of the United Nations (UN), the United Nations Economic Commission for Europe (UNECE) or of its member states.

References

African Centre for Technology Studies (2002) 'The plan of action for the development of guidelines for regional environmental impact assessment of shared ecosystems of East Africa: Project summary', http://pdf.usaid.gov/pdf_docs/PDACF675.pdf, accessed July 2010

Albrecht, E. (2005) 'SEA in binding land-use plan procedures with special focus on transboundary consultation', paper for the IAIA SEA Conference, Prague

Bonvoisin, N. and Horberry, J. (2005a) 'Transboundary SEA: Position paper', paper presented at the IAIA SEA Conference, Prague

Bonvoisin, N. and Horberry, J. (2005b) 'Transboundary SEA: Session report', paper presented at the IAIA SEA Conference, Prague

Brecht, E. (2007) 'Transboundary consultations in strategic environmental assessment', in *Impact Assessment and Project Appraisal*, Special issue on environmental assessment and transboundary impact assessment, edited by Wiek Schrage and Nick Bonvoisin, vol 26, no 4, pp289–298.

Commission for Environmental Cooperation (1997) 'Expert group recommendations on a North American agreement on transboundary environmental impact assessment', www.cec.org/Page.asp?PageID=122&ContentID=1906&SiteNodeID=366, accessed July 2010

Czech Republic (2005) 'Submission by the Ministry of Environment to Espoo Convention information exchange', 27 April, www.unece.org/env/eia/documents/database/Czech_Republic_info_EIA-SEA_27April2005_en.pdf, accessed July 2010

de Groote, M. (2005) 'SEA for the Scheldt Estuary Development Plan 2010: Flanders and the Netherlands work together on a large-scale water project of international importance', presentation to eighth meeting of the Working Group on EIA under the Espoo Convention, www.unece.org/env/eia/documents/WG08_april2005/transboundary_project_workshop/Schedlt%20Estaury%20-%20technical.pdf, accessed July 2010

DTI (Department of Trade and Industry) (2001) 'Strategic environmental assessment of the mature areas of the offshore North Sea – SEA 2', consultation document, www.offshore-sea.org.uk/consultations/SEA_2/SEA2_Assessment_Document.pdf, accessed June 2006

DTI (2002) 'Strategic environmental assessment of parts of the central and southern North Sea – SEA 3', consultation document, August, www.offshore-sea.org.uk/consultations/SEA_3/SEA3_Assessment_Document_Rev1_W.pdf, accessed June 2006

EPA (Environmental Protection Agency) (2006) 'Northwest Area Water Supply Project, North Dakota', in Federal Register Environmental Documents, 6 March, www.epa.gov/fedrgstr/EPA-IMPACT/2006/March/Day-06/i3102.htm, accessed June 2006

EU (European Union) (1985) 'Council Directive of 27 June 1985 on the assessment of the effects of certain public and private projects on the environment (85/337/EEC), amended by Council Directive 97/11/EC of 3 March 1997', http://eur-lex.europa.eu/LexUriServ/site/en/consleg/1985/L/01985L0337-19970403-en.pdf, accessed June 2006

EU (2001) 'Directive 2001/42/EC of the European Parliament and the Council on the assessment of the effects of certain plans and programmes on the environment', http://eur-lex.europa.eu/LexUriServ/LexUriServ.do?uri=CELEX:32001L0042:EN:NOT, accessed July 2010

European Commission, Directorate-General for Energy and Transport (2005a) *The SEA Manual: A Sourcebook on Strategic Environmental Assessment of Transport Infrastructure Plans and Programmes*, http://ec.europa.eu/environment/eia/sea-studies-and-reports/beacon_manuel_en.pdf, accessed July 2010

European Commission, Directorate-General for Energy and Transport (2005b) 'The SEA Manual – factsheets', http://ec.europa.eu/environment/eia/sea-studies-and-reports/beacon_manuel_factsheet_en.pdf, accessed July 2010

Horberry, J. (2004) 'EIA capacity building in a transboundary setting', presentation to the third Meeting of the Parties to the Espoo Convention, www.unece.org/env/eia/documents/cavtat/John%20Horberry.pdf, accessed July 2010

Leibniz Institute of Ecological and Regional Development (2006) 'Project 165: Strategic environmental assessment for regional planning – development of a transnational assessment and practice concept for Saxony, Poland and Czech Republic', www.tu-dresden.de/ioer/internet_typo3/index.php?id=683&L=1, accessed July 2010

Mercier, J.-R. (2003) 'Strategic environmental assessment (SEA): Recent progress at the World Bank', http://info.worldbank.org/etools/docs/library/86287/Reading%201.4%20%282%29.doc, accessed June 2006

Moore, D. and Knausenberger, W. (2000) 'USAID/REDSO/ESA Strategy: Environmental threats and opportunities assessment, with special focus on biological diversity and tropical forestry', for USAID, Regional Economic Development Support Office (REDSO), Eastern and Southern Africa (ESA), http://pdf.dec.org/pdf_docs/Pdabs862.pdf, accessed June 2006

MRC (Mekong River Commission) (2004) *The People's Highway: Past, Present and Future Transport on the Mekong River System*, Mekong Development Series No 3, www.mrcmekong.org/download/free_download/Mekong_Development_No3.pdf, accessed June 2006

Nile Basin Initiative, Global Environment Facility, United Nations Development Programme and World Bank (2001) *Nile River Basin: Transboundary Environmental Analysis*, May

Phare, M.-A. (2005) 'SEA as a transboundary watershed management tool', paper presented at the IAIA SEA Conference, Prague

UNECE (United Nations Economic Commission for Europe) (1991) *Convention on Environmental Impact Assessment in a Transboundary Context*, Espoo, Finland, 25 February

UNECE (2003) *Protocol on Strategic Environmental Assessment*, Kiev, 21 May

UNECE (2006) *Report of the Ninth Meeting*, Working Group on EIA, Meeting of the Parties to the Espoo Convention, document symbol ECE/MP.EIA/WG.1/2006/2

World Bank (1991) *Environmental Assessment Sourcebook*, http://web.worldbank.org/WBSITE/EXTERNAL/TOPICS/ENVIRONMENT/EXTENVASS/0,contentMDK:20282864~pagePK:148956~piPK:216618~theSitePK:407988,00.html, accessed June 2006

World Bank (1996) 'Regional environmental assessment', in *Environmental Assessment Sourcebook*, Update No 15, http://siteresources.worldbank.org/INTSAFEPOL/1142947-1116495579739/20507383/Update15RegionalEnvironmentalAssessmentJune1996.pdf, accessed June 2006

World Bank (1999) *Environmental Assessment*, Operational Policy 4.01, http://wbln0018.worldbank.org/Institutional/Manuals/OpManual.nsf/023c7107f95b76b8852570 5c002281b1/9367a2a9d9daeed38525672c007d0972?OpenDocument, accessed June 2006

26
Planning in Tiers? Tiering as a Way of Linking SEA and EIA

Jos Arts, Paul Tomlinson and Henk Voogd[1]

Introduction

The idea of tiering can be considered as one of the major drivers for the development of strategic environmental assessment (SEA) (see, for example, Thérivel et al, 1992; UNECE, 1992; Wood and Djeddour, 1992; Thérivel and Partidário, 1996; Sadler and Verheem, 1996; Partidário, 1999; Fischer, 2002a; Wood, 2003). Many decisions that have a bearing on environmental quality are taken at a higher level of decision-making than the project level. As Partidário (1999, p60) indicates: 'The reasons [for SEA] are various but initially related to the *timing* of project [environmental impact assessment] EIA, i.e. it enters the decision-making process at too late a stage to be able the final decision in a satisfactory way.' Tiering means that, by preparing a sequence of environmental assessments (EAs) at different planning levels and linking them, foreclosure may be prevented, postponement of detailed issues may be permitted and assessments can be better scoped. A tiered approach minimizes the problem of EIA being only a 'snapshot in time'. Accordingly, the European SEA Directive (2001/42/EC) explicitly assumes tiering of SEAs and EIAs at different planning levels and the SEA and EIA Directives are directly linked.

Although tiering is an important notion to SEA and EIA in academic literature, it is hardly discussed in a critical manner (Tomlinson and Fry, 2002). The concept of tiering might provide a means to address the complexity of planning and decision-making, which EAs must operate. However, its implicit assumption of a linear planning process does not fit well with the dynamic nature of planning and decision-making in practice. In planning practice, all too often project decisions and EIAs may precede strategic plans and the SEAs that should provide the framework for project decision-making. It is clear that good coordination between planning levels and between SEA and EIA is needed to achieve planning for sustainability, efficient and effective decision-making. The question is: how can the link between SEA and EIA that is too often missing be made operational and what is the actual and potential role of tiering?

The concept of tiering

A major impetus for the development of SEA is the awareness that EIA at project level is intrinsically limited in complex and dynamic practice of planning and decision-making. Crucial decisions that imply impacts on the environment are constantly made throughout the planning process such that the context in which plans and projects are developed is often highly dynamic (changes in the environment, society, policies, regulations, scientific insights, and so on) with numerous parties often involved in the process. Moreover, multiple projects and events in an area may have synergistic interactions and may result in cumulative impacts, indirect effects and large-scale effects. Finally, a common criticism of EIA is that the essential decisions on the scope of the project are made before an environmental study has been carried out. For achieving sustainability objectives, a broader perspective is needed than a project EIA generally will provide.

Two major views on SEA are related to the tiering concept: first, SEA as an extension of project EIA applied at strategic levels; and second, SEA as a means for policy development and a process for 'trickling down' sustainability ideas (Annandale et al, 2001). In addition to this, literature and also legislation (see, for example, the EU SEA Directive), distinguishes various strategic decision-making levels relevant to SEA, each tier of decision-making being the result of a separate planning process (see, for example, Lee and Wood, 1978; Wood and Djeddour, 1992; Sadler and Verheem, 1996; Thérivel, 1998; Partidário, 1999; EC, 1999; Nooteboom, 2000; Annandale et al, 2001; Partidário and Fischer, 2004; Dalal-Clayton and Sadler, 2005):

- **Policy:** General course overall direction that is pursued and functions as inspiration and guidance for action and ongoing decision-making.
- **Plan** (with subdivision of spatial plan SEA and sectoral plan SEA): A purposeful forward-looking strategy often with coordinated priorities, options, measures for implementation.
- **Programme:** A schedule of proposed commitments, activities, instruments (a group of projects) within a particular sector or area.

In addition to policies, plans and programmes (PPPs), a fourth planning tier can be distinguished at the project level, comprising development and implementation of an activity (for example, construction, modification, operation of infrastructure works), which is subject to EIA (see Figure 26.1).

Various definitions of tiering exist. The European Commission (EC, 1999) defines the concept as distinguishing different levels of planning – PPPs – that are prepared consecutively and influence each other. The US Council on Environmental Quality describes tiering as the coverage of general matters in broader environmental impact statements (such as national programme or policy statements) with subsequent narrower statements or environmental analysis (such as regional or basin-wide programme statements or ultimately site-specific statements) incorporating by reference the general discussions and concentrating solely on the issues specific to the statement subsequently

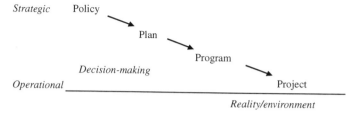

Source: See, for example, Wood (2003)

Figure 26.1 *The concept of tiering as it usually is depicted in SEA literature*

prepared (see Tomlinson and Fry, 2002). Tomlinson and Fry (2002) consider tiering as a process that ensures that the environmental implications of an action are addressed at appropriate levels within the decision-making process and with an appropriate amount of effort to provide robust information for decision-makers. Here we define tiering as:

> *The deliberate, organized transfer of information and issues from one level of planning to another, which is being supported by EAs.*

Tiering is about EAs that are prepared consecutively at different levels of planning (tiers) and that influence each other. The relationship between different levels of planning may vary. Consequently, various types of tiering can be distinguished depending on the dimension chosen (planning, administrative, geographical, sectoral; see also Figure 26.2):

Vertical tiering between a hierarchy of levels:

- Planning levels (in a restricted sense as mentioned before): PPPs and projects (for example, national transport and traffic plan, national programme for infrastructure and transport, national road development projects).
- Administrative, government levels: supranational, national state, provincial, municipal (for example, national spatial planning report, provincial spatial plan, municipal land-use plan).
- Geographical levels: global, continental, national, regional, local (for example, national waste management plan, regional waste management plan, local waste management plan).

Horizontal tiering at the same (administrative) level:

- Tiering across sectors (for example, housing, transport, water management, waste management, spatial planning and so on).
- Tiering of sector plans between different government bodies at the same administrative level (for example, coordination of policy plans and EAs within adjacent municipalities).

Diagonal tiering, a combination of vertical and horizontal tiering, for instance, a national spatial policy influencing local transport plans.

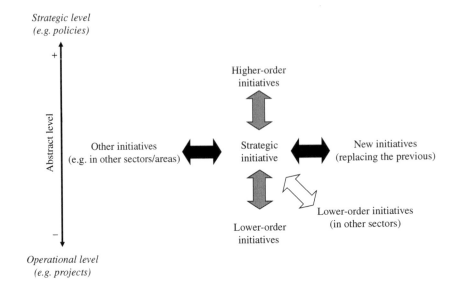

Source: After Partidário and Arts (2005)

Figure 26.2 *The multidirectional nature of strategic initiatives*

The dimension of time is essential to tiering, in other words EAs at whatever level should be attuned to the preceding assessments. In literature, tiering is assumed to minimize various limitations of EIA, including:

- Prevention of foreclosure of assessing important environmental issues.
- Better focused EAs, for instance, relating to the scope (in issues, time, geographical area), the type of alternatives assessed, the types of impacts assessed, and the abstract level of analysis (broad-brush methods, expert opinions versus advanced quantitative and detailed methods, and so on).
- Efficiency gains for (S)EA at lower levels by undertaking EAs at higher levels, for example, by indicating major issues that need further elaboration (or not), providing guidelines for subsequent EAs.
- Better fit with the ongoing nature of decision-making and planning processes by tiering of EAs.
- Improvement of plans and projects that are developed and implemented.

Issues related to tiering in planning practice

Much SEA literature focuses on various possible forms of SEA tiers and definitions. However, remarkably little literature discusses critically the concept of tiering. At first glance, the concept of tiering seems very rational, but the implicit and rather naïve assumption behind the concept of tiering of SEAs is that planning is seen as a linear process. Like the rational planning background of EIA, the concepts of SEA and tiering also seem to be grounded in this approach, which assumes hierarchic mechanisms and clear means-ends relations. The underlying idea is that, first an SEA is carried out for a plan or a programme followed by an EIA for the project that is developed to implement the policies of the strategic plan/programme. The plan/programme and the SEA set the framework for the project and the EIA (see also Figure 26.1).

As extensively discussed in planning literature, planning in the real world does not conform to neatly arranged process structures and other assumptions of rationality (see, for example, De Roo, 2000, 2003; Linden and Voogd, 2004). More recently, attention to the complexity of concepts such as SEA and tiering in practice is growing in EIA and SEA literature (see, for example, Noble, 2000; Nooteboom, 2000; Thissen, 2000; Tomlinson and Fry, 2002; Bina, 2003; Partidário and Arts, 2005; Fischer, 2005). Problems of the tiering concept in planning practice include issues such as:

- Differences in conceptualization of PPPs in practice.
- Ordering of PPPs and projects that may differ in practice.
- Limited shelf-life of EA information.
- SEA and EIA are undertaken in different planning arenas.
- Limited influence of governmental planning agencies.
- Aligning SEA and EIA with each other.

Differences in conceptualization of PPPs in practice

The terms 'policies', 'plans' and 'programmes' as well as 'projects' may have a rather different meaning in different countries depending on the political and institutional context (Dalal-Clayton and Sadler, 2005). In addition, there are institutional gaps in the PPP-cascade. Many planning systems do not always have a fully tiered system with all three SEA types, and if so, they are rarely applied in a systematic manner. For instance, the programme level may be missing in the planning system of a certain sector, such as planning for industrial estates. Hybrid forms of strategic initiatives can also be found, such as a transport plan that includes a programme for operational road development projects (see also Fischer, 2005). Furthermore, (elements of) strategic initiatives subject to SEA may be approved but never fully implemented in practice and/or result in concrete projects subject to EIA.

A strategic initiative – either a policy, plan or programme – will establish multiple effects that may require some form of follow-up but not only 'downwards' as the 'traditional' tiering concept seems to suggest (see Figure 26.1). Figure 26.2 depicts the various relationships that a strategic initiative may have vertical tiering relationships as well as horizontal and also diagonal tiering. In reality, a strategic initiative may potentially cause reactions in all these directions – a 'splash effect' – and therefore it may be useful to establish explicit tiering relationships to these different levels of planning in order to become effective (see Partidário and Arts, 2005).

Ordering of PPPs and projects may differ in practice

In practice, often projects are proposed which precede or indeed induce the generation of plans and programmes. For example, in Dutch infrastructure planning, many such 'strategic' projects have been developed – one could think of the high-speed railway from Amsterdam to Belgium of the Betuweroute freight railway from Rotterdam harbour to Germany (Niekerk and Voogd, 1999). Also, national level plans do not necessarily precede provincial government plans and a regional programme does not always precede local project development. Strategic plans can be replaced by new plans before the policies laid down in those plans have been implemented through projects. The cumulative impacts of individual projects (and the issues raised in the accompanying EIA) may result in the preparation of a new strategic plan and in SEA addressing cumulative, synergistic, indirect and/or large-scale impacts.

So instead of impact information 'trickling down' like rain along a neat sequence of planning tiers, information generated by various projects may 'evaporate' and 'condensate' at strategic levels, clarifying the need for more comprehensive (strategic) impact assessments (see Box 26.1). For instance, the cumulative impacts generated by the development of waste management facilities (subject to operational level EIA) may be addressed in an SEA for a waste management policy plan at national level (see Arts, 1998; Figure 26.3). With respect to this, not only are impacts assessments ex ante (such as SEA and EIA) relevant but also monitoring and evaluation ex post (EIA and SEA follow-up). In addition, such EIA and SEA follow-up studies may clarify the need for new plans or projects and thus subsequent SEAs and EIAs. Tiering is not one-way traffic down the hill, but comprises two-way traffic, top-down and bottom-up.

Projects may be well linked to plans, especially where an agency has plan to project responsibility, for example, waste management, water management or planning of national road infrastructure (see Alton and Underwood, 2005;

Box 26.1 *An analogy: Strategic plans as clouds*

For strategic plans the image of a cloud may be used (Arts, 1998; Figure 26.3). Like clouds, strategic plans often have a rather ethereal quality. Nevertheless, they are real in that they can influence social and biogeophysical reality. Strategic plans cast their shadow upon reality as clouds do. Analogously, projects can be seen as the result – precipitation, raindrops – of the clouds that actually change reality. Trickling down, they cause concrete effects. You cannot 'feel' the cloud, but you become wet from the rain falling from it. Moreover, strategic plans, like clouds, may pass over the physical environment they oversee. New clouds may be formed and old ones may evaporate over time – thereby losing their relevance for the environment below. Also, the 'project drops' do not circulate back into the 'strategic plan cloud' but are implemented downwards. However, when many such droplets – operational and spatial decisions – have fallen, they may cause the formation of a new 'strategic plan cloud' when the humidity – their combined impact – has become so high that they condensate and there is need for a new plan.

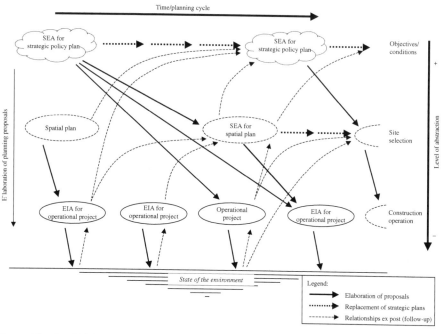

Source: After Arts (1998)

Figure 26.3 *'Trickling down and evaporating up': The various relationships between different planning levels, decisions and EAs that can be seen in planning practice*

Marshall and Arts, 2005). In practice, however, links between SEA and EIA prove to be rather weak. Vertical and horizontal tiering across different administrations proves to be difficult between different administrations and jurisdictions (James and Tomlinson, 2005).

Limited shelf-life of EA information

SEA literature often assumes that information can endlessly cascade from one assessment level to another, despite EA information having a 'limited shelf-life' (Tomlinson and Fry, 2002; Nooteboom, 2000). For some fast-moving topics, an assessment may be out of date in a few years, while in a slowly developing region, some assessments may possibly be valid for five or more years. So every subsequent assessment must first undertake an examination of the validity of earlier assessments before building upon it. Such validity checks do not involve only physical and biological change in the study area, but also legislative and, most importantly, changing societal values. Would some of today's problems exist if different values had been in place in the past? A key difficulty is the time-lag between plan, project and impacts. Prior assessments may prove to be very weak in defining this timeline, such that subsequent assessments disregard the forecasts of environmental change.

Different planning arenas

It should be recognized that SEA and EIA are carried out in rather different planning arenas (Kørnøv and Thissen, 2000; Deelstra et al, 2003; Partidário and Arts, 2005). Policy SEAs are prepared in a political context in which discussions are usually about normative, subjective arguments instead of (only) objective facts. This policy process is rather fluid, not linear, usually contains many feedback loops and may be subject to sudden changes. PPPs are usually developed in a cyclic and iterative process. EIAs are prepared for project development in which quantitative data and analysis are important, as well as optimizing the proposal through designing construction and mitigation measures.

Limited influence of governmental planning agencies

Formal planning frameworks may allow for the tiering of EAs, but this may not be sufficient to ensure that environmental responsibilities are cascaded to other parties and plans. Moreover, according to Bache and Flinders (2004), another constraint for tiering is the limited competencies and influencing power of government bodies, for example, due to the shift from government to governance. For instance, in the Netherlands, strategic plans and the accompanying SEA are mainly self-binding for government and usually do not have direct juridical consequences for private persons or companies, in contrast to environmental permits at operational level. This situation limits the potential for preventing foreclosure by tiering as environmental measures proposed in SEAs are not enforceable.

The distribution of responsibilities and tasks over different levels of government also impacts upon tiering. It is usually argued, based on the subsidiarity principle, that decision-making authority should reside at the level most appropriate to the problem being addressed. Unfortunately, the subsidiarity principle is not an unambiguous criterion, as discussions in and about the EU clearly illustrate (see, for example, Toulemonde, 1996; MacCormick, 1997). Does the subsidiarity principle have any meaning for tiering? We think it may do, as tiering involves influencing planning and decision-making at subsequent planning levels. The institutional framework determines the extent to which binding, imperative means or only 'softer' means (such as persuasion and communication) can be used for implementing the policies laid down in a strategic initiative.

Aligning SEA and EIA with each other

Because of their different nature, assessments undertaken at the various planning tiers are different in terms of (see Sadler and Verheem, 1996; EC, 1999; Jansson, 2000; Fischer, 2002b):

- **Type of information:** More qualitative information is available and used at policy level and more concrete, quantitative information at programme level.
- **Types of methods and techniques used:** At strategic level, broad-brush, often qualitative methods based on judgement tend to dominate, whereas at programme and project levels, quantitative methods tend to dominate.

For instance, in the transport planning sector use is made of scenario-modelling, intermodal simulation analysis, workshops at policy level, overlay mapping geographical information systems (GISs), impact matrices at plan level, and checklists, multicriteria analysis or cost-benefit analysis at programme level. Also methods for participation by other parties may be used (use of internet, brainstorm sessions, design workshops, formal consultation, review, and so on). The approaches to public consultation also differ with interest groups dominating the PPP levels, whereas the general public often show an interest only when their interests are immediately affected by the project.

- **Types of questions addressed** in the decision-making on a strategic initiative: 'whether', 'why' and 'what' questions may be more relevant to policies, 'what' and 'where' questions to plans, and 'when' and 'how' questions to programmes. Regarding this, however, one should bear in mind that the 'how' question may also be considered in a SEA for a strategic plan, while 'where' questions may be addressed in an EIA for a project (though within a small area) (Nooteboom, 2000).

- **Risk and uncertainty** are inevitably greater at more strategic level SEA than at project level EIA, not least since the ultimate project is only defined at a reference level of detail in SEA (Tomlinson and Fry, 2002). In addition, the appreciation of the environmental context is inevitably not to the same level of detail as during project level EIA (see before). For example, it is unlikely that effects upon protected species can be assessed when site selection issues have not been resolved. Instead, it is only practical to adopt a risk-based approach taking account of the occurrence of suitable habitats. Such uncertainty makes it difficult to be definitive regarding the actual effects that would result. It is, therefore, important that SEA focuses upon those elements on which the assessment can be seen to be robust and provides mechanisms to address such uncertainty.

In order to achieve effective tiering, the differences described above must be taken into account when undertaking a subsequent EA. There is a desire that broadly the same answer should be delivered at the SEA as at the EIA level (Tomlinson and Fry, 2002). At least, the answers need to be aligned in the same direction. The SEA/EIA system would come in for tremendous criticism if the SEA promotes a particular strategy only for the EIA to find that the projects generated deliver unacceptable environmental impacts. The EIA should always refine rather than confound the SEA. However, can this be ensured with the emphasis upon an objectives-led approach towards SEA in which vague objectives set the arena in which significant environmental impacts have to be assessed? This contrasts with the evidence-based approach to SEA in which the traditions of seeking significant impacts are paramount. Furthermore, the differences in predictive techniques also mean that the results of the assessment often do not scale from one level of assessment to another. What is unacceptable is for the SEA to miss a critical impact that would threaten the viability of the project, especially if that project is crucial to the delivery of the plan's strategy.

Dealing with tiering in practice

The development of SEA for PPPs should eventually strengthen the role of EA throughout the planning and decision-making process. However, the links between the various assessments at different planning levels are rather complex and rarely addressed in practice. As previously described, one can find both vertical tiering between planning, administrative or geographical levels and horizontal tiering across sectors or between different agencies at the same level, as well as combinations of these (diagonal tiering). In addition, the relationships are not only downwards or sideways but also upwards (for example, a project/EIA that influences others or a strategic initiative/SEA). Such examples, in practice, are all too often weak, implicit, *ad hoc* or are just lacking.

Isolated islands of EAs in sea of decisions?

Here the image may be used of a turbulent sea of decision-making in which rather isolated islands of EAs exist (see Figure 26.4). Undertaking SEA and EIA does not ensure that the various planning levels will be connected. Also, many activities and decisions are taken without formal EAs and are 'under the waterline'.

Linking decision-making through tiering is fundamental to delivering upon the objectives of SEA such as: strengthening the EAs; preventing foreclosure of alternatives and issues; addressing cumulative and large-scale effects; enhancing stakeholder engagement; and incorporating sustainability considerations

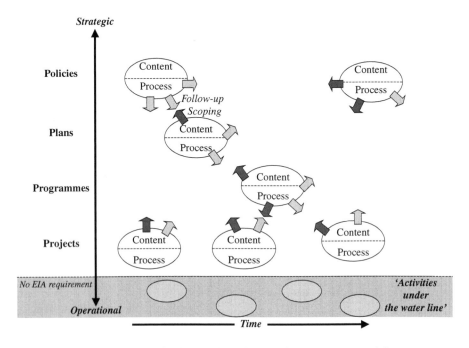

Figure 26.4 *Tiering bridging the islands of EAs in a sea of decisions*

into planning and decision-making (Sadler and Verheem, 1996; EC, 1999; Tomlinson and Fry, 2002).

Although tiering is often seen as a rather theoretical concept not readily found in complex planning practice, we suggest that it can be a guiding principle. Without tiering, the effectiveness of SEA is limited to quality checking of the proposed PPP to the neglect of the deliverables. Tiering might provide a useful way to deal with uncertainty throughout the planning process and helping to safeguard sustainable development. In other words, tiering might bridge the islands of EA (Figure 26.4).

In order to safeguard a structured, systematic approach, as well as to allow for sufficient flexibility throughout the planning implementation process, attention is needed for both the content and process side of decisions and assessments. Uncertainty is inherent in SEA and needs to be recognized, although not necessarily solved at that stage. Tiering can help to deal with uncertainty in a structured manner by determining what needs to be known now and what could/should be addressed later. Holling's principles of adaptive environmental management are relevant here; without some form of adaptive management throughout the planning process, policy/planning implementation failures can be expected (Holling, 1978; Noble, 2000; Morrison-Saunders and Arts, 2004). As a consequence, to establish bridges between subsequent EAs, tiering needs to employ a two-way approach consisting of:

- **Follow-up** of the prior (strategic) initiative and EA (either a SEA or EIA). The prior initiative should inform/set the agenda for subsequent plans/projects and EAs and the follow-up programme should hand on the 'baton'.
- **Scoping** of the subsequent plans/projects needs to take account of the issues handed on by the previous strategic initiative/project and EA.

In this way, the scope of the EA (content) is focused to the appropriate level of planning and decision-making (not too much information, level of detail, and so on, not overlooking essential issues). The postponement of issues to the next steps in the planning process is acceptable, provided that the decision being taken remains robust and that the issues are actually addressed in a follow-up programme and later EAs. The process element builds on follow-up by providing flexibility in managing risk and uncertainty intrinsic to planning where a content-oriented approach of assessing environmental impact is not possible – flexing as well as hedging (see Morrison-Saunders and Arts, 2004).

Follow-up and tiering

SEA follow-up may play an important role in the adequate transfer of issues between SEAs at various planning tiers and importantly between the SEA and EIA tiers (discussed in Chapter 32 of this book, see also Partidário and Arts, 2005; Partidário and Fischer, 2004; Arts, 1998). Relevant institutional frameworks and regulations for SEA related follow-up are found in, for example, Finland, the Netherlands, Canada, South Africa, Hong Kong and the EU (see Partidário and Fischer, 2004). The EU SEA Directive (2001/42/EC) explicitly assumes tiering of SEAs and EIAs at different planning levels through Article 3(2) of the Directive. Article 10 of the same Directive requires member states to 'monitor the significant environmental effects of the implementation of plans and programmes'.

SEA follow-up can be seen as a potential aid within tiering, one that allows the proponent to check and set in place the initial parameters for post-SEA developments through monitoring, evaluation and management. In addition, at specific time points, it may be used to communicate these processes or findings with the various stakeholders. Preparation of such follow-up should start early (preferably in the pre-decision stage) in order to provide for adequate screening for the need and scoping of the content of the follow-up programme. In this way the SEA follow-up programme can link with the PPP approval, decision-making and public review stages. In the consideration of the role of follow-up for linking SEA and EIA, relevant points to address comprise (Marshall and Arts, 2005):

- Transfer of identified PPP objectives (retaining continuity of direction between tiers).
- Transfer of knowledge (for example, impact information).
- Transfer of responsibilities (within a governmental organization or between different parties).
- Risk management (follow-up as a tool for managing risks).
- Transfer of agreed arrangements (such as design principles, project alternatives, critical issues, and so on).

More specifically, issues that may require follow-up include:

- Environmental and sustainability objectives.
- Decisions regarding the elaboration of alternatives.
- Uncertainties and gaps in knowledge (regarding impacts, measures).
- Risks of implementation failures.
- Sensitivity (of the area, society, politics) or public concerns.

To ensure careful tiering with subsequent decision-making and EA, monitoring and/or evaluation activities as part of SEA follow-up should start after approval of the strategic initiative and should preferably cover the full period in which the strategic initiative is in place. However, SEA follow-up may become redundant as subsequent EIA(s) are performed.

In order to fulfil a process management function for linking SEA and EIA, it is necessary to track environmental indicators that provide feedback on developments and the performance of the SEA (monitoring, evaluation) and to track post-SEA decision-making, management and communication actions that enable transfer of issues to the next tier of activity (feed forward). Management responses could be related to (Cherp et al, 2007):

- Decisions on revising and amending the strategic initiative itself.
- Actions prescribed in the strategic initiative.
- Decisions and actions for which the initiative sets a formal framework.

- All other decisions and actions ('under the waterline', see Figure 26.4), possibly using environmental management systems employed by the planning agency (see Cherp et al, 2007; Marshall and Arts, 2005).

To achieve this, SEA follow-up must take on the role of a managed process, a method or procedure that defines the required course of action. Specifically, it should include a route map indicating the way the strategic initiative will or should be implemented. Also, residual risks and interests of the various stakeholders need to be identified in order to enable proactiveness and flexibility in adaptive management responses. This process mapping should help to inform where responsibility should rest in subsequent stages. Lack of leverage or ability to bind other parties can constrain effectiveness of tiering unless consensus or collaboration already exists, for example, in relation to the 'not in my backyard' (NIMBY) attitude and subsidiarity issues. Public pressure may help in ensuring adequate transfer of issues to the next tiers. The assessment community also may provide continuity between different planning levels (PPPs and projects). In general, delegation not abdication of responsibility must be the watchword in tiering – no 'buck passing'.

The issue of public involvement is important to tiering, especially as the cooperation of other parties is needed in order to implement the strategic initiative (as well as for undertaking SEA follow-up). There is a need for transparency and process control between the tiers of SEA and EIA. Confidence in SEA (and subsequently in EIA) should reinforce transparency and accountability in the responsible agency, while clearly communicating to third parties the role and contribution the process of SEA has made to subsequent planning and EA. Communication processes can also be assisted through transfer of public concerns or issues of relevance to EA activities and to capture and transfer ideas presented by stakeholders that are of greater relevance for activities at subsequent tiers.

Ultimately, components of the SEA process, notably the SEA report, must clearly set out for all parties what is being applied and what is being transferred (through follow-up mechanisms) to subsequent planning tiers. In relation to this, a SEA follow-up programme could provide the map to direct the issues to the correct address (an 'island of EA' in Figure 26.4) in a timely manner. This would allow the early warning of issues to be addressed in subsequent tiers.

Scoping and tiering

At the subsequent tier, scoping of the plan/project and EA will be essential to identify the relevant issues, alternatives, effects, level of detail, methods. In practice, tiering might be considered as the 'art of ongoing scoping' throughout the planning and decision-making process. First of all, such scoping needs to take account of the issues handed over. To this end, the results of the follow-up programme of the preceding strategic initiative and SEA are leading.

Theoretically, SEA and the subsequent EIA should be consistent with and reinforce each other, with the former providing the framework for setting the scope of the latter and the prospect of a more focused and efficient EIA. Consequently, the scope of the subsequent EIA can be better circumscribed and hence SEA could shorten project delivery timescales. Moreover, it may be possible to remove or focus the burden of project assessment if the findings of a previous SEA or SEA follow-up indicate little environmental impact, for example, class approvals or changes in EIA thresholds/categories.

When tiering PPP SEAs to project EIAs, there is a need to recognize the differences in planning levels, the sectors and arenas where the plan/project and EA operate (political, financial and technical contexts). Not every issue can or should be addressed in the SEA. As noted earlier, postponement of issues to a next stage is acceptable provided that decision-making remains robust and the issues are actually addressed in later EAs. As Nooteboom (2000) argues, strategic tiers may refine and reduce the scope of EAs at later tiers (impacts and alternatives considered).

Tiering can make it easier to identify the issues that the next tier should consider and that tier can be focused on the impacts that really need to be influenced by decision-making. According to Nooteboom (2000) three mechanisms are relevant here:

- The 'funnelling effect' whereby the strategic initiative subject to SEA, in turn, influences the range of alternatives that are taken into consideration at the next tier (for example, by excluding certain alternatives).
- SEAs can be used to develop an environmental planning framework against which the effects of decisions at next tiers can be identified, monitored and evaluated (linking with SEA follow-up).
- SEA provides useful information and experience that gives EA at the next tier a 'head start'.

When tiering is done properly and SEA and EIA are combined as one assessment process, the benefits identified in Table 26.1 can be delivered.

Table 26.1 *Scoping of impacts during SEA and EIA*

Issue	Potential benefits
Focus on significant impacts	Some projects do not require an EIA ('under the waterline') but have cumulative effects and hence are appropriate to consider in the SEA. EIA is not good at addressing large-scale (national or global) impacts so these might be assessed in SEA.
Some impacts can only be assessed at a later stage	While some impacts cannot be assessed until after decisions are made, their early identification remains important as it helps to inform the scope of EIA.
Some impacts are the domain of other sectors or SEAs	Regulations may require some impacts to be addressed later in the process or by other organizations.
Some impacts are not significant or are too localized	Thresholds may suggest that impacts be discounted for later assessment, but consider potential for cumulative effects and if in doubt, assess it.
Some impacts can only be mitigated at higher decision-making levels	As well as addressing significant impacts, potential exists to mitigate or avoid many small or indirect impacts.

Source: After Tomlinson and Fry (2002)

However, in scoping an EA at the next tier, some important aspects (from earlier discussion) include: the issue of time-lag; aligning SEA and EIA information; the formal relationship of the proposed initiative to the preceding PPP (competencies, subsidiarity, the institutional framework); and stakeholder involvement. It remains to be seen whether the positions of stakeholders supporting given strategies during the SEA actually are translated into support at those tiers when issues become more concrete and the consequences are directly felt (Tomlinson and Fry, 2002).

Follow-up of the previous EA and scoping of the next assessment are closely related. The image of the 'Italian flag' may summarize this. In careful SEA follow-up, a distinction can be made between 'green' issues that do not need attention in the next stages (for example, issues only relevant at the preceding strategic tier) and 'red' issues that do need attention in the follow-up (for example, known uncertainties and risks). Good scoping at the next tier needs an eye on especially those issues that are in the 'blank' area (for example, new developments unknown beforehand). Here, careful definition of the problem and objectives of a plan or project is essential (see Arts and Van Lamoen, 2005).

The cumulative impacts of combined projects and activities deserve special attention. The SEA at the preceding tier analyses should address the cumulative (and synergistic) impacts of multiple projects and activities. Appropriate alternatives should also have been sought to reduce adverse effects. A potential problem may arise when subsequent planning and decision-making approves various projects and activities until the last one exceeds limits. That project then cannot be admitted even if its contribution to the cumulative total is small (last one in pays). As Nooteboom (2000) states it becomes 'a victim' of the rules. In such situations, it might be very tempting to amend the original strategic PPP especially if (external) pressure is strong.

Conclusions

Tiering may play the following roles (see also Marshall and Arts, 2005):

- It may allow proponents to safeguard for controlled implementation of plan promises, critical data and findings (of SEAs) and management decisions that are of a recognized value for subsequent environment assessment tiers.
- It may act as an early warning device in mitigation management that seeks to prevent negative impacts and ensure positive actions before actual impacts on the environment occur.
- It may serve as a tool for quality assurance, control and management in subsequent EIA activities to ensure continuity with earlier SEA processes, to allow for adequate scoping of EA at subsequent planning tiers and to safeguard congruence between SEAs and EIAs.
- It may enhance effectiveness of EAs throughout the planning and decision-making process. Tiering can provide opportunities to introduce 'class' approvals (reducing the burden of project assessments) as well as better focused EAs in subsequent planning stages. Also it may lead to institutional strengthening and better inter-organizational cooperation.

- It allows practitioners to retain a route map through the complexities presented through evolving PPP and ultimately project formation and/or development of other activities in order to keep track of the implementation of environmental and sustainability goals.

Effective tiering means building bridges between different planning tiers or 'islands' of EA through process management using follow-up and scoping as 'bridgeheads' for feed forward and feedback. Major potential constraints to tiering are issues such as: the complex ordering of PPPs and projects in planning practice; time-lag or the limited shelf-life of EA information; differences in the planning arenas in which SEA and EIA are undertaken and operate; the limited influence of government bodies (due to competency and subsidiarity issues); and ensuring the content of SEA and EIA are in line with each other.

Favourable conditions for tiering are:

- The existence of strong functional links between PPPs and projects.
- The availability of a formal planning system that is hierachically organized, and comprises legal/binding requirements for tiering of PPPs (institutionalization). However, this will not be a sufficient condition.
- Also cultural aspects are relevant – effective tiering depends on the possibility and willingness to coordinate EAs at different tiers and to use the lessons learned at the previous tiers.
- Bridges of tiering might be easier to build if PPP and project planning and decision-making lie in the hand of one agency/authority. Tiering will be more difficult to achieve across administrative boundaries.

Authorities need to actively address tiering. The danger is that we bury ourselves in assessment tasks with an ever-increasing array of topics and forget that the aim of the process is to communicate to and inform decision-makers. Unless decision-makers are engaged in the process of EA, they may react adversely to the loss of flexibility to make decisions and also question the cost-effectiveness of the process. In this context, it is important to engage with those that have to deal with the issues that a plan generates and to hand over and 'cascade' environmental responsibilities and action to other sectors/tiers. Otherwise, tiering will not work effectively. Within a well-functioning tiered system, the postponement of issues is acceptable, provided the decision remains robust – and issues are actually addressed elsewhere.

In order to allocate issues to different tiers, mapping of issues, interests and stakeholders is essential. The importance of such mapping is especially relevant as not all PPPs lead to projects with EA but also to other formal or informal activities without EA but with environmental consequences. Therefore, in tiering, consideration needs to be given not only to the legal system and formal and informal requirements, but also the culture of PPP formulation, the political and economic system and how communication and interaction happens. This involves speaking the language of those who you want to influence.

To conclude, it can be argued that tiering has three main characteristics:

- Tiering is not easily found in practice, often absent or lacking at certain planning levels. The relationships between planning levels are not simply downwards but far more complex.
- Tiering is useful as a guiding principle for EA practice. It can be argued that systematic tiering of EA is a prerequisite for decision-making for sustainable development. Large-scale, cumulative environmental problems need structured and systematic approaches to decision-making and assessment from the most strategic level to concrete, operational level. Tiering may provide a vehicle for explicit transference of planning objectives to other PPP or project levels of planning.
- Tiering can be seen as a test of the quality of (S)EA. Adequate tiering can prevent foreclosure of issues, support assessment of issues at the appropriate planning level (prevention of *ad hoc* and *pro forma* assessments), and may help to stimulate more environmentally responsive planning and adaptive management. Finally, tiering requires – but also may enhance – stakeholder engagement and provides transparency not only of EAs but also of strategic decision-making.

Note

1 In memory of Henk Voogd, a great academic, who died 8 March 2007. Henk was Professor in Planning and Urban Geography at the University of Groningen, the Netherlands. He has made important contributions to the development of evaluation methods and rationality in environmental and infrastructure planning.

References

Alton, C. C. and Underwood, P. B. (2005) 'Successful tiering of policy-level SEA to project-level environmental impact assessments: Building a strong foundation for tiering decisions', paper presented at the IAIA SEA Conference, Prague

Annandale, D., Bailey, J., Ouano, E., Evans, W. and King, P. (2001) 'The potential role of strategic environmental assessment in the activities of multi-lateral development banks', *Environmental Impact Assessment Review*, vol 21, pp407–429

Arts, J. (1998) *EIA Follow-Up: On the Role of Ex Post Evaluation in Environmental Impact Assessment*, Geo Press, Groningen

Arts, J. and Van Lamoen, F. (2005) 'Before EIA: Defining the scope of infrastructure in the Netherlands', *Journal of Environmental Assessment and Project Management*, vol 7, no 1, pp51–80

Bache, I. and Flinders, M. (eds) (2004) *Multi-level Governance*, Oxford University Press, Oxford

Bina, O. (2003) 'Re-conceptualising strategic environmental assessment: Theoretical overview and case study from Chile', PhD thesis, geography department, University of Cambridge

Cherp, A., Partidário, M. R. and Arts, J. (2007) 'From formulation to implementation: Strengthening SEA through follow-up', Chapter 32 in this volume

Deelstra, Y., Nooteboom, S. G., Kohlmann, H. R., Van den Berg, J. and Innanen, S. (2003) 'Using knowledge for decision-making purposes in the context of large projects in the Netherlands', *Environmental Impact Assessment Review*, vol 23, no 5, pp517–541

EC (European Commission) (1999) *Manual on Strategic Environmental Assessment of Transport Infrastructure Plans*, drafted by DHV Environment and Infrastructure, DG VII Transport Brussels

EU (European Union) (2001) *Directive 2001/42/EC of the European parliament and of the Council, of 27 June 2001 on the assessment of the effects of certain plans and programmes on the environment*, vol L197, pp30–37

Dalal-Clayton, B. and Sadler, B. (2005) *Strategic Environmental Assessment: A Sourcebook and Reference Guide to International Experience*, Earthscan, London

De Roo, G. (2000) 'Environmental conflicts in compact cities: Complexity, decision-making, and policy approaches', *Environment and Planning B: Planning and Design*, vol 27, pp151–162

De Roo, G. (2003) *Dutch Environmental Planning: Too Good to be True*, Ashgate, Aldershot

Fischer, T. B. (2002a) *Strategic Environmental Assessment in Transport and Land Use Planning*, Earthscan, London

Fischer, T. B. (2002b) 'Towards a more systematic approach to policy, plan and programme assessment: Some evidence from Europe', in Marsden, S. and Dovers, S. (eds) *SEA in Australasia*, Federation Press, Sydney

Fischer, T. B. (2005) 'Rationality and SEA, effective tiering: Useful concept or useless chimera?', paper presented at the IAIA SEA Conference, Prague

Holling, C. (ed) (1978) *Adaptive Environmental Impact Assessment and Management*, John Wiley, Chichester

James, E. and Tomlinson, P. (2005) 'SEA of multiple plans: Can it work?' paper presented at the IAIA SEA Conference, Prague

Jansson, A. H. H. (2000) 'Strategic environmental assessment for transport in four Nordic countries', in Bjarnadottir, H. (ed) *Environmental Assessment in the Nordic Countries*, Nordregio, Stockholm, pp39–46

Kørnøv, L. and Thissen, W. A. H. (2000) 'Rationality in decision and policy-making: Implications for strategic environmental assessment', *Impact Assessment and Project Appraisal*, vol 18, no 3, pp191–200

Lee, N. and Wood, C. M. (1978) 'EIA: A European perspective', *Built Environment*, vol 4, pp101–110

Linden, G. and Voogd, H. (eds) (2004) *Environmental and Infrastructure Planning*, Geo Press, Groningen

MacCormick, N. (1997) 'Democracy, subsidiarity and citizenship in the European Commonwealth', *Law and Philosophy*, vol 16, pp331–356

Marshall, R. and Arts, J. (2005) 'Is there life after SEA? Linking SEA to EIA', paper presented at the IAIA SEA Conference, Prague

Morrison-Saunders, A. and Arts, J. (eds) (2004) *Assessing Impact, Handbook of EIA and SEA Follow-up*, Earthscan, London

Niekerk, F. and Voogd, H. (1999) 'Impact assessments for infrastructure planning: Some Dutch dilemmas', *Environmental Impact Assessment Review*, vol 19, no 1, pp21–36

Noble, B. F. (2000) 'Strategic environmental assessment: What is it? And what makes it strategic?', *Journal of Environmental Assessment and Project Management*, vol 2, no 2, pp203–224

Nooteboom, S. (2000) 'Tiered decision-making – environmental assessments of strategic decisions and project decisisons: Interactions and benefits', *Impact Assessment and Project Appraisal*, vol 18, no 2, pp151–160

Partidário, M. R. (1999) 'Strategic environmental assessment: Principles and potential', in Petts, J. (ed) *Handbook on Environmental Impact Assessment*, vol 1, Blackwell Science, Oxford, pp60–73

Partidário, M. R. and Arts, J. (2005) 'Exploring the concept of strategic environmental assessment follow-up', *Impact Assessment and Project Appraisal*, vol 23, no 3, pp246–257

Partidário, M. R. and Fischer, T. B. (2004) 'Follow-up in current SEA understanding', in Morrison-Saunders, A. and Arts, J. (eds) *Assessing Impact: Handbook of EIA and SEA Follow-up*, Earthscan, London, pp224–247

Sadler, B. and Verheem, R. (1996) *Strategic Environmental Assessment: Status, Challenges and Future Directions*, Ministry of Housing, Spatial Planning and the Environment, The Hague

Thérivel, R. (1998) 'Strategic environmental assessment in the transport sector', in Banister, D. (ed) *Transport Policy and the Environment*, E. and F. N. Spon, London, pp50–71

Thérivel, R. and Partidário, M. R. (eds) (1996) *Practice of Strategic Environmental Assessment*, Earthscan, London

Thérivel, R., Wilson, E., Thompson, S., Heartly, D. and Pritchard, D. (1992) *Strategic Environmental Assessment*, Earthscan, London

Thissen, W. (2000) 'Strategic environmental assessment at a crossroads', *Impact Assessment and Project Appraisal*, vol 18, pp174–176

Tomlinson, P. and Fry, C. (2002) 'Improving EIA effectiveness through SEA', paper presented at the 22nd Annual Meeting of the IAIA, The Hague, 15–21 June

Toulemonde, J. (1996) 'Can we evaluate subsidiarity? Elements of answers from the European practice', *International Review of Administrative Sciences*, vol 62, pp49–62

UNECE (United Nations Economic Commission for Europe) (1992) *Application of Environmental Impact Assessment Principles to Policies, Plans and Programmes*, UNECE, Geneva, Environmental Series no 5

Wood, C. (2003) *Environmental Impact Assessment – A Comparative Overview*, Prentice Hall, Pearson Education, Harlow

Wood, C. and Djeddour, M. (1992) 'Strategic environmental assessment: EA of policies, plans and programmes', *Impact Assessment Bulletin*, vol 10, no 1, pp3–21

PART V

SEA PROCESS DEVELOPMENT AND CAPACITY-BUILDING

27
SEA Process Development and Capacity-building – A Thematic Overview

Maria R. Partidário

Introduction

The use of strategic environmental assessment (SEA) worldwide has been greater and faster than expected when discussions on its possible relevance and need first took place between the late 1980s and early 1990s. A multiple-purpose and multiple-shape instrument has evolved, as currently observed in international practice. Some consider this diversity in SEA to be quite confusing and troubling for its efficient and pragmatic application. Others see this diversity as an opportunity to develop an instrument that can be well adapted to the policy-making and planning characteristics of different countries and organizations.

While much experience already exists, SEA is still far from a mature stage. An efficient instrument will result eventually once sufficient evidence becomes available, well-argued and related to the different contexts in which it developed, supported by the necessary debate between problems and advantages of the different approaches. Process development to increase practice, and capacity-building to develop know-how, are both needed for that purpose. Many authors already argue against the one-size-fits-all type of SEA, but there is still much divergence as to what are acceptable forms of SEA, concerning their rationale, scope, process development, relationship with the decision-making processes, timing, tools, institutional frameworks and many other aspects.

Part V of this book includes many different themes that share a common objective of SEA improvement through process development and capacity building. It covers SEA theory and research (Chapter 28), professional and institutional capacity-building (Chapter 29), institutional challenges (Chapter 30), guidance (Chapter 31), SEA follow-up (Chapter 32) and knowledge-based systems for better information (Chapter 33). All represent different angles and contain elements that can contribute to the consolidation of SEA, conceptually and empirically.

This chapter provides a thematic overview of these areas and aspects and related concerns that have been debated at different conferences and professional meetings. It draws particularly on the chapters themselves and on the intensive discussion on improving standards and building capacity for SEA at the International Association for Impact Assessment (IAIA) Prague meeting. This thematic overview highlights key messages for SEA capacity-building and process development and concludes with actions that IAIA and other professional bodies can take to contribute to improve these areas.

Key themes

The discussion in this section focuses on four main issues (suggested at the Prague conference):

1 What are the main trends in each theme?
2 What progress has been made in taking forward the aspects and areas discussed?
3 What else needs to be done and what are the priorities for future action?
4 How might IAIA contribute to that agenda?

In the paragraphs that follow, the two strongest ideas and main conclusions resulting from each theme are highlighted. Chapters 28–33 address the key questions in this agenda.

In Chapter 28, Bina, Wallington and Thissen consider SEA theory and reflect on the intensive debate regarding the scientific bases of SEA. The two strongest ideas revolve around (a) the need for a strategic use of the instrument and (b) the discussion and clarification of the core business of SEA; in other words, should SEA go into policy, plan or programme to improve it or is SEA supposed to improve the systems and organizations that determine the context of development?

The authors propose a distinction between the fundamental purpose of SEA and its delivery mechanisms, and also distinguish between institutionalizing SEA systems and individual applications (procedures and tools). They conclude that SEA research needs to focus on three core issues: the substantive purpose of SEA; the strategy adopted to achieve this purpose; and the specific mechanisms (procedures, techniques and tools) for operationalizing SEA.

Research needs and priorities include:

- Seeking greater clarity on the above core issues.
- Promoting interdisciplinarity and cross-fertilization of theoretical contributions from a range of disciplines, such as communication, collaborative and rational planning, strategy formation theories, policy analysis and theories of learning and institutional change.
- Exploring whether SEA ought to adapt to the existing decision-making process or attempt to transform it.
- Encouraging SEA practitioners to attend to the wider context in which SEA operates.

In Chapter 29, Partidário and Wilson address SEA professional and institutional capacity-building, widely recognized as being of fundamental importance to process development and particularly to enabling its effective impact on decision-making. The two strongest ideas developed under this theme confirm that (a) capacity for SEA is yet not in place and is far from ideal and (b) principles and forms of building capacity need to be adapted to each country's needs and realities.

Key issues to be considered in building capacity include: the tiers at which this is needed and their relationship to national, organizational, individual actions; and the need to acknowledge the SEA context (policy and planning practice, institutional set-up, openess of political system, collaborative and constructive relationships), considering both intangible factors (for example, trust, power relationships, willingness to share) and tangible factors (for example, resources availability, in-built knowledge). These factors relate strongly to other themes discussed in the papers in Part V.

Recognizing that current experience with building professional and institutional capacity is relatively diverse, Partidário and Wilson conclude this activity should address national SEA systems, contexts and institutional frameworks and illustrate forms (methods, initiatives) whereby such capacity can be improved while being made context-specific. Other key conclusions point to the importance of better understanding and clarification of the purpose of SEA, making it more strategic and ensuring it is decision-focused and results-oriented rather than process-oriented, and enhancing the strategic role and impact of SEA in decision-making (adapting to it and possibly changing it).

In Chapter 30, Schijf reviews the purpose, role and diversity of SEA guidance to improve practice. The two strongest ideas are (a) that best practice principles are not always good practice and (b) that the use of SEA guidance can promote a shift in SEA development. Schijf makes a case for improved harmonization of guidance to promote better, less rigid, purpose-driven practice.

Concluding that most SEA guidance is internet-based, she considers that technological advances enable more flexible and adaptive SEA guidance, which is layered, supported by a wide array of examples and regularly updated. The chapter further lists a number of additional key lessons for the process of developing SEA guidance and improving its content.

In Chapter 31, Kørnøv and Dalkmann review appropriate organizations and institutional frameworks for SEA. Two strong ideas are (a) the need to consider actor constellation models and (b) the role and effect of political culture in influencing decisions and the implications for the organizations involved. They identify four key actors in the organizational structures for SEA, namely politicians, public administrators, the general public and researchers/consultants, and enunciate performance criteria of good practice for each group.

In their view, the knowledge and tools necessary for undertaking SEA generally exist in practice already but organizational aspects, such as non-value free, rational and linear decision-making processes, established routines and mechanisms and different institutional and political culture preconditions, are still weak or missing. This calls for better recognition of key challenges, such as dealing with formal and informal organizational structures, strengthening communication, understanding existing power constellations and recognizing that stakeholders have different rationalities (norms, values, attitudes) and require specific formats and timings for involvement.

In Chapter 32, Cherp, Partidário and Arts address SEA follow-up and discuss the meaning, importance, potential and benefits of implementing this stage of the process. The two strongest points are (a) that SEA follow-up is much more complex than EIA follow-up and adopts multiple forms and (b) that SEA should be undertaken throughout the life-time of a strategic initiative.

Key challenges for SEA follow-up include the notions of 'organizational anchoring' or 'institutional ownership' (who should undertake SEA follow-up) and its interaction with other environmental policy tools and instruments, such as environmental management strategies undertaken by public authorities. The authors argue that SEA should influence not only the formal content of strategic documents but also their practical implementation, which may be affected by uncertainties during the planning stage, unforeseen circumstances and/or significant deviation of implementation from original plans. SEA can perform this role using a variety of instruments: monitoring, evaluation, management and communication – collectively referred to here as 'SEA follow-up'. Recent progress in the conceptualization of SEA follow-up notes that it should follow several 'tracks' in monitoring and evaluation and concern not only the impact of strategic initiatives but also their performance, goal achievement, changes in the underlying assumption and related activities.

In Chapter 33, van Gent provides a synopsis of current SEA knowledge centres and their potential importance for overall capacity-building and process development. The two strongest ideas are that (a) there is too much SEA information available for those that have access to these sources but too little for those that do not and (b) there should be more than one kind of knowledge centre.

Key challenges pointed out by van Gent include the increased development of digital and web information (likely to increase in the future), supported by personal contacts and written materials. This is where universities can play an important role, particularly in developing countries, but research and practice still need to find better ways and opportunities to learn from each other. The author envisages a knowledge exchange system, anchored in country nodes and linked to regional and wider networks.

Core messages on capacity-building and process development

Theme highlights

A reasonable degree of consistency can be found across each theme and major conclusions can be extracted to highlight core messages on the overall theme of SEA process development and capacity-building. These fall under three main headings: improving standards for SEA, better capacity for decision-making towards sustainable development and acknowledging diverse interpretations of the *raison d'être* of SEA. These aspects are briefly addressed below.

Improving standards for SEA

SEA is context-specific. That is a strong message that comes across all themes. Ways to improve standards for SEA are suggested through:

- Establishing simple, complementary and practical guidance.
- Accrediting courses (both educational and professional training).
- Undertaking empirical and theoretical research.
- Developing legal and regulatory capacities, particularly in developing countries.
- Implementing follow-up systems that enable knowledge-building based on empirical evidence.

It is evident that the context-specific nature of SEA may conflict with the notion of universal standards. Therefore, it would be unadvisable to choose one particular context as the basis for the purpose of developing standard practices and targets for SEA. Guidance itself will hardly be able to impose standard practices and must be made specific to each SEA context, as Schijf contends in Chapter 30. Standards may be considered only if they can be made context-specific.

Countries need to agree on their SEA good practice before standards are imposed on SEA practice and evaluation of performance. The concept of static standards for SEA was rejected by those debating this issue at Prague. At a general level, the agenda for SEA good practice will be shaped by the context. This is bottom-line in the process of improving standards for SEA.

Specifically, the context will determine:

- SEA purposes (for example, in relation to other available policy assessment tools or planning practices).
- The nature and features of national systems (depending, for example, on the organization of institutional frameworks, constellation of actors and power sharing regarding environmental issues).
- The participating sectors and how they will be involved (depending, for example, on existing levels of environmental integration and also the SEA ownership of sectors in relation to the role played by environmental authorities).
- The appropriate professionals for delivering adequate approaches to SEA (for example professionals with expertise in policy science, land-use planning, engineering and technology, which use different approaches and tools).

Better capacity for decision-making towards sustainable development

Capacity-building is fundamental to create conditions for more effective SEA as many authors and organizations have pointed out. For example, Partidário and Wilson (Chapter 29) introduce capacity-building for SEA as a means to: improve the structures of governance and institutional frameworks that provide the context for SEA; strengthen the organizations that conduct SEA; produce guidance documents; and provide training to individuals who perform SEA.

SEA is a means, not an end in itself. When thinking of improving SEA, attention must be directed at environmental issues, sustainable development and decision-making, not at SEA *per se*. The questions are: is SEA helping to ensure full consideration of environmental issues as well as other sustainable development considerations? Is SEA contributing to achieve sustainable development processes, goals and targets? Is SEA assisting and informing strategic decision-making (Kørnøv and Dalkmann in Chapter 31)? Is SEA checking on policies, plans and programmes (PPPs) or contributing to improving the systems and the organizations that create the context for SEA (Bina, Wellington and Thissen in Chapter 28)?

Building capacity for SEA should follow key principles but in all circumstances should be directed at what SEA is needed for. It will involve developing technical contents as well as setting up appropriate institutional and organizational frameworks, and also helping with the better use of communication facilities and technologies (such as the web-based, training, learning and knowledge centres described by van Gent in Chapter 33). The question of whether there is sufficient SEA capacity should be complemented by the questions of who needs capacity and capacity for what? Developing capacity to address SEA effectively involves further integrating environmental assessment in national institutions and systems of policy-making, as well as maintaining the link and direction for sustainability.

Diversity in interpretation of what SEA is and what it should do

As mentioned, and widely debated, SEA is multi-purpose and context-specific and there is a high diversity of existing forms of SEA. Many consider this situation to be highly confusing and inefficient for the purpose of understanding the leading motivations for SEA. However, even though the current situation appears to be chaotic, it may be seen as a sign of progress towards improvement (Hilding-Rydevik, personal communication, 2005). This paradox means that we are looking at the bigger picture, testing different forms of SEA and seeking improvement instead of crystallizing on a single form of SEA that may not be entirely accepted.

SEA has a large potential yet to be fully explored and linked to dimensions such as strategy formation, organizational frameworks and sustainable development approaches (Box 27.1). It would represent a major inefficiency to allow SEA to crystallize before its full potential is realized and while its practice still falls far behind its full capacity.

IAIA's contribution to the agenda

The debates at Prague contributed insights on the possible role for IAIA and other such organizations in helping to set the agenda for improving process development and capacity-building in SEA. Elements include:

- **Contribute to empirical and theoretical research:** IAIA can assist by promoting thematic, workshop-oriented conferences and conceptual 'brain-storming' sessions on SEA of the type that took place at Prague. It is also critical to capture these in publications, such as the current handbook, which share ideas and experiences and should be taken as multipliers of SEA thinking.

Box 27.1 *Building SEA capacity*

The apparent chaotic situation of multiple purposes and forms referred to in the text can be seen as a catalyst for:

Capacity-building to focus on
How to
Achieve improvement in
Organizational frameworks for
Sustainable development

SEA will lead to better informed decision-making processes and better informed decision-makers.

Source: Designed by Tadhg O'Mahony

- **Engage other non-impact assessment professional areas:** Often, IAIA is speaking to IAIA. Although important to nest and consolidate ideas, it will not lead us too far with respect to innovation and dissemination of SEA. IAIA needs to establish strong and effective links with other professional organizations that represent areas of application of SEA, as well as with other disciplines that contribute to advancing the knowledge-base of SEA. It needs to move beyond its own boundaries and seek to influence the practice of other related professionals. It will be important to develop and establish relationships and joint events with other professional organizations, particularly those that are users of SEA.
- **Contribute to clarification of SEA:** IAIA also has an important role to play in helping to clarify the role of SEA in the constellation of impact assessment instruments. It is not only the forms of SEA that multiply. Over the years, the variety of impact assessment instruments has been replicating at a considerable speed and IAIA acknowledges all of them. Perhaps this requires some analysis, discussion and a consolidated approach to clarify the differences in purpose and outcomes of multiple impact assessment tools and, most importantly, to focus on the difference between EIA and SEA. A key point (widely made at Prague) was that SEA should not be used to replace the malfunctions of EIA. Yet, often, it is hard to draw the line between what is an EIA and what is an SEA.

It is important to determine the integrity of each instrument and be clear about the key role and contribution that each one brings or can potentially bring, if well used, to the evolving body of knowledge and practice of impact assessment. This means, for example, improving EIA to clarify SEA, by promoting discussion regarding the theory, quality and potential in EIA and helping to clarify why EIA is failing to meet its original purposes and full potential. This will streamline the distinction between EIA and SEA, and may well release SEA to deal with actual strategic notions and scales instead of simply making up for the deficiencies of EIA.

Conclusions

There is still much to learn about SEA. More empirical and theoretical research is needed to gain a better understanding of how SEA can be useful, effective and efficient. A key bottom-line is that SEA is context-specific. This point has been repeatedly made in the SEA literature and is evident in Chapters 28–33 in this volume. It means that the issues of what SEA is and what it should do must be understood from a wide array of experiences in multiple contexts, reflecting a diversity of contexts and practices.

SEA is a tool for sustainability. Sustainability is the ultimate purpose and SEA is a means to achieve it. While the focus of SEA should remain centred on environmental issues in strategic development, SEA needs to be undertaken through integrated approaches that incorporate physical, ecological, social, cultural, institutional and economic dimensions of sustainability. The clarification of the purpose of SEA requires action beyond and outside SEA frontiers. This involves engaging other non-impact assessment related disciplines in the development of SEA, for example planning and policy development, decision theory and institutional learning, governance and participatory approaches. All are strongly related to SEA but each is associated with well-established fundamental knowledge.

Improving SEA also strongly implies the need to improve EIA. There is too much overlap between the two tools and that is undermining the full-shaping and effectiveness of both EIA and SEA. Much SEA practice could be replaced by good EIA, leaving SEA to deal with strategic decisions that need to be questioned on environmental grounds and that require dedicated and appropriate inquiry. In sum, we need to avoid the trend of using SEA to replace ineffective EIA.

Acknowledgements

This chapter is based on the papers prepared for Part V of this Handbook and the discussions that took place at the IAIA Conference on Strategic Environmental Assessment (Prague, 2005).

28
SEA Theory and Research: An Analysis of the Early Discourse[1]

Olivia Bina, Tabatha Wallington and Wil Thissen

Introduction

Since the inception of strategic environmental assessment (SEA), scholars and practitioners have devoted much attention to the development of techniques to facilitate its implementation in the upstream decision contexts that characterize strategic initiatives. As such, significant attention has been given to documenting practical experiences with case studies, establishing so-called 'best practice' guidelines, and making comparisons of SEA implementation rules across different nations. In contrast, despite regular calls to that end, very little attention has been paid to the conceptual development of SEA (Cashmore, 2004; Cashmore et al, 2004). While SEA has drawn significant lessons from the experience with project-level environmental impact assessment (EIA), it faces a number of fundamentally different challenges at higher levels of decision-making. In particular, uncertainty and value conflict associated with developments ranging from transport planning to energy policy indicate that the knowledge and techniques traditionally relied upon to 'solve' environmental problems are no longer adequate to the task (Wallington, 2003). These challenges suggest that SEA must move beyond the 'impact assessment mindset' (Bina, 2003), which in turn indicates the need for renewed attention to be paid to the theoretical development of SEA.

The aim of this chapter is to first outline some of the most prominent features of discussions regarding the development and status of SEA generally, and of SEA theory in particular. Next, we propose three themes as a conceptual framework for organizing the different theoretical issues raised by debates in the SEA literature that may support the development of a more solid theoretical basis for SEA practice. These themes – namely, the purpose associated with SEA, the strategies chosen to achieve that purpose, and the mechanisms for operationalizing SEA – were further developed through contributions to the SEA Theory and Research workshop held as part of the SEA conference in Prague, 2005.[2] The Prague workshop provided an invaluable opportunity for SEA scholars to discuss these issues,[3] particularly where they had been presented in the literature from apparently polarized viewpoints. We conclude by highlighting the remaining tensions regarding the theoretical grounding of SEA, and their implications for further research.

Situation and trends

Since the first specific use of the term 'SEA' by Wood and Djeddour (1992),[4] this form of assessment has been conceived of as a structured means of introducing and safeguarding environmental consequences at the level of policies, plans and programmes (Sadler and Verheem, 1996; Thérivel and Partidário, 1996). First, SEA was seen as a 'tool' to deal with some of the perceived shortcomings of project-level EIA, where the timing of analysis had constrained its capacity to deal proactively with environmental problems. Second, it was argued that giving attention to the environmental consequences of policies, plans and programmes (PPPs) would enable SEA to contribute more effectively to the international environmental policy agenda of 'sustainable development' (Sadler and Verheem, 1996; Partidário, 1999).

Supported by claims that the philosophy and principles of EIA could be effectively translated 'upstream' in the context of SEA (Clark, 2000) and the tools and techniques of EIA could be applied at higher levels of decision-making (Thérivel and Partidário, 1996), implementing SEA was considered of paramount importance. As Wood and Djeddour (1992, pp10–11) stated, 'there is no fundamental methodological reason why SEA should not be introduced in any country... utilizing a form of SEA basically similar in its basic nature to that employed for projects'. Thus, a promotional tone clearly permeates much of the SEA literature to date as scholars have striven to articulate SEA objectives, role, benefits, and practical achievements (see also Fischer, 1999; Partidário and Clark, 2000; Jones et al, 2005).

In practical terms, the institutionalization of SEA has been realized in a number of countries, as well as in the European Union (EU) and the United Nations Economic Commission for Europe (UNECE, 2003). Despite these significant initiatives, however, the recent proliferation of new assessment methods and processes also aimed at strategic-level planning – including, among other things, sustainability appraisal, sustainability impact assessment, integrated assessment and territorial impact assessment – has caused confusion among practitioners, policy-makers and scholars regarding the particular role of SEA. At the same time, scholars and practitioners have made multiple pleas for change in the practice of SEA, including: the need for a better analysis of, and integration into, policy processes (Caratti et al, 2004); more and stricter formal requirements; more communicative approaches; and better tools and techniques. Moreover, although the formal institutionalization of SEA addresses specific proposals for (public) decision-making processes, there are increasing calls to consider the 'wider context', notably institutional habits and values, and the 'environmental capacity' of the organizations and actors involved (Bina, 2003).

As a consequence of these myriad expectations, there are no clearly identifiable or commonly agreed upon directions for the future development of

SEA. This conceptual confusion presents a very real threat to the future of SEA unless the relevant academic and practitioner communities are capable of making a clear case for its existence. We are convinced that making this case demands renewed attention to the theory of SEA[5] to complement the prevailing emphasis on developing better techniques. The relatively recent opening of environmental assessment (EA) discourse to contributions from theories of decision-making (Lindblom, 1971; Weiss, 1982; Faludi, 1987; Rapoport, 1989; March and Olsen, 1989), planning (Lawrence, 2000), policy analysis (Torgerson, 1986; Thissen, 1997; Majone, 1989), social and organizational learning (Argyris, 1992; Owen and Lambert, 1995), and democracy and governance (Grove-White, 1999; van Eeten, 2001) are a welcome development in this regard. This paper aims to explore and illuminate some of these developments – and ensuing debates – in SEA theory, as well as to articulate a framework to guide future discussion and research in this important field of inquiry and practice.

Toward a conceptual framework for analysing the debate

Scholarly debate on the theory and methodology of SEA may be grouped under three (tightly connected) issues: (a) the substantive purpose associated with SEA; (b) the strategy adopted to achieve this purpose; and (c) the specific mechanisms (procedures, techniques, tools) for operationalizing SEA. These three issues may be considered vital elements of a conceptual framework for SEA.[6]

The first element concerns the substantive purpose(s)[7] of SEA. By this we mean the ultimate end or purpose of SEA; its *raison d'être*. Debates regarding the substantive purpose of SEA have centred on the primacy of protecting and enhancing the natural environment versus the need to address social and economic values alongside this traditional focus (the 'triple bottom line' interpretation of sustainable development). Originally, SEA was conceived to address the environmental consequences of planning and policy decisions (for example, EC, 2001; Sheate et al, 2001; Thérivel et al, 1992), a focus that was later translated into the concept of environmental sustainability in which SEA 'can and should … facilitate the design of environmentally sustainable policies and plans' (Dalal-Clayton and Sadler, 2005, p19). Gradually, however, attention has shifted to a broader understanding of sustainability, which involves the balancing of a much wider set of values (including at least social, economic and environmental values) informed by a diversity of worldviews. Thus, the purpose given to SEA, which relates to the ultimate implications of societal decision processes, has become increasingly diverse since the mid-1990s as proponents of SEA argue for its contribution to a range of (potentially conflicting) values (Brown and Thérivel, 2000; Dalal-Clayton and Sadler, 2005; Eggenberger and Partidário, 2000; Fischer, 2003; Noble and Storey, 2001).

The second element of the proposed conceptual framework concerns the strategies invoked to contribute to SEA's ultimate purpose.[8] These strategies are closely associated with the object of inquiry of SEA.[9] By 'object', we refer to the entity (thing or process) that SEA activities focus on, and that SEA is intended to directly and indirectly influence. Where risk assessment, for example, takes its central object of inquiry to be (undesirable) events, SEA has traditionally taken its object to be programmes, plans and policies, or PPPs. This focus accords with early definitions of SEA (see for example Sadler and Verheem, 1996; Thérivel et al, 1992). The common interpretation of such definitions has been that the term 'strategic'[10] EA suggests that SEA is intended to influence the 'strategies'[11] that constitute higher levels of decision-making, as compared to the site-specific development proposals (projects) that are the object of EIA attention. The primary intended target of SEA activities, then, was to influence the outcome of specific decision processes by informing decision-makers about the potential environmental impacts associated with particular PPPs.

In order to exert such influence, however, it was recognized that the provision of information would not be sufficient and that SEA professionals may also may need to focus attention on the context in which 'traditional' SEA would be embedded. Here, we make a distinction between the 'immediate' and 'wider' context (Figure 28.1). Initially, attention focused on the immediate context: the planning and policy-making processes that SEA seeks to influence (the set of squares at the centre of Figure 28.1), in recognition of the need to better understand 'how policy-making works' in order to adapt and tune SEA to existing policy processes (see Nitz and Brown, 2000). This has led to more effective assessment processes, capable of influencing decisions within the timeframe of policy, plan or programme formulation (see, for example, CSIR, 2003; Devon County Council, 2004; and several examples in Dalal-Clayton and Sadler, 2005).

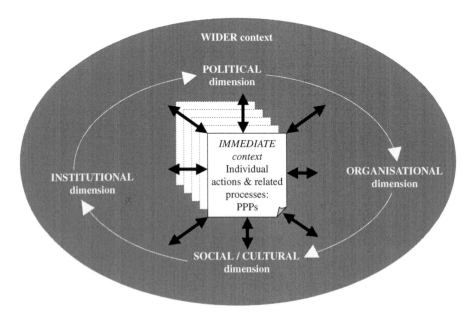

Source: Bina (2003, p93)

Figure 28.1 *The immediate and wider contexts relevant to SEA theory*

Furthermore, scholars have increasingly highlighted the need for SEA practitioners to attend to the *wider* context in which it operates (Audoin and Lochner, 2000; Bina, 2003; Hilding-Rydevik and Bjarnadóttir, 2005). Rather than assuming that SEA – and the decision-making process it seeks to influence – operate in a vacuum, scholars have recognized that these processes are embedded in policy (legislative, regulatory) and societal (political, cultural) contexts. As such, SEA practitioners need to understand these contextual dimensions, for the same reasons that they need to pay attention to the immediate context; namely, being more effective in influencing decisions and changing the habits and frames of mind of decision-makers. Figure 28.1 depicts this wider context, which includes the organizational and institutional location of the decision-making process (the institutional and organizational dimensions), which are themselves situated within and influenced by a given society and its broader social, cultural and political values (the political and social/cultural dimensions).

The immediate and wider contexts are interdependent, as symbolized by the black arrows in Figure 28.1. On the one hand, the wider context affects decision processes (and thus SEA) in many ways, most notably by influencing the decision agenda and the implementation of the decision outcome. On the other hand, the introduction of SEA can affect decision processes and elements of their immediate and wider contexts. Over a longer time period, by repeated application at the individual PPP level, SEA may induce social learning, and possibly change dominant values within a given organization, which may in turn translate into the formulation and adoption of more environmentally sustainable policies and plans (Bina, 2003).

This range of influence highlights the potential of SEA to affect the decision-making process associated with a specific PPP in the short term and to transform the institutional, organizational, and societal contexts in the longer term, as a means of achieving SEA's substantive purpose. From this perspective, SEA, while focusing on specific PPP processes, aims to influence the dominant habits, beliefs and values of the actors and institutions in the immediate and/or wider contexts in order to make them more amenable to (environmental) sustainability. In the language used earlier, these contextual factors have increasingly been taken as an additional object of inquiry in SEA.

The third element of the proposed conceptual framework relates to the specific mechanisms for operationalizing SEA.[12] How can SEA achieve any of the above? In line with trends in planning and policy analysis (see Thérivel and Partidário, 2000), proponents increasingly argue for a broader variety of approaches, methods and techniques in SEA practice (for example, by including more deliberative approaches to public participation, and by introducing scenario workshops to aid alternatives design) to complement the more traditionally quantitative techniques of the SEA 'toolbox' (Owens et al, 2004).

The conceptual framework for SEA outlined above aims to distinguish among:

• The substantive purposes underlying the need for SEA.
• The strategies chosen to achieve those purposes.

- The delivery mechanisms (methods, techniques and tools) chosen at the operational level.

In the remainder of this chapter, we explore a range of contributions within the SEA discourse as they relate to the above three areas of conceptual development. No attempt is made to outline a complete picture of this discourse, rather, we focus on selected issues that proved to be of central interest to contributors to the Prague workshops.

The substantive purpose and values associated with SEA

The purpose of SEA, as conceived in the early 1990s, was closely linked to that of EIA, namely to secure the protection and enhancement of natural systems by ensuring that the environmental consequences of proposals were appropriately considered. This principle, however, soon gave way to a much more diverse (and often confused) set of priorities. Some commentators continued to stress the environmental focus of SEA, warning that the inclusion of social and economic issues on the SEA agenda could dilute the role of SEA in safeguarding environmental sustainability and drawing attention to the limits of natural systems (for example, Sadler, 1999; Audoin and Lochner, 2000; among other South African scholars and practitioners). Others enthusiastically adopted the sustainability agenda in a variety of interpretations, most notably the focus on environmentally and socially sustainable development advocated by the World Bank (Mercier and Kulsum, 2005; World Bank, 2005).

Support for the idea that SEA should contribute to achieving sustainable development has become increasingly widespread (see EC, 2001; Lee and Walsh, 1992; Partidário, 1999; Sadler and Verheem, 1996; Thérivel et al, 1992), albeit without a clear articulation of what this means for the original focus on the biophysical environment. The sustainability concept thus brings complications: some prefer to limit it to environmental sustainability; others take it to include economic and social aspects. These debates regarding the substantive purpose of SEA, in turn, have created new debates about the theoretical orientation of SEA, reflecting the necessarily political dimension of its increasingly more complex remit – requiring difficult trade-offs between environmental, economic and social concerns (particularly as 'objective' indicators of sustainability cannot be established) – compared to its traditional environmental focus and technocratic orientation.

At the same time, the numerous alternative processes and methods being proposed and adopted to assess strategic initiatives (for example, sustainability appraisal and sustainability impact assessment) all favour the broader concept of sustainability (see Dalal-Clayton and Sadler, 2005, for an overview), suggesting a widespread preference for the adoption of sustainability as the ultimate purpose of such interventions. These developments trigger questions regarding the differences between SEA and these other approaches (in particular where these are promoted by the same people), as well as questions about the relevance of environmental concerns as the core value of SEA.

There are arguments both for and against the sustainability shift. On the one hand, a sustainability mantle promises to be politically advantageous, and may extend the influence of EA more broadly. The strategic nature of the issues being addressed by SEA will often require an analytical framework that is more interdisciplinary, and this could be leading some advocates to uphold the sustainability shift. On the other hand, renouncing the 'environment' and the 'institutionalization of ecological rationality' (Bartlett, 1997, p57) as the core value of SEA could equate to a radical departure from the original *raison d'être* of SEA, and threaten to undermine the future of the natural environment as a focus of political attention (see, for example, Wood, 2003). The Royal Commission on Environmental Pollution (RCEP) has raised similar concerns in the context of sustainability appraisal in the UK, suggesting that 'it can in fact marginalize the very social and environmental appraisals it is supposed to bolster as a counterpoint to dominant financial and economic assessments'. The RCEP goes on to recommend that the government needs to 'strengthen the environmental component' (RCEP, 2002, cited in Jackson and Illsley, 2005, p5). Without the purpose of improving the environment and its positive effect on the quality of life, SEA is just a method that could be applied for any conceivable aim. Importantly, actively embracing its environmental purpose would help to distinguish SEA from all other forms of strategic assessment whose scope often tends to overlap, giving SEA a clear purpose and role in modern governance: environmental sustainability (Sadler, 1999).

Contributions to the workshops were based on advocacy of both environmental sustainability and the wider understanding of sustainable development as the substantive purpose of SEA. However, there were repeated and strong warnings against adopting the broader sustainability purpose, or as Tony Jackson phrased it, *'floating down the misty river of sustainability'*. Most of those present, in the end, concluded that it might be more *'strategic'* to focus SEA on the environment *'rather than on a general sustainability scope'*. The conclusion of this debate was that *'we should keep the environmental dimension central to SEA'*. Thus, the dominant opinion among participants was that the ultimate purpose of SEA should be the promotion of environmental sustainability, maintaining the environment as the primary value.

SEA strategies and their object of inquiry

The strategies proposed to achieve the substantive purpose of SEA may be classified according to the differing assumptions made about the object of SEA and the context in which SEA operates. Basically, two points of view are evident in the discussion:

1   **Traditional 'procedural' strategy:** SEA activities are meant to directly affect the outcome of a specific policy or decision process (such as a decision or recommendations for action) and this outcome, after implementation, affects the (primarily physical) state of the world. This is the traditional focus of EA in general and is most notably associated with a 'rational',

procedural approach. The policy and institutional context are assumed to be given, providing boundary conditions for SEA.

2 **Transformative strategy:** In the short term, SEA aims to change the way decisions are made – rather than adapting to a given context – by introducing environmental considerations into decision arenas dominated by economic and other values.[13] SEA activities are also intended to contribute to (medium to long-term) changes in the range of values, worldviews, behaviour and practices of actors and institutions in the immediate and, crucially, in the wider contexts; for example, by raising environmental awareness at the political level, contributing to organizational learning, and so on. This more 'indirect' contextual change then affects the setting of policy agendas, the outcomes of policy processes, the implementation of their outcomes, and ultimately the state of the world. This latter strategy is often referred to as a 'learning' strategy, as its aim is to permanently change values, worldviews and practices, as opposed to what often happens in immediate decision contexts where *ad hoc* compromises are made and nothing is changed in the views or values of participants (which, however, does not mean that no learning could take place in individual decision situations).

Procedural versus transformative strategies: Current debates

The first approach, based on a 'rational' model of planning and policy-making processes, seeks to influence the formulation of a specific PPP proposal. It assumes that the environmental information introduced by SEA will be given due weight alongside the economic and social values that traditionally guide planning and policy-making. This procedural strategy implicitly assumes that events proceed in a linear (deterministic) fashion: that the provision of better 'objective' information will automatically lead to an improved decision, and will therefore improve the prospects of a better, more environmentally sustainable policy, plan or programme proposal (see Bailey, 1997, p320; Caratti et al, 2004). This assumption remains dominant in models of EIA (Nitz and Brown, 2000) and SEA (Kørnøv and Thissen, 2000) alike. It is an assumption that can be challenged on empirical grounds; the practice of EA rarely lives up to this ideal rational model, a conclusion supported by virtually all empirical research in policy analysis (Kørnøv and Thissen, 2000). In pursuing this first strategy, those responsible for SEA should therefore become more cognizant, as Leknes (2005) has argued, of the multiplicity of logics that actually inform public decision-making processes. Thus, echoing the assumption that the decision-making context is given, Leknes (2005) suggested that: 'Understanding principle types of public decision-making processes and the characteristics of these is important as [it provides critical] boundaries for SEA.'

The second approach is based on the conviction that, rather than simply adapt to prevailing ways of doing things, SEA should, in the long run, also contribute to transforming policy and planning processes (see Wallington, 2003), and the way development is thought of in the first place (see, for example, Caldwell, 1989; Taylor, 1984; Culhane et al, 1987; Weston, 2000; Nilsson and Dalkmann, 2001; Lawrence, 2000; Caratti et al, 2004). This approach is also recommended in recognition of the far-reaching implications of pursuing the substantive purpose of SEA, and in response to warnings about uncritically adapting to prevailing policy processes, which operate according to established development-oriented values. As Boggs explained:

> *Congress designed NEPA to help **reform** institutional realities with deeply embedded values and world views. Paradoxically, these same entrenched views and perspectives often govern how agencies implement NEPA. (Boggs, 1993, p29, emphasis added)*

At a minimum, SEA strategies might focus on the 'traditional' role of identifying the environmental consequences of development plans, informing and forcing governments to come to terms with the environmental implications of their decisions. In turn, the institutionalization of SEA could trigger longer-term changes in the wider context of institutional and social values. For example, at the Prague workshop, Nooteboom (2005) noted that the repeated application of EIA at the project level has led to social learning in the Netherlands, and SEA could achieve similar, possibly greater, influence given its more strategic scope (see also Cashmore and Nieslony, 2005; World Bank, 2005).

A number of arguments also support a more proactive but indirect form of SEA's transformative role (see d'Ieteren and Godart, 2005; Cashmore and Nieslony, 2005; Jackson and Illsley, 2005; Hilding-Rydevik and Bjarnadóttir, 2005). For example, Bina (2003) proposes improving the 'environmental capacity' – the combination of political will and availability of means to promote environmental protection and sustainability – as a way to reframe the contribution of SEA to sustainability. She argues that by 'improving the environmental capacity of the policy process and its wider context,' SEA holds the promise of 'progressively reducing the gap between current practices of policy-making, and those more conducive to environmentally sustainable decision-making' (Bina, 2003, p332).

Another argument relates to problems with the concept of 'tiering' (Bailey and Dixon, 1999), and the implications of these problems for the traditional object of SEA, namely PPPs. The tiering principle is based on the assumption that there is a hierarchical nesting of decision levels, and that assessment at higher levels reduces the need for assessment at lower levels. However, these assumptions may be challenged; indeed, there is reason to question whether policies, plans and programmes exist in any concrete sense (see Markus, 2005). Evidence from developed and developing countries has demonstrated the absence of policies, and so the absence of clear tiering, so that projects are often developed in a policy vacuum, and PPPs are formulated without the necessary 'capacity for strategic thinking and planning' (Bina, 2003, p331).

This argument was supported by Cherp (2005) who stressed that:

> *Policies, plans and programmes (PPPs) addressed by SEA are rarely 'strategic' ... because they do not guide future activities: They reflect past patterns of thinking and action. They do not necessarily relate to any new significant activities ... They do not necessarily result in any activities at all. Thus, SEA applied to PPPs may be less (rather than more) 'strategic' than project-level EA.*

As a result, SEA strategies may need to address the weaknesses of planning, as much as – or even instead of – plans themselves. In doing so, SEA may be addressing aspects of the wider context such as promoting inter-sectoral dialogue to help produce a coherent river-basin plan, or defining long-term data gathering strategies for land-use plans, or helping to set up new committees and other formal institutions for improved environmental governance. Such activities would provide support for a weak planning process that lacks methodological capacity to address environmental sustainability consider-ations, the introduction of which may have longer-term effects on the way planners and policy-makers think and act. In Belgium, for example, existing arrangements for tourism planning do not include mechanisms for anticipating environmental impacts (positive or negative), highlighting the importance of SEA as a driver for the development of environmentally sustainable tourism strategies (d'Ieteren and Godart, 2005).

However, there were also more cautious contributions. Nilsson's (2005) research highlighted the limited influence of the expertise provided by SEA on the formation of policy preferences and policy learning processes, suggesting that this depended more on the institutional rules of decision-making. He suggested that SEA might also have a limited influence in changing such rules. Leknes' (2005) research found that Norway's Ministry of Finance relies exclusively on its own analyses, and suggested that such mainstream actors are unlikely to be interested in the contribution of SEA to the debate on development (sustainable or otherwise).

Nooteboom (2005) also argued that decision-makers form their opinions and obtain their expertise outside the formal decision-making processes:

> *The reality is that the minds of key players are made up in informal networks. They make use of the environmental expertise that has developed in 30 years. Since these networks are informal, they cannot easily be observed as being influential, but they are. The networks must be informal because otherwise they become politically hijacked.*

Therefore, the effect of environmental information on planning and decision-making is '*totally dependent*' on these wider networks, which pose 'contextual' constraints on the influence of the environmental information provided by SEA. Targeting the formation of opinions in such networks may therefore be much more effective than directing efforts at influencing the formal process, and would result in a role for SEA both within the immediate and wider contexts. What remains to be explored is the potential of SEA strategies designed more explicitly to address the problems or weaknesses of key elements of the wider context, and whether learning can result from their long-term application.

In this sense, we note that this discussion, as well as some of the presentations at the Prague conference (Williams, 2005; McPhail, 2005), point to an interpretation of SEA's transformative strategy that would directly target the wider context with the aim of improving environmental governance. This could relate to the SEA transformative strategies described earlier, in the sense that SEA could draw on (or be integrated into) current innovative practices such as environmental auditing, backcasting activities focusing on sustainable technology development (Weaver et al, 2000), or climate change (Van de Kerkhof et al, 2002, 2005), and efforts at managing energy transitions (Rotmans et al, 2001), none of which are directly related to a formal PPP decision process.

However, by broadening the reach of SEA to the wider context it may become difficult for decision-makers to differentiate SEA from other sustainability-oriented initiatives. Thus, rather than directly targeting the wider context, it may be argued that SEA should be formally institutionalized as a contribution to the formulation and evaluation of PPPs, ideally in association with processes of regulatory and legislative authority, as traditionally understood. Its contribution to improve elements of the wider context should be the result of its repeated and systematic application. Transformative strategies could help to ensure such longer-term contribution. One possibility is to seek to maximize each individual assessment by establishing mechanisms and processes that aim to strengthen environmental governance (including, for example, development organizations' environmental capacity) beyond the lifetime of the specific planning process and its implementation. By systematically introducing the use of methods – such as informal discussions, scenario workshops, back-casting exercises, state-of-the-environment reports, and similar approaches – that aim to stimulate critical reflection on a policy, plan or programme and its consequences for environmental sustainability, SEA strategies could contribute to raising environmental awareness at the level of a sector or of society as a whole. Where the kind of innovative practices noted above are absent or weak (especially, but by no means exclusively, in developing countries), SEA transformative strategies could be the lever for their introduction.

Toward a reconciliation of procedural and transformative strategies

Given the diverse contextual influences on SEA, Prague workshop participants emphasized that there is no single 'best' strategy for SEA to achieve its ultimate purpose; rather, the choice will depend upon the nature of the institutional (for example, legal, regulatory, administrative), political and other contextual circumstances in question. Tuija Hilding-Rydevik (2005) stressed that in the Nordic countries, for example, the objective of sustainability is already well-established so that discussions regarding the added value of SEA point to its more traditional role of providing 'good environmental information'. The situation would be different in other parts of Europe, where the sustainability objective remains relegated to the introductory sections of policy documents or laws with little evidence that this objective informs the design and implementation of PPPs.

There was general agreement among Prague workshop participants regarding the relevance of attempts to change critical attributes of the immediate context (the planning and decision-making processes) to achieve the purpose of SEA. There was also a certain amount of agreement on the 'potential' of SEA to improve the wider context alongside its primary focus on PPPs. In the end, the general view among workshop participants was that authorities responsible for introducing SEA – guided by the expertise and counsel of SEA practitioners – should take a pragmatic approach, defining SEA strategies according to the particular characteristics of the country, sector, and organizations in question. Strategies could thus be drawn in response to the specific nature of 'the gap' between current practices of policy-making, and those more conducive to environmentally sustainable decision-making, as well as in response to specific weaknesses in the wider context. A transformative strategy would potentially enable SEA to 'compensate' for the context's weaknesses (see Bina, 2003), strengthening its environmental capacity and thus promoting the active pursuit of sustainable development planning in the medium and longer term.

Based on this discussion, it is clear that the 'object' of SEA will vary, depending on the circumstances. The context will define the nature and character of PPPs and these can range widely. Moreover, actors (including SEA experts) can understand planning and decision-making in narrow or broad terms, considering different logics of decision processes. Ultimately, the question of whether SEA should adapt to the existing decision-making process and its wider context (its existing institutions, established values and worldviews that might limit its effectiveness and influence) or attempt to transform these through a long-term strategy (for example, strengthening the environmental capacity of key organizations) may not be a fruitful one. Rather, both strategies seem to be complementary and both should be used to foster the ultimate purpose of SEA. We discuss this further in terms of SEA mechanisms.

Mechanisms for operationalizing SEA

Having explored the purpose, object and strategies for SEA, the third element of the proposed conceptual framework considers the mechanisms that could ensure SEA will actually 'add value' through the chosen strategies, and bring its end purpose(s) closer to realization. Here, we address the question of what techniques, methods and procedures can or should be used by SEA practitioners to put preferred strategies into effect, and ultimately to contribute to the fundamental purpose of SEA?

The mechanisms recommended to operationalize SEA relate closely to the stance taken by commentators on questions of purpose and strategy and to the theoretical views on the various (decision-making, political, social) processes to be influenced. Thus, for example, where the rational decision model is used as a starting point to characterize decision processes, the traditional tools and techniques of EIA tend to be promoted. These concentrate, primarily, on systematic inquiry to provide information on the expected environmental consequences of proposed PPPs. In contrast, where decision processes are seen as inherently political and communicative and closely interlinked with elements of the wider context, deliberative processes are increasingly recommended. The following discussion will outline key elements of workshop contributions along these two lines – namely, information-oriented (substantive) and communicative mechanisms – followed by a discussion on the desirability and potential of a synthesis of the two.

Substantive analysis

Traditional themes such as the need for better models with more integrative capabilities, the need for better ways to deal with uncertainties, and explorations into an appropriate balance of quantitative and qualitative methods and tools, were all raised at the Prague workshop but were not central to the discussions. Two other issues were thought to be of greater salience: the need to broaden the scope of SEA to include issues beyond environmental impacts; and the desirability of broadening analytic efforts to encompass problem definition and the design of alternatives.

First, if SEA is to improve the environmental dimension of strategic development initiatives, this requires that SEA practitioners are cognizant of the values and methodological assumptions that inform related sectoral, political, economic and social discourses so as to relate (and integrate) the environmental dimension into prevailing thinking and planning processes. Therefore, irrespective of whether environmental or broader sustainability purposes are fundamental, workshop participants thought it desirable that SEA practitioners pay due attention to these additional aspects in their analyses. Second, attention was drawn to the desirability of broadening analytical attention to problem definition and alternatives design. Theoretically, if SEA is to be effective in a context of planning, it should explicitly combine the prediction and evaluation tasks that are traditionally associated with EA with activities traditionally linked to planning. Central tasks here are problem definition (Thérivel and Brown, 1999; Bailey and Renton, 1997) and the proposal of alternatives. Practically, involvement in processes of problem definition and the conceptualization of alternatives provides a more proactive and potentially more effective way of influencing the decision process in question.

Mechanisms for communication and learning

The SEA community is increasingly engaging with arguments regarding the relevance and nature of communicative and learning approaches as a means of facilitating SEA. Participative approaches have generally been advocated based on the belief that they contribute to general qualities of decision processes, such as their democratic nature, and their efficiency and effectiveness (for example, by contributing to a richer knowledge and ideas base and by generating support for the outcomes of the process). In the SEA context, the assumption that deliberation and interaction among participants enables learning, and stimulates a creative redefinition of problems and solutions, is particularly relevant. As Cashmore and Nieslony (2005) point out, the lessons of EIA suggest that SEA holds the potential to foster learning and institutional reform if it is capable of stimulating debate and exchange of ideas. Recent World Bank (2005) guidance also placed learning at the centre of SEA for policies, and João (2005) reinforced the importance of dialogue for achieving common understandings:

> SEA is about people working together to achieve common good and for that dialogue is crucial. Any stumbling blocks that prevent this dialogue taking place in an effective manner can therefore be stumbling blocks of the SEA process itself.

The emphasis on communication can be formulated in different ways, highlighting the need for interactions between different types of actors. Harashina (2005) stressed that, from the perspective of Japan, the balance between 'rational and emotional' concerns needs careful attention. The inclusion of both experts and stakeholders, facilitated through meeting-like procedures as a vehicle to structure the discourse, has provided empirical support for the promotion of both rationality and fairness through SEA (Harashina, 2005). Vicente and Partidário (2005) emphasized reciprocal learning between SEA professionals and decision-makers:

> *Affecting decision-makers perception on environmental problems should be at the forefront of environmental assessors' priorities ... communication plays an important role for SEA since it is through dialogue about different problem interpretations and value judgements that the common meanings arise and strategic decision-making can be readjusted to better environmental decisions.*

Kørnøv and Nielsen (2005, p4) provide an organizational learning perspective, which draws on the work of Argyris and Schön (1978), to distinguish between single-loop learning and double-loop learning. In single-loop learning, actors or organizations stick to their underlying norms, routines, goals or preferences (also called 'frames'). In double-loop learning, individuals, groups and organizations question the values, assumptions and policies that led to the action in the first place, leading to so-called 'frame reflection' (Schön and Rein, 1994). It is through double-loop learning that individuals and groups develop their perspective and adapt their dominant habits and beliefs to include environmental concerns more prominently. Discursive, communicative or argumentative approaches to policy or strategy development are believed to be a key to fostering double-loop learning and frame reflection (Schön and Rein, 1994; Fisher and Forester, 1993; Hoppe, 1998). Various contributions, however, pointed to a variety of unresolved issues related to communicative approaches. No clear guidelines exist so far as to when and how to set up communication between what parties and for which purpose.

There remain a number of unresolved issues related to communicative approaches. At the Prague workshop, Jiliberto Rodriguez suggested that *'learning may be obstructed by the tendency to distrust or even fear collaboration'*. Other authors emphasize the critical importance of trust as a condition for open discourse, and point to the limitations of discursive approaches in conditions where strategic behaviour dominates (for example, van der Riet, 2003; de Bruijn and ten Heuvelhof, 2002). In the Prague discussion, Tony Jackson noted that *'many advocates for using SEA solely as a discursive planning tool overlook the limitations of deliberative approaches when attempting to bridge gaps created by fundamentally different world views.'* Fischer (2005) pointed to these and other unresolved issues and unfulfilled promises of communicative approaches, and warned against prematurely abolishing rational elements in SEA. Indeed, there is evidence that discussions can expose deeply rooted tensions between dominant worldviews within organizations responsible for sectoral development (Bina, 2003).

Toward a synthesis of rational and communicative approaches?

Various contributions emphasized the need for a creative synthesis of analytical, information-oriented mechanisms and communicative mechanisms. Different views remain regarding the best way of achieving this, however. One view, articulated by Fischer (2005) and based on the logic of 'tiering', was that 'communicative strategies are more appropriate at the policy level, whilst an EIA-based approach [for example, systematic, technical] should be taken to SEA at plan and programme levels.' Others looked to the role of SEA as a vehicle for achieving environmental justice as a means of preserving 'useful aspects of the rational decision-making attributes of EA, but also exploiting the technique's potential for promoting discursive democratic decision-making on environmental policy' (Jackson and Illsley, 2005).

Rather than seeing SEA as either a technical-rational or a discursive-communicative process, it has been argued that SEA should facilitate the interaction between the kind of critical reflection associated with a 'political' or dialogical approach and the systematic, disciplined inquiry that has always characterized the 'technical', or analytical/descriptive, role of SEA (NRC, 1996; Owens et al, 2004; RCEP, 1998; Wallington, 2003). In this way, SEA would facilitate moments of learning throughout policy-making processes, integrating its traditional analytic role, which leads to a 'corrective' learning style, with one that promotes argumentative and dialogical moments, leading to 'cognitive' and 'social' learning (Van der Knaap, 1995, p203) – a synthesis that relies on both the single- and double-loop organizational learning strategies described earlier. Integrating these complementary dimensions of inquiry in SEA demands the creation of institutionalized forums that foster dialogue and the kind of critical reflection necessary to facilitate opportunities for learning in decision-making, organizational and wider societal contexts. As noted earlier, designing SEA strategies that integrate with other initiatives aimed at strengthening environmental governance is increasingly rec-ommended as a promising way forward. A more direct way of facilita-ting cognitive and social learning through SEA is to embrace interactive methodologies for SEA that facilitate creativity in the evaluation of a proposal and its context through the inclusion of multiple interests and discipli-nary perspectives. For Brown (2000), the Environmental Overview process employed by the OECD epitomizes this kind of strategy because 'interactive process ... is the heart of the technique' (Brown, 2000, p133).

In general, despite their divergent rationalities, workshop participants felt that the appropriate mix of information- and communication-oriented mechanisms needs to be tuned to the particular context. This conclusion reinforces that of Owens et al (2004, p1951), who state that 'technical and deliberative processes need not be mutually exclusive, but the context in which appraisal occurs should be a crucial determinant of which approach, or combination of approaches, to adopt'. Reflecting on the variety of approaches and styles that have been developed in the field of policy analysis, Mayer et al (2004) came to a similar conclusion. In addition to technical, research-based, and argumentative activities, they identify activities directed at strategic advice (of one actor), mediation and democratization. Each of these different activities corresponds to a different style of analysis and is associated with different values. They conclude that, 'in practice, policy analysis consists of creatively combining these activities and styles' (Mayer et al, 2004, p169).

Concluding remarks

In this chapter, we emphasize that developing better techniques for SEA must be complemented by renewed attention to its conceptual development. The Prague workshops provided an opportunity to clarify debates with regard to the substantive purpose and role of SEA, as well as to make explicit some of the theoretical assumptions informing the proliferation of mechanisms and approaches proposed to operationalize SEA. This chapter on SEA theory and research has attempted to illuminate some of these issues, as well as to articulate a framework to guide the development of a more solid theoretical basis for this important field of inquiry and practice.

We have suggested that a promising way to structure debates concerning SEA's conceptual foundations is to distinguish between: (a) the substantive purpose and values of SEA; (b) the strategies invoked to achieve the substantive purpose; and (c) the specific mechanisms that may be employed to operationalize SEA.

Regarding substantive purpose, the debate among those favouring environmental sustainability and those favouring broader ('triple bottom line') sustainability concerns as SEA's *raison d'être* remains unresolved. At the Prague workshops, however, a clear preference for retaining a focus on environmental sustainability was expressed.

With respect to the strategies that should be employed toward the achievement of the purpose of SEA, two main approaches can be discerned: 'procedural' strategies, which reproduce the traditional, EIA-based approach to the assessment of individual policies, plans and programmes; and 'transformative' strategies, which also aim to change contextual characteristics (including decision-making, organizational, institutional and wider societal contexts). Where the procedural approach accepts a given context of policy and planning processes, transformative approaches aim to influence the way decisions are made, either directly or indirectly, by stimulating learning and change in institutional and societal perspectives and values in the longer term.

The debate about the strategy of SEA, which finds its roots in different models of decision-making, is reflected at the operational level. Based on the rational decision model, refinement and quality improvement of the analytic information produced by SEA studies is advocated, alongside a broadening of the analytic focus to include problem formulation and formulation of alternatives. The latter would also stimulate learning. Viewed from the perspective that policy-making is an essentially deliberative process, and driven by the desire to stimulate institutional and societal learning, communicative approaches are proposed. These may be targeted at specific PPP decision processes, but may also serve to influence the broader policy networks in which the opinions of decision-makers develop, such as formal and informal sectoral networks, parliamentary committees and so forth.

There is general agreement regarding the need to adapt the choice of strategy and operational methods to the needs of the specific situation. There also seems to be a certain level of agreement on the need for a creative synthesis of systematic and critical approaches at both the strategic and the operational level. However, little if any guidance has been produced by the SEA community to aid in this process. Here, insights from the rich range of theories and associated empirical studies increasingly drawn upon in discussions on SEA (for example, deliberative democracy, collaborative and rational planning, strategy formation theories, policy analysis, political science, theories of learning and institutional change, and so on) hold valuable lessons for SEA.

Scholars of SEA theory have identified a variety of additional challenges for further research. Clearly, comparative case studies would be a valuable empirical contribution towards illuminating the differences across contexts, informed by recent developments in SEA theory. Much remains to be learned about the practical implementation and effects of the variety of methods and techniques that are discussed. Retrospective reviews of practice (for example, by using existing case studies) through various theoretical lenses may serve to make explicit the assumptions informing current SEA practice. Conversely, enrichment of theories may provide the basis for innovative (combinations of) methods and techniques, which could then be tested in practice. Challenges in terms of research methods remain open for debate: is qualitative analysis sufficient? How can in-depth case-studies illuminate wider theoretical thinking?

The importance of long-term research was also highlighted, which challenges the prevailing focus of SEA research on single cases of SEA application. Nilsson (2005) argued, for example, that the direct causal links between EA and learning are difficult to establish through short-term empirical research: 'While policy learning appears to be a theoretically appealing concept, it is problematic as an analytical concept. My study confirms that it is difficult to distinguish empirically, you need to have access to at least ten years of empirical work.' Research difficulties relate to both the long time scale at which detailed information must be available, and to the impossibility of setting up controlled experiments in which some of these causalities would be excluded.

While research can illuminate many of the issues and questions raised by SEA scholars and practitioners, a number of key dilemmas remain on the table that can only be resolved by agreement within the SEA community. The choice of the substantive purpose of SEA is one such issue. Without some degree of consensus on the purpose of this decision-aiding process, decision-makers will be understandably confused about the point of SEA. A similar issue concerns the scope of what is called SEA. Is it wise to include all deliberate activities directed at fostering (environmental) sustainability, including those

Table 28.1 *SEA theory and research: Summary statement*

Main trends and issues	The authors noted a confusion between means and ends, in the literature and during the debate at the Prague workshop. Confusion that is also reflected in the inaccurate or misleading use of terms that are fundamental to this field of research and practice: purpose, objective, role, function, strategic, context, object, tool, process, to quote the most important.
	The authors propose a distinction between the fundamental purpose of SEA and its delivery mechanisms, for example, providing environmental information (which has sometimes been considered as the aim of SEA). They also distinguish between institutionalizing SEA systems and individual applications (procedures and tools).
	They conclude that scholarly debate on the theory and methodology of SEA may be grouped under three (tightly connected) issues:
	1. The **substantive purpose** associated with SEA, which relates to the ultimate implications of societal decision processes. 2. The **strategy** adopted to achieve SEA's purpose. 3. The specific **mechanisms** (procedures, techniques, tools) for operationalizing SEA.
	Substantive purpose: Regarding the purpose of SEA there are two elements causing tension:
	1. Keep the environmental dimension central to SEA. 2. Focus on broader sustainability needs (socio-economic and environmental).
	Contributions to the workshops were based on advocacy of both environmental sustainability and the wider understanding of sustainable development as the substantive purpose of SEA. However, there were repeated and strong warnings against adopting the broader sustainability purpose.
	Strategy: The strategies proposed to achieve SEA's substantive purpose may be classified according to the differing assumptions made about the object of SEA and the context in which SEA operates. Basically, two points of view are evident in the discussion:
	1. Traditional 'procedural' strategy. 2. Transformative strategy.
	In practice, the authors argue that boundaries between these categories tend to blur, depending on the context of application. Context is increasingly central in SEA discourse.
	Mechanisms: What techniques, methods and procedures can or should be used by SEA practitioners to put preferred strategies into effect, and ultimately to contribute to the fundamental purpose of SEA? Two broad categories are proposed:
	1. Substantive analysis. 2. Mechanisms for communication and learning.
Main perspectives	The authors identify a myriad of expectations attached to SEA. A significant consequence of this is that there are no clearly identifiable or commonly agreed upon directions for the future development of SEA. This conceptual confusion presents a very real threat to the future of SEA. The authors of this chapter are of the conviction that making this case demands renewed attention to the theory of SEA to complement the prevailing emphasis on developing better techniques.

(continued)

Table 28.1 *(continued)*

The workshop and subsequent analysis of the state of the art in this area revealed that there is a growing body of theory being applied to SEA and that this is changing the trend of the 1990s where theory had been lagging behind practice.

Most scholars are drawing from and building on existing theories and do not feel the need for a new theory. The relatively recent opening of the EA discourse to contributions from theories of decision-making (Lindblom, 1971; Weiss, 1982; March and Olsen, 1989), planning (Lawrence, 2000), policy analysis (Torgerson, 1986; Thissen, 1997; Majone, 1989), social and organizational learning (Argyris, 1992), and democracy and governance (Grove-White, 1999) are a welcome development for SEA.

Key lessons	Scholarly debate on the theory and methodology of SEA may be grouped under three (tightly connected) issues:

1. The *substantive purpose* associated with SEA, which relates to the ultimate implications of societal decision processes.
2. The *strategy* adopted to achieve SEA's purpose.
3. The specific *mechanisms* (procedures, techniques, tools) for operationalizing SEA.

These three issues may be considered vital elements of a conceptual framework for SEA. They can also help practitioners, especially those responsible for the development of SEA systems for a sector, ministry or country, to structure such systems in a more reflexive way.

In terms of applying SEA in practice, scholars have increasingly highlighted the need for SEA practitioners to attend to the wider context in which it operates. Rather than assuming that SEA – and the decision-making process it seeks to influence – operates in a vacuum, scholars have recognized that these processes are embedded in policy (legislative, regulatory) and societal (political, cultural) contexts. As such, SEA practitioners need to understand these contextual dimensions, for the same reasons they need to pay attention to the immediate context: being more effective in influencing decisions and changing the habits and frames of mind of decision-makers.

Future directions	Research priorities for developing/strengthening SEA theory:

- There is a need for greater clarity of scholars' assumptions on the three core issues proposed here as a conceptual framework for the development of SEA: purpose, strategy (and object) and mechanisms.
- There is a general need for more interdisciplinarity and cross-fertilization of theoretical contributions from a range of disciplines (directly and indirectly relevant to SEA, such as communicative, collaborative and rational planning, strategy formation theories, policy analysis, theories of learning and institutional change, and so on), to address the above three elements of the conceptual framework.
- Questions such as whether SEA ought to adapt to the existing decision-making process or attempt to transform it, should be addressed both conceptually and through the analysis of practice.
- More empirical research is required to support the recent developments in the theory. Challenges in terms of research methods remain open for debate: is qualitative analysis sufficient? How can in-depth case-studies illuminate wider theoretical thinking? The importance of long-term research was also highlighted, which challenges the prevailing focus of SEA research on single cases of SEA application.

(continued)

Table 28.1 *(continued)*

Challenges for SEA (for example, for legislation, practice, linkages, cross-cutting issues or improving standards and building capacity):

- Clarifying the purpose of SEA remains a challenge, and is critical in defining the skills and capacity-building needed to institutionalize SEA systems, to design and carry out SEA processes and tools. It is considered an essential action to advance the profession.
- There is a need for guidance regarding how to adapt the choice of strategy and operational methods to the needs of the specific situation/context.
- Comparative case studies would be a valuable empirical contribution toward illuminating the differences across contexts, informed by recent developments in SEA theory.
- There is a need to learn about the practical implementation and effects of the variety of methods and techniques that are discussed. Retrospective reviews of practice (by using existing case studies, for example) through various theoretical lenses may serve to make explicit the assumptions informing current SEA practice.
- Conversely, enrichment of theories may provide the basis for innovative (combinations of) methods and techniques, which could then be tested in practice.

directly targeting what we called the immediate and wider context of PPP decision-making processes, under the SEA umbrella? Or, should the use of the term SEA be limited to those activities directly linked to specific, formal decision processes (as in the European Directive 2001/42/EC, for example)?

The authors of this chapter, with many workshop participants and others (see Sadler, 1999), believe that affirming environmental sustainability[14] as the substantive purpose of SEA is a key to carving out a definitive space for it in planning and policy-making arenas. Along with many SEA scholars, we would recommend a strategy for SEA that does not limit its scope to the assessment of individual PPPs but also facilitates longer-term change by challenging decision processes to embrace environmental sustainability goals – a strategy that creatively combines interactive, communicative processes alongside the systematic, disciplined analysis that has traditionally underpinned SEA. A range of processes and techniques are available for application and adaptation by SEA scholars and practitioners, which should be utilized according to the needs of the particular situation.

In all, it is clear that SEA scholars and practitioners alike are increasingly embracing the quest for strong conceptual foundations in SEA and for communicating the lessons of practice or knowledge-in-action toward that end. The revolutionary success of EIA was due in no small part to its purpose of improving the 'environmental quality of life' (Caldwell, 1989, p9) and its role both as a democratizing influence and as a 'worm in the brain' of the administrative state (Torgerson, 1997). These goals are pronounced in the professional aspirations of the International Association for Impact Assessment (IAIA), where EA is described as a process in which 'sound science and full public participation provide a foundation for equitable and sustainable development' in order to 'enhance the quality of life for all' (see www.iaia.org).

The contemporary task is to reinforce these lessons and to embrace these aspirations at higher levels of decision-making and to creatively apply them in the range of organizational and institutional locations of SEA that often exist beyond the state, but that increasingly influence the future of environmental governance and thus of environmental sustainability.

Acknowledgements

We sincerely thank the contributors to the SEA Theory and Research workshops for their diligent and thoughtful contributions to the discussion on which this chapter is partly based. Important issues raised by workshop participants have inevitably been left out of the discussion reported here, for which we apologise but hope that the chapter stimulates reflection and further debate. We would also like to thank Maria R. Partidário for her comments and suggestions on an earlier draft of this chapter.

Notes

1 This chapter draws on literature published until 2005. The unique value of this chapter is the account it provides of the critical debates, key observations and conclusions arising from workshop discussions at a special conference on 'International Experience and Perspectives in SEA' hosted by the International Association for Impact Assessment, and held in Prague in September 2005. As we have stressed elsewhere, 'the unique value of the Prague workshops was to provide a forum for double-loop learning amongst SEA scholars: a process of critical reflection on the norms and assumptions which inform SEA theory and practice' (Wallington et al, 2007, p577).

2 Paper contributions to the SEA Theory and Research workshops cited in the body of this chapter are formally referenced in the bibliography. Fourteen contributions were submitted to the Prague workshops, and at least 50 participants contributed to the workshop discussions. Several workshop papers were subsequently revised and published as a special journal issue (see Thissen et al, 2007).

3 Where discussions at these workshops helped to clarify issues – and the extent of agreement on an issue – they are referred to directly. Given the limited attention to the conceptual development of SEA in the literature, these debates are an important contribution to the 'state of the art' in SEA theory and research. Where comments from the workshop discussions are cited in the chapter, the format used is to cite only the name of the contributor (no date). Direct quotes of participants are in italics, to differentiate them from citations sourced in conference papers and the published literature.

4 The appearance of the expression 'strategic environmental assessment' probably occurs only in the early 1990s; however, several authors have stressed that forms of SEA have taken place in the US and elsewhere since the late 1960s and increasingly during the 1980s (Dalal-Clayton and Sadler, 2005, p6).

5 We follow Bartlett and Kurian's (1999) rationale in suggesting that SEA theorizing must begin with, and make sense of, the implicit and explicit assumptions of existing models of SEA (both normative and operational), as well as the normative claims made about the *raison d'être* of SEA.

6 The conceptual framework presented here has subsequently been developed further, and the revised version published in Wallington et al (2007).

7 Definitions of 'substantive' that convey our meaning here are 'real rather than apparent'; 'expressing existence'. A definition of 'purpose' is 'something set up as an ... end to be attained'. Purpose therefore suggests a settled determination. Relatedly, 'end' stresses the intended effect of action, in distinction or contrast to the action or means as such, in contrast to the 'strategy' described below. All definitions given in this chapter are taken from *Merriam-Webster Online* (www.m-w.com).

8 These strategies might also be thought of as 'instrumental' or 'intermediate' goals, since they are instrumental to the achievement of the primary purpose of SEA. However, we have chosen not to use the term goal or purpose here so as not to confuse these strategies with the substantive purpose of SEA. These strategies – such as the provision of environmental information to decision-makers – have often been considered to represent the ultimate purpose of SEA. It is our view, rather, that such strategies are better thought of as means to the ultimate end of SEA, rather than ends in themselves.

9 We use the term 'inquiry' here because we conceive of SEA as a process of inquiry – a systematic investigation – the aim of which is to provide an assessment of the environmental consequences of a given strategy, the traditional 'object' of inquiry. Assessment, in turn, involves a determination of the 'importance, size, or value' of these environmental consequences.

10 A definition of 'strategic' is 'necessary to or important in the initiation, conduct, or completion of a strategic plan'.

11 A definition of strategy is 'a careful plan or method; the art of devising or employing plans toward a goal'.

12 A definition of mechanism is 'a process or technique for achieving a result'.

13 We might recall Caldwell's comment that 'environmental impact analysis in its broader context represents a fundamental change in perceptions of how propositions regarding how society's environmental future should be evaluated and how political and economic decisions regarding the environment should be made' (Caldwell, 1989, p7).

14 The authors' understanding of the term 'environmental sustainability' follows that of Lynton K. Caldwell, a principal architect of NEPA. As Bartlett and Gladden (1995) point out, Caldwell's work represents the first call for making human-environmental relationships the focus of public policy. The interdependence of the social and biophysical ('natural') worlds clearly anticipates later sustainability discourses. The political implications of understanding humans as part of nature is a consistent theme in Caldwell's work, and the term 'environment' was meant to be an integrating concept for viewing reality. Far from a view of 'environment' as 'the substance of things', the idea of relationships is implicit in the term 'environmental', which should be understood as constitutive of the interactive relationships between ecological, political, physical, aesthetic and ethical aspects (e.g. Caldwell, 1989).

References

Argyris, C. (1992) *On Organisational Learning*, Blackwell, Cambridge, MA

Argyris, C. and Schön, D. (1978) *Organizational Learning: A Theory of Action Perspective*, Addison-Wesley Reading, MA

Audouin, M. and Lochner, P. (2000) *SEA in South Africa: Guideline Document*, report prepared for the Department of Environmental Affairs and Tourism (DEAT), Pretoria

Bailey, J. (1997) 'Environmental impact assessment and management: An underexplored relationship', *Environmental Management*, vol 21, no 3, pp317–327

Bailey, J. and Dixon, J. (1999) 'Policy environmental assessment', in Petts, J. (ed) *Handbook of Environmental Impact Assessment*, Blackwell Science, Oxford, pp251–272

Bailey, J. and Renton, S. (1997) 'Redesigning EIA to fit the future: SEA and the policy process', *Impact Assessment*, vol 15, pp319–334

Bartlett, R. V. (1997) 'The rationality and logic of NEPA revisited', in Clark, R. and Canter, L. (eds) *Environmental Policy and NEPA: Past, Present and Future*, St Lucie Press, Boca Raton, FL

Bartlett, R. V. and Gladden, J.N. (1995) 'Lynton K. Caldwell and environmental policy: What have we learnt?' in Caldwell, L.K., Bartlett, R.V. and Gladden, J.N. (eds) *The Environment as a Focus for Public Policy*, Texas A & M University Press, College station

Bartlett, R. V. and Kurian, P. A. (1999) 'The theory of environmental impact assessment: Implicit models of policy making', *Policy and Politics*, vol 27, no 4, pp415–433

Bina, O. (2003) *Re-conceptualising Strategic Environmental Assessment: Theoretical overview and case study from Chile*, unpublished PhD thesis, geography department, University of Cambridge

Boggs, J. P. (1993) 'Procedural vs substantive in NEPA law: Cutting the Gordian knot', *The Environmental Professional*, vol 15, pp25–34

Brown, A. L. (2000) 'SEA experience in development assistance using the environmental overview', in Partidário, M. R. and Clark, R. (eds) *Perspectives on Strategic Environmental Assessment*, Lewis Publishers, London, pp131–139

Brown, A. and Thérivel, R. (2000) 'Principles to guide the development of strategic environmental assessment methodology', *Impact Assessment and Project Appraisal*, vol 18, pp183–189

Caldwell, L. K. (1989) 'Understanding impact analysis: Technical process, administrative reform, policy principle', in Bartlett, R. V. (ed) *Policy Through Impact Assessment: Institutionalized Analysis as a Policy Strategy*, Greenwood Press, New York, Westport, Connecticut and London, pp7–16

Caratti, P., Dalkmann, H. and Jiliberto, R. (eds) (2004) *Analytical Strategic Environmental Assessment: Towards Better Decision-Making*, Edward Elgar Publishing Ltd, Cheltenham

Cashmore, M. (2004) 'The role of science in EIA: Process and procedure versus purpose in the development of theory', *Environmental Impact Assessment Review*, vol 24, no 4, pp403–426

Cashmore, M. and Nieslony, C. (2005) 'The contribution of environmental assessment to sustainable development: Towards a richer conceptual understanding', paper presented at the IAIA SEA Conference, Prague

Cashmore, M., Gwilliam, R., Morgan, R., Cobb, D. and Bond, A. (2004) 'The interminable issue of effectiveness: Substantive purposes, outcomes and research challenges in the advancement of EIA theory', *Impact Assessment and Project Appraisal*, vol 22, no 4, pp295–310

Cherp, A. (2005) 'From three Ps to five Ps: SEA and strategy formation schools', paper presented at the IAIA SEA Conference, Prague

Clark, R. (2000) 'Making EIA count in decision-making', in Partidário, M. R. and Clark, R. (eds) *Perspectives on Strategic Environmental Assessment*, Lewis Publishers, London, pp15–28

CSIR (Council for Scientific and Industrial Research) (2003) *Strategic Environmental Assessment: Port of Cape Town Sustainability Framework*, report no ENV-S-C

2003-074, prepared by S. Heather-Clark and M. Audoin for the National Port Authority Cape Town, Stellenbosch, South Africa

Culhane, P. J., Friesema, H. P. and Beecher, J. A. (1987) *Forecasts and Environmental Decisionmaking: The Content and Predictive Accuracy of Environmental Impact Statements*, Westview Press, Boulder, CO

Dalal-Clayton, B. and Sadler, B. (2005) *Strategic Environmental Assessment: A Sourcebook and Reference Guide to International Experience*, Earthscan, London

de Bruijn, H. and ten Heuvelhof, E. (2002) 'Policy analysis and decision making in a network: How to improve the quality of analysis and the impact on decision making', *Impact Assessment and Project Appraisal*, vol 20, no 4, pp232–242

Devon County Council (2004) *Strategic Environmental Assessment for the Devon Local Transport Plan 2006–2011: Scoping Report*, Devon County Council, Environment Directorate, Exeter

d'Ieteren, E. and Godart, M. (2005) 'Contextual issues in ensuring an added value of strategic environmental assessment to tourism planning: The case of the Walloon Region', paper presented at the IAIA SEA Conference, Prague

EC (European Commission) (2001) *Directive 2001/42/EC of the European Parliament and of the Council on the Assessment of the Effects of Certain Plans and Programmes on the Environment*, Luxembourg, 27 June 2001, http://europa.eu.int/comm/environment/eia/sea-support.htm

Eggenberger, M. and Partidário, M. R. (2000) 'Development of a framework to assist the integration of environmental, social and economic issues in spatial planning', *Impact Assessment and Project Appraisal*, vol 18, pp201–207

Faludi, A. (1987) *A Decision-Centred View of Environmental Planning*, Pergamon Press, Oxford

Fischer, T. B. (1999) 'Benefits arising from SEA application', *Environmental Impact Assessment Review*, vol 19, pp143–173

Fischer, T. B. (2003) 'Strategic environmental assessment in post-modern times', *Environmental Impact Assessment Review*, vol 23, pp155–170

Fischer, T. B. (2005) 'Effective tiering: Useful concept or useless chimera?', paper presented at the IAIA SEA Conference, Prague

Fisher, F. and Forester, J. (eds) (1993) *The Argumentative Turn in Policy Analysis and Planning*, Duke University Press, Durham, NC

Grove-White, R. (1999) 'Environment, risk and democracy', in Jacobs, M. (ed) *Greening the Millenium*, Blackwell, Oxford, pp44–83

Harashina, S. (2005) 'A communication theory of strategic environmental assessment', paper presented at the IAIA SEA Conference, Prague

Hilding-Rydevik, T. and Bjarnadóttir, H. (2005) 'Understanding the SEA implementation context and the implications for the aim of SEA and the direction of SEA research', paper presented at the IAIA SEA Conference, Prague

Hoppe, R. (1998) 'Policy analysis, science and politics: From speaking truth to power to making sense together', *Science and Public Policy*, vol 23, no 3, pp201–210

Jackson, T. and Illsley, B. (2005) 'An examination of the theoretical rational for using strategic environmental assessment of public sector policies, plans and programmes to deliver environmental justice, drawing on the example of Scotland', paper presented at the IAIA SEA Conference, Prague

João, E. (2005) 'SEA as a platform for dialogue and a springboard for innovation?', paper presented at the IAIA SEA Conference, Prague

Jones, C., Baker, M., Carter, J., Jay, S., Short, M. and Wood, C. (eds) (2005) *Strategic Environmental Assessment and Land Use Planning*, Earthscan, London

Kørnøv, L. and Nielsen, E. (2005) 'Institutional change: A premise for impact assessment integration', paper presented at the IAIA SEA Conference, Prague

Kørnøv, L. and Thissen, W. (2000) 'Rationality in decision and policy-making: Implications for strategic environmental assessment', *Impact Assessment and Project Appraisal*, vol 18, pp191–200

Lawrence, D. P. (2000) 'Planning theories and environmental impact assessment', *Environmental Impact Assessment Review*, vol 20, pp607–625

Lee, N. and Walsh, F. (1992) 'Strategic environmental assessment: An overview', *Project Appraisal*, vol 7, pp126–136

Leknes, E. (2005) 'SEA and types of decision-making processes: A decision-taker's perspective', paper presented at the IAIA SEA Conference, Prague

Lindblom, C. E. (1971) 'Defining the policy problem', in Castles, F. G., Murray, D. and Potter, D. C. (eds) *Decisions, Organizations and Society*, Penguin Books in association with The Open University Press, Harmondsworth

Majone, G. (1989) *Evidence, Argument and Persuasion in the Policy Process*, University Press, New Haven

March, J. G. and Olsen, J. P. (1989) *Rediscovering Institutions: The Organizational Basis of Politics*, The Free Press, New York

Markus, E. (2005) 'SEA and alternatives', paper presented at the IAIA SEA Conference, Prague

Mayer, I. S., Els van Daalen, C. and Bots, P. W. G. (2004) 'Perspectives on policy analyses: A framework for understanding and design', *International Journal of Technology, Policy and Management*, vol 4, pp169–191

McPhail, I. (2005) 'Strategic environmental auditing', paper presented at the IAIA SEA Conference, Prague

Mercier, J.-R. and Kulsum, A. (2005) 'World Bank', in Jones, C., Baker, M., Carter, J., Jay, S., Short, M. and Wood, C. (eds) *Strategic Environmental Assessment and Land Use Planning*, Earthscan, London, pp261–274

Nilsson, M. (2005) 'The role of assessments and institutions for policy learning: A study on Swedish climate and nuclear policy formation', paper presented at the IAIA SEA Conference, Prague

Nilsson, M. and Dalkmann, H. (2001) 'Decision making and strategic environmental assessment', *Journal of Environmental Assessment Policy and Management*, vol 3, pp305–327

Nitz, T. and Brown, A. L. (2000) 'SEA must learn how policy-making works', paper presented at the IAIA annual meeting, Hong Kong, 19–23 June

Noble, B. F. and Storey, K. (2001) 'Towards a structured approach to strategic environmental assessment', *Journal of Environmental Assessment Policy & Management*, vol 3, pp483–508

Nooteboom, S. (2005) 'Impact assessment procedures as incentive for social learning: Signs of a new Dutch polder model', paper presented at the IAIA SEA Conference, Prague

NRC (National Research Council) (1996) *Understanding Risk*, National Academy Press, Washington, DC

Owen, J. and Lambert, F. (1995) 'Roles for evaluation in learning organizations', *Evaluation*, vol 1, pp259–273

Owens, S., Rayner, T. and Bina, O. (2004) 'New agendas for appraisal: Reflections on theory, practice and research', *Environment and Planning A*, vol 36, pp1943–1959

Partidário, M. R. (1999) 'Strategic environmental assessment: Principles and potential', in Petts, J. (ed) *Handbook of Environmental Impact Assessment*, vol 1, Blackwell, Oxford

Partidário, M. R. and Clark, R. (eds) (2000) *Perspectives on Strategic Environmental Assessment*, Lewis Publishers, London

Rapoport, A. (1989) *Decision Theory and Decision Behaviour: Normative and Descriptive Approaches*, Kluwer Academic Publications, Dordrecht

RCEP (Royal Commission on Environmental Pollution) (1998) *Twenty-First Report. Setting Environmental Standards*, Cm 4053, The Stationery Office, London

Rotmans, J., Kemp, R. and van Asselt, M. (2001) 'More evolution than revolution: Transition management in public policy', *Foresight*, vol 3, pp1–17

Sadler, B. (1999) 'A framework for environmental sustainability assessment and assurance', in Petts, J. (ed) *Handbook of Environmental Impact Assessment*, vol 1, Blackwell, Oxford, pp12–32

Sadler, B. and Verheem, R. (1996) *Strategic Environmental Assessment: Status, Challenges and Future Directions*, Ministry of Housing, Spatial Planning and the Environment, The Hague

Schön, D. A. and Rein, M. (1994) *Frame Reflection: Toward the Resolution of Intractable Policy Controversies*, Basic Books, New York

Sheate, W., Dagg, S., Richardson, J., Aschermann, R., Palerm, J. and Steen, U. (2001) 'SEA and integration of the environment into strategic decision-making', vol 1, report to the European Commission, http://europa.eu.int/comm/environment/eia/sea-support.htm

Taylor, S. (1984) *Making Bureaucracies Think: The Environmental Impact Statement Strategy of Administrative Reform*, Stanford University Press, Stanford

Thérivel, R. and Brown, A. L. (1999) 'Methods of strategic environmental assessment', in Petts, J. (ed) *Handbook of Environmental Impact Assessment*, vol 1, Blackwell, Oxford, pp441–464

Thérivel, R. and Partidário, M. R. (eds) (1996) *The Practice of Strategic Environmental Assessment*, Earthscan, London

Thérivel, R. and Partidário, M. R. (2000) 'The future of SEA', in Partidário, M. R. and Clark, R. (eds) *Perspectives on Strategic Environmental Assessment*, Lewis Publishers, London, pp271–280

Thérivel, R., Wilson, E., Thompson, S., Heany, D. and Pritchard, D. (1992) *Strategic Environmental Assessment*, Earthscan, London

Thissen, W. (1997) 'From SEA to integrated assessment: A policy analysis perspective', *Environmental Assessment*, vol 5, no 3, pp24–25

Thissen, W., Bina, O. and Wallington, T. (eds) (2007) Special issue on Strategic Environmental Assessment Theory, *Environmental Impact Assessment Review*, vol 27, no 7

Torgerson, D. (1986) 'Between knowledge and politics: The three faces of policy analysis', *Policy Sciences*, vol 19, pp3–59

Torgerson, D. (1997) 'Green political thought and the nature of politics', paper presented at the Environmental Justice Conference, University of Melbourne, Australia, 1–3 October

UNECE (United Nations Economic Commission for Europe) (2003) *Protocol on Strategic Environmental Assessment to the Convention on the Environmental Impact Assessment in a Transboundary Context*, UNECE, Kiev, www.unece.org/env/eia/sea/_protocol.htm

Van de Kerkhof, M. and Wieczorek, A. (2005) 'Learning and stakeholder participation in transition processes towards sustainability: Methodological considerations', *Technological Forecasting and Social Change*, vol 72, pp733–747

Van de Kerkhof, M., Hisschemöller, M. and Spanjersberg, M. (2002) 'Shaping diversity in participatory foresight studies: Experiences with interactive backcasting in a stakeholder dialogue on long term climate policy in the Netherlands', *Greener Management International*, vol 37, pp85–99

Van der Knaap, A. (1995) 'Policy evaluation and learning', *Evaluation*, vol 1, pp189–216

van der Riet, O. (2003) *Policy Analysis in Multi-Actor Setting: Navigating between Negotiated Nonsense and Superfluous Knowledge*, Eburon, Delft

van Eeten, M. J. G. (2001) 'The challenge ahead for deliberative democracy: In reply to Weale', *Science and Public Policy*, vol 28, pp423–426

Vicente, G. and Partidário, M. R. (2005) 'Role of SEA in fostering better decision-making', paper presented at the IAIA SEA Conference, Prague

Wallington, T. (2002) *Civic Environmental Pragmatism: A Dialogical Framework for Strategic Environmental Assessment*, PhD thesis, Institute for Sustainability and Technology Policy, Murdoch University, Perth

Wallington, T., Bina, O. and Thissen, W. (2007) 'Theorising strategic environment assessment: Fresh perspectives and future challenges', *Environmental Impact Assessment Review*, vol 27, no 7, pp569–584

Weaver, P., Jansen, L., Van Grootveld, G., van Spiegel, E. and Vergragt, P. (2000) *Sustainable Technology Development*, Greenleaf Publishing, Sheffield

Weiss, C. (1982) 'Policy research in the context of diffuse decision-making', *Policy Studies Review Annual*, vol 6, pp19–36

Weston, J. (2000) 'EIA, decision-making theory and screening and scoping in UK practice', *Journal of Environmental Planning and Management*, vol 43, pp185–203

Williams, J. M. (2005) 'Strategic environmental assessment: Looking at the bigger picture', paper presented at the IAIA SEA Conference, Prague

Wood, C. (2003) 'Rose-Hulman Award acceptance speech', annual meeting of the IAIA, Marrakech, Morocco, 14–20 June

Wood, C. and Djeddour, M. (1992) 'Strategic environmental assessment: EA of policies, plans and programmes', *Impact Assessment Bulletin*, vol 10, pp3–22

World Bank (2005) *Integrating Environmental Considerations in Policy Formulation – Lessons from Policy-Based SEA Experience*, Environment Department, World Bank, Washington, DC

29
Professional and Institutional Capacity-building for SEA

Maria R. Partidário and Lee Wilson

Introduction

The concept of capacity-building is founded on principles of democracy, participation, development and continuous improvement of skills, shared learning processes and equal access to opportunities. The debate on sustainable development preceding and following the 1992 United Nations Conference on Environment and Development (UNCED) placed capacity-building at the top of priorities for international development assistance, as a condition to enable the achievement of effective and sound development in all regions. Currently, it is also recognized that this activity is about ensuring technical and decision capacities that will lead to ways of making better decisions and environment and social issues are integral parts of economic development.

Building capacity means creating conditions for effective and efficient performance and improved capabilities to do something. In strategic environmental assessment (SEA), capacity-building refers: (a) to the improvement of structures of governance and institutional frameworks for SEA; (b) to the strengthening of organizations that conduct SEA; and (c) to the production of guidance documents and training of individuals who perform SEA. The particular objective of capacity-building for SEA is to develop and improve its process and methodology; it involves a broad, long-term focus and thinking that informs professionals, decision-makers and the general public on the consequences and sustainability of strategic decisions.

The specific needs for SEA capacity-building depend on country-specific cultural and decision-making contexts but the general trend is one of unprecedented growth in demand and a response that is both uncoordinated and falls far short of satisfying this demand. Although training can provide benefits, the more pressing need is to develop coherent institutional frameworks and basic approaches to governance that support and promote interaction and dialogue among key organizations and individuals, accountability processes and a sound SEA system that is adapted to country-specific context and needs.

In this chapter, we illustrate current efforts toward professional and institutional capacity-building for SEA and argue that these should influence decision-making as a key and ultimate purpose. Based on discussions, experiences and success stories presented at the 2005 International Association for Impact Assessment (IAIA) Prague Conference on SEA, we conclude with principles and forms for improving capacity to influence decision-making, both in terms of governance and professional performance. The chapter also further provides an incomplete consideration of current international and national project and professional guidance documents directed towards SEA capacity-building.

Background: Recent developments towards SEA capacity-building

SEA is a strategic, comprehensive and integrated assessment approach that has a distinctive role to play in relation to other tools such as project environmental impact assessment (EIA), cumulative impact assessment (CIA), policy analysis or planning. While sharing common roots with other impact assessment tools, SEA follows integrative, holistic and systemic principles and approaches and assumes the role of facilitating planning and policy decision-making. SEA falls under the strategic and integrative thinking type of tools, with the particular aim of helping planning and policy-making strategies to focus on the key environmental and sustainability issues and on the appropriate strategic options, including the opportunities and risks of undertaking such options. SEA does this by adopting multidimensional and multi-stakeholder approaches, in a rather complex framework of analysis, yet acting at the appropriate scale according to its object of assessment (Partidário, 2007a). Strategic thinking and integration thus underlie the essence of SEA, in support of new modes of development that aim at sustainability.

A number of cases presented at Prague illustrate experience with building capacities for SEA and forms (methods, initiatives) whereby such capacity can be improved, however context-specific these may be (Ferdowsi et al, 2005; Fleming and Campbell, 2005; Ghanimé, 2005; O'Mahoney et al, 2005; Susani, 2005). Among the experiences, some have a greater focus on environmental issues, others move from an environmental to a sustainability focus as a result of capacity-building efforts. The policy and planning culture, and the range and type of instruments (for example, EIA, policy, plan, auditing) to which SEA relates all influence how this process is used and the efforts that must be made to improve professional and institutional capacities.

Overall, the cases indicated a general lack of SEA knowledge and experience with insufficient capacities in leading institutions or lack of awareness of authorities. Under the circumstances, it is hard to judge the effectiveness of SEA while there is a need to improve knowledge on SEA and educate decision-makers.

Ghanimé (2005) documented recent global assessments that show that progress towards environmental sustainability has been disappointingly weak. The lack of progress is attributed, in part, to inefficient and inadequate institutional capacities, from enforcing environmental legislation to monitoring environmental indicators. Developing capacity to effectively address the global lag of environmental sustainability involves further integrating environmental assessment in national institutions and systems of policy making. For Ghanimé (2005), SEA offers the potential to develop capacity for making complex development choices in relation to policies, plans and programmes (PPPs) and major public investments. Capacity development for SEA is an ongoing process of transformation that requires resources, a willingness to learn and the use of existing capacities.

An example of institutional support is *Good Practice Guidance on SEA in Development Cooperation*, from the Organisation for Economic Co-operation and Development (OECD) Development Assistance Committee (DAC) (see Table 29.2). Support for capacity development in SEA processes includes linking poverty alleviation strategies to environmental assets and constraints and assessing the needs and opportunities for using SEA in the poverty-environment process.

Ferdowsi et al (2005) reviewed the model of SEA capacity-building programme initiated in Iran, in which a 'core group' of national professionals from various sectors – including non-governmental organizations (NGOs) – was brought together. The core group was provided with technical and conceptual assistance from an international expert in the field of SEA. The national team was charged with assessing the needs for SEA, devising a national SEA model and developing technical guidelines that ensure effective application of SEA to PPPs in Iran. Project outputs are intended to contribute to and promote ongoing government activities regarding the Sustainable Development Strategy.

Susani (2005) identified the consultative role of the Environment Agency of England and Wales in specific stages of the SEA process as an opportunity to guide, monitor and influence the SEA process since approximately 100–200 SEA per year are expected to be completed. Susani also referred to the Environmental Agency's responsibility in providing environmental relevant data and to a number of initiatives to facilitate and maximize its role as an effective consultee. These include the following:

- Identification of a suite of SEA objectives, to be offered as part of the Environmental Agency's consultation response and reflective of key drivers for the agency.
- Compilation of in-house baseline data packages useful for SEA preparation, to be distributed electronically to plan/programme makers.
- A dedicated internal guidance document on SEA and the consultation process to ensure that responses are consistent, effective and representative of Environmental Agency concerns.
- A one-page 'dos and don'ts' guide as a memorandum for plan-makers.

Similarly in Ireland, the Environmental Protection Agency (EPA) must be consulted by competent authorities when screening for or undertaking SEA. O'Mahoney et al (2005) addressed this role and the guidance developed for plan/programme-makers and SEA practitioners. They indicate that air and water monitoring programmes provide relevant background information on the current state of the environment and assist in the identification of environmental problems and issues, while geographical information systems (GIS) have been a key tool in screening and identifying key issues in scoping exercises.

Fleming and Campbell (2005) highlighted the importance of cultural heritage in SEA, noting that many SEA directives, conventions and national policies include this aspect as well as biophysical and social issues. Cultural heritage can be a key factor in strategic development because it constitutes an actual or potential socio-economic asset in many countries. Ignoring it can jeopardize the sustainability of policies, programmes and strategies and a special effort is required to ensure that cultural heritage is fully covered in SEA and that the concerned institutions participate in the process. The professional and institutional capacity-building requirements for this purpose are substantial, especially as the concerned institutions are marginalized in national decision-making in many countries.

In the case of EIA, a number of methods and instruments are being developed to improve coverage of cultural heritage. In the case of SEA, further developments are required; for example, at the strategic level, an entire cultural landscape may be affected. Similarly, biophysical and social impacts, such as changes in settlement patterns, can affect the use and physical status of cultural heritage by changing the basic character of an area. Furthermore, the socio-economic value of heritage may change as a result of policies such as the decision to promote tourism. Therefore, new models, databases, training strategies and capacity-building approaches are required.

Professional training

Professional training is the dominant component in SEA capacity-building. Every year, dozens of professional training events on SEA take place in different parts of the world. Many of these are more supply-driven than demand-driven. Even in major capacity-building programmes, the training activity is not only the first to be developed but often the only one. Very little feedback is available so far on changes that result to governance structures such as institutional redesign or reform of decision-making towards sustainability.

Professional development and institutional reform

Tables 29.1 and 29.2 provide an illustration of major capacity-building programmes that have been conducted to date internationally and offer a view of a sounder approach, including traditional training, on-the-job training and institutional reform. For example, in Eastern Europe, initiatives led by the Regional Environmental Centre (REC), United Nations Development Programme (UNDP), United Nations Environment Programme (UNEP) and multi-financial institutions offer what appears to be a larger consistent approach to SEA capacity-building. The World Bank experience with the Structured Learning Programme to develop in-house SEA capacity is an outstanding example for a major world organization.

Table 29.1 *Projects directed at professional development and institutional reform*

Project	Date(s)	Delivering institution(s)	Recipient institution(s)	Context
Capacity-Building in SEA of the Hydropower Project, Vietnam	2005	Asian Development Bank (ADB)	Vietnamese agencies	ADB technical assistance – institutional capacity – assessment of needs, on-the-job training, follow-up of staff's capacity-building results SEA power sector development
Conflict-Affected Areas	2005	World Bank		Paper addressing how to build capacity for an SEA in conflict-affected areas
Strategic Environmental Assessment Information Service		Centre for Sustainability		Provide a gateway to the latest information on SEA in the UK
SEA Network Website		UNDP	Support to Africa, Arab States, Asia and the Pacific, Europe and the Commonwealth of Independent States	SEA Network and Guidance and SEA and National Sustainable Development Strategies
SEA Capacity Development in EECCA Countries		United Nations Economic Commission for Europe (UNECE)	Eastern Europe, Caucasus and Central Asia (EECCA) countries	Activities under the Espoo EIA Convention and its Protocol on SEA
ENEA Capacity-Building Working Group	2004	European Commission (EC) Unit D3 and REC	European Union (EU) member states and accession countries	Improve capacity-building for integration of environment in Structural Funds and Cohesion Fund programme and projects
Structured Learning Programme		World Bank	World Bank staff and countries	Increasing World Bank capacity-building on SEA

Source: ADB (2005); World Bank (undated, 2005); EC (undated); www.sea-info.net; www.seataskteam.net

Guidance for professional development

The development of professional guidance is an important element for on-the-job capacity-building. The rationale for the development of guidance is developed in Chapter 31, but Table 29.1 provides an illustration of some recent activities to support professional development and institutional reform. Currently, SEA guidance is the province not only of multilateral and bilateral organizations, such as those indicated in Table 29.2, but also of several countries that are developing national, regional and sectoral guidance.

Table 29.2 *Professional guidance for SEA capacity-building*

Published guidance	Date(s)	Delivering institution(s)	Recipient institution(s)	Context
SEA Guidance		UK Environment Agency	UK institutions	European Directive 2001/42/EC General and Specific guidance (land-use and spatial planning and transport planning, climate change, biodiversity)
SEA Open Educational Resource	2001	United Nations University (UNU)		Initiated with a Distance Learning Course in collaboration with Oxford Brookes University, now also includes a SEA wiki
SEA Distance Learning Course	2002	World Bank/IAIA/ State Environmental Protection Administration (SEPA)	China government relevant officials	Request from China for SEA Training
EIA Training Resource Manual	2002	UNEP	Developing countries and countries in transition to market economies	Capacity-building and the environment
Guidance on the Implementation of Directive 2001/42/EC	2003	European Commission (EC) Directorate General Environment (DGENV)	European member states and accession countries	European Directive 2001/42 on the assessment of the effects of certain plans and programmes on the environment
Guidance for Strategic Impact Assessment in Land-Use Planning	2003	DGOTDU-Portugal	Portugal Land-use planning	
Canadian International Development Agency (CIDA) Handbook on SEA	2004	CIDA	CIDA's operations in developing countries	Guides CIDA employees through the Agency's SEA process
EIA and SEA Manual	2004	UNEP	Developing countries and countries in transition to market economies	UNEP's Economics and Trade Branch EIA and SEA Programme

(continued)

Table 29.2 *(continued)*

Published guidance	Date(s)	Delivering institution(s)	Recipient institution(s)	Context
Coastal Erosion	2004	DGENV		EU Coastal Management Policy + SEA
Training Manual: SEA of Plans and Programmes in Lebanon	2004	UNDP	Lebanese land-use planning	UNDP Energy and environment, European Commission, LIFE Third Countries Programme project entitled Strategic Environmental Assessment and Land Use Planning in Lebanon
SEA Transports Manual (Beacon)	2005	EU Directorate General Energy and Transports	EU member states and worldwide	EU Transports Policy + SEA
Hong-Kong SEA Manual (interactive edition)	2005	Environmental Protection Department, Hong Kong	Hong Kong	
SEA for Cohesion Policy 2007–2013	2006	EU	EU member states	EU Regional Development Policy + SEA
SEA Toolkit	2006	Scottish Executive	Scottish institutions	Directive 2001/42/EC
Resource Manual to support the application of the Protocol on SEA	2006	UNECE/REC		UNECE Convention on Transboundary Impacts – SEA Protocol
SEA Good Practice Guidance for Development Cooperation	2006	OECD-DAC Envir-onet Task Team		SEA for development assistance
Guidance for Strategic-based Approach to SEA	2007	APA – Portuguese Environment Agency	All spatial planning and sectoral organizations	Assist the implementation of national legislation pursuant to European Directive 2001/42
Integrated Assessment – Mainstreaming Sustainability into Policy-making – A Guidance Manual	2009	UNEP	Market economies, developing countries and countries in transition to market economies	Integrated assessment

Source: CIDA (2004); DGOTDU (2003); EC (2003, 2004, 2005); EU (2006); Hong Kong Environmental Protection Department (2005); OECD (undated); Partidário (2007b); Scottish Executive (2006); UK Environment Agency (undated); UNDP (2005); UNECE (2006); UNEP (2002, 2004); UNU (undated)

Drivers in SEA capacity-building

Partidário (2004) identified three priorities for improving current problems and enhance the strategic nature of SEA:

1 **Improve the relationship between SEA and decision-making:** This issue requires presenting decision-makers with information that is timely, short, concise, relevant and focused. It is a change in emphasis from the tradition of providing thick reports with comprehensive documentation of impacts, which are often overly complex and filed too late in the decision process. To address this issue, it is critical to understand how the decision process functions, what information is needed and when.
2 **Improve communication skills and mechanisms in SEA:** This issue addresses the many different barriers to effective communication such as diverse and unclear nomenclature and artificial boundaries that separate sectors, disciplines or regions. Communication across a network of actors is seen as a fundamental condition for the effectiveness of SEA (see Chapters 28 and 30). At least part of the solution is to develop a simple, uniform, common-sense language for SEA (Partidário, 2007a; Vicente and Partidário, 2006).
3 **Make SEA attractive and increase win-win opportunities:** This is a marketing issue and requires documenting and disseminating success stories that demonstrate real benefits and/or reduced costs from modest effort.

Development is about realities, expectations, priorities and choice. Together, these make up the context in which SEA operates and the leading motive of decision-making. Increased capacities for SEA are therefore inherently linked to improvement in decision frameworks, including policy design, political engagement, leadership (motivation, prioritization, governance) and institutional architecture.

Policies are, or should be, masters of development. In strategic approaches, policies are the strings that operate the mechanisms and the design of policies becomes a sensitive dimension, while the absence of policies can leave medium to long-term development without direction (Partidário, 2004). Political engagement and commitment provides the master energy and leadership provides the direction, ensuring motivation, long-term perspectives, coherent and transparent priorities and rules of governance. Vicente and Partidário (2006) and Genter (2004) argue that SEA should be about 'working together' and 'avoiding inter-sectoral or geographical conflicts'. Therefore, the institutional architecture and engineering that characterizes the context of decision-making is critical to the success of SEA (Partidário, 2004).

Based on the needs for improved decision-making frameworks and the components of capacity-building suggested by George (2001), Box 29.1 suggests essential drivers in the process of creating capacity for SEA. These include policy, institutional and technical drivers but also financial and human resources, as introduced by Partidário (2004). Such drivers and resources relate strongly to key issues in SEA that have been advanced by many authors at

---

Box 29.1 *Key drivers in SEA capacity-building*

Policy drivers:

- Policy framework for sustainability, environment, development.
- Policy interactions, priorities, policy tools to operate the essential policies.
- Decision-making structure, whether formal and informal, but focused, open and effective, marked by political engagement and inter-sectoral cooperation.
- Leadership in mastering processes of involvement, of dialogues, of prioritization, of values management and consensus-building to get choices that make up decisions.

Institutional drivers:

- Institutional framework, relationships, interactions, mechanisms.
- Accountibilities, essential in decisions quality control.
- Power relationship – sharing and strengthening power.

Technical drivers:

- Cultural mind-set.
- Typical tools (planning, evaluation, decision).
- Needs assessment, both in substance and in process.
- Guidance.
- Communication capacities.
- Participation tools, dialogues.
- Consensus-building traditional knowledge – a pool of essential rules-of-thumb and good common sense.

Financial and human drivers:

- Availability of financial resources.
- Cost-effectiveness practices.
- Expertise and competence of human resources.

Source: Partidário (2004)

---

various times (Partidário, 1996; Sadler and Verheem, 1996). Such key issues must be adopted and put in place as part of capacity-building approach for SEA.

Improving capacity-building for SEA

Discussions at the Prague conference identified trends and issues that help to understand the reasons why SEA capacity-building is important (Table 29.3). The need to develop knowledge on SEA and to share such knowledge and experience across PPP-making and with environmental and sectoral authorities and public decision-makers were among the priority issues. Process issues were also highlighted, including the need to apply the SEA and planning processes as coordinated and simultaneous actions that share several aspects, such as the engagement of different stakeholders and the consideration of options in both process.

Current trends indicate that both state of environment reporting at European, national and regional contexts and GIS are important tools in SEA. However, they need to be tailor-made for SEA, while resources need to be harmonized across countries that share transboundary issues to help fulfill the UNECE SEA Protocol.

The challenges that face planning and environmental authorities and decision-makers are numerous in relation to the issues identified above, particularly the need to develop and tailor environmental reporting and resource tools and to ensure ongoing review of SEA quality and successes in order to learn from experience. Other key challenges for improving SEA include: the need to develop joint SEA teams within and between planning and environmental authorities, web-based dissemination of experiences and guidance, research, professional training and undergraduate education on SEA. A future challenge is the need to focus SEA on strategic issues at any decision-level with project-related and detailed level impacts being addressed under EIA.

Based on such issues and challenges, ten principles for improving the capacity of SEA to impact decision-making process and decision-makers were

---

Box 29.2 *Ten principles for improving the capacity of SEA to impact the decision-making process and decision-makers*

1 Proactive leadership.
2 Institutional systems – oversight of process and implementation.
3 Transparency – evaluation and monitoring.
4 Results-oriented.
5 Follow-up processes: monitoring, evaluation, management and communication.
6 Provision for early and continuous information to decision-makers.
7 Simple and explicit environmental report and recommendations for decision-makers.
8 Building trust.
9 Promotion of SEA as a platform for dialogue exchange (with decision-makers and key stakeholders).
10 Acknowledgement of the variation in the political economy.

Box 29.3 *Professional and institutional forms of improving SEA capacity to impact decision-making*

- Knowledge-sharing.
- Decision-maker brought on board and encouraged to engage in the SEA process from day one.
- Sensitization of all stakeholders involved.
- Mediation processes.
- Training for plan-makers and decision-makers on SEA process and links with plan-making process.
- Understanding of policy system.
- Considering levels of information for public/decision-makers according to the respective level of decision-making.
- Recognizing the added value to plan/programme following SEA.
- Ability/opportunity to impact/influence decision-making process.
- More systematically influence people and organizational systems.
- Potential for recommendations of SEA environmental report to impact decision-making process through planning process.
- Need for SEA to be totally integrated into decision-making system/process taking into account policy context.

Table 29.3 *SEA capacity-building: Summary statement*

Main trends and issues	Recognition of the fundamental role and importance of building capacity for SEA, particularly to enable effective impact on decision-making. Examples of capacity-building efforts are increasing, namely those driven by international development efforts, although public organizations also reveal internal efforts for increased capacity. Building professional and institutional capacity is taking place at national, organizational and individuals levels, envisaging national SEA systems, SEA-contexts and internal institutional frameworks. Key issues relate to: • Levels ('tiers') at which capacity-building is needed, and how they relate (national, organizational, individual). • SEA context (policy and planning practice, institutional set-up, openess of political system, collaborative and constructive relationships). • Intangible factors (for example, trust, power relationships, willingness to share). • Tangible factors (for example, resources availability, in-built knowledge).
Main perspectives	Current status shows that SEA capacity-building is yet not in place, and what is being developed is still far from ideal. However, it is also recognized that it is hard to judge the effectiveness of SEA. Current experiences focus on building capacities for SEA and illustrate forms (methods, initiatives) whereby such capacity can be improved, however context-specific these may be.

(continued)

Table 29.3 *(continued)*

	Focus is on environmental issues in some cases, others move from environmental to sustainability focus of SEA as a result of capacity-building efforts. The policy and planning culture, and the range and type of instruments (for example, EIA, policy, plan, auditing) to which SEA relates, influence the way SEA is used and the efforts that must be made to improve professional and institutional capacities. There is lack of knowledge and experience in SEA. There are insufficient capacities in leading institutions or lack of awareness in authorities. There is a need to learn for better SEA. Education of decision-makers is needed.
Key lessons	Key lessons are driven from the two key questions raised for discussion: principles and forms of improving the capacity of SEA to impact decisions. As principles for improving the capacity of SEA to impact decision-making: • Strong leadership. • Building trust. • Institutional oversight (internal and external). • Knowledge-sharing. • SEA as a learning process and a platform for exchanged dialogue. • Transparency and accountability. • Results-oriented. • Early and continuous information to decision-makers. • Simple and explicit in view of the audience. • Acknowledgement of the variation in the political economy. • Continuity of the SEA process and adaptibility to planning changes. As forms of improving: • Decision-maker brought on board and encouraged to engage in the SEA process from day one. • Set institutional systems to oversight process and implementation (internal and external). • Awareness. • Mediation processes. • Training for plan-makers and decision-makers on SEA process and links with plan-making process. • Understanding of policy system. • Promote knowledge-sharing across professional individuals and institutions. • Consider 'tiering' – levels of information for public/decision-makers/level of decision-making. • Recognition of added value to plan/programme following SEA. • Ability/opportunity to impact/influence decision-making process through the planning process. • Follow-up (evaluation and monitoring) for increased transparency and accountability. • More systematically influence people and organizational systems. • Need for SEA to be totally integrated into decision-making system/process taking into account policy context.
Future directions	Move towards better understanding and clarification of the purpose of SEA, demystifying the concept, making it more strategic and ensuring it is decision-focused and results-oriented, rather than process-oriented. Demonstrate the added-value of SEA to decision-making and ensure future capacity to enhance such value. Lead capacity-building through sharing knowledge, for example the role of websites and inherent links. Educate decision-makers. Enhance the strategic role of SEA to impact decision-making.

put forward by Prague workshop participants (Box 29.2), along with actions for improvement (Box 29.3).

Conclusions

As discussed at the Prague conference, SEA capacity-building is linked to the need to improve organizational frameworks for sustainable development (see Chapter 30). It was also recognized that capacity for SEA is yet not in place and what is being developed is far from ideal. Principles and forms of building capacity need to be adapted to each country's needs and realities, not driven by standard approaches developed in particular political and institutional contexts and sometimes driven by commercial or business purposes.

At the end of the day, capacity-building for SEA should lead to better informed decision-making processes and better informed decision-makers. It would benefit from a systematic effort to identify specifically: the conditions that prevent SEA from being optimally accomplished; the types of actions that would benefit from SEA capacity; the experiences in accomplishing such actions; and a synopsis of good practice in SEA capacity-building. Such a systematic analysis could lead to an action plan for SEA capacity-building that could be implemented by those who require, oversee or conduct SEA.

References

ADB (Asian Development Bank) (2005) 'Technical assistance Socialist Republic of Vietnam: Capacity building in the strategic environmental assessment of the hydropower project', ADB, Manila, www.adb.org/Documents/TARs/VIE/39536-VIE-TAR.pdf, accessed March 2007

CIDA (Canadian International Development Agency) (2004) *Strategic Environmental Assessment of Policy, Plan, and Program Proposals: CIDA Handbook*, CIDA, Ottawa, www.acdi-cida.gc.ca/INET/IMAGES.NSF/vLUImages/Environmental%20assessment/$file/SEA-Handbook.pdf, accessed March 2007

DGOTDU (Direcção-Geral do Ordenamento do Território e Desenvolvimento Urbano) (2003) 'Guidance for strategic impact assessment in land-use planning', DGOTDU, Lisbon

EC (European Commission) (undated) 'ENEA Capacity-Building Working Group', http://ec.europa.eu/environment/integration/pdf/capacity_building.pdf, accessed March 2007

EC (2003) 'Implementation of Directive 2001/42/EC on the assessment of the effects of certain plans and programmes on the environment', EC Directorate General Environment, Brussels, http://ec.europa.eu/environment/eia/sea-support.htm, accessed September 2010

EC (2004) 'Development of a guidance document on strategic environmental assessment (SEA) and coastal erosion, EC Directorate General Environment, Brussels, http://ec.europa.eu/environment/iczm/pdf/coastal_erosion_fin_rep.pdf, accessed March 2007

EC (2005) *The SEA Manual: A Sourcebook on Strategic Environmental Assessment of Transport Infrastructure Plans and Programmes*, EC Directorate General for Energy and Transport and Building Environmental Assessment and Consensus (BEACON), http://ec.europa.eu/ten/transport/studies/doc/beacon/beacon_manuel_en.pdf, accessed March 2007

Environment Agency (undated) 'Environment Agency', www.environment-agency.gov. uk, accessed March 2007

EU (European Union) (2006) *Handbook on SEA for Cohesion Policy 2007–2013*, GRDP, Interreg IIIC, EU, http://ec.europa.eu/regional_policy/sources/docoffic/working/sf2000_en.htm, accessed September 2010

Ferdowsi, S., Hakimian, A. H., Monavari, S. M., Partidário, M. R. and Rad, H. F. (2005) 'Sustainable development and strategic environmental assessment capacity building in Iran', paper presented at the IAIA SEA Conference, Prague

Fleming, A. and Campbell, I. (2005) 'Professional and institutional capacity for cultural heritage in SEA', paper presented at the IAIA SEA Conference, Prague

Genter, S. (2004) 'Evaluating the consideration of biodiversity in NRM policy through PEA', MPhil dissertation, Murdoch University, Perth

George, C. (2001) 'Sustainability appraisal for sustainable development: Integrating everything from jobs to climate change', *Impact Assessment and Project Appraisal*, vol 19, no 2, pp95–106

Ghanimé, L. (2005) 'Professional and institutional forms of improving SEA capacities on impact decision making', paper presented at the IAIA SEA Conference, Prague

Hong Kong Environmental Protection Department (2005) *SEA Manual*, www.epd. gov.hk/epd/SEA/eng/index.html accessed September 2010

OECD (Organisation for Economic Co-operation and Development) (undated) 'Environment and development', www.oecd.org/department/0,2688,en_2649_34421_1_1_1_1,00.html, accessed March 2007

O'Mahoney, T., Byrne, G. and Donnelly, A. (2005) 'The Environment Protection Agency's SEA experience in Ireland – the first twelve months', paper presented at the IAIA SEA Conference, Prague

Partidário, M. R. (1996) 'Strategic environmental assessment: Key issues emerging from recent practice', *EIA Review*, vol 16, pp31–55

Partidário, M. R. (2004) 'Capacity building and SEA', in Schmidt, M., João, E., Knopp, L. and Albrecht, E. (eds) *Implementing Strategic Environmental Assessment*, Springer Verlag, Berlin

Partidário, M. R. (2007a) 'Scales and associated data – what is enough for SEA needs?', *EIA Review*, vol 27, no 5, pp460–478

Partidário, M. R. (2007b) *Strategic Environmental Assessment Good Practice Guidance: Methodological Guidance*, Agência Portuguesa do Ambiente, Lisboa, www. iambiente.pt/divulgacao/publicacoes/outrossuportes/documents/SEA-guide.pdf, accessed November 2010

Sadler, B. and Verheem, R. (1996) *Strategic Environmental Assessment: Status, Challenges and Future Directions*, Ministry of Housing, Spatial Planning and the Environment, The Hague

Scottish Executive (2006) 'Strategic environmental assessment tool kit', www.scotland. gov.uk/Publications/2006/09/13104943/1, accessed September 2010

Susani, L. (2005) 'Building capacity for SEA consultation response', paper presented at the IAIA SEA Conference, Prague

UNDP (United Nations Development Programme) (2005) 'Training manual: Strategic environmental assessment of plans and programmes in Lebanon', www.undp.org/fssd/priorityareas/sea.html, accessed September, 2010

UNECE (United Nations Economic Commission for Europe) (2006), Convention on Environmental Impact Assessment (EIA) in a Transboundary Context – Resource

Manual to Support Application of the Protocol on SEA, www.unece.org/env/eia/sea_manual/links.html, accessed March 2007

UNEP (United Nations Environment Programme) (2002) 'Section B: Capacity building', *Environmental Impact Assessment Training Resource Manual*, Environmental Impact Assessment Training Resource Manual, www.unep.ch/etu/publications/EIA_2ed/EIA_B_body.pdf, accessed March 2007

UNEP (2004) 'Environmental impact assessment and strategic environmental assessment: Towards an integrated approach', UNEP, Geneva, www.unep.ch/etu/publications/text_ONU_br.pdf, accessed March 2007

UNEP (2009) *Integrated Assessment:Mainstreaming Sustainability into Policymaking: A Guidance Manual*, UNEP, Geneva, www.unep.ch/etb/ publications/AI%20guidance%202009/UNEP%20IA%20final.pdf

UNU (United Nations University) (undated) 'Online learning', www.onlinelearning.unu.edu/sea/index.html, accessed March 2007

Vicente, G. and Partidário, M. R. (2006) 'SEA: Enhancing communication for better environmental decisions', *EIA Review*, vol 26, no 8, pp696–706

World Bank (undated) 'Strategic environmental assessment (SEA)', World Bank, Washington, DC, http://web.worldbank.org/WBSITE/EXTERNAL/TOPICS/ENVIRONMENT/0,contentMDK:20885949~menuPK:549265 ~ pagePK:148956 ~ piPK:216618 ~ theSitePK:244381,00.html, accessed March 2007

World Bank (2005) 'Strategic environmental assessments: Capacity building in conflict-affected countries', World Bank, Washington, DC, http://go.worldbank.org/BCVLZDDAG0, accessed March 2007

30
Developing SEA Guidance

Bobbi Schijf

Introduction

The increase in strategic environmental assessment (SEA) application around the world has been accompanied by a proliferation of guidance material. Typically, when SEA is introduced, be it at international, regional, national or district level, some sort of manual or practical advice document on how to undertake SEA will follow. In addition to documents that deal with the SEA process generally, there is also an array of guidance that addresses SEA for a specific level of planning, such as the policy level, for a particular sector, such as transport, or for a certain topic, such as health or climate change.

Considering the effort that has gone into the development of SEA guidance, it is perhaps surprising that there has been little systematic analysis of the guidance that is available. This chapter makes a start. It first looks at the range of SEA guidance that is available at the international level and highlights a few key differences. Subsequently, the chapter discusses whether and to what degree harmonization of SEA guidance development is possible or indeed desirable. It concludes with a number of lessons learned for the future development of SEA guidance.

This chapter relies heavily upon the practical experience and opinions of a number of SEA professionals who have been involved in drafting and using SEA guidance material and who took part in discussion sessions at the International Association for Impact Assessment (IAIA) Prague Conference. The limited literature on this topic is also drawn in.

Overview of different types of SEA guidance

SEA guidance can be found in different guises. Besides the documents that are clearly labelled as SEA guidance, guidelines or manuals, there are also instructions on how to do SEA integrated into various capacity-building/training resources and academic and professional publications on SEA. In some cases, SEA guidance is embedded in legislative or procedural interpretation. For example, the European Commission (EC) document on the implementation of the SEA Directive was drafted to assist member states in interpreting the directive's requirements and translating these into national legislation, but it also provides some practical suggestions and references to SEA examples (EC, 2003).

Taking a broad interpretation of SEA guidance then, what kind can be found worldwide, and what is driving the production of guidance? The most common form of SEA guidance is country-specific and generic, meaning that it explains the SEA concept and process for a specific jurisdiction. Such guidance is usually commissioned by the government authority responsible for SEA and driven by national requirements or international agreements. The European Directive on SEA (2001/42/EC), in particular, has been an important impetus for new guidance materials. All European Union (EU) member states have either introduced or adapted existing strategic assessment processes to meet the requirements of the directive in law and practice, followed by SEA guidance in most countries. Thérivel et al (2004) reviewed five such national SEA guidance documents in their article on writing SEA guidance. They looked at the early guidance documents for the implementation of the European SEA Directive in England, Scotland, Iceland, Portugal and the Lombardy region of Italy. Their conclusions have been integrated into this text.

In tandem with the increase in the amount of generic SEA guidance material, the number of specialized SEA guidance documents is growing as well. This is a reflection of the multiplication of SEA use in various sectors, for different types of planning, and at varying levels. Territorial planning and transportation are well represented in sectoral SEA guidance materials, and particularly among the SEA manuals of EU member states. Specific topical SEA guidance is also on the rise, as recognition is growing that SEA might prove a useful vehicle to address issues such as biodiversity, health and climate change in strategic decision-making.

Besides the national authorities mentioned above, international development cooperation agencies are also key contributors to SEA guidance. The World Bank, for example, has developed an online SEA Toolkit, which includes information on how to prepare assessments and on sector-specific good practices (World Bank, 2007). Similarly, the United Nations Economic Commission for Europe (UNECE) SEA Protocol to the Espoo Convention is accompanied by an SEA capacity-building manual and a number of dedicated webpages with SEA examples and links to other resources (UNECE, 2007).

National and international non-governmental organizations (NGOs) involved in supporting SEA capacity have also published guidance. UICN Meso America, for example, has prepared an SEA manual for the Central American Commission on Environment and Development. This manual targets SEA practitioners in the seven countries in the Central American region (UICN/ORMA, 2007). In the same vein, the Royal Society for the Protection of Birds has collaborated with English authorities to prepare a practical guide on SEA and biodiversity (2004).

Much of the existing SEA guidance material has been funded by public money, and consequently is widely available, in print and on the internet. A quick online investigation yields many guidance documents. Box 30.1 contains an

Box 30.1 *Examples of SEA guidance material available online*

Overarching SEA guidance:

- **SEA Performance Criteria:** One-page checklist for a good quality SEA process, issued by the International Association for Impact Assessment (IAIA, 2002).

Guidance related to SEA in international cooperation:

- **Resource Manual to Support Application of the Protocol on SEA:** Capacity-building manual which incorporates guidance on how to undertake SEA, including chapters on how to apply SEA to different plans and programming processes and an overview of SEA tool and methods (UNECE, 2007).
- **World Bank:** Developed a structured learning programme to support the application of SEA approaches in World Bank and client operations and to clarify how SEA relates to other Bank instruments. It maintains a SEA Toolkit website with information on how to undertake SEA, on sector applications, and with links to other online SEA resources (World Bank, 2007). The World Bank has also developed SEA guidance specifically for the application of SEA to policies (World Bank, 2010). SEA applied at the policy level requires a particular focus on the political, institutional and governance context underlying decision-making processes. This guidance provides instructions on how to analyse this context and develop suitable SEA approaches.
- **Canadian International Development Agency (CIDA):** Produced a SEA handbook that guides employees through the Agency's SEA process and its application to the development of a policy, plan or programme proposal. The handbook includes instructions on how to screen for SEA, how to conduct an SEA and prepare a SEA report (CIDA, 2004).

Topical or sector-specific SEA guidance:

- *Strategic Environmental Assessment and Adaptation to Climate Change*, publication from a series of guidance notes on SEA practice by the Organisation for Economic Co-operation and Development (OECD, 2008).
- *Voluntary Guidelines on Biodiversity-Inclusive Impact Assessment*, a background document to the Convention on Biodiversity (Slootweg et al, 2006).
- *Reference Manual for the Integrated Assessment of Trade-Related Policies*, UNEP (2001).
- *The SEA Manual: A Sourcebook on Strategic Environmental Assessment of Transport Infrastructure Plans and Programmes*, European Commission Directorate General for Energy and Transport (EC, 2005).

> Guidance on specific SEA methodologies that integrate content or process considerations:
>
> - Strategic environmental analysis (SEAN) methodology for integrated sustainability analysis consisting of ten steps, developed with the support of the Dutch Directorate General for International Cooperation (SEAN Platform, 2007).

indicative overview of a number such resources. This list is by no means exhaustive, not least because it is limited to documents available in English.

Variation in SEA guidance

A brief review of SEA guidance material shows a variation in SEA concepts and approaches. This variation is meaningful because it follows the differentiation in how SEA is understood, and how SEA is interpreted within existing planning practices and procedures.

One area of variation in guidance is whether SEA is introduced as a more technical tool or with a stronger emphasis on the dialogue aspects of SEA. The Ghanaian SEA manual is an example of guidance that focuses on the participative side of SEA (EPA, 2007). It is light on technical methods, relying on a limited set of checklists and matrices. Instead, the manual presents strategic assessment as the result of multiple rounds of discussions with a range of stakeholders. The Abu Dhabi SEA manual, on the other hand, concentrates more on the technical methods that should be used for identification and mitigation of impacts, and indicators for monitoring (EAD, 2010).

Another key distinguishing feature in SEA guidance is the degree to which SEA is framed as a sustainability tool. Although most guidance documents refer to sustainable development as a goal to which SEA should contribute, only a few integrate sustainability concerns into the instructions. At one end of the scale are manuals that take a narrow approach to SEA and focus on effects on the biophysical environment. The middle range is occupied by guidance material that explicitly suggests the inclusion of social and economic factors in SEA but does not detail how this should be done. Guidance that strongly emphasizes sustainability seems to come from two directions. It is either prepared for planning contexts in which systems of sustainability appraisals are already established, such as in England and Scotland, or it is related to SEA application in development cooperation. In their review of experience in this latter area, Dalal-Clayton and Sadler (2005) explain that more integrated assessment suits the development cooperation context because it more clearly identifies contributions to poverty alleviation and sustainable development.

Different SEA guidance documents also present different models for the SEA process. This is notable even in SEA guidance issued by EU member states, where the SEA process must meet the same set of basic requirements as set out in Directive 2001/42/EC. For example, English guidance reviewed by Thérivel et al

(2004) refers to ten sequential stages, while Portuguese guidance organizes the process into a circular approach with four main planning phases (Thérivel et al, 2004).

A case for harmonizing SEA guidance development?

There are good arguments for making guidance material specific to a given planning system, a certain planning level or a particular type of policy, plan or programme. First, there are often legal and procedural requirements that have to be met in an SEA process, and these will differ with each administration. Second, guidance needs to be attuned to the level of experience in the system, both with planning and assessment. If planning practice is not well-developed, SEA guidance has to give more explicit direction to the planning process itself. On the other hand, if planning practice is more evolved, the integration of SEA into existing planning processes can be given more prominence in guidance documents. Similarly, if there is limited SEA experience within a country or region, there should arguably be more emphasis on basic SEA, while practitioners with more advanced SEA experience can be expected to handle more sophisticated SEA methods and techniques. The political context of a given planning system can also limit possibilities for SEA. For example, there may be inadequate commitment to SEA as a planning instrument, public participation in governmental planning may be problematic or the concept of sustainable development may not be widely accepted. General SEA guidance needs to be attuned to such factors.

There are, of course, also solid reasons for developing sector-specific guidance on SEA. Arguably, such guidance can be complementary general forms of SEA guidance. It provides a level of detail for sector application of SEA that general guidance cannot give. It is also convenient for users, taking them directly and immediately to information and instructions needed for the type of SEA process in which they are involved.

While there is logic to developing SEA guidance according to its context and target group, there is certainly also a case to be made for improved harmonization of guidance. For one thing, much confusion among new practitioners can be avoided if SEA guidance consolidates and promotes the same principles of SEA good practice. Secondly, the production of guidance would be more efficient and the guidance produced more effective, if it built on previous experience. Although there may be copyright issues to resolve, new guidance could certainly incorporate material from existing guidance if and where appropriate. This argument is especially valid for materials that are produced for SEA processes that follow from a common set of SEA requirements, such as given by the EU SEA Directive which requires all member states to have similar scope of application of SEA, comparable provision of opportunities for participation and the same minimum requirements for the content of the SEA report.

How might better harmonization of SEA guidance be achieved? The SEA task team of the Organisation for Economic Co-operation and Development, Development Assistance Committee (OECD DAC) provides a good example. This task team was set up with the expressed purpose to develop SEA guidance that would harmonize the way in which the various task team members propagated SEA in their development cooperation initiatives throughout the world. After an extensive process, the task team produced a SEA guidance document that provides a unified explanation of SEA, but also respects the need for variable applications in practice. This guidance starts with the principles and concepts, benefits and contexts of SEA, and then identifies 12 key potential entry-points for SEA application and provides more detailed instruction for each (OECD DAC, 2006).

Lessons learned from developing SEA guidance

In this spirit of improved harmonization, the participants of the SEA guidance workshop in Prague drew out a series of lessons learned from their collective experience with the development of such guidance

The process of developing guidance

One of the key points from this session was that effective SEA guidance starts with the design of a sound process for development of this guidance. Thérivel et al (2004) describe in some detail how the manuals they reviewed were put together. By and large, the process involves the development of draft guidance, either by an organization, often a government authority, with some interest or responsibility in SEA, or a consultant commissioned by that organization. When a draft is completed, the guidance is reviewed, revised and finalized. The review process can be quite extensive and includes multiple rounds of consultation with a range of stakeholders, and even test applications of the guidance. In some cases, the whole process is overseen by a steering committee of individuals with planning and/or assessment expertise.

The workshop participants had positive experiences with such consultative processes, which have the added benefit of building capacity among those involved. Involving the guide's users also creates greater recognition and support for the guidance. Furthermore, a participative process provides an opportunity to improve cooperation between different governmental authorities involved in SEA (Thérivel et al, 2004).

A sound process for SEA guidance development would include the following elements:

- Broad agreement on the nature of any proposed guidance and on its intended audience, at the outset.
- A working group to oversee the development process and the quality of the guidance material.
- Use of workshops and/or seminars to consult with a wide range of stakeholders involved in SEA, including authorities, consultancies and public participants.
- Testing of draft guidance in pilot applications.
- Involvement of experts who are well-connected to the international SEA community and have a good grasp of recent developments in this area.

One size does not fit all, but common principles apply

The main conclusions of the Prague discussion was that SEA guidance should strike a balance between context-specific, detailed instructions and overriding basic SEA principles. The participants concluded that it makes sense to tailor SEA guidance to the specific type of planning into which it should be integrated. This does of course require a sound analysis of this planning context before designing the SEA instructions (Fischer, 2006). The guidance should also be clear on what context it was written for. According to Thérivel et al (2004), it is generally easier to write practical guidance for countries with existing SEA-type experience than for those with less experience. This is especially true if planning processes in a given system are not well-defined or understood. In such situations, it is challenging to identify the decision windows that SEA should support, as well as the consultation requirements that the SEA process should incorporate, for example.

Because the context within which SEA is applied changes over time, SEA guidance needs to be regularly updated. It should follow the evolution of planning and SEA experience within a given system (see also Chapter 29). However, the workshop participants did not agree on the kind of guidance that should be available when SEA is first introduced. Differentiated guidance that is catered to sectors, planning levels or roles in the SEA process could provide a good starting point, since it will help to make the concept of SEA more concrete and demonstrate its value to specific target groups. Alternatively, general guidance could also precede more detailed guidance, in order to first promote a common view on SEA before widening its application. Ultimately, there was wide agreement that some sort of guidance, even if interim, should be available when SEA is introduced.

The key to good guidance is that the general concept and principles are not lost in the detailed SEA instructions. The Prague workshop participants felt strongly that guidance should expressly propagate a best practice 'way of thinking' about SEA; an understanding that goes beyond procedure and technique. Key messages that should be transmitted in guidance are that SEA is a flexible instrument that should be adapted to the planning process and context to which it is applied, and that SEA can serve different purposes and lead to different outputs at different decision stages in a planning process. Guidance should also demystify SEA by identifying the basic principles that underlie often complex procedural requirements and by emphasizing that clear, focused reports are better than more elaborate ones. Essentially, SEA guidance should work to promote a shift in practice towards less rigid, more responsive and purpose-driven SEA. Even in advanced SEA systems, the need to stress these overriding principles remains (see Box 30.2).

Additional tips on developing guidance

In addition to what has been set out above, the Prague workshop generated a number of generally applicable tips on developing on SEA Guidance (see also Box 30.3). Many of the pointers below are common sense, but the list can nonetheless serve as a useful reminder.

Box 30.2 *Highlighting key SEA principles*

Within the context of the UK, a number of SEA guidance documents have been prepared. These documents range in length from 8 to more than 80 pages and, although thorough, can sometimes prove overwhelming. To combat SEA 'information overload', the Environment Agency of England and Wales has developed a one-page guide summarizing key SEA principles, in particular for local development documents prepared by responsible authorities.

The *SEA Dos and Don'ts Guide* was designed for accessibility and user-friendliness. On the document, a flow diagram indicates the key stages of SEA: screening, baseline, scoping, assessment and reporting, consultation and decision-making and monitoring. For each stage, there is a list of relevant 'dos' and 'don'ts', which reflect SEA principles.

For example, for baseline development, plan-makers are urged, 'do stick to relevant issues; don't collect excessive detail'. In scoping, 'do consider a range of options; don't be afraid of being creative'. For assessment and reporting, 'do ensure assessment is evidence-based; don't hide uncertainties'. A handful of process-wide 'dos and don'ts' are also suggested.

The one-page document was distributed widely and made available electronically. A positive response was received on the effectiveness and accessibility of the information. The importance of brevity, visual clarity, and immediacy in guidance documents is highlighted.

Source: Contributed by Lucia Susani (Environmental Assessment Policy and Process Manager, Environment Agency of England and Wales). The guide is available at www.environment-agency.gov.uk.

- It is important to consider SEA from the perspective of the guide's intended audience and, in developing guidance, authors should not attempt to impose their own preconceived notions of the SEA process.
- Although guidance should be clearly explained, it should not be too prescriptive so as to stifle innovation. There is a danger of SEA guidance lowering the bar so that practitioners will simply aim to meet the requirement rather than creatively design a fit-for-purpose SEA process.
- It has proven useful to include case study material in SEA guidance. Such examples make the SEA process more tangible and can illustrate innovative practices. If case examples from the planning context for which the guidance is issued are not available, there are likely to be useful cases from elsewhere.
- Lengthy, unattractive guidance is not likely to become widely used, therefore the presentation of guidance material should receive some consideration. The possibility of web-based guidance offers many advantages, especially since it can be layered, with prominent key messages supported by more detailed methodological descriptions. Web-based guidance can also direct users to other resources on the internet and can

---

Box 30.3 *Lessons from experience in developing European Directive-compliant guidance*

For each country, the SEA guidance has to deal with remarkably similar issues, these include:

- How to integrate SEA with existing planning systems.
- How to make SEA manageable and practical.
- How to ensure that SEA is as effective and powerful as possible.

There is also inherent tension in developing country guidance, because:

- One guidance document cannot be oriented to all users.
- A guidance document cannot be concise and comprehensive at the same time.
- A guidance document cannot work optimally in all formats.

Source: Contributed by Riki Thérivel, Oxford Brookes University

---

be easily updated. However, this medium is not appropriate for all regions and other means, such as a CD-Rom, need to be used in places where internet access is problematic.

- Guidance should not promote unrealistic expectations regarding what SEA can or should achieve; there are many examples of good assessments serving as input for bad decisions. An SEA is only one of several factors determining a planning outcome (the political context being a notable other). SEA can certainly influence decision processes, particularly if it is attuned to the key issues at hand, but it does not provide insurance against unsustainable plans or policies.
- Similarly, a note of caution in guidance is warranted regarding the detail and complexity of the information in SEA. An effective SEA process need not require detailed technical assessment and the quality of information is not dependant on the complexity of the methods applied. Indeed, if financial resources are limited, quantitative methods such as geographical information systems (GIS) may even be out of reach. The methods and approaches suggested in guidance should be realistic and appropriate.
- Finally, guidance should give some attention to the expertise required for the assessment and for the management of the SEA process. It should be clear that technical expertise alone is not sufficient. Complex assessments, especially, require multidisciplinary teams of people.

In terms of the content of guidance material, it is recommended that all SEA guidance material should:

- Identify where a specific plan and the SEA process fit into the planning hierarchy, particularly what level of impacts are being considered.

- Cover SEA methods but not necessarily describe them in detail. It is important to explain how to select the best method for a specific SEA purpose and also to note the importance of (expert) judgement in SEA practice. Guidance might also outline common problems that result from the application of some types of methods for certain uses.
- Deal with uncertainty as an inherent aspect of SEA, outlining ways and means of dealing with this issue and emphasizing that these are not necessarily restricted to technical solutions.
- Address presentation of the SEA report and suggest that different SEA outputs are possible to support different planning and policy decision moments, and different target groups.

Using online options

There are quite a few good practice examples of SEA guidance that use the internet to provide access to information. The online Hong Kong SEA Manual (see Figure 30.1) is an excellent example of innovation in SEA guidance (EPD, 2005). Although prepared for a specific jurisdiction, the manual has a chapter on worldwide trends in SEA and links to guidance materials of other countries and regions. The online manual is an interactive, layered resource, with clear and concise explanations of SEA basics, supported by range of case study examples and other more detailed documents that can be downloaded separately.

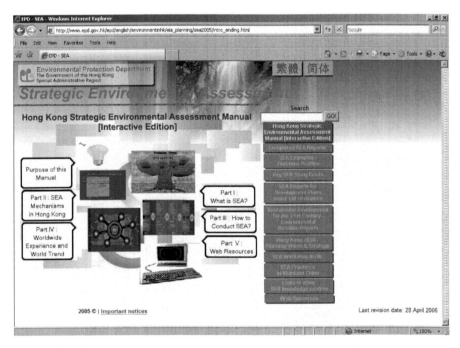

Source: EPD (2005)

Figure 30.1 *The interactive Hong Kong SEA Manual*

Table 30.1 *SEA guidance: Summary statement*

Main trends and issues	The range of available SEA guidance material is large and increasing steadily, but there is little systematic analysis of the scope or effectiveness of SEA guidance. Existing SEA guidance can be found under a variety of guises, and from a range of sources, including national government authorities and international development agencies. Much SEA guidance is widely available through the internet.
Main perspectives	Several differences can be identified in the SEA guidance material available: • Key differences are the conceptualization of SEA as a more technical or a dialogue instrument, and the degree to which SEA is framed as a sustainability tool. • There is also variation in how the SEA process is divided into stages and activities, the division usually corresponding with the planning process to which SEA is to be applied. • A good deal of the guidance produced is of a general nature, but there is also guidance specific to a given planning system, a certain planning level or a particular sector.
Key lessons	The most effective SEA guidance is the result of an iterative and consultative process, which includes broad agreement on the nature of the guidance and its intended audience at the outset. It is also important that SEA guidance is attuned to the level of planning practice and SEA experience in the context to which it will be applied. Keeping a practical focus, using examples and case studies leads to better guidance. This chapter lists a number of additional key lessons for the process of developing SEA guidance, as well as for the content of SEA guidance.
Future directions	This chapter makes a case for improved harmonization of guidance development. There are lessons to be learned from previous SEA guidance experiences that should be taken on board in future SEA guidance development. Since SEA guidance can set the tone for SEA practice, guiding material should work to promote a shift towards best practice, which suggests less rigid and more responsive, purpose-driven SEA. Finally, technological advances make for more flexible and adaptive web-based SEA guidance, which is layered, supported by a wide array of examples, and can be regularly updated.

Another example is the comprehensive online resource on SEA Good Practice Guidelines that the Environment Agency of England and Wales maintains (Environment Agency, 2005). Although produced for UK practitioners, it provides meta-guidance that places a range of sectoral and topical guidance and cases in a wider SEA context and has direct links to these documents. This is particularly helpful in the UK, where a wide range of SEA guidance products exists.

As SEA guidance material continues to be developed, overview websites will become increasingly useful to practitioners searching for advice on specific SEA issues, as well as to those drafting SEA guidance. Currently, there are a number of such sites For example, there is the UK gateway to SEA and sustainability appraisal (www.sea-info.net), which gives an overview of UK and

European guidance in an exceptionally user-friendly format. Similarly, the Netherlands Commission on Environmental Assessment has an online database that is searchable and gives access to a range of online guidance and case study documents, which are in Spanish, Portuguese and French as well as English (www.eia.nl).

Conclusion

SEA guidance can be a determining factor of the quality of SEA practice and its development deserves close attention from the SEA community. It is important that guidance documents propagate a widely shared and up-to-date understanding of SEA good practice. Since this understanding evolves, so should any piece of SEA guidance. Recurrent assessment of the relevance and performance of SEA guidance material are needed to ensure it is still pertinent to practice. Regular updating of guidance material will also be required to incorporate technological and methodological advances in SEA. The use of the internet to disseminate guidance facilitates regular updating of documents, components and sources and allows cross-referencing between different materials and sites, which does not occur often enough. More in-depth and comparative analysis of existing SEA guiding material would reveal where and how guidance materials might supplement each other.

Another key priority for action is analysis of the effectiveness of SEA guidance. There has been little systematic evaluation of guiding documents on SEA, and there are undoubtedly still lessons to be learned regarding what works well and what does not. It would also help to frame conclusions from studies into the effectiveness of SEA itself in terms of consequences for guidance.

Finally, SEA guidance should provide clearer direction on how to incorporate the concept and goals of sustainability into SEA practice. Above all, the instructions given should be practical and deal with concrete issues, such as making trade-offs and setting sustainability objectives and indicators.

References

This chapter is largely based on presentations and discussion on SEA guidance (stream E3) at the IAIA SEA Conference 'International experience and perspectives in SEA', held in Prague, 26–30 September 2005.

CIDA (Canadian International Development Agency) (2004) *Strategic Environmental Assessment of Policy, Plan, and Program Proposals: CIDA Handbook*, CIDA, Ottawa, www.acdi-cida.gc.ca/acdi-cida/acdi-cida.nsf/eng/EMA-218131145-PHA, accessed September 2010

Countryside Council for Wales, English Nature, Environment Agency, Royal Society for the Protection of Birds (2004) *Strategic Environmental Assessment and Biodiversity: Guidance for Practitioners*, www.rspb.org.uk/Images/SEA_and_biodiversity_tcm9-133070.pdf, accessed September 2010

Dalal-Clayton, B. and Sadler, B. (2005) *Strategic Environmental Assessment, A Sourcebook and Reference Guide to International Experience*, Earthscan, London

EAD (Environment Agency of Abu Dhabi) (2010) *Technical Guidance Document for Strategic Environmental Assessment*, www.ead.ae/_data/global/tgds%20new/tgd_sea_final.pdf, accessed September 2010

EC (European Commission) (2003) *Implementation of Directive 2001/42/EC on the Assessment of the Effects of Certain Plans and Programmes on the Environment*, EC Directorate General Environment, http://ec.europa.eu/environment/eia/pdf/030923_sea_guidance.pdf, accessed September 2010

EC (2005) *The SEA Manual: A Sourcebook on Strategic Environmental Assessment of Transport Infrastructure Plans and Programmes*, European Commission Directorate General for Energy and Transport, http://ec.europa.eu/environment/eia/sea-support.htm, accessed April 2007

Environment Agency (2005) *Good Practice Guideline for Strategic Environmental Assessment*, Environment Agency, UK

EPA (Ghana Environmental Protection Agency) (2007) *Strategic Environmental Assessment of the Ghana Poverty Reduction Strategy*, EPA, Ghana

EPD (Environmental Protection Department) (2005) *Hong Kong Strategic Environmental Assessment Manual*, Environmental Protection Department, Government of Hong Kong, www.epd.gov.hk/epd/SEA/eng/sea_manual.html, accessed September 2010

Fischer, T. B. (2006) 'Strategic environmental assessment and transport planning: Towards a generic framework for evaluating practice and developing guidance', *Impact Assessment and Project Appraisal*, vol 24, no 3, pp183–197

IAIA (International Association for Impact Assessment) (2002) *Strategic Environmental Assessment Performance Criteria*, IAIA Special Publications series No 1, www.iaia.org/publicdocuments/special-publications/sp1.pdf, accessed September 2010

OECD (Organisation for Economic Co-operation and Development) (2008) *Strategic Environmental Assessment and Adaptation to Climate Change*, OECD DAC Network on Environment and Development Co-operation (ENVIRONET), www.oecd.org/dataoecd/0/43/42025733.pdf, accessed September 2010

OECD DAC (Organisation for Economic Co-operation and Development, Development Assistance Committee) (2006) *Good Practice Guidance on Applying Strategic Environmental Assessment (SEA) in Development Co-operation*, OECD DAC Task Team on Strategic Environmental Assessment, www.oecd.org/dataoecd/4/21/37353858.pdf, accessed April 2007

SEAN Platform (2007) 'SEAN Home Strategic Environmental Analysis', www.seanplatform.org, accessed April 2007

Slootweg, R., Kolhoff, A. and Verheem, R. (eds) (2006) *Biodiversity in EIA and SEA. Background Document to CBD Decision VIII/28: Voluntary Guidelines on Biodiversity-Inclusive Impact Assessment*, http://docs1.eia.nl/os/bibliotheek/biodiversityeiasea.pdf, accessed September 2010

Thérivel, R., Caratti, P., Partidário, M. R., Theorsdottir, A. H. and Tyldesly, D. (2004) 'Writing strategic environmental assessment guidance', *Impact Assessment and Project Appraisal*, vol 22, no 4, pp259–270

UICN/ORMA (Unión Mundial para la Naturaleza/Unidad de política y gestión ambiental) (2007) *Lineamientos para la Aplicación de la Evaluación Ambiental Estratégica en Centroamérica*, UICN, San José, Costa Rica

UNECE (United Nations Economic Commission for Europe) (2007) *Draft Resource Manual to Support Application of the Protocol on SEA*, www.unece.org/env/eia/sea_manual/welcome.html, accessed April 2007

UNEP (United Nations Environment Programme) (2001) *Reference Manual for the Integrated Assessment of Trade-Related Policies*, UNEP, Geneva

World Bank (2007) *SEA Toolkit*, http://go.worldbank.org/XIVZ1WF880, accessed April 2007

World Bank (2010) *Policy SEA: Conceptual Model and Operational Guidance for Applying Strategic Environmental Assessment in Sector Reform*, Report No 55328 The World Bank Sustainable Development Network Environment Department, http://go.worldbank.org/H711VPS9D0, accessed September 2010

31

Institutional Challenges for SEA Implementation and Decision-making: Search for Appropriate Organizations

Lone Kørnøv and Holger Dalkmann

There is no such thing as 'good organization' in any absolute sense. Always it is relative; and an organization that is good enough in one context or under one criterion may be bad under another. (W. Ross Ashby, 1968)

Introduction

During the development and use of strategic environmental assessment (SEA), it has become more and more obvious that SEA could not be defined as a technical instrument operating in a social vacuum. It is widely recognized that continuing social, political and organizational processes influence the form of SEA and determine whether and how SEA results are used. With increasing practical experience with SEA, the relation with policy, programme and planning (PPP) processes has come into sharper focus in the international discourse on this subject (for example, Nilsson and Dalkmann, 2001; Bina, 2003; Renton and Bailey, 2000; Fischer, 2003; Kørnøv and Thissen, 2000; Cashmore, 2004).

SEA can be viewed as being another component in an already complex set of mechanisms, characterized by loose-coupled organizations that have to live up to contradictory considerations, whereby each actor or group of actors bring their own goals and understanding of environmental problems and solutions, preferences change and most attempts at social control are unpredictable. This is not to say that one should loose faith in the systematic way that knowledge about the environment is produced through SEA. However, this process has to be applied in a way that recognizes existing institutional structures, including the formal and informal decision-making process, actor involvement and organizational arrangements.

The 2005 Prague workshop titled Search for Appropriate Organizations used the above aspects as a starting point. In this chapter, the aim is to identify the key factors for SEA from the perspective of decision-making, actor constellations and process organization. This review will draw on a literature review as well as workshop discussions to examine the current situation, in which new SEA procedures often meet old decision-making structures with existing routines and formal as well as informal processes.

Background

Even though frequently mentioned, the strategic character of SEA needs to be stressed. As a flexible instrument, which has to be adapted to the decision-making process, it is crucial to have an early recognition and defined inter-relations with the policy and planning process. On this basis, different organizational models of how to implement SEA can be identified (João, 2005; Dalkmann, 2005).

Planning and decision-making processes are neither rational nor linear, nor are they value-free and only technical. This raises central questions regarding the development and use of SEA, bearing in mind that there are different types and frameworks of approach that provide different opportunities for the integration of SEA processes and results. How can a more nuanced and non-rational understanding of political decision-making processes and organizational aspects bring us closer to the purpose of SEA to establish a sound environmental basis for decision-making? What factors are crucial for successful implementation?

The following discussion will highlight some of the threats and opportunities regarding the organizational aspects of SEA, which must be dealt with proactively through the search for appropriate organizations.

SEA within formal and informal organizational structures
SEA takes place within:

- Formal organizational structures (explicated rules, division of responsibility and competence).
- Informal structures of a more psychological nature (attitudes, norms, traditions, and so on).

Formal organizational structures consist of explicated rules, specialization and hierarchy framing of the formal decision-making process, namely who can/should participate, when and how?

Informal organizational structures can be coded in everyday behaviour through routines, norms and standards (March and Olsen, 1989). This informal structure encapsulates our perceptions of reality or what Berger and Luckmann (1972) called 'the world taken for granted'. One example of an informal power structure is the decoupling of health and environment in organizations. As long as health is viewed (unconsciously) as another department's responsibility, SEA will have a limited impact in that respect. An understanding of the influence of structure on decision-making can supplement our understanding of power as being only actor-oriented.

The informal structure is not directly visible when it takes form of routines, myths and norms. However, it can be very strong and influential both in relation to how decisions are reached and to which decisions are made (Kørnøv and Thissen, 2000). Notably, when rules within the informal structure are so strong that they lead to path dependence, they are difficult and often costly to change (Campell, 2004). Only by questioning the informal structure is there an opportunity to challenge the structural power, which raises the question of how the SEA process can cope with formal and informal organizational structures and decision-making processes?

SEA as a communicative action

In general, specialization and division of responsibility and competence are presented as a way of securing efficient organizations. However, there are some potential downsides of a very divided and specialized organizational structure. One important concern is the limited sharing of information, preferences and understanding. Division of responsibility and specialization affects the information that various actors receive. This may contribute to the differentiation of sub-goals with the risk that other organizational sub-goals tend to be ignored (March and Simon, 1993). Actors select, organize and perceive information based upon both their organizational and their professional identification.

To support the development of perceptions, preferences and understanding of complex environmental systems, there is a need to view SEA as a communicative action. Assessing complex environmental issues often demands a well-coordinated effort between different groups of professionals or between different parts of the organization. It also demands an effort to involve stakeholders from outside the organization. Differences in their rationalities (covering different norms, values, professional attitudes, and so on) bring the need to develop a structured and qualified dialogue. The way in which this effort is organized may be crucial for the success of SEA, reflecting the capability for mutual understanding. It raises the question of how the organization of the SEA work can support the dialogue and exchange of expertise and challenge different perceptions and preferences.

SEA as used by decision-makers and the public

The findings of the SEA are produced to inform decision-makers and the public. Whether the basis for decision-making is sound or not depends upon the level of detail and timing being appropriate for decision-makers and the public. Specifically, the public needs to appreciate that their participation in the SEA process matters, and politicians need to receive and understand the information as it relates to opportunities for development (Elling, 2003). Since experts primarily perform environmental assessment (EA), there may be considerable differences in the level of knowledge and understanding among officials, decision-makers and the public. It is crucial that officials and experts recognize that SEA is necessary for democratization in society and is not just a tool to get information for solving their own problems (Elling, 2003).

When undertaking this process, there is a need for awareness of the cognitive limitations in decision-making, covering limitations in attention, memory, comprehension and communication (March, 1994) and how cognition affects decision-making (as discussed by Simon, 1957; Lindblom, 1959; March and Olsen, 1976, 1986; Dawes, 1988). In organizing SEA work, how can knowledge be produced at the right time and at the right level of detail for decision-makers and the broader public to ensure transparency and use of the results?

SEA function in political systems

Organizations are a loose coupling of individuals and groups with different interests that build coalitions to support their objectives. Power is both a resource in the political game and an important result of the same, which is why political processes always continue and never end. SEA cannot avoid being part of the ongoing game of power and interest brokerage. It is, by definition, politically loaded because it contributes to the selection of activities, decides which need attention, contributes to the formulation of the alternatives, selects which should be taken into account and how positive and negative impacts are assessed. Furthermore, SEA is also influenced by the way resources are divided in the organization.

The use and influence of political power can be understood in relation to direct and indirect power. Direct power is linked to a specific choice in the decision-making process that involves, for example, two groups of actors with conflicting interests with one using resources (money, position or knowledge) to retain or gain power (Dahl, 1957). Indirect power is exercised when actors hinder cases from being put on the agenda and from reaching the decision-making process (Bachrach and Baratz, 1962, 1963).

This raises other questions. When organizing SEA work, how can direct and indirect power in the political system be coped with and support transparency in relation to the decision-making process? Which role could or should public participation play in relation to the political processes?

If SEA is to affect policy processes and their outcome, we have to consider the organizational aspects in relation to the decision-making process. Guided by insight into the nature of decision-making, different organizational models can be recognized, which will be explored in the following analysis.

Review of actor constellation

SEA is reflected as an overarching philosophy, rather than a procedural prescription (Thérivel and Brown, 1999). Therefore, different legislative frameworks in numerous countries and different applications for dissimilar sectors and spatial level can be identified (Dalal-Clayton and Sadler, 2005;

Schmidt et al, 2005). All that SEAs have in common is the use of the instrument in an institutional arena where different actor groups interact.

For an effective and efficient SEA, the institutional framework and the power constellation of stakeholders should be taken into account (Fischer, 2003; Kørnøv and Thissen, 2000). For successful implementation of a SEA, the organization of the different actors involved and their influence in the decision-making process is crucial. Obviously, the stakeholders differ, based on, for example, cultural values and the political system, and their interactions reflect the role and relation of formal and informal processes.

Researchers have recognized the decision-making perspective as an important issue for an effective and efficient SEA (Sheate et al, 2001; Caratti et al, 2004). In reviewing actual SEA processes, it is necessary to simplify the constellation of actors. The following four actor groups can be identified as the key players: politicians, public administrators, consultants and the public. Industry is often mentioned as a further participant and uses SEA in corporate decision-making. However, industry sectors play a minor role for purposes of discussion of the organization and institutionalization of the process and consequently they are not referred to in the following analysis, although their influence in business-related SEA should be a subject for future research. In some cases, the media play a role in the SEA process, for example, in informing the public about the process and the issues, aspects that are not analysed here.

The following analysis describes the role of the four actor groups identified above in the SEA process (from the legislative as well as from the decision-centred perspective). It is based on a review of the literature as well as on presentations at the session titled Search for Appropriate Organizations at the Prague Conference on SEA. Some initial hypotheses on the future role for a more efficient and more effective SEA also are presented.

Politicians

Although many authors stress the importance of SEA on the policy level (Schmidt et al, 2005; World Bank, 2005), only a few countries, such as Canada, Denmark and New Zealand, include policies under an assessment regulation (Canadian Environmental Assessment Agency, 2004; Ministry of the Environment and Energy, 1995; World Bank, 2005). Most national legislation refers to plans and programmes as does the European Directive 2001/42/EC.

In democratic political systems, politicians set the general targets for future development. Therefore, they play a major role in providing the framework condition and often define the tasks for public administration including obligations on their own actions. Under Directive 2001/42/EC, the results of an environmental report shall be taken into account, in the final stage of the decision-making process. There is an implied acknowledgement of the existence of two processes – the formal SEA process and a non-technical political process – and to bridge them, van Dyck (2005) proposed organizing interactive policy planning.

In comparing the political system and political culture of Belgium and the Netherlands, van Dyck (2005) identified major differences that influence the SEA process. While there is an interactive policy planning approach in the Netherlands, he concluded that poor policy planning takes place in Belgium, which is generally more election driven. He argues, that the planning system – and consequently the SEA process – should be aligned with political requirements, otherwise it will receive no recognition or lead to false consequences that will reflect badly on the image of the instrument and have poor public acceptance.

The World Bank (2005) has identified SEA as an evolving tool to improve its influence on policy-making by more directly addressing institutional and governance dimensions. It would strengthen prioritizing of environmental issues, bring together different viewpoints through formulation and implementation processes, ensure social accountability and provide a mechanism where social learning can occur.

For an efficient and effective SEA, the future role of the politicians and their involvement in SEA has to be discussed. Some initial themes for improvement of the SEA process in decision-making include the following:

- Politicians have a democratic right to participate in the SEA process and their early involvement in the process might secure political ownership.
- There is a need for an analysis of the political situation in each case to tailor the organization of the SEA process to secure political involvement.
- There is no guarantee, however, that politicians will want to be involved in the process and use the results. Politicians have different roles and interests and therefore they enter the SEA process and use the results differently.
- SEA is a long-term learning process with a broadening of understanding and perceptions for all stakeholders including politicians.

Public administrators

Public administration aims are changing rapidly as the role of the government moves from providing services and infrastructure to only setting the framework for these. For example, many environmental impact assessments (EIAs) are carried out by consultants and only scoped and reviewed by the responsible public agency. For SEA, this body decides if this process should be carried out and defines the scope of the study. While the government makes the general decision regarding which plans and programmes should be subject to SEA, the operational responsibilities and tasks are in the hands of public administrators.

The system established for SEA administration differs from country to country and sometimes from municipality to municipality (for example, in a federal system such as in Germany or in a centralized model such as in France). It also changes when new legislative requirements are imposed on an existing public body, such as the Netherlands EIA Commission, or when national or local authorities implement completely new administrative structures, such as in most of the developing countries or in Eastern Europe where, under the framework of the United Nations Economic Commission for Europe (UNECE) Protocol on SEA, national and subregional capacity-building action plans are carried out (Jurkeviciute et al, 2005).

Another organizational feature of SEA is the structural division of departments and groups responsible for different environmental aspects and well-defined sub-targets. With a broad concept of the environment, SEA requires knowledge and experience from several disciplines and fields and inter-departmental and cross-professional organizations are therefore essential. A positive case from Austria reflects the value of openness of the SEA process. Through a proactive participative and moderated stakeholder process, the responsible Federal Environmental Agency developed a stepwise process for a national waste management plan, which was governed by a consensus group consisting of officials from different departments, non-governmental organizations (NGOs) and members from scientific communities (Mayer, 2005).

Public administrators have a major influence on the incorporation of the SEA into the decision-making process. For their future role, the following requirements are suggested:

- SEA calls for both vertical and horizontal, cross-professional and cross-departmental communication and organization.
- The administration should strive for an ethical and sound SEA process, one that meets principles of free access to information, accountability, transparency and participation beyond the level of just informing the public and including consultation or even mediation.

The public

The involvement of the public with regard to SEA is typically equated with the organization of public participation. Compared to bottom-up processes, such as local Agenda 21, where the public plays a major role in future development, SEA takes a more top-down approach to public participation that is not yet well-developed. In theory, public participation should take place from the beginning of the SEA and decision-making processes, but cases of early influential public involvement are rare. Although Article 6 of the European Directive requires participation (or 'consultation'), it is mainly at the level of information and occurs relatively late in the assessment process after a draft report is written. Participation should occur earlier and on a higher level of public involvement such as cooperation or even mediation (Arbter, 2004).

An issue for consideration here centres on the legitimacy of the representatives of the different stakeholder groups. Many pressure groups define themselves as representatives of a segment of the public but often lack direct legitimacy reflected, for example, in membership or signature lists. A proactive approach to identify and include different social groups and interests in SEA would lead to a stronger democratic process.

The Austrian case quoted above is a positive example of public involvement in SEA. On the one hand, there are criticisms that public participation in SEA processes is not manageable or that higher levels of decision-making are too abstract for the general public (Heiland, 2005). On the other hand, the government is concerned that too many people will react when active participation is required, for example via the internet. Experience shows that, in most cases, the contribution from the public has a manageable scope and a representative approach via stakeholders of different societal groups can be used in addition or as another opportunity (Arbter, 2004).

By taking an active role in inviting the different groups with qualified cross sectional opinions and positions early in the decision-making process, the 'world of knowledge' and 'world of decision-making' could be better connected (Deelstra et al, 2003). In the Austrian case, the identification was proactive and subject-driven. A balanced proportion of scientists, lobby groups and practitioners were engaged in a consensus-oriented process and through different workshops prepared a draft of the future Waste Management Plan for the National Ministry of Environment. The European Commission (EC, 2005) suggests that to 'concretely disseminate the information and reach the target groups, specialized agencies may be entrusted to facilitate the circulation of draft documents and organize venues where debates and verbal communication (e.g. bilateral meetings, round-table meetings and informal discussions)'. It also identifies good practice examples such as the Milan-Bologna High Speed Railway and the extension of the Port of Rotterdam.

In practice, the role of the public within SEA processes is a minor one in comparison to politicians and public administrators. Nevertheless, public participation is often identified as a major pillar for SEA – based upon the rationalities of improved planning, strengthened democracy, better implementation and, in some cases, conflict resolution (Elling, 2003; Thérivel, 2004; World Bank, 2005). As a consequence, the following thesis is advanced for defining the role of the public in the future:

- There is a need for a case-specific public participation regarding who to involve, at what level and by which participation techniques.
- There is a need for transparency regarding the selection procedure when using a stakeholder approach.

Consultants

The fourth group of key actors in the SEA process are consultants – although in legal frameworks they have neither standing as a specific group nor as contractors on behalf of public authorities. Yet by providing contracted services, the private sector plays an increasing role in SEA. At the same time, the role of the public sector may be reduced. In engaging consultants and deciding their level of involvement, public authorities can follow at least two models:

- The first model calls for consultants to carry out the SEA in part or in full. In this case, public authorities can use consultants to address issues when in-house resources or competences are not available. Normally, the public authority will determine the scope of analysis for consultants to prepare the environmental report in part or in full.
- The second model involves consultants to support the assessment process itself. It is based on the assumption that the public authority has the necessary knowledge and competence regarding knowledge on environmental cause and effect relations, local circumstances and solutions.

The first model is viewed by the authors as potentially problematic in cases where consultants mainly provide the environmental report and are not part of the full process. The model might lead to SEA being decoupled from the decision-making process, for example, by providing reports that are not understandable to decision-makers or resulting in two separate processes with the risk that SEA will not influence ongoing decision-making. Furthermore, in this model, consultants work separately from the public participation process and address the concerns of the public only second-hand or through the administrative agency.

Experience shows that that a key success factor for SEA is the involvement of different stakeholders, including consultants, policy-makers and the wider public, so that the process becomes educational for all parties (Thérivel, 2004; Sheate et al, 2001). It is also highly important that the public administrators themselves develop knowledge and competence regarding SEA and in that way build their own institutional capacity and memory. This approach is consistent with the second model, in which the consultants are involved in the SEA process in order to help public authorities to 'perceive, understand, and act upon the process events that occur in the client's environment in order to improve the situation as defined by the client' (Schein, 1969).

This sort of process consultancy is one way of setting up a learning arena that facilitates sharing knowledge and perceptions (Schein, 1987). Besides giving guidance during the SEA process, the process consultant's role can be to secure cooperation and assessment across disciplines and understandings. The following suggestions are made for a new role for consultants in the SEA process:

- When consultants are used to undertake a SEA in part or in full, they should have a close working relationship with the public authority, which includes clear terms of reference.
- Consultants involved in SEA need to perform more as process consultants rather than as technical experts who provide final solutions and statements. This requires the 'process consultant' to recognize and understand the political and planning cultures.

Conclusion: Organization of interaction and communication

The chapter has emphasized the importance of awareness and understanding of the organization of the SEA process and the consequence of the power relationships among key actors. For SEA to have an impact on decision-making, it needs to address at least four important institutional challenges:

- SEA takes place in organizations consisting of both formal and informal structures.
- SEA needs to communicate across organizational and professional divisions.
- SEA results will be used by different actors.
- SEA functions in political systems in which both direct and indirect power are exercised.

Table 31.1 *Search for appropriate organizations: Summary statement*

Main trends and issues	Practice shows that, in general, the necessary knowledge on the SEA process and more or less the necessary tools for undertaking SEA exist. However, regarding the organizational aspects, practice shows that SEA often meets: • Decision-making processes that are not value-free, rational and linear. • Established routines and mechanisms in organizations. • Different institutional preconditions. • Not 'one' established solution for organizing the process. • Different political cultures. Therefore, there are different challenges for SEA, such as: • Dealing with formal and informal organizational structures. • Strengthening communication between and within organizations. • Dealing with stakeholders having different rationalities (norms, values, attitudes). • Timing (when to involve which actors in the process). • Understanding the power constellation.
Main perspectives	The following strengths and weaknesses of SEA process and practice were identified: • Existing organization with established working routines is a strength for SEA (for example, EIA Commission, the Netherlands). • Informal 'bodies' and informal discussions could support the assessment process (for example, Hong Kong, the Netherlands) and lead to more acceptance by all actors. • Improvement for SEA through public participation with round table stakeholder meetings and a proactive search for participants (for example, Austria). • Ambitious legislation beyond the Directive (for example, Scotland, the Czech Republic). • Different interest and awareness of politicians is a premise for SEA.
Key lessons	The main lessons and implications for SEA development regarding the organizational structure are related to four actors; politicians, the public administration, the public and research/consulting. Performance criteria of good practice are listed in the following. **Politics:** Politicians have a democratic right to participate in the SEA process and involvement early in the process might secure political ownership. However, politicians differ, have different roles and interests and therefore enter the SEA process and use the results differently. Therefore, it is necessary: • To analyse the political situation in each case to tailor-make the organization of the SEA process to secure political involvement. • To view SEA as a long-term learning process with a broad understanding and perceptions for all stakeholders – including politicians. **The public administration:** Public administration plays the major role in the organizational structure of an SEA process and defines the relationship with the planning process in most cases. Therefore, there is a need for: • Both vertical and horizontal, cross-professional and cross-departmental organization. • Ethical and sound SEA processes; meeting the principles of free access to information, accountability and transparency. **The public:** Public participation is often formally required, however, most of the time.

Table 31.1 (*continued*)

	it is seen as a minimum approach. As a consequence, the following issues should be strengthened: • A case-specific public participation regarding both who to involve and by which techniques. • Transparency regarding the selection procedure while using a stakeholder approach. **Research and consulting:** Scientific evaluations as well as consultant inputs often focus on the outcome and neglect the needs to focus more on the assessment process and institutional aspects. So there is a need for: • Consultants involved in SEA to perform more as process consultants than as experts providing final solutions and statements. • Political and planning cultures to be understood and recognized by the 'process consultant'.
Future directions	Core priorities for future research and development of SEA regarding the organizational aspects are: • A need for an improved understanding of the political structure while implementing SEA and organizing the SEA process. • A need to define the role of environmental democracy in the organization of the SEA process. • Discussion of the potential of independent bodies and the different roles they can play in the SEA process such as, for example, quality control/auditing, information management and process management. • Research into how different organizational set-ups and processes have an impact on SEA and on decision-making. • Research and experiments into how to organize and use the benefit of informal processes.

SEA is considered a long-term learning process that broadens understanding and perceptions of all actors. For optimal integration, both a vertical as well as a horizontal approach involving cross-professional and cross-departmental organizations are important. Knowledge, norms and practices differ from one actor to another and SEA is dependent on their interaction and on external actors/organizations. Given that not all SEA actors have an environmental background, a strong communicative process is needed. Analysis of different cases of ecological disaster indicates that most of them could have been avoided through better communication and information policy (Luhmann, 2001; EEA, 2001).

To solve that problem, it is necessary to deal issues related to subsystems, which may be defined as a differentiation among societal groups (for example, specific networks) or at least improve the communication between the different functional subsystems (Luhmann, 1986). Interpreting Luhmann's theory on environmental communication, the stakeholders involved in a SEA process could be identified as one subsystem separately from the policy and planning process. Within the policy and planning process, there are different sub-systems consisting of professional disciplines. In this chapter, we advocate the organization of 'communication arenas' in the SEA process that facilitate exchanging and developing knowledge, preferences and perceptions for all stakeholders involved, using process consultancy and expert teamwork.

In each case, a decision must be made on whether the arena should be a new institution or based upon the roles and interaction of actors within an existing institution. As an example of a new institution, McLauchlan and João (2005) identified the possibility of having an independent body to communicate, coordinate, to secure access to information and to review and provide guidelines. Such a decision must be based upon the actual formal and informal institutional structures.

Further research and discussion is needed on the potential of independent bodies and the different roles that they can or should play in the SEA process, such as quality control and auditing, information management and process management. Other issues for research work include: the impact of different organizational systems and processes for communication and interaction on SEA and decision-making; and how to organize and use the benefit of informal communication processes, such as exchange forums between different professions and departments.

References

Arbter, K. (2004) *SUP – Strategische Umweltprüfung für die Planungspraxis von Morgen*, Neuer Wissenschaftlicher Verlag, Graz

Bachrach, P. and Baratz, M. S. (1962) 'The two faces of power', *American Political Science Review*, vol 56, pp947–952

Bachrach, P. and Baratz, M. S. (1963) 'Decisions and non-decisions', *American Political Science Review*, vol 57, no 3, pp632–642

Berger, P. L. and Luckmann, T. (1972) *Den Samfundsskabte Virkelighed*, Lindhardt & Ringhof, Copenhagen

Bina, O. (2003) *Re-conceptualising Strategic Environmental Assessment: Theoretical Review and Case Study from Chile*, PhD thesis, geography department, University of Cambridge

Campell, J. L. (2004) *Institutional Change and Globalization*, Princeton University Press

Canadian Environmental Assessment Agency (2004) *Sustainable Development Strategy 2004–2006*, www.ceaa-acee.gc.ca/017/0004/001/SDS2004_e.pdf

Caratti, P., Dalkmann, H. and Jiliberto, R. (2004) *Analysing Strategic Environmental Assessment*, Edward Elgar Publishing Limited, Cheltenham

Cashmore, M. (2004) 'The role of science in environmental impact assessment: Process and procedures versus purpose in the development of theory', *Environmental Impact Assessment Review*, vol 24, pp403–426

Dahl, R. A. (1957) 'The concept of power', *Behavioural Science*, vol 2, pp201–215

Dalal-Clayton, B. and Sadler, B. (2005) *Strategic Environmental Assessment: A Sourcebook and Reference Guide to International Experience*, Earthscan, London

Dalkmann, H. (2005) 'Die integration der strategischen umweltprüfung in entscheidungsprozesse', *UVP-report*, vol 19, no 1, pp31–34

Dawes, R. W. (1988) *Rational Choice in an Uncertain World*, Brace College Publishers, Orlando

Deelstra, Y., Nooteboom, S. G., Kohlmann, H. R., Van den Berg, J. and Innanen, S. (2003) *Using Knowledge for Decision-Making Purposes*, DHV Management Consultants, Leusden

EC (European Commission) (2005) *The SEA Manual: A Sourcebook on Strategic Environmental Assessment of Transport Infrastructure Plans and Programmes*, EC Directorate General for Energy and Transport, Brussels

EEA (European Environmental Agency) (2001) *Late Lessons from Early Warnings: The Precautionary Principle 1896–2000*, EEA, Copenhagen

Elling, B. (2003) *Modernitetens miljøpolitik (Modernity and Environmental Politics)*, Roskilde University Centre, Denmark

Fischer, T. (2003) 'Strategic environmental assessment in post-modern-times', *Environmental Impact Assessment Review*, vol 23, pp155–170

Heiland, S. (2005) 'What does participation mean?', in Schmidt, M., João, E. and Albrecht, E. (eds) *Implementing Strategic Environmental Assessment*, Springer Verlag, Berlin

João, E. (2005) 'Key principles of SEA', in Schmidt, M., João, E. and Albrecht, E. (eds) *Implementing Strategic Environmental Assessment*, Springer Verlag, Berlin

Jurkeviciute, A., Dusik, J. and Martonakova, H. (2005) 'Regional Overview', prepared for the Capacity Building Needs Assessment for the UNECE SEA Protocol, first outline of regional report, United Nations Development Programme and The Regional Environmental Centre for Central and Eastern Europe

Kørnøv, L. and Thissen, W. A. H. (2000) 'Rationality in decision and policy-making: Implications for strategic environmental assessment', *Impact Assessment and Project Appraisal*, vol 18, no 3, pp191–200

Lindblom, C. (1959) 'The science of muddling through', *Public Administration Review*, vol 19, pp79–88

Luhmann, H-J. (2001) *Die Blindheit der Gesellschaft: Filter der Risikowahrnehmung*, Gerling Akademie Verlag, Munich

Luhmann, N. (1986) *Ökologische Kommunikation: Kann die moderne Gesellschaft sich auf ökologische Gefährdungen einstellen?*, Westdeutscher Verlag, Opladen

March, J. G. (1994) *A Primer of Decision-Making*, The Free Press, New York

March, J. G. and Olsen, J. P. (1976) *Ambiguity and Choice in Organizations*, Scandinavian University Press, Oslo

March, J. G. and Olsen, J. P. (1986) 'Garbage can models of decision making in organizations', in March, J. G. and Weissinger-Baylon, R. (eds) *Ambiguity and Command: Organizational Perspectives on Military Decision Making*, HarperCollins, Cambridge

March, J. G. and Olsen, J. P. (1989) *Rediscovering Institutions: The Organizational Basis of Politics*, The Free Press, New York

March, J. G. and Simon, H. (1993) *Organizations*, Blackwell Publishers, London

Mayer, S. (2005) 'Actors' teamwork developing a National Strategy for waste prevention and processing for Austria – a proactive step towards bridging the gap between experts work and political decision-making', paper presented at the IAIA SEA Conference, Prague

McLauchlan, A. and João, E. (2005) 'An independent body to oversee SEA: Bureaucratic burden or efficient accountable administration?', paper presented at the IAIA SEA Conference, Prague

Ministry of the Environment and Energy (1995) *Strategic Environmental Assessment of Bills and other Governmental Proposals: Examples and Experience*, The Ministry of the Environment and Energy, Copenhagen

Nilsson, M. and Dalkmann, H. (2001) 'Decision making and strategic environmental assessment', *Journal of Environmental Assessment Policy & Management*, vol 3, pp305–327

Renton, S. and Bailey, J. (2000) 'Policy development and the environment', *Impact Assessment and Project Appraisal*, vol 18, no 3, pp245–251

Schein, E. (1969) *Process Consultation: Its Role in Organization Development*, vol 1, Addison-Wesley, New York

Schein, E. (1987) *Process Consultation: Lesson for Managers and Consultants*, vol 2, Addison-Wesley, New York

Schmidt, M., João, E. and Albrecht, E. (2005) *Implementing Strategic Environmental Assessment*, Springer Verlag, Berlin

Sheate, W., Dagg, S., Richardson, J., Aschemann, R., Palerm, J. and Stehen, U. (2001) *SEA and Integration of the Environment into Strategic Decision-Making*, vol 1, European Commission

Simon, H. (1957) *Models of Man*, John Wiley and Sons, New York

Thérivel, R. (2004) *Strategic Environmental Assessment in Action*, Earthscan, London

Thérivel, R. and Brown, A. L. (1999) 'Methods of strategic environmental assessment', in Petts, J. (ed) *Handbook of Environmental Impact Assessment*, vol 1, Blackwell Science, Oxford, pp74–92

van Dyck, M. (2005) 'Political decision making and the influence of an SEA-process', paper presented to the IAIA SEA Conference, Prague

World Bank (2005) *Integrating Environmental Considerations in Policy Formulation: Lessons from Policy-Based SEA Experience*, Environment Department, Washington, DC

32
From Formulation to Implementation: Strengthening SEA through Follow-up

Aleh Cherp, Maria R. Partidário and Jos Arts

Introduction: Rationale for SEA follow-up

This chapter deals with strategic environmental assessment (SEA) follow-up, which we define as:

> *Monitoring and evaluation of the implementation of a strategic initiative and relevant environmental factors for management of, and communication about, the environmental performance of that strategic initiative.*[1]

Although SEA follow-up is substantially different from environmental impact assessment (EIA) follow-up, they are based on similar principles and rationale. This rationale stems from the observation that impact assessment predictions are uncertain, that unexpected circumstances may emerge during implementation, and that execution may deviate from original plans. EIA follow-up aims to reduce such uncertainties, account for such new circumstances and keep the project in line with the EIA recommendations.

The need for SEA follow-up is dictated by similar factors, which assume larger importance and impose greater challenges at the strategic level. These comprise:

- **Uncertainties** in determining environmental implications of a strategic initiative are typically more profound than those found with regard to environmental impacts of an individual project.
- **New circumstances** are more likely to emerge in relation to a strategic initiative whose implementation arena is much less controlled by the proponent than project operation is controlled by the developer.
- **Deviations** from initial designs are more usual for strategic initiatives than for projects, which normally tend to follow more closely the original plans.

The last point is especially important. The rationale for SEA follow-up is linked to its promise to promote strategic change towards environmental sustainability. This means that SEA should be able to help shape not only the formulation of strategic initiatives but also their implementation. At the same time, the link between formulation and implementation of strategic initiatives is often much weaker than is the case at the project level. Thus, follow-up is needed to expand the focus of SEA from merely ensuring 'green rhetoric' in policies, plans and programmes (PPPs) to safeguard environmentally sound patterns of activities arising from PPPs.

Given such a convincing rationale for SEA follow-up, it is surprising that the discussion of this topic has been rather limited so far. Although the need for SEA follow-up was noted in early SEA publications (for example, Lee and Walsh, 1992; Sadler and Verheem, 1996; Thérivel and Partidário, 1996), since then there has been only a handful of research papers on this topic,[2] most notably Partidário and Fischer (2004) and Partidário and Arts (2005). In practical guidance, SEA follow-up has also been less emphasized than other SEA elements. Both legislation and guidance tend to address monitoring to a greater extent than evaluation, management and communication.

There are two reasons for this relative neglect of SEA follow-up. First of all, the SEA discourse has been strongly influenced by impact assessment (IA) thinking, historically shaped by the conviction that decision precedes and guides action. The centrality of this view is reflected in the IA motto: 'Think first – act second.' Operationally, this meant the focus of IA and SEA on attaining environmental ends through shaping environmentally significant decisions, resolutions regarding future actions. The idea of SEA was largely based on the assumption that once a 'strategic decision' is made it is then implemented until superseded by another strategic decision. By influencing 'strategic decisions', the SEA process also influences a range of lower-level decisions and 'implementation' activities without focusing on their details. Thus, in the SEA discourse, shaping decisions 'as early as possible' is traditionally given more importance (see, for example, Thérivel, 2004) than examining what happens to these decisions (and the environment) after they have been made.

The second reason for neglecting SEA follow-up has had less to do with SEA and more with the nature of strategic initiatives themselves. The relationship between formulation and implementation of such initiatives is much more complex (see Partidário and Arts, 2005, for an extended discussion). Many strategic initiatives do not presume much implementation activities to speak of. They may be more about articulating and communicating commitments or principles than about action. If there are little or no implementation activities and if the institutional frameworks created for formulation of strategic initiatives cease to exist after the initiative has been endorsed, SEA follow-up may lose its 'organizational anchoring' or 'ownership'. Even when this is not the case, the links between formulation and implementation of strategic initiatives are much more complex than, for example, the links between design and implementation of projects. Understanding the nature of these links is a necessary step in conceiving effective SEA follow-up.

Conceptually, the relationship between formulation and implementation of strategic initiatives has been extensively scrutinized by corporate 'strategy formation' theories, policy and organizational studies. All these disciplines clearly point out that the connection between the two is not linear, straightforward and one-way as often depicted by formal and rational planning theories (see, for example, Mintzberg, 1994). In particular, there is significant evidence that actual implementation often dramatically differs from formally conceived plans even in successful strategies. Moreover, in so-called 'emergent' strategies, action does not follow formal decisions, but instead decisions articulate learning gained from action. 'Implementation' here is as important (if not more important) as 'formulation'. This reasoning is reflected in the ongoing debate regarding strategies for sustainable development, which are now sometimes pictured as such 'emergent' strategies – processes for learning, capacity-building, debate, and so on – rather than 'new plans' (for example, OECD, 2001).

The EA discourse has partially reflected these developments, often connecting them to the fact that environmental impacts of proposed activities can rarely be predicted or managed with certainty. EIA follow-up recognizes that flexibility is needed in managing environmental impacts of individual projects. Adaptive environmental assessment and management (AEAM) aims to overcome key weaknesses of EIA by suggesting a focus on creating interactive management systems instead of attempting to formulate 'environmentally sound decisions' (Holling, 1978).

The SEA thinking has also evolved to become more receptive to the concept of 'emergent' strategies (see an overview of this evolution in Cherp et al, 2007). If at the early stages of the IA evolution the focus was on getting one key decision 'right', more recent SEA thinking recognized that strategic initiatives are shaped not by one single decision, but by series of connected decisions (see, for example, Deelstra et al, 2003). That is why SEA guidance stresses integration of SEA with planning or policy-making processes rather than simply producing a one-point 'assessment' of a proposed decision. However, decision-making does not stop with the adoption of a strategic initiative. Indeed, in some cases, it becomes more complex and strategically significant as the strategic initiative goes through revision and adjustment cycles. In parallel, there are also processes of interpretation, application and implementation of the strategic initiative. In order to support sustainable development, any strategic initiative in principle needs to integrate sustainability considerations into all of these post-adoption activities.

SEA scholars increasingly recognize that 'decision-making processes [are] neither linear nor phase-wise' (Nooteboom and Teisman, 2003) and thus, revisiting once adopted decisions may become necessary not only during formulation of strategies, but also during their implementation. These theories, both within and outside the SEA field, argue for shifting the weight from shaping strategy formulation to integrating environmental considerations into strategy implementation, in other words, for SEA follow-up. As this thinking strengthens and disseminates, SEA follow-up will inevitably become a more important element of the SEA discourse. The question will then become: how can it be practically implemented?

From EIA to SEA follow-up

The emerging theories and practice of SEA follow-up are largely shaped by those of project-level EIA follow-up. EIA follow-up is a relatively well-established field covered in at least two dedicated books (Arts, 1998; Morrison-Saunders and Arts, 2004a) and a special issue of *Impact Assessment and Project Appraisal* (September 2005). Most of the principles for EIA follow-up (such as those formulated by Marshall et al, 2005) are relevant to SEA follow-up. There is also a general consensus that, similarly to EIA follow-up, SEA follow-up should include the following key elements: monitoring, evaluation, management and communication (Morrison-Saunders and Arts, 2004c).

As already mentioned, not all of these elements are equally emphasized in legislation and guidance. For example, the 'SEA' Directive 2001/42/EC includes a requirement:

> To monitor the significant environmental effects of the implementation of plans and programmes in order, inter alia, to identify at an early stage unforeseen adverse effects, and to be able to undertake appropriate remedial action. (Article 10)

It explicitly stipulates monitoring, but only indirectly refers to evaluation (implied in 'identification of unforeseen adverse effects') and management (implied in 'the ability to undertake appropriate remedial action') and does not mention communication at all.

Not all approaches to EIA follow-up will be universally applicable or effective for SEA follow-up. We shall illustrate this statement in relation to the four follow-up elements listed above, but first we make two general observations on the differences between EIA and SEA follow-up.

The first concerns the focus on impacts within EIA follow-up. The SEA focus has been shifting from environmental impacts of strategic initiatives to (sustainability) implications of their goals, objectives, agendas and implementation measures. This means that SEA follow-up should also address all these aspects rather than merely environmental impacts. For example, the 'multi-track approach' proposed by Partidário and Arts (2005) expands from the initial focus on impacts towards checking validity of underlying assumptions, goal-achievement, performance of the strategic initiative and consistency of other activities linked to it as described in Box 32.1. This echoes the shift of focus from verifying 'what was expected' to 'what was wanted', from impacts to objectives, as suggested by Noble and Storey (2005) based on empirical evidence of EA follow-up in Canada.

The second difference between EIA and SEA follow-up concerns the implementation mechanisms to which they are linked. EIA follow-up and project implementation are often undertaken by the same proponent (also responsible for the project proposal and the EIA). As already mentioned, the relationship between formulation and implementation of strategic initiatives is much more complex. The type of implementation activities depends upon the nature of a particular strategic initiative. Implementation activities may not envision specific actions leading to the declared goals of strategic activities. The actors in implementation may be not the same as proponents of the strategic initiative.

For example, a programme may prescribe specific actions, which are funded and controlled by the proponent. In this case, programme implementation is not significantly different from operation of a project. In many cases, however, programmes might envision actions that are dependent on other actors. Land-use plans may set up conditions for developments and, thus, 'implementation' of such plans may not presume any proactive actions by the planning authorities that draft them. At the same time, regular revision and updating of such plans, as well as issuing planning permits may be viewed as implementation activities. Policies may envision only periodic evaluations and amendments.

Many strategies are adopted because they set agendas, articulate commitments, or promote certain principles. Their implementation occurs through information, communication and learning rather than through any specific development activities. Some policies are more exercises in rhetoric than

---

Box 32.1 *A multi-track approach in SEA follow-up*

Track 1: Monitoring and evaluating actual changes in the state of the environment, socio-economical situation, institutional structures, and so on, to detect and assess factors with implications for the strategic initiative in question. Examples of such factors may include:

- Trends indicating actualization of specific scenarios considered during the formulation of the strategic initiative.
- New emerging factors that affect the underlying assumptions or baseline analysis, the choice of objectives, alternatives and implementation measures made during the formulation of the strategic initiative.

Track 2: Evaluating achievement of stated objectives of the strategic initiative (so-called 'goals achievement evaluation')

Track 3: Evaluating performance of the strategic initiative, with a focus on 'implementation' activities.

Track 4: Evaluating conformance of subsequent decision-making with the strategic initiative and the SEA, the focus here is on consistency in decision-making, especially relevant for hierarchical planning systems.

Track 5: Monitoring and evaluating of the actual impacts of the strategic initiative on the environment and sustainability, the focus being to understand the causal link between an observable fact and the strategic initiative.

Source: Partidário and Arts (2005)

action-inducing mechanisms. Often, but not always, the more 'strategic' the initiative (for example, policy) the less specifically defined is its implementation. Thus, SEA follow-up will always need to face the need to integrate into these sometimes complex, sometimes unclear and sometimes absent implementation mechanisms.

Expanding the focus beyond impacts and untangling complex links between formulation and implementation are at heart of developing all four elements of SEA follow-up as described in the next section.

Elements of SEA follow-up

Monitoring

The International Association for Impact Assessment (IAIA) SEA Performance Criteria (IAIA, 2002) prescribe that good SEA should provide information on the 'actual impacts of implementing a strategic decision'. Likewise, the European Commission 'SEA' Directive requires monitoring of effects (see above). This focus on effects (impacts) has faced both practical and conceptual challenges. From the practical angle, effects of strategic initiatives are difficult to both trace and attribute. On the one hand, strategic initiatives may have complex and indirect effects through their influence on other initiatives of different levels. Partidário and Arts (2005) refer to this as a 'splash effect'. Consequently, impacts may become difficult to trace through complex chains of causality. Furthermore, tracking impacts that are not based on tiering are hardly feasible or necessary at the current development stage of SEA follow-up practice (Gachechiladze, 2010). On the other hand, when changes in environmental conditions are observed, their attribution to a specific strategic initiative may be problematic, as such changes usually also result from many other factors.

From the conceptual angle, the very focus of SEA on impacts, originally inherited from IA, has been questioned in the SEA literature. It has been argued that SEA should concentrate not only on impacts, but on the validity of the objectives, soundness of the underlying analysis and various other features of strategic initiatives (for example, Dalal-Clayton and Sadler, 2005). All such information obtained during SEA is characterized by the same uncertainty and dynamism as prediction of environmental impacts and therefore should be a focus of SEA follow-up to the same (if not a larger) degree as environmental impacts.

In accordance with the multi-track approach proposed by Partidário and Arts (2005), SEA follow-up monitoring may be broadly divided into the following three types:

- A) Monitoring of actual environmental, socio-economic and institutional changes relevant to: (a) the broader context of formulation and implementation of a strategic initiative (such as envisioned scenarios, underlying assumptions, and so on); (b) progress towards strategic goals ('goal-achievement'); and/or (c) actual impacts of a strategic initiative.

- B) Monitoring of implementation activities within a strategic initiative.
- C) Monitoring of other activities related to the implementation of a strategic initiative.

The first type of monitoring is required by some national legislation (for example, in Finland, the Netherlands and Hong Kong). Directive 2001/42/EC specifically focuses on the third subcomponent of monitoring (A(c) actual impacts). In other systems, monitoring focuses both on impacts and objective-related indicators. For example, Table 32.1 lists selected parameters proposed for monitoring environmental aspects of transport infrastructure in Nordthüringen regional plan in Germany. Canadian legislation focuses (S)EA follow-up monitoring on: (a) the accuracy of prediction of environmental impacts; and (b) effectiveness of mitigation measures (Noble and Storey, 2005).There is considerable guidance on choice of indicators for SEA follow-up monitoring (for example, Barth and Fuder, 2002). In order for the monitoring to be relevant, such indicators should be selected with reference to the evaluation tasks, for instance, according to the 'multi-track approach' described below.

As with the other elements of SEA follow-up, assigning responsibilities for monitoring may be challenging. The proponent of the strategic initiative may not have adequate capacities or a mandate for required monitoring. Thus, existing monitoring systems may need to be utilized, especially for monitoring of environmental and sustainability changes (type A in the list above). In countries such as the Netherlands, Germany and England, the authority responsible for SEA is also responsible for monitoring; other authorities are obliged to provide relevant information and existing monitoring systems should be utilized as much as possible (Hanusch, 2005; Arts, 1998; Gachechiladze, 2008).

Directive 2001/42/EC encourages use of existing systems for SEA monitoring (Article 10 (2)). However, reliance on external monitoring systems

Table 32.1 *Selected monitoring parameters for environmental aspects of transport infrastructure in the Nordthüringen regional plan, Germany*

	Environmental objective	Monitoring parameter
The road and railway network should be developed in a way that:		
1.1	Reduces traffic-related noise and pollutants including CO_2	Trends in traffic-related noise and pollution
1.2	Preserves large non-fragmented areas	Trends in fragmentation in the region
1.3	The continuity of biotope networks is maintained or recovered	Length of selected roads in particularly sensitive areas/areas with high
1.4	The traffic density in ecologically sensitive areas is reduced	environmental and technical risks (for example, flooding areas)
1.5	It sustains a high stability against environmental and technical risks	Development of species particular sensitive for fragmentation
1.6	It results in a lower increase of traffic areas including the share of seating	Development of the share of traffic areas in the region

Source: Hanusch (2005)

may create a challenge in linking the monitoring component of the SEA follow-up to evaluation and management of the strategic initiative and relevant communication. In particular, other types of monitoring (B and C) will often need to be conducted by the proponent of the strategic initiative. There also should be special provisions for transferring monitoring data collected by external agencies to those actors who can evaluate and act upon the information in the context of SEA follow-up (see Marshall and Arts, 2005). Thus, an important role of SEA processes is to establish such provisions and foster linkages between external monitoring agencies and actors involved in the implementation of the strategic initiative.

In addition to using existing systems, special arrangements can be made for SEA follow-up monitoring. For example, the SEA of Vienna Waste Management Plan established a special monitoring team including representatives of the waste management authorities, environmental authorities, and a non-governmental organization (NGO). The monitoring team drafts a yearly monitoring report which is then sent to the SEA team and the Vienna city environmental department who can make necessary adjustments to the plan (reported in Barth and Fuder, 2002; see also Box 32.2). Thus, the responsibility for monitoring should be considered in a broader context of ensuring institutional ownership and anchoring of SEA follow-up efforts.

Box 32.2 *Issues addressed in the annual monitoring report of the Vienna Waste Management Plan (WMP) SEA*

- Is there sufficient progress to realistically implement the WMP by 2010?
- Do the current waste flows correspond to the ones forecasted?
- Which measures of avoidance have been implemented? Which avoidance effects have been thereby achieved?
- Will the waste flow still correspond to the forecast in 2010?
- Will the assumptions concerning the emission standards of the planned facilities be still valid in 2010?
- Have the provisions of the Viennese WMP for the construction and operation of the agreed facilities (such as emission standards) been met?
- Have there been essential technological developments since the WMP was agreed on which make it necessary to adjust the plan?
- Have essential framework conditions changed since the WMP has been agreed in, which make it necessary to consider new alternatives (scenarios)?
- Is it necessary to adjust the capacities of the treatment facilities, which were agreed on?
- Have the predicted numbers and types of buildings been connected to district heating? Have the predicted emission reductions taken place?

Source: Adapted from Barth and Fuder (2002)

Evaluation

In the context of SEA follow-up, evaluation, simply stated, means making sense of the monitoring data and especially linking them to management decisions. While noting that 'it is unhelpful to view monitoring and evaluation as very distinct and mutually exclusive activities' (Persson and Nilsson, 2007, p477), Persson and Nilsson (2007, p483) point out key differences between evaluation and monitoring:

> *(a) evaluations are undertaken less frequently, but are broader and deeper in scope, (b) evaluations involve ... making a value judgement rather than just measuring; and (c) evaluation may question underlying intervention rationales and strategies to deal with a problem rather than focusing on operation aspects [only].*

In EIA follow-up practice, evaluation usually focuses on two sets of questions (as, for example, in the Canadian system described by Noble and Storey, 2005):

- Are the actual impacts of development in line with EIA predictions? Do they conform to environmental quality standards, functional thresholds, permits or other reference values?
- Is the project, especially its environmental mitigation components, implemented in accordance with the original design, EIA recommendations and permit conditions?

In case of non-conformance or significant undesirable impacts, EIA follow-up evaluation may result in management recommendations, for example, on changing operation conditions or implementing additional mitigation measures. In principle, the evaluation element of SEA follow-up should pursue the same action-triggering function in relation to the unfolding strategic initiative. However, the complex and strategic nature of SEA follow-up presumes that the scope of evaluation should extend beyond accuracy of SEA predictions and conformity of mitigation measures as suggested, for example, in the 'multi-track approach' (Box 32.1).

The relative importance of these tracks depends upon the nature of strategic initiative in question. For instance, as stated by Partidário and Arts (2005), a strategic initiative around a highly sensitive issue of much public concern may adopt an extensive monitoring programme with no direct focus on causal relationships (Track 1), use headline-sensitive indicators in order to inform the public about the state of affairs and whether objectives are being achieved (Tracks 1 and 2), and also aim to demonstrate if the strategy is performing well (Track 3) as well as its subsequent decisions (Track 4).

A highly abstract national policy, which focuses mainly on decision-making at other planning levels, may use: evaluation of achievement of objectives (Track 2); performance evaluation (Track 3); and/or conformance check of subsequent decision-making (Track 4) to review plan implementation. A concrete strategic initiative that unfolds directly into an operational project and involves huge environmental risks may employ monitoring and evaluation of the impacts on the environment and sustainability (Track 5).

Strategic initiatives with notable legal and procedural implications (such as land-use plans, regulations, and so on) may need particular evaluation according to Tracks 3 and 4. At the same time, most strategic initiatives may, to a certain extent, benefit from evaluation along all of the five tracks. Moreover, in reality, various evaluation tracks may overlap as illustrated by the example of the Vienna Waste Management Plan (Box 32.2). In addition to biophysical indicators and criteria used in evaluation, Persson and Nilsson (2007) suggest the possible use of institutional criteria common in policy evaluation, such as 'flexibility', 'legitimacy' and 'transparency'.

Whatever track is pursued, evaluation in SEA follow-up is likely to deal with vast data arrays (often collected for different purposes), complex issues, new phenomena and emerging factors. Compared with EIA follow-up, it is much more likely to encounter unexpected and unforeseen circumstances and the need for a strategic rather than incremental response, such as revisiting the assumptions underlying the strategic initiative (deep or 'double-loop learning' (Schön, 1983) as discussed in Morrison-Saunders and Arts, 2004a). This is partially recognized in Directive 2001/42/EC, which states that the purpose of monitoring should be 'identifying unforeseen adverse effects'.[3]

For example, the Integrated Assessment of the Tomsk Regional Development Strategy recommended creating a 'Strategic Radar' mechanism. The 'Radar' would regularly test the validity of assumptions on which the Strategy has been based, particularly which of the underlying scenarios is actually followed. It will also detect and assess new factors, which may affect the implementation of the Strategy. The 'Strategic Radar' data would be fed into 'strategic conversations', a forum of Strategy's stakeholders who will be able to discuss these new trends and make decisions on potential changes to the strategy (Ecoline and REC, 2006).

Consequently, SEA follow-up evaluation potentially may become as complex as the original SEA. Unsurprisingly, Persson and Nilsson (2006) call SEA follow-up 'ex post SEA' to stress its equal importance to the mainstream 'ex ante SEA' and to emphasize that it can be conducted even in the absence of the latter.

While monitoring may often use external systems for data collection, evaluation should be directly connected to the strategic initiative in question. It may be conducted within the same organizational and procedural framework as the strategic initiatives themselves. For example, formal regular evaluations of policies or reviews and revisions of plans may provide convenient time-points for SEA follow-up evaluation ('evaluative moments' in the planning process, see Arts,1998). Persson and Nilsson (2006) follow Vedung (1997) in outlining advantages and disadvantages of internal (conducted by the proponent of the strategic initiative) versus external evaluation. Due to potential complexity of SEA follow-up evaluation, there may be merits for assembling 'SEA follow-up evaluation teams' to prepare evaluation reports much in the same way as SEA reports are prepared.

Management

Management is probably the most important and challenging yet least discussed component of SEA follow-up that ensures continuous integration of sustainability considerations into unfolding strategic initiatives. The management component should ensure that SEA and SEA follow-up recommendations are translated meaningfully into decisions and actions implementing the strategic initiative and protecting the environment. Two questions arising here are: (a) which 'decisions and actions' should be targeted; and (b) how can these be influenced? The first question relates to the already discussed complex implementation of strategic initiatives. In general terms, several types of actions and decisions may be relevant to implementation of strategic initiatives (Figure 32.1).

- **Type I:** Decisions on revising and amending a strategic initiative. For example, land-use plans undergo periodic reviews and renewals. Monitoring and evaluations according to Tracks 1, 2, 3 and 4 (Box 32.1) are especially relevant in the context of such revisions.
- **Type II:** Actions directly prescribed in a strategic initiative and often implemented by the proponent. For example, a transport plan may prescribe road construction. Evaluation of goal-attainment (Track 2), performance (Track 3) and actual impacts (Track 5) are especially relevant here.
- **Type III:** Decisions and actions implemented by other actors but controlled by a strategic initiative through formal frameworks. For example, a land-use plan may restrict certain type of developments in particular zones. Checking conformance of subsequent decision-making on development proposals is especially relevant here (Track 4).
- **Type IV:** All other decisions and actions, which are affected by a strategic initiative. For example, a national energy policy may influence consumer

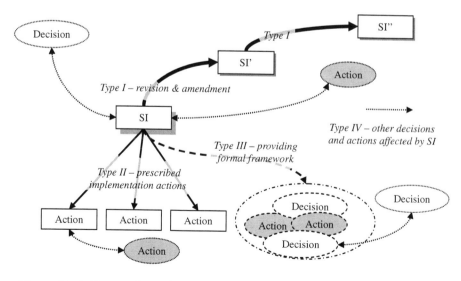

Figure 32.1 *Types of 'implementation activities' for a strategic initiative (SI)*

and investor behaviour without directly controlling it. Such effects are mainly achieved through price signals, 'soft' incentives and other information-based or similar indirect mechanisms.

The importance of different types of actions and decisions depends upon the nature of a strategic initiative. Types II–III management and control responses may be more relevant for plans and programmes, Type IV actions and decisions might be especially relevant for policies, whereas Type I decisions are for all types of strategic initiatives undergoing revision cycles. It should also be noted that all four types overlap to a certain degree.

At this point, we address the second question: how can all these decisions and actions be influenced by SEA follow-up? For decisions and actions of Types I–III, there may be legal, administrative or other institutional conditions that directly support such an influence. For example, SEA follow-up may play a relatively straightforward role in Type I decisions. The proponent of a strategic initiative will most likely also be responsible for its revision and amendment. The original SEA findings as well as the results of SEA follow-up (which should ideally be timed so as to correspond to the revisions cycle) in principle may be directly linked to the renewal decisions, in the same way that SEA is used at other 'evaluative moments' of planning processes.

The role of SEA follow-up in Type II and III actions may be related to the concept of tiering (described in Chapter 26 of this book, see also Lee and Wood, 1987). Tiering focuses on decisions that are 'nested' within or hierarchically linked to the strategic initiative. The mechanism of tiering suggests that SEA follow-up should shape such decisions by linking their environmental assessments (SEAs or EIAs) to the original ('higher-level') SEA findings and recommendations. The concept of tiering features in most SEA texts and principles, but empirical evidence on its practical implementation remains, so far, scarce. Tiering is naturally more common and effective in formal hierarchically organized planning systems, such as transport or waste management planning (see Fischer, 2002; Arts et al, 2011).

The SEA community has been increasingly coming to terms with the fact that many actions and decisions relevant to the implementation of strategic initiatives belong to Type IV, they lack *a priori* known, formal and easily traceable links with the original initiative. This is very well described by the 'splash' metaphor mentioned earlier (Partidário and Arts, 2005). The 'splash' effect means that a strategic initiative may affect decisions and actions at the same, lower or higher levels across sectors and administrative jurisdictions. The question is: how can these actions and decisions be possibly tracked and shaped by SEA follow-up?

The problem of influencing Type IV actions and decisions is closely related to the challenge of institutional ownership of SEA follow-up. Actors behind Type IV decisions are rarely 'owners' of the original SEA. Thus, their participation in the SEA follow-up should be assured by specific organizational, communication or other arrangements. In certain cases, such arrangements may be provided by an environmental management system (EMS). Then, the EMS is part of the overall management system that supports formulation and implementation of the organization's environmental policy. In principle, SEA follow-up may be linked to EMS in much the same way as EIA follow-up is often linked with EMS or environmental management plans (Marshall and Arts, 2005). If the project-level EIA links with EMS for a company-developer, the SEA for public sector strategic initiatives may be linked to EMS in public authorities.

So far, this approach to SEA follow-up seems to be little used in the public sector and it is merely at the stage of discussion and testing (for example, in the framework of the MiSt research programme in Sweden). Despite certain potential, it may face serious obstacles. The first obstacle concerns the role of EMS in (local) authorities. Worldwide research has shown that authorities most often employ EMS to deal with their own affairs (use of energy, paper, production of waste, and so on), but not with their PPPs (which are subject to SEA). This observation was made in Sweden (Naturvårdsverket, 2004), New Zealand (Cockrean, 2000), Japan (Srinivas and Yashiro, 1999) and the Netherlands.

In other words, EMS in authorities is not strategic (Cherp, 2004) and it is not certain whether EMS as currently set-up can address strategic issues dealt with by SEA. The second challenge is that appropriate management responses within SEA follow-up may be needed outside of the organizational boundaries from those in which an original strategic initiative was adopted (and the SEA conducted). Thus, even if adequate approaches to linking SEA follow-up with EMS are developed, they are not likely to encompass Type IV decisions and actions taken by other stakeholders outside of the responsible authority. It is nevertheless important for an effective SEA follow-up to at least identify key Type IV decisions and attempt to shape them by available means.

To summarize, the management component of SEA follow-up:

- Should concentrate on those decisions and actions that are most significant for implementing the strategic initiative (especially achievement of stated environmental goals and avoidance or mitigation of negative environmental effects); and that can be reasonably influenced by SEA follow-up. This is analogous to a key principle of EIA follow-up as stated by Morrison-Saunders and Arts (2004a).
- During the SEA and SEA follow-up, continuous identification of such decisions and actions should be undertaken. This 'scoping' process should involve institutional analysis of the arena in which the strategic initiative unfolds.
- This identification should describe: (a) the actions and decisions that are relevant; (b) their relationship to the implementation of the strategic initiative; (c) the key actors and stakeholders involved in these actions and decisions; and (d) the mechanisms by which they can potentially be influenced within the SEA follow-up.
- Identification should also cover those decisions and actions that are not formally articulated (for example, informal decisions, actions, behaviour patterns) but nevertheless strategically significant.

Communication

At the project level, EIA follow-up communication may be primarily designed to provide information about the actual impacts and conformance to those who are affected by or have a statutory responsibility to oversee the development. EIA follow-up can also be communicated much wider to ensure continuous improvement in EIA systems and capacities. Marshall et al (2005) also emphasize the importance of using local knowledge and learning as an outcome of effective communication within EIA follow-up. In general, SEA follow-up should perform similar tasks, although its audiences may be even wider and more diverse than at the project level.

As we mentioned in the previous section, communication and especially learning within SEA follow-up is closely linked to its management component. Management of Types I–III actions may be supported by information flows within formally established channels, whereas influencing Type IV decisions may require wider and less traditional communication dissemination strategies. This is because many of the relevant decisions and actions will be carried out by actors that were not originally involved in the formulation of a strategic initiative or the SEA. In order to bring these actions in line with SEA recommendations, all these actors should be informed both about the original SEA and about the SEA follow-up.

In the context of SEA follow-up, communication should be two-way. An open process that includes all relevant stakeholders is important since strategic plan formation and implementation often involves not only enforcement actions but also processes of negotiation, learning and persuasion (Woltjer, 2004; Deelstra et al, 2003). It is important to clarify the intentions, values, needs, wishes, knowledge and views of the network of actors for effective implementation of a strategic initiative. SEA follow-up communication with, and participation of, stakeholders should go beyond just informing, and include consultation, or even partnership (analogous to Arnstein's (1969) 'ladder of citizen's participation'). For an approach to the role of SEA in communication between evaluators and decision-makers, see Vicente and Partidário (2006).

Thus, communication can be considered as both a separate element and a component of monitoring, evaluation and management of SEA follow-up. Communication plays an important role in learning, formation of cultures, networks and institutions, which are key components of societal change. Moreover, SEA follow-up might provide a useful mechanism for ongoing communication and learning. Therefore, communication should be the central element of SEA follow-up if SEA aims to achieve strategic change for sustainable development.

Conclusions and outlook

Views on the importance of SEA follow-up depend upon perception of the overall purpose of SEA. If SEA primarily aims to influence the formal content of PPPs then SEA follow-up may have relatively little importance. If, on the other hand, the purpose of SEA is to promote strategic change towards sustainable development then follow-up may be viewed as one of its central elements, because it is implementation of strategic initiatives, not their formal articulation that shapes such change.

In comparison with EIA follow-up, SEA follow-up has a wider scope arising from complexity of implementation of strategic initiatives. The key elements of SEA follow-up (monitoring, evaluation and management elements) and essential relationships between them are shown on Figure 32.2. This figure should be taken as only a very simplified representation since various 'elements', 'tracks' and 'types' would often overlap in reality. Despite this complexity, a number of practical points can be made about SEA follow-up:

- SEA follow-up should be undertaken throughout the life cycle of the strategic initiative.
- An SEA follow-up programme should be elaborated and endorsed during the SEA process and before the strategic initiative is launched.
- SEA follow-up should include monitoring, evaluation, management and communication components.
- SEA follow-up should extend beyond mere monitoring and managing impacts of the strategic initiative and ensuring its conformance to the original plan. It should also verify goal-achievement, identify unforeseen circumstances and periodically validate the original assumptions of strategic initiative.
- It should be integrated with implementation (in a broader sense) of the strategic initiative and tailored to specifics of such implementation.
- Monitoring, evaluation and management of environmental implications of a strategic initiative may start during its implementation, even in the absence of SEA at an earlier stage.

Such 'ex post' SEA, mentioned in the last point, may serve as an entry point to prepare the ground and apply the SEA process to future revisions of the strategic initiatives or linked strategic decisions. In our experience, such an approach

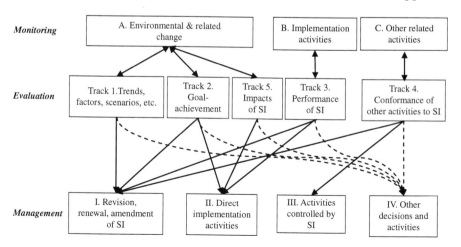

Figure 32.2 *Key elements of SEA follow-up monitoring, evaluation and management of strategic initiatives (SI)*

may be especially suitable in recent SEA systems where some pilot SEA projects may need to start in the middle of the planning cycle.

Table 32.2 can provide a template for planning SEA follow-up in connection with untangling implementation actions. For the preparation of a SEA follow-up programme, it may be useful to start with recording the envisioned implementation activities for the strategic initiative, possibly dividing them into monitoring, evaluation, management and communication. SEA follow-up activities should be aligned, to the extent possible, with these implementation

Table 32.2 *Planning SEA follow-up of strategic initiatives (SI)*

SEA follow-up element	Elements in implementation of the SI	SEA follow-up activities	Responsibilities	Issues to consider
Monitoring	Monitoring as part of implementation of SI. Other related monitoring systems.	Systematic data collection, processing, storage, publication.	May be linked with existing monitoring systems.	Address: A. Environmental and related factors. B. Implementation activities. C. Other relevant activities. Choice of indicators to support evaluation.
Evaluation	For example, regular reviews, evaluations, performance assessments, audits.	Periodic in-depth (monitoring) data analysis. Evaluation reports.	Internal or external SEA (follow-up) team.	Scanning for emergent and strategic issues related to basic assumptions. Multi-track approach.
Management	Regular revisions and renewal of SI (Type I). Direct implementation activities (Type II). Controlled decisions and actions (Type III). Other decisions and actions (Type IV).	For example, (formal) tiering systems, EMS, communication with or partici- pation of key actors.	For example, proponent of SI, relevant organizations, stakeholders.	Systematic identification of relevant actions and decisions, including those that are not formally articulated, implementation of management response/actions.
Communication	For example, negotiation, learning, persuasion.	For example, informing, consultation, discussion, mediation, partnerships Should be included in monitoring, evaluation, management activities.	For example, proponent of SI, relevant organizations, actors.	Intentions, interests, perceptions, also relevance of (local) knowledge.

Table 32.3 *SEA follow-up: Summary statement*

Main trends and issues	It is increasingly recognized that SEA should influence not only formal content of strategic documents, but also their real-life implementation, which may be affected by uncertainties during the planning stage, unforeseen circumstances and/or significant deviation of implementation from original plans. It is therefore believed that SEA should not end with the adoption of the strategic initiative but should rather be linked with a variety of instruments: monitoring, evaluation, management and communication – collectively referred to as 'SEA follow-up'.
Main perspectives	At present, SEA follow-up is relatively underdeveloped. There is little theoretical and empirical research in this area. Legislation requiring SEA follow-up in some jurisdictions primarily focuses on its monitoring component and interprets this component rather narrowly. At the same time, existing insights into practice demonstrate that SEA follow-up is an effective tool of increasing the impact of SEA in real-life activities rather than just 'on paper'. Recent progress in conceptualization of SEA follow-up notes that it should follow several 'tracks' in monitoring and evaluation, concerning not only the effects of strategic initiatives but also their performance, goal achievement, changes in the underlying assumption and related activities. In relation to its management component, the SEA follow-up should explicitly address diverse decisions ranging from revisions of the strategic initiative in question to implementation of directly or indirectly controlled or influenced activities.
Key lessons	SEA follow-up should be undertaken throughout the life cycle of the strategic initiative. An SEA follow-up programme should be elaborated and endorsed during the SEA process and before the strategic initiative is launched. SEA follow-up should include monitoring, evaluation, management and communication components. SEA follow-up should extend beyond mere monitoring and managing impacts of the strategic initiative and ensuring its conformance to the original plan. It should also verify goal-achievement, identify unforeseen circumstances and periodically validate the original assumptions of strategic initiative. SEA follow-up should be integrated with implementation (in a broader sense) of the strategic initiative and tailored to specifics of such implementation. The activities which form SEA follow-up may be carried out even if no SEA was conducted (a suitable term for such activities in this case may be 'ex post SEA').
Future directions	The key challenges for SEA follow-up are 'organizational anchoring' or 'institutional ownership' (who should undertake SEA follow-up) and its interaction with other environmental policy tools and instruments such as EMS in public authorities.

activities, but may also have additional elements. Responsibilities for SEA follow-up should be carefully identified, because in most cases the proponent of the strategic initiative will play only a limited role in its implementation (Marshall and Arts, 2005). Most importantly, SEA follow-up should be prepared to deal with a wide variety of actors, actions and decisions beyond the organizational context of the original strategic initiative (Table 32.3).

Although there is emerging legislation and practice of SEA follow-up (especially in relation to monitoring and 'Type I' management elements), most of the discussed ideas and models are yet to be tested empirically. Empirical evidence and lessons on SEA follow-up should be systematically collected and related to emerging conceptual frameworks. Further work is needed for refining and disseminating SEA follow-up concepts, particularly their links with relevant SEA discourse on tiering, 'evolutionary' public participation, communication strategies, adaptive management and integration with various environmental management tools such as EMS. In this way, SEA follow-up may become an important tool in achieving strategic change for sustainable development.

Notes

1 In this definition we follow the structure of the definition of EIA follow-up by Morrison-Saunders and Arts (2004b, p4): 'The monitoring and evaluation of the impacts of a project or plan (that has been subject to EIA) for management of, and communication about, the environmental performance of that project or plan.'
2 See Partidário and Fischer (2004), Persson and Nilsson (2007), Gachechiladze et al (2009), Gachechiladze (2010), Hanusch and Glasson (2008) for a review.
3 EC guidance interprets this rather narrowly by suggesting 'unforeseen adverse effects is better interpreted as referring to shortcomings of the prognostic statements in the environmental report (e.g. regarding the predicted intensity of an environmental effect) or unforeseen effects resulting from changes of circumstances, which have led to certain assumptions in the environmental assessment being partly or wholly invalidated' (EC, 2003, p45).

Acknowledgement is given to Maia Gache chiladze-Bozhesku for her contribution to the update of this chapter in 2010.

References

Arnstein, S. (1969) 'A ladder of citizen participation', *Journal of the American Institute of Planners*, pp216–223
Arts, J. (1998) *EIA Follow-up: On the role of Ex-post Evaluation in Environmental Impact Assessment*, GeoPress, Groningen
Arts, J., Tomlinson, P. and Voogd, H. (2011) 'Planning in tiers? Tiering as a way of linking SEA and EIA', Chapter 26 in this volume
Barth, R. and Fuder, A. (2002) *Implementing Article 10 of the SEA Directive 2001/42: Final Report*, IMPEL Network, http://ec.europa.eu/environment/impel, accessed 12 June 2006
Cherp, A. (2004) *The Promise of Strategic Environmental Management*, Blekinge Tekniska Högskola, Karlskrona
Cherp, A., Watt, A. and Vinichenko, V. (2007) 'SEA and strategy formation theories: From 3 Ps to 5 Ps', *Environmental Impact Assessment Review*, vol 27, no 7, pp624–644
Cockrean, B. (2000) 'Success and failures: National guidance on ISO 14001 for New Zealand local authorities', in Hillary, R. (ed) *ISO 14001: Case Studies and Practical Experiences*, Greenleaf, Sheffield, pp39–50
Dalal-Clayton, B. and Sadler, B. (2005) *Strategic Environmental Assessment: A Sourcebook and Reference Guide to International Experience*, Earthscan, London

Deelstra, Y., Nooteboom, S. G., Kohlmann, H. R., Van den Berg, J. and Innanen, S. (2003) 'Using knowledge for decision-making purposes in the context of large projects in the Netherlands', *Environmental Impact Assessment Review*, vol 23, no 5, pp517–541

EC (European Commission) (2003) *Implementation of Directive 2001/42 on the Assessment of the Effects of Certain Plans and Programmes on the Environment*, http://ec.europa.eu/environment/eia/pdf/030923_sea_guidance.pdf, accessed November 2010

Ecoline and REC (2006) *Russia: Integrated Assessment of the Tomsk Oblast Development Strategy*, Ecoline, Moscow, www.unep.ch/etb/areas/pdf/Russia%20FINAL%20Report.pdf, accessed November 2010

Fischer, T. B. (2002) *Strategic Environmental Assessment in Transport and Land Use Planning*, Earthscan, London

Gachechiladze, M. (2008) 'Potential of SEA follow-up for institutional learning and collaboration: The case of the Merseyside Local Transport Plans, UK', paper presented at the EASY-ECO 2005-2007 Conference 'Governance by Evaluation', Vienna

Gachechiladze, M. (2010) 'Strategic environmental assessment follow-up: From promise to practice. Case studies from the UK and Canada', doctoral dissertation, Environmental Sciences and Policy, Central European University, Budapest

Gachechiladze, M., Noble, B. F. and Bitter, B. W. (2009) 'Following-up in strategic environmental assessment: A case study of 20-year forest management planning in Saskatchewan, Canada', *Impact Assessment and Project Appraisal*, vol 27, no 1, pp45–56

Hanusch, M. (2005) 'SEA Monitoring of spatial plans in Germany', paper presented at the IAIA SEA Conference, Prague

Hanusch, M. and Glasson, J. (2008) 'Much ado about SEA/SA monitoring: The performance of English regional spatial strategies, and some German comparisons', *Environmental Impact Assessment Review*, vol 28, pp601–617

Holling, C. S. (1978) *Adaptive Environmental Assessment and Management*, Wiley, New York

IAIA (International Association for Impact Assessment) (2002) *Strategic Environmental Assessment Performance Criteria*, Special Publications Series No1, IAIA, Fargo, ND

Lee, N. and Walsh, F. (1992) 'Strategic environment assessment: An overview', *Project Appraisal*, vol 7, pp126–136

Lee, N. and Wood, C. (1987) 'EIA: A European perspective', *Built Environment*, vol 4, pp101–110

Marshall, R. and Arts, J. (2005) 'Is there life after SEA? Linking SEA to EIA', paper presented at the IAIA SEA Conference, Prague

Marshall, R., Arts, J. and Morrison-Saunders, A. (2005) 'International principles for best practice EIA follow-up', *Impact Assessment and Project Appraisal*, vol 23, no 3, pp175–181

Mintzberg, H. (1994) *The Rise and Fall of Strategic Planning*, Free Press, New York

Morrison-Saunders, A. and Arts, J. (eds) (2004a) *Assessing Impact: Handbook of EIA and SEA Follow-up*, Earthscan, London

Morrison-Saunders, A. and Arts, J. (2004b) 'Introduction to EIA follow-up', in Morrison-Saunders, A. and Arts, J. (eds) *Assessing Impact: Handbook of EIA and SEA Follow-up*, Earthscan, London, pp1–21

Morrison-Saunders, A. and Arts, J. (2004c) 'Exploring the dimensions of EIA follow-up', paper presented to the IAIA Annual Conference, Vancouver, Canada

Naturvårdsverket (2004) *Environmental Management in Central Government Authorities: Sweden's Experience*, Naturvårdsverket, Stockholm

Noble, B. and Storey, K. (2005) 'Towards increasing the utility of follow-up in Canadian EIA', *EIA Review*, vol 25, no 2, pp163–180

Nooteboom, S. and Teisman, G. (2003) 'Sustainable development: Impact assessment in the age of networking', *Journal of Environmental Policy and Planning*, vol 5, no 3, pp285–309

OECD (Organisation for Economic Co-operation and Development) (2001) *Strategies for Sustainable Development: Practical Guidance for Development Co-operation*, OECD, Paris

Partidário, M. R. and Arts, J. (2005) 'Exploring the concept of strategic environmental assessment follow-up', *Impact Assessment and Project Appraisal*, vol 23, no 3, pp246–257

Partidário, M. R. and Fischer, T. B. (2004) 'Follow-up in current SEA understanding', in Morrison-Saunders, A. and Arts, J. (eds) *Assessing Impact: Handbook of EIA and SEA Follow-up*, Earthscan, London, pp225–247

Persson, A. and Nilsson, M. (2006) 'Towards a framework for ex post SEA: Theoretical issues and lessons from policy evaluation', in Emmelin, L. (ed) *Effective Environmental Assessment Tools: Critical Reflection on Concepts and Practice*, Blekinge Institute of Technology Research Report 2006:03, Karlskrona, Sweden

Persson, A. and Nilsson, M. (2007) 'Towards a framework for SEA follow-up: Theoretical issues and lessons from policy evaluation', *Journal of Environmental Assessment Policy and Management*, vol 9, no 4, pp473–496

Sadler, B. and Verheem, R. (1996) *Strategic Environmental Assessment: Status, Challenges and Future Directions*, Ministry of Housing, Spatial Planning and the Environment, The Hague

Schön, D. (1983) *The Reflective Practitioner: How Professionals Think in Action*, Basic Books, New York

Srinivas, H. and Yashiro, M. (1999) *Cities, Environmental Management Systems and ISO 14001: A View from Japan*, International Symposium on Sustainable City Development, United Nations University, Seoul, South Korea

Thérivel, R. (2004) *Strategic Environmental Assessment in Action*, Earthscan, London

Thérivel, R. and Partidário, M. R. (eds) (1996) *The Practice of Strategic Environmental Assessment*, Earthscan, London

Vedung, E. (1997) *Public Policy and Program Evaluation*, Transaction Publishers, New Brunswick

Vicente, G. and Partidário, M. R. (2006) 'SEA: Enhancing communication for better environmental decisions', *Environmental Impact Assessment Review*, vol 26, no 8, pp696–706

Woltjer, J. (2004) 'Consensus planning in infrastructure and environmental development', in Linden, G. and Voogd, H. (eds) *Environmental and Infrastructure Planning*, GeoPress, Groningen, pp37–57

33
SEA Knowledge and Its Use in Information Sharing, Training and Learning

Petrie van Gent

Introduction

The use of strategic environmental assessment (SEA) has increased rapidly in recent years, not only in number but also in modes of application. It is important to understand developments in introducing or improving the use of SEA in countries and institutions. At the Prague SEA Conference, the dissemination of SEA information and how this can be facilitated through SEA knowledge centres was discussed. This chapter reviews the status of SEA knowledge centres and documents their services, users and aspects of interest. Specific details on the type of information and guidance available from selected SEA knowledge centres can be found in the boxes included in this chapter.

Background

At present, SEA is a hot topic in the impact assessment community, reflecting a gradual shift in focus away from environmental impact assessment (EIA) and towards strategic assessment instruments for policies, plans and programmes (PPPs). At country level, the interest is in SEA application for national, regional or sector planning. SEA procedures, application and experiences vary from country to country and also between institutions. There is also a wide variation in experiences, often reflecting their geographical distribution. A worldwide blueprint for SEA does not exist, although there is much discussion regarding what constitutes SEA good practice (or its obverse) and how SEA can be implemented most effectively.

Given these trends, it is important to know what is happening in the SEA world. This information has to be made explicit and made available to take advantage of other experiences. It can be conveyed through networks such as the International Association for Impact Assessment (IAIA), conferences such as IAIA annual meetings, personal meetings (for example, in the day-to-day work), websites, publications, SEA training and education and/or SEA helpdesks. In that regard, SEA knowledge centres can play an important coordinating role.

Just as there are different forms and scales of SEA, there is a wide spectrum of SEA knowledge centres. They may be defined as a focal point for the collection and dissemination of knowledge about SEA, covering a local, organizational, country, regional or wider perspective. A knowledge centre may have a web presence, a physical presence or both. It can be operated by any type of organization (for example, government, academic or research institutions, non-governmental organizations (NGOs), and so on). Such centres need to deliver quality and demonstrate an impartial outlook and lack of bias in order to maintain credibility with stakeholders.

Main issues

The discussions in Prague drew attention to different issues in SEA knowledge centres and information sharing, including the focus of SEA knowledge centres,

---

Box 33.1 *EIA Transportation Centre (ETC) in the Netherlands*

The ETC gives advice and undertakes studies and evaluations for the various divisions within the Netherlands Ministry of Transport, Public Works and Water Management. It aims to improve the quality of planning and of EIA/SEA processes for infrastructure projects, which are carried out within different divisions of the ministry. Independent reviews by the Netherlands Commission for Environmental Assessment (NCEA) of EIA and SEA reports show a considerable improvement has occurred in the quality of environmental impact statements prepared by the ministry.

The ETC offers the following services:

- Internal quality reviews and consultancy, focusing the content of EIA/SEA of the infrastructure projects on what is relevant for decision-making.
- Transferring knowledge regarding decision-making, environmental issues and infrastructure by training-courses, EIA-manuals, a website and a newsletter.
- Translating technical issues to the procedural and process elements of infrastructure planning and vice versa.
- Integrating the various technical and environmental disciplines through an interdisciplinary approach, creating added value for project managers and EIA/SEA study teams.
- Acting as an intermediary between decision-makers (policy aspects) and proponents of infrastructure (implementation aspects).

ETC information is disseminated internationally through conferences and papers (www.english.verkeerenwaterstaat.nl/english).

Source: Summary of contribution by Roel Nijsten

---

access to information and its price, quality of information, emphasis on theoretical and practical knowledge and the relationship to sustainability.

Many SEA knowledge centres are focused on the interests of their own staff and clients, and only to a limited extent on sharing information with others outside this network. Examples are shown in Boxes 33.1 and 33.2. These describe the activities of the EIA Transportation Centre (ETC) in the Netherlands, which is focused on decision-makers and proponents, and the Swedish helpdesk on EIA and SEA good practice, which is funded by the Swedish International Development Cooperation Agency (Sida) to provide support for its activities in developing countries.

Box 33.2 *Sida's Expert Advice for Environmental Assessment*

Since 1998, the Swedish EIA Centre has maintained a working expert advice function (helpdesk) to provide EIA and SEA information and support on request of Sida. The EIA centre is located at the Swedish University of Agricultural Sciences; Sida is a government agency within the Ministry for Foreign Affairs. The helpdesk assists agency staff in Sweden and some 50 country offices on the mainstreaming of environmental concerns and the conduct of EIA and SEA in particular

The helpdesk offers the following services:

- Advice on environmental integration in all types of supports.
- Review and assessment of EIA and SEA documents related to Sida-supported projects and programmes as well as policy documents.
- Review of and advice on terms of reference for EIA and SEA.
- EIA and SEA training for Sida staff, cooperating partners and consultants.
- Development of tools, guidance and factsheet material.
- Baseline, review and state-of-the-art studies.
- Support in the area of capacity-building to regional and national EIA centres in Sida's partner countries.
- Assistance in identifying and formulating environmental issues for discussions.

The helpdesk's aim is to assist Sida programme officers with the integration of sustainability and environmental aspects into dialogue with partners, to address pressing environmental challenges in the project and programme preparation cycle, and to support internal capacity development and provide guidance material. The helpdesk pursues to establish good working relations with their clients and to be seen as a coach rather than as an auditor. They share knowledge through discussions, written comments, training sessions and a website. Worldwide, Sweden is an important player in the field of environmental assessment in international cooperation, for example, in Central America and southeast Africa (http://mkb.slu.se/helpdesk/index.asp).

Source: Summary of contributions by Eva Stephansson and Lisa Åhrgren

Their activities reflect the practical realities of funding of knowledge centres; it takes time and money to make materials available to, and useful for, clients and more so for the SEA community at large. To a lesser extent, and more so in the academic world, information and knowledge are not always readily shared, because they mean power or publications.

Access to information and knowledge comes at a price. Sufficient financing is needed for technical facilities such as computers and internet providers and both are conditions for exchange of information. The gap is becoming smaller between developing countries in Africa on the one hand, and many Western countries on the other hand, but it will take some time before the situation becomes comparable. In Africa, for example, there has been the emergence of centres such as the Southern African Association for Impact Assessment (SAIEA) and the Eastern African Association for Impact Assessment (EAAIA) (Box 33.3). In Asia and Latin America, similar developments are taking place.

Box 33.3 *Eastern Africa Association for Impact Assessment (EAAIA)*

EAAIA was established in 2001. This was in response to a statement of political commitment on the use of EIA, made at the African Ministerial Conference on the Environment conference in Durban, South Africa in 1995. Its purpose is to support EIA capacity-building in Eastern Africa through exchange, networking and strengthening of EIA policies and practice. Membership of the association is open to researchers, practitioners, decision-makers, organizations and others interested in environmental assessment in Eastern Africa.

EAAIA seeks to provide:

- A forum for exchange of information and ideas on EIA regionally and globally, through its quarterly e-newsletters and EIA database.
- Opportunities for individual EIA capacity enhancement. This is facilitated through the established resource centre at its secretariat; supporting members to participate in regional, subregional and international EIA forums and networks; implementing the Professional Development (PD) Fellowship programme, including other relevant EIA trainings. Various development partners have financially supported these professional trainings. They include USAID through its Environmental Capacity Building Program (ENCAP), the Swedish International Development Agency (Sida) and more recently, funding has been provided through the Partnership for Environmental Assessment for Africa (PEAA) funding framework mechanism.
- Support services and coordination in linkages and partnerships with, for example, the Capacity Development and Linkages for Environmental Assessment in Africa (CLEAA) and IAIA. Coordination of the CLEAA secretariat was facilitated by EAAIA between 2003 and 2009.

Source: Summary of contribution by Maureen Babu

For developing countries especially, funds for travelling to partner centres, to SEA meetings and to learn first-hand of SEA experiences and practices are important components of capacity building (see also Chapter 29).

Quality of information has much to do with the source. If you know the SEA arena, the individual or institution behind the information is an indicator of its quality or utility. Databases within well-known institutions can be a source of good information. Examples include the SEA-info.net at the Centre for Sustainability in the UK and the SEA/EIA database on the website of the Netherlands Commission for Environmental Assessment (NCEA), which focuses especially on SEA practice.

In addition to their role in training and education of SEA professionals, university-based centres in both developed and developing countries are important for the advancement of theoretical knowledge, although the link to practice should always be borne in mind. Many also serve as a focal point for information exchange and networking, as well as research and field development. The EIA Centre of the University of Manchester is a good example; it maintains contacts with former students and other SEA professionals through what is now an immense network.

Apart from staying in touch with trends and developments in SEA practice, the SEA community should also foster closer links with professionals in other sectors. For example, knowledge centres on governance, planning and water management have a wealth of information on tools, methodologies and processes that are instrumental to informed decision-making. In many cases, these have proven value in practice and can supplement or reinforce the work of SEA practitioners.

Knowledge centres are more likely to be sustainable if they already have a remit relating to SEA activity and information gathering. An example is the NCEA, which has mandated responsibilities for the review of EIA and SEA reports in the Netherlands and undertakes services and activities in developing countries under an agreement with the Minister of International Cooperation. The NCEA's practical work and experience has enhanced its capacity and effectiveness as a focal point in SEA for the geographical areas it serves. A web-based knowledge platform is an important means of information sharing (Box 33.4).

Recent initiatives

Based on the Prague discussion of practice and experience of SEA knowledge centres, national level information is considered to be particularly useful. Ideally, the coverage of information (web and/or physical) for each country should be similar in content, encompassing the following key areas: legislation; guidance, manuals and procedures; list or copies of SEA reports; key case studies and lessons learned; and training materials and facilities. Preferably, this information should be available online, in English and with links to other such websites. In this way, a regional network could be established, and may form the basis for wider networks for information exchange. First steps in this direction were taken following the IAIA conference in Prague through the update of the website of the Environmental Protection Department in Hong Kong (Box 33.5).

Box 33.4 *NCEA knowledge platform*

The NCEA is an independent expert body that provides advice on scoping guidelines for EIA and SEA processes and undertakes review of assessment reports. Internationally, the NCEA has provided advisory services on environmental and social impact assessment since 1993. Additionally, it assists countries in establishing effective systems for impact assessment, as a means of contributing to sustainable development, good governance and poverty alleviation. In carrying out this mandate, the NCEA has dealt with some 2450 EIA and SEA cases in the Netherlands and issued more than 260 advisory reports internationally.

In 2002, with the assistance of the Ministry of Foreign Affairs, the NCEA developed a knowledge platform for sharing its practical experience with others, in the first instance to support our international counterparts. The knowledge platform provides:

- A website with information on NCEA's activities and advisory reports, news items in four languages and a large resources section with:
  - An EIA/SEA database with manuals, SEA approaches, guidelines and case studies.
  - A project database with NCEA's advisory reports and capacity development activities.
  - A country profile database with EIA/SEA legislation per country, searchable on a vast set of criteria.
  - Case studies, key sheets and other publications on methodologies and the NCEA's approach.
- A helpdesk service for environment and sector ministries, environmental assessment entities and others who work in the practice of SEA (and EIA) in developing countries including services to international donors, NGOs, development banks and Netherlands Embassies.
- Training, presentations and guest lectures on themes within EIA/SEA context in relation to international cooperation (www.eia.nl).

In 2009, the Netherlands Ministry of Housing, Spatial Planning and the Environment decided to substantially expand the knowledge platform of the NCEA in the Netherlands in order to also reach Dutch parties with no experience of environmental assessment. They provide:

- A website with databases containing notifications of intent, advisory reports by the NCEA, project descriptions, jurisprudence.
- Regular e-newsletters, handouts and factsheets.
- Presence of NCEA staff at public participation and information meetings.
- Some of the key projects and articles, for example on SEA and structural design planning, in English. They are available through a special website (www.eia.nl/netherlands/).

> **Box 33.5** *Hong Kong's bilingual SEA knowledge centre*
>
> Subsequent to the publication of the Hong Kong SEA Manual in 2004, the Environmental Protection Department of Hong Kong Special Administrative Region (SAR) government developed a web-based SEA knowledge centre in order to further promote the sharing of SEA experiences and information The centre was jointly launched by the Permanent Secretary for the Environment and the Director of Environmental Protection Department of Hong Kong SAR Government, the Director General of the State Environmental Protection Administration of China (in charge of EIA matters), and the Chairman of the Hong Kong Advisory Council on the Environment (December 2005).
>
> The website offers:
>
> - The latest edition of the Hong Kong SEA Manual, an interactive version, which includes a theoretical introduction to SEA, experiences in Hong Kong and Mainland China and much guidance material.
> - Information on relevant SEA matters including developments in Mainland China.
> - SEA reports completed in Hong Kong.
> - Hyperlinks to other related international SEA resources and websites.
>
> This webpage will be further enhanced to provide a useful network and platform for exchange and sharing as well as international collaboration and promotion of the application of SEA in China, in Asia and internationally (www.epd.gov.hk/epd/sea).
>
> *Source:* Summary of contribution by Elvis Au

Without funding, SEA databases for external users are difficult to develop or keep up-to-date. For example, the EIA Centre at the University of Manchester experienced this difficulty when EU funding for its database ended. The United Nations University (UNU) developed an SEA database and distance learning resource, which is kept updated by the users (mostly partner universities) using a wiki format and based on the principle that users take but also give. As it is a fully open system, it is difficult to guarantee quality. Therefore, access restrictions for editing of information may be necessary (Box 33.6). Students following SEA modules can be valuable contributors, as shown by experience in Oxford Brookes University and the Ecole Polytechnique Fédérale de Lausanne.

Future steps

At the Prague workshop, it was agreed that there is no one type of SEA knowledge centre. Existing centres serve different target groups and provide different services, some open to all, others specific to particular users. Another conclusion was that national or regionally-focused SEA centres seem to be most useful and in demand.

> ## Box 33.6 *SEA database and distance learning*
>
> In 2003, UNU and Oxford Brookes University began work on an interactive distance and online learning resource based on an existing course. The new course was available for use at Oxford Brookes University and as part of the UNU Global Virtual University. Following feedback from learners and from UNU partners, the course module was subsequently redesigned and completed in 2006. It was showcased at the IAIA SEA Conference in 2005, and at the Learning Centre for the United Nations Commission on Sustainable Development in New York in 2006. This learning resource is currently used is several masters degree programmes, including the online Master in Development Management run by the University of Agder in Norway (http://sea.unu.edu).
>
> As with any online resource, continuous updating is essential, including the fixing or removal of broken links to other websites and resources. It was concluded that the best way to proceed would be to create a wiki on SEA. The user community takes responsibility for updating and adding new information; in return, they have access to what may become one of the most comprehensive information resources on SEA (however the user community is currently restricted to partner universities, who update upon request, mainly for student assignments). UNU sees it as a challenge to develop greater synergies between their initiative and those of IAIA, World Bank and the United Nations Environment Programme (UNEP) in order to provide materials that meet their own needs, individual learning or group training requirements (http://sea.unu.edu/wiki).
>
> *Source:* Summary of contribution by Brendan Barrett

Table 33.1 *SEA knowledge and its use: Summary statement*

Main trends and issues	Current situation: • SEA information and experiences are increasing rapidly. • Quantity: there is much for those who have access to the different sources (websites, conferences, publications); there is much less for those with limited access, for example, from developing countries; • Quality: what you find is not necessarily what you are looking for; references are necessary.
Main perspectives	SEA knowledge centres: • SEA knowledge is in different centres and for different user groups; there should not be just one centre. • Many centres are just focused on their own organization and clients. • The centres should develop as well as disseminate SEA information. • This knowledge should be practical as well as theoretical. • There should be incentives for those who contribute. • Sustainability is a problem.
Future directions	Key challenges:

Table 33.1 (*continued*)

- Digital and web information is the future; however this should/will always be supported by personal contacts and written materials.
- Universities can play an important role, also in developing countries.
- Research and practice should find better opportunities to learn from each other.
- Develop a knowledge exchange system, starting country nodes with the most relevant information, which can be linked to regional and wider networks.

The larger challenge is to keep information up-to-date and to tap available knowledge in an efficient way. Even though digital information is becoming more and more important, the physical component of knowledge exchange, between SEA practitioners, scientists, decision-makers, affected persons and others, still remains necessary, at least for the foreseeable future.

A number of SEA training programmes are in place around the world including those supported by the World Bank, the United Nations Development Programme (UNDP), UNEP and IAIA (see Chapter 29). The challenge for the future is to create synergies between these initiatives. One potentially important way forward may be the promotion of content sharing through new licensing schemes that allow people to copy, remix and publish SEA-related content in order to meet their own needs and their individual or group training requirements.

Acknowledgements

The author thanks all representatives of the various knowledge centres who contributed the original information in 2005 and updates in 2010 for the boxes in this chapter. She also thanks her successor at NCEA, Anne Hardon, for the afterword and her help with updating the boxes.

Afterword:

The information in the boxes on the different organizations has been edited to the current situation in August 2010. Since the SEA Knowledge sharing workshop in 2005, new initiatives are being developed. To name two of them with a world wide focus:

- The SEA Task Team was established in 2004 under the Network on Environment and Development Cooperation (ENVIRONET) – a subsidiary body of the OECD Development Assistance Committee (DAC). The Task Team developed the Good Practice Guidance on SEA in Development Cooperation (published in 2006) and continues to engage in dialogue, exchange experiences and sharing resources on SEA. The website provides several SEA resources (www.seataskteam.net).

- The IAIA Wiki, developed in 2009 by the IAIA contains definitions, explanations, and information on topics related to impact assessment. Everyone is welcome to view the IAIA Wiki pages. However, at this time, only IAIA members may contribute to the wiki (www.iaia.org/iaiawiki).

Part VI

Toward Integrated Sustainability Assessment

34
From SEA to Sustainability Assessment?

Jenny Pope and Barry Dalal-Clayton

Introduction

Sustainability assessment (SA)[1] has emerged as the third generation of impact assessment, following environmental impact assessment (EIA) and strategic environmental assessment (SEA). For the purposes of this chapter, we will define SA broadly as an 'ex ante'[2] process that seeks to identify the future consequences of a proposed action in a manner that directs planning and decision-making towards sustainability.[3] SA is therefore not a prescribed process as such, but rather an orientation of practice.

There are two important points arising from this definition, both of which relate to the relationship between SEA and SA, which, as the title of this chapter indicates, is of particular interest. The first point is that SA may be applied at any level of decision-making, from the most strategic to the most project-specific, and this is a point of distinction between SEA and SA. The second point is that the concept of sustainability is fundamental to the practice of SA, and we will explore in detail the implications of the adopted interpretation of sustainability on the SA process. A 'three pillar' approach is common, in which the SA attempts to reconcile and integrate economic, social and environmental considerations. We will consider the various ways in which this conceptualization might be applied within decision-making, its limitations and emerging alternatives to this approach. Of particular concern here is the relationship between sustainability and the environment, and we argue that SA must ensure the protection of environmental assets within its broader mandate.

A review of current international practice found that there is already considerable practical experience with SA processes in different jurisdictions and sectors around the world (Dalal-Clayton and Sadler, 2011, in press). This chapter seeks to outline the current themes of discussion and debate. It draws mainly upon the contributions to and lessons of the Prague SEA Conference, but also attempts to reflect some of the more recent contributions to this rapidly evolving field.

No attempt is made to provide a 'one-size-fits-all' manual for conducting SA, as such a thing can never exist. Instead, the aim is to raise the issues that must be addressed in the process of clarifying what it is that we seek to achieve through SA and then to design processes that are fit for purpose within their specific application and context (Govender et al, 2006). We commence by providing some background to locate SA within the context of EIA and SEA, from which many applications of SA have evolved, and discussing the relationships between the three forms of assessment. Since the overriding goal of our work as SA theorists and practitioners should always be to contribute to the shift towards a more sustainable society, we devote some time and space to exploring the concept of sustainability.

At the heart of our discussion is the argument for an integrated approach to SA. We explore what integration means in relation to sustainability and its interpretation within a decision-making context, and then look more broadly at an integrative approach to the design and implementation of SA processes. As Gibson (2006) notes, 'the package is not easily at hand but is within reach'.

Background: SEA and SA

SA is evolving simultaneously from both SEA and EIA, as well as from other processes such as land-use planning, resource management, technology assessment and from broader sustainability debates in development assistance practice and elsewhere. However, in keeping with the theme of this book we will focus in this section upon the relationships between EIA, SEA and SA.

The evolution and practice of SA

Various forms of SA have emerged through different mechanisms and different drivers in different parts of the world. One of the most established is the UK process of sustainability appraisal of spatial plans, which has integrated the requirements of the European Directive on SEA (Bond and Morrison-Saunders, 2009). In contrast, some non-European jurisdictions, such as Australia, Canada and South Africa, have applied SA to both public and private project proposals as part of an approvals process, building upon existing EIA regimes (Hacking and Guthrie, 2006; Pope and Grace, 2006). Many businesses, particularly large industrial corporations, now apply forms of integrated assessment to their internal decision-making processes (Hacking and Guthrie, 2006); while sustainability impact assessment is also increasingly applied to trade agreement and development strategies (Lee and Kirkpatrick, 2001; Hugé and Hens, 2007).

The result of this incremental development of SA from a variety of sources, including both EIA and SEA, is that there is now a diverse and significant body of experience with SA around the world from which lessons can be learnt and conclusions drawn. This 'learning by doing' is certainly occurring within specific contexts, is deliberate policy in some cases, and is inevitable insofar as different cases and places raise different problems and possibilities. For example, Western Australia is one jurisdiction where the former government adopted a deliberate 'learning by doing' approach to SA (Pope and Grace, 2006).

Relationships between EIA, SEA and SA

Interestingly, there is a recently discernible convergence between project and strategic level approaches to SA, as project level practice matures far beyond 'EIA with social and economic considerations added in' (Pope et al, 2004). Consequently, many of the criticisms directed at what has become common EIA practice, for example, its reactivity, lack of effective consideration of alternatives and focus on the minimization of negative impacts, do not automatically apply to project-level SA. Instead, SAs of project proposals are becoming more proactively integrated with proposal development and thus are exerting a far greater influence on decision-making. They are guiding the consideration of more sustainable alternatives, for example, in infrastructure site selection processes, and actively seeking positive project outcomes guided by the concept of sustainability. Some go even further and consider strategic and policy issues that extend well beyond the immediate project and its operations (Dalal-Clayton and Sadler, 2005; Gibson et al, 2005; Hacking and Guthrie, 2008; Pope and Grace, 2006).

If the suggestion of a linear evolution from SEA to SA is simplistic and not representative of reality, then what is the true nature of the relationship between SEA and SA? Firstly, as might be expected, many topics of current debates within SEA described in other chapters of this volume are also emerging as challenges and ambiguities in the context of SA. For example:

- What is an appropriate process framework for SA and should it graft onto existing decision-making processes or impose a methodology of its own to align decision-making with sustainability?
- What is the relationship between the environment and other potentially competing objectives that fall under the concept of sustainability and are also increasingly addressed in SEA processes?
- Is tiering a useful concept and what is the relationship between an assessment and its broader context?
- What institutional arrangements are appropriate?

With respect to such concerns, to some of which we will return later, there is much that SEA and SA can learn from one another. But perhaps the most debated aspect of the relationship between SEA and SA is their point of difference, and whether or not they are the actually the same thing (not withstanding that, unlike SEA, SA may also be applied to project proposals). This may be the case in some applications but it depends upon the conceptual basis of each form of assessment.

Although there is debate in SEA literature on whether and when SEA should shift towards a comprehensive sustainability agenda or should be a process of purely biophysical/ecological evaluation and (at least implicitly) advocacy (Kørnøv and Thissen, 2000; Govender et al, 2006; Morrison-Saunders and Fischer, 2006), SA is less ambiguous on this point. We argue, supported by the general consensus at the Prague conference, that the defining characteristic of SA is that it must be sustainability-oriented (Dalal-Clayton and Sadler, 2011, in press; Hacking and Guthrie, 2006; Pope, 2006).

Therefore, the extent to which SEA and SA may be considered analogous depends upon the extent to which an SEA process embeds the concept of sustainability.

Sustainability: The conceptual basis of SA

The concept of sustainability is fundamental to SA as defined here. However, sustainability is an ambiguous and contested concept (McManus, 1996; Dobson, 1996; Jacobs, 1999). Many alternative theoretical formulations have been developed, which are founded upon common concerns and principles but have different emphases depending upon the decision-making context, the disciplinary orientations and any number of other factors (Gibson, 2001; Hermans and Knippenberg, 2006).

In the following discussion, we highlight some of these conceptual complexities and challenges by comparing the prevailing 'three pillar' approach with alternative, more holistic conceptualizations, leading into a discussion in the following section of how this abstract concept might be 'operationalized' for practical decision-making.

The 'three pillars'

One of the most common conceptualizations of sustainability involves the 'three pillar' integration of environmental, social and economic considerations, and correspondingly most SA processes are based upon a three pillar approach (Eales and Twigger-Ross, 2003; Pope et al, 2004). In jurisdictions in which environment is broadly defined to encompass socio-economic as well as biophysical issues, EIA and SEA processes may already provide a platform for SA based upon the three pillars. However, sustainability and the environment have an uneasy relationship that is heightened within an assessment context. The main argument against three pillar approaches to SA is that they frustrate integrated, systems-based thinking and encourage trade-offs between the pillars by emphasizing the traditional conflict between economic and environmental concerns, usually to the detriment of the environment (Gibson, 2001; Lee, 2002; Jenkins et al, 2003; Sheate et al, 2003; Morrison-Saunders and Fischer, 2006).[4]

From the three pillar perspective, the term 'integration' typically refers to a process of weighing up environmental versus social versus economic issues at some stage of a SA process. This has led to debates about whether this should occur during the process or at the final decision point (see, for example, Jenkins et al, 2003). In practice, multi-criteria analysis (MCA) techniques are often utilized to integrate the various dimensions of SA processes to determine an overall 'score' by which various alternatives can be compared (see for example Kain and Söderberg, 2008). Integration of the three pillars can also mean recognizing the relationships between different factors, for example, noting that protecting a conservation area may have economic benefits through increased tourism and social benefits in terms of community recreation opportunities, as well as direct environmental benefits.

The three pillar concept may be applied differently in different approaches to SA, with correspondingly different purposes and intentions (Pope et al, 2004). Morrison-Saunders and Thérivel (2006) distinguish eight different aims that might underpin SA processes, six of which are based upon a three pillar conceptualization of sustainability. These range from the minimization of adverse impacts, to the maximization of objectives, to the delivery of net overall gains, to the achievement of mutually beneficial win/win/win outcomes across the three pillars. In a world in which current behaviour is not sustainable and key trends are negative, SA should go beyond the identification, evaluation and mitigation of the negative impacts of a proposal to at least promote positive outcomes and contributions towards aspirational objectives (Gibson, 2001; Pope et al, 2005). For example, in Canada, there is increasingly a requirement to demonstrate 'contribution to sustainability' (Gibson et al, 2005), which is more aligned with attempts to achieve 'win/win/wins', 'net gains' or to 'maximize objectives'. These more positive approaches also commonly underpin spatial planning assessment processes (Morrison-Saunders and Thérivel, 2006). In contrast with the three pillar approach, Morrison-Saunders and Thérivel's two highest level conceptions interpret sustainability as a more inherently integrated concept as considered in the following section.

Alternatives to the three pillars

The view that the three pillar approach is an inappropriately reductionist interpretation of sustainability is gaining momentum and was strongly endorsed in the Prague conference. Alternatives for the purposes of assessment have been espoused (Pope et al, 2004; Gibson, 2006; Morrison-Saunders and Thérivel, 2006). George (1999, 2001) was among the first to consider how alternative interpretations of sustainability might guide SA. Using the UK's sustainability appraisal as a starting point, he argues that it attributes too many factors to the concept of sustainability, which more appropriately belong in the realm of planning. Instead, he advocates SA based upon criteria derived from the Rio Declaration sustainable development principles of inter-generational and intra-generational equity where the former is characterized by the preservation of environmental systems for future generations.

Others have promoted models of sustainability based on principles that cross the three pillars. Hermans and Knippenberg (2006) propose a model based upon the principles of justice, resilience and efficiency. At first glance these may appear to align with the three pillars, but they are inherently more integrative. Gibson (2001, 2006; Gibson et al, 2005) also presents a set of inherently integrative principles for sustainability which, he argues, are generally accepted at their highest level (see Box 34.1),[5] serve as 'driving objectives and consequent evaluation and decision criteria to avoid the three conventional categories', and are fundamental to an approach to SA that recognizes the essentially integrated nature of the concept of sustainability.

Sustainability as an integrative concept

As well as blurring the demarcation lines of the three pillars and intrinsically linking the human and the biophysical, sustainability principles such as those

---

Box 34.1 *Integrated sustainability principles*

- Socio-ecological system integrity.
- Livelihood sufficiency and opportunity.
- Intra-generational equity.
- Inter-generational equity.
- Resource maintenance and efficiency.
- Socio-ecological civility and democratic governance.
- Precaution and adaptation.
- Immediate and long term integration.

Source: Gibson (2006)

---

listed in Box 34.1 begin to suggest some of the other linkages inherent within the notion of sustainability. Sustainability also links 'present and future, local and global, active and precautionary, critique and alternative vision, concept and practice, and universal and context-specific' (Gibson, 2006). An integrated concept of sustainability requires recognition and consideration of these many facets and layers.

It has also been argued that sustainability should be conceptualized in a way that integrates its concrete and quantitative dimensions with characteristics that are less tangible and qualitative (Bradbury and Rayner, 2002). In practice, it is often observed that the latter category, which includes concepts such as equity, justice and democracy, is often marginalized and given scant consideration in decision-making processes (Davison, 2001; Owens and Cowell, 2002). Consultation and engagement processes (discussed in the following section) may help to redress this imbalance. For example, Bradbury and Rayner (2002) highlight the dominance of descriptive social sciences approaches in SAs that focus on job creation, public infrastructure and the like, and call for further attention to the interpretive social sciences and the importance of social meaning and values. Similarly, Knippenberg and Edelmann (2005) highlight the 'strong qualitative undertone' and 'process-like character' of social considerations within SA, and offer an alternative conceptual model for the social-cultural domain of sustainability.

More recently, there has been an increasing interest among SA practitioners in the first of the sustainability principles listed in Box 34.1: the notion of socio-ecological system integrity, together with the associated concepts of complexity and resilience (Audouin and de Wet, 2010; Gaudreau and Gibson, 2010; Grace, 2010). The systems approach, exemplified by the Millennium Ecosystem Assessment (2005) takes as its starting point the interrelatedness of socio-economic and ecological system components, usually within a defined geographical area. It seeks firstly to understand the dynamics of the socio-ecological system, particularly the points at which the resilience of the overall system might already be under pressure, as the basis for assessing the impacts of proposed activities on the area. The over-riding objective of SA is then to ensure that the health and resilience of the socio-ecological system is maintained (Grace, 2010).

As Gibson (2006) suggests: 'Sustainability is an essentially integrative concept. It seems reasonable, then, to design SA as an essentially integrative process and framework for decision-making on undertakings that may have lasting effects.' But what might an integrative SA process look like in practice? In the following section we explore the contours of a framework for integrative SA that is based upon an integrated, holistic concept of sustainability as well as other, more process-orientated forms of integration.

Integrative SA processes

Gibson (2006) argues that sustainability is an essentially integrated concept and SA must consider the global as well as the local, the qualitative and abstract as well as the quantitative and concrete, the future as well as the present and the particular as well as the conceptual. He goes further to argue that integration should be the guiding principle for SA, relating not just the interpretation of sustainability itself, but extending into every aspect of the process design and the overall system of governance for sustainability. One particularly important form of process integration is the integration of SA with the process of developing a proposal. This means that the assessment is applied proactively rather than reactively at a time when most important decisions have already been made (Lee, 2002).

In this section, we examine the application of a holistic, integrated concept of sustainability to decision-making in practice, present a broad methodological framework designed to promote integration, and discuss important aspects of processes affecting integration, including governance and institutional structures and consultation and engagement processes.

Applying the concept: sustainability for SA

While the starting point for integrated SA must be an holistic conceptualization of sustainability that avoids the reductionism of the three pillars, the risk remains that, when applied to a specific decision, the concept will become reduced, and mechanistic, and in spite of best efforts will revert to something approximating the three pillars (Hacking and Guthrie, 2006). Some of the counters against this tendency are the design of the process and particularly the relationship between the assessment and the process of developing the proposal in the first instance, as well as the effective use of consultation and engagement, and potentially also institutional reform (which are addressed in the following section). For now, the focus is upon how the concept of sustainability might be applied to decision-making in a way that remains true to its essentially holistic and integrative nature.

Sustainability decision criteria

On a practical level, the concept of sustainability must be 'operationalized' in the form of criteria for sustainability decision-making (Gibson, 2001; Hacking and Guthrie, 2006). Dalal-Clayton and Sadler (2011, in press) argue that SA 'is an impact assessment carried out against or within an explicit framework of goals, principles, rules and indicators'. Similarly, Pope and Grace (2006) discuss the concept of a 'sustainability decision-making protocol' that guides decision-making and also provides a basis for the evaluation of the sustainability implications of a proposal, whether by internal decision-makers or external regulators.

The first step in the development of decision criteria is the identification of the sustainability factors that should be considered in decision-making. These must be relevant to the decision at hand, but also guided by a holistic suite of sustainability principles such as those reproduced in Box 34.1, as well as reflective of the dynamics of the socio-ecological system in question. The higher-level principles help to ensure the inclusion of aspects of an holistic sustainability discourse that may otherwise be neglected, particularly less tangible concepts such as equity and justice (Gibson, 2006). Like Gibson, Verheem (2002) reminds us that when we are considering sustainability, impacts go beyond the local and the foreseeable future and that 'at the heart of SA is the question of whether a plan or project will lead to improvements on all fronts, or whether there is a risk of *transfer of impacts* into another domain – either in *time* or *place*' (Verheem, 2002, p10, emphasis in original).

Thus, the integrated concept of sustainability means something for assessment and decision-making that goes beyond identifying linkages between aspects of a proposal and seeking beneficial synergistic relationships between outcomes. SA must also find ways to recognize and incorporate the full breadth and depth of the sustainability concept, including its global dimensions, and resist any temptation for a narrow focus and short-sightedness. Hacking and Guthrie (2006) explore a variety of ways in which sustainability decision criteria might be developed. Along with Gibson (2006), they acknowledge the challenges associated with aligning high-level, generic principles for sustainability with local considerations to guide a specific decision and they consider the contribution of stakeholder engagement, backcasting and tiering, through which higher level decisions provide the boundaries for lower level ones.

Sustainability decision criteria should not be viewed as another attempt at reductionism, whereby sustainability is mechanically converted into a series of quantitative indicators and targets. Rather, it should be conceived as a framework within which decision-making occurs, decision-making that is inclusive and deliberative and that acknowledges the value-based and subjective dimensions of sustainability. It provides the catalyst for debates between opposing views, a focus for discussions in which underlying assumptions and worldviews are exposed, and in which learning occurs and system understanding is developed. Box 34.2 provides an example of how this has worked in practice.

Decision criteria for sustainability should include both aspirational objectives and acceptability limits, where the latter represent the line of demarcation between what is sustainable and what is unsustainable (Devuyst, 2001; Hacking and Guthrie, 2006), ideally derived through an understanding of system dynamics and resilience (Grace, 2010). The articulation of

---

Box 34.2 *South West Yarragadee Water Supply Development*

The SA of the South West Yarragadee Water Supply Development was conducted in 2004–2006 as part of finalizing the proposal to extract 45 gallons of water per year from the south-west region of Western Australia and supply it to the integrated scheme serving the capital city of Perth. The proposal was controversial, due to the perception by the regional, rural communities that 'their' water was being taken away, thus potentially denying them future options to use the water for private agricultural purposes.

The assessment was guided by a 'sustainability decision-making protocol' that defined relevant sustainability factors, objectives and acceptability criteria. Impact data was then collected and evaluated against the protocol. The economic goal of maximizing the economic value of the water implied that the water should be supplied to an integrated public water supply, which meant supplying the city, since the rural communities are not connected to an integrated scheme, and the economic analysis thus favoured the broad proposal. This, however, was in conflict with the social goal of ensuring that the rural communities' reasonable needs for water were met, since an interpretive approach to the social impact analysis identified a prevailing storyline of 'futures foregone'.

Deliberations around this tension between the two objectives led to a reframing of the proposal itself in a way commensurate with both objectives: in addition to supplying the city, the integrated water supply scheme could be extended to also serve the rural communities. This would ensure the best economic use of the water and also meet social objectives.

Source: Pope and Grace (2006)

---

acceptability limits or bottom lines is particularly important to prevent the erosion of achievements over the past 30 years towards ensuring the consideration of ecological concerns in decision-making (Sadler, 1999; Sippe, 1999). These may otherwise remain vulnerable to trade-offs, whether the SA is based upon the three-pillar or an integrated concept of sustainability, and as Gibson (2006) argues: 'Sustainability assessment must not be introduced in a way that threatens them.'

Trade-offs

One dimension of integration already discussed is the relationship between different sustainability factors or objectives. These might be mutually supportive, potentially leading to 'win/wins'; or may be opposing, leading to trade-offs. Gibson et al (2005) point out that trade-offs are often unavoidable, and may have to be accepted in the identification of best overall options, since 'trade-offs allow some adverse effects in the interests of securing important gains'. Although the focus should always be on avoiding trade-offs, guidance for determining which trade-offs might be acceptable would help where it is not possible to avoid them (Gibson, 2006).

Because development is rarely possible without some adverse impact on the natural environment, mechanisms are often needed to achieve a net positive environmental outcome from a development. Such mechanisms include the concept of 'net conservation benefits' or 'environmental offsets'. Offsets can be considered as a special kind of trade-off, made within a pillar rather than between pillars.

Trade-off rules proposed to guide decision-making seek to protect the components of the sustainability discourse, such as the environment, that might be vulnerable if potential trade-offs are not specifically identified and evaluated (Gibson et al, 2005; Gibson, 2006). These rules are based upon the principles of: ensuring maximum net gains; placing the burden of argument on the trade-off proponent; avoidance of significant adverse effects; protecting the future by rejecting the displacement of significant negative effects to the future; and requiring explicit justification and open process.

Integrative process frameworks and methodologies

It has been argued extensively in SEA literature that assessment methodologies which commence early in the process of developing a proposal and inform every stage of decision-making achieve better outcomes for the environment than those applied more reactively (Thérivel and Pártidario, 1996; Brown and Thérivel, 2000; Eggenberger and Partidário, 2000; Noble and Storey, 2001). The same is true for SA where a proactive approach not only delivers better outcomes, but is more consistent with a holistic interpretation of sustainability and less likely to lead to trade-offs being made (Morrison-Saunders and Thérivel, 2006).

The relationship between the assessment and the decision-making processes is defined by the question framing a SA process as discussed in Morrison-Saunders and Thérivel (2006) and Pope and Grace (2006). They contrast strategic, open questions (such as 'what should the future of area X be?') with questions of acceptability (such as 'is proposal X acceptable at site Y?). The former encourage proactive assessment methodologies in which a desired outcome is defined and alternative means of achieving this outcome are proposed and assessed (Noble and Storey, 2001; Thérivel, 2004). By its nature, the latter defines an assessment that is reactive to a proposal. An example of the relationship between the question and integration are presented in Box 34.3.

In both SEA and SA, different questions and correspondingly different process methodologies, may be relevant in different applications. For example, project SAs based on EIA may be more reactive, although, as noted in the background section, even project-level SAs are beginning to become more proactive and to play a greater role in shaping the proposal. In contrast, the generation of development plans for a region are, by their nature, likely to be more proactive and strategic (Morrison-Saunders and Thérivel, 2006).

A generic framework for an integrated, proactive SA process might consist of the following broad steps (see also Noble and Storey, 2001):

- Define the issue to be addressed and the desired outcome, ensuring that this is defined as openly and strategically as possible.

Box 34.3 *The Gorgon gas development in Western Australia*

This case study relates to the integrated assessment of the proposed Gorgon gas development on Barrow Island, a Class A nature reserve in Western Australia, which was conducted in 2002–2003.

Question: Can Gorgon gas processing facilities be located on Barrow Island? This defined an essentially reactive assessment of the proponent's preferred option.

Approach: Initially win/win/win – the assessment applied a three pillar approach with an emphasis on achieving simultaneous environmental, social and economic gains, with the application of 'net conservation benefits' or environmental offsets designed to achieve an overall positive environmental outcome. It eventually proved impossible to achieve the desired win/win/win, due to the high environmental risks and hence the approach reverted in effect to 'minimize impacts'.

Integration: The assessment of impacts was conducted in two separate sections: the environment and the social and economic, which reached opposing conclusions. 'Integration' was thus limited to a trade-off decision at the level of the cabinet decision to approve the proposal.

Conclusion: The potential for integration and win/win/win outcomes was hindered by a closed, non-strategic framing question, a reactive assessment process and the separate consideration of environmental, social and economic implications.

Source: Adapted from Morrison-Saunders and Thérivel (2006).

- Define the sustainability decision criteria.
- Identify alternative means of achieving the desired outcome.
- Analyse the sustainability implications of each alternative.
- Select the most desirable alternative.
- Refine the preferred alternative to maximize potential benefits and minimize potential adverse effects.

It has recently been argued that this simple framework can be enhanced by (Grace, 2010):

- Taking a systems approach that commences with defining the socio-ecological system and seeking to understand its dynamics and resilience as the basis for the identification of appropriate sustainability decision criteria and the assessment of alternatives.
- Undertaking the SA in the context of a range of future scenarios of conditions to which the system might be subjected.
- Acknowledging the uncertainties inherent to the process and developing an adaptive management strategy to ensure that system integrity is maintained into the future.

Governance and institutional arrangements for integration

From a governance perspective, integration means that a specific SA should link with other decisions at all levels (the concept of tiering) and with decision-making processes beyond assessment (for example monitoring and follow-up). Unfortunately, governance and institutional structures that might support these forms of integration remain rare in practice. Recent experiences with SAs conducted for the purpose of project approvals have emphasized that decision-making based upon the integrated and holistic concept of sustainability often sits uncomfortably with traditional bureaucratic structures in which environmental, social and economic mandates are separated (Gibson, 2006). Such cases can degenerate into conflicts between agencies, with little chance of an integrated approach to assessing sustainability or the achievement of positive sustainability outcomes (Pope et al, 2005). In jurisdictions such as Canada and Western Australia, attempts have been made to overcome this fragmentation through the use of 'sustainability panels' charged with presenting integrated advice on the sustainability of a proposal to government decision-makers (Gibson et al, 2005; Gibson, 2006; Pope and Grace, 2006). The systems approach in particular highlights the interrelatedness of all system components, some of which may full within the jurisdiction of various government agencies and others within the remit of a proponent, and calls for a high level of cooperation and sharing of responsibilities.

The influence and purpose of SA may go beyond making better decisions into another form of integration. Hacking and Guthrie (2006) and Pope and Grace (2006) have described how individual project-level SAs have influenced aspects of their policy and institutional contexts, and how they have raised more fundamental questions regarding the way society is structured through a process of social learning. Similar observations have been made in relation to SEA (Owens and Cowell, 2002; Bina, 2003). An integrative approach calls for governance systems that capture and implement such learning outcomes (Jenkins et al, 2003). Furthermore, the extent to which private project proponents can be encouraged to adopt a proactive sustainability approach to the development of a proposal will also depend upon the legislative and governance structures in place. It therefore seems likely that institutional and perhaps legislative reform may be required in some jurisdictions in the future to enhance the degree of integration of SA processes (Pope and Grace, 2006).

Consultation and engagement

Many authors note the increasing emphasis on public participation and engagement in impact assessment and decision-making generally throughout the history of environmental assessment (EA) and cite the potential advantages of this trend in enhancing the following aspects: social responsibility and learning; procedural fairness; the integration of social values into analytical decisions; increased public trust and confidence in decisions and decision-makers; and the quality of technical assessment processes through lay interrogation and challenging of expert assumptions (Kørnøv and Thissen, 2000; Monnikhof and Edelenbos, 2001; Scrase and Sheate, 2002; Petts, 2003).

Table 34.1 *From SEA to SA: Summary statement*

Main trends and issues	A rapid growth of SA reflecting a wide range of approaches across the world, and recognition of the opportunity and need to collectively reflect and learn from practical experiences.
	Recognition that the interpretation of sustainability implicit to a SA process has a significant influence over the process and its potential outcomes, and that, ideally, sustainability should be recognized as an integrative concept that informs every stage of the process.
	Emergence of SA processes underpinned by the concepts of socio-ecological system integrity and resilience.
	Debate about the appropriate relationship between SA and the decision-making process itself, and recognition that this is shaped by the question framing the decision and the nature of the application.
	Increasing calls for both practical guidance in the form of process frameworks, tools and techniques, underpinned by conceptual understanding.
Main perspectives	**Current status**: The practice of SA is occurring in different contexts, applications and jurisdictions around the world. While much has been learnt already from these experiences, there is a need for further cross-jurisdictional sharing and learning, underpinned by a conceptual understanding of different practices, their roles and aims. There is a particular focus on integration and what this means in terms of sustainability itself and in the design and implementation of SA processes. Systems approaches to SA are emerging.
	Strengths and weaknesses: The current variety of approaches to SA is a strength – it reflects the evolution of SA practices that are appropriate to the context in which they are conducted; and it provides a rich base of experience from which to learn. But is also a weakness, since it creates difficulties in comparing different practices as context-dependent assumptions are often built into particular processes.
	Many applications of SA build upon existing practices, particularly in EIA and SEA, which again is both a strength and a weakness. The strength is that processes can evolve appropriately through a learning by doing approach; the weaknesses are that: the specific and potentially distinguishing conceptual and theoretical basis for SA has received little attention to date; and the legacy of impact assessment with its focus on specific issues, and the institutions that support it, may limit the ability of SA processes to contribute to the essentially integrative and holistic concept of sustainability.
	A further related weakness is that, depending upon the interpretation of sustainability applied within an assessment process, there is a risk that environmental protection may be undermined. This is particularly true of assessment processes based upon the 'three pillars' of environmental, social and economic considerations and which are not essentially integrative.
	Information and inputs: The quality of information and inputs will vary according to the particular application. In general, however, SAs, by virtue of their broad scope, tend to generate vast amounts of data.

(continued)

Table 34.1 (*continued*)

	Outcomes and benefits: SA that is an integral part of the decision-making process has been demonstrated to improve individual decisions, including project proposals. It is also becoming apparent that such processes also have the potential to influence and change aspects of the prevailing policy and institutional context in a process of 'trickle-up' and ultimately to enhance the whole socio-ecological system. Additionally, SA processes that involve collaborative decision-making can support social learning that may make an important contribution to sustainability.
Key lessons	An integrative approach to SA should be guided by the holistic and integrative concept of sustainability, should be inherent to the process of developing a proposal, should be supported by appropriate governance and institutional systems, and should embrace community engagement and deliberation.
	Reflection upon the conceptual basis and intent of a SA is essential to good practice. Such reflection will also facilitate learning among practitioners working in different sectors and different jurisdictions. This, in turn, is vital to the continued development of SA.
Challenges for the further development of SA	The development of an increasingly integrative approach to SA, as defined above, in particular, the further development of SA processes that take account of socio-ecological systems and resilience.
	The relationship between SA and the broader context within which it is conducted, and the potential for each to influence the other.
	The potential for SA to contribute to a process of social learning through deliberation and engagement.
	The challenges associated with operationalizing sustainability in the context of a specific decision and establishing appropriate decision criteria.
	The development of practical guidance informed by reflections on these conceptual aspects.

However, Bradbury and Rayner (2002, p23) have observed that consultation and engagement processes are often limited to 'instrumental' approaches in which 'information from the agency is a commodity (input) causing change (response) in a passive, public recipient' and the main aim is to legitimate decisions that are well on the way to being made. This approach has been repeatedly proven to be entirely inadequate and to escalate rather than limit conflict. Consequently, it is increasingly being recognized that it is better to engage the wider community early in the decision-making process, including the framing of the assessment, the identification of alternatives and the modelling of the socio-ecological system (Enserinck, 2000; Monnikhof and Edelenbos, 2001; Petts, 2003; Partidário et al, 2009).

Extending this argument, Owens and Cowell (2002, p51) believe that consultation and engagement processes should facilitate a process of social learning, using the potential of assessment processes to raise 'searching questions about policies and development strategies' (see also Sinclair et al, 2008). This phenomenon has been observed in relation to project SA in Western Australia. Here, participation and open deliberation have identified gaps and anomalies in the immediate policy and institutional context and have also posed challenges to deeply embedded societal and political assumptions affecting sustainability (Pope and Grace, 2006).

Providing deliberative space within SA processes may be one of the most powerful facets of integrative SA processes. It may help to ensure a holistic approach to sustainability in which values and different worldviews are not only respected but play a part in shaping the decision in the antithesis of a reductionist and mechanistic approach to sustainability. Furthermore, allowing the kinds of deep challenges discussed above has the potential to generate growing societal awareness of what global sustainability might require, thus integrating the decision at hand with its context in a deep and fundamental way.

Conclusion

Although SA has much in common with SEA, its distinguishing feature is that it is grounded in the societal goal of sustainability, the complexity and ambiguity of which has been briefly outlined in this chapter. This deceptively simple distinction has broad implications and bestows upon the practice of SA a mandate that extends beyond an individual decision and seeks to contribute to a more sustainable society.

We have explored the contours of an integrative framework for SA, examining how the assessment process should be integrated with the process of developing the proposal; the relationship between the decision and its broader governance and institutional context; and the potential power of deliberative consultation processes to promote integration. We have attempted to briefly introduce the emerging thinking around systems approaches to SA. We do not claim that our picture is complete. Rather, we hope that pitching our discussion largely at a conceptual level has provided a basis for two important activities: the sharing of experiences from different contexts and the development of good and effective SA practices. Both require us to reflect upon the conceptual underpinnings of our practice.

In continuing to develop and refine SA processes that might contribute to a shift towards a more sustainable society, we must ask:

- How do we understand sustainability?
- How might the proposal at hand contribute to sustainability?
- By what criteria might sustainability be defined within this socio-ecological system?
- What is the question that the assessment process is to help answer?
- What process methodology will answer this question most effectively?
- What are the institutional and governance implications?
- How can we incorporate the views and values of the broader community?

Only when these questions have been addressed can we consider which analytical tools and techniques might enable us to gather and analyse the data upon which the assessment process depends.

If SA is to effectively contribute to this global agenda, its practitioners must engage fully with the concept of sustainability and explore its contours and meaning in relation to assessment and decision-making. Sustainability calls for us to challenge our own notions of what impact assessment is and should be, and how our field of practice might evolve to contribute to a better future.

Acknowledgements

We are grateful to Barry Sadler, Robert Gibson, Theo Hacking and Angus Morrison-Saunders for their comments and contributions.

Notes

1 While the alternative term 'sustainability appraisal' has a specific meaning in the UK, we will use 'sustainability assessment' as a more general term, and one that reflects the preferred terminology of most contributors to our session in Prague.
2 We use the term 'ex ante' here to mean assessment that is conducted prior to the implementation of a proposal or action, in contrast with 'sustainability assessments' that seek to determine the 'state of sustainability' in a particular area and that are 'ex post' monitoring tools.
3 This definition is derived from one suggested by Theo Hacking (personal communication). We have modified it by choosing the term 'sustainability' over 'sustainable development', following Davison (2001) in suggesting that the former has more holistic and integrative connotations.
4 In the development sector, the potential for trade-offs is viewed in a more positive light. The integrated triple bottom line approach to sustainability appraisal is seen as a process for striking an appropriate balance between environmental, social and economic outcomes, and therefore perhaps providing the means to make acceptable a proposal that would otherwise be considered unacceptable if viewed only in environmental terms (Pope et al, 2004).
5 There is considerable variation in terminology evident in the recent literature: for example, Hacking and Guthrie (2006) use the term 'objectives' for both aspirational and threshold criteria (in our terminology); Gibson (2006) uses 'criteria' to refer to what Hacking and Guthrie (2006) and Pope and Grace (2006) term 'principles'.

References

Audouin, M. A. and de Wet, B. (2010) *Applied Integrative Sustainability Thinking (AIST): An Introductory Guide to Incorporating Sustainability Thinking into Environmental Assessment and Management*, CSIR, Pretoria

Bailey, J. and Dixon, J. (1999) 'Policy environmental assessment', in Petts, J. (ed) *Handbook of Environmental Impact Assessment*, vol 2, Blackwell, Oxford

Bina, O. (2003) 'Reconceptualising strategic environmental assessment: Theoretical overview and case study from Chile', unpublished PhD thesis, geography department, University of Cambridge

Bond, A. and Morrison-Saunders, A. (2009) 'Sustainability appraisal: Jack of all trades, master of none?', *Impact Assessment and Project Appraisal*, vol 27, no 4, pp321–329

Bradbury, J. and Rayner, S. (2002) 'Reconciling the irreconcilable', in Abaza, H. and Baranzini, A. (eds) *Implementing Sustainable Development: Integrated Assessment and Participatory Decision-Making Processes*, Edward Elgar, Cheltenham

Brown, A. L. and Thérivel, R. (2000) 'Principles to guide the development of strategic environmental assessment methodology', *Impact Assessment and Project Appraisal*, vol 18, no 3, pp183–189

Dalal-Clayton, B. and Sadler, B. (2005) *Strategic Environmental Assessment: A Sourcebook and Reference Guide to International Experience*, Earthscan, London

Dalal-Clayton, B. and Sadler, B. (2011, in press) *Sustainability Appraisal: A Sourcebook and Reference Guide to International Experience*, Earthscan, London

Davison, A. (2001) *Technology and the Contested Meanings of Sustainability*, State University of New York Press, Albany

Devuyst, D. (2001) 'Sustainability reporting and the development of sustainability targets', in Devuyst, D., Hens, L. and De Lannoy, W. (eds) *How Green is the City? Sustainability Assessment and the Management of Urban Environments*, Columbia University Press, New York

Dobson, A. (1996) 'Environmental sustainabilities: An analysis and a typology', *Environmental Politics*, vol 5, no 3, pp401–428

Eales, R. and Twigger-Ross, C. (2003) 'Emerging approaches to integrated appraisal', paper presented to IAIA annual meeting, Marrakech, Morocco

Eggenberger, M. and Partidário, M. (2000) 'Development of a framework to assist the integration of environmental, social and economic issues in spatial planning', *Impact Assessment and Project Appraisal*, vol 18, no 3, pp201–207

Enserinck, B. (2000) 'A quick scan for infrastructure planning: Screening alternatives through interactive stakeholder analysis', *Impact Assessment and Project Appraisal*, vol 18, no 1, pp15–22

Gaudreau, K. and Gibson, R. (2010) 'Illustrating integrated sustainability and resilience based assessments: A small-scale biodiesel project in Barbados', *Impact Assessment and Project Appraisal*, vol 28, no 3, pp233–243

George, C. (1999) 'Testing for sustainable development through assessment', *Environmental Impact Assessment Review*, vol 19, no 2, pp175–200

George, C. (2001) 'Sustainability appraisal for sustainable development: Integrating everything from jobs to climate change', *Impact Assessment and Project Appraisal*, vol 19, no 2, pp95–106

Gibson, R. (2001) 'Specification of sustainability-based environmental assessment decision criteria and implications for determining "significance" in environmental assessment', Canadian Environmental Assessment Agency Research and Development Program, Ottawa

Gibson, R. (2006) 'Beyond the pillars: Sustainability assessment as a framework for effective integration of social, economic and ecological considerations in significant decision-making', *Journal of Environmental Assessment, Policy and Management*, vol 8, no 3, pp259–280

Gibson, R., Hassan, S., Holtz, S., Tansey, J. and Whitelaw, G. (2005) *Sustainability Assessment: Criteria, Processes and Applications*, Earthscan, London

Grace, W. (2010) 'Healthy and resilient socio-ecological systems: Towards a common approach to sustainability assessment and management', paper presented at Sustainfability Assessment Symposium 2010: Towards Strategic Assessment for Sustainability, Fremantle, Western Australia, 25–26 May 2010, http://integral-sustainability.net/sas-2010-programme-updates/papers/bill-grace, accessed 30 June 2010

Govender, K., Hounsome, R. and Weaver, A. (2006) 'Sustainability assessment: Dressing up SEA, experiences from South Africa', *Journal of Environmental Assessment, Policy and Management*, vol 8, no 3, pp320–340

Hacking, T. and Guthrie, P. (2006) 'Sustainable development objectives in impact assessment: Why are they needed and where do they come from?', *Journal of Environmental Assessment, Policy and Management*, vol 8, no 3, pp341–371

Hacking, T. and Guthrie, P. (2008) 'A framework for clarifying the meaning of triple bottom-line, integrated, and sustainability assessment', *Environmental Impact Assessment Review*, vol 28, no 1, pp73–89

Hermans, F. and Knippenberg, L. (2006) 'A principle-based approach for the evaluation of sustainable development', *Journal of Environmental Assessment, Policy and Management*, vol 8, no 3, pp299–319

Hugé, J. and Hens, L. (2007) 'Sustainability assessment of poverty reduction strategy papers', *Impact Assessment and Project Appraisal*, vol 25, no 4, pp247–258

Jacobs, M. (1999) 'Sustainable development as a contested concept', in Dobson, A. (ed) *Fairness and Futurity: Essays on Environmental Sustainability and Social Justice*, Oxford University Press, New York

Jenkins, B., Annandale, D. and Morrison-Saunders, A. (2003) 'Evolution of a sustainability assessment strategy for Western Australia', *Environmental Planning and Law Journal*, vol 20, no 1, pp56–65

Kain, J.-H. and Söderberg, H. (2008) 'Management of complex knowledge in planning for sustainable development: The use of multi-criteria decision aids', *Environmental Impact Assessment Review*, vol 28, no 1, pp7–21

Knippenberg, L. and Edelmann, E. (2005) 'A framework for the assessment of the social-cultural domain of sustainable development', paper presented to the IAIA SEA Conference, Prague

Kørnøv, L. and Thissen, W. (2000) 'Rationality in decision and policy-making: Implications for strategic environmental assessment', *Impact Assessment and Project Appraisal*, vol 18, no 3, pp191–200

Lee, N. (2002) 'Integrated approaches to impact assessment: Substance or make-believe?', *in Environmental Assessment Yearbook 2002*, Institute for Environmental Management and Assessment, Lincoln, and the EIA Centre, University of Manchester

Lee, N. and Kirkpatrick, C. (2001) 'Methodologies for sustainability impact assessments of proposals for new trade agreements', *Journal of Environmental Assessment, Policy and Management*, vol 3, no 3, pp395–412

McManus, P. (1996) 'Contested terrains: Politics, stories and discourses of sustainability', *Environmental Politics*, vol 5, no 1, pp48–73

Millennium Ecosystem Assessment (2005) *Millennium Ecosystem Assessment Synthesis Report*, Island Press, Washington, DC

Monnikhof, R. and Edelenbos, J. (2001) 'Into the fog? Stakeholder input in participatory impact assessment', *Impact Assessment and Project Appraisal*, vol 19, no 1, pp29–39

Morrison-Saunders, A. and Fischer, T. (2006) 'What's wrong with EIA and SEA anyway? A sceptic's perspective on sustainability assessment', *Journal of Environmental Assessment, Policy and Management*, vol 8, no 1, pp19–39

Morrison-Saunders, A. and Thérivel, R. (2006) 'Sustainability, integration and assessment', *Journal of Environmental Assessment, Policy and Management*, vol 8, no 3, pp281–298

Noble, B. and Storey, K. (2001) 'Towards a structured approach to strategic environmental assessment', *Journal of Environmental Assessment, Policy and Management*, vol 3, no 4, pp483–508

Owens, S. and Cowell, R. (2002) *Land and Limits: Interpreting Sustainability in the Planning Process*, Routledge, London and New York

Partidário, M., Sheate, W., Bina, O., Byron, H. and Augusto, B. (2009) 'Sustainability assessment for agriculture scenarios in Europe's mountain areas: Lessons from six study areas', *Environmental Management*, vol 43, no 1, pp144–165

Petts, J. (2003) 'Barriers to deliberative participation in EIA: Learning from waste policy, plans and projects', *Journal of Environmental Assessment, Policy and Management*, vol 5, no 3, pp269–293

Pope, J. (2006) 'Editorial: What's so special about sustainability assessment?', *Journal of Environmental Assessment, Policy and Management*, vol 8, no 3, ppv–ix

Pope, J. and Grace, W. (2006) 'Sustainability assessment in context: Issues of process, policy and governance', *Journal of Environmental Assessment, Policy and Management*, vol 8, no 3, pp373–398

Pope, J., Annandale, D. and Morrison-Saunders, A. (2004) 'Conceptualising sustainability assessment', *Environmental Impact Assessment Review*, vol 24, no 6, pp595–616

Pope, J., Morrison-Saunders, A. and Annandale, D. (2005) 'Applying sustainability assessment models', *Impact Assessment and Project Appraisal*, vol 23, no 4, pp293–302

Sadler, B. (1999) 'A framework for environmental sustainability assessment and assurance', in Petts, J. (ed) *Handbook of Environmental Impact Assessment*, vol 1, Blackwell, Oxford

Scrase, I. and Sheate, W. (2002) 'Integration and integrated approaches to assessment: What do they mean for the environment?', *Journal of Environmental Policy and Planning*, vol 4, no 4, pp275–284

Sheate, W., Dagg, S., Richardson, J., Aschemann, R., Palerm, J. and Steen, U. (2003) 'Integrating the environment into strategic decision-making: Conceptualizing policy SEA', *European Environment*, vol 13, no 1, pp1–18

Sinclair, J., Diduck, A. and Fitzpatrick, P. (2008) 'Conceptualizing learning for sustainability through environmental assessment: Critical reflections on 15 years of research', *Environmental Impact Assessment Review*, vol 28, no 7, pp415–428

Sippe, R. (1999) 'Criteria and standards for assessing significant impact', in Petts, J. (ed) *Handbook of Environmental Impact Assessment*, vol 1, Blackwell, Oxford

Thérivel, R. (2004) *Strategic Environmental Assessment in Action*, Earthscan, London

Thérivel, R. and Partidário, M. (1996) *The Practice of Strategic Environmental Assessment*, Earthscan, London

Verheem, R. (2002) 'Environmental Impact Assessment in the Netherlands: Views from the Commission for EIA in 2002, Commission for EIA, Netherlands

35
Assessment for Sustainable Development: Theoretical Framework and Application to the Mining Sector

Theo Hacking and Peter Guthrie

Introduction

With particular reference to mining projects, this chapter discusses how assessment should be undertaken to ensure that the planning and decision-making process is directed towards sustainable development (SD)/ sustainability[1]. It is organised into two main parts. First, the literature is reviewed to identify the features commonly promoted for enhancing impact assessment as a decision-support tool in support of SD, in other words, sustainability assessment (SA). Second, this theoretical framework is evaluated in relation to the mining sector by establishing the extent to which its features have been applied to mining projects in Canada, Namibia and South Africa. In this analysis, particular lessons are drawn with regard to the concept of 'strategicness', which, together with 'comprehensiveness' and 'integratedness', is a key feature that distinguishes SA from established forms of assessment.

Features of sustainability assessment

A literature survey was undertaken to identify the features commonly promoted for 'sharpening' or redirecting assessment in support of SD. The review covered a range of sectors and assessment at policy, plan and programme (PPP) and project levels. The literature encapsulates a wealth of experience in the use of environmental impact assessment (EIA), strategic environmental assessment (SEA) and other forms of assessment. Through critical evaluation of historical experience, researchers have formulated normative proposals; however many of these are largely untested, since they have been used to a limited extent, if at all. Furthermore, many years (or decades) must typically elapse before it becomes apparent whether or not decisions supported by assessments have achieved the desired outcomes.

In the case of mining projects, the results of effective planning and decision-making only become fully apparent after closure when, for example, the success of rehabilitation and attainment of durable benefits can be confirmed. There are no mining projects where the approval was supported by SAs that are sufficiently mature to judge the attainment of positive contributions to SD objectives and, hence, to judge the effectiveness of the original assessments. However, there is a robust body of evidence that indicates the use of EIA and other forms of assessment have contributed to the attainment of desired outcomes, which include important elements of SD. This experience underpins the use of impact assessment to support the attainment of SD as the desired outcome.

Among the wide range of SA features that are proposed, theoretical saturation[2] was only achieved for features within the assessment process. It was not possible to isolate process and context features that distinguish SA. The features that are promoted for enhancing the effectiveness of established forms of assessment are also relevant to SA. While these features are unquestionably important, it was decided to focus on the features that distinguish SA from established forms of assessment. It is reasonable to assume that SA will face at least the same challenges as those that have constrained the effectiveness of EIA and SEA, in particular. Questions that have been raised regarding whether or not EIA and SEA have influenced substantive decisions can certainly be raised against enhanced forms of assessment, which may challenge even further politically-sensitive decision-making.

Convergence of features within the assessment process occurred under three main categories, namely the degree to which: SD 'themes' are covered ('comprehensiveness'); the assessment techniques that are used and/or the themes that are covered are aligned, connected, compared and/or combined ('integratedness'); and the focus is broad and forward-looking ('strategicness'). As shown in Figure 35.1, these categories can form the axes of a three-dimensional space within which various types of assessment can be located by analysing the features that they encompass rather than the 'labels' that they have been given (Hacking and Guthrie, 2008). The discipline of 'unpacking' the features according to the axes enables comparison on the basis of substance rather than semantics, which is helpful in a field where the use of terminology is inconsistent and, sometimes, confusing.

SA is sometimes used to refer to specialized forms of strategic assessment, which only encompass features in the most 'advanced' corner of the framework (see Figure 35.1). The authors favour the use of the term to refer to the spectrum covered by the overall framework. This is consistent with the definition of SA proposed by Dalal-Clayton and Sadler (2004, p3), namely: 'Approaches that are used to integrate or interrelate the environmental, social and economic (ESE) pillars of sustainability into decision-making on proposed initiatives at all levels, from policy to projects and particularly within or against a framework of sustainability principles, indicators or strategies.' They contend that integrated assessment is a necessary but not sufficient condition for SA, which is consistent with the distinction proposed here (Dalal-Clayton and Sadler, 2004, p12).

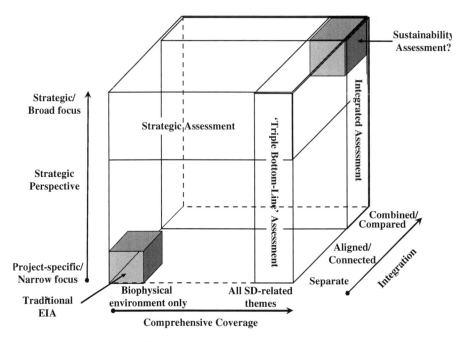

Source: Adapted from Hacking and Guthrie, 2008, p75

Figure 35.1 *Spectrum of features within sustainability assessment*

At times, discussions concerning SA are at crossed purposes, since the perspective of some is informed by the UK's system of sustainability appraisal of regional plans; whereas the experience of others was gained in countries such as Australia, Canada and South Africa where the most prominent SA experience has been at the project level or in response to projects (Dalal-Clayton and Sadler, 2005, pp256–258; Gibson et al, 2005, Grace and Pope, 2005). In the UK, the term 'sustainability appraisal' is used to distinguish 'conventional' SEA with a biophysical focus from a form of strategic assessment that also covers social and economic impacts (Dalal-Clayton and Sadler, 2005, pp101–102). Govender et al (2005) argue that what is called SA in some countries is essentially the same as SEA in South Africa, where a broad definition of 'environment' is used.

In the literature there is considerable overlap between the features described under the cumulative effects assessment (CEA), SEA and SA 'labels'. CEA has been widely promoted as means to enhance project-level EIA and features in most 'good practice' guidelines (Bisset, 1996; IFC, 2009, Annex C; Shell, 2002, p28). However, many commentators have recognized that CEA is most effective when undertaken at a strategic level, since it requires consideration of a wide range of activities within wider spatial and longer time scales, (Bisset, 1996; Sadler, 1996, p161, Stinchcombe and Gibson, 2001, pp353–354; MMSD North America, 2002, p9; Dalal-Clayton and Sadler, 2005, pp20–21). The authors of a South African guideline observe that there appears to be consensus that CEA should be integrated into existing EIA and SEA processes

(DEAT, 2004, p1). Following her review of the CEA literature, Stiff (2001, p85) concludes that: 'CEA should be undertaken both at the project-specific level and on a regional planning basis, in order to develop a complete picture of the environmental effects of human activities. Linkages need to be established between these processes.'

The remainder of this chapter is focused on the strategicness axis, since it encompasses among the greatest challenges in the pursuit of SA. Perhaps due to its overuse in the impact assessment literature, the term 'strategic' has lost much of its meaning and is widely used merely as a label for assessment at the PPP levels. In this chapter, 'strategic' is used in a more conventional sense to refer to the features that characterize the degree of 'emphasis on strategy' within assessment at any level (Noble, 2000, p206).

The strategicness axis of Figure 35.1 has intentionally not been subdivided into the idealized planning levels favoured in much of the normative assessment literature. A distinction is typically made between project-level assessment and strategic assessment at the PPP levels. At some point along the strategicness axis, the boundary is crossed between project and PPP-level assessment and planning, and some form of 'tiering' is necessary for the axis to be continuous. However, 'tiering' has been criticized for being an unrealistic representation of reality (Dalal-Clayton and Sadler, 2005, p18; Gibson et al, 2005, p90; Lee and Kirkpatrick, 2000, p10; Pope et al, 2004, p600; Scrase and Sheate, 2002, p280). In particular, the normative literature on 'tiering' has not addressed adequately the challenge of linking projects initiated by the private sector with strategic planning (Goodland and Mercier, 1999, p25; MMSD North America, 2002, p22).

By avoiding the idealized distinction between assessment at the PPP and project levels, the framework can be applied to contexts ranging from well-developed system of 'tiering', to the virtual absence of assessment at higher planning levels. In jurisdictions with well-developed assessment and planning at the PPP levels, the strategicness axis may well be covered by a tiered system. Hence, it should be emphasized that the framework does not represent the coverage of a single assessment technique but rather the net effect of all the assessment and para-assessment techniques used in a particular context. In that vein, Vanclay (2004, p268) defines 'assessment' as 'a generic term that can mean either an integrated approach or the composite/totality of all forms of impact assessment'.

There is growing consensus that a strategic perspective is a necessary, but not sufficient, requirement for SA. When considering the framework in relation to project-level assessment a difficult question that arises is the extent to which shifting along the strategicness axis can (or should) be achieved. The corollary of this is to question the extent to which project-level assessments can be SAs.

EIA is the most commonly used process for evaluating the wider implications of mining projects. Social impact assessment (SIA) and other specialized types of assessment are also increasingly used. In situations where assessment and planning at the PPP levels is ineffective, project-level assessment may be 'pushed' up the strategicness axis. The independent reviewers of an EIA for a mining project in Canada's Northwest Territories (NWT) observed that, while project-specific assessment is arguably not the appropriate forum to address cumulative impacts and land-use planning, it becomes a focal point for them when higher level planning processes are absent (CIRL, 1997, p52). Similarly, Couch (2002, p267) concludes that in Canada's north 'EIA reviews have on occasion been the "only show in town"'; hence:

> By default, the EIAs of mega-projects have had characteristics ascribed to strategic environmental assessment [...]. They have been thrust into the breech to fill gaps for policy and/or regional planning of areas larger than many European countries, and have served as a catalyst for broader government initiatives.

Mining and sustainable development

The Plan of Implementation endorsed at the 2002 World Summit on Sustainable Development (Johannesburg Summit) acknowledges the importance of mining, stating that (UN, 2002b): 'Mining, minerals and metals are important to the economic and social development of many countries. Minerals are essential for modern living.' However, detractors highlight poor health and safety records, ecological damage and social upheaval associated with some mining projects, the poor economic performance of certain mining-dependent countries, and instances where mines are associated with corruption or have financed conflicts (MMSD, 2002; Weaver and Caldwell, 1999; Weber-Fahr, 2002).

Leading companies in the mining sector were proactive in their efforts to improve occupational health, safety and environmental performance, and to contribute to community development well before these issues became an integral part of the SD agenda, which has become a focus of attention in recent years. Three-quarters of respondents to a PricewaterhouseCoopers (2001, p11) survey of the sector cited enhanced shareholder value and survival of the business in the long-term as factors motivating the adoption of SD strategies. However, operational-phase management systems and public 'ex post' reporting on SD performance by sector leaders are well in advance of 'ex ante' SA of projects. This is akin to putting the 'cart is before the horse' and efforts are needed to reverse this. One commentator has noted that SD reporting and assessment currently operate in 'parallel universes' (Heather-Clark, 2004).

Thus, far, the sector's most prominent SD-related collaborative effort is the establishment of the Global Mining Initiative in 1999 by ten international mining companies (ICMM, 2010). The GMI launched an initiative to examine the role of the mining and minerals sector in contributing to SD, and how that contribution could be increased. They contracted the International Institute for Environment and Development through the World Business Council for Sustainable Development to undertake a two-year independent process of research and consultation, known as the Mining, Minerals and Sustainable Development (MMSD, 2002) project.

The MMSD project included regional partnerships in Southern Africa, South America, Australia and North America; national projects in some 20 countries; 23 global workshops attended by approximately 700 people from diverse backgrounds; and some 175 pieces of commissioned research. The MMSD final report is supported by an extensive database of literature. Dalal-Clayton and Sadler (2005, p35) suggest that this process 'can be considered a global-scale sustainability assessment of this sector'.

The GMI concluded in May 2002 with a conference attended by a broad range of stakeholders with an interest in the sector. The GMI orchestrated the formation of a new industry association, the International Council on Mining and Metals (ICMM, 2010), to act as a conduit for implementing some of the MMSD project's recommendations. The ICMM (2003) has adopted a set of ten principles that underpin an SD framework and its corporate membership have committed to measuring performance against these principles.

It is sometimes argued that mining is incompatible with SD, since it entails the extraction of non-renewable resources and because mines have finite lives. However, MMSD North America (2002, p8) concluded that 'the fact that minerals are non-renewable (or stock) resources ... turns out to be relatively unimportant from a sustainability perspective – at least at the macro scale ... the focus is now on mining as an activity and its implications for the communities and renewable resources within which minerals are imbedded'. It also makes no sense to refer to the 'sustainability' of an individual mining (or any other) project. Little and Mirrlees (1994, p213) point out that if 'unsustainability were really regarded as a reason for rejecting a project, there would be no mining, and no industry ... [and the] world would be a primitive place'.

What matters is the contribution that mining can make to SD (MMSD, 2002, p24):

> *Applying the concept of sustainable development to the mineral sector does not mean making one mine after another 'sustainable' – whatever that means. The challenge for the sustainable development framework is to see that the mineral sector as a whole contributes to human welfare and wellbeing today without reducing the potential for future generations to do the same.*

If SD is defined as the integration of social, economic and environmental considerations, then a mining project that is developed, operated and closed in an environmentally and socially acceptable manner could be seen as contributing to SD. Critical to this goal is ensuring that benefits of the project are employed to develop the region in a way that will survive long after the mine is closed (UN, 2002a, p6).

Robinson et al (1996, p34), who reject the notion of sustainability as mere persistence over time, explain that 'it is first necessary to identify the overall system of interest, and then to identify the sustainability of that system as a whole'.

Mining sector case studies

In this section, six mining projects that are considered 'best practice' in their respective jurisdictions were analysed to establish the extent to which the SA features proposed in the literature were used, and to identify any additional features that may have been used in practice. Evidence of the use of a feature is a step towards endorsing its practicality, at least within a particular context. The intention was also to analyse mining-specific experience, which is not obtainable from the general literature or literature from other sectors or planning domains. 'Best practice' case studies were selected, since they are most likely to contain sustainability features. To gain insight from a range of economic and governance contexts, case studies were selected in Canada, Namibia, and South Africa (see Table 35.1). Context-specific opportunities and limitations were explored through cross-case comparisons.

Skorpion Zinc

The Skorpion Zinc mine and refinery was officially opened in September 2003. It is in a remote and inhospitable part of southwestern Namibia, 40km north of the border with South Africa. The nearest settlement is Rosh Pinah, approximately 25km to the southeast, which was established more than 30 years ago to serve the adjacent Rosh Pinah zinc mine. The site is between two important conservation areas – the Sperrgebiet ('Forbidden Area') to the west and the Ai-Ais Richersveld Transfrontier Park to the east. The area lies at the northern end of the Succulent Karoo biome, the world's most diverse arid environment and the only desert biome in the International Union for Conservation of Nature (IUCN) list of biodiversity 'hotspots'; it is also one of Southern Africa's least protected and most threatened biomes.

Table 35.1 *Case studies*

Name	Location	Main owner proponent	Key references
Skorpion Zinc Project	Karas Region, Southern Namibia	Anglo Base Metals	Bannon and Morrall (2003); eco.plan (2000); Kilbourn Louw and Green (2003); WEC (1998, 2001)
Rössing Uranium Mine	Erongo Region, Central Namibia	Rio Tinto plc	Middleditch (2004); *Mining Journal* (2004, 2005); RUL (2003a, b)
Gamsberg Zinc Project	Northern Cape Province, South Africa	Anglo Base Metals	Brownlie et al (2005, pp217–219); Envirolink (2000a, b, c); IUCN and ICMM (2004, pp42–43); Joughin (2000)
Der Brochen Platinum Project	Mpumalanga Province, South Africa	Anglo American Platinum Corporation	Coombes (2004b); SRK (2002)
Voisey's Bay Nickel Project	Labrador, Canada	Inco Limited	CEAA (1999); Gibson (2000, 2001, 2002, 2005); Gibson et al (2005); VBNC (1997)
Snap Lake Diamond Project	NWT, Canada	De Beers Canada Inc	Couch (2002); De Beers (2002); Ednie (2004); Morgan (2004, 2005); MVEIRB (2003)

Rössing Uranium Mine

Since 1976, Rössing Uranium Limited (RUL) has operated a large-sale, open pit uranium mine in the Erongo Region of central-western Namibia. The mine is in the Namib Desert, 65km northeast of Swakopmund on the Atlantic coast. The nearest town to the mine is Arandis, 5km to the west, which was established in 1970s to house the mine's semi-skilled and unskilled employees and their families. In 1990, RUL opted to relinquish control of Arandis due to negative market conditions and changed political circumstances following Namibia's independence. After operating at a loss in 2003, the company issued statements warning that the mine would close in 2007, when ore accessible via the existing open pit geometry would be depleted, or earlier unless circumstances improved. Mine closure would result in the loss of around 1000 direct jobs, and Namibia would lose its 4 per cent contribution to gross domestic product (GDP) and 10 per cent to exports. Of particular concern was the impact on Arandis, since the town is unlikely to have a viable future if the mine were to close in the short-term. The closure warnings were accompanied by the announcement that options for prolonging the mine's life were being explored. Due to improved global uranium prices, the mine has not closed and a number projects that would further extend the mine's life are under investigation (RUL, 2007). However, like all mines, Rössing will eventually close and the planning for possible closure by 2007 will contribute greatly to the mine's preparedness when it does eventually close.

Gamsberg Zinc Project

The zinc deposit is located just beneath the surface of the Gamsberg inselberg ('island mountain') in Northern Cape Province, South Africa, between the towns of Springbok and Pofadder, near the border with Namibia. The nearest town is Aggeneys some 20km to the west, which belongs to the existing Black Mountain zinc and lead mine. The Northern Cape is rich in minerals and its economy has been dominated by mining for many decades; however, the sector has been in decline, aggravating the widespread poverty and high unemployment. The Gamsberg project represented a stereotypical 'trade-offs dilemma', since urgently needed socio-economic development could be achieved only by sacrificing part of a unique ecosystem (Brownlie and Wynberg, 2001, p28). A combination of isolation, unusual topography, extreme and variable climatic conditions and a variety of soil types combine to produce unique habitats for a spectacular array of endemic and rare succulents. As an outlier of Succulent Karoo within the Nama-Karoo biome at its upper elevation, the Gamsberg inselberg is considered the single most important site for conservation in the region. In 1998, the property was acquired by what is now Anglo American plc, which initiated a feasibility study of the project. Towards the end of 2000, the Gamsberg received authorization; however, in 2001, the company postponed the implementation of the project due to the unfavourable market outlook for zinc. In early 2010 the project was sold to Vedanta Resources plc and it was announced that they intend to 'rapidly develop' the project (Anglo American, 2010).

Der Brochen Platinum Project

Anglo American Platinum Corporation (AAPC) is investigating the establishment of the Der Brochen platinum group metal mine in Mpumalanga Province, South Africa. The towns of Burgersfort, Lydenburg, Dullstroom and Rossenekal surround the site at straight-line distances of approximately 30–45km. Poverty and unemployment levels in the district are among the highest in the country, and a shortage of water has severely constrained development. The area lies within what is known as the Sekhukhuneland Centre of Endemism (SCE). A combination of irregular topography, diverse microclimates and varied geological and physical features has resulted in high levels of biodiversity and endemism. The area where the mine site is situated is of considerable conservation importance, since it is relatively undisturbed compared to more accessible parts of the SCE where disturbance by agriculture, settlements and subsistence activities is prevalent. In 2001–2002, AAPC applied for mining authorization for Der Brochen. The government were initially reluctant to process the applications at a time when mining policy developments aimed at Black Economic Empowerment (BEE) were pending. The hiatus ended when AAPC agreed to split the Der Brochen area into two separate mines, one wholly owned by AAPC and another owned as a 50:50 joint venture with a BEE partner. After gaining authorization, AAPC pressed on with designing a large-scale mine against a backdrop of rapidly deteriorating economic circumstances, primarily caused by the strengthening South African currency. In 2003, AAPC reviewed its expansion programme and opted to slow down the implementation of projects, including Der Brochen.

Voisey's Bay Nickel Project

In 2003, the Voisey's Bay Nickel Company, a wholly owned subsidiary of Inco Ltd, started construction of the Voisey's Bay nickel mine in northern Labrador on the north-eastern coast of Canada. The mine is 350km north of Happy Valley-Goose Bay, 35km south of Nain, and 79km north of Utshimassits. A succession of Aboriginal peoples has occupied the region over the past 6000 years. In Canada, Aboriginal title is upheld by the constitution and reinforced by a number of legal precedents. Voisey's Bay was within an area of overlapping land claims by two Aboriginal groups and the project raised the stakes in the land claims negotiations as expectations regarding self-government and revenue sharing focused on the high-profile development. Northern Labrador is an inhospitable region with a harsh Arctic to sub-Arctic climate. It is an area of stark beauty and is one of the world's few remaining expansive wildernesses. It covers much of the range of the largest herd in North America, the George River caribou herd. The region also has significant populations of other wildlife, such as black and polar bears.

Snap Lake Diamond Project

In 2005, De Beers Canada started construction of the Snap Lake Diamond Project. It will be the third diamond mine in the NWT, Canada's first fully underground diamond mine, and De Beers' first mine outside of Africa. Snap Lake is a small lake located some 220km northeast of Yellowknife in a part of the NWT aptly known as the 'barrenlands'. The Snap Lake area is within

Aboriginal traditional land and was covered by a land claim submitted by an Aboriginal group. An agreement in principle for a comprehensive land claim with self-government provisions was signed in January 2000, but the final agreement was only signed in August 2003, two months prior to the approval of the environmental assessment (EA) of the project. A number of other Aboriginal groups are located within the project's socio-economic zone of influence and are potentially affected by (actual or perceived) impacts on traditional resources. Similar to Northern Labrador, the NWT is a vast wilderness with a harsh climate and rugged natural beauty. Snap Lake is just north of the 'tree line', the approximate boundary between the treeless Arctic and the sub-Arctic. All of the NWT diamond mines are located within the range of the Bathurst caribou herd, but indications are that relatively few caribou migrate through the Snap Lake area due to the boulder-strewn terrain. The area also provides habitat for other wildlife, such as grizzly bears and wolves.

The case study assessments

The case study assessments were built around a social and environmental impact assessment (SEIA)[3] undertaken by the proponents with the assistance of a lead consultant and input from a range of specialists. The assessments were carried out in parallel and interactively with the technical and financial feasibility studies and followed, as a minimum, a good practice SEIA process, including stakeholder consultation (UNEP, 2003, pp113–115). In this chapter, 'assessment' does not only refer to SEIA, it is rather used as 'a generic term that can mean either an integrated approach or the composite/ totality of all forms of impact assessment' (Vanclay, 2004, p268). Figure 35.2 summarizes the main assessment techniques employed and the terminology used.

The development of projects is evolutionary, especially prior to construction. Lengthy delays, which are common in the mining sector, are a key reason why impact assessments seldom unfold in a 'textbook' fashion but rather progress in fits and starts. The core SEIA processes for the case studies were all completed prior to May 2005.

Noteworthy enhancements to and/or variations from 'standard' SEIA are the use of SA (Rössing), CBA (Gamsberg), SEA (Der Brochen), IBAs and panel/board reviews (Voisey's Bay and Snap Lake).

Sustainability assessment (Rössing)

This was 'an intuitive approach taken by members of the project team' (RUL, 2003a, p169). Objectives for the SD of the town of Arandis were established and the 'base case' and various expansion scenarios were then compared by considering their ability to satisfy the objectives. The study hoped to establish whether it would be preferable to close the mine, which would cause many negative impacts, or to extend its life to prolong the positive impacts. The approach entailed establishing an overall vision and then defining the strategic objectives, strategic actions and management contributions needed to achieve the vision. The alternatives were evaluated to determine the extent to which they satisfy these requirements. Objectives–actions–contributions hierarchies were developed for quality of life values of: social acceptance, physiological or

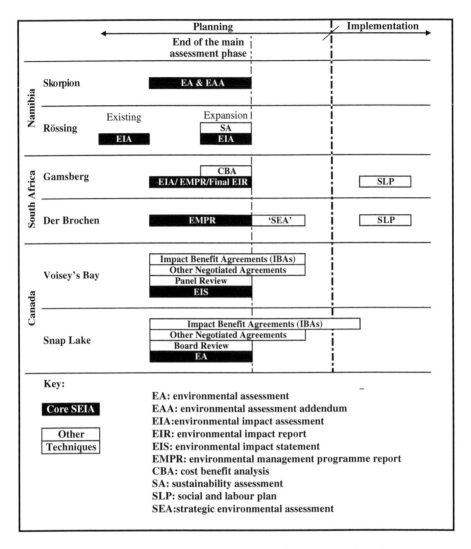

Figure 35.2 *Main assessment techniques employed*

basic needs, safety and security needs, self-esteem and self-actualization. These values were used to structure the analysis, and a final 'sustainability test' was applied to determine the durability beyond mine closure.

Cost-benefit analysis (Gamsberg)

The Gamsberg proponent commissioned this analysis in response to escalating concerns regarding the potential adverse impact of mining on tourism, and the suggestion that ecotourism could be a viable alternative to mining (Joughin, 2000, p99; KPMG, 2000, pp1–3). The aim of the CBA was to 'determine the net benefit or cost to society and the environment of the proposed investment, over and above the net private benefit by way of company profits' (KPMG, 2000, p3).

Only the two items considered material were quantified. The consultants calculated the net present value of the anticipated tax revenues, and valued the biodiversity loss by applying the willingness to pay and replacement cost methods KPMG, 2000, pp21–25). No willingness to pay surveys were available; instead government expenditure on conservation at a nearby nature reserve was taken and adjusted to accommodate differences between the areas. The replacement cost was based on a botanist's estimate of the cost of purchasing 1000 km² of land with similar botanical merit. The CBA concluded that the benefits of the project exceed the costs. Conservation non-governmental organizations (NGOs) and authorities were unimpressed by the findings, and were particular dissatisfied with the estimate of the valuation of the biodiversity loss (Envirolink, 2000b).

SEA (Der Brochen)

In the light of the Der Brochen project's location 'within a sensitive biophysical environment and a poor and underdeveloped socio-economic environment', and AAPC's policy of applying international best practice, company environmental specialists recommended that a SEA should be undertaken (Coombes, 2004b, p1). In presenting the case to AAPC senior management, the SEA approach was presented as fundamentally different to EIA in that 'SEA fits mining into the environment as contrary to the EIA approach, which considers the impact of mining on the environment' (Heymann, 2004, p1). This recommendation was accepted and the SEA was undertaken during the first half of 2004 and completed approximately a year after obtaining approval via the statutory SEIA process. In September 2004, AAPC management endorsed the strategy developed thorough the SEA process, which was largely an objectives-driven land-use planning exercise. As AAPC owned a much larger area of land than would be needed for mining, it recognized that (Coombes, 2004a, p13): 'This presents the opportunity to integrate the broader area owned by Anglo Platinum, with the proposed mine in a manner that achieves the socio-economic benefits of mining but not at the expense of the Sekhukhuneland Centre of Endemism.'

The purpose of the land-use planning as the key output of the SEA was to guide the location of infrastructure by demarcating zones where preference should, as far as possible, be given to varying intensities of land-use (Coombes, 2004b, pp19–20). A primary mining development zone was located within larger conservation and socio-economic zones. Management goals, objectives and operational rules were established for each zone.

IBAs and panel/board reviews (Voisey's Bay and Snap Lake)

Canada has a well-developed system of EA; however in parts of the country where Aboriginal peoples are present there has evolved what Couch (2002, p265) calls a 'two-step process', and Klein et al (2004, p2) describe as 'two distinct but linked processes'. EA is the one process and the other is the negotiation of quasi-judicial or supraregulatory agreements (CIRL, 1997, p1). Galbraith and Bradshaw (2005, p4) define the latter as:

> *Legally binding, project-specific agreements that are not described in existing legislation. Typically, they are used in*

tandem with EA and are negotiated between a company that is planning a resource development and a stakeholder group that is considered to be impacted by this proposed development (i.e. often an aboriginal group, but may include government).

A distinction can be made between agreements negotiated with the authorities and, sometimes, Aboriginal groups and IBAs, which are negotiated exclusively with Aboriginal groups. Both Inco and De Beers opted to negotiate IBAs even though in the absence of settled land claims there was no requirement for them (MVEIRB, 2003, p23; CEAA, 1999). However, based on the precedent set by earlier projects, it would have been difficult to gain approval without committing to IBAs (CIRL, 1997, p1). There are two obstacles to the effective integration of SEIA and IBA, namely: timing, and confidentiality of the IBAs (Klein et al, 2004, p2; MVEIRB, 2003, pp23–24). At Voisey's Bay, IBAs were only agreed some three years after the EIS was approved. At Snap Lake, the non-IBA agreements were signed shortly after the EA was approved; however the IBAs had still not been concluded, despite more than two years of negotiations. (The last of the four IBAs was eventually agreed in 2007.)

A key feature of the Canadian case studies is the involvement of a panel or board in coordinating the assessment process through detailed scoping up-front and review – including public hearings – at the end. Its review reports provide an overview of the submissions by the proponent and other parties, an analysis of these submissions, and recommendations and suggestions targeted at the proponents and authorities. In contrast, the approvals granted by the Southern African authorities are not supported by any substantive reports; hence their rationale is opaque. In Canada, as is the case in Southern Africa, the responsibility for undertaking and funding the assessment still rests predominantly with the proponent, which can 'put the developer into the powerful position of speaking on behalf of communities' (MVEIRB, 2002, p39). The Canadian public hearings provide the opportunity for submissions via an avenue not controlled by the proponent.

Strategicness of the case study assessments

Planning at the project level can be informed by a strategic perspective either by 'pushing' project assessments up the strategicness axis, or by cascading the results of assessments and/or planning at higher levels. It might be less challenging and/or more appropriate to incorporate strategic features at higher planning levels; however, project-level assessment may – to varying degrees – adopt a strategic perspective, especially in the absence of well-developed planning at higher levels. Strategicness should be determined by the features of the assessment rather than the level at which the assessment is initiated. As noted by Couch (2002, p267), assessments initiated at the project level can have features normally attributed to SEA, and assessments at the PPP level may be undeserving of the 'strategic' label (Noble, 2000).

Figure 35.3 summarizes the relationship between the case study assessments and planning initiatives at higher levels, if any. The chronology has been approximately normalized around the ends of the main pre-approval

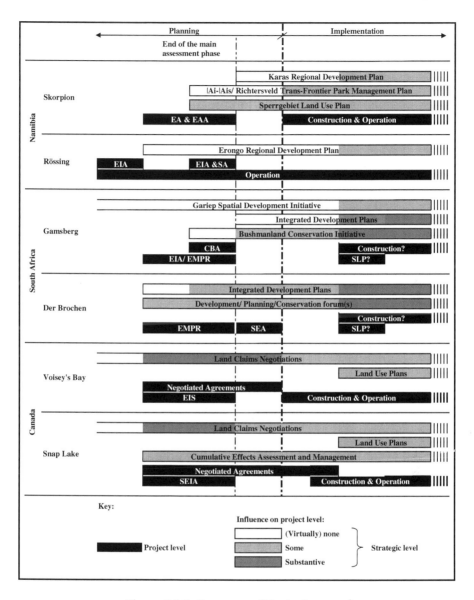

Figure 35.3 *Summary: 'Tiering' strength*

assessment phases to enable comparison of the planning sequences. Its main purpose is to reveal any 'tiering' during and/or following the main assessment phase, and how this is likely to evolve. The case studies revealed no evidence of substantive 'tiering' during their assessments. Strategic planning initiatives have only gained momentum after the projects were approved and, in most cases, their emergence is – at least in part – in response to the project and/or other similar projects.

Table 35.2 *Strategicness features and 'best practice' case study evidence*

Strategicness features	'Best practice' case study evidence
Explicit assessment goal: Aim to enhance positive impacts in addition to avoiding negative impacts.	Enhancing positive impacts set as an explicit assessment goal.
Aim to achieve a positive contribution to SD.	SD set as an explicit assessment goal.
The assessment 'benchmark': Use of SD objectives developed using stakeholder opinion.	Used issues identified during stakeholder consultations to scope the assessment.
Use of SD objectives derived from the baseline.	Used land-use planning objectives based on maintaining the ecology, as far as possible, in the baseline condition, while achieving positive trends against the socio-economic baseline.
Use of SD objectives determined using backcasting.	Used objectives that define the desired quality of life to select the alternative(s) most likely to achieve the objectives.
Use of SD objectives derived from SD principles.	Used broad principles as the basis for a 'sustainability test', and multi-stakeholder deliberations to establish conformity.
Use of SD objectives obtained via 'tiering'.	Referenced existing/evolving regional development plans, land use plans and/or other strategic planning initiatives.
	Committed to contribute to strategic planning by the authorities.
	Catalysed the establishment of strategic planning forums.
Use of thresholds for unsustainability.	Used best estimates of thresholds for 'acceptable' ecological damage.
Spatial and temporal coverage: Use of large spatial scales for the assessment of socio-economic impacts.	Assessed socio-economic impacts on communities/ towns within the project's area of influence.
	Assessed economic aspects and some impacts at the regional or country level.
Use of large spatial scales for the assessment of biophysical impacts.	Used baseline surveys and analysis at the regional-scale to establish the context.
	Established boundaries for each valued ecosystem component (VEC) based on ecological/physical characteristics.
	Used 'spatial scale' as a significance rating criterion.
Use of a spatial planning model.	Used a 'nested' planning model to locate the mine within the larger ecological and socio-economic context.
Assessment of long-duration impacts.	Used 'duration' as a significance rating criterion.
Assessment of far-future impacts, especially impacts at closure.	Assessed, in general terms, adverse socio-economic impacts at closure and propose mitigation measures, especially for avoiding 'boom-bust'.
	Referred to experience at similar operations.
Assessment of post-closure situation.	Assessed residual post-closure impacts on each VEC.
	Committed to restoring, as far as possible, the pre-mining biophysical conditions.
	Established a general post-mining vision.

(continued)

Table 35.2 (*continued*)

Strategicness features	'Best practice' case study evidence
Consideration of alternatives:	
Assessment of the 'no project' option.	Outlined the benefits that will not be realized.
Assessment of substantive technical and/or location alternatives.	Avoided, as far as possible, ecologically sensitive areas.
	Compared underground versus open pit mining.
	Considered technical and location alternatives from an early stage via dynamic interactions between the SEIA and project teams.
Use more strategic analysis methods to select technical and/or location alternatives.	Selected alternatives based on rating by an 'expert panel' comprising the multidisciplinary SEIA team.
	Demarcated land use zones, based on ecological sensitivity, where preference should be given to varying intensities/categories of use.
Assessment of project life alternatives.	Analysed a range of project lengths (such as varying production rates) and selected the preferred option by also considering socio-economic factors.
Assessment of accommodation, transport and shift-rotation alternatives.	Analysed in general terms, the benefits of long-distance commuting versus establishing/expanding a mine-dependent town.
	Investigated alternative workforce pick-up points/sources, and shift-rotations.
Assessment of land-use alternatives.	Provided a general overview of economic sectors in the region and their opportunities and constraints.
Assessment of timing alternatives.	Allowed sufficient time for planning and/or communities to prepare by delaying project implementation, if necessary.
Assessment of cumulative impacts:	Assessed the overall impact of the project itself on each VEC.
	Undertook a CEA of activities that could act in combination with the proposal.
	Developed a land-use plan to constrain future developments and sought buy-in from other stakeholders.
Treatment of uncertainty:	
Reveal areas of uncertainty.	Revealed uncertainties due to lack of knowledge/data, unforeseen project changes, complexity/analytical limitations and/or the unknown/unpredictable future.
Reduce/eliminate uncertainty.	Undertook 'ex ante' research to increase knowledge before designs/management plans/decisions were finalized.
	Used design/management to eliminate aspects that could cause uncertain impacts.
Accommodate uncertainty.	Used conservative assumptions and 'worst case' scenarios.
	Used monitoring and adaptive design and management.

The case studies reinforce the findings of researchers who assert that: there is an iterative relationship between the project and strategic planning levels; the strategic level is as likely to informed by 'evaporating-up' from the project level; and that in many countries 'tiering' is still in its infancy and there are still many difficulties to overcome (Sadler, 1996, p155; Lee and George, 2000, p5; Noble, 2000, p217; Stinchcombe and Gibson, 2001, p363). This is especially the case in developing countries and regions where priorities and/or resource constraints are such that planning is often only initiated when there are pressing reasons, usually problems. Der Brochen most obviously contradicts the normative model, since a proponent-initiated SEA was undertaken *after* the SEIA.

Key features that determine the strategicness of assessments are: the explicit goal; the 'benchmark' used; the spatial and temporal coverage; and the extent to which alternatives, cumulative impacts, and uncertainty are considered. Table 35.2 contains the best evidence that was found in the case studies for the use of these features.

Progress along the strategicness axis is such that, in many respects, the case studies have characteristics normally attributed to assessments at the PPP levels. Areas of progress are: the use of wider spatial and time scales, consideration of substantive alternatives, the assessment of cumulative impacts, and efforts towards accommodating uncertainty. While there have been attempts to use SD objectives as the assessment 'benchmark', this is an area that requires further development through experience and research (Hacking and Guthrie, 2006).

The Rössing SA was considered sufficiently strategic to feature as a case study in a review of international SEA experience. It was noted that the SA 'included strategic aspects and options that focused on far more than the sustainability aspects of mine operations' (Dalal-Clayton and Sadler, 2005, p256). An interviewee who contributed to the SA observed that, unlike conventional EIA, SA 'takes a strategic view of how the project will fit into ... the bigger picture'.

There are disadvantages to using project-level assessments as a vehicle for addressing wider issues of concern. Stinchcombe and Gibson (2001, p351) observe that 'typically the experiences have been frustrating for all concerned', since most project-level assessments are 'too reactive and too narrowly mandated to deal effectively with larger policy and planning matters'.

Conclusions

It is unfeasible to 'stretch' project-level assessments to the extent that they become fully strategic. Private sector project proponents will, in particular, be reluctant to consider alternatives that lie outside their areas of business interest. In addition, developments by the private sector are not intended primarily to satisfy societal needs; although it is reasonable for societies to expect that they contribute to such needs. At some point along the strategicness axis the boundary is crossed between project and PPP-level assessment and planning, and some form of 'tiering' is necessary for the axis to be continuous. In the case study jurisdictions, as is likely to be the case in all but the most developed regions, assessment by the leading private sector proponents is well in advance of strategic planning by the authorities.

If it is accepted – as the framework developed through this research suggests – that a fully strategic perspective is a necessary requirement, then a project-level assessment will only be truly an SA when informed by strategic assessment at higher planning levels. However, the case studies demonstrate that considerable progress can be achieved in the absence of authorities with the necessary capacity, inclination or mandate to plan for SD; although much of the burden then falls on the leading proponents. In the case study jurisdictions, there are encouraging signs of progress towards planning for SD coordinated by the authorities, which may serve to better guide the assessment of future projects.

While the shortcomings of 'tiering' have been acknowledged, the SEA and SA literature still tends to be dominated by this idealized model. Further progress in these forms of assessment should take greater account of the iterative relationship between planning at the project and PPP levels and the potential for projects to act as catalysts for strategic planning, especially in developing regions.

Notes

1 Distinctions are sometimes made in the literature between sustainable development and sustainability (Piper, 2002, p18); however in this chapter the terms are used synonymously.
2 'Theoretical saturation' describes the point at which no new properties, dimensions, or relationships emerge (Strauss and Corbin, 1998, p143).
3 To avoid ambiguity, social and environmental impact assessment (SEIA) is used to refer to EIA-type assessment techniques that also cover socio-economic 'themes'.

References

Anglo American (2010) 'Anglo American announces sale of Zinc portfolio to Vedanta for $1,338 million', Press releases, 10 May 2010, www.angloamerican.com/aal/media/releases/2010pr/zinc_portfolio, Accessed 20 April 2010

Bannon, J. and Morrall, A. (eds) (2003) *The Skorpion Zinc Project: A Unique Development in a Unique Environment*, Portiva Mining, Liverpool

Bisset, R. (1996) *UNEP EIA Training Resource Manual – EIA: Issues, Trends and Practice*, Scott Wilson Resource Consultants for United Nations Environment Programme (UNEP)

Brownlie, S. and Wynberg, R. (2001) *The Integration of Biodiversity into National Environmental Assessment Procedures: South Africa*, UNEP Biodiversity Planning Support Programme, UNEP

Brownlie, S., De Villiers, C., Driver, A., Job, N., von Hase, A. and Maze, K. (2005) 'Systematic conservation planning in the Cape Floristic region and Succulent Karoo, South Africa: Enabling sound spatial planning and improved environmental assessment', *Journal of Environmental Assessment Policy and Management*, vol 7, no 2, pp201–228

CEAA (Canadian Environmental Assessment Agency) (1999) 'Voisey's Bay mine and mill environmental assessment panel report', CEAA, Ottawa, (Accessible at www.ceaa.gc.ca/default.asp?lang=En&n=0A571A1A-1&xml=0A571A1A-84CD-496B-969E-7CF9CBEA16AE&offset=&toc=show)

CIRL (Canadian Institute of Resources Law) (1997) 'Independent Review of the BHP Diamond Mine Process', University of Calgary for Department of Indian Affairs and Northern Development (Accessible at www.ainc-inac.gc.ca/nth/mm/pubs/bhp/bhp-eng.pdf)

Coombes, P. J. (2004a) *Der Brochen Mine State of the Environment Report*, Anglo Technical Division for Anglo Platinum, unpublished report, Johannesburg

Coombes, P. J. (2004b) *Strategic Environmental Report for Mining in a Sustainable Development Context in the Der Brochen Valley*, Anglo Technical Division for Anglo Platinum, unpublished report, Johannesburg

Couch, W. J. (2002) 'Strategic resolution of policy, environmental and socio-economic impacts in Canadian Arctic diamond mining: BHP's NWT diamond project', *Impact Assessment and Project Appraisal*, vol 20, no 4, pp265–278

Dalal-Clayton, B. and Sadler, B. (2004) 'Sustainability appraisal: A review of international experience and practice', first draft, International Institute for Environment and Development (Accesible at www.iied.org/pubs/display.php?o=G02194)

Dalal-Clayton, B. and Sadler, B. (2005) *Strategic Environmental Assessment: A Sourcebook and Reference Guide to International Experience*, Earthscan, London

De Beers (2002) *Snap Lake Diamond Project Environmental Assessment*, De Beers Canada Mining Inc, unpublished report, Toronto

DEAT (Department of Environmental Affairs and Tourism) (2004) 'Cumulative Effects Assessment (IEM Series No.7)', In Integrated Environmental Management Information Series, Pretoria

eco.plan (2000) *The Skorpion Zinc Project Environmental Assessment Addendum*, for Anglo Base Metals, unpublished draft, Windhoek

Ednie, H. (2004) 'De Beers Canada: Building a Canadian empire', *CIM Bulletin*, vol 97, no 1080, pp17–24

Envirolink (2000a) *Gamsberg Zinc Project Addendum to the Draft EMPR and EIA*, Anglo American Technical Services, unpublished report, Johannesburg

Envirolink (2000b) *Gamsberg Zinc Project Environmental Impact Assessment*, Anglo American Technical Services, unpublished report, Johannesburg

Envirolink (2000c) *Gamsberg Zinc Project Environmental Management Programme Report*, Anglo American Technical Services, unpublished report, Johannesburg

Galbraith, L. and Bradshaw, B. (2005) 'Towards a new supraregulatory approach for environmental assessment in Northern Canada', paper to IAIA Annual Meeting, Boston

Gibson, R. (2000) 'Favouring the higher test: Contributions to sustainability as the central criterion for reviews and decisions under the Canadian Environmental Assessment Act', *Journal of Environmental Law and Practice*, vol 10, no 1, pp39–54

Gibson, R. (2001) *Specification of Sustainability-based Environmental Assessment Decision Criteria and Implications for Determining 'Significance' in Environmental Assessment*, Canadian Environmental Assessment Agency Research and Development Program (Accessible at www.sustreport.org/downloads/Sustainability,EA.doc)

Gibson, R. (2002) 'From Wreck Cove to Voisey's Bay: The evolution of federal environmental assessment in Canada', *Impact Assessment and Project Appraisal*, vol 20, no 3, pp151–159

Gibson, R. (2005) 'Sustainability assessment and conflict resolution: Reaching agreement to proceed with the Voisey's Bay nickel mine', *Journal of Cleaner Production*, vol 14, no 3–4, pp225–462

Gibson, R. B., Hassan, S., Holtz, S., Tansey, J. and Whitelaw, G. (2005) *Sustainability Assessment: Criteria, Processes and Applications*, Earthscan, London

Goodland, R. and Mercier, J-R. (1999) *The Evolution of Environmental Assessment in the World Bank: From "Approval" to Results*, World Bank, Washington, DC

Govender, K., Hounsome, R. and Weaver, A. (2005) 'Sustainability assessment: Dressing up SEA?', paper presented to the IAIA SEA Conference, Prague

Grace, W. and Pope, J. (2005) 'Sustainability assessment: Issues of process, policy and governance', paper presented to the IAIA SEA Conference, Prague

Hacking, T. and Guthrie, P. M. (2006) 'Sustainable development objectives: Why are they needed and where do they come from?', *Journal of Environmental Assessment Policy and Management*, vol 8, no 3, pp341–371

Hacking, T. and Guthrie, P. M. (2008) 'A framework for clarifying the meaning of Triple Bottom-Line, Integrated, and Sustainability Assessment', *Environmental Impact Assessment Review*, vol 28, no 2–3, pp73–89

Heather-Clark, S. (2004) 'Letter to the editor: Reconsidering IAIAs vision and mission', *IAIA South Africa Newsletter*, December 2004, pp2

Heymann, E. (2004) *Sustainable Development Strategy for the Der Brochen Valley*, Anglo Platinum, unpublished report, Johannesburg

ICMM (International Council on Mining and Metals) (2003) 'ICMM Sustainable Development Framework: ICMM Principles', *ICMM Newsletter*, vol 2, no 3, pp4–6

ICMM (2010) 'Our History', ICMM, www.icmm.com/about-us/icmm-history, Accessed 18 September 2010

IFC (International Finance Corporation) (2003) 'Environmental and Social Review Procedure', (Accessible at www.ifc.org/ifcext/sustainability.nsf/AttachmentsByTitle/pol_ESRP2009/$FILE/ESRP2009.pdf)

IUCN and ICMM (2004) *Integrating Mining and Biodiversity Conservation Case Studies from Around the World*, (Accessible at www.icmm.com/page/1155/integrating-mining-and-biodiversity-conservation-case-studies-from-around-the-world)

Joughin, J. (2000) *Gamsberg Zinc Project Final Environmental Impact Report*, SRK Consulting, unpublished report, Johannesburg

Kilbourn Louw, M. and Green, N. (2003) *The Skorpion Zinc Project IAIAsa Awards Submission 2003*, Skorpion Zinc Project, unpublished report, Johannesburg

Klein, H., Donihee, J. and Stewart, G. (2004) 'Environmental impact assessment and impact and benefit agreements: Creative tension or conflict?', paper presented to the IAIA Annual Meeting, Vancouver

KPMG (2000) *Cost Benefit Study on Eco-tourism: Gamsberg Feasibility Study*, KPMG Tourism and Leisure Unit, unpublished report, Johannesburg

Lee, N. and George, C. (2000) 'Introduction', in Lee, N. and George, C. (eds) *Environmental Assessment in Developing Countries and Countries in Transition: Principles, Methods and Practice*, John Wiley and Sons, Chichester and New York

Lee, N. and Kirkpatrick, C. (2000) 'Integrated appraisal, decision making and sustainable development: an overview', in Kirkpatrick, C. (ed) *Sustainable Development and Integrated Appraisal in a Developing World*, Edward Elgar, Cheltenham, pp1–19

Little, I. M. D. and Mirrlees, J. A. (1994) 'The cost and benefits of analysis: Project appraisal and planning twenty years on', in Layard, R. and Glaister, S. (eds) *Cost-Benefit Analysis*, Cambridge University Press

Middleditch, D. (2004) 'Energy from the desert', *Mining Magazine*, May 2004, pp6–13

Mining Journal (2004) 'New closure warning from Rössing Uranium', *Mining Journal* 2 January 2004, p7

Mining Journal (2005) 'Revised mining plan reprieves Rössing', *Mining Journal*, 13 May 2005, p3

MMSD (Mining, Minerals, and Sustainable Development Project) (2002) *Breaking New Ground: Mining, Minerals, and Sustainable Development: The Report of the MMSD Project*, Earthscan, London

MMSD North America (2002) *Seven Questions to Sustainability: How to Assess the Contribution of Mining and Minerals Activities*, International Institute for Sustainable Development (IISD), Winnipeg, Manitoba

Morgan, R. (2004) 'What goes around…', *Mining Journal*, 4 June 2004, p2

Morgan, R. (2005) 'A thickening wedge', *Mining Journal*, 1 April 2005, p2

MVEIRB (Mackenzie Valley Environmental Impact Review Board) (2002a) 'Issues and recommendations for social and economic impact assessment in the Mackenzie Valley', MVEIRB, Yellowknife, (Accessible at www.reviewboard.ca/upload/ ref_library/SEIA-Nontech_summary.pdf)

MVEIRB (2003) *Report of Environmental Assessment and Reasons for Decision on the Snap Lake Diamond Project*, MVEIRB, Yellowknife, (Accessible at www. reviewboard.ca/registry/project_detail.php?project_id=6&doc_stage=11)

Noble, B. F. (2000) 'Strategic environmental assessment: What is it and what makes it strategic?', *Journal of Environmental Assessment Policy and Management*, vol 2, no 2, pp203–224

Piper, J. M. (2002) 'CEA and sustainable development: Evidence from UK case studies', *Environmental Impact Assessment Review*, vol 22, no 1, pp17–38

Pope, J., Annandale, D. and Morrison-Saunders, A. (2004) 'Conceptualising sustainability assessment', *Environmental Impact Assess Review*, vol 24, no 6, pp595–616

PricewaterhouseCoopers (2001) *Mining and Minerals Sustainability Survey 2001*, PricewaterhouseCoopers and MMSD. (Accessible at www.iied.org/pubs/pdfs/ G00741.pdf)

Robinson, J. B., Francis, G., Lerner, S. and Legge, R. (1996) 'Defining a sustainable society', in Robinson, J. B. (ed) *Life in 2030: Exploring a Sustainable Future for Canada*, University of British Columbia Press, Vancouver

RUL (Rössing Uranium Limited) (2003a) *Sustainability Assessment for the Life Extension of Rössing Uranium Mine*, RUL, unpublished report, Swakopmund

RUL (2003b) *Sustainability Assessment for the Life Extension of Rössing Uranium Mine: Integrated Executive Summary*, RUL, unpublished report, Swakopmund

RUL (2007) *Rössing Uranium Mine Expansion Project Social and Environmental Impact Assessment Public Information Document*. Swakopmund, (Accessible at www.rossing.com/files/mine_expansion/9_lom_expansion_20Aug07.pdf)

Sadler, B. (1996) *Environmental Assessment in a Changing World: Evaluating Practice to Improve Performance*, final report of the International Study of the Effectiveness of Environmental Assessment, Canadian Environmental Assessment Agency (CEAA) and International Association for Impact Assessment (IAIA), Ottawa

Scrase, J. I. and Sheate, W. R. (2002) 'Integration and integrated approaches to assessment: what do they mean for the environment?', *Journal of Environmental Policy and Planning*, vol 4, no 4, pp275–294

Shell (2002) *Guidance on Integrated Impact Assessment*, Shell International Exploration and Production BV, unpublished

SRK (2002) *Environmental Management Programme Report for the Der Brochen Mine: Volume 1 (Final Draft)*, SRK Consulting for Anglo Platinum, unpublished report, Johannesburg

Stiff, K. (2001) 'Cumulative effects assessment and sustainability: Diamond mining in the slave geological province', master's thesis, University of Waterloo

Stinchcombe, K. and Gibson, R. B. (2001) 'Strategic environmental assessment as a means of pursuing sustainability: Ten advantages and ten challenges', *Journal of Environmental Assessment Policy and Management*, vol 3, no 3, pp343–372

Strauss, A. L. and Corbin, J. M. (1998) *Basics of Qualitative Research: Techniques and Procedures for Developing Grounded Theory*, Sage, Thousand Oaks, London

Stueck, W. (2004) 'Natives hope for big gains from Inco's nickel riches', *The Globe and Mail*, 17 June 2004

UN (United Nations) (2002a) 'Berlin II Guidelines for Mining and Sustainable Development', (Accessible at http://commdev.org/content/document/detail/903/)

UN (2002b) 'World Summit on Sustainable Development Plan of Implementation', (Accessible at www.un.org/esa/sustdev/documents/WSSD_POI_PD/English/WSSD_PlanImpl.pdf)

UNEP (United Nations Environment Programme) (2003) *UNEP Environmental Impact Assessment Training Resource Manual*. Second Edition, (Accessible at www.unep.ch/etu/publications/EIAMan_2edition_toc.htm)

Vanclay, F. (2004) 'The triple bottom line and impact assessment: How do TBL, EIA, SIA, SEA and EMS relate to each other?', *Journal of Environmental Assessment Policy and Management*, vol 6, no 3, pp265–288

VBNC (Voisey's Bay Nickel Company Limited) (1997) *Voisey's Bay Mine and Mill Project Environmental Impact Statement*, VBNC, unpublished report

Weaver, A. and Caldwell, P. (1999) 'Environmental impact assessment of mining projects', in Petts, J. (ed) *Handbook of Environmental Impact Assessment*, vol 2, Blackwell, Oxford

Weber-Fahr, M. (2002) *Treasure or Trouble? Mining in Developing Countries*, International Finance Corporation, Washington, DC

WEC (Walmsley Environmental Consultants) (1998) *Skorpion Zinc Environmental Assessment – Volume 1: Final Report*, unpublished report for Reunion Mining Namibia (Pty) Ltd

WEC (2001) *The Sperrgebiet Land Use Plan*, unpublished report for the Ministry of Lands Resettlement and Rehabilitation and the Ministry of Mines and Energy

Index

Page numbers in *italics* refer to figures, tables and boxes